The Principles and Practice of Banking
by James William Gilbart

*The principles
and practice of banking*

James William Gilbart

Gilbert
THD

THE

PRINCIPLES AND PRACTICE OF

BANKING.

FROM A PHOTOGRAPH BY T. R. WILLIAMS.   ENGRAVED BY S. HOLLYER.

Yours faithfully,

W. Gilbart

THE

PRINCIPLES AND PRACTICE OF

BANKING.

BY THE LATE

JAMES W. GILBART, F.R.S.,

ONE OF THE DIRECTORS OF THE LONDON AND WESTMINSTER BANK, .
AND FORMERLY GENERAL MANAGER.

NEW EDITION.

THOROUGHLY REVISED AND ADAPTED TO THE PRACTICE OF
THE PRESENT DAY.

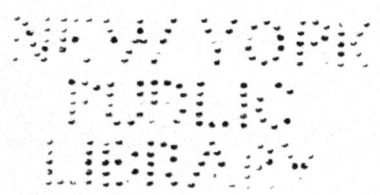
LONDON:

BELL & DALDY, YORK STREET, COVENT GARDEN.
1871.

LONDON:
PRINTED BY W. CLOWES AND SONS, STAMFORD STREET
AND CHARING CROSS.

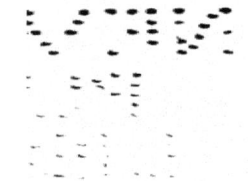

PREFACE.

———•◦•———

THE public appreciation of the late Mr. Gilbart's works on banking has been testified by their frequent reissues. Of his various publications, the "History and Principles of Banking," and the "Practical Treatise on Banking," have been the most popular, and still rank as standard text-books. In the present volume they are combined, with the double view of preserving the more valuable characteristics of both, and, by lessening the cost, of bringing them within the reach of the many.

Entrusted by the publishers with the preparation of this combined edition, I have laboured to do them justice, if not intelligently, at least assiduously. In one respect I have been singularly fortunate. Wheresoever, or to whomsoever, I have applied for information—to the Bank of England, the Clearing House, Joint-Stock Banks, Country Banks—to directors, managers, stock-brokers, clerks—I have been received courteously, answered unreservedly (confidential matters of course excepted), and have been afforded the information I sought, rather as if I were conferring a favour on my informants, than as if I were the party benefited and honoured. One honourable peculiarity, common to all, especially struck me, namely, the ready frankness with which each confessed his inability to enlighten me on matters unconnected with his own department.

Would I were at liberty to give the names of these highly informed and cultivated gentlemen to whom I owe so much, but to whom I must only return, generally, my sincere and grateful thanks. Yet, however pleasurable this would be to my sense of obligation, I doubt its turning to my editorial repute. Their names, like "the King's," would, indeed, be "a tower of strength;" but, on the credit of them, it would naturally be presumed that the following pages were free from errors; an exemption which, from the very nature of the subject matter, not to speak of my own "shortcomings," is impossible.

They who are familiar with Mr. Gilbart's writings will see at a glance that numerous alterations have been made in the present edition. Almost the entire section on "Banking Calculations" has been expunged, many "tables" omitted, the "reports of the joint-stock banks" left out, the excellent advice (which would now be considered "old-fashioned") contained in the section, "The Duties of Public Companies," much abridged, and forms of letters, guarantee bonds, prospectuses, legal undertakings, &c. &c., ruthlessly excised.

Not one omission of the kind, however, has been made unauthorized by the best authorities—bankers themselves.

En revanche, if, under advice, I have omitted much, I have added not a little; to wit, an account of the panics of 1857 and 1866, a description of the present admirable system pursued at the Clearing House, the existing rules for regulating the Scotch exchanges, and many minutiæ respecting the Bank of England, and the Scotch and Irish banks. Some of these additions are distinguished from the original text by brackets, and some of the additional notes by the word "editor" after them. I say "some," because the distinguishing signs just mentioned have not been invariably inserted, and because the minor corrections rendered necessary since Mr. Gilbart's last revision of his writings have been so numerous, that to have made them otherwise than silently would have seemed, as well as have been, an ostentation of labour—"great cry, and little wool."

It is well known that Mr. Gilbart held decided opinions as to the effects of the Act of 1844, and as to the natural laws of Exchange and Currency. His opinions have stood the test of a long experience, and are now generally received. His masterly disquisitions on these subjects are given verbatim, and deserve the serious attention, not only of the banking world, but of the legislature.

The present edition being chiefly intended for the use of the student, especially of those younger clerks in banks who aspire to a knowledge of their business beyond its mere mechanism, which may enable them to pioneer their way to new truths, and to the realization of those truths by elevating sound theory into sound practice after the example set by Mr. Gilbart, I would respectfully recommend a preliminary study of that portion of the " History and Principles " embodied herein, and suggest that on proceeding to the " Practice of Banking,"* they should revert, as they read the sections, to the corresponding sections in the " History and Principles."

I must note that although in the latter, the history of banking is not brought down later than 1833, yet that such details as refer to banking operations, *ex. gra.*, " the facilities

---

* The original title is, " A Practical Treatise on Banking."

granted by the Bank of England," p. 92—are corrected to the present time, and that the further history is continued in the " Practice of Banking."

A summary or abstract of the principal Banking Acts, not detailed in the body of the work, as well as some changes which have occurred since the text has been printed, will be found in the Appendix.

It only remains for me to solicit that indulgence from reader and critic, which no one can more unaffectedly feel that he needs than

THE EDITOR.

CONTENTS.

viii   *Contents.*

HISTORY AND PRINCIPLES

OF

BANKING.

SECTION I.

THE ORIGIN AND PROGRESS OF BANKING.

AN eminent historian observes, that " it is a cruel mortification, in searching for what is instructive in the history of past times, to find that the exploits of conquerors who have desolated the earth, and the freaks of tyrants who have rendered nations unhappy, are recorded with minute and often disgusting accuracy, while the discovery of useful arts, and the progress of the most beneficial branches of commerce are passed over in silence, and suffered to sink into oblivion." * This remark is strictly applicable to the origin and progress of banking. We have but little information as to what kind of banks existed in the earlier ages, or on what system they conducted their business. As most of the nations of antiquity subsisted chiefly on agriculture, they probably had little occasion for banks ; for it is only in commercial countries that these institutions have attained to any high degree of prosperity. And as even the commercial nations of antiquity were unacquainted with joint-stock companies, or commercial corporations, and had not discovered the use of paper-money or bills of exchange, the business of a banker, even among them, must have been somewhat different from that of a banker of the present day. The merchants of those early times employed as money, gold and silver bullion ; and received it and paid it away by weight.

* Robertson's Historical Disquisition on India, page 46.

B

It is probable that the merchants would require that the precious metals they received should be of a certain degree of fineness. We read of Abraham * weighing unto Ephron 400 shekels of silver, *current money with the merchant*—a phrase which implies that the money current with the merchant was different from that in ordinary use.

After bullion was superseded by coin, and each nation had a coin of its own, the merchants would necessarily in the course of their business receive coins belonging to different nations, and hence would be applied to by strangers who wished to exchange their own money for the money of the country in which they sojourned. This would take place more particularly in those oriental countries whose inhabitants were accustomed in certain seasons to meet together for the celebration of public festivals. We read in the New Testament † of money-changers who had tables in the Temple of Jerusalem. It is probable they attended for the purpose of giving Jewish money in exchange for those various coins which persons coming from the neighbouring countries might have brought with them. Whether the business of money-changing was carried on as a separate employment, or united with the general business of a merchant, we are not informed ; but it is stated, that the exchangers allowed interest for money lodged in their hands. " Thou wicked and slothful servant, thou oughtest to have put my money to the exchangers, and then at my coming I should have received mine own with usury." ‡ From the circumstance of their allowing interest on money, we may infer that they also lent money on interest ; otherwise they would have had no use for the money they borrowed. This scanty information forms the whole of our knowledge respecting the mode of banking practised by the ancient Babylonian, Egyptian, and Jewish nations.

With respect to the Bankers of Greece we have more ample details :

In Greece the first banks were the temples.

" The wealth and growing estimation of Delphi had also another source, of which information remains only so far as to assure us of the fact with far less explanation of circumstances than for its importance might be desired. In the general insecurity of property in the early ages, and especially in Greece, it was highly desirable to convert all that could be

---

* Genesis xxiii. 16.   † Matthew xxi. 12.   ‡ Matthew xxv. 27.

spared from immediate use into that which might more easily be removed from approaching danger. By a compact, understood among men, with this view the precious metals appear to have obtained their early estimation. Gold, then, and silver having acquired their certain value as signs of wealth, a deposit secure against the dangers continually threatening, not individuals only, but every town and state in Greece, would be a great object of the wealthy. Such security offered nowhere in equal amount as in those temples, which belong not to any single state, but were respected by the common religion of the nation. The priesthood, not likely to refuse the charge, would have a large interest in acquiring the reputation of fidelity to it. Thus Delphi appears to have become the great bank of Greece, perhaps before Homer, in whose time its riches seem to have been already proverbial. Such then was found the value of this institution, that when the Dorian conquerors drove so large a part of the Greek nation into exile, the fugitives who acquired new settlements in Asia, established there their own national bank in the manner of that of their former country, recommending it to the protection of the same divinity. The Temple of Apollo, at Branchidæ, became the great depository of the wealth of Ionia." *

Afterwards the temple of Olympia, like that at Delphi, became an advantageous repository for treasure. But although the temples discharged one of the offices of banks, by being places of security, yet as they did not grant interest on the money deposited, they did not supersede banks of deposit established by private individuals. At Athens especially, banking was a flourishing trade.

"The greater part of the Athenians employ their money in trade, but they are not permitted to lend it for any place but Athens. They receive an interest for the use of it which is not fixed by the laws, but stipulated in a contract, deposited either in the hands of a banker or some friend to both parties. If, for instance, a voyage is to be made to the Cymmerian Bosphorus, the instrument specifies the time of the departure of the vessel, the kind of commodities with which she is to be freighted, the sale which is to be made of them in the Bosphorus, and the merchandize which she is to bring back to Athens; and as the duration of the voyage is uncertain, some agree that their money shall not be payable till the return of the vessel, while others, more timid, and contented with a less profit, require that it shall be repaid at the Bosphorus immediately after the sale of the goods carried out; in which case they either themselves repair to the place where they are to receive it, or send thither some person in whom they can confide, and whom they empower to act for them.

"The lender has his security, either on the merchandize or the goods of the borrower; but as the dangers of the sea are in part risked by the former, and the profit of the latter may be very considerable, the interest of money thus lent may rise as high as thirty per cent., more or less, according to the length and hazards of the voyage.

* Mitford's History of Greece, vol. i. page 193.

" The usury of which I have spoken is known by the name of maritime; that called landed is more oppressive, and no less variable.

"Those who, without risking the dangers of the sea, wish to derive profit from their money, lend it to bankers at the rate of twelve per cent per annum, or rather one per cent. for every new moon. But as the laws of Solon do not prohibit those who have money from demanding the most extravagant interest for it, some persons receive more than sixteen per cent., and others, especially among the lower classes of people, exact every day the quarter of the principal. These extortions are not concealed, and cannot be punished, except by the public opinion, which condemns, but does not sufficiently despise those who are guilty of them.

" Commerce increases the circulation of wealth, and this circulation has given birth to the occupation of bankers, which facilitates it still more. A person who is about to make a voyage, or who fears to keep by him too great a sum of money, lodges it in the hands of these bankers, sometimes only as a trust, and without requiring any interest, and sometimes on condition of sharing with them the profit it shall produce. They advance money to generals who go to take on them the command of armies, or other individuals who stand in need of their assistance.

" In the greater part of bargains made by them, no witness is required ; they content themselves with entering in a register that such a person has deposited in their hands such a sum, which they must repay to such another, if the former should happen to die. It would sometimes be very difficult to prove that they have received a sum of money, were they to deny it ; but if they should expose themselves to such a charge more than once, they would lose the confidence of the public, on which depends their success in the business in which they are engaged.

" By employing the money deposited in their hands, and lending it at a greater interest than they are to pay for it, they amass riches which gain them friends, whose protection they purchase by assiduous services. But all is lost when, unable to call in their money, they are incapable of fulfilling their engagements. They are then obliged to conceal themselves, and can only escape the severity of justice by surrendering all their remaining property to their creditors.

" Those who wish to exchange foreign moneys apply to the bankers, who by different means, as the touchstone and the balance, examine whether they are not adulterated or deficient in weight." *

In a treatise published by Xenophon, upon the Athenian revenue, we meet with the first suggestion for the establishment of a joint-stock bank.

"A very remarkable project, which seems to have been original with Xenophon, next occurs—the establishment of a bank by subscription, open to all the Athenian people. The interest of money, it appears, was enormous at Athens, an unavoidable consequence of the wretched insecurity of person and property. Throughout modern Europe, land is, of

* See Travels of Anacharsis in Greece, by the Abbé Barthelemy, and the authorities there referred to.

all property, esteemed the safest source of income; but in Greece it was held that the surest return was from money lent at interest. For in the multiplied division of Greece into small republics with very narrow territories, the produce of land was continually liable to be carried off or destroyed by an invading enemy, but a moneyed fortune, according to Xenophon's observation, was safe within the city walls. In proportion, then, to the interest of money, and the insecurity of all things, the profits of trade will always be high, and thus numbers would be induced to borrow, even at a high interest. Xenophon therefore proposed, by lending from the public stock, and encouraging commercial adventure by just regulations, to raise a great revenue, and, by the same means, instead of oppressing to enrich individuals. As a corollary, then, to his project, when the amount of the subscription or its profits might allow, he proposed to improve the ports of Athens, to form wharves and docks, to erect halls, exchanges, warehouses, market-houses, and inns; for all which tolls and rents should be paid, and to build ships to be let to merchants. Thus, while numbers of individuals were encouraged and enabled to employ themselves for their private benefits, the whole Athenian people would become one great banking company, from whose profits every member, it was expected, would derive at least an easy livelihood." [*]

At Rome, the bankers were called *Argentarii, Mensarii, Numularii,* or *Collybistæ.* The banking-houses or banks were called *Tabernæ Argentariæ,* or *Mensæ Numulariæ.* Some of these bankers were appointed by the government to receive the taxes, others carried on business on their own account. Their mode of transacting business was somewhat similar to that which is in use in modern times. Into these houses the state or men of wealth caused their revenues to be paid, and they settled their accounts with their creditors by giving a draft or cheque on the bank. If the creditor also had an account at the same bank, the account was settled by an order to make the transfer of so much money from one name to another. To assign over money or to pay money by a draft, was called *perscribere,* and *rescribere;* the assignment or draft was called *attributio.* These bankers, too, were money-changers. They also lent money on interest, and allowed a lower rate of interest on money deposited in their hands. In a country where commerce was looked upon with contempt, banking could not be deemed very respectable. Among most of the ancient agricultural nations, there was a prejudice against the taking of interest for the loan of money. Hence the private bankers at Rome were sometimes held in disrepute, though those whom the government had established as public cashiers,

[*] Mitford's History of Greece, vol. iv. page 22.

or receivers-general, as we may term them, held so exalted a rank, that some of them became consuls.*

The Romans had also loan banks, from which the poor citizens received loans without paying interest. We are told that the confiscated property of criminals was converted into a fund by Augustus Cæsar, and that from this fund sums of money were lent without interest to those citizens who could pledge value to double the amount. The same system was pursued by Tiberius. He advanced a large capital, which was lent for a term of two or three years to those who could give landed security to double the value of the loan. Alexander Severus reduced the market-rate of interest by lending sums of money at a low rate, and by advancing money to poor citizens to purchase lands, and agreeing to receive payment from the produce.

After commerce and the arts had revived in Italy, the business of banking was resumed. The word bank is derived from the Italian word *Banco*, a *bench*—the Jews in Lombardy having benches in the market-place for the exchange of money and bills.† When a banker failed, his bench was broken by the populace; and from this circumstance we have our word *bank-rupt*. Though the States of Venice and Genoa made the most rapid advances in commerce, and established public banks, yet the department of banking appears to have fallen more particularly into the hands of the Florentines. " As the Florentines did not," like the Venetians and the Genoese, " possess any commodious seaport, their active exertions were directed chiefly towards the improvement of their manufactures and domestic industry. About the beginning of the fourteenth century, the Florentine manufacturers of various kinds, particularly those of silk and woollen cloth, appear, from the enumeration of a well-informed historian, to have been very

---

* See Beckmann's History of Inventions, vol. iii. page 19.

† This is the commonly received derivation. A more accurate etymology is that which derives the word from the Italian *Monte* (Latin, *Mons*), a mound, heap, or bank. Thus the Italian *Monte di Pietà* and the French *Mont de Piété* signify " A Charity Bank." Bacon and Evelyn use the word in the same sense. Bacon says, " Let it be no *Bank* or common stock, but every man be master of his own money." Evelyn, adverting to the *Monte di Pietà* at Padua, writes, " There is a continual *bank* of money to assist the poor." Blackstone also : " At Florence, in 1344, government owed 60,000l., and being unable to pay it, formed the principal into an aggregate sum called, metaphorically, a *Mount* or *Bank*."—(Vol. i.)

considerable. The connections which they formed in different parts of Europe, by furnishing them with the productions of their own industry, led them to engage in another branch of trade, that of banking. In this they soon became so eminent, that the money transactions of almost every kingdom in Europe passed through their hands, and in many of them they were intrusted with the collection and administration of the public revenues. In consequence of the activity and success with which they conducted their manufactures and money transactions—the former always attended with certain though moderate profit, the latter lucrative in a high degree, at a period when neither the interest of money nor the premium on bills of exchange were settled with accuracy—Florence became one of the first cities in Christendom, and some of its citizens extremely opulent."[*] Cosmo di Medici was reckoned the most wealthy merchant ever known in Europe, and in a treaty whereby Louis XL engaged to pay Edward IV. fifty thousand crowns annually, it was expressly stipulated that the king of France should engage the partners of the Bank of Medici to become bound for the faithful and regular performance of this agreement on the part of himself and his heirs.[†]

Although the business of banking has probably always been carried on by private individuals before it has been carried on by a public company, yet most countries have found it useful to establish a public or national bank. Some of these banks have been founded for the purpose of facilitating commerce, others to serve the government.

The most ancient bank was that of Venice. It is supposed to have been established in 1157.[‡] The State being involved in debt, through a long and severe war, the public creditors were formed into a corporation, with peculiar privileges, and the debts were allowed to be transferred from one name to another, much in the same way as our public funds, or the stock of our public banks. It was made a particular regulation that all payments of wholesale merchandise, and bills of exchange, should be in bank money; and that all debtors and creditors should be obliged, the one to carry their money to the bank, the other to receive their payments in banco, so that payments

[*] Robertson's Disquisition on India, page 113.
[†] Macpherson's History of Commerce, vol. i. page 698.
[‡] Anderson's History of Commerce, vol. i. page 156.

were made by a simple transfer of stock from one account to the other. This bank may be deemed a wonder for the twelfth century, but requiring much alteration to adapt it to the modes and manners of the nineteenth.*

So early as the year 1349 the business of banking was carried on by the drapers of Barcelona, who were probably the most wealthy class of merchants in that city. But by an ordinance of the king of Arragon, they were not allowed to commence this branch of trade until they had first given sufficient security. In the year 1401 a public bank was established by the magistrates, and the city funds were responsible for the money placed in the bank. They exchanged money, received deposits and discounted bills of exchange, both for the citizens and for foreigners.†

The bank of Genoa was established in 1407. This bank, like that of Venice, owed its origin to the debts of the State. Considerable confusion had arisen from the multitude of loans which the republic had contracted with its citizens. These various loans were now formed into one total amount, and made the capital of the bank. This bank was called the Chamber of St. George, and its management was intrusted to eight directors, elected by the proprietors of the stock. As a security for the debt, the State made over to the bank several cities and territories, among which were the port of Caffa and the little kingdom of Corsica.

The bank of Amsterdam was founded in the year 1609. It was occasioned by the vast quantity of worn and clipped coins then in circulation, in consequence of which the value of the currency was reduced above nine per cent. below that of good money fresh from the mint. The bank received these deficient coins at nearly their intrinsic value, and made all its issues in coin of the standard weight and fineness. At the same

---

* See Montefiore's Commercial Dictionary, Article *Bank.* It was not until 1587 that the Bank of Venice became a bank in the modern sense of the word. The extensive foreign trade of the city brought thither coins of all countries, and in every state of wear. To remedy the loss and inconvenience thus caused, the merchants were ordered to bring their coins to the Bank, where they were weighed, the merchants receiving notes, promising to pay the bearer on demand bullion of the proper or standard fineness, equal to the value of the coins paid in. The Bank was a Bank of Deposit solely—exchanging notes for bullion, and bullion for notes.

† Macpherson's History of Commerce, vol. i. pp. 540, 612.

time a law was made that all foreign bills of exchange should be paid in bank money. This law raised the value of bills on Holland in foreign countries, and compelled every merchant to keep an account at the bank, in order that he might at all times have legal money to pay his foreign bills. The premium (called the Agio) on bank money was regulated by the market price of gold, and was subject to considerable fluctuations. To prevent the gambling to which these fluctuations gave rise, the bank at length determined to sell bank money for currency at five per cent. agio, and to buy it again at four per cent. From this and other sources of profit the bank is supposed to have gained a considerable revenue. It was the entire property of the city of Amsterdam, and was placed under the direction of four burgo-masters, who were changed every year.*

The bank of Amsterdam was the model on which were formed most of the European banks now in existence; but they have varied very considerably from each other, according to the circumstances of the respective countries in which they have been established.

SECTION II.

THE RISE OF BANKING IN ENGLAND.

THE exchanging of money; the lending of money; the borrowing of money; the transmitting of money, are the four principal branches of the business of modern banking. and in most countries they seem to have taken their rise in the order in which they are here named.

MONEY-CHANGING.

For several centuries the only coin current in England was made of silver, and the highest denomination was the silver penny. This coin contained about half as much silver as one of our sixpences. There were also silver half-pence and silver farthings, and frequently the silver pennies were cut into halves and quarters to serve the purpose of half-pence and farthings, until laws were made to prohibit the practice. Copper was not coined in England until the year 1609, and then the small

* Adam Smith's Wealth of Nations, vol. ii. p. 220. Edition 1812.

leaden tokens previously issued by private individuals were suppressed.

Gold was first coined in England in 1257, but soon went out of circulation, and did not enter permanently into currency until 1344, when Edward III. issued gold nobles,* half nobles, and farthing nobles; the noble to pass for 6s. 8d., the half noble for 3s. 4d., and the farthing noble for 1s. 8d. This coinage seems to have given rise to the office of Royal Exchanger :—

"It was not so easy a matter in the times we are now considering to exchange gold and silver coins for each other as it is at present, and, therefore, Edward III. and several of his successors took this office into their own hands, to prevent private extortion as well as for their own advantage, and they performed it by appointing certain persons, furnished with a competent quantity of gold and silver coins, in London and other towns, to be the only exchangers of money, at the following rate :—When these royal exchangers gave silver coins for a parcel of gold nobles, for example, they gave one silver penny less for each noble than its current value, and when they gave gold nobles for silver coins they took one penny more, or 6s. 9d. for each noble, by which, in every transaction, they made a profit of 1 1-5th per cent. These royal exchangers had also the exclusive privilege of giving the current coins of the kingdom, in exchange for foreign coins, to accommodate merchant-strangers, and of purchasing light money for the use of the mint. As several laws were made against exporting English coin, the king's exchangers, at the several seaports, furnished merchants and others who were going beyond seas with the coins of the countries to which they were going, in exchange for English money, according to a table which hung up in their office for public inspection. By these various operations they made considerable profits, of which the king had a certain share. The house in which the royal exchanger of any town kept his office was called the *Exchange*, from which it is probable the public structures where merchants meet for transacting business derive their name." †

This institution continued until the middle of the reign of Henry VIII., when it fell into disuse. It was re-established in 1627, by Charles I., who then issued the following proclamation :—

"Whereas the exchange of all manner of gold and silver current in moneys or otherwise, as the buying, selling, and exchanging of all manner of bullion, in species of foreign coins, billets, ingots, &c., fine, refined, or allayed howsoever, being fit for our mint, hath ever been and ought to be our sole right, as part of our prerogative, royal and ancient revenue, wherein none of our subjects of whatever trade or quality soever, ought at all, without any special licence, to intermeddle, the same being prohibited by divers Acts of Parliament and Proclamations, both ancient and modern.

* So named from the noble nature of the metal they were made of.
† Henry's History of England, vol. viii. page 347.

And whereas ourself and divers of our royal predecessors have, for some time past, tolerated a promiscuous kind of liberty to all, but especially to some of the mystery and trade of goldsmiths in London and elsewhere, not only to make the said exchanges, but to buy and sell all manner of bullion, and from thence some of them have grown to that licentiousness, that they have for divers years presumed, for their private gain, to sort and weigh all sorts of money current within our realm, to the end to cull out the old and new moneys, which, either by not wearing or by any other accident, are weightier than the rest, which weightiest moneys have not only been molten down for the making of plate, &c., but even traded in and sold to merchant-strangers, &c., who have exported the same, whereby the consumption of coins has been greatly occasioned, as also the raising of the silver even of our own moneys to a rate above what they are truly current for, by reason whereof no silver can be brought up to our mint but to the loss of the bringers, &c.—For the reforming of all which abuses we have, by the advice of our Privy Council, determined to assume our said right, for our own profit and the good of the realm, and for this end we do now appoint Henry Earl of Holland and his deputies, to have the office of our changes, exchanges, and out-changes whatsoever, in England, Wales, and Ireland.—And we do hereby strictly charge and command that no goldsmith nor other person whatsoever, other than the said Earl of Holland, do presume to change, &c." *

As this measure occasioned some dissatisfaction, the king authorized, in the following year, the publication of a pamphlet, entitled " Cambium Regis, or the Office of his Majesty's Ex-changer Royal." In this pamphlet it was attempted to be shown :—

" That the prerogative of exchange of bullion for coin has always been a flower of the Crown, of which instances are quoted from the time of King Henry I. downwards. That King John farmed out that office for no smaller a sum than five thousand marks—that the place or office where the exchange was made in his reign was near St. Paul's Cathedral in London, and gave name to the street still called the Old 'Change—that in succeeding reigns there were several other places for those exchanges besides London—that this method continued to Henry the Eighth's time, who suffered his coin to be so far debased that no regular exchange could be made—that the same confusion made way for the London goldsmiths to leave off their proper trade of *goldsmithrie*, *i. e.*, the working and selling of new gold and silver plate, and manufacture, the sole intents of all their charters, and to turn exchangers of plate and foreign coins for our English coins, although they had no right to buy any gold or silver for any other purpose than for their manufacture aforesaid, neither had any other person but those substituted by the Crown a right to buy the same. The king, therefore, has now resumed this office, not merely to keep up his right so to do, but likewise to prevent those trafficking goldsmiths from culling and sorting all the heavy coin, and selling the same to the mint of Holland,

* Anderson's History of Commerce, vol. ii. page 324.

which gained greatly thereby, or else by melting those heavy coins down for making of plate, witness the pieces of thirteenpence-halfpenny, old shillings of Queen Elizabeth, ninepenny and fourpenny-halfpenny pieces, which, being weighty moneys, none of them were now to be met with, whereby they have raised the price of silver to twopence per ounce above the value of the mint, which thereby has stood still ever since the eleventh of King James—that for above thirty years past it has been the usual practice of those exchanging goldsmiths to make their servants run every morning from shop to shop to buy up all weighty coins for the mints of Holland and the East countries, whereby the king's mint has stood still."

Not only the Goldsmiths' Company of London, but the lord mayor, court of aldermen, and common council, petitioned against the revival of the office of the Royal Exchanger. They were not, however, successful, and on a second application of the Goldsmiths' Company, the king told them " to trouble him no farther, since his right to the office was undoubtedly clear." After the death of Charles I. this office was not continued, and the business of money-changing fell again into the hands of the Goldsmiths. Their shops were situated chiefly on the south row of Cheapside, and extended from the street called the Old 'Change unto Bucklersbury.*

MONEY-LENDING.

That part of the business of banking which consists in the lending of money lay, during the Middle Ages, under severe restraints. The taking of interest for the loan of money was deemed sinful, and stigmatized with the name of usury. This opinion appears to be wholly unwarranted, either by the principles of natural equity or the enactments of the Mosaic law. " The taking of interest from Israelites was forbidden by Moses ; not, however, as if he absolutely and in all cases condemned the practice, for he expressly permitted interest to be taken from strangers, but out of favour to the poorer classes of the people. The farther we go back towards the origin of nations, the poorer do we commonly find them, and the more strangers to commerce ; and where this is the case, people borrow, not with a view to profit, but from poverty, and in order to procure the necessaries of life ; and there it must be, no doubt, a great hardship to give back more than has been got. The taking of

* See Maitland's History of London, page 826.

interest from *strangers*, Moses has not only nowhere forbidden, but even expressly authorized it. Hence it is clear that he does by no means represent interest as in itself sinful and unjust. Any such prohibition of interest in our age and country would, without doubt, be unjust towards lenders, and destructive to trade of every description. Among all the remnants of ancient laws, it would be difficult to find one which, in the present state of society, it would be more foolish and hurtful to revive and enforce. It could only suit a state so constituted as was that of the Israelites by Moses."* The taking of interest for the loan of money was first prohibited in England by Edward the Confessor. This law, however, appears to have become obsolete; for, in a council held at Westminster, in the year 1126, usury was prohibited only to the clergy, who, in case they practised it, were to be degraded; and in another Council, held twelve years afterwards, it was decreed that, "such of the clergy as were usurers and hunters after sordid gain, and for the public employments of the laity, ought to be degraded." The earliest mention we find in the English history, of a certain yearly allowance for the usury or interest of money, is in the year 1199, the tenth and last year of Richard the First. In this case the rate of interest was 10 per cent. This appears to have been the ordinary or market-rate of interest from that period until the time of Henry VIII., but there are many instances on record of a much higher rate of interest being taken, especially by the Jews and the Lombards, who, in those times, were the principal money-lenders. The exorbitant interest taken by them is supposed by eminent writers to have been the effect of the prohibition of usury.

The Jews, who were previously famous in foreign countries for their "egregious cunning in trade and in the practice of brokerage," arrived in England about the time of the Conquest, and soon became remarkable for wealth and usury. "The prejudices of the age," says Hume, "had made the lending of money on interest pass by the invidious name of usury; yet the necessity of the practice had still continued it, and the greater part of that kind of dealing fell everywhere into the hands of the Jews, who, being already infamous on account of their religion, had no honour to lose, and were apt to exercise a profession odious in itself by every kind of rigour, and even some-

* See Michaelis's Commentaries on the Laws of Moses. vol. ii. pp. 324 to 342.

times by rapine and extortion. The industry and frugality of this people had put them in possession of all the ready money, which the idleness and profusion common to the English with the European nations enabled them to lend at exorbitant and unequal interest." *   Henry III. prohibited the Jews taking more than twopence a week for every 20s. they lent to the scholars at Oxford.†   This is after the rate of 43l. 6s. 8d. per cent. per annum.   Peter of Blois, Archdeacon of Bath, writes thus to his friend the Bishop of Ely, "I am dragged to Canterbury to be crucified by the perfidious Jews amongst their other debtors, whom they ruin and torment with usury. The same sufferings await me also at London, if you do not mercifully interpose for my deliverance, I beseech you, therefore, O most Rev. Father and most loving friend, to become bound to Samson the Jew for 6l. which I owe him, and thereby deliver me from that cross."‡   The wealth and the rapacity of the Jews occasioned the most cruel proceedings against them on the part of both the populace and the Government.   These persecutions terminated by their expulsion from England in the year 1290.   They were not readmitted until the time of Oliver Cromwell.   On this occasion the Protector summoned an assembly to debate two questions: 1st, whether it were lawful to tolerate the Jews; and 2nd, if it were, on what conditions?   The assembly consisted of two judges, seven citizens of London, among whom were the lord mayor and the sheriffs, and fourteen divines. The judges considered toleration merely as a point of *law*, and declared they knew of no law against it, and that if it were thought useful to the State, they would advise it.   The citizens viewed it in a *commercial* light, and they were divided in their opinions about its utility.   Both these, however, despatched the matter briefly; but the divines violently opposed it by text after text for four whole days. Cromwell was at length so weary that he told them he had hoped they would have thrown some light on the subject to direct his conscience, but, on the contrary, they had rendered it more obscure and doubtful than before; that he desired, therefore, no more of their reasonings, but lest he should do anything rashly, he begged a share in their prayers.

Previous to the expulsion of the Jews, the Lombards had

---

* Hume's History of England, chap. 10.
† Henry's History of England, vol. vi. page 280.
‡ Ibid.

settled in England, and they soon became as great usurers as the Jews themselves. By *Lombards* were generally understood Italian merchants from the four republics of Genoa, Lucca, Florence, and Venice. The foreign commerce of those times was usually carried on by companies of merchants who, on payment of certain duties, were invested by the government with a monopoly of the trade to those countries of which they were natives, and they also possessed peculiar privileges. " As the Lombards engrossed the trade of every kingdom in which they settled, they soon became masters of its cash. Money of course was in their hands not only a sign of the value of their commodities, but became an object of commerce itself. They dealt largely as bankers. In an ordonnance A.D. 1295, we find them styled *mercatores* and *campsores*. They carried on this, as well as other branches of their commerce, with somewhat of that rapacious spirit which is natural to monopolizers who are not restrained by the concurrence of rivals : an opinion which prevailed in the Middle Ages was, however, in some measure the cause of their exorbitant demands, and may be pleaded in apology for them. Commerce cannot be carried on with advantage, unless the persons who lend a sum are allowed a certain premium for the use of their money, as a compensation for the risk which they run in permitting another to traffic with their stock. This premium is fixed by law in all commercial countries, and is called the legal interest of money. But the Fathers of the Church absurdly applied the prohibitions of usury in Scripture to the payment of legal interest, and condemned it as a sin. The schoolmen, misled by Aristotle, whose sentiments they followed, implicitly and without examination adopted the same error and enforced it. Thus the Lombards found themselves engaged in a traffic which was deemed criminal and odious. They were liable to punishment if detected. They were not satisfied, therefore, with that moderate premium which they might have claimed, if their trade had been open and authorized by law. They exacted a sum proportional to the danger and infamy of a discovery. Accordingly we find it was usual for them to demand twenty per cent. for the use of money in the thirteenth century. About the beginning of that century the Countess of Flanders was obliged to borrow money in order to pay her husband's ransom. She procured the sum requisite, either from Italian merchants or from Jews. The lowest interest which she paid to them was above twenty per cent., and some of them exacted near thirty.   In the fourteenth century, A.D. 1311, Philip IV. fixed the interest which might be legally exacted in the fairs of Champagne at twenty per cent.   The interest of money in Arragon was somewhat lower.   James I., A.D. 1242, fixed it by law at eighteen per cent.   As late as the year 1490, it appears that the interest of money in Placentia was at the rate of forty per cent.   This is the more extraordinary, because at that time the commerce of the Italian states was become considerable.   It appears from Lud. Guicciardini that Charles V. had fixed the rate of interest in his dominions in the Low Countries at twelve per cent., and at the time when he wrote, about the year 1560, it was not uncommon to exact more than that sum.   He complains of this as exorbitant, and points out its bad effects both on agriculture and commerce.   This high interest on money is alone a proof that the profits on commerce were exorbitant.   The Lombards were also established in England in the thirteenth century, and a considerable street in the city of London still bears their name.   They enjoyed great privileges, and carried on an extensive commerce, particularly as bankers." *

The English monarchs frequently borrowed money of the Lombards, as well as of other public bodies and of private individuals.   The companies of foreign merchants made advances of money, which were repaid by the duties on their merchandise.   The oldest and wealthiest of these companies, the Steel-Yard Company, was a kind of bank to our kings, whenever they wanted money on any sudden emergency, but the company was sure to be well paid in the end for such assistance.†

In the year 1546 the taking of interest for money was made legal in England, and the rate was fixed at ten per cent.   This Act was repealed in the year 1552, but it was re-enacted in 1571.   The legal rate of interest was reduced to eight per cent. in 1624, and to six per cent. in 1651.   In the year 1714 it was reduced to five per cent. ‡   After the taking of interest was sanctioned by law, the term USURY, which was previously applied to interest in general, became limited, to denote a rate of interest higher than that which the law allowed.

* Robertson's History of Charles V. vol. i., page 257.
† Anderson's History of Commerce, vol. ii. page 192.
‡ Since repealed.

MONEY BORROWING.

That part of the business of banking which consists in the borrowing of money, with a view of lending it again at a higher rate of interest, does not appear to have been carried on by bankers until the year 1645, when a new era occurred in the history of banking. The goldsmiths, who were previously only money-changers, now became also money-lenders. They became also money-borrowers, and allowed interest on the sums they borrowed. They were agents for receiving rents. They lent money to the king on the security of the taxes. The receipts they issued for the money lodged at their houses circulated from hand to hand, and were known by the name of "Goldsmiths' notes." These may be considered as the first kind of bank notes issued in England. The following account of these banking goldsmiths is taken chiefly from Anderson's 'History of Commerce.' *

When our merchants became enriched by commerce, they wished for a place of security in which they might deposit their wealth. Hence they usually sent their money to the mint in the Tower of London, which became a sort of bank. The merchants left their money here when they had no occasion for it, and drew it out as they wanted it. But in 1640, King Charles I. took possession of 200,000*l.* of the merchants' money that had been lodged in the mint,† and from that period the merchants kept their money in their own houses, under the care of their servants and apprentices. On the breaking out of the civil war between Charles I. and the Parliament, it became very customary for the apprentices to rob their masters, and then run away and join the army. As the merchants could now place no confidence either in the public authorities or in their own servants, they were under the necessity of employing bankers.

These bankers were the goldsmiths. Previous to this period, the business of the goldsmiths was similar to what it is in our own time. They bought and sold plate and foreign coins; they procured gold to be coined at the mint, and supplied refiners, plate-makers, and others, with the precious metals. To deal in gold and silver bullion to any large extent, implies the possession of considerable wealth; and as all the money in the country

* Vol. ii. page 402.
† This money was in no long time repaid.

then consisted of gold and silver coin, it was natural enough that the goldsmiths should become the bankers of those who had money for which they had no immediate use.

An account of the bankers of those days is related in a curious pamphlet, published in the year 1676, and entitled, 'The mystery of the new-fashioned Goldsmiths or Bankers discovered.' The author observes:—

"That this new banking business soon grew very considerable. It happened," says he, " in those times of civil commotion, that the Parliament, out of plates and old coins brought into the mint, coined seven millions into half-crowns; and there being no mills then in use at the mint, this new money was of a very unequal weight, sometimes twopence and threepence difference in an ounce, and most of it was, it seems, heavier than it ought to have been in proportion to the value in foreign parts. Of this the goldsmiths made naturally the advantage usual in such cases, by picking out or culling the heaviest, and melting them down and exporting them.

" Moreover, such merchants' servants as still kept their masters' running cash, had fallen into a way of clandestinely lending the same to the goldsmiths at fourpence per cent. per diem, who, by these and such-like means, were enabled to lend out great quantities of cash to necessitous merchants and others, weekly or monthly, at high interest, and also began to discount the merchants' bills at the like or higher interest.

" Much about the same time, the goldsmiths (or new-fashioned bankers) began to receive the rents of gentlemen's estates remitted to town, and to allow them and others who put cash into their hands some interest for it, if it remained but a single month in their hands, or even a lesser time. This was a great allurement for people to put money into their hands, which would bear interest till the day they wanted it; and they could also draw it out by one hundred pounds or fifty pounds, &c., at a time, as they wanted it, with infinitely less trouble than if they had lent it out on either real or personal security.

" The consequence was, that it quickly brought a great quantity of cash into their hands, so that the chief or greatest of them were now enabled to supply Cromwell with money in advance, on the revenues, as his occasion required, upon great advantages to themselves.

" After the Restoration, King Charles II. being in want of money, the bankers took ten per cent. of him barefacedly and by private contracts; on many bills, orders, tallies, and debts of that king, they got twenty, sometimes thirty per cent., to the great dishonour of the government.

" This great gain induced the goldsmiths more and more to become lenders to the king, to anticipate all the revenue, to take every grant of Parliament into pawn as soon as it was given; also to outvie each other in buying and taking to pawn bills, orders, and tallies, so that in effect all the revenue passed through their hands."

The " new-fashioned bankers" were also attacked by Sir

Josiah Child, in his 'New Discourse of Trade,' in the following terms :—

"And principally this seeming scarcity of money proceeds from the trade of bankering, which obstructs circulation, advanceth usury, and renders it so easy, that most men, as soon as they can make up a sum of from 50*l.* to 100*l.*, send it in to the goldsmith, which doth and will occasion, while it lasts, that fatal pressing necessity for money visible throughout the whole kingdom, both to prince and people.

"A seventh accidental reason why land doth not sell at present at the rate it naturally should in proportion to the legal interest, is that innovated practice of *bankers* in London, which hath more effects attending it than most I have conversed with have yet observed; but I shall here take notice of that only which is to my present purpose, viz. :—

"The gentlemen that are bankers, having a large interest from his Majesty for what they advance upon his Majesty's revenue, can afford to give the full legal interest to all persons that put money into their hands, though for never so short or long a time, which makes the trade of usury so easy and hitherto safe, that few, after having found the sweetness of this lazy way of improvement (being by continuance and success grown to fancy themselves secure in it), can be led (there being neither ease nor profit to invite them) to lay out their money in land, though at fifteen years' purchase; whereas before this way of private banking came up, men that had money were forced often times to let it lie dead by them until they could meet with securities to their minds, and if the like necessity were now of money lying dead, the loss of use for the dead time being deducted from the profit of six per cent. (*communibus annis*) would in effect take off 1*l.* per cent. per annum of the profit of usury, and consequently incline men more to purchase lands, because the difference between usury and purchasing would not, in point of profit, be so great as now it is, this new invention of cashiering having, in my opinion, clearly bettered the usurer's trade one or two per cent. per annum. And that this way of leaving money with goldsmiths hath had the aforesaid effect, seems evident to me from the scarcity it makes of money in the country; for the trade of bankers being only in London, doth very much drain the ready money from all other parts of the kingdom." *

In the year 1667 occurred the first RUN of which we have any account in the history of banking. The business of the new-fashioned bankers had increased so fast, and they had become so numerous, that their trade was supposed to be at its height in this year; when, during the time that a treaty of peace was under consideration, the Dutch fleet sailed up the Thames, blew up the fort of Sheerness, set fire to Chatham, and burned four ships of the line. This disaster occasioned great alarm in London, particularly among those who had money in

* Page 45.

o 2

their bankers' hands, as it was imagined that the king would not be able to repay the bankers the money they had lent him. To quiet the fears of the people, the king issued a proclamation, declaring that the payments to the bankers should be made at the Exchequer the same as usual.

In 1672, five years afterwards, a much greater calamity befel the bankers: for King Charles II. shut up the Exchequer, and would not pay the bankers either the principal or the interest of the money which he had borrowed. The amount then due by the king was 1,328,526*l*., which he had borrowed of the bankers at eight per cent., and which he never repaid.

The mode in which the bankers transacted their loans with the king was this: as soon as the parliament had voted to the king certain sums of money out of particular taxes, the bankers advanced at once the money voted by the parliament, and were repaid in weekly payments at the Exchequer as the taxes were received. The mode of making the repayments and the rate of interest were agreed upon at the time of making the loan.

The shutting up of the Exchequer occasioned great distress among all classes of the people. Persons not in trade had then no way of employing their money with advantage but by placing it out at interest in the hands of a banker. Hence, not merchants only, but widows, orphans, and others, became suddenly deprived of the whole of their property. They came in crowds to the bankers, but could obtain neither the principal nor the interest of the money they had deposited. The clamour became so great, that the king granted a patent to pay six per cent. interest out of his hereditary excise ; but he never paid the principal. But, about forty years afterwards, the parliament made arrangements by which the debt was assumed to be discharged.*

The business of banking remained entirely in the hands of the new-fashioned bankers until the establishment of the Bank of England, in the year 1694.

The TRANSMISSION OF MONEY was in ancient times effected by sending a messenger with the coin. During the Middle Ages, it was accomplished by means of bills of exchange, which were purchased by merchants. Ultimately, a class of persons carried on this kind of traffic, and purchased or sold bills to suit the convenience of parties who wished to deal with them. The

---

* That is, it still forms part of the National Debt. The creditors never received a farthing.

pecuniary transactions of independent nations are still adjusted in the same way. But the transmission of money from one part of the country to another part, is more frequently effected upon the principle of transfers, without the passing of any bill. I have explained this mode of operation in my 'Practical Treatise on Banking.'

SECTION III.

THE HISTORY OF THE BANK OF ENGLAND.

THE Bank of England was first projected by Dr. Hugh Chamberlain, but the plan actually adopted was proposed by Mr. William Paterson. The object was to raise money for the use of the government. After the scheme had received the sanction of the ministry, it was brought before the parliament. Here it underwent a long and violent discussion. One party expatiated upon the national advantages that would accrue from such a measure; they said it would rescue the nation out of the hands of extortioners and usurers, lower interest, raise the value of land, revive and establish public credit, extend the circulation, consequently improve commerce, facilitate the annual supplies, and connect the people more closely with the government. The opposition party affirmed that it would become a monopoly, and engross the whole money of the kingdom ; that as it must infallibly be subservient to government views, it might be employed for the worst purposes of arbitrary power ; that instead of assisting, it would weaken commerce, by tempting people to withdraw their money from trade and employ it in stock-jobbing; that it would produce a swarm of brokers and jobbers to prey upon their fellow creatures, encourage fraud and gambling, and thus corrupt the morals of the nation.* Notwithstanding these objections, the Act passed both houses of parliament, and received the royal assent. The following observations upon the establishment of the Bank of England, are taken from Bishop Burnet's ' History of his own Times :'—

"Some thought a bank would grow to be a monopoly, all the money in England would come into their hands, and they would, in a few years, become masters of the wealth and stock of the nation ; but those that were for it argued that the credit it would have must increase trade, and the circulation of money, at least in bank notes. It was visible that all the

* See Smollett's History of England, chap. iv.

enemies of the government set themselves against it with such a vehemence of zeal that this alone convinced all people that they saw the strength that our affairs would receive from it. I had heard the Dutch often reckon up the great advantages they had from their banks; and they concluded that as long as England continued jealous of the government, a bank could never be settled among us, nor gain credit enough to support itself; and upon that, they judged that the superiority in trade must still lie on their side.

"The advantages the king and all concerned in tallies had from the bank were soon so sensibly felt that all people saw into the secret reasons that made the enemies of the constitution set themselves with so much earnestness against it."

The Act of Parliament by which the bank was established, is entitled, "An Act for granting to their Majesties several duties upon tonnage of ships and vessels, and upon beer, ale, and other liquors, for securing certain recompenses and advantages in the said Act mentioned, to such persons as shall voluntarily advance the sum of fifteen hundred thousand pounds towards carrying on the war with France." After a variety of enactments relative to the "duties upon tonnage of ships and vessels, and upon beer, ale, and other liquors," the Act authorizes the raising of 1,200,000*l.* by voluntary subscription, the subscribers to be formed into a corporation, and be styled "The Governor and Company of the Bank of England." The sum of 300,000*l.* was also to be raised by subscription, and the contributors to receive instead annuities for one, two, or three lives. Towards the 1,200,000*l.* no one person was to subscribe more than 10,000*l.* before the first day of July next ensuing, nor at any time more than 20,000*l.* The corporation were to lend their whole capital to government, for which they were to receive interest at the rate of eight per cent. per annum, and 4,000*l.* per annum for management; being 100,000*l.* per annum in the whole. The corporation were not allowed to borrow or owe more than the amount of their capital, and if they did so the individual members became liable to the creditors in proportion to the amount of their stock. The corporation were not to trade in any "goods, wares, or merchandise whatsoever;" but they were allowed to deal in bills of exchange, gold or silver bullion, and to sell any goods, wares, or merchandise upon which they had advanced money, and which had not been redeemed within three months after the time agreed upon.

The whole subscription having been filled in ten days, a charter was issued on the 27th day of July, 1694.

The charter declares—

" That the management and government of the corporation be committed to the governor, deputy-governor, and twenty-four directors, who shall be elected between the 25th day of March and the 25th day of April each year, from among the members of the company duly qualified.

" That no dividend shall at any time be made by the said governor and company, save only out of the interest, profit, or produce arising out of the said capital, stock, or fund, or by such dealing as is allowed by Act of Parliament.

" They must be natural born subjects of England, or naturalized subjects; they shall have in their own name and for their own use, severally, viz., the governor at least 4,000*l.*, the deputy-governor 3,000*l.*, and each director 2,000*l.*, of the capital stock of the said corporation.

" That thirteen or more of the said governors or directors (of which the governor or deputy-governor shall be always one), shall constitute a court of directors for the management of the affairs of the company, and for the appointment of all agents and servants which may be necessary, paying them such salaries as they may consider reasonable.

" Every elector must have, in his own name and for his own use, 500*l.* or more, capital stock, and can only give one vote; he must, if required by any member present, take the oath of stock, or the declaration of stock if it be one of those people called Quakers.

" Four general courts to be held in every year, in the months of September, December, April, and July. A general court may be summoned at any time, upon the requisition of nine proprietors duly qualified as electors.

" The majority of electors in general courts have the power to make and constitute by-laws and ordinances for the government of the corporation, provided that such by-laws and ordinances be not repugnant to the laws of the kingdom, and be conformed and approved, according to the statutes in such case made and provided."

1694. Aug. 8. The rate of discount charged on foreign bills was six per cent., which was the highest legal interest. Aug. 30. The bank discounted foreign bills at four and a half per cent.; and Oct. 24, the discount on inland bills was six per cent.

1695. Jan. 16. The following rates of interest were charged at the bank : foreign bills, having three months to run, six per cent. ; but to those who keep accounts at the bank, foreign bills were discounted at three per cent., and inland bills at four and a half per cent. May 19. Running notes and bills were discounted at three per cent. May 6. The following advertisement appeared in the ' London Gazette :'—" The Court of Directors of the Bank of England give notice, that they will lend money on plate, lead tin, copper, steel, and iron, at four per cent. per annum."

1697. Bank notes were from fifteen to twenty· per cent.

discount. During the recoinage in 1696, the bank had issued their notes in exchange for the clipped and deficient coin previously in circulation, and they were not able to procure from the mint a sufficient quantity of the new coins to discharge the notes presented to them for payment. This compelled them to make two calls of twenty per cent. each upon their stockholders. They paid some of their notes by bills, bearing interest at six per cent. They also advertised, that while the silver was recoining, " such as think it fit, for their convenience, to keep an account in a book with the bank, may transfer any sum under five pounds from his own to another man's account."

Exchequer tallies and orders for payment having, in 1696, been at a discount of forty, fifty, and sixty per cent., and bank notes at a discount of twenty per cent., the bank was empowered to receive subscriptions for the enlargement of their stock ; four-fifths in tallies and orders, and the remaining one-fifth in bank notes. The sum subscribed was 1,001,171*l.* 10*s.*, which, with the original capital of 1,200,000*l.*, raised the capital to the sum of 2,201,171*l.* 10*s.*

The bank charter was extended or renewed until the expiration of twelve months, notice to be given after the first day of August, 1710, and until payment by the public to the bank of the demands therein specified ; being an extension or renewal for five years (8 and 9 William III. c. 20). It was also enacted, " that the common capital and principal stock, and also the real fund of the governor and company, or any profit or produce to be made thereof, should be exempted from any rates, taxes, assessments, or impositions whatever, during the continuance of the bank ;" and that the forgery of the company's seal, or of any of their notes or bills, should be felony without benefit of clergy. The dividend on bank stock this year was nine per cent.

1704. Feb. 28. Foreign bills *made payable at the bank* were charged discount at the rate of four per cent., but if not payable at the bank they were charged five per cent.

1707. The subscription of 1,001,171*l.* 10*s.*, raised in the year 1697, was restored. This reduced the bank capital to the original sum of 1,200,000*l.*

1708. The bank charter was extended or renewed until the expiration of twelve months' notice, to be given after the first day of August, 1732, and until payment by the public to the bank of the demands therein specified ; being an extension or renewal of the said charter for twenty years (7 Anne, c. 7). By this Act it is provided, " That during the continuance of the said corporation of the Governor and Company of the Bank of England, it shall not be lawful for any body politic or corporate whatsoever, created or to be created (other than the said Governor and Company of the Bank of England), or for any other persons whatsoever, united or to be united in covenants or partnership, *exceeding the number of six persons*, in that part of Great Britain called England, to borrow, owe, or take up any sum or sums of money on their bills or notes, payable at demand, or at a less time than six months from the borrowing thereof."

From this year until the year 1729, the annual dividends varied from nine to five and a half per cent.

1709. In this year there was a new subscription of 1,001,171*l.* 10*s.*, another of 2,201,171*l.* 10*s.*, and a call upon the proprietors of fifteen per cent., 656,204*l.* 1*s.* 9*d.* ; altogether making the total capital of the bank, 5,058,547*l.* 1*s.* 9*d.* This increase of capital became necessary, from the bank having in the preceding year lent the government 400,000*l.* without interest, and agreed to cancel one million and a half exchequer bills in their possession, amounting, with interest, to 1,775,027*l.* 17*s.* 10½*d.*

1710. A further call of 501,448*l.* 12*s.* 11*d.*, which increased the bank capital to 5,559,995*l.* 14*s.* 8*d.*

The interest on foreign bills raised from four to five per cent., the same as the inland bills.

1713. The bank charter was extended or renewed until the expiration of twelve months' notice, to be given after the first day of August, 1742, and until payment by the public to the bank of the demands therein specified ; being an extension or renewal of the said charter for ten years (12 Anne, Stat. I. c. ii.). In consideration of receiving this privilege, the bank undertook to circulate 1,200,000*l.* in exchequer bills. In this year the legal rate of interest was reduced from six to five per cent.

1716. July 26. The bank rate of discount on foreign and inland bills reduced to four per cent.

1717. The bank cancelled 2,000,000*l.* exchequer bills, and received interest from the government at five per cent. on the amount.

1718. Subscriptions for government loans were first received at the bank. From this period the government have found it

more convenient to employ the bank as their agents in all
operations of this nature, than to transact them at the treasury
or the exchequer.   The bank, becoming by degrees more closely
connected with the government, began to make advances of
money in anticipation of the land and malt taxes, and upon
exchequer bills and other securities.

1719. April 30. The rate of discount at the bank upon bills
and notes was raised from four to five per cent.

1720. THE SOUTH SEA BUBBLE commenced April 7.

"The directors opened their books for a subscription of one million, at
the rate of 300*l.* for every 100*l.* capital.   Persons of all ranks crowded to
the house in such a manner, that the first subscriptions exceeded two
millions of original stock.   In a few days this stock advanced to 340*l.*, and
the subscriptions were sold for double the price of the first payment.   The
infatuation prevailed till the 8th day of September, when the stock began
to fall.   Then did some of the adventurers awake from their delirium.
The number of the sellers daily increased.   On the 29th day of the month,
the stock had sunk to one hundred and fifty.   Several eminent goldsmiths
and bankers, who had lent great sums upon it, were obliged to stop
payment, and abscond.   The ebb of this portentous tide was so violent,
that it bore down everything in its way, and an infinite number of
families were overwhelmed with ruin; public credit sustained a terrible
shock; the nation was thrown into a dangerous ferment; and nothing was
heard but the ravings of grief and despair.   Some principal members of
the ministry were deeply concerned in these fraudulent transactions.
When they saw the price of stock sinking daily, they employed all their
influence with the bank to support the credit of the South Sea Company.
That corporation agreed, though with reluctance, to subscribe into the
stock of the South Sea Company, valued at 400*l.* per cent., 3,500,000*l.*,
which the company was to repay to the bank on Lady-day and Michaelmas
of the ensuing year.   This transaction was managed by Mr. Robert
Walpole, who with his own hand wrote the minute of agreement, afterwards known by the name of the Bank Contract.   Books were opened at
the bank to take in a subscription for the support of public credit, and
considerable sums of money were brought in.   By this expedient the
stock was raised at first, and those who contrived it, seized the opportunity to realise.   But the bankruptcy of goldsmiths and the sword-blade
company, from the fall of South Sea stock, occasioned such a run upon
the bank, that the money was paid away faster than it could be received
from the subscription.   Then the South Sea stock sunk again, and the
directors of the bank, finding themselves in danger of being involved in
the company's ruin, renounced the agreement; which, indeed, they were
under no obligation to perform, for it was drawn up in such a manner as
to be no more than the rough draft of a subsequent agreement, without
due form, penalty, or clause of obligation." *

* Smollett.

The directors of the South Sea Company took legal advice, with a view to compel the bank to perform their contract; but the matter was arranged through the intervention of the government, who remitted to the South Sea Company two millions sterling as a compensation for the non-performance of the bank contract.

1721. By the 8th Geo. I. c. 21, the South Sea Company were authorized to sell 200,000*l.* per annum, government annuities; and corporations purchasing the same at twenty-six years' purchase were allowed to add the amount to their capital stock. The bank purchased the whole of this 200,000*l.* per annum, at twenty years' purchase, making 4,000,000*l.*

1722. The bank capital increased 3,400,000*l.* by a new subscription. This made the amount of capital 8,959,995*l.* 14*s.* 8*d.* April 23. The rate of discount on bills, reduced from five to four per cent.

1726. The stock called three per cents. 1726, was created this year by the means of a lottery.

1727. The bank advanced to government, 1,750,000*l.* upon the coal and culm duties, at four per cent. interest (1 Geo. II. c. 8).

1728. The bank advanced to government, 1,250,000*l.* upon the lottery, at four per cent. (2 Geo. II. c. 3).

1730. The half-yearly dividend at Lady-day was at the rate of six per cent. per annum, and that at Michaelmas at the rate of five and a half per cent. per annum.

1731. The dividends were the same as in the preceding year.

1732. The dividends were the same as in the preceding year. From this year until the year 1747, the dividends were at the rate of five and a half per cent. per annum.

Thursday, 3rd of August, about one o'clock, the governor, sub-governor, and several of the directors of the bank, came to see the first stone laid of their new building, in Threadneedle Street; and after they had viewed the stone, on which his Majesty's and their several names were engraved, the same was covered with a plate of lead, and that, with the base of a pillar. They then gave twenty guineas to be distributed among the workmen. The following are the names of the directors in this year :—

Sir EDWARD BELLAMY, Governor.

HORATIO TOWNSEND, Deputy-Governor.

ROBERT ALSOP, Alderman.	MATHEW RAPER.
ROBERT ATTWOOD.	MOSES RAPER.
JOHN BANCE.	JOHN RUDGE.
Sir GER. CONYERS, Knt., Ald.	WILLIAM SNELLING.
DELILLERS CARBONELL.	BRYAN BENSON.
Sir JOSEPH EYLES.	STAMP BROOKSBANK.
NATHANIEL GOULD.	CLEMENT BOEHM.
Sir GIL. HEATHCOTE, Knt., Ald.	WILLIAM FAUKENER.
JOHN HANGER.	JAMES GAULTIER.
SAMUEL HOLDEN.	CHRISTOPHER LETHIEULLIER.
WILLIAM HUNT.	HENRY NEAL.
JOSEPH PAICE, Jun.	ROBERT THORNTON.

The last eight were not in the direction the preceding years.

1734. Thursday, 5th of June. The directors began to transact business at their new house in Threadneedle Street. The business of the bank had previously been carried on at Grocers' Hall, in the Poultry. In the hall of the new building was erected a curious marble statue of King William III., with a Latin inscription, of which the following is a translation :—

> For restoring efficacy to the laws,
> Authority to the courts of justice,
> Dignity to the parliament,
> To all his subjects their religion and liberties,
> And
> For confirming these to posterity,
> By the succession of the illustrious House
> Of Hanover
> To the British Throne,
> To the best of Princes, WILLIAM III.,
> Founder of the Bank,
> This Corporation, from a sense of gratitude,
> Has erected this statue,
> And dedicated it to his Memory,
> In the year of Our Lord MDCCXXXIV.,
> And the first year of this building.

1737. Considerable public discussion about the propriety of again renewing the bank charter. The following extracts from the 'London Magazine' of this year will show the sentiments which different writers entertained upon this subject :—

"The bank have power to lend money on land, and no doubt might have put out prodigious sums that way, and have had a better interest for their money than most private people. Had the bank, then, lent out their money on land, they would have strengthened their CREDIT and their

INTEREST, and also extended their usefulness by relieving the landed property, of which there is a great deal at this time in mortgage, most unaccountably, at five per cent., while inferior securities bear a premium at three per cent.

" Another branch of business which the bank have power to transact, but yet never meddle with, is the remittance of money backwards and forwards to London from all the chief trading cities in England, for which they should have proper offices or inferior banks erected in all such cities and towns as they intend to manage a remittance with;—this, besides what profit might be expected upon the remittances, would naturally bring great part of the cash which is circulated in the country to be lodged in their hands.

" I must next observe that in that branch of business in which they do employ themselves, which is that of a *London banker*, they very much contract and narrow their dealings, by refusing to take in payment *the foreign coins*, for which reason it is impracticable with many traders to keep their cash with them.

" This very privilege which the bank has for so long enjoyed, I could demonstrate to be a most heavy burthen upon the people, and a great prejudice to the landed interest as well as the trading interest of this kingdom; for if it had not been for this privilege, we should have had a bank, perhaps, in every county in England, and probably half a dozen different banks in London, by which means no merchant of tolerable credit could ever have been straightened for want of ready money at a low interest when he had occasion for it, nor would any landed gentleman who had a good title to his estate have been obliged to pay such premiums to brokers, or such an interest to mortgagees as they have now generally to pay;—whereas our present bank has never, so far as I have heard, assisted any landed gentleman, nor any merchant, except in and about London only.

" I am of opinion that with respect to the banking trade and the trade to the East Indies, neither the one nor the other can be carried on with such success, or in such an extensive manner, by private adventurers, as by a public company with such an exclusive privilege as our present companies have. The circulating of bank bills or cash notes must certainly increase the current cash of any country, and must, therefore, be of great use in trade; consequently, the more extensive and the more general such a circulation is, the better will it be for the inland trade of that country. It is true, a private man or set of men may, by a long series of good management, gain a very extensive credit, but that credit can never come to be so extensive or near so general as the credit of a rich public company, that has supported itself with honour, perhaps, for some ages ; because the credit of a private man always depends upon himself, so that when he dies, his credit, as to any further circulation, generally dies with him, for it must require some time before those who succeed can revive or regain it ; whereas a public company never dies, nor can their credit meet with any such interruption ; and as their managers are always chosen annually by the company, there is a greater security for its being under good management than a private bank, whose chief managers are appointed by the chance of natural or legal succession: therefore, I shall always think it better for a trading country to have a public bank than to trust entirely to private bankers.

"There certainly never was a body of men that contributed more to the public safety than the Bank of England. This flourishing and opulent company have, upon every emergency, always cheerfully and readily supplied the necessities of the nation, so that there never have been any difficulties—any embarrassments—any delays in raising the money which has been granted by parliament for the service of the public; and it may very truly be said that they have, in very many important conjunctures, relieved the nation out of the greatest difficulties, if not absolutely saved it from ruin."

1738. Dec. 14. The bank commenced issuing post bills, payable seven days after sight, that in case the mail was robbed the parties might have time to stop payment of the bills. Highway robberies appear to have been very frequent at this period.

1742. The bank charter was extended or renewed until the expiration of twelve months' notice, to be given after the first day of August, 1764, and until payment by the public to the bank of the demands in this Act specified, being an extension or renewal of the said charter for twenty-two years (15 Geo. II. c. 13). In consideration of obtaining this charter, the bank lent to government 1,600,000*l.* without interest. To raise this sum the bank made a call upon the proprietors of 840,004*l.* 5*s.* 4*d.*, which increased their capital to 9,800,000*l.* Oct. 18. The rate of discount on bills drawn within the kingdom was raised to five per cent.; bills drawn without the kingdom were still discounted at four per cent.

1745. A RUN upon the bank, occasioned by the rebellion in Scotland, and supposed to be for the purpose of supplying the rebels with gold. A public meeting was held, and one thousand one hundred and forty merchants signed a declaration expressing their readiness to take bank notes.

1746. May 1. The rate of discount on foreign bills reduced from five to four per cent.: inland bills and notes were still charged five per cent. These rates continued until the year 1773. By the 19 Geo. II. c. 6, the bank delivered up to be cancelled 986,000*l.* exchequer bills, in consideration of an annuity of 39,472*l.*, being three per cent. per annum. To raise the above sum the bank made a call of ten per cent. upon their proprietors; this increased the bank capital from 9,800,000*l.* to 10,780,000*l.*

1747. The bank dividend was at the rate of five per cent. per annum. It continued at this rate until the year 1753.

1750. A reduction took place in the interest of part of the national debt. The bank held a court at Merchant-Taylor's Hall, and consented to receive a reduced rate of interest upon 8,486,800*l.* of the debt due to them by the government. The bank also agreed to advance to the government a sum of money to pay off the dissentients.

1751. In order to raise the sum promised to be lent to the government, the bank established what was called "Bank Circulation." Books were opened to the public, and any person might enter his name and the sum he was willing to lend to the bank, *in case it should be called for.* The books being closed, the bank had the power of calling for the whole or any part of the sum subscribed at any time they pleased. The subscribers were to receive 2*s.* per cent. on the total amount of their subscription, and 4*l.* per cent, on the sum actually advanced.

1752. By 25 Geo. II. the balance of annuities granted by 8 Geo. I. was carried to a three per cent. stock, formed in 1731, and they were consolidated into one stock—the new stock is still called "Three per cent. *consols.*" The word *consols* is a contraction for consolidated.

1753. The bank dividend this year was at the rate of four and three-quarters per cent.

1754. The bank dividend was at the rate of four and a half per cent. It continued at this rate until the year 1764.

1757. The government stock, called "Three per cent. reduced," derives its name from the operation of this year. This stock had borne four per cent. until the year 1750; from that time it paid three and a half per cent., and this year it was *reduced* to three per. cent.

1758. It was legally determined that those persons who had given value for bank notes stolen from the mail, had a right to receive payment of them from the bank.

In this year occurred the first instance of the forgery of a bank note. It was committed by a person named R. W. Vaughan, who had been a linendraper at Stafford. The note was for 20*l.*, the smallest amount then in circulation. He was convicted and executed.

1759. The bank commenced issuing notes and post bills of

15*l.* and 10*l.* It was proved by experiment, that five hundred and twelve 10*l.* bank notes weighed one pound.

1764. The bank charter was extended or renewed until the expiration of twelve months' notice, to be given after the first day of August, 1786, and until payment by the public to the bank of the demands therein specified; being an extension or renewal of the said charter for twenty-two years (4 Geo. III. c. 25).

In consideration of obtaining this charter the bank advanced 1,000,000*l.* on exchequer bills until the year 1766, and paid into the exchequer 110,000*l.*

The dividends this year were raised to five per cent. per annum, at which rate they continued until the year 1767.

1767. The bank dividend was raised to five and a half per cent., and was continued at that rate until the year 1781.

1773. The rate of discount on foreign bills raised from four to five per cent. The discount on both foreign and inland remained at five per cent., until the year 1822.

1775. Bankers were prohibited to issue notes of a less amount than 20*s.* (15 Geo. III. c. 51).

1777. Bankers were prohibited to issue notes of a less value than 5*l.* (17 Geo. III. c. 30).

1781. The bank charter was extended or renewed until the expiration of twelve months' notice, to be given after the first day of August, 1812, and until payment by the public to the bank of the demands therein specified; being an extension or renewal of the said charter for twenty-six years (21 Geo. III. c. 60). In consideration of obtaining this renewal of their charter, the bank advanced to the government 2,000,000*l.*, for three years, at three per cent.

The bank dividend raised to six per cent., at which rate it continued till the year 1788.

It is legally decided that the bank is not liable to pay forged notes.

1782. A call of 862,400*l.*, making the total capital of the bank 11,642,400*l.* There was no further increase of capital until the year 1816.

1786. Previous to this year the bank received an allowance from the government on account of the management of the public debt; that is, for trouble in paying the dividends, superintending the transfer of stock, &c., of 562*l.* 10*s.* a million.

It was now reduced to 450*l.* a million; the bank being at the same time entitled to a considerable allowance for trouble in receiving contributions on loans, lotteries, &c. This scale of allowance was continued until the year 1808.

1788. The bank dividend raised to seven per cent., at which rate it continued until the year 1807.

1791. A bill was brought into parliament to render 500,000*l.* of the unclaimed dividends on the public funds available for the service of the public; but the bank agreed to lend that sum to the government without interest, and the bill was withdrawn.

1792. A calculation was made with a view to ascertain the number of days that a bank note of each denomination remained in circulation in this year. The following are the results:—

£			£		
Notes of 10 each, 236 days.			Notes of	50 each, 124 days.	
„ 15	„	114 „	„	100 „	84 „
„ 20	„	209 „	„	200 „	81 „
„ 25	„	74 „	„	300 „	24 „
„ 30	„	95 „	„	500 „	24 „
„ 40	„	65 „	„	1000 „	22 „

1793. An Act of Parliament was passed (33 Geo. III. c. 32), declaring that the bank should not be subject to any penalties for advancing money to the government for the payment of bills of exchange, accepted by the commissioners of his Majesty's treasury, and made payable at the bank. The amount of sums so advanced was required to be annually laid before parliament. According to their original charter, the bank were prohibited lending money to the government without the consent of parliament, under a penalty of three times the sum lent: one-fifth part of which was to go to the informer.

This was a year of great commercial distress: twenty-two commissions of bankruptcy were issued against country bankers.

1794. The bank commenced issuing notes for 5*l.*

1795. The bank having resolved to reduce their discounts, placed the following notice in the discount office:—

" Bank of England, 31st December, 1795.
" Pursuant to an order of the Court of Directors:
" Notice is hereby given,
" That no bills will be taken in for discount at this office after 12 o'clock at noon, or notes after 12 o'clock on Wednesday.
" That in future, whenever the bills sent in for discount shall in any day amount to a larger sum than it shall be resolved to discount on that day, a

D

pro ratâ proportion of such bills in each parcel as are not otherwise objectionable, will be returned to the person sending in the same, without regard to the respectability of the party sending in the bills, or the solidity of the bills themselves.

"The same regulation will be observed as to the notes."

1797. THE SUSPENSION OF CASH PAYMENTS.

This took place on Monday, Feb. 27th, in consequence of an order in council, which ran in the following terms :—

"Upon the representation of the Chancellor of the Exchequer, stating that from the results of the information which he had received, and of the inquiries which it has been his duty to make, respecting the effects of the unusual demand for specie that has been made upon the metropolis, in consequence of ill-founded or exaggerated alarms in different parts of the country; it appears, that unless some measure is immediately taken, there may be reason to apprehend a want of a sufficient supply of cash to answer the exigencies of the public service. It is the unanimous opinion of the Board, that it is indispensably necessary for the public service, that the directors of the Bank of England should forbear issuing any cash in payment, until the sense of parliament can be taken on that subject, and the proper measures adopted thereupon, for maintaining the means of circulation and supporting the public and commercial credit of the kingdom at this important conjuncture; and it is ordered that a copy of this minute be transmitted to the directors of the Bank of England, and they are hereby required, on the grounds of the exigency of the case, to conform thereto until the sense of parliament can be taken as aforesaid."

Among the crowd assembled at the bank, with a view of demanding gold, handbills were distributed, of which the following is a copy :—

                                       "Bank of England, Feb. 27th, 1797.

"In consequence of an order of his Majesty's Privy Council, notified to the bank last night, a copy of which is hereunto annexed, the governor, deputy-governor, and directors of the Bank of England think it their duty to inform the proprietors of the bank stock, as well as the public at large, that the general concerns of the bank are in a most affluent and prosperous situation, and such as to preclude every doubt as to the security of its notes. The directors mean to continue their usual discounts for the accommodation of the commercial interest, paying the amount in bank notes, and the dividend warrants will be paid in the same manner."

On the same day was held a meeting of merchants, bankers, and others, the Lord Mayor in the chair, when the following resolution was unanimously passed :—

"That we, the undersigned, being highly sensible how necessary the preservation of public credit is at this time, do most readily declare, that we will not refuse to receive bank notes in payment of any sum of money to be paid to us, and we will use our utmost endeavours to make all our payments in the same manner.

This resolution was left for signature at several of the most respectable taverns, and a similar resolution was subsequently adopted by other public assemblies.

Immediately afterwards, the House of Commons appointed a committee to enquire into the affairs of the bank. The committee reported, that " The total amount of outstanding demands on the bank, on the 25th of July, was 13,770,390*l.*; and that the total amount of the funds for discharging those demands (not including the permanent debt due from government of 11,686,800*l.*, which bears an interest of three per cent.) was 17,597,280*l.*; and the result is, that there was, on the 25th day of February last, a surplus of effects belonging to the bank, beyond the amount of their debts, amounting to the sum of 3,825,890*l.*, exclusive of the above-mentioned permanent debt of 11,684,800*l.*, due from government." From accounts since published, it appears that the amount of gold and silver in possession of the bank was reduced by the previous run to 1,086,170*l.*

1797. March 3. The bank was authorized to issue notes under 5*l.*; 37 Geo. III. c. 28. It is entitled " An Act to remove doubts respecting promissory notes of the Governor and Company of the Bank of England, for payment of sums of money under 5*l.*" Accordingly, on the 10th of March the bank issued, for the first time, notes for 1*l.* and 2*l.*

May 3. THE BANK RESTRICTION ACT PASSED. It is the 37 Geo. III. c. 45, and is entitled, " An Act for continuing, for a limited time, the restriction contained in the minute of council of the 26th of February, 1797, on payment of cash by the bank." By this Act the bank directors were indemnified against any legal proceedings on account of having complied with the order of council. They were not permitted to issue cash, except for any sum under twenty shillings. But if any person lodged *cash* in the bank, he might be repaid in cash to the extent of three-fourths of the sum lodged; but the sum lodged must not be less than 500*l.* The bank was also allowed to advance to the bankers of London, Westminster, and Southwark, any sum of cash not exceeding in the whole 100,000*l.*; and also 25,000*l.* each to the Bank of Scotland and the Royal Bank of Scotland,

D 2

during the continuance of this Act. The bank could not be sued for payment of any of their notes for which they were willing to give other notes; and no person could be held to special bail upon any process issuing out of any court, unless the affidavit made for the purpose stated, also, that the party had made no offer to pay in bank notes. This Act was to be in force till the 24th day of the following June, a duration of fifty-two days.

1797. June 22. Another Act was passed, continuing the bank restriction until one month after the commencement of the then next session of parliament.

Nov. 30. A third Act passed, continuing the restriction until six months after the conclusion of the war.

An Act was also passed (37 Geo. III. c. 32) suspending the Acts passed in 1777, which prohibited bankers issuing notes below the amount of 5*l.*, and the country bankers commenced issuing notes of 1*l.*

1799. Jan. 3. The bank gave notice, " That on and after the 14th instant, they would pay in cash all fractional sums under 5*l.*; and that on and after the 1st day of February next, the bank will pay cash for all notes of 1*l.* and 2*l.* value that are dated prior to the 1st day of July, 1798, or exchange them for new notes of the same value, at the option of the holders."

This year the bank proprietors received a bonus of ten per cent. on their capital. The bonus was made in five per cents., 1797.

1800. The bank charter was extended or renewed until the expiration of twelve months' notice, to be given after the 1st day of August, 1833, and until payment by the public to the bank of the demands therein mentioned; being an extension or renewal of the said charter for twenty-one years (40 Geo. III. c. 28). In consideration of obtaining this renewal of their charter, the bank agreed to lend the government the sum of 3,000,000*l.* without interest for six years.

The 40 Geo. III. c. 36, was enacted to enable courts of equity to compel a transfer of stock in suits, without making the Bank of England, or the East India Company, or the South Sea Company, partners in the sales.

1801. 41 Geo. III. c. 57, was enacted " For the better prevention of the forgery of the notes and bills of exchange of persons carrying on the business of bankers."

" After July 10th, 1801, no person shall use or make any frame or mould for making paper, with the name or firm of any persons or body corporate appearing in the substance of the paper, without a written authority for that purpose: or shall make or vend such paper, or cause such name or firm to appear in the substance of the paper, whereon the same shall be written or printed,—on penalty of being imprisoned for the first offence, not exceeding two years, nor less than six months; and for the second offence, transported for seven years.

" No person shall engrave, &c., any bill or note of any person or banking company, or use any plate so engraved, or any device for making or printing such bill or note, nor shall knowingly have in his custody such plate or device, or shall utter such bill or note, without a written authority for that purpose, under a like penalty.

" No person shall engrave, &c., on any plate, any subscriptions subjoined to any bill or note of any person or banking company, payable to bearer on demand, or have in his possession any such plate, on penalty, for the first offence, of being imprisoned not exceeding three years, nor less than twelve months; and for the second, transported for seven years."

1801. The proprietors of bank stock received a bonus of five per cent. on their capital in navy five per cents.

1802. The war having been concluded by the peace of Amiens, the Bank Restriction Act would have expired six months afterwards, but it was by a new Act continued in force till the 1st day of March, 1803.

The bank proprietors received a bonus of two and a half per cent. on their capital in navy five per cents.

1803. Feb. 28. The Bank Restriction Act was continued until six weeks after the commencement of the next session of parliament.

Dec. 15. War having recommenced, the Bank Restriction Act was continued until six months after the conclusion of a definitive treaty of peace.

The bank is said to have lost this year no less a sum than 300,000*l.*, through a fraud committed by one of their principal cashiers, Mr. Astlett.

1804. The bank proprietors received a bonus in cash of five per cent. on their capital.

In consequence of the scarcity of silver, the bank issued five-shilling dollars. These dollars had on the obverse side an impression of his Majesty's head, and the following superscription: " Georgius III. Dei Gratia Rex;" and on the reverse side, the impression of Britannia and the following: " Five shillings dollar. Bank of England, 1804." The bank subsequently issued silver tokens for three shillings, and for one shilling and sixpence. By an Act passed in 1812, the counterfeiting these dollars and tokens was liable to a punishment of fourteen years' transportation.

By 44 Geo. III. c. 98, the following duties were imposed upon the notes of country bankers :—

						£	s.	d.
Not exceeding £1	1s.	. . .	. . .			0	0	3
Exceeding . .	1	1	not exceeding £2	2s.		0	0	6
,, . .	2	2	,,	5	5	0	0	9
,, . .	5	5	,,	20	0	0	1	0

These duties continued until the year 1808.

1805. The bank proprietors received another bonus of five per cent. in cash.

1806. Another bonus of five per cent. in cash.

1807. The dividend on bank stock was raised from seven to ten per cent., at which rate it continued until the year 1823.

1808. The allowance from the government to the bank for managing the public debt, reduced from 450l. a million to 340l. a million, on six hundred millions of the debt, and to 300l. a million on all that it exceeded that sum. This was exclusive of some separate allowances on annuities, &c.

By 48 Geo. III. c. 149, the following duties were imposed upon country bank notes :—

						£	s.	d.
Not exceeding £1	1s.	. . .	. . .			0	0	4
Exceeding . .	1	1	not exceeding £2	2s.		0	0	8
,, . .	2	2	,,	5	5	0	1	0
,, . .	5	5	,,	20	0	0	1	6
,, . .	20	0	,,	30	0	0	3	0
,, . .	30	0	,,	50	0	0	4	6
,, . .	50	0	,,	100	0	0	7	6

These duties remained the same until the year 1815.

1810. THE BULLION COMMITTEE, appointed by the House of Commons for the purpose of inquiring into the causes of the high price of gold bullion, and its effect on the circulating medium.

The committee delivered a very long report, in which they discussed a variety of matters connected with the currency, and concluded by recommending that the bank should resume cash payments at the end of two years. The following are extracts :—

" Your committee have found that the price of gold bullion which, by the regulation of his Majesty's mint, is 3*l*. 17*s*. 10½*d*. per ounce of standard fineness, was, during the years 1806, 1807, and 1808, as high as 4*l*. in the market. Towards the year of 1808 it began to advance very rapidly, and continued very high during the whole year 1809, the market price of standard gold fluctuating from 4*l*. 9*s*. to 4*l*. 12*s*. per oz. The market price at 4*l* 10*s*. is about 15½ per cent. above the mint price.

" Your committee have likewise found, that towards the end of the year 1808 the exchanges with the continent became very unfavourable to this country, and continued still more unfavourable through the whole of 1809, and the three first months of the present year.

" Mr. Whitmore, the late governor of the bank, stated to the committee, that in regulating the general amounts of the loans and discounts, he did ' not advert to the circumstance of the exchanges, it appearing upon a reference to the amount of our notes in circulation, and the course of the exchange, that they frequently have no connection.'

" Mr. Pearse, now governor of the bank, agreed with Mr. Whitmore in this account of the practice of the bank, and expressed his full concurrence in the same opinion. Mr. PEARSE,—' In considering this subject with reference to the manner in which bank notes are issued, resulting from the applications made for discounts to supply the necessary want of bank notes, by which their issue in amount is so controlled that it can never amount to an excess; I cannot see how the amount of bank notes issued can operate upon the price of bullion, or the state of exchanges ; and therefore I am individually of opinion that the price of bullion or the state of the exchanges can never be a reason for lessening the amount of bank notes to be issued, always understanding the control which I have already described.'

" The bank directors, as well as some of the merchants who have been examined, showed a great anxiety to state to your committee a doctrine, of the truth of which they professed themselves to be most thoroughly convinced; that there can be no possible excess in the issue of Bank of England paper, so long as the advances in which it is issued are made upon the principles which at present guide the conduct of the directors —that is, so long as the discount of mercantile bills is confined to paper of undoubted solidity, arising out of real commercial transactions, and payable at short and fixed periods. That the discounts should be made only upon bills growing out of real commercial transactions, and falling due in a fixed and short period, are sound and well established principles. But that while the bank is restrained from paying in specie, there need be no other limits to the issue of their paper than what is fixed by such rules of discount; and that during the suspension of cash payments, the discount of good bills falling due at short periods cannot lead to any excess in the amount of bank paper in circulation, appears to your committee to be a doctrine wholly erroneous in principle, and pregnant with dangerous consequences in practice.

" Upon a review of all the facts and reasonings, which have been submitted to the consideration of your committee in the course of this inquiry, they have formed an opinion, which they submit to the House— That there is at present an excess in the paper circulation of this country, of which the most unequivocal symptom is the very high price of bullion; and, next to that, the low state of the continental exchanges : that this excess is to be ascribed to the want of a sufficient check and control in the issues of paper from the Bank of England, and originally to the suspension of cash payments, which removed the natural and true control.

" Your committee would suggest, that the restriction on cash payments cannot safely be removed at an earlier period than two years from the present time ; but your committee are of opinion that early provision ought to be made by Parliament for terminating, at the end of that period, the operation of the several statutes which have imposed and continue that restriction."

This report was delivered late in the session, and was not taken into consideration by the House until the following year.

1811. The commercial distress of the country had become so great, that Parliament authorized the sum of six millions to be advanced to merchants on their giving sufficient security ; but such had been the fall in the price of mercantile property, that not many could give the required security, and bankruptcies were numerous. Whether this distress arose from any preparations of the bank to return to cash payments, from the American embargo, or from Buonaparte's Berlin and Milan decrees, was a matter of much controversy. From the accounts since published, it does not appear that the bank had taken any measures to increase their stock of gold ; but during the years 1810, 1811, and 1812, they considerably reduced their private securities and increased the amount of their public securities. Thus on the last day of February, 1810, their public securities were 14,322,634*l.*, and their private securities 21,055,946*l.* On the same day in 1813, their public securities were 25,036,626*l.*, and their private securities 12,894,324*l.* This progressive reduction of the discounts no doubt occasioned great distress, though it was in some degree counteracted by an increase in the same period of above two millions in the circulation.

The report of the Bullion Committee was taken into consideration by the House of Commons, and after much discussion rejected. Instead of the measures recommended by the committee, the House adopted certain resolutions proposed by Mr. Vansittart (afterwards Lord Bexley), declaring that the value of bank notes was not depreciated, but that the value of gold was enhanced ; and that the political and commercial relations of Great Britain with foreign states were sufficient to acc00nt for the unfavourable state of the foreign exchanges and the high price of bullion.*

July 24. Lord Stanhope's Act passed. This Act (51 Geo. III. c. 127) is entitled, "An Act for making more effectual provision for preventing the current gold coin of the realm from being paid or accepted for a greater value than the current value of such coin ; for preventing any note or bill of the Governor and Company of the Bank of England from being received for any smaller sum than the sum therein specified ; and for staying proceedings upon any distress by tender of such notes." It enacts that the taking of gold coin at more than its value, or Bank of England notes for less than their value, shall be deemed a misdemeanour. This Act was to be in force until the 25th of March, 1812. It was introduced by the Earl of Stanhope, in consequence of the following notice having been addressed by Lord King to his tenantry :—

"By lease, dated 1802, you have contracted to pay the annual rent of 47*l.* 5*s.* in good and lawful money of Great Britain. In consequence of the late great depreciation of paper money, I can no longer accept any bank notes at their nominal value in payment or satisfaction of an old contract. I must, therefore, desire you to provide for the payment of your rent in the legal gold coin of the realm ; at the same time, having no other object than to secure payment of the real intrinsic value of the same, stipulated by agreement, and being desirous to avoid giving you any unnecessary trouble, I shall be willing to receive payment in either of the manners following, according to your option :—1st. By payment in guineas : 2nd. If guineas cannot be procured, by a payment in Portugal gold coin, equal in weight to the number of guineas requisite to discharge the rent : 3rd. By a payment in bank paper, of a sum sufficient to purchase (at the present market price) the weight of standard gold requisite to discharge the rent. The alteration in the value of paper money is estimated in this manner : the price of gold, in 1802, the year of your agreement, was 4*l.* an ounce ; the present market price is 4*l.* 14*s.*, arising from the diminished value of paper. In that proportion an addition of 17*l.* 10*s.* per cent. in paper money will be required as the equivalent for the payment of rent in paper."†

* Thus repudiating the principles laid down in the report, now universally accepted, that when the market or paper price of gold bullion exceeds the mint price (3*l.* 17*s.* 10½*d.*), it is not gold which has risen in value, but paper which has become depreciated ; that the difference between the two prices is the measure of this depreciation ; and the only sound mode of rectifying the exchanges is the timely contraction of its discounts by the bank as the drain of bullion for exportation sets in, the creation and confirmation of public confidence by liberality at seasons of severe pressure, and enlargement of its issues as the exchanges become favourable.

† A cutting sarcasm on the resolutions proposed and carried by Mr. Vansittart.

1812. "An Act passed for the further prevention of the counterfeiting of silver tokens issued by the Governor and Company of the Bank of England, called *dollars*, and of silver pieces issued and circulated by the said Governor and Company, called *tokens*, and for the further prevention of frauds practised by the imitation of the notes or bills of the said Governor and Company" (52 Geo. III. c. 138).

Lord Stanhope's Act continued, by 52 Geo. III. c. 5, until three months after the commencement of the next session of parliament.

1814. Lord Stanhope's Act revived and continued, by 54 Geo. III. c. 52, during the continuance of the Bank Restriction Act.

1815. The following stamp duties were imposed upon the notes of country bankers (55 Geo. III. c. 184):—

	£	s.			£	s.			s.	d.
Not exceeding	1	1	. . . .			. .	.	0	5
Exceeding . .	1	1	and not exceeding	2	2	. .		0	10
„ . .	2	2	„	5	5	. .		1	3
„ . .	5	5	„	10	0	. .		1	9
„ . .	10	0	„	20	0	. .		2	0
„ . .	20	0	„	30	0	. .		3	0
„ . .	30	0	„	50	0	. .		5	0
„ . .	50	0	„	100	0	. .		8	6

1815. Peace being restored, the Bank Restriction Act would have expired six months afterwards, but it was continued by a new Act until the 5th July, 1816.

1816. The Bank Restriction Act continued from July, 1816, to July, 1818.

The bank was authorized to increase its capital from 11,642,400*l.* to 14,553,000*l.*, being an addition of twenty-five per cent. to the stock of the several proprietors. This addition was made out of the surplus profits without any further call (56 Geo. III. c. 96). In consideration of obtaining this privilege, the bank agreed to lend the government the sum of 3,000,000*l.* at three per cent.

1817. April 17. The bank gave notice that on and after the second day of May then next ensuing, they would pay cash for all notes of 1*l.* and 2*l.* value dated prior to the first day of January, 1816, or exchange them for new notes of the same value, at the option of the holders.

Sept. 18. The bank gave notice that on and after the first day of October then next ensuing, they would be ready to pay cash for their notes, of every description, dated prior to the first day of January, 1817.

1818. The Bank Restriction Act continued from the 5th July, 1818, to 5th July, 1819.

A calculation was made this year, to ascertain the number of days that a bank note of each denomination remained in circulation. The following are the results:—

£			£		
Notes of 1 and 2*l.*.	147 days.	Notes of	40	. .	38 days.
„ 5 . . .	148 „	„	50	. .	72 „
„ 10 . . .	137 „	„	100	. .	49 „
„ 15 . . .	66 „	„	200	. .	18 „
„ 20 . . .	121 „	„	300	. .	14 „
„ 25 . . .	43 „	„	500	. .	14 „
„ 30 . . .	55 „	„	1000	. .	13 „

The bank had always been in the practice of detaining the forged notes offered for payment. But two persons, who had forged notes returned to them by the bank, paid the amount and kept the notes. They were charged with having forged notes in their possession, and tried on this charge, but the juries acquitted them. In consequence of this decision the bank have since returned all forged notes to the parties presenting them, after having stamped them in several places with the word "forged."

1819. A bill passed through parliament in the course of two nights to restrain the bank paying away any more gold under its notice of September, 1817, or any previous notice. A committee of the House of Commons had reported that the bank had paid away above five millions in gold; the greater part of which had been taken to the continent, and there re-coined into foreign money.

From an account submitted to parliament, of the total amount of outstanding demands on the Bank of England, and the funds for discharging the same, it appears that there was a surplus in favour of the bank of 5,202,320*l.*, independently of their capital of 14,686,800*l.*

MR. PEEL'S BILL PASSED. This bill (59 Geo. III. c. 49) contains the following provisions :—

1. The Bank Restriction Act was continued, absolutely, from the 5th of July, 1819, to February 1, 1820.

2. Between February 1 and October 1, 1820, the bank were required to pay their notes in gold bullion of standard fineness at the rate of 4*l.* 1*s.* per ounce, but not to be liable to a demand for a less quantity than sixty ounces at one time.

3. Between October 1, 1820, and May 1, 1821, the bank were required to pay their notes in gold bullion upon the same plan, at the rate of 3*l.* 19*s.* 6*d.* per ounce.

4. Between May 1, 1821, and May 1, 1823, the bank were to pay in gold bullion upon the same plan, at the rate of 3*l.* 17*s.* 10½*d.* per ounce, which was the mint price of gold.

5. From May 1, 1823, the bank were to pay their notes in the gold coin of the realm.

6. But between February 1 and October 1, 1820, the bank might make payments at a less rate than 4*l.* 1*s.*, and not less than 3*l.* 19*s.* 6*d.* per ounce; and between October 1, 1820, and May 1, 1821, the bank might pay at any rate less than 3*l.* 19*s.* 6*d.*, and not less than 3*l.* 17*s.* 10½*d.*, on giving three days' notice in the Gazette. Such payments to be made in ingots or bars of gold, of the weight of sixty ounces. The bank were also permitted to pay in gold coin on or after May 1, 1822.

7. All the laws which restrained the exportation of gold and silver coin were repealed, and the coin was allowed to be exported or melted without incurring any penalty.

The bill did not give satisfaction to the bank directors. They wished to be allowed to pay their notes in gold bullion at the market price of the day.

The 59 Geo. III. c. 76, was passed to prohibit the bank making advances to government without the authority of parliament. But the bank were allowed to purchase exchequer bills, or to advance money on them, but the amount of such bills was to be laid annually before parliament.

1820. An Act passed for the further prevention of forging and counterfeiting of bank notes (1 Geo. IV. c. 92). It also enacted, that the names of persons authorized by the bank directors to sign the notes, might be impressed by machine instead of being subscribed in the handwriting of such persons.

1821. The bank commenced paying off their notes under 5*l.* in gold. The directors had procured an Act of Parliament, 1 & 2

Geo. IV. c. 26, permitting them to do so from the first day of May, 1821. The gold coins issued by the bank were not guineas, but sovereigns of the value of twenty shillings, which were now first coined. The gold coined at the mint this year amounted to 9,520,758*l.*, and the silver to 433,686*l.*

1822. In this year an Act was passed permitting the country bankers to continue the issuing of notes under 5*l.* until the expiration of the bank charter in 1833. As the law previously stood, their notes were prohibited on the resumption of cash payments by the bank. The directors made the following reference to this subject, in a memorandum they delivered to the parliamentary committee of 1832 :—

" By the resolution of the House of Commons of 1819, the bank were required, within four years, to pay off in gold the amount of their one-pound notes then in circulation (about 7,500,000*l.*) ; further, to provide the coin for paying off the country small notes in 1825 (about seven or eight millions more) ; in addition to which the necessity was imposed of providing the requisite surplus bullion for insuring the convertibility of all their liabilities, which addition of bullion to their then stock could not be estimated at less than 5,000,000*l.*; making in the aggregate 20,000,000*l.* of gold as necessary to be provided from foreign countries, within the space of four years from 1819.

" That supply of gold could only be purchased by reduced prices of commodities ; the bank withdrawing a given amount of securities, in the first instance, the notes for which might be reissued in payment of the-gold as imported. The low prices and general state of trade, from 1819 to 1821, and the withdrawal of the bank's securities, enabled the bank to cancel their small notes in the latter year; and in the following (1822) three years prior to the time fixed by parliament, they were in a situation to furnish the gold for paying off the country small notes, when, without any communication with the bank, the government thought proper to authorize a continuance of the circulation of the country small notes until 1833. The consequence of that measure was, to leave in the possession of the bank an inordinate quantity of bullion (14,200,000*l.* in January, 1824); and further, to afford the power of extension to the country bankers' issues, which it is believed were greatly extended, from 1823 to 1825."

By a return from the Stamp Office, it appears that the number of country banks this year was five hundred and fifty-two, and the number of persons in those firms was one thousand six hundred and seventy-three.

1822. June 22. The bank reduced the rate of interest upon bills of exchange from five to four per cent., and extended the time of such bills from sixty-one to ninety-five days.

In this year the government reduced the interest of the navy five per cents. to four per cent. Each holder of 100*l.* stock received 105*l.* new stock, bearing four per cent., with a guarantee that the interest should not be farther reduced until the year 1829. This new stock was distinguished by the name of "new fours." The bank agreed to advance the money to pay off the dissentients.

1822. In consequence of the abolition of the notes under 5*l.*, the bank found they had many more clerks than was necessary. A good number were, therefore, discontinued ; the bank giving them either a pension, or the value of a pension in ready money, at the option of the clerks. The conduct of the bank on this occasion was highly liberal, and met with universal approbation.

1823. Lady-day. The dividend on bank stock was reduced from ten to eight per cent.

The bank engaged to advance to government, between April, 1823, and April, 1828, the sum of 13,089,419*l.*, for the purpose of defraying the charge of military and naval pensions, and to receive in lieu of this sum 585,740*l.* per annum ; to commence from the 5th of April, 1823, and to continue for a term of forty-four years, and then to cease. This charge is commonly called " the dead weight."

In the latter end of this year the bank commenced advancing money upon the security of government stock. They also lent 1,500,000*l.* to the East India Company.

1824. The bank extended their advances upon stock, and commenced lending money on mortgage.

The old four per cents. were reduced to three and a half per cent. The new stock is called "Three and a half per cent. reduced."

This and the subsequent year were remarkable for the commencement of a great number of joint-stock companies. The total number of projects was six hundred and twenty-four, and to carry them all into effect would have required a capital of 372,173,100*l.* They have been thus classified :—*

		Capital. £
74	Mining Companies	38,370,000
29	Gas ditto	12,077,000
20	Insurance ditto	35,820,000
29	Investments ditto	52,600,000
54	Canal Railroad ditto	44,051,000
67	Steam ditto	8,555,500
11	Trading ditto	10,450,000
26	Building ditto	13,781,000
24	Provision ditto	8,360,000
292	Miscellaneous ditto	148,108,600
624		£372,173,100

The above companies are divided by Mr. English into four classes. First, companies which continued to exist in the year 1827 ; secondly, companies whose shares had been sold in the market, but were afterwards abandoned ; thirdly, companies which published prospectuses, or which were announced in the papers, but which are not known to have issued shares ; fourthly, companies the formation of which was noticed in the public papers, but the particulars not specified.

The following is the general summary :—

Companies.	Capital required. £	Amount actually advanced. £
127 Companies existing in 1827	102,781,600	15,185,950
118 ditto abandoned	56,606,500	2,419,675
236 ditto projected	143,610,000	
143 ditto ditto not particularized	69,175,000	
624	£372,173,100	£17,605,625

Besides the capital required for the above companies, large sums of money were granted as loans to foreign powers, as appears from the following table :—

---

* See A Complete View of the Joint-stock Companies formed during the years 1824 and 1825, by Henry English.

A list of the foreign loans contracted in England, with the amounts of the same, the names of the contractors, the years in which the contracts were made, and the prices at which they were issued.

	£	Per Cent.			Per Cent.
Austrian . . .	2,500,000	5	N. M. Rothschild . .	1823	82
Brazilian . . .	3,200,000	,,	T. Wilson & Co . .	1824	75
Ditto	2,000,000	,,	N. M. Rothschild . .	1825	85
Buenos Ayres .	1,000,000	6	Baring Brothers . . .	1824	85
Chili	1,000,000	,,	Hullett Brothers . .	1822	70
Columbian . .	2,000,000	,,	Herring, Graham, & Co.	1822	84
Ditto	4,750,000	,,	B. A. Goldschmidt & Co.	1824	88¼
Danish	5,500,000	3	T. Wilson & Co . .	1825	75
Greek	800,000	5	Loughnan & Co . .	1824	59
Ditto	1,000,000	,,	Ricardos.	1825	56½
Guatemala . .	1,428,571	6	I. & A. Powles . . .	1825	73
Guadaljava . .	600,000	5	W. Ellward, Jun. . .	1825	60
Mexican . . .	3,200,000	,.	B. A. Goldschmidt & Co	1824	58
Ditto	3,200,000	6	Barclay, Herring, & Co.	1825	89¼
Neapolitan. . .	2,500,000	5	N. M. Rothschild . .	1824	92¼
Prussian . . .	5,000,000	,,	Ditto	1818	72
Ditto	3,500,000	,,	Ditto	1822	84
Portuguese . .	1,500,000	,,	B. A. Goldschmidt & Co.	1823	87
Peruvian . . .	450,000	6	Frys and Chapman . .	1822	88
Ditto.	750,000	,,	Ditto	1824	82
Ditto	616,000	,,	Ditto	1825	78
Russian . . .	3,500,000	5	N. M. Rothschild . .	1822	82
Spanish . . .	1,500,000	,,	A. F. Haldimand . . .	1821	56
Ditto	1,500,000	,,	J. Campbell & Co. . .	1823	30¼

1825. At the commencement of this year there was every appearance of general prosperity, but in December occurred "THE PANIC."

The course of exchange being unfavourable, had occasioned a demand for gold for exportation. The bank became under the necessity of restraining its issues.

The house of Sir Peter Pole and Co., who were agents to several country banks, stopped payment. This occasioned a general alarm, and the notes of private bankers became discredited throughout the country. As the bank had ceased to issue notes under 5*l*., they were obliged to find gold to the country bankers to pay off their notes; but their gold failing, they reissued their 1*l*. notes, some of which, happily, had not been destroyed. Notwithstanding the great liberality of the bank, several London bankers, and a much greater number of country bankers, were obliged to suspend their payments. Most of the joint-stock companies, that had been formed in the season of speculation, fell to the ground.*

The following is the opinion of J. H. Palmer, Esq., the governor of the bank, as to the causes of the wild spirit of speculation which had preceded the panic :—

" Will you state to the committee what, in your opinion, was the nature and the march of the crisis in 1825 ?—I have always considered that the first step towards the excitement was the reduction of the interest upon the government securities ; the first movement in that respect was, I think, upon 135,000,000*l.* of five per cents., which took place in 1823. In the subsequent year, 1824, followed the reduction of 80,000,000*l.* of four per cents. I have always considered that reduction of interests, one-fifth in one case, and one-eighth in the other, to have created the feverish feeling in the minds of the public at large, which prompted almost everybody to entertain any proposition for investment, however absurd, which was tendered. The excitement of that period was further promoted by the acknowledgment of the South American republics by this country, and the inducements held out for engaging in mining operations, and loans to those governments, in which all classes of the community in England seem to have partaken almost simultaneously. With those speculations arose general speculation in commercial produce, which had an effect of disturbing the relative values between this and other countries, and creating an unfavourable foreign exchange, which continued from October, 1824, to November, 1825, causing a very considerable export of bullion from the bank, about seven millions and a half. Commercial speculations had induced some bankers, one particularly, to invest money in securities not strictly convertible, to a larger extent than was prudent ; they were also largely connected with country bankers. I allude to the house of Messrs. Pole and Co., a house originally possessed of very great property, in the persons of the partners, but which fell with the circumstances of the times. The failure of that banking-house was the first decisive check to commercial and banking credit, and brought at once a vast number of country bankers, which were in correspondence with it, into difficulties. That discredit was followed by a general discredit throughout London and the interior."

Some of the other witnesses considered the panic to have arisen from an over-issue of notes on the part of the Bank of England and the country bankers. But whatever may have

---

* The crisis was at its height from Monday, the 12th, to Saturday, the 17th December. Up to the night of Wednesday the bank restricted its issues, to the ruin of houses of first-rate importance. Becoming sensible of its error, it discounted liberally the three last days of the week, issuing upwards of 5,000,000*l.* of notes ; otherwise, the ruin would have been universal.

F.

been the cause, the bank certainly acted with great liberality at the period of the alarm, even at the risk of its own stoppage of payment.

" Will you describe the manner in which the bank lent its assistance at that time ?—We lent it by every possible means, and in modes that we never had adopted before.   We took in stock as security, we purchased exchequer bills, we made advances on exchequer bills, we not only discounted outright, but we made advances on deposit of bills of exchange to an immense amount ; in short, by every possible means consistent with the safety of the bank ; and we were not, upon some occasions, over nice ; seeing the dreadful state in which the public were, we rendered every assistance in our power.

" Did any communication take place between the bank and the government respecting an order in council to restrain payments in gold at that period ?—Yes ; it was suggested by the bank.

" What answer did his Majesty's government give to that ?—They resisted it from first to last.

" The Bank of England issued one-pound notes at that period.   Was that done to protect its remaining treasure ?—Decidedly ; and it worked wonders, and it was by great good luck that we had the means of doing it : because one box containing a quantity of one-pound notes had been overlooked, and they were forthcoming at the lucky moment.

" Had there been no foresight in the preparation of these one-pound notes ?—None whatever, I solemnly declare.

" Do you think that issuing of the one-pound notes did avert a complete drain ?—As far as my judgment goes, it saved the credit of the country."

Evidence of Jeremiah Harman, Esq. (p. 154.)

On the last day of December, 1825, the coin and bullion in the bank amounted to only 1,260,890*l.*

Dec. 13. The bank raised the rate of discount from four to five per cent. upon bills not having more than ninety-five days to run.   This rate continued until July, 1827.

1826. Jan. 13. The government made a communication to the bank directors, stating their intention, in order to prevent a recurrence of panic, to propose to parliament the gradual abolition of country bank notes under 5*l.* ; and also proposing to the bank,

" First, That the Bank of England should establish branches of its own body in different parts of the country.

" Secondly, That the Bank of England should give up its exclusive privilege as to the number of partners engaged in banking, except within a certain distance from the metropolis."

The directors were at first unwilling to establish branches, but ultimately they acceded to both the above propositions.

The government also induced the bank to make advances upon the security of goods, and accordingly the bank established boards for this purpose at the following places, and advanced to the undermentioned amounts :—

	£			£
Manchester	115,490	Huddersfield	. .	30,300
Glasgow	81,700	Birmingham	. .	19,600
Sheffield.	59,500	Dundee	. . .	16,500
Liverpool	41,450	Norwich	. . .	2,400

To carry these measures into effect several Acts of Parliament were passed, viz :—

"An Act to facilitate the advancing of money by the Governors and Company of the Bank of England, upon deposits and pledges" (7 Geo. IV. c. 7). It was enacted that persons in possession of bills of lading, warrants, &c., should be deemed owners of the goods therein mentioned, so far as to make valid any contracts for the advance of money thereupon by the Bank of England.

"An Act to limit, and after a certain period to prohibit, the issuing of promissory notes, under a limited sum, in England" (7 Geo. IV. c. 6). By this Act, no further notes under 5*l.* were allowed to be stamped, and those already stamped could not be issued or reissued after the 5th of April, 1829, under a penalty of 20*l.* The Bank of England were required to make monthly returns to the treasury, of the weekly amounts of their notes in circulation under 5*l.*, to be published in the Gazette, and laid before parliament. And after the 5th of April, 1829, all bankers' notes under 20*l.* were to be made payable at the place of issue, though they might also be made payable at other places.

"An Act for the better regulating copartnerships of certain bankers in England," &c. (7 Geo. IV. c. 46.) According to this Act—

1. Banks having more than six partners might carry on business in England at a greater distance than sixty-five miles from London, provided they have no establishment as bankers in London, and that all the partners are liable for the whole debts of the bank.

2. The banks shall not issue their notes at a place within

E 2

sixty-five miles from London, nor draw any bills on London for a less amount than 50*l.*

3. The banks may sue, and be sued, in the name of their public officers; and when judgment is obtained against such public officers, execution may be issued against any member of the copartnership.

4. Previous to issuing notes, the bank shall deliver to the Stamp Office, schedules containing the name or title of the bank —the names and places of abode of all the partners—the names of the places where the banks are established—and the names and descriptions of the public officers in whose name the bank wishes to sue and be sued.

5. These banks are allowed to compound for the stamp duties on their notes, at the rate of seven shillings per annum for every 100*l.* in circulation.

By the fifteenth clause of this Act, the Bank of England was expressly authorized to establish branches. This was enacted to "prevent any doubts that might arise" upon the subject. The bank accordingly opened branches this year at Gloucester, Manchester, and Swansea.

1827. July 5. The bank reduced the rate of discount from five to four per cent.

The extension of the branches of the Bank of England this year occasioned great dissatisfaction among the country bankers. The establishment of rival banks in their own neighbourhood, was a circumstance that the country bankers could not view with indifference. They declared that the Bank of England, and not themselves, had been the cause of the previous spirit of speculation; that the Bank of England, by their advances to government and loans on mortgage, had made excessive issues, and that now to extend their influence, at the expense of the country bankers, was to reward the guilty and to punish the innocent. The country bankers had been accustomed to charge five per cent. on the bills they discounted, and at some places five or six shillings commission besides the discount, but the branches of the Bank of England charged only four per cent. without any commission. The country bankers were of course compelled to do business on the same terms, or to permit their customers to go to the branch. The chief advantage the country bankers possessed over the branch banks was, that they continued to allow interest on deposits, which the branch banks did not. But the additional confidence which was then possessed by the branch banks may, notwithstanding, have induced some depositors to give them a preference to the country bankers.

On December 7, the country bankers held a meeting at the London Tavern, Bishopsgate Street, where they passed several resolutions, and appointed a deputation to wait upon Lord Goderich, the first Lord of the Treasury, and Mr. Herries, the Chancellor of the Exchequer. Among other resolutions were the following:—

" That the late measures of the Bank of England in the establishment of branch banks have the evident tendency to subvert the general banking system that has long existed throughout the country, and which has grown up with, and been adapted to the wants and conveniences of the public.

" That it can be distinctly proved that the prosperity of trade, the support of agriculture, the increase of general improvement, and the productiveness of the national revenue, are intimately connected with the existing system of banking.

" That the country bankers would not complain of rival establishments, founded upon equal terms; but they do complain of being required to compete with a great company, possessing a monopoly and exclusive privileges.

" That should this great corporation, conducted by directors who are not personally responsible, succeed, by means of these exclusive advantages, in their apparent object of supplanting the existing banking establishments, they will thereby be rendered masters of the circulation of the country, which they will be enabled to contract or expand according to their own will, and thus be armed with a tremendous power and influence, dangerous to the stability of property and the independence of the country."

At a meeting held at the same place, on the 16th of December, Sir John Wrottesley, Bart., M.P., the chairman, reported to the meeting the result of the interview of the deputation with Lord Goderich and the Chancellor of the Exchequer on that day, and read their answer as follows: "Lord Goderich and the Chancellor of the Exchequer stated to the deputation, that they were fully sensible of the great importance of the subjects which were brought before them by the deputation; and that, although it was obviously impossible that they could undertake, on the part of the government, to express upon that occasion any opinion upon the matters under consideration, they could assure the deputation that all that had been communicated should receive the most deliberate and serious attention."

The country bankers complained, too, that the branch banks, instead of meeting them on the footing of equality, had refused to take their notes, unless the bankers had previously opened accounts with the branch banks, and provided funds for the purpose.

1828. Another subject of complaint on the part of the country bankers.—The Bank of England had always issued their notes and post-bills unstamped, in consideration of paying, as a composition for the stamp duties, 3500*l*. per annum on every 1,000,000*l*. in circulation. When the branches were established they issued bills, drawn upon the parent establishment in London, at twenty-one days after date, without being stamped, alleging that these were included in their composition. At the same time the country bankers could not draw bills upon London without paying the stamp duty. In a memorial, presented to the government by the bankers in the town and neighbourhood of Birmingham, it was shown that the stamp duty on a bill drawn at twenty-one days on London, is three shillings and sixpence, while under the composition the Bank of England would pay but fivepence; and that a circulation throughout the year of 10,000*l*., in bills of exchange of 20*l*. each, would subject the Bank of England to a payment, in lieu of stamp duty, of only 35*l*., while other banks would have to pay 650*l*. An Act of Parliament (9. Geo. IV. c. 23) was accordingly passed, to enable country bankers to compound for their stamp duties on the same terms as the Bank of England, and to include bills drawn upon London at twenty-one days' date in the composition. By this law the country bankers have the advantage of paying duty only on the amount of notes in circulation.

1828. May 9. "The humble memorial of the country bankers in England and Wales," was presented to "the Lords Commissioners of his Majesty's Treasury" against the branch banks. It concludes thus :—

"Your memorialists therefore deeply regret that your lordships do not feel justified in adopting measures for the withdrawal of the branch banks, and they hope that your lordships will be pleased, as far as lies in your lordships' power, to prevent any interference with the business of your memorialists; and that your lordships will be pleased to institute an inquiry into the system of country banking, and take into your lordships' consideration the claims of the country bankers to be regarded as parties in the intended application for the renewal of the bank charter, and that no special privilege or monopoly be granted or continued to the governor and company of the Bank of England; but that they may be placed on a perfect equality with country bankers in the competition which, by means of their branches, they are now carrying on with your memorialists."

The government replied, " that the interests of the country bankers should not be neglected in any negotiation between the government and the Bank of England for the renewal of the bank charter."

1830. The government reduced the interest on the new four per cent. stock to three and a half per cent. This stock was formed in the year 1822, by the reduction of the navy five per cents. to four per cent. The holders had the option of receiving for every 100*l.* new four per cents. either 100*l.* stock at three and a half per cent., not redeemable until the year 1840, or 70*l.* at five per cent., not redeemable until the year 1873. Most of the holders chose the former. This stock is called " *new* three and a half per cent.," and amounts to above 139,000,000*l.* The other stock, formed by those who chose the 70*l.*, is called the new five per cents., and amounts to little more than 466,000*l.*

1831. "An account of the amount of silver coin melted; also the loss sustained by the Bank of England thereby, in 1831."

	£
Amount of silver coin melted in bars	565,000
Ditto, melted and re-coined.	35,000
	£600,000

	£	s.	d.
Loss on sixpenny pieces	4,601	1	3
Loss on other denominations	62,982	19	2
	£67,584	0	5

1832. May 22. A committee of secrecy was appointed by the House of Commons, to inquire into the expediency of renewing the charter of the Bank of England, and into the system on which banks of issue in England and Wales are conducted.

The committee was composed of the following members :—

Lord Viscount Althorp	Mr. J. Smith	Mr. Haywood
Sir R. Peel, Bart.	Mr. Robarts	Lord Visct. Ebrington
Lord John Russell	Sir M. Ridley, Bart.	Mr. Lawley
Mr. Goulburn	Mr. Attwood	Sir. J. Wrottesley, Bart.
Sir J. Graham, Bart.	Sir J. Newport, Bart.	Lord Cavendish

Mr. Herries	Mr. Baring	Mr. Alderman Wood
Mr. Poulett Thomson	Mr. Irving	Mr. Strutt
Mr. Courtenay	Mr. Warburton	Mr. Bonham Carter
Colonel Maberly	Mr. G. Phillips	Mr. E. J. Stanley
Sir H. Parnell, Bart.	Mr. J. Morrison	Mr. Ald. Thompson
Mr. Vernon Smith	Lord Viscount Morpeth	

On the 11th day of August the committee delivered the following report :—

" The secret committee appointed to inquire into the expediency of renewing the charter of the Bank of England, and into the system on which banks of issue in England and Wales are conducted, and to whom the petition of certain directors of joint-stock banking companies in England was referred, and who were empowered to report the minutes of evidence taken before them, have agreed upon the following report :—

" Your committee have applied themselves to the inquiry which the House has committed to them, by calling for all the accounts which appeared to them necessary for the purpose of elucidating the affairs of the Bank of England, and have examined evidence for the purpose of ascertaining the principles on which it regulates the issues of its notes, and conducts its general transactions. They feel bound to state that the directors of the Bank of England have afforded to them every facility in their power, and have most readily and candidly answered every question which has been put to them, and produced every account which has been called for. The committee have also examined such witnesses as appeared to them, from their practical knowledge and experience, most likely to afford information on the important subjects under their consideration, who have all been ready to give the committee the most ample information.

" The principal points to which they have directed their attention are—

" *First.*—Whether the paper circulation of the metropolis should be confined, as at present, to the issues of one bank, and that a commercial company ; or whether a competition of different banks of issue, each consisting of an unlimited number of partners, should be permitted.

" *Secondly.*—If it should be deemed expedient that the paper circulation of the metropolis should be confined, as at present, to the issues of one bank, how far the whole of the exclusive privileges possessed by the Bank of England are necessary to effect this object.

" *Thirdly.*—What checks can be provided to secure for the public a proper management of banks of issue, and especially whether it would be expedient and safe to compel them periodically to publish their accounts.

" With respect to the circulation of paper in this country, the committee have examined,—*First*, into the effect produced by the establishment of the branch banks of the Bank of England; and *secondly*, into the expediency of encouraging the establishment of joint-stock banks of issue in the country.

" On all these, and on some collateral points, more or less information will be found in the minutes of evidence; but on no one of them is it so complete as to justify the committee in giving a decided opinion.

" The period of the session at which the committee commenced their labours, the importance and extent of the subjects, and the approaching close of the session, will sufficiently account to the House for the limited progress of the inquiry, and for the incompleteness of the materials which have been collected for the purpose of forming an opinion;—they have thought it better, therefore, to submit the whole of the evidence which they have taken, with a very few exceptions, to the consideration of the House.

" In their opinion, no public inconvenience will arise from this publication. The only parts of the evidence which they have thought it necessary to suppress, are those which relate merely to the private interests of individuals.

" The House will perceive that the committee have presented, as part of the evidence which they have taken, the actual amount of bullion at different times in the hands of the Bank of England. This information has never before been given to the public; it is, however, very essential to a complete knowledge of the subject, and if it had been suppressed by the committee, many parts of the evidence would have been unintelligible, and a false impression would have been produced in the minds of the public, that the bank were not so well provided with bullion as is desirable, which might have a very injurious effect. The House will, however, observe that the bank is amply provided with bullion at the present time; and it does not, therefore, appear to the committee that this information being now given to the public can be productive of any injurious consequences.

" The committee, however, by no means wish it to be understood, from their having felt themselves called upon to include this evidence in their report, that they have formed any opinion as to the propriety of periodically publishing the affairs of this or of any other bank of issue. There appears to be a difference between a publication of the affairs of the bank when an inquiry is instituted for the purpose of deciding whether the bank charter shall be renewed or not, and a periodical publication during the course of its ordinary transactions.

" Of the ample means of the Bank of England to meet all its engagements, and of the high credit which it has always possessed and which it continues to deserve, no man who reads the evidence taken before this committee can for a moment doubt; for it appears that, in addition to the surplus rest in the hands of the bank itself, amounting to 2,880,000*l.*, the capital on which interest is paid to the proprietors, and for which the state is debtor to the bank, amounts to 14,553,000*l.*, making no less a sum than 17,433,000*l.* over and above all its liabilities."

The following years were remarkable for a great increase in the profits of the bank—1786, 1796, 1800, 1805, 1806, 1814, 1815, 1816, 1822.

1786. In the year ending February, 1786, the profits were 976,194*l.*;

being an increase of 124,970*l.* over that of the preceding year, and 122,540*l.* over the following year. We find that between the last day of February, 1785 and 1786, the circulation of notes had increased from 5,923,090*l.* to 7,581,960*l.* : this no doubt was the main cause of the profits ; for the deposits, the public securities, and the private securities had all decreased ; and what was also unfavourable, a considerable increase had taken place in the stock of bullion. It seems likely that this increase of bullion did not occur till the latter end of the year, and the diminution of profits in the following years arose from keeping up this large amount of bullion.

1796. This year the profits had increased from 887,668*l.* to 1,114,028*l.* A great reduction had taken place in the circulation in the course of this year, but this decrease had probably been gradual, so that there was a profit for a good part of the year on the large amount ; and on the other hand, there was an increase of above 500,000*l.* in the private securities or discounts, and a much larger decrease in the stock of bullion. The diminution in the amount of bullion was about the same amount as the diminution of the circulation, and was no doubt occasioned by a demand for gold upon the bank, in consequence of the unfavourable state of the foreign exchanges. This issue of gold, while confined to the amount the bank had previously on hand, would not diminish their profits. The gold might as well be in circulation as be confined in the coffers of the bank.

1800. This year the profits increased from 942,568*l.* to 2,129,048*l.* By reference to Table II. we find there was a great increase in the circulation —the public securities and the private securities,— and a diminution in the amount of bullion. All these are favourable to an increase of profits.

1805. In this year the profits were much larger than those of the preceding year, having increased from 1,109,938*l.* to 1,371,038*l.* This arose from a great increase in the deposits, and also in the public securities.

1806. The profits again increased from 1,371,038*l.* to 1,674,038*l.* The cause of this is not very evident. The circulation, and the private securities, and the amount of bullion, were about the same as the preceding year. A reduction of 2,000,000*l.* had also taken place in the public securities. We should imagine there would be a reduction of profit, rather than an increase. Possibly, however, the public securities which were parted with were sold at a much higher price than they cost, and hence might arise a considerable profit.

1814. The profits advanced from 1,494,620*l.* to 1,765,700*l.*, arising from an increase in the circulation, an increase in the deposits, and a considerable increase in the private securities.

1815. An increase of profits, arising from an increase in the circulation and in the public securities.

1816. An increase of profit, from 1,857,950*l.* to 2,172,410*l.* This profit seems to have risen chiefly from an increase in the private securities. Possibly some profit was also realized from the large reduction of the public securities. The profit on the increase in the deposits was not equivalent to the loss upon the increase of bullion.

1822. Here the profits rose from 1,092,780*l.* to 1,971,880*l.*, while every source of profit appears diminished. The circulation, the deposits, the public and the private securities, were all considerably less than in the preceding year, and the average stock of bullion much increased. The only way of accounting for this extraordinary profit, is to suppose that it was realized by the sale of public securities. They were reduced from 16,010,990*l.* to 12,478,133*l.*

I shall now notice those years in which there was a diminution of profits.

1790. In this year the profits were only 671,438*l.*; and this, with an increase in the circulation, the deposits, and the public securities. But, on the other hand, there was a great falling off in the private securities, and an increase in the amount of bullion.

1798. The profits were only 841,068*l.*, while the preceding year they amounted to 924,988*l.*, and the following year to 942,568*l.*, while there was a great increase in the circulation and the deposits. But there was also a great increase of bullion; from 1,086,170*l.* it was raised to 5,828,940*l.* This year, it will be recollected, was the period of the Bank Restriction Act being passed, and no doubt the bank went to great expense in order to obtain gold.

1804. The profits fell from 1,359,828*l.* to 1,109,938*l.*, notwithstanding an increase in the circulation, the deposits, and the public securities. There was, however, a diminution in the private securities.

1809. A fall in the profits from 1,481,670*l.* to 1,156,600*l.*, in consequence, it would appear, of a fall in the deposits.

1817. A fall of profit from 2,172,410*l.* to 1,316,780*l.*, in consequence of a fall in the deposits, and an immense fall in the private securities. There was also an increase in the amount of bullion. This was the first year after the termination of the war.

1818. In this year the profits fell still lower, being only 911,480*l.* There was a further fall in the deposits, and a still greater fall in the private securities; and also an increase in the average stock of bullion.

1819. The profits this year appear to be only 362,580*l.*, notwithstanding a considerable increase in the private securities, and a great reduction in the stock of bullion. The bank returns are not sufficiently minute to enable us to account for this falling off. It may have been occasioned by losses, expenditure on bank buildings, &c., but we have no *data* upon which to form any conjecture on the subject.

: 0. The profits, though still below the average, were a considerable advance on the preceding year, notwithstanding a reduction in the deposits and in the private securities. It appears, however, that there was a considerable reduction in the average stock of bullion.

1828. The profits were reduced from 1,186,280*l.* to 917,670*l.*, in consequence of a reduction in the private securities, and an increase of bullion.

1830. An apparent fall of profits from 1,209,490*l.* to 930,790*l.* This, however, is only apparent; as a portion of the losses by Fauntleroy's forgeries, amounting to 250,000*l.*, were passed to the debit of the profit and loss account this year.

The profits of the bank are derived from the following sources:—First, The interest on their capital, which is lent to the public at three per cent. Secondly, the use of the rest, or surplus capital. Thirdly, the use of the capital raised by the circulation and the deposits. Fourthly, the allowance they receive as agents for transacting the business of the government. There is another source of profit, arising from the accidental destruction of notes that are in circulation. The amount cannot be ascertained, but it may be presumed, from the following account, that the sum is not inconsiderable:—

An account of the amount of bank notes in circulation, of dates beyond five, ten, fifteen, and twenty years respectively:—

	£
Bank notes of 5*l.* and upwards, and post bills outstanding, dated prior to 1st January, 1812	280,380
Ditto, dated between 1st January, 1812, and 1st January, 1817	95,600
Ditto, dated between 1st January, 1817, and 1st January, 1822	149,860
Ditto, dated between 1st January, 1822, and 1st January, 1827	511,490
Bank notes of 5*l.* and upwards, and post bills	1,037,330
The bank are unable to state what amount of 1*l.* and 2*l.* notes is outstanding of the dates above specified, but the present amount is	297,000

An account of all distributions made by the Bank of England amongst the proprietors of bank stock, whether by money payments, transfer of five per cent. annuities, or otherwise, under the heads of bonus, increase of dividend, and increase of capital, betwixt the 25th February, 1797, and 31st March, 1832, in addition to the ordinary dividend of seven pounds per cent. on the capital stock of that corporation existing in 1797 ; including therein the whole dividend paid since June, 1816, on their increased capital, stating the period when such distributions were made and the aggregate amount of the whole :—

	£
In June, 1799, 10l. per cent. bonus in Five per Cents. 1797, on 11,642,400l. is	1,164,240
May, 1801, 5l. ditto Navy Five per Cents. ditto	582,120
Nov., 1802, 2½l. ditto ditto ditto	291,060
Oct., 1804, 5l. ditto Cash ditto	582,120
Oct., 1805, 5l. ditto ditto ditto	582,120
Oct., 1806, 5l. ditto ditto ditto	582,120
From April, 1807, to Oct., 1822, both inclusive · · Increase of dividend at the rate of 3l. per cent. per annum, on 11,642,400l., is 16 years	5,588,352
From April, 1823, to Oct., 1831, both inclusive · Increase of dividend at the rate of 1l. per cent. per annum, on 11,642,400l., is 9 years	1,047,816
In June, 1816, increase of capital at 25l. per cent. is	2,910,600
From Oct., 1816, to Oct., 1822, both inclusive · Dividend at the rate of 10l. per cent. per annum, on 2,910,600l. increased capital is 6½ years . .	1,891,890
From April, 1823, to Oct., 1831, both inclusive · Dividend at the rate of 8l. per cent. per annum on 2,910,600l. increased capital is 9 years . . .	2,095,632
Aggregate amount of the whole	17,318,070
Annual dividend payable on Bank Stock in 1797, on a capital of 11,642,400l., at the rate of 7l. per cent. per annum . . .	814,968
Annual dividend payable since June, 1816, on a capital of 14,553,000l. to October, 1822, inclusive, at the rate of 10l. per cent. per annum	1,455,300
Annual dividend payable from April, 1823, to 31st March, 1832, both inclusive, on a capital of 14,553,000l., at the rate of 8l. per cent. per annum	1,164,240

1833. May 31. A meeting of the proprietors of bank stock was held at the Bank of England, to receive a communication from the court of directors, of the result of the negotiation with his Majesty's government, respecting the renewal of the bank charter. The following letter from Lord Althorp, the Chancellor of the Exchequer, was read by the secretary :—

"Downing Street, May 2, 1833.

" GENTLEMEN,

"After duly considering the conversation I have had with you, the substance of which I have reported to my colleagues, his Majesty's government have directed me to make the following proposals to you for the purpose of renewing the bank charter.

" 1. We propose to renew the charter for twenty-one years, subject, however, to this condition :—that if at the end of ten years the then existing government should so think fit, they may give a twelvemonth's notice to the bank that the charter shall expire at the end of eleven years.

" 2. That no banking company consisting of more than six partners shall issue notes payable on demand within the metropolis, or within sixty-five miles from the metropolis. Banking companies, however, consisting of any number of partners established at a greater distance from the metropolis than sixty-five miles, shall have the right to draw bills on London without restriction as to their amounts, and to issue notes payable in London.

" 3. Bank of England notes shall be a legal tender, except at the Bank of England, or at any of its branches.

" 4. Bills not having more than three months to run before they become due, shall not be subject to the usury laws.

" 5. An account, similar to that laid before the bank committee, of the amount of bullion and securities in the hands of the bank, and of the amount of notes in circulation, and of the deposits in the hands of the bank, shall be transmitted, as a confidential paper, weekly, to the Chancellor of the Exchequer : these accounts shall be consolidated at the end of each quarter, and the average state of the bank accounts for the preceding quarter published quarterly in the Gazette.

" A bill will also be introduced into Parliament, with the view of regulating country banks. The provisions of this measure will be such as to hold out an inducement to the establishment of joint-stock banks who will not issue their own notes.

" His Majesty's government desire me to call your attention to the advantages which these different propositions are likely to confer upon the bank. Their tendency must be to extend the circulation of its notes, and by relieving bills at short dates from the usury laws to facilitate its operations. While, on the other hand, the only relaxation in its exclusive privileges, as they at present exist, which is required—is the permission given to joint-stock banks, established at a greater distance than sixty-five miles from the metropolis, to draw bills and to issue notes payable in London. His Majesty's government, therefore, think that they have a right to expect some considerable pecuniary advantages from the bank in the management of the government business. They consequently propose that government should repay to the bank twenty-five per cent. of the debts of 14,500,000*l.* now due, and that the bank should deduct from the payments made to them from the government for the transaction of the government business the annual sum of 120,000*l.*

" I hope that this proposal will be satisfactory to the bank directors, and that by making this arrangement an end may be speedily put to the suspense now existing.

" I have the honour to be,
" Gentlemen,
" Your most obedient humble Servant,
" ALTHORP.

" To the Governor and Deputy-Governor
　　of the Bank of England."

After some discussion, the further consideration of this letter was adjourned to a future meeting.

In the same evening Lord Althorp brought forward the subject in the House of Commons. Besides the measures that were connected with the Bank of England, he announced the measures for regulating country banks. These were—

1. That government should have the power of granting charters to joint-stock banks issuing notes beyond sixty-five miles from London, and to joint-stock banks within the sixty-five miles, provided they issued only the notes of the Bank of England.

2. That the joint-stock banks which issued notes should be required to pay up one half of their capital, and all the shareholders be answerable individually to the full extent of their property.

3. That the joint-stock banks which did not issue their own notes should be required to pay up only one fourth of their capital, and the shareholders be responsible only to the amounts of their shares.

4. That the government when granting the charter should have the power to decide whether the amount of capital subscribed was a sufficient amount for the place in which the bank was situated.

5. That each private bank should be required to send a statement of its accounts to the government in London, as a strictly confidential paper, which was not to be published in a separate form, but, the accounts being added together, the total results should be given to the public periodically.

6. That to enable the government to know the total amount of notes in circulation, each private bank, as well as each joint-stock bank, should be compelled to compound for the stamp duties.

The Bank of England proprietors agreed, at a subsequent meeting, to the measures which had a reference to them.   But the country bankers expressed great dissatisfaction ; and on the 12th of June they presented a memorial to Earl Grey, the first Lord of the Treasury, and to Lord Althorp, the Chancellor of the Exchequer, upon the subject.   In consequence of the opposition of the country bankers, Lord Althorp postponed his measures for the regulation of the private and joint-stock banks, and carried forward his plan for the renewal of the charter of the Bank of England.   The following bill was ultimately passed into a law :—

An Act for giving to the corporation of the Governor and Company of the Bank of England certain privileges, for a limited period, under certain conditions, was passed August 29, 1833.

" Whereas an Act was passed in the 39th and 40th years of the reign of his Majesty King George III., intituled, An Act for establishing an agreement with the Governor and Company of the Bank of England, for advancing the sum of 3,000,000*l*. towards the supply for the service of the year 1800: and whereas it was by the said recited Act declared and enacted, that the said governor and company should be and continue a corporation, with such powers, authorities, emoluments, profits, and advantages, and such privileges of exclusive banking, as are in the said recited Act specified, subject nevertheless to the powers and conditions of redemption, and on the terms in the said Act mentioned : and whereas an Act passed in the 7th year of the reign of his late Majesty King George IV., intituled, An Act for the better regulating co-partnerships of certain bankers in England, and for amending so much of an Act of the 39th and 40th years of the reign of his late Majesty King George III., intituled, An Act for establishing an agreement with the Governor and Company of the Bank of England for advancing the sum of 3,000,000*l*. towards the supply for the service of the year 1800, as relates to the same: and whereas it is expedient that certain privileges of exclusive banking should be continued to the said governor and company for a further limited period, upon certain conditions : and whereas the said Governor and Company of the Bank of England are willing to deduct and allow to the public, from the sums now payable to the said governor and company for the charges of management of the public unredeemed debt, the annual sum hereinafter mentioned, and for the period in this Act specified, provided the privilege of exclusive banking specified in this Act is continued to the said governor and company for the period specified in this Act."

Bank of England to enjoy an exclusive privilege of banking upon certain conditions :—

" May it therefore please your Majesty that it may be enacted, and be it enacted by the King's most excellent Majesty, by and with the advice and consent of the lords spiritual and temporal, and commons, in this present Parliament assembled, and by the authority of the same, that the said Governor and Company of the Bank of England shall have and enjoy such exclusive privilege of banking as is given by this Act, as a body corporate, for the period and upon the terms and conditions hereinafter mentioned, and subject to termination of such exclusive privilege at the time and in the manner in this Act specified."

During such privilege, no banking company of more than six persons to issue notes payable on demand, within London or sixty-five miles thereof :—

"And be it further enacted, that during the continuance of the said privilege, no body politic or corporate, and no society, or company, or persons united or to be united in covenants or partnerships, exceeding six persons, shall make or issue in London, or within sixty-five miles thereof, any bill of exchange or promissory note, or engagement for the payment of money on demand, or upon which any person holding the same may obtain payment on demand, provided always, that nothing herein or in the said recited Act of the 7th year of the reign of his late Majesty King George IV. contained shall be construed to prevent any body politic or corporate, or any society or company, or incorporated company or corporation, or co-partnership, carrying on and transacting banking business at any greater distance than sixty-five miles from London, and not having any house of business or establishment as bankers in London, or within sixty-five miles thereof (except as hereinafter mentioned), to make and issue their bills and notes, payable on demand or otherwise, at the place at which the same shall be issued, being more than sixty-five miles from London, and also in London, and to have an agent or agents in London, or at any other place at which such bills or notes shall be made payable for the purpose of payment only, but no such bill or note shall be for any sum less than 5*l.*, or be re-issued in London, or within sixty-five miles thereof."

Any company or partnership may carry on the business of banking in London, or within sixty-five miles thereof, upon the terms herein mentioned :—

"3. And whereas the intention of this Act is, that the Governor and Company of the Bank of England should, during the period stated in this Act (subject, nevertheless, to such redemption as is described in this Act), continue to hold and enjoy all the exclusive privileges of banking given by the said recited Act of the 39th and 40th years of the reign of his Majesty King George III. aforesaid, as regulated by the said recited Act of the 7th year of his late Majesty King George IV., or any prior or subsequent Act or Acts of Parliament, but no other or further exclusive privilege of banking : and whereas doubts have arisen as to the construction of the said Acts, and as to the extent of such exclusive privilege; and it is expedient that all such doubts should be removed, *be it therefore declared and enacted,*

F

that any body politic or corporate, or society, or company, or partnership,
although consisting of more than six persons, may carry on the trade or business
of banking in London, or within sixty-five miles thereof, provided that such
body politic or corporate, or society, or-company, or partnership, do not borrow,
owe, or take up in England, any sum or sums of money on their bills or notes
payable on demand, or at any less time than six months from the borrowing
thereof, during the continuance of the privileges granted by this Act to the said
Governor and Company of the Bank of England."

All notes of the Bank of England, payable on demand, which
shall be issued out of London, shall be payable at the place
where issued, &c. :—

" 4. Provided always, and be it further enacted, that from and after the
1st day of August, 1834, all promissory notes payable on demand of the
Governor and Company of the Bank of England, which shall be issued at
any place in that part of the United Kingdom called England, out of
London, where the trade and business of banking shall be carried on for
and on behalf of the said Governor and Company of the Bank of England,
shall be made payable at the place where such promissory notes shall be
issued ; and it shall not be lawful for the said governor and company, or
any committee, agent, cashier, officer, or servant of the said governor and
company, to issue, at any such place out of London, any promissory note
payable on demand which shall not be made payable at the place where the
same shall be issued, anything in the said recited Act of the seventh year
aforesaid, to the contrary notwithstanding."

Exclusive privileges hereby given, to end upon one year's
notice, given at the end of ten years after August, 1834 ; and
what shall be deemed sufficient notice :—

" 5. And be it further enacted, that upon one year's notice given within
six months after the expiration of ten years from the 1st day of August,
1834, and upon repayment by Parliament to the said governor and company, or their successors, of all principal money, interest, or annuities,
which may be due from the public to the said governor and company at
the time of the expiration of such notice, in like manner as is hereinafter
stipulated and provided, in the event of such notice being deferred until
after the 1st day of August, 1855, the said exclusive privileges of banking
granted by this Act shall cease and determine at the expiration of such
year's notice ; and any vote or resolution of the House of Commons,
signified by the Speaker of the said House in writing, and delivered at the
public office of the said governor and company, or their successors, shall
be deemed and adjudged to be a sufficient notice."

Bank notes to be a legal tender, except at the bank and
branch banks :—

" 6. And be it further enacted, that from and after the 1st day of
August, 1834, unless and until Parliament shall otherwise direct, a tender
of a note or notes of the Governor and Company of the Bank of England,

expressed to be payable to bearer on demand, shall be a legal tender, to the amount expressed in such note or notes, and shall be taken to be valid as a tender to such amount for all sums above 5*l.* on all occasions on which any tender of money may be legally made, so long as the Bank of England shall continue to pay on demand their said notes in legal coin : provided always, that no such note or notes shall be deemed a legal tender of payment by the Governor and Company of the Bank of England, or any branch bank of the said governor and company ; but the said governor and company are not to become liable or be required to pay and satisfy, at any branch bank of the said governor and company, any note or notes of the said governor and company not made specially payable at such branch bank ; but the said governor and company shall be liable to pay and satisfy at the Bank of England in London all notes of the said governor and company, or of any branch thereof."

Bills not having more than three months to run, not to be subject to usury laws :—

"7. And be it further enacted, that no bill of exchange or promissory note made payable at or within three months after the date thereof, or not having more than three months to run, shall, by reason of any interest taken thereon or secured thereby, or any agreement to pay, or receive, or allow interest in discounting, negotiating, or transferring the same, be void, nor shall the liability of any party to any bill of exchange or promissory note be affected by reason of any statute or law in force for the prevention of usury, nor shall any person or persons drawing, accepting, indorsing, or signing any such bill or note, or lending or advancing any money, or taking more than the present rate of legal interest in Great Britain and Ireland respectively for the loan of money on any such bill or note, be subject to any penalties under any statute or law relating to usury, or any other penalty or forfeiture; anything in any law or statute relating to usury in any part of the United Kingdom to the contrary notwithstanding."

Accounts of bullion, &c., and of notes in circulation to be sent weekly to the Chancellor of the Exchequer, &c. :—

"8. And be it further enacted, that an account of the amount of bullion and securities in the Bank of England belonging to the said governor and company, and of notes in circulation, and of deposits in the said bank, shall be transmitted weekly to the Chancellor of the Exchequer for the time being, and such accounts shall be consolidated at the end of every month, and an average state of the bank accounts of the preceding three months, made from such consolidated accounts as aforesaid, shall be published every month in the next succeeding London Gazette."

Public to pay the bank one-fourth part of the debt of 14,686,800*l.* :—

"9. And be it further enacted, that one-fourth part of the debt of 14,686,800*l.* now due from the public to the Governor and Company of the Bank of England, shall and may be repaid to the said governor and company."

Capital stock of the bank may be reduced :—

"10. And be it further enacted, that a general court of proprietors of the said Governor and Company of the Bank of England shall be held at some time between the passing of this Act and the 5th day of October, 1834, to determine upon the propriety of dividing and appropriating the sum of 3,638,250*l*., out of or by means of the sum to be repaid to the said governor and company as hereinbefore mentioned, or out of or by means of the fund to be provided for that purpose, amongst the several persons, bodies politic or corporate, who may be proprietors of the capital stock of the said governor and company on the said 5th day of October, 1834, and upon the manner and the time for making such division and appropriation, not inconsistent with the provisions for that purpose herein contained ; and in case such general court or any adjourned general court, shall determine that it will be proper to make such division, then, but not otherwise, the capital stock of the said governor and company shall be, and the same is hereby declared to be reduced from the sum of 14,553,000*l*., of which the same now consists, to the sum of 10,914,750*l*., making a reduction or difference of 3,638,250*l*. capital stock, and such reduction shall take place from and after the said 5th day of October, 1834 ; and thereupon out of or by means of the sum to be repaid to the said governor and company as hereinbefore mentioned, or out of or by means of the fund to be provided for that purpose, the sum of 3,638,250*l*. sterling, or such proportion of the said fund as shall represent the same, shall be appropriated and divided amongst the several persons, bodies politic or corporate, who may be proprietors of the said sum of 14,553,000*l*. bank stock on the said 5th day of October, 1834, at the rate of 25*l*. sterling for every 100*l*. of bank stock which such persons, bodies politic and corporate, may then be proprietors of, or shall have standing in their respective names in the books kept by the said governor and company for the entry and transfer of such stock, and so in proportion for a greater or lesser sum."

Governor, deputy-governor, or directors, not to be disqualified by reduction of their share of the capital stock :—

"11. Provided always, and be it enacted, that the reduction of the share of each proprietor of and in the capital stock of the said Governor and Company of the Bank of England, by the repayment of such one-fourth part thereof, shall not disqualify the present governor, deputy-governor, or directors, or any or either of them, or any governor, deputy-governor, or director who may be chosen in the room of the present governor, deputy-governor, or directors at any time before the general court of the said governor and company, to be held between the 25th day of March and the 25th day of April, 1835 : provided that at the said general court, and from and after the same, no governor, deputy-governor, or director of the said corporation shall be capable of being chosen such governor, deputy-governor, or director, or shall continue in his or their respective offices, unless he or they respectively shall at the time of such choice have, and during such his respective office continue to have, in his and their respective names, in his and their own right, and for his and their own use, the respective sums or shares of and in the capital stock of the said corporation in and by the charter of the said governor and company prescribed as the qualification of governor, deputy-governor, and directors respectively."

Proprietors not to be disqualified :—

"12. Provided also, and be it enacted, that no proprietor shall be disqualified from attending and voting at any general court of the said governor and company, to be held between the said 5th day of October, 1834, and the 25th day of April, 1835, in consequence of the share of such proprietor of and in the capital stock of the said governor and company having been reduced by such repayment as aforesaid below the sum of 500*l.* of and in the said capital stock : provided such proprietor had in his own name the full sum of 500*l.* of and in the said capital stock on the said 5th day of October, 1834; nor shall any proprietor be required, between the said 5th day of October, 1834, and the 25th day of April, 1835, to take the oath of qualification in the said charter."

Bank to deduct the annual sum of 120,000*l.* from sum allowed for management of national debt :—

"13. And be it further enacted, that from and after the said 1st day of August, 1834, the said Governor and Company, in consideration of the privileges of exclusive banking given by this Act, shall, during the continuance of such privileges, but no longer, deduct from the sums now payable to the said governor and company, for the charges of management of the public unredeemed debt, the annual sum of 120,000*l.*, anything in any Act or Acts of Parliament or agreement to the contrary notwithstanding : provided always that such deduction shall in no respect prejudice or affect the right of the said governor and company to be paid for the management of the public debt, at the rate and according to the terms provided in an Act passed in the 48th year of his late Majesty King George III., intituled ' An Act to authorise the advancing for the public service, upon certain conditions, a proportion of the balance remaining in the Bank of England, for payment of unclaimed dividends, annuities, and lottery prizes, and for regulating the allowances to be made for the management of the national debt.' "

Provisions of Act 39 and 40 Geo. III. to remain in force, except as altered by this Act :—

"14. And be it further enacted, that all the powers, authorities, franchises, privileges, and advantages given or recognised by the said recited Act of the 39th and 40th years aforesaid, as belonging to or enjoyed by the Governor and Company of the Bank of England, or by any subsequent Act or Acts of Parliament, shall be and the same are hereby declared to be in full force and continued by this Act, except so far as the same are altered by this Act, subject, nevertheless, to such redemption upon the terms and conditions following; (that is to say), that at any time, upon twelve months' notice, to be given after the 1st day of August, 1855, and upon repayment by Parliament to the said governor and company, or their successors, of the sum of 11,015,100*l.*, being the debt which will remain due from the public to the said governor and company after the payment of the one-fourth of the debt of 14,686,800*l.* as hereinbefore provided, without any deduction, discount, or abatement whatsoever, and upon payment to the said governor and company and their successors of all arrears of the sum of 100,000*l.* per annum, in the said Act of the 39th and 40th years aforesaid mentioned, together with the interest or annuities payable upon the said debt or in respect thereof, and also upon repayment of all the principal and interest which shall be owing unto the said governor and company and their successors, upon all such tallies, exchequer orders, exchequer bills, or parliamentary funds which the said governor and company or their successors shall have remaining in their hands, or be entitled to at the time of such notice to be given as last aforesaid, then and in such case, and not till then (unless under the proviso hereinbefore contained), the said exclusive privileges of banking granted by this Act shall cease and determine at the expiration of such notice of twelve months."

Act may be amended this session :—

" 15. And be it further enacted, that this Act may be altered, amended, or repealed by any Act to be passed in this session of Parliament."

The government of the bank rests entirely with the court of directors, who may, if they please, change the whole system of management. The only check upon their proceedings consists in the publicity of their measures, the half-yearly meetings of their proprietors, and the communications between the court and the government. The directors are elected by the proprietors of bank stock at a general meeting. Eight directors go out and eight come in every year. The eight that come in are commended by the whole court—that is, a " house list " is sanctioned by the court ; and though the proprietors are not required to vote for the names included in the list, yet these persons have always been elected. The qualification for governor is 4000*l.* bank stock ; deputy-governor, 3000*l.* ; director, 2000*l.* The directors are not usually large holders of bank stock : none of them hold more than the qualification. The governor and deputy-governor are appointed by the directors, and usually continue in office for a year. The senior directors of the bank, who have passed the chair, form a select committee :

to these are added, the director immediately succeeding by rotation to the deputy chair. The governor and the select committee have the management of the bank in the intervals between the sittings of the court, but nothing of consequence is done without the knowledge and concurrence of the court of directors.

At the weekly meeting of the court of directors there is a statement read of the actual position of the bank in every department, of its securities, of its bullion, and of its liabilities. There is a committee of treasury, who may suggest any measure they think fit for the consideration of the court. The daily transactions of the bank are conducted by a committee of three, assisted by the governor or deputy-governor: no responsible action is taken by the committee without reference to the governor. All bills presented for discount are presented before that daily committee, and they determine upon the bills to be discounted. The bullion is purchased by the governor, who considers that he has no power to refuse the issue of notes for gold bullion brought to him at the bank. The purchasing price of gold has been fixed at 3*l*. 17*s*. 9*d*. per ounce. The price of silver is regulated by the course of the foreign exchanges.

SECTION IV.

THE LONDON BANKERS.

AFTER the establishment of the Bank of England, the goldsmiths or " new-fashioned bankers " continued their business in the same manner as before. In the year 1705 they obtained greater facilities, from an alteration in the laws respecting promissory notes. It had been held that promissory notes, whether issued by bankers or others, could not be legally transferred to a third party, and that no action at law could be sustained against the issuer, unless brought by the person to whom the note was originally granted. But, by 3 and 4 Anne, c. 9, all doubts were removed; and it was enacted, that after the 1st of May, 1705, all notes in writing made and signed by any person or persons, bodies politic or corporate, or by the servant or agent of any corporation, banker, goldsmith, merchant.

or trader, who is usually entrusted to sign such promissory notes, shall be assignable or endorsable over, in the same manner as inland bills of exchange.

In the year 1714, the legal interest of money was reduced from six to five per cent. The reduction of the rate of interest was probably the effect of the abundance of money produced by the issue of Bank of England notes, and the increase of deposits with the private bankers. The various small sums of money which had remained idle in the hands of individuals were collected into large deposits in the hands of the bankers. Hence the supply of capital was increased, and the rate of interest consequently fell.

About the year 1775, the London bankers who lived in the city, established what is called "the Clearing House," for the purpose of facilitating their exchanges with each other. By this means each banker is enabled to pay the cheques drawn upon himself by the cheques he holds upon other bankers. And hence he is not under the necessity of keeping so large an amount of money unemployed in his till.*

The London banks have long ceased to be banks of circulation: they are now banks of deposit, banks of discount, and banks of agency to country bankers.

The oldest banking houses in London are Messrs. Child & Co., of Temple Bar, and Messrs. Hoares, of Fleet Street; these were established previous to the Bank of England. The others are comparatively of recent date. In the year 1810 the number of banking houses who settled their accounts with each other at the Clearing-House was forty-six.

SECTION V.

COUNTRY BANKS.

WE have no authentic details of the rise and progress of country banking. It is generally understood that very few country banks existed previous to the American war; that they rapidly increased after the termination of that war; that they received a severe check in the year 1793, when twenty-two became

---

* A full account of the operation of *Clearing*, and of the London bankers' system of book-keeping, will be found in the "Practical Treatise on Banking."

bankrupt; and that they increased with wonderful rapidity after the passing of the Bank Restriction Act.

The country banks are banks of deposit, banks of discount, and banks of remittance; many of them are also banks of circulation.

As banks of deposit, they allow interest upon deposits; as banks of discount, they discount for parties who do not keep with them a current account; as banks of remittance, they conduct their business through the agency of the London bankers; they also receive through the London agents the dividends on the public funds, on account of the stockholders in the neighbourhood. The holders of stock grant in the first instance to the London banker a power of attorney to receive the dividends, which, when received, are placed to the credit of the country banker, by whom they are paid to the holders. This facility of receiving dividends in all parts of the country, has, no doubt, induced many persons to become holders of government securities, and thus the country banks have assisted in supporting public credit.

The country banker pays his London agent either by a *balance*, by a *commission*, or by an *annual fixed amount*. In the case of a balance, the country banker agrees to keep in the hands of the London banker a certain sum, for which he is to receive no interest. The amount of this deposit varies, according to the extent of the business. If the country banker keeps less than the stipulated amount, he is charged interest for the deficiency, as upon an overdrawn account. If he keeps more than this amount, he is usually allowed interest at a rate per cent. which is agreed upon by the parties. In the case of a commission, the country banker pays at the end of each year a certain rate of commission on the transactions of the year; the charge is made upon the amount of the debit side of his account. Some country bankers, instead of a commission, prefer paying a fixed sum per annum. In this case the charge does not vary with the amount of transactions as in the case of commission, but whether the transactions be great or small the payment remains the same.

By 3 and 4 William IV. c. 83, passed in 1833, banks issuing promissory notes are required to make returns to the Stamp Office of the average amount of notes in circulation in the quarters ending the first day of January, April, July, and

October in each year.   The quarterly average is to be formed
from the amount in circulation at the end of each week.

In the memorial presented by the committee of country
bankers to Earl Grey and Lord Althorp, June 12, 1833, they
make the following observations upon the circulation of the
country banks :—

"Your memorialists are prepared to prove that the issues of country
bankers have less tendency to promote fluctuations in the country than
those of the Bank of England; and that their effect in throwing the
exchanges against the country is comparatively insignificant.   The
slightest attention to facts would indicate the truth of these positions.
It has been established by parliamentary evidence that the issues of
country bankers fluctuated much less between the years 1817 and 1826
than those of the Bank of England ; and it is indisputable that adverse
exchanges, which endanger the bank, always succeed great importations
of foreign produce, and that they never can be occasioned by large exportations of domestic productions.   Now it is notorious that the circulation of country bankers acts almost exclusively in promoting these
productions: and that, when it is in an extended state, the direct and
proper influence even of an alleged excess of that circulation, would be
to provide the means of paying for the importations of foreign produce
without causing so great an export of gold as to derange and endanger
the monetary system of the country.   This is looking at the separate
and distinctive character of the issues of country bankers; if regarded as
a part of a whole, any excess in which must bear its relative proportion of
effect in producing derangement, that proportion can never exceed one-
tenth ; because, assuming that all paper currency has an equal bearing
upon depreciation and appreciation, the issues of country bankers never
amounted to one-tenth part of that which is used for effecting the
interchanges of commodities and property in the country.   All experience
shows that great fluctuations have originated in the speculations of
influential merchants, and never originated in the channels to which the
issues of country bankers are confined ; their source is in great mercantile
cities, and they are promoted by the issues of the Bank of England.   That
this is the invariable course which fluctuations resulting in excess and
derangement take, is proved by the evidence of Mr. Ward and others,
before the bank charter committee, and is fully explained by the speeches
of the king's ministers in the year 1826.   The debts of a few speculative
merchants who failed in a single year in the town of Liverpool, where
country bankers' notes never circulated, amounted to between seven and
eight millions sterling, and their bills were either lodged in the Bank of
England for loans, or were current in all parts of the country, stimulating
circulation and promoting excess.

"Then, with regard to the alleged tendency of many sources of issue to
promote fluctuation—the rivalry of numerous banks of issue was set up
by the government of 1826 as a principle which insures solidity and
equability to the circulation, ' from the constant exchange of notes between

the different banks, by which they become checks upon each other, and by which any over-issue is subject to immediate observation and detection.' That was the report of the lords' committee, after full and complete investigation. The government of 1833 is proceeding with a measure founded on the principle that rival banks of issue promote fluctuation; this, however, is before investigation. Deposits and cash credits were declared by the witnesses from Scotland to be absolutely dependent on local bank issues, and the government of 1826 admitted the validity of the plea; the government of 1833 concludes that the system of deposits and cash credits may be maintained in England without local issues, but this conclusion is adopted without any inquiry into the case. It would be fruitless to dwell on this contradictory conduct in two administrations professing to be guided, in dealing with the currency, by the same policy. Admitting that by one source of issue, the actual amount of notes payable on demand might be kept more equal than by many, it does not follow that their distribution would not be infinitely more unequal—every man possessed of practical information who understands the subject knows that by giving the exclusive circulation of notes to the Bank of England abundance will be created in the money market, and in the great commercial emporiums—raising the price of public securities, and stimulating the produce markets—while unexampled scarcity will be the consequence in the country, producing embarrassment and discontent among the cultivators of the soil and all who are dependent upon them. Therefore the real practical point to be determined concerning the tendency of different issues is, whether 2,000,000*l.*, or any given sum, laid out in purchasing French rentes in Paris, and indigo in Calcutta, or in replenishing with stock the exhausted corn and pasture fields of England, have the most effect in drawing gold out of the country. It is hardly possible to imagine any measure of greater danger than the projected plan of government. The present bank directors may be men of unimpeachable integrity; but others less scrupulous may succeed them; and it is within the range of possibility for a man of influence who had obtained a seat at their board, to make a speculation by purchasing indigo in Calcutta, and then proceed to stimulate the market for that commodity in London just before the sale at the East India House, by discounting the bills of favoured connexions; then, at nearly the same period, he might cause instructions to be given to the manager of the branch bank in Manchester to contract the customary and stipulated discounts; which would have the effect of depressing the market for cotton twist and piece goods, which are the principal commodities transmitted to India in exchange for the produce of that country. By this double operation the produce of a director's capital employed in Hindostan might be temporarily raised in price in the London market, and the produce of English capital and labour sunk to favour the interests of one bank director or of several. The same result might be produced by the importer of Baltic produce: indeed, the importation of corn in 1831 probably created that state of things, which suggested to the government the plan of suppressing all local issues as the remedy for an alleged evil in the country bank system. It is hardly necessary to disclaim all personal imputation in this illustration. The Chancellor of the Exchequer has taken the self-interest of country bankers to be an element of so much danger, from its tendency to induce them to extend their issues, as to adopt it as a principle in framing a legislative measure of the most hazardous character. Is the danger of the operation of the same principle to be disregarded when it might be exercised, not in a manner where it would be open to 'immediate operation and correction,' but in secret, where it could not be detected and challenged? The history of national banks proves that their funds may be applied by their directors to far more daring private speculations than is described by this supposititious case.

" If all bankers should be compelled to supply their customers with the notes of the Bank of England, a charge of seven per cent. for the interest of loans to graziers, farmers, and dealers in agricultural produce, would not remunerate the country bankers so well as four or five per cent. does now upon the present system. The contemplated change in the usury laws, which if intended to afford to your memorialists some advantage for that which it is intended to deprive them, would give them some satisfactory compensation, because its tendency is to disorder or change that system upon which loans are made by country bankers with promptitude, facility, and comparative· uniformity and cheapness; the distinctive characteristics of their business are regularity and the absence of extortionary charges. In the event of the subversion of that system it would be impossible·for a great corporation, forming rules of conduct in London, and thence directing their application, to appoint agents competent to conduct the pecuniary affairs of the productive portion of the community. Those affairs, as far as banks are concerned with them, always demand peculiar local knowledge, and are in a great measure based on the confidential intercourse of fellowship and neighbourhood; they frequently require personal knowledge of the circumstances and character of individuals, and the closest sympathy with feelings arising from family difficulties, or family expectations and prospects. The governing principles, therefore, for conducting those important pecuniary affairs are totally incompatible with any that can govern the conduct of an hired agent in attempting to conduct the same. From these premises it results that the free application of labour to land would be prevented, the cost of cultivation enhanced, markets and the sale of produce impeded, and the pursuits of agriculture deeply injured.

" Then with respect to miners and manufacturers, any system which would bring them into immediate contact with the operation of the bank for regulating the foreign exchanges, without that protection and defence from those convulsive changes which the local circulations afford, would be a system pregnant with indescribable hazard. Many of the bank directors are connected by friendship or commercial dealings with the great speculators in London and the populous towns, whose transactions mainly cause excess of circulation and an adverse state of the exchanges. In this class any contraction of the paper currency for the rectification of derangement, upon the present system, acts; but upon the projected plan, parliamentary evidence, as well as the nature of things, shows that the contracting force will be put into operation by the branch bank

·

managers at a distance from London, and produce confusion in the affairs of mining and manufacturing industry, and discontent among a dense and excitable population. It may, under such a state of things, be rationally apprehended that occasions will arise when workmen will be suddenly dismissed for the want of the power to pay them their wages, shopkeepers deprived of their weekly receipts, and the regular custom at markets for the supply of agricultural produce, impaired."

In reply to a question, "What effect do you suppose that an increase or decrease of London bank notes has upon the issues of country bankers?" J. H. Palmer, Esq., replied:—

" A material increase of the bank in London tends, in the first instance, to reduce the value of money, and, consequently, the rate of interest, upon all negotiable securities. That abundance of money renders it difficult for the country bankers to find beneficial investment for that part of the country money sent up to the capital for employment, consequently they are forced to resort to their immediate neighbourhoods for new channels for investing their surplus money; and which tends to create additional issues in the country at an early period after the London increase has taken place. But it does not follow that a diminution of issues has an equally rapid effect in reducing the issues of the interior."

SECTION VI.

JOINT-STOCK BANKS.

In the year 1708, a clause was inserted in the charter of the Bank of England, prohibiting the establishment of any other bank having more than six partners. This clause prevented the formation of any other joint-stock bank ; and, as the increasing wealth and commerce of the nation occasioned a demand for banks, a great number, each having no more than six partners, rose into existence, as they were successively required by the wants of the country. The charter of the Bank of England had no reference to Scotland, which, at the period of the grant of the charter, was a separate kingdom. Hence, with the increasing wealth of Scotland, joint-stock banking companies were formed ; and at present they conduct nearly the whole of the banking business of that country. But with every renewal of the charter of the Bank of England, this clause was retained, and hence has arisen the difference which subsists between the Scotch and the English systems of banking. In the year 1826, an Act of Parliament was passed to permit the formation of banks having more than

six partners, at a greater distance than sixty-five miles from
London; with a provision, however, that such banks should
not make their notes payable in London, nor draw bills upon
London for a less amount than 50*l.* By an Act passed in 1833,
these banks have the privilege of drawing bills on their London
agents, either on demand or otherwise, and for sums less than
50*l.*

The advocates of joint-stock banks allege that they possess
the following advantages over private banks:—

1. Joint-stock banks possess greater security than private
banks.

Security is of the first importance to a bank. One branch of
the business of a banker is to take charge of money committed
to his care. But who will entrust money to a banker who is not
known to be, or, at least, supposed to be rich? And if a banker
be rich, but afterwards, by mismanagement or misfortune, become poor, and fail, what dreadful misery *is* inflicted upon those
who have money in his hands. How many respectable individuals may be suddenly bereft of their whole dependence. How
many industrious tradesmen may become bankrupts. What
distrust, what inconvenience, what interruption of business is
occasioned, even to those who can bear the loss. But by a
joint-stock bank all these evils are avoided. Another branch of
the business of a bank is to remit money from one part of the
country to another; but who will trust them with money to
remit when they may fail before they have executed their trust?
Banks, too, issue their own notes, and thus supply the circulating
medium of the country. Here wealth and security are more
necessary than ever. In the former cases, the creditors of the
banker may have had some opportunity of judging of his safety,
and would probably make previous inquiries upon the subject.
But when the notes of a banker have become the circulating
medium of a neighbourhood, they are readily taken without any
inquiries about his solvency. And, indeed, in some cases, if the
notes were suspected, they could not be refused. If a tradesman will not deliver goods to his customers for such notes as
they offer him, they will take the notes to some other tradesman.
Men who receive wages must receive them in such notes as the
master chooses to pay. Since then, each banker supplies the
circulating medium of a large district, and the notes are thus
circulated among all classes, some of whom have not the option

of refusing them, nor the ability to judge of their value, it is of the utmost importance that banks should be established on those principles which will prevent their failure.

That a bank having a great number of partners should be more secure than a bank consisting of only a few partners, seems a very obvious proposition; and it has received abundant confirmation from the numerous failures that have occurred among the bankers in England, and the few failures that have occurred in Scotland. This is a fact that demonstrates the superior security of joint-stock banks. If a bank of this kind has a charter, it must previously possess a large fund, which forms a guarantee for the punctual payment of its notes or deposits. If the bank have no charter, then every individual shareholder is answerable for all the debts of the bank to the whole extent of his property, as fully as though he had incurred those debts himself. In either case the security is greater than can be offered by any one individual, or by any four or five individuals, however respectable they may be.

2. A joint-stock bank is less liable to runs.

A run is a sudden and general demand for the payment of notes or deposits. It is not sufficient that a banker be safe: it is also necessary that he should be believed to be safe. He derives the larger portion of his gains from the confidence which is placed in him by others. Confidence is money. However wealthy or respectable a banker may be, he may not always be believed to be so. The misfortunes of others may cause him to be suspected. But no banker has always in his coffers all the sums necessary to pay all the claims that may be made upon him. If he were to do this, from what quarter would he obtain his profits? What, then, is he to do in case of a run? He must at all events obtain money to meet the demands made upon him; for if he once suspend his payments, all his credit is destroyed, and his business is broken up. Hence he may be compelled to borrow money at a high rate of interest, or to sell stock or estates below their value, and to incur great expense, in order that the money may arrive in time to meet the demand. But the effects of a run are not confined to the banker himself. One run is over, but another may come. He will be anxious to be better provided next time. He will be more cautious. He will call in the money he has lent. He will lend no more. He will discount fewer bills. Those tradesmen and others who have been accustomed to obtain from the banker facilities for carrying on their business, can obtain them no longer. Some have depended on these facilities, and will now fail ; others will circumscribe their business ; labourers will be thrown out of work, and trade will be obstructed and depressed.

Such are the effects of a run when the banker is solvent, and the run is met with promptitude. But the banker may be good, and yet the run may cause him to stop payment. In this case, though the banker may ultimately pay the whole of his debts, yet this stoppage will produce for a while the same effects as though he were insolvent. But it is possible that he might have been solvent before the run, and have been rendered insolvent by the run. The sacrifices he may have been compelled to make for the purpose of raising the money in time to meet the demand, may have absorbed the whole of his property.

Now, what is it that causes a run ? It is merely an apprehension that the banker cannot discharge the whole of his obligations, and hence each creditor tries to be first, that he may secure the full amount of his own claim. But no apprehension of this kind can exist in reference to a joint-stock bank. Everybody knows that all the partners are liable for the debts of the bank to the full extent of their property ; and each creditor feeling assured that even should the bank fail his property is secure, abstains from engaging in a run whereby he can gain no advantage.

3. Another advantage which joint-stock banks are alleged to possess, consists in the prudence of their management.

A joint-stock bank is managed by a board of directors, men of character and ability, who are chosen to fill the office from their superior knowledge of mercantile and banking business. The united knowledge and wisdom of a number of individuals must be greater than that of two or three individuals. They are not so liable to be imposed upon by false representations, to be deluded by false reasonings, or to be biassed by personal attachments. As among many persons there is sure to be a difference of opinion on almost every question brought before them, it is certain that no measure will be adopted without having first received a full discussion.

On the other hand, the management of a private bank is too frequently intrusted to one or two of the partners ; men who cannot be expected to act with the caution and prudence of an elected body, answerable for their conduct to the great body of proprietors; men, too, who have their prejudices to indulge, their friends to please, and their partialities to gratify. Not so with the directors of a joint-stock bank, where the follies of an individual would be checked, and his deficiencies supplied by his colleagues. It often happens, too, that the partners of a private bank are engaged in some branch of manufactures or commerce; and in this case the bank will be made subordinate to the trading concern. The banking merchant or manufacturer will extend his business, or engage in speculation, under the consciousness of being able to make good his purchases. The trading concern will have an account at the bank, and will always be overdrawn. The money which ought to be employed by the bank in discounting bills for their customers, will be absorbed by the trade of the partners. If the trading concern fails, the bank too must fail : the one involves the ruin of the other. Perhaps, indeed, the bank, by supplying money in the first instance for the parties to speculate with, may have been the cause of the ruin. Even when the partners of a private bank are not themselves engaged in any other employment, the bank often becomes connected with some large manufacturing or commercial establishments. Such establishments are useful to the bank, by enabling them to circulate a considerable amount of their notes. Hence the bank is induced to make large advances to them. Afterwards a further advance is necessary. A run upon the bank compels them to call in the money they have advanced. The money cannot suddenly be replaced. Hence all the parties become bankrupts. From all these evils joint-stock banks are alleged to be free.

Whatever the opinion, whether for or against, that may be entertained respecting joint-stock banks, the fact is undeniable that competition is, in most cases, good for the public. And hence, perhaps, the best system of banking is, when private banks and joint-stock banks are intermingled with each other. The rivalry of the private banks may induce the public banks to act with promptness and liberality : while the rivalry of the public banks may induce the private banks to guard against any measure that might shake their credit, and tend to weaken the public confidence in their stability.

SECTION VII.

BRANCH BANKS.

THE establishment of branch banks may be considered as the effect of the formation of joint-stock banks. A bank consisting of only six partners is seldom sufficiently well known over a great extent of country, to be able to open many branches. The credit of such a bank would be liable to be shaken at one or other of its branches, and this might throw a suspicion on the whole establishment. But a joint-stock bank, possessing undoubted credit, may extend its branches with confidence whereever adequate business can be obtained. The comparative merits of an independent private bank, and a branch of a joint-stock bank, and the effects they are adapted to produce in any town in which they may be introduced, form a useful subject of inquiry.

In the first place, the branch bank may be supposed to possess greater security. The branch, however small, would possess all the security that belonged to the whole establishment. The notes issued at the branch would be as valid as notes issued at the head office ; and deposits made at the branch would be recoverable from all the partners in the whole bank. In case a run were upon even the smallest branch, the directors would be as anxious to meet the demand as though the run were directed against the largest. A small private bank, on the other hand, would have its only resource within itself. Its own capital would form its only guarantee ; and, in case of a sudden demand, it must expect but little assistance from its neighbours.

Secondly, A branch bank would command the use of greater capital.

Every joint-stock bank would call upon its shareholders for a supply of capital equal to the carrying on of the business. This capital would be kept in a disposable form, and, not like the capital of some private banks, locked up in loans upon inconvertible security. The confidence the bank possessed would create more banking capital, by attracting deposits and facilitating the issue of notes. Some banks create more capital than they can employ ; such is the case when the amount of notes and deposits is greater than that of the loans and discounts.

Others employ more than their banking capital. And some banks employ more at one season of the year, and less at another. In such cases a branch bank would be fed with capital from the parent bank, as its wants might demand. If it yielded more capital than it required, the parent bank would employ it elsewhere. If it wanted capital the parent bank would grant an ample supply. But in these cases a private bank would be troubled with an excess of capital which it might not be able to employ advantageously for a short period, or it might be distressed to raise capital to meet the wants of its customers.

Thirdly, A branch bank would probably do business with the public on lower terms.

A bank having many branches usually charges the same rate of interest at all the branches. The Bank of England discounts at all its branches on the same terms as in London. This cheapness of discount occasioned a great reduction of profits to the private bankers. A branch bank, too, conducted on the principle of allowing interest on deposits, will probably allow a higher rate, because the money can always be employed at some one or other of the branches, and it will return the deposits at a shorter notice, because the funds of the whole bank are ready to meet the call. In the transmission of money, a system of branch banks has a decided advantage, because the branches draw direct upon each other, and discount bills, payable at all the branches respectively. In a system of independent banks the transmission of money from one to another is usually effected by a bill on London; and bills drawn by one town on another are obliged to be made payable in London.

Branch banks are enabled to charge less than private bankers, from their expenses and their expected profits being less. If a country bank, having many branches, employs a London agent, the charge for agency will be much less than though the branches were all independent banks. A branch bank is not under the necessity of keeping in its coffers so large a stock of gold as though it were an independent bank, because, in case of emergency, it is sure of obtaining supplies. The rate of profit, too, expected from a branch bank is much less than would be expected by a private banker. A banking company would be induced to establish a branch, could they be assured of obtaining a clear profit of one or two per cent. on their capital above the market rate of interest.   But a private banker, who may be supposed already a wealthy man, would not consider that amount a sufficient remuneration for his own trouble and superintendence.   Hence, his charges must be higher, to meet this increased rate of profit.   Were the profits of a private banker, in proportion to the amount of capital employed, to be reduced to the average rate of profit of joint-stock banks, he would very soon think of retiring from business.

A branch bank may thus be established in a place where a private bank could not exist.   It may also be opened in places not sufficiently wealthy to furnish capital for a joint-stock bank, and, where the people have no banking facilities; branches being opened in such places, prevent the formation of banks with insufficient capital.   For, to be without a bank is felt to be so great an inconvenience that, if a good bank cannot be obtained, a bad one will, for a while, be supported.   Hence, shopkeepers and others have become bankers ; and, having but a small capital, and being unacquainted with their business, they have, ultimately, involved themselves and others in irretrievable ruin.

I have hitherto only compared a branch bank with an independent private bank.   I will now compare it with an independent joint-stock bank.   Several of the advantages already specified will apply as justly in this case as in the other. The branch may in this case also be supplied with a greater amount of capital if it could be profitably employed, or it may have better means of disposing of its surplus capital.   The charges of the branch, especially for the transmission of money by letters of credit, or by discounting bills, may also be less at the branch.   In point of security, the two banks may be considered as on an equality; though, perhaps, in some cases, the advantage may be in favour of the branch.

The expense of managing a branch must be less than that of managing an independent bank, as a less number of directors would be necessary.   The directors or managers of a branch, too, acting under the direction of a superior board, are less liable to be involved by indiscreet advances of loans from personal friendship or imperfect information.   The transactions are more thoroughly sifted, and no important measure adopted without full discussion.   The very circumstance of being accountable to a superior board would render the agents at the branch more scrupulous and cautious than they might otherwise be. And the periodical returns made to the head office would constantly bring all the business of the branch under the notice of experienced and unbiassed inspectors.

There are, however, some disadvantages attending a branch bank. As a branch bank is a mere colony, the agents must be directed by the commands they receive from the seat of government. And the branch may be directed, in some cases, to adopt measures more adapted to promote the welfare of the whole establishment than to advance the interest of that particular branch. The Bank of England, for instance, may engage to lend, on advantageous terms, a certain sum of money to the government; and, for the purpose of raising this money, they may direct their agents at the branches to limit their discounts. As it is the duty of the directors to consult the interest of the whole establishment, they might consider themselves justified, as commercial men, in adopting this line of conduct. At the same time, it would be a great inconvenience to the persons resident at the places where the branches are established to be deprived of their usual discounts.

Another possible inconvenience to a branch arises from the circumstance, that most cases of importance are necessarily referred for the consideration of the head office; not that these cases are more difficult than ordinary cases, but because they are deviations from the usual course of business, or they belong to a class of transactions which is reserved for the decision of the highest authority. Hence, persons who have dealings with the branch may be obliged to wait the return of post, or a still longer term, before they can obtain answers to important inquiries. This inconvenience may, however, be largely diminished by giving to the managers or agents a high degree of discretionary power, reserving as few cases as possible for the decision of the board of directors, and by recourse to the telegraph.

The respective claims of these three different kinds of banks as far as regards any particular place, must depend on local circumstances. It is easy to imagine cases wherein a private bank of undoubted wealth and judicious management is superior to either a branch bank or an independent joint-stock bank. But private banks depend entirely upon the persons by whom they are managed. And these persons, whatever other endowments they may possess, are not endowed with immortality, nor with the power of bequeathing their good qualities to their successors. Leaving private banks out of the question, a branch bank seems best adapted for a small town : and an independent joint-stock bank for a large one. When banking is left perfectly free, the natural force of competition will soon enable each town to provide itself with that kind of bank which is best adapted to its own wants and circumstances.

The Bank of England has several branches. The business of the branches consists in discounting bills; in receiving deposits; in issuing bills on the London bank, at seven, fourteen, and any greater number of days after date ; and in the transmission of money to and from London. Each branch issues its own notes, which are payable at the place of issue, and in London. The rate of discount is the same as in London ; no interest is allowed on deposits; no charge is made for a fourteen day bill on the parent establishment : but if money be lodged at the branch, to be received the following day in London, or lodged in London, to be received at the branch, a charge is made for commission. The charge to parties who have accounts at a branch, or in London, is at a reduced rate.

SECTION VIII.

BANKS OF DEPOSIT.

BANKING is a kind of trade carried on for the purpose of getting money. The trade of a banker differs from other trades, inasmuch as it is carried on chiefly with the money of other people.

The trading capital of a bank may be divided into two parts : the invested capital, and the banking capital. The invested capital is the money paid down by the partners for the purpose of carrying on the business. This may be called the real capital. The banking capital is that portion of capital which is created by the bank itself in the course of its business, and may be called the borrowed capital.

There are three ways of raising a banking or borrowed capital. First, by receiving deposits ; secondly, by the issuing of notes; thirdly, by the drawing of bills. If a person will lend me 100*l.* for nothing, and I lend that 100*l.* to another person at four per cent. interest, then, in the course of a year, I shall gain 4*l.* by the transaction. Again, if a person will take my "promise to pay," and bring it back to me at the end of the year, and pay me four per cent. for it, just the same as though I had lent him 100 sovereigns, then I shall gain 4*l.* by that transaction; and again, if a person in a country town brings me 100*l.* on condition that, twenty-one days afterwards, I shall pay the same amount to a person in London, then whatever interest I can make of the money during the twenty-one days, will be my profit. This is a fair representation of the operations of banking, and of the way in which a banking capital is created by means of deposits, notes, and bills.

The profits of a banker are generally in proportion to the amount of his banking or borrowed capital. If a banker employ only his real or invested capital, it is impossible he should ever, in the ordinary course of business, make any profits. Bankers can seldom attain more upon their advances than the market-rate of interest; and that may be obtained upon real capital, without the expense of maintaining a banking establishment. If, after deducting the expenses, the profits amount to nothing more than the market-rate of interest upon the invested capital, the bank may be considered to have made no profits at all. The partners have received no higher dividend upon the capital invested in the bank than they would have received if the same money had been laid out in government securities. To ascertain the real profit of a bank, the interest upon the invested capital should be deducted from the gross profit, and what remains is the banking profit.

A bank that receives lodgments of money, is called a bank of deposit. A bank that issues notes, is called a bank of circulation. Each bank attempts to procure a banking capital, but by different means. When a bank of deposit is opened, all the people in the district, who have money lying idle in their hands, will place the money in the bank. This will be done by the merchants and tradesmen, who are in the habit of keeping by them a sufficient sum of money to answer daily demands; by the gentry, and others out of business, who receive their rents, dividends, or other moneys, periodically, and disburse them as they have occasion. The various small sums of money which were lying unproductive in the hands of numerous individuals, will thus be collected into one sum in the hands of the banker. The banker will retain a part of this sum in his till, to answer the cheques the depositors may draw upon him; and with the other part he will discount bills, or otherwise employ it in his business. But if, instead of a bank of deposit, a bank of circulation *only* be established, then the several small sums of money will remain unproductive as before in the hands of various individuals; and the banker, in discounting bills, will issue his own promissory notes.

Now, it is obvious that these two kinds of banking are adapted to produce precisely the same effects. In each case a banking capital is created, and each capital is employed in precisely the same way; namely, in the discounting of bills. To the parties who have their bills discounted, it matters not from what source the capital is raised,—the advantage is the same to them,—the mode in which they employ the money is the same,—and the effects upon trade and commerce will be the same. Let us suppose that in each case the banking capital created is 50,000*l*. Now, the bank of circulation will have increased the amount of money in the country by 50,000*l*. The bank of deposit will not have increased at all the amount of money in the country, but it will have put into motion 50,000*l*. that would otherwise have been idle. Here, then, is a proof, that to give increased rapidity to the circulation of money, has precisely the same effects as to increase the amount. Here, too, is a proof of the ignorance of banking, on the part of those writers who consider that the banks which issue notes are the sole cause of high prices, over-trading, and speculation; whereas it is obvious, that if those effects are to be attributed to banking at all, they may as fairly be ascribed to banks of deposit as to banks of circulation.

Even those bankers who do not issue notes, create a banking capital by the discounting of bills. They render their discounts subservient to the increase of their deposits. The London bankers will not discount except for those persons who have deposit accounts with them. A party who has had bills discounted, and has paid interest on the whole amount, must leave some portion of that amount in the hands of the banker without interest. By this means the banker obtains more than the current rate of interest on the money actually advanced, and raises a banking capital to the amount of the balance left in his hands. " A good account," in the language of the London bankers, is an account on which there is a large deposit—a bad account is that on which the sum deposited is small. A person who keeps a good account may have his bills discounted readily, but a person who keeps a bad account will have his bills more severely scrutinized. The depositors are aware of this; and therefore they endeavour to keep a fair account with the banker, that they may at all times be able to obtain such accommodation in the way of discounts as they may require. This mode of raising a banking capital by means of discounts, without allowing interest on the deposits, appears to be less advantageous to the borrower than by means of notes. In the one case, the borrower has to lodge some portion of his money in the hands of the banker, but in the other case he has only to take the banker's notes, which are probably as serviceable to him as gold. Hence, such banks appear adapted for the service of the rich rather than the poor—a young tradesman who is commencing business with a slender capital, will hardly find it worth his while to open an account at a banker's unless he has always by him a certain portion of his capital, which he is obliged to keep unemployed.

The London private bankers usually grant no interest for money placed in their hands, nor charge any commission upon the amount of the transactions. Their customers pay them for the trouble of conducting their accounts by keeping a certain balance to their credit. The amount of the balance is never definitely fixed, but is regulated very much by the good sense and proper feeling of the parties. The number of cheques a party draws—the degree of accommodation he receives by discount or otherwise, these and other circumstances are taken into consideration; and though the amount of the balance is not expressly stipulated, yet few people of business habits are at a loss to judge whether the average balance of their account throughout the year is sufficient to remunerate the banker.

By the Scotch banks, deposit accounts are divided into two classes—" accounts current," and " deposit receipts;" the " accounts current " are similar to the " current accounts " kept by merchants, traders, and others in the English banks. The party pays his money into the bank, and makes all his payments by cheques upon the bank. The deposit receipts are similar to what the English bankers call " dead accounts." The depositor pays his money into the bank, and there it lies " dead " until he has occasion for it, and then he produces his receipt and withdraws the whole amount, or takes a new receipt for any part he wishes to leave. The deposit receipts are chiefly for the use of those who lodge their money in the bank merely for the purpose of security and interest. The accounts current are for those who, in addition to security and interest, wish to make use of the bank as a means of facilitating their pecuniary transactions. As far as regards the circulation of the bankers' notes, each kind of account has the same effect; but as the operations on the current accounts are more frequent, they put into circulation a larger amount.

When a banker's own notes are lodged on a deposit account, they do not diminish the amount of his banking capital. The banking capital raised by his notes is diminished, but that raised by his deposits is in the same proportion increased. If, however, the interest he allows upon the deposits is greater than the expense of the wear and tear of his notes, then will his banking capital be diminished in the more profitable, and increased in a less profitable direction. But when a deposit consists of notes of other banks, his banking capital is increased by that amount. Hence, if a banker could know that all the money deposited in his hands would consist chiefly of his own notes, it might not be for his advantage to allow any interest on deposits. It would be better for him that his notes should remain in circulation.

It will be observed that the amount of notes issued on deposit accounts, depends not on the banker but upon the depositors. They lodge money in his bank, and draw it out when they please. The deposit system, therefore, cannot place in circulation any additional amount of money. The depositors cannot draw out of the bank more money than they had deposited. After the deposits are made, the amount of money in existence is precisely the same as before. The only difference is, that what was previously in the hands of many individuals, is now in the hands of the banker—and until he has made use of this money in the way of discounts or loans, or in some other mode, no effect whatever can be produced upon the trade and commerce of the district. All the advantage the people of the neighbourhood obtain by the deposit system, considered by itself, consists in having a place of security in which they may lodge their money —in receiving interest for the sums thus deposited—and in the saving of time and trouble in effecting their pecuniary transactions. But although the deposit system does not affect the amount of the currency, it changes its character. As the lodgments will be made in the previously existing currency—whether gold, or silver, or notes of other banks—and all the issues will be in the banker's own notes—the effect will be, that in course of time all the previous currency will have passed into the bank, and all the existing currency will consist exclusively of the banker's own notes—and the more frequent and heavy are the operations on the deposit accounts, the more rapidly will this effect be produced.

Banks of deposit serve to economize the use of the circulating medium. This is done upon the principle of transfer. The principle of transfer was one of the first which was brought into operation in modern banking. The bank of Amsterdam was founded upon this principle. Any person who chose, might lodge money in the bank, and might then transfer it from his own name to that of another person. All foreign bills of exchange were required, by law, to be paid by such transfers. Although the money might at any time be drawn out, either by the original depositor or by the party into whose name it had been transferred, yet, in fact, this was seldom done, because the bank money was more valuable than the money in common use, and consequently bore a premium in the market. The transfer of lodgments is extensively practised in our own times. If two persons, who have an account in the same bank, have business transactions with each other, the debtor will pay the creditor by a cheque upon the bank. The creditor will have this cheque placed to his credit. The amount of money in the bank remains the same, but a certain portion is transferred into a different name in the banker's books. The cheque given by the debtor is an authority from the debtor to the banker to make this transfer.

Here the payment between the creditor and debtor is made without any employment of money. No money passes from one to the other: no money is paid out or received by the banker. Thus it is that banks of deposit economize the use of the circulating medium, and enable a large amount of transactions to be settled with a small amount of money. The money thus liberated, is employed by the banker in making advances, by discount or otherwise, to his customers. Hence the principle of transfer gives additional efficiency to the deposit system, and increases the productive capital of the country. It matters not whether the two parties who have dealings with each other, keep their accounts with the same banker or with different bankers; for, as the bankers exchange their cheques with each other at the clearing-house, the effect, as regards the public, is the same. The deposit system might thus, by means of transfers, be carried to such an extent as wholly to supersede the use of a metallic currency. Were every man to keep a deposit account at a bank, and make all his payments by cheques, money might be superseded, and cheques become the sole circulating medium. In this case, however, it must be supposed that the banker has the money in his hands, or the cheques would have no value.

Since 1825, the following facilities have been granted by the Bank of England to those who have deposit accounts; or, as they are called, "drawing accounts" at the bank :—

1. The bank receives dividends, by power of attorney, for all persons having drawing accounts at the bank.

2. Dividend warrants are received at the drawing office for ditto.

3. Exchequer bills and other securities are received for ditto—the bills exchanged, the interest received, and the amount carried to their respective accounts.

4. Cheques may be drawn for 5*l*. and upwards, instead of 10*l*. as heretofore.

5. Cash boxes taken in, contents unknown, for such parties as keep accounts at the bank.

6. Bank notes are paid at the counter, instead of drawing tickets for them on the pay clerks as heretofore.

7. Cheques on city bankers, paid in by three o'clock, are received and passed to account the same evening.

8. Dividend warrants taken in at the drawing office until four in the afternoon, instead of till three as heretofore.

9. Credits paid into account are received without the bank book, and are afterwards entered therein without the party claiming them.

10. Bills of exchange, payable at the bank, are paid with or without advice; heretofore with advice only.

11. Notes of country bankers, payable in London, are sent out the same day for payment.

12. Cheques are given out in books, and not in sheets as heretofore.

SECTION IX.

BANKS OF REMITTANCE.

In the infancy of commerce, all trade was carried on with ready money. Before good roads are formed, and posts are established, trade between distant places is carried on by merchants, who associate together in considerable numbers, and meet at fixed times at particular places, whence they commence their journey to the country with which they intend to traffic. When arrived at the place where the market is held, they dispose of their goods for ready money ; they then lay out their money in the purchase of other goods, with which they return. Such was the practice with the merchants of the East, who formed the immense caravans that formerly traded between Europe and India ; and such is the practice of similar caravans that now trade between Egypt and Mecca. In such cases all the transactions are carried on with ready money. The bankers, if such they may be called, are mere money changers, who exchange the money of the country in which they live, for the money of other countries.

The labour of carrying money from one country to another was considerably diminished by the invention of bills of exchange ; but the same mode of remittance was continued even in England, until a very recent period, with regard to the transmission of money through the provinces. When a country is considerably improved, good roads are established, and places hitherto obscure become seats of manufacturing, and agricultural industry ; an interchange of commodities will take place between the provinces ; the produce of one district will be transported to another, hence will arise the necessity of having some means of transmitting money in payment of these respective commodities, and banks will consequently be established. It is not the banks that give rise to the trade, it is the trade that gives rise to the banks : though, after the trade is established, the introduction of a bank extends the trade.

The most effectual means of transmitting money throughout a country is by an extensive establishment of banks ; banks transmit money by means of their agencies, by means of their branches, and by means of the circulation of notes.

First.—Banks transmit money by means of their agencies. This is the way in which it is carried on by the country bankers. Each country banker employs a London agent to pay his notes or bills, and to make payments in London; and, on the other hand, to receive sums that may be lodged by parties residing in London for the use of parties residing in the country. As each country bank is thus connected with London, it is virtually connected with all the other banks in the country; as far, at least, as concerns the transmission of money.

Money is remitted from London to a country town, by being paid into a London bank, to the credit of the country bank, for the use of the party who resides in the country. Money is remitted from a country town to London, by being paid into a country bank, to the credit of their London agents, for the use of the party who resides in London, or by remitting to the party a bill drawn by the country upon the London bank. Money is remitted from one country town to another by paying the money into the country bank, to be paid by their London agents to the London agent of the country bank established in the town to which the money is to be remitted, or by sending direct to the party a bill drawn by the country upon the London bank, which bill will be discounted by the bank established in the place to which the bill is sent.

Secondly.—Banks remit money from one place to another by means of their branches. Money is received at the head office for the credit of any branch; and money is received at each of the branches for the credit of the head office; and letters of credit are also granted at every branch upon all the other branches. The Bank of England transmits money from London to a branch; and, *vice versâ*, for only the charge of postage. The branches also draw bills upon the parent establishment at fourteen days' date, without any charge.

Thirdly.—Banks remit money from one place to another by means of their circulation. Every bank of circulation will necessarily become a bank of remittance, whether it carry on the remitting of money as a branch of business or not. Some of the notes which are issued, will be sent as payments from one place to another. This will be more frequently the case if the notes are payable at any place besides the place of issue, or if the bank that issues them has credit over a great extent of country: thus, Bank of England notes serve the purpose of remittance all over the kingdom. They are usually cut in halves and sent by post, one half being retained till the receipt of the first is acknowledged. The issue of bank post bills, payable seven days after sight, and granted in favour of the party to whom the payment is made, has still farther increased the efficiency of the Bank of England as a bank of remittance.

The extent of the remittance of any place must depend in a great degree upon its trade—that is, upon its exports and its imports. Money must be sent *from* a place to pay for its imports, and money must be *received* in exchange for exports. Both these branches of remittance, as far as regards provincial towns, are effected through the banks. Exporters and importers, residing in a city or town, do not meet together, like the merchants engaged in foreign trade, and traffic from their bills, but both parties go to the bank. The exporter draws bills, which he discounts with the bank ; the importer obtains from the bank bills or letters of credit, which he remits in payment of his imports. The amount of this kind of business must, of course, depend upon the amount of the trade. Where the imports are great, there will be demand for bills, or other modes of remittance, upon the banker. When the exports are great, bills will be brought to him for discount, or lodgments will be made to his credit at his agents. By comparing the sums which are thus transmitted in different directions, a banker can, merely by a reference to his own books, ascertain the balance of trade between the place in which he resides, and any other place with which it may have commercial inter-course. If he finds his exchanges with the neighbouring bankers are unfavourable, he may infer that the balance of trade is against the place in which his bank is established. And if, on the other hand, the exchanges are in his favour, he may infer the balance of trade is favourable. It will generally be found, that the trade between seaport and inland towns is always in favour of the former. Manufacturing towns and large cities have usually the balance in their favour. It may be observed, however, that the balance of remittances will not *always* show the balance of trade. With regard to places of fashionable resort for instance, there must be a great consumption of commodities imported from other places, and at the same time there is no commodity exported,—here the balance of trade is unfavourable : at the same time there must be great remittances, in money, to the parties residing there, to enable them to pay for the commodities they consume. Thus, too, when large sums are remitted from England to absentee landlords, or as loans to foreign powers, the balance of remittance may be against England, while the balance of trade may be in her favour.

The remitting of money to London by a country bank, diminishes the currency to that amount in the place where the bank is established. If a person at Birmingham takes one hundred sovereigns to the branch of the Bank of England, and obtains a bill at fourteen days on the parent establishment in London, then there is a banking capital created for fourteen days. If, when the bill becomes due, the Bank of England pay the bill in gold, the banking capital is destroyed. The currency of Birmingham is now one hundred sovereigns less, and that of London is one hundred sovereigns more. During the existence of the bill there were one hundred sovereigns less in circulation, and these one hundred sovereigns were represented by the bill. Some country bankers, instead of drawing bills upon their London agents, reissue the bills they have discounted. By this means the banker saves the expense of remitting the discounted bill to London, and the person taking it saves the expense of the stamp for a new bill.

Banks of remittance encourage the trade of a district in two ways: First, by diminishing the prices of commodities. The facility of conveying money has the same effect upon trade as a facility of conveying commodities. The opening of good roads diminishes the expense of the conveyance of goods. This cheapness in the conveyance causes the commodities to be sold at a lower price. As the imports into the town are sold at a cheaper rate, and the exports are also sold at a lower price at the place of consumption, the increased cheapness in both cases increases the demand, and hence trade is advanced. The cheapness of conveying money operates in the same way as cheapness in the conveyance of goods. After the goods are sold, the money must be transmitted. The expense of remitting the money, like the expense of conveying the goods, must be regarded as an item in the cost of production, and be taken into account in fixing the price at which the goods must be sold. Banks remit money at a less expense than it can be remitted in any other way. Hence the merchants are enabled to sell their merchandise at a lower price, and thereby consumption is increased and trade is extended.

The second way in which banks of remittance promote trade, is by enabling capital to revolve more rapidly. They cause money to be remitted in a shorter space of time. For instance, —an Irish butter merchant may purchase of a farmer a quantity of butter, and ship it for London. He may, on the same day, draw a bill for the value of the butter, and have it discounted at the bank. With this money he may purchase a further quantity of butter, against which he may draw another bill, and have it discounted. This operation, if he be in good credit, may be repeated as often as he pleases. Now, if there be no bank in the district, he could not get the money for the first shipment of butter until the return of post from London, and then he would receive large Bank of England notes, which he might not easily be able to get changed. During this interval he can make no purchases for want of money, and the farmer has no sale for his butter. Thus the banks enable the merchants' capital to revolve several times more rapidly than it could otherwise do. To increase the rapidity of the returns of capital has the same effect as to increase its amount. If any given amount of capital, that now revolves once in a year, be made to revolve twice in a year, it will have the same effect upon trade as if the amount of capital were doubled, and its progress remained the same.

Banks of *deposit* encourage the trade and wealth of a district by collecting together the various small amounts of money that previously lay idle in the hands of the depositors, and employing this sum in advances, by way of loan or discount, to the productive classes of the community. The commodities thus produced are remitted to a distant place for sale. But in the interval, between the transmission of the goods and the return of the money for which they may be sold, the manufacturer is deprived of the use of this amount of capital. Banks of *remittance* guard against this inconvenience, and advance immediately to the manufacturer the value of the goods, by discounting his bill upon the party to whom they are consigned. By this means he has all the advantage to be gained from the higher prices of a distant sale, in connexion with that prompt payment he would obtain from a home market. Thus it is, that while banks of deposit enable the capital of any district to

H

revolve more rapidly *within the district,* banks of remittance enable it to revolve more rapidly with reference to other places.   Both produce the same effect as that positive increase of capital which is introduced by banks of circulation.

SECTION X.

BANKS OF CIRCULATION.

A BANK that issues notes is called a bank of circulation.   The amount of notes that any bank has in circulation is usually called by bankers *" the circulation."*   Banks of circulation, both in England and Scotland, have all of them had to sustain heavy accusations.   I shall notice some of these charges, not with a view of rebutting them in regard to any individual bank, but in order to discuss the general principles by which we should be guided, in judging of the effects produced by banks of circulation.

The most common charge against banks of circulation is, that they have issued an excessive amount of their notes ; and thus have encouraged speculation, raised the price of commodities, and led to commercial convulsions similar to that of December, 1825.

Before entering upon the consideration of these charges, I shall point out the checks that operate against an over-issue of notes.

I have already stated, that similar accusations may be as justly advanced against banks of deposit as against banks of circulation ; for to give increased motion to the currency has the same effect as to increase its amount.   If a million of money be taken from the counting-houses of the merchants, and the tills of the shopkeepers, and lodged in the hands of a London banker, for him to employ in advancing loans or discounting bills, this has the same effect as though he issued for the same purposes a million of his own promissory notes. There is, however, one difference.   The advances of a London banker are limited by the amount of his lodgments.   If the money be not placed in his hands, he cannot issue it ; and hence he may be regarded as merely an agent regulating the distribution of the previously existing currency.   But the country banker having the power of making money, the amount of his advances is not subject to this restraint.

But the amount of notes issued by a bank must be limited by the demand of its customers. No banker is so anxious to put his notes into circulation, that he gives them away. He advances them either by way of loan or discount; and he always believes that the security on which he makes his advances is sufficiently ample. He expects that the money will be repaid with interest. It is true, that like other commercial men, he is sometimes deceived in his customers; and by placing too much confidence in them, he sustains losses. But this is a misfortune against which he is always anxious to guard. The issues of bankers are limited, therefore; on the one hand by the wants of the public, and on the other by the bankers' desire to protect their own interests.

A further check upon the issues of banks is, that all their notes are payable on demand. Although a banker has the power of issuing his notes to excess, either by advancing them as dead loans or on slender security, yet he has not the power of keeping them out: their remaining in circulation depends not on him, but on the public; and the uncertainty as to the time of their return for payment compels him to keep at all times a sufficient stock of money to meet the most extensive demand that is likely in the ordinary course of business to occur.

Another check upon an excessive issue of notes, is the system of exchanges that is carried on between the banks. Every banker that issues notes has an interest in withdrawing from circulation the notes of every other banker, in order to make more room for his own. When a banker receives the notes of another banker, he never reissues them. If the two bankers live in the same place, they meet once or twice a week, as they may find convenient, and exchange their notes. The balance between them, if any, is paid by a draft on London payable on demand; or, which amounts to the same thing, the London agent of the one party is directed to pay the amount to the London agent of the other party. If the country banker lives at a distance from the banker whose notes he has received, he sends them to his London agent to present for payment. Hence it is that country notes seldom travel far from the place of issue: they are sure to be intercepted by some of the rival

H 2

banks; and in a country where banks are so numerous as in England, it is obvious that the notes of any individual bank must move in a very limited circle. If a banker attempts to force out a higher amount of notes than the wants of this circle require, he will soon find that the notes will be returned to him in the exchanges with neighbouring bankers, or else they will speedily find their way for payment to his London agent.

Another check upon an over-issue on the part of the banks is their practice of allowing interest upon money lodged in their hands. No man will keep money lying idle in his hands if he can obtain interest for it, and have it returned to him upon demand. If a banker attempts to force out a large amount of notes, they will get into the hands of somebody. And those who do not employ them in their trade will take them back to the bank and lodge them to their credit, for the purpose of receiving the interest. Thus, if the notes of a banker are put in motion by the operations of commerce, they are soon intercepted by rival bankers; and if they attain a state of rest, they are brought back and lodged upon interest; so that in either case they are withdrawn from circulation.

Banks of circulation have also been accused of encouraging a spirit of speculation.

To obtain clear ideas as to the justice of this charge, it will be necessary to define accurately the nature of speculation, and to view the circumstances by which it is governed.

Between the producer and the consumer of any commodity, there are generally two or more parties, who are merchants or dealers. The demand for any commodity is either a speculative or a consumptive demand. The demand by the consumers who purchase for immediate use, is always a consumptive demand. But if the commodity purchased be not intended for immediate use, but is purchased at any given time, merely because the purchaser apprehends that its price will advance, then is that demand a speculative demand. So, if a merchant purchase of a manufacturer, or a farmer, such a quantity of commodities as in the ordinary course of his trade he is likely to require, that demand may be considered a consumptive demand; but if, in expectation of a rise in price, he fills his warehouses with goods for which he has no immediate sale, then is that demand a speculative demand. A speculation, then, is that kind of traffic in which the dealer expects to realize a profit, not by the ordinary course of trade, but by the intervention of some fortuitous circumstance that shall change the price of the commodity in which he deals.

A speculation in any commodity, therefore, is occasioned by some opinion that may be formed of its future price. It is well known that the price of commodities is governed by the proportion that may exist between the supply and the demand. Whatever increases the supply, or diminishes the demand, will lower the price; and, on the contrary, whatever diminishes the supply, or increases the demand, will advance the price. The greater part of our food, and the materials of most of our clothing, are produced by the seasons; and the quantity produced in each year depends, in a great degree, upon the most uncertain of all things,—the weather. Here, then, is a wide field for speculation. If our food, like the manna in the wilderness, were supplied to us day by day, in exactly the quantity that each individual required, it would furnish no subject for speculation. But as long as the seasons are variable in the quantity of their productions, so long will speculation exist. Many commodities, too, besides being influenced by the seasons, are influenced by several other circumstances,—as a state of peace or war,—the opening of new markets,—the discovery of cheaper modes of production,—or the substitution of a rival commodity; all these circumstances have an effect upon price, and the dealer who buys or sells any commodity in expectation, than an alteration in price will be produced by such causes, is a speculator.

Now, it is obvious that no system of banking can prevent speculation, and that speculations would be formed, even were there no bank in existence. We learn from Holy Writ, that the owners of corn sometimes refused to sell, in expectation of an advance of price. These were speculations, though Judæa had neither banks nor paper money. If it be said that the country banks are the cause of speculation, I will ask how it is that speculations exist in countries where there are no country banks? If it be said that the issuing of country notes is the cause of speculation, I will ask how it is that Liverpool is the most speculative place in England, although the Liverpool bankers do not issue notes? If it be said that the speculations of 1825 were produced by the country banks, I will ask, what produced similar speculations in 1720, when there was not a single country bank in the kingdom?

It must not, however, be denied that all banking gives to speculation facilities that would not otherwise be so easily supplied. It is the object of banking to give facilities to trade, and whatever gives facilities to trade gives facilities to speculation. Trade and speculation are in some cases so nearly allied, that it is impossible to say at what precise point trade ends and speculation begins. When a banker discounts a bill, he does not usually ask the party how he intends to employ the money; and, for aught he knows, it may be employed in speculation. Wherever there are banks, capital is more readily obtained, and at a cheaper rate. The cheapness of capital gives facilities to speculation just in the same way as the cheapness of beef and of beer gives facilities to gluttony and drunkenness.

The legitimate operations of banking, however, are such as to place speculation under some degree of restraint. As to men of large capital and immense wealth, they may speculate as much as they please; over *them* the bankers have no control. But if men of moderate means engage in speculation beyond their capital, it is not the interest of the banker to support them. For such persons to carry speculation to any great extent, it is necessary either that they raise money on slender security, or that the money be advanced for a considerable length of time. It is not the interest of a banker to meet their wishes in either of these respects. It is not his interest to advance his money on insufficient security. It is not his interest to advance money as a dead loan. The security a banker requires ought to be both ample and convertible. It is contrary to all sound principles of banking for a banker to advance money on dead security. In the first place, such loans do not create any banking capital; and, in the second place, they cannot be suddenly called up, in case any contraction of the banking capital should render it necessary.

In admitting that banking, by granting facilities to trade, necessarily grants facilities, to a certain extent, to speculation, it is not admitted that bankers generally have granted facilities to speculation beyond the fair operations of their trade. All speculation, by increasing the number and amount of commercial transactions, puts into motion a greater quantity of money. This money is supplied by the bankers either in the way of repayment of deposits, or of discounting of bills, or by loans. Now as increased issues on the part of the banks are almost simultaneous with a spirit of speculation, it has been inferred that the issues of the notes have excited the spirit of speculation, whereas it has been the spirit of speculation that has called out the notes. In the years 1824 and 1825, as the speculations increased, the issues of notes increased; and when the speculations were over, the notes returned. This was the case not merely in England, but also in Scotland, though none of the Scotch banks sustained the least diminution of public confidence.

Another charge that has often been preferred against banks of circulation is, that by an increased issue of their notes they have caused a general rise in prices.

In investigating this charge, it will be proper to inquire what are the cases in which an increased issue of notes may produce a rise in prices.

It cannot be denied that if any bank have the privilege of issuing notes, not convertible into gold—that is, not payable in gold on demand—the notes may be issued to such an amount as to cause a considerable advance in prices. It is now generally believed that the issues of the Bank of England during the operation of the Restriction Act did produce this effect. It may also be admitted that in a country where there is one chief bank, possessing an immense capital and unbounded confidence, the notes of such a bank, even if payable in gold, may be issued to such an extent as to cause an advance of prices, until an unfavourable course of the exchange shall cause payment of the notes to be demanded in gold. For gold will not be demanded until the course of the exchange is so unfavourable as to cause the exportation of gold to be attended with profit. Hence the issues of the Bank of England being at present under no other restraint than liability to pay in gold on demand, may for a time cause an advance in prices.

In cases where the increased issue of notes is caused by the increased quantity of commodities brought to market, the additional amount of notes put into circulation does not cause any advance of prices. In all agricultural districts there is a great demand for notes about the season of harvest, to pay for the produce then brought to market. In the south of Ireland the amount of notes in circulation is much greater in the winter, when corn and bacon are being exported, than in the summer months. Almost every trade and every kind of manufacture is carried on with more activity at some periods of the year than at others; and during the active seasons when money is in demand, more notes are in circulation. These notes are at such periods drawn out of the banks, either as repayments of money lodged, or by discount of the bills drawn against the exported commodities.

An increased issue of notes often causes the production of an additional quantity of commodities, and in this case does not produce an advance of prices. The issue of notes will be either in the form of discounts, or loans, or the repayment of deposits. In either case the parties receiving the money will spend it, and a demand will thus be occasioned for a certain class of commodities. If this demand should not exceed the quantity that can be readily supplied, there will be no advance of price. The parties who receive the money from the banker may give it to the dealer in exchange for the articles they purchase. The dealer wishes to replace the goods he has sold, and passes the money for more goods to the manufacturer. The manufacturer consequently buys more raw material and employs more labourers. An increased quantity of goods is thus produced, and exchanged against the increased quantity of money. But while the supply can keep pace with the demand, the price will remain the same; it is only when the demand exceeds the supply, and the commodities are consequently comparatively scarce, that the price will advance.

In many cases, an increased issue of notes is not the *cause*, but the *effect* of an advance of prices. If a Yorkshire clothier sells a thousand pounds' worth of goods to a London merchant, he will draw a bill for a thousand pounds, and take it for discount to a country banker, whose notes for a thousand pounds may thus be put into circulation; but if, in consequence of a scarcity of wool, or from any other cause, the goods that were sold for a thousand pounds are now worth two thousand pounds, then will the banker discount a bill for two thousand pounds, and put into circulation two thousand pounds of his notes. In this case it is obvious that the issue of notes is not the cause of the high price of wool; but that the high price of wool is the cause of the increased issue of notes. Such is often the case with many other commodities; a real or apprehended scarcity causes an advance in price. The same commodity exchanges for a greater quantity of money. The bills are drawn for higher sums, and the bankers who discount these bills issue, of course, a greater amount of notes. The rise in price, too, renders more capital necessary to carry on the same extent of business. Many persons who had money in the bank on interest will now draw it out, to employ it in their trade, and these operations will occasion a still farther issue of notes. A rise in the price of one commodity will sometimes advance the price of other commodities, and hence similar banking operations are affected by persons engaged in other branches of trade. The process by which high prices cause an increase in the amount of notes in circulation, can thus be easily and obviously traced.

In cases where an increased issue of notes does cause an advance of price, the advance can be but temporary, and this advance may generally be ascribed to a spirit of speculation on the part of the dealers, and not to an excessive issue on the part of the banks. As the prices of all commodities are regulated by the proportion that may exist between the demand and the supply, whenever an increased issue of notes raises prices, it must be either by increasing the demand for commodities, or diminishing the supply. The cases in which an increased issue of notes may cause an advance of prices, are chiefly those in which the money is employed in purchasing such commodities as cannot be readily produced by human labour. Thus, if a banker lend money to a corn merchant to purchase a stock of corn, he increases the demand for corn. If he lend money to a farmer to enable him to pay his rent without selling his corn, he diminishes the supply. In both cases he may cause an advance in price. But even in this case, the most unpopular that can well be imagined, the effect on price will be but temporary ; for these speculations do not diminish the quantity of corn in the country. The supplies now withheld must ultimately be sold, and in proportion as they advance the price when withheld, will they lower the price when brought to market. A degree of speculation in some commodity or other is always on foot, and occasions fluctuations in the price. The banks have no control over these speculations, and ought not to be deemed answerable for the changes they occasion. To suppose that the banks can so regulate their issues as to maintain permanent prices, is to ascribe to them a power which they do not possess, and which, if they did possess, they ought never to use.

There are various cases wherein an increased issue of notes causes a reduction of prices. The speculations which advance prices are chiefly those carried on by *dealers*. The speculations of *producers* who invest their capital in new undertakings, with the view of producing any given commodities at a less cost, will, if successful, reduce the price to the consumer, and so far as such speculations are assisted by the banks, the issue of notes thus occasioned tends to the reduction of prices. An advance of money which enables a farmer to bestow a higher degree of cultivation on his land—which enables a manufacturer or a tradesman to extend his business—has the effect of increasing the quantity of commodities offered for sale, and consequently to reduce the price. The banks, too, by advancing capital on lower terms than it could be otherwise obtained, diminish the cost of production, and, consequently, the price. The banks still farther reduce prices by destroying monopoly. In towns where there are no banks, a few moneyed men have all the trade in their own hands; but when a bank is established, other persons of character are enabled to borrow capital of the bankers. Thus monopoly is destroyed, competition is produced, and prices fall. Hence it is obvious, that *in the ordinary course of business* the issues of the banks tend not to advance but to lower prices.

The effect which the amount of notes in circulation has upon the foreign exchanges has been the subject of much discussion. One party contended, that as the amount of notes increases, the exchange must become unfavourable. Another party maintained, that the exchanges were not at all affected by the issue of notes, but by the state of foreign trade. The authors of the Report of the Bullion Committee expressed the former opinion, some of the Bank Directors maintained the latter.

It is obvious that the exchanges are regulated by the amount of gold that is required to be sent abroad, either to pay the balance of trade, or to pay our armies, or to subsidize foreign powers, or as rents to absentees, or for some other purpose. Now it is clear that an increased or diminished issue of notes will in no way diminish the amount of gold that is to be sent abroad, and, therefore, can have no *direct* effect upon the exchanges. If we owe the gold, we must pay it. We may diminish our issues of notes, but that will not pay our debts.

If, then, the issues of notes have any effect upon the exchanges, it must be in an *indirect* way.

I have already stated that an increased issue of notes can have no effect upon the prices of commodities at home, but by influencing either the supply or the demand. If the increased quantity of money raises the demand for commodities beyond a certain point, it will advance the price. And if it increases the supply, it will lower the price; but in no way can the quantity of money in circulation affect the price of commodities but through the channels of supply and demand. Just so with the foreign exchanges. An unfavourable course of exchange arises generally from our owing a sum of money which we have to pay in consequence of our imports having exceeded our exports. An increased quantity of money, therefore, to affect the exchanges, must diminish the amount of our foreign debt, and it can do this only by either increasing our exports or diminishing our imports. When money is abundant our merchants can import more than formerly. This increases our debt. The importers are disposed to lay in stocks of goods, and the competition between the importers raises the price they give to the foreigner. Hence there are heavy sums to be sent abroad. It is true that when money is abundant our manufacturers and exporters can also export more goods, but the competition among exporters diminishes the price to the foreigner, and hence we have a less proportionate sum to receive. The exporter, too, having abundance of money, gives the foreigner long credit, and hence the money is not received in England for a considerable time after the goods have been shipped. In the mean time the exchanges become unfavourable, and gold must be sent abroad. Now suppose in this state of things the bank contract their issues; money becomes scarce—bills cannot be discounted, and trade is dull. Now, then, the importer, having already a heavy stock of goods, will buy no more; he is anxious to sell, for he has not now sufficient capital to keep so large a stock. A general desire of selling will cause a fall of price. Fewer commodities will now be imported, and these obtained at a less price, hence there is less money due to the foreigner. The exporters, on the other hand, deprived also of their usual accommodation, cannot carry on business to the same extent—the supply will be reduced—the competition is less, and prices rise to the foreigner. The exporters, too, cannot give such long credit as formerly; they will call in the sums due to them, and hence more money must come in from abroad. As, then, we have to pay other nations a less amount of money for our imports, and they have to pay us a greater amount for our exports, the exchanges will become favourable. It is obvious that this operation will cause great embarrassment in trade; in fact, it is only by producing embarrassment that a contraction of the currency can affect the exchanges.

The amount of notes in circulation affects the foreign exchanges in another way. When an increased issue takes place, money becomes more abundant; the lenders are more numerous, and the supply of capital is increased. Hence the price given for the loan of money, that is, the rate of interest, falls. Persons who have money to employ will find they cannot obtain the same interest as formerly; hence they will be disposed to invest it in the foreign funds, where it can be employed to greater advantage. In order to remit this money they will purchase foreign bills; this demand for foreign bills will advance their price, and the exchanges will consequently be unfavourable. On the other hand, when the circulation is considerably reduced, money becomes scarce, a higher price will be given for the use of it, the rate of interest rises; persons who have property abroad will be disposed to bring it home, where it can be more profitably invested; they will draw bills against it and sell them in the market. This new supply of bills will lower the price, and make the exchanges favourable.

It should always be recollected that the transmission of money as subsidies, loans, or for investment in the foreign funds, will have the same effect upon the exchanges as though it were transmitted in payment of commodities imported. Whenever, therefore, the issue of notes shall, directly or indirectly, cause a transmission of money from one country to another, the exchanges will be affected. But when this shall not be the case, the expansion or contraction of the currency will have no effect upon the foreign exchanges.

SECTION XI.

BANKS OF DISCOUNT.

A CONSIDERABLE branch of the business of modern banking consists in discounting bills of exchange. As they have only a short time to run before they fall due, the capital advanced soon returns; and being transferable, they can, if necessary, be re-discounted. Hence they are admirably adapted for the purposes of the bankers: for, as the advances of bankers to their customers are made with other people's money, and that money may at any time be withdrawn, it becomes necessary that the securities on which those advances are made should rapidly revolve and be at all times convertible. By means of bills of exchange bankers can easily extend or diminish their advances in proportion to the capital they may have to employ. If they find that the amount of their deposits or the amount of their circulation is diminishing, they will diminish their discounts. If these increase, they may increase their discounts.

I. *Nature and Origin of Bills of Exchange.*—Bills of exchange are said to have been invented in the fourteenth century by the Jews or the Lombards, for the purpose of withdrawing their property from the countries from which they were expelled. The drawer and the acceptor of a bill were two persons, residing at two distant places, and the bill was probably nothing more than a written order delivered to a third person, who was going to visit the place where the debtor resided, and who would return with the money to the drawer. But it might happen that this person might not be going to return; in this case he might advance to the creditor the amount of the order, and receive the money again from the debtor when he arrived at his journey's end. But this third person might not be going to the place where the debtor resided, he might be going only a part of the way, and he might then fall in with some other person who was going the other part; he would then request this other person to advance him the money in exchange for the order he had received from the creditor, and the order would then be transferred. It would thus be discovered that as a creditor might give an order upon his debtor to a third person, this third person might transfer the order to a fourth, the fourth to a fifth, and so on. To effect these transactions it would be necessary that each person receiving the order, or bill, had confidence in the drawer or some of the endorsers, and also that each person receiving it should have some compensation for the trouble it occasioned him. If the order were not payable on demand, but at some months after date, the compensation would be increased by the amount of interest for the time the order had to run before it would be payable.

Such is at present the case. The drawer of a bill on a person residing in the country *sells* it on the exchange. Foreign bills are never said to be *discounted*, but to be *sold*; for the person who gives the drawer the amount, is supposed to deduct not only the interest on the bill, but also the expense of its transmission. The buyer of a bill is a person who owes a sum of money to a person in another country (say in France), and who wants a bill to remit thither to pay his debt. The seller of a bill is a person who has exported a quantity of goods to France, and who draws a bill for the amount: it will be for the convenience of these two people to deal together: the buyer will give his money in exchange for the bill, which he will send to his creditor in France, and the seller will give his bill in exchange for the buyer's money, by which he is paid for the goods he has exported. If this money is equal to the amount of the bill, minus only what may be deemed equal to the discount and the expense of transmission, the exchange is said to be at par; but there are various circumstances which may cause the exchange to be either above or below par, and the price given for bills of exchange will vary accordingly.

When two nations exchange their commodities with each other to exactly the same amount, the buyers will be just as numerous as the sellers. The demand for bills and the supply of bills will be equal; the exchange will now be at par; but it rarely or never happens that the exports and imports between any two countries are precisely the same; and as gold is the medium of traffic between nations as well as between individuals, the balance or difference between the purchases and the sale must be remitted in that metal. Now the expense in freight and insurance of sending a quantity of gold from one country to another will not be inconsiderable. If, then, I owe a sum of money to a merchant in France, I would be willing to give something more than that sum for a bill, rather than submit to the expense and trouble of remitting gold. But if the bill would cost more than the expense at which I could send the gold, why, then the gold should go. It is evident, then, that in that nation which is in debt to another nation, and which, consequently, has to send gold to pay its debts, the demand for bills of exchange will be greater than the supply. These bills will be sold for more than the amount of the money for which they are drawn; they are then at a premium, but this premium never can rise higher than the expense of remitting an equal amount in gold: for if it were cheaper to remit gold, the gold would be remitted.

The price of bills in the market is usually called the rate of exchange, and when the balance of trade is against a country, and gold must be remitted to pay that balance, and, consequently, the price of foreign bills rises beyond their real value or par, then the course of exchange is said to be against that country: thus, for instance, if in London I can sell a bill on Paris for more than the amount for which it is drawn, then the course of exchange is said to be against England and in favour of France; but if I am obliged to sell my bill for less than the amount, then the exchange is against France and in favour of England. The price of bills is regulated entirely by the proportion that may exist between the demand and the supply, and the demand and the supply are regulated chiefly by the state of trade between the respective countries.

The trafficking in bills of exchange is now a distinct branch of business. When bills, say on France, are at a high premium in our market, a house in London will draw bills upon a house in Paris, and the bills will be sold at a good price. On the other hand, when bills on England are at a high premium in the Paris markets, a house in Paris will draw upon a house in London, and sell the bill in the Paris market. This seems to be a very honourable kind of business, but it is said that some inferior persons engaged in this traffic sometimes have recourse to unjustifiable means of raising or lowering the price of bills, in the same way as stockjobbers are said to do to affect the value of the public funds.

Not only are bills employed as the means of transmitting money from one country to another, but also as the means of

making remittances from one town to another.   If a person in
a country town wishes to send money to London, he can go to
the bank and procure a bill upon a banker in London.   If he
wants to receive money from London, he will draw a bill upon
his debtor, and get the money for it at the bank.   If he wish to
send money from one provincial town to another, he will get
from the bank a bill upon a London banker and send it to his
correspondent by post.   When the country banker discounts, or,
as it is called in the foreign market, *buys* a bill, he usually
charges, in addition to the discount, a commission to pay the
expense of its transmission and collection.   And when he issues
or sells a bill, he usually gives in exchange for cash a bill at a
certain number of days after date.   Hence the number of days
at which a provincial banker is in the habit of drawing upon his
London agent is usually called the *par of exchange* between that
place and London.

II. *Advantages of Bills.*—Besides their utility as a means of
transferring money from one place to another, bills have the
following advantages :—

1. Bills are a means of transferring debts from one person to
another.   If I owe a man 100*l*. and another man owes me 100*l*.,
I will draw a bill for that amount on my debtor and give it to
my creditor.   I have thus transferred the debt from my debtor
to my creditor, and my own debt is liquidated.   My debtor,
instead of paying me the money he owed me, will pay it to the
holder of the bill.   My creditor will now look for payment to
my debtor, and consider me simply as a guarantee for the payment of the bill.   If he wishes to make use of the bill he will
again transfer the debt to another party, placing his own name
on the bill as an additional guarantee.   The bill may thus pass
through a variety of hands, and liquidate a great number of
debts, before it becomes due.   When due, it will be paid by the
acceptor, who was the original debtor, and all these intermediate
transactions will be closed.   Hence, in Lancashire, bills of
exchange have served the purpose of a circulating medium, in
the same way as bank notes.   The only difference is, that in
transferring a bank note you are not responsible for its ultimate
payment ; but in passing a bill of exchange you place your
name on it as a guarantee.   A bill of exchange, too, cannot
always be passed for its full amount, but you will have to pay a

discount according to the time it has to run before it will fall due.

2. Bills fix the period for the payment of debts, and in case of litigation they afford an easy proof of the debt. A person will have little scruple in putting off a tradesman to whom he owes money, and the creditor dares not be urgent lest the debtor should no longer deal with him, hence the time of payment can never be calculated upon with certainty. But if the customer has given a bill for the amount he owes, that bill will circulate into the hands of other persons who will be more peremptory in demanding payment, and whose applications cannot be disregarded with impunity. Besides, if a man dishonour his acceptance, his character is stamped at once in the commercial world as being either very poor, very negligent, or very unprincipled, and at no future time will he be able to raise money upon the credit of his name. Hence many persons who are very tardy in paying a book debt, are very punctual in paying their bills. In case, too, a tradesman is under the necessity of bringing an action at law against his customer, he will have to prove the actual delivery of every article mentioned in his account. This, at a distance of time, is often difficult to do; but if a bill has been accepted for the amount, it is only necessary to prove that the acceptance is in the defendant's handwriting,

3. Bills enable a tradesman to carry on a more extensive business with the same amount of capital. If, by the custom of trade, a dealer gives his customers three months' credit, he can, during that period, make no use of that portion of his capital which is invested in the commodities they have purchased; but if they accept his bills, drawn at three months after date, he can, if in good credit, get those bills discounted at the bank in his town, and then employ this money in the further extension of his business. He will thus, while selling on credit, obtain nearly the same advantages as though he sold for ready money. Should he, instead of having these bills discounted, pay them to the manufacturer or wholesale house of whom he makes his purchases, it will amount to nearly the same thing. The whole of his capital is thus kept in motion, and is not diminished by any amount of outstanding debts. To give credit without drawing bills requires that a tradesman should have a large capital. To give no credit will restrict his business. By means

I

of bills he is enabled to give credit and to extend his business, without requiring any addition to his capital.

4. Bills afford an easy way of giving a guarantee. A person may wish to borrow money of me, and I may be unwilling to lend it to him unless he procure a more wealthy person to guarantee the repayment at a given time. If he has a friend that will do this, the most easy way of effecting the guarantee is by means of a bill drawn by the borrower upon his friend. This, in point of security, is the same thing as a letter of guarantee; but it has also this additional advantage, that if I should want the money before the time fixed for its repayment, I can get this bill discounted and reimburse myself the money I have advanced. Bills of this description are called accommodation-bills, or wind-bills, or kites. When employed only as a means of affording occasional assistance to a needy friend, or for raising a sum of money for a short time, to meet an unexpected call, they do not appear to be very objectionable; but when systematically pursued for the purpose of raising a fictitious capital whereon to trade, they uniformly indicate the folly and effect the ruin of all the parties concerned.

5. Bills are the means of facilitating the removal of capital from one branch of trade to another as circumstances may require. When the demand for any commodity increases, the price advances, and more capital is put into requisition to increase the supply. When the demand for any commodity declines, the price falls, the trade is bad, and capital will be withdrawn to be invested in a more profitable employment. Every branch of trade is liable to fluctuations from an alteration in the proportion between the demand and the supply, and hence capital is continually undergoing a transfer from the production of those articles for which there is a less demand to the production of those articles for which there is a greater demand. But in what way is this transfer effected? Is it by a manufacturer leaving one employment for another? No. The manufacturer in the declining trade will reduce his capital, while the manufacturer in the prosperous trade will augment his capital; and the transfer of capital from one trade to the other is effected chiefly by bills of exchange. The manufacturer who has sold a less quantity of commodities will have fewer bills for his banker to discount; the other, having sold a greater quantity of commodities, has more bills for discount. The banker's

capital, which he employs chiefly in the discount of bills, is thus easily transferred from one branch of manufacture to another, in exact proportion to the circumstances of the respective parties. On this subject we quote Mr. Ricardo:

" In all rich countries there is a number of men forming what is called a moneyed class. These men are engaged in no trade, but live on the interest of their money, which is employed in discounting bills, or in loans to the more industrious part of the community. The bankers, too, employ a large capital on the same objects. The capital so employed forms a circulating capital of a large amount, and is employed in larger or smaller proportions by all the different trades of a country. There is, perhaps, no manufacturer, however rich, who limits his business to the extent that his own funds alone will allow; he has always some portion of this floating capital increasing or diminishing according to the activity of the demand for his commodities. When the demand for silks increases, and that for cloth diminishes, the clothier does not remove with his capital to the silk trade, but he dismisses some of his workmen, and he discontinues his demand for loans from bankers and moneyed men: while the case of the silk manufacturer is the reverse; he wishes to employ more workmen, and thus his motive for borrowing is increased; he borrows more, and thus capital is transferred from one employment to another without the necessity of a manufacturer discontinuing his usual occupation."*

III. *Classes of Bills.*—The bills presented to a bank for discount may generally be divided into the following classes:

1. Bills drawn by producers or manufacturers upon wholesale dealers.

2. Bills drawn by wholesale dealers upon retail dealers.

3. Bills drawn by retail dealers upon consumers.

4. Bills not arising out of trade, but yet drawn against value, as rents, &c.

5. Kites, or accommodation bills.

The first two classes of bills are the best, and are fair legitimate bills for bankers to discount.

The third class ought not to be too much encouraged. They are for comparatively small amounts, and are drawn by shopkeepers and tradesmen upon their customers. To discount

* Ricardo's Principles of Political Economy, page 84.

these bills freely would encourage extravagance in the acceptors; and ultimately prove injurious to the drawers. When a man accepts bills to his butcher, baker, tailor, upholsterer, &c., he may fairly be suspected of living beyond his income. Solvent and regular people pay their tradesmen's accounts with ready money.

The fourth class of bills, though sometimes proper, ought not to be too much encouraged. Persons out of trade have no business with bills.

The last class of bills should almost always be rejected. To an experienced banker, who knows the parties, the discovery of accommodation bills is by no means difficult. They are usually drawn for even amounts, for the largest sum that the stamp will bear, and for the longest term that the bank will discount, and are presented for discount soon after they are drawn. The parties are often relations, friends, or parties, who, from their avocations, can have no dealings with each other.

Not only the parties and the amounts of bills are matters of consideration to a banker, but also the time they have to run before they fall due. A bill drawn for a long term after date, is usually styled, not perhaps very properly, *a long dated bill.* A bill drawn at a short term, is styled a short dated bill.

Query.—Is it most for the interest of a bank to discount long dated bills or short dated bills?

Short Bills versus *Long Bills.*—First, There is more safety in discounting short bills, because the parties may fail before the long ones become due. Secondly, If any given amount of capital be employed in discounting bills, it will accumulate more rapidly by discounting short bills than long bills, operating in the same way as money placed at compound interest, which increases the faster, as the times of paying the interest are more frequent. Thirdly, If a bank charges commission on the amount of the bills discounted, the commission will be more in the course of a year upon any given amount of capital employed in discounting short bills than employed in discounting long bills. Fourthly, If a bank issues notes, a greater amount of notes will be issued in discounting a succession of short bills, than by discounting long bills. Thus if I discount a bill for 1,000*l.* drawn at twelve months after date, I issue only 1,000*l.* of notes; but if I discount in succession four bills each, having only three months to run, I issue, in the course of the year, 4,000*l.* of notes. Fifthly, Long dated bills lock up the funds of a bank so that they cannot be discounted with safety but from the bank's own capital : for if a bank employs its deposits or its circulation in discounting long dated bills, and payment of the notes or deposits should be demanded, the long dated bills could not be re-discounted, and the bank must stop. Sixthly, Long bills may encourage speculation. Persons may purchase large quantities of commodities in the expectation that the price will advance before the long bills which they accept in payment shall fall due. But if the bills are of short date, the speculation will be prevented.

Long Bills versus *Short Bills.*—First, The amount of discount is greater on a long bill than on a short bill. If, therefore, a gentleman out of business wants a temporary advance, and proposes to draw a bill on his friend, it is better to advise him to draw a long bill than a short one. Secondly, Long bills will employ a larger amount of capital. If a banker discounts any given amount per week, he will always have twice the amount of bills current, if they are drawn at four months' date, than he will have if they are drawn at two months. And, as bankers wish to employ their capital, it will be more for their advantage to discount such bills as will employ the largest amount. Thirdly, The discounting of long dated bills, being a more permanent advance of capital, is more beneficial to the commercial and agricultural classes in the district. If a retail dealer can get long bills discounted, he can afford to give longer credit, and this will induce his customers to buy more goods of him, and he will do more business. If a manufacturer or wholesale dealer can get his long bills discounted, he also can give longer credit, and will sell more goods. If a landlord can get a long bill on his tenant discounted, he need not urge him for rent, and the money may, in the interim, be employed in improving the land. The discounting of long bills is similar to a permanent advance of capital. The money may be profitably employed, and be reproduced before the long bill may become due, but if the bill be short this cannot be done.

IV. *Notaries Public.*—" A notary was anciently a scribe that only took *notes* or minutes, and made short drafts of writings and other instruments, both public and private. But, at this day, we call him a notary public who confirms and attests the truth of any deeds or writings, in order to render the same authentic."* This part of the business of a public notary must have been very necessary before the discovery of the art of printing, and when many of the first men in the state were unable to read or write. We find that some public documents have been attested by notaries in the following form :—" As my Lord Bishop is unable to write, I do hereby certify, that the above is his mark." These notaries were appointed by the Archbishop of Canterbury, and took an oath of fidelity on receiving their appointment. All instruments made by them were considered public instruments, and were received as evidence in the courts of law.

The business of a notary includes the making of wills, drawing up powers of attorney, bonds of arbitration, bills of sale, charter parties, and attestations. The drawing of instruments of this description constitutes almost the sole employment of some few notaries; while the chief, indeed, the sole business of the majority, consists in noting and protesting bills of exchange. Some notaries are translators of languages, but more frequently they employ a foreigner for this purpose.

The difference between the noting and the protesting of a bill of exchange for non-payment, is this: In noting, the notary, after having presented the bill at the proper place, and demanded payment, attaches to it a small piece of paper, on which he writes the amount of his charge and the reason why the bill is not paid—such as " no effects," " no advice," " out; no orders," " will be paid to-morrow," &c. This piece of paper is called " the notary's ticket," and the writing on it is called " the notary's answer." Some notaries have their name and address printed on their tickets. The notary also places on the bottom part of the bill, in front, the initials of his name, the amount of his fee, and the date of the noting. The same form is used in noting a bill for non-acceptance.

The practice of noting bills of exchange is not recognized by the laws of England. It is said to have taken its rise from the following circumstance : After the modern system of banking was established, and bills of exchange became numerous, it was customary for one of the clerks of the banking-house to act as a notary. If the bill had been presented in the morning and was not paid, he called in the evening to ask the reason of its non-

---

* Burns' Ecclesiastical Law, vol. iii. page 1.

payment, and he charged a small fee for this additional trouble. By degrees this practice became established, and, ultimately, a notary public was employed for the purpose.

A protest is a legal instrument, drawn on stamped paper, generally according to the following form :—

On this day, , the day of , one thousand eight hundred and , I, *A. B.*, Public Notary, by legal authority, admitted and sworn, dwelling in the city of , did present for *payment* the original bill (a true copy whereof is within written), to a *woman* at , who replied, *that said bill could not then be paid.*

Wherefore, I, the said notary, do solemnly protest against the drawer and endorsers of the said bill, and all others therein concerned, for all exchange, re-exchange, losses, costs, interest and damages, suffered and to be suffered, for want of *payment* of said bill. Thus done in my office, the day and year aforesaid,

Which I attest,

A. B., Not. Pub.

If a bill has been protested for non-acceptance, it must, when due, be again protested for non-payment. The holder of a protested bill should immediately send the protest to the party of whom the bill had been received. If the bill was only noted, the party should receive due notice.

If an action be brought upon a bill which has been only noted, it will be necessary to produce a witness in court, to prove that the bill was duly and properly presented for payment : but if the bill has been protested, the production of the protest will be sufficient evidence. No action can be brought upon a foreign bill, unless it has been protested. But if the bill has been duly noted, a protest may be drawn up at any time previous to the commencement of a suit, without a second presentation of the bill at the place where it was payable.

An inland bill may be protested for non-acceptance if it be above 5*l.*, if drawn after date, and if the value is stated therein to be received. Inland bills, in such cases, may also be protested for non-payment, if they have been accepted. No other inland bills can legally be protested. This excludes bills drawn after sight, or for a less sum than 5*l.*

Although every foreign bill must be protested, yet it is not considered absolutely necessary that an *inland* bill should be either noted or protested, in order to sustain an action for the amount.

A bill is usually noted or protested for non-payment after

bank hours, on the evening of the day on which it falls due. But if not done then, it may be noted or protested at any subsequent time. The omission of the noting or protesting by the holder does not nullify his claims upon any of the antecedent parties, provided they received due notice of the dishonour. Foreign bills should be noted on the day that acceptance or payment was refused. Inland bills may also be noted on that day, but a protest for non-payment of an inland bill cannot be made out until the day after it is due.

If a bill be refused acceptance by the drawee, and another party accept it for honour of the drawer or of an endorser, it must again be protested for non-payment by the drawee before an action can be sustained against the acceptor.

In London it is not the custom to protest inland bills at all. And in case of non-acceptance, they are not even noted, unless drawn after sight. It is then necessary that they should be noted in order to fix the time on which they fall due. Inland bills are always noted for non-payment. Foreign bills are protested both for non-acceptance and for non-payment. Bills drawn from Ireland or from Scotland are regarded as foreign bills. The notary's charge for noting a bill within the site of the ancient walls of the city of London, is 1s. 6d. Beyond those limits the charges are 2s. 6d., 3s, 6d., 5s., and 6s. 6d., &c., according to the distance. The charge for protesting a bill under 20l. is 5s. 6d.,—from 20l. to 100l. it is 6s. 6d.,—100l. to 500l. it is 7s. 6d.—500l. to 2000l. it is 10s., and for every additional thousand, 1s. extra. The charges of notaries in London are not fixed by law, but are regulated by a society which they have established themselves, and which issues printed rules, a copy of which is given to each notary. Mr. Justice Bayley has stated positively, that if a bill be paid when presented by the notary, the acceptor is not bound to pay the expense of noting. But this is contrary to the usual practice. In such cases, the notaries always refuse to take the money for the bill, unless they are paid the noting fees at the same time.

It is customary for the country bankers to re-issue the London bills they have discounted. In this case they always endorse the bills, and place on them a "case of need." A case of need is a reference for payment to a merchant or banker in London if the bill should not be paid by the party on whom it is drawn. This reference is made by writing on the back of the bill at bottom *—" In case of need apply to Messrs. A. B. & Co." If, then, the bill should not be paid, Messrs. A. B. & Co. will pay it for honour of the endorser. The advantage of placing a case of need upon a bill is, that the party endorsing it receives it back sooner in case of non-payment. It also makes the bill more respectable, and secures its circulation. The notaries always observe these " cases of need," and after having noted the bill apply to the referee.

In the year 1801, an Act of Parliament was passed for the better regulation of public notaries in England. It enacts, that from and after the first day of August, 1801, no person shall be admitted as a notary, unless he shall have served as an apprentice for seven years to a public notary, or to a scrivener, being also a public notary. Within three months after the date of the indenture of apprenticeship, one of the subscribing witnesses must make an affidavit of the fact before the Master of the Faculties of his Grace the Lord Archbishop of Canterbury, in London, his surrogate, or commissioner. This affidavit is to be entered in a book, for which the clerk may charge the sum of 5s., and this book may be searched by any person on paying the sum of 1s. for each search. Every person, previous to being enrolled as a notary, must also make an affidavit that he has served an apprenticeship of seven years, and that during the whole of that time he has been actually employed in the business. No public notary can have an apprentice but while he actually practises. Persons applying for a faculty to become notaries within the jurisdiction of the company of scriveners, must previously take their freedom of that company. Any person doing anything belonging to the office of the notary, without being enrolled, shall forfeit the sum of 50l.

In the year 1833, an Act was passed to alter and amend the Act of 1801. It limits the operation of the former Act to the city of London and liberties of Westminster, the borough of Southwark, and the circuit of ten miles from the Royal Exchange, in the said city of London. Beyond those limits the Archbishop of Canterbury may authorize attorneys, solicitors, and proctors, to practise as notaries within any district in which it shall be made to appear to the master of the Court of Faculties, that

---

* A foreign case of need is generally written on the front of the bill, and the notary presents it the day after due.

there is not (or shall not hereafter be) a sufficient number of such notaries public (3 & 4 Will. IV. c. 70).

In default of a notary public, a bill may be protested for non-acceptance or non-payment by any other substantial person of the city, town, or place where such bill or note shall be so dishonoured, in the presence of two or more credible witnesses, which protest shall be made and written under a fair written copy of such bill or note.

V. *The Rate of Discount.*—During the middle ages it was believed that all interest taken for the loan of money was unjust and unscriptural, and the lender was stigmatized as a usurer.

Though this notion has been altogether discarded in modern times, it may not have been either pernicious or absurd at the time it was introduced. It originated when the population was purely agricultural. That a man who borrows money with a view of making a profit by it, should give some portion of his profit to the lender, is a self-evident principle of natural justice. A man makes a profit usually by means of traffic. But in a country purely agricultural, and under such a government as was the feudal system, there can be but little traffic, and hence but little profit. Besides, in an agricultural country a person seldom wants to borrow money except he be reduced to poverty or distress by misfortune. Now for a rich man who has money which he cannot profitably employ, to charge interest for a loan to a man in distress, appears to be consistent with neither justice nor benevolence.

Erroneous views are often entertained of the Mosaic laws, from neglecting to consider the state of the people to whom those laws were given. It was the object of the Jewish legislator to make the Jews a purely agricultural people. The promotion of agriculture was, as Montesquieu would say, the SPIRIT of his laws. Hence he prohibited the taking of interest for the loan of money. By this means he interdicted commerce. His design was to prevent the Israelites associating with the surrounding nations and learning their idolatrous practices. But even Moses permitted the Jews to take interest for money lent to strangers; a circumstance which proves that the prohibition was only a political and not a moral precept. If the taking of interest for money were morally wrong, it would have been forbidden in all cases. But in the Middle Ages the political and the moral laws of Moses were confounded together, and all of them were supposed to be of perpetual obligation upon all nations. These opinions, which might have been useful in a purely agricultural state, were still indulged when a change of manners required that this country should become commercial. If we admitted the unlawfulness of taking interest for money we might on the same principle condemn all kinds of commerce, and even all profitable investment of capital. Where is the difference between taking money for the use of money, and taking money for the use of commodities that are purchased with money? If I lay out 100*l.* in the purchase of a house, I am allowed to take rent for the use of that house. Why, then, if I lend to a friend the 100*l.* with which he purchases a house, am I to receive no remuneration? If we are not allowed to receive any money for the loan of money, why are we allowed to receive money for the loan of a house or a coach, or any other article? An exorbitant charge for interest is certainly unjust, but so is an exorbitant charge for anything else.

After it had been admitted that it was lawful to take interest for the loan of money, the government thought proper to limit the amount. In the reign of Henry VIII. interest was limited to 10 per cent. James I. reduced it to 8 per cent.; at which rate it remained till the reign of Charles II., when it was reduced to 6 per cent.; and finally, in the reign of Queen Anne, it was reduced to 5 per cent., in Ireland the legal rate of interest being higher. However inapplicable these laws may be to our own times, they were probably beneficial at the time they were enacted. In our time capital has accumulated, money is abundant, the lenders are numerous, hence competition is sure to take place, and the value of money will be regulated in the same way as that of any other commodity in the market. But, in those times, the lenders were few, and might easily combine to fix the rate of interest as they pleased. They had, in fact, though not a legal, yet an actual monopoly, and hence it was necessary that they, like other monopolists, should be placed under restraint. In our times, it is the rate of profit which regulates the rate of interest. In those times, it was the rate of interest which regulated the rate of profit. If the money-lender charged a high rate of interest to the merchant, the merchant must have charged a high rate of profit on his goods. Hence, a large sum of money would be taken from the pockets of the purchasers to be put into the pockets of the money-lenders. This additional price, too, put upon the goods, would render the public less able and less inclined to purchase them. The laws, therefore, which restricted the rate of interest were, probably, in those times, friendly to trade.

Sir Josiah Child, in his excellent Essay on Trade, accuses the "new-fashioned bankers" of being "the main cause of keeping the interest of money at least two per cent. higher than otherwise it would be ; for, by allowing their creditors six per cent , they make monied men sit down lazily with so high an interest, and not push into commerce with their money, as they certainly would do, were it at four or three per cent., as in Holland. This high interest also keeps the price of land at so low as fifteen years' purchase. It also makes money scarce in the country, seeing that the trade of bankers being only in London, it very much drains the ready money from all other parts of the kingdom."

That we may be able to judge of the truth of these accusations, it will be necessary to make some observations upon those circumstances which influence the rate of interest.

It has been the opinion of most of our political economists, that the rate of interest is regulated by the rate of profit. This sentiment has, however, been attacked. It has been contended, that the rate of interest is not influenced by the average rate of profit, but by the quantity of moneyed capital in the market, compared with the wants of the borrowers. In other words, that the price of money is influenced by the proportion between the demand and the supply.

This sentiment is undoubtedly right ; but it does not overthrow the proposition against which it is advanced. The price of money, or of the loan of money, is no doubt, like the price of every other commodity, regulated *at any particular time* by the proportion between the supply and the demand. But does not the rate of profit regulate the supply and the demand ? Will any commercial man borrow money when he must give a higher interest for it than he can make profit by its use ? Or will any man lend money at a very low interest when, by engaging in business, he can make a very high profit ? It is true that, on particular occasions, and under particular circumstances, some individuals may do this, but not permanently and universally. It is obvious, then, that a high rate of interest, in proportion to profits, increases the supply of money, and diminishes the demand; and a low rate of interest, in proportion to profits, increases the demand for the loan of money, and diminishes the supply. The rate of interest, therefore, is ultimately regulated by the rate of profits.

When we say the price of cotton is regulated by the cost of production, we do not mean to deny that the market price of cotton is fixed by the proportion between the demand and the supply. On the contrary, this is admitted; but then it is contended, that the supply itself is regulated by the cost of production. If the market price of cotton were so low as not to furnish to the grower a fair average of profit on the capital employed, then would capital be removed, after a while, from the cultivation of cotton to some other employment. And if the price of cotton were so high as to furnish more than a fair average of profit, then, after a while, more capital would find its way into that employment, the supply would be increased, and the prices would fall; but it is only by influencing the supply that the cost of production has any effect upon the price. Thus, although the cost of production may be the same for a number of years, the price may be perpetually varying. The price may, from a variety of causes, be in a state of constant vibration : but it cannot *permanently* deviate on one side or the other much beyond the line marked out by the cost of production.

It is the same with the interest of money. It is subject to perpetual fluctuation from the proportion between the demand and the supply, but it will not deviate far from the line marked out by the rate of profit. For the rate of profit not only influences the supply (as with cotton) but also influences the demand.

The above reasoning is founded on the supposition that those who borrow money, borrow it for the purpose of investing it in trade, or of making a profit by its use. But this is not always the case; and is never the case with the government of a country, who always borrow for the purpose of spending. Now we can form a judgment as to what portion of his profits a merchant is willing to give for the loan of a sum of money, but we can form no judgment as to the conduct of a profligate rake who wants money to spend on his follies. A king or a government is in the same state. They will borrow money as cheap as they can ; but, at all events, money they will have. We cannot, therefore, infer that, because Charles II. gave, at times, to the new-fashioned bankers, thirty per cent. for money, the average rate of profit exceeded thirty per cent. May not, then, these advances to the king have had the effect of raising the interest of money, and thus justify the accusations of Sir Josiah Child ?

When a number of commercial men borrow money of one another, the *permanent* regulator of the rate of interest is the rate of profit ; and the *immediate* regulator is the proportion between the demand and the supply. But when a new party comes into the market, who has no common interest with them, who does not borrow money to trade with, but to spend, the permanent regulator (the rate of profit) loses its influence, and the sole regulator is then the proportion between the demand and the supply. The loans to the king created a much greater demand for money, and the rate of interest consequently rose. These demands were to so great an amount, and were so frequently repeated, that the rate of interest became permanently high. Many individuals would, no doubt (as Sir Josiah Child states they did) withdraw their capitals from trade, and live upon the interest of their money. And others, who were in business, would employ their superfluous capital in lending it at interest, rather than in extending their business. Those commercial men who now wanted to borrow money must give a higher interest for it than they did before. To enable themselves to do this, they must charge a higher profit on their goods. Thus then, in this artificial state of the money market, it appears reasonable to suppose that the rate of interest may have regulated the rate of profits, instead of the rate of profits regulating the rate of interest, which is the natural state.

As the rate of interest is regulated by the proportion between the demand and the supply of money, it will vary, not only in different countries, but in different provinces of the same country, according to the proportions found to exist. In the London money market the rate of interest is usually much less than in the country. The price of any commodity when purchased in large quantities at a wholesale warehouse, is always less than that at which it is retailed to the consumer. So the price of the loan of money at the Stock Exchange, where it is advanced in large masses upon government security, will always be less than when advanced in small sums upon individual security. A low rate of interest in London, however, will, after a while, have the effect of lowering the rate of interest in the country *upon those securities which are negotiable in London.* For if the country banker insists on a high rate of discount for bills drawn upon good London houses, the drawer will send them to a bill broker in London, who will get them discounted and remit the money to the drawer. But with regard to those bills which are not payable in London, a higher rate of discount may be obtained.

The cheapness of money in London has the effect of diminishing the number of bills drawn upon London. A London merchant who sends an order for goods to a country manufacturer, instead of saying, " Draw upon me at two months," will say, " Allow me the discount, and I will send you the cash." If he can get an allowance of four per cent. discount, and borrow the money in London at two per cent., he will make an additional profit on this transaction. As the surplus quantity of money in London thus becomes diffused throughout the country, the rate of discount will gradually advance in London and fall in the country.

Although a low rate of interest indicates the abundance of capital, and hence may be considered as a favourable circumstance in the condition of any nation, yet it produces some injurious effects : it occasions the removal of capital to foreign countries ; it weakens the inducements to frugality and accumulation ; and it encourages speculative and hazardous undertakings. Persons who can obtain but a low rate of interest for their money, are often induced to engage in speculations which promise to yield a more profitable return. All seasons of speculations have been preceded by a low rate of interest.

In the year 1818, a select committee of the House of Commons was appointed to consider of the effects of the laws which regulate or restrain the interest of money, and to report their opinion thereupon to the House. After examining twenty-one witnesses upon the subject, the committee delivered the following report :—

" 1. *Resolved,*—That it is the opinion of this committee, that the laws regulating or restraining the rate of interest have been extensively evaded, and have failed of the effect of imposing a maximum on such rate; and that of late years, from the constant excess of the market rate of interest above the rate limited by law, they have added to the expense incurred by borrowers on real security; and that such borrowers have been compelled to resort to the mode of granting annuities on lives,—a mode which has been made a cover for obtaining higher interest than the rate limited by law, and has further subjected the borrowers to enormous charges, or forced them to make very disadvantageous sales of their estates.

" 2. *Resolved*,—That it is the opinion of this committee, that the construction of such laws, as applicable to the transactions of commerce as at present carried on, has been attended with much uncertainty as to the legality of many transactions of frequent occurrence; and, consequently, been productive of much embarrassment and litigation.

" 3. *Resolved*,—That it is the opinion of this committee, that the present period, when the market rate of interest is below the legal rate, affords an opportunity peculiarly proper for the repeal of the said laws."

In the Bill passed in 1833 for the renewal of the charter of the Bank of England, a clause was introduced, which exempted bills not having more than three months to run, from the operations of the laws against usury.*

VI. *Effect of Discounts on the Circulation.*—The discounting of bills, by banks of circulation, will have the same effect in changing the currency as the deposit accounts, but will not operate so rapidly. When a bill is discounted, the banker issues his own notes to that amount; and when the bill is paid, he receives a part of the amount in gold, or silver, or in notes of other banks. If, however, the bill be not a local bill, that is, if it be not payable in the place in which the bank is established, it will be paid in the currency of the place where it is payable, and its payment will not have the effect of diminishing the local currency.

While the issue of notes upon the deposit accounts depends altogether upon the depositors, the issues in the way of discount depend altogether upon the banker—he may discount, or not discount, as he pleases. If he discounts with real capital, he does not thereby increase the amount of the currency—for that capital must, in some way or other, have been previously employed. If he discounts with that portion of his banking capital which is raised by deposits, he does not increase the amount of the currency, but gives it increased rapidity. If he discounts with that portion of his banking capital which is

---

* The laws against usury have been repealed.

raised by notes, he increases the amount of the currency. As banks of circulation always issue their own notes, it would seem that their discounting business was carried on exclusively with this last description of capital, but it is not so. It is very possible for a banker to issue his own notes for all the bills he discounts, and yet nine-tenths of the bills in his possession shall represent real capital. For, although in the first instance, the banker's notes are given for the bill, yet these notes may not stay in circulation until the bill becomes due: the bill may have three months to run, the notes may return in three days. If the notes given in exchange for the bills remain in circulation until the bills become due, then do the discounts create a banking capital equal to their own amount. But if the bills have three months to run, and the notes remain out only one month, then they create a capital to only one-third of their amount, and the other two-thirds must consist of capital derived from other sources. If the notes remain out beyond the time the bill falls due, then do the discounts create a banking capital beyond their own amount.

It may be observed, that in order to trace the effects of banking, it is necessary to mark particularly the way in which the bankers employ their money. It is not by the creation of a banking capital, but by the way in which that capital is applied, that the greatest effects are produced upon the currency, and upon the trade and commerce of a country. Money employed in discounting bills drawn for value will encourage trade—if employed in discounting accommodation bills, it will promote speculation—if advanced as dead loans to persons out of trade it may lead to extravagance—if invested in the funds, it will raise their price and reduce the market rate of interest—if kept in the till, it will yield no profit to the banker, and be of no advantage to the community.

SECTION XII.

CASH CREDIT BANKS.

A CASH credit is an understanding on the part of the bank to advance to an individual such sums of money as he may from time to time require, not exceeding in the whole a certain definite amount ; the individual to whom the credit is given entering into a bond, with securities, generally two in number, for the repayment, on demand, of the sums actually advanced, with interest upon each issue from the day upon which it is made.

A cash credit is, in fact, the same thing as an overdrawn current account, except that in a current account the party overdraws on his own individual security, and in the cash credit he finds two securities who are responsible for him. Another difference is, that a person cannot overdraw his current account without asking permission each time from the bank, whereas the overdrawing of a cash credit account is a regular matter of business ; it is, in fact, the purpose for which the cash credit has been granted.

The following considerations will show that a person who has occasion for temporary advances of money will find it more advantageous to raise these sums by a cash credit than by having bills discounted :—

First. In a cash credit the party pays interest only for the money he actually employs.

If a person wants to make use of 100*l*., and has a bill for 150*l*., he will get the bill discounted, and thus pays interest for 50*l*. for which he has no use. But if he has a cash credit, he draws only 100*l*., and pays interest for that amount.

Secondly. In a cash credit he can repay any part of the sum drawn whenever he pleases.

If a trader has a bill for 150*l*. discounted to-day, and should unexpectedly receive 150*l*. to-morrow, he cannot rediscount the bill, but has actually paid interest for money he does not want. But if he draws 150*l*. upon his cash credit account to-day, and to-morrow receives 150*l*., he takes this money to the bank, and will have to pay the interest upon 150*l*. for only one day.

Thirdly. In a cash credit he has the power of drawing whenever he pleases, to the full amount of his credit ; but in the case of discounting bills, he must make a fresh application to the bank to discount each bill, and if the bank have at any time more profitable ways of employing their money, or if they suspect the credit of the applicant, they may refuse to discount, but this would not be the case if he had a cash credit.

Fourthly. In a cash credit the party does not pay the interest until the end of the year ; whereas, in the other case, he pays the interest at the time the bill is discounted.

Cash credits are granted not only upon personal security, but also upon the security of the Public Funds.

This furnishes great facilities of raising money to those who possess property which they are not disposed to sell. A person who is a holder of government stock may sell out a portion to supply his temporary necessities; and when he wishes to replace it he finds the price of stock has risen, and it will cost him more money to repurchase than he received when he sold. But if he transfers the stock to a bank as a security for a cash credit, he may repay the money whenever he pleases; and if, in the mean time, the value of the security should have risen, all the advantage will be his own.

The effects of cash credits are thus described by Adam Smith :—

" The commerce of Scotland, which at present is not very great, was still more inconsiderable when the two first banking companies were established, and those companies would have had but little trade had they confined their business to the discounting of bills of exchange. They invented, therefore, another method of issuing their promissory notes, by granting what they call cash accounts, that is, by giving credit to the extent of a certain sum (two or three thousand pounds, for example) to any individual who could procure two persons of undoubted credit and good landed estate to become surety for him, that whatever money should be advanced to him within the sum for which the credit had been given should be repaid upon demand, together with the legal interest. Credits of this kind are, I believe, commonly granted by banks and bankers in all different parts of the world. But the easy terms upon which the Scotch banking companies accept of repayment are, so far as I know, peculiar to them, and have perhaps been the principal cause both of the great trade of those companies, and of the benefits which the country has received from it.

" Whoever has a credit of this kind with one of those companies, and borrows a thousand pounds upon it, for example, may repay this sum piecemeal, by twenty and thirty pounds at a time, the company discounting a proportional part of the interest of the great sum, from the day on which each of those small sums is paid in, till the whole be in this manner repaid. All merchants, therefore, and almost all men of business, find it convenient to keep such cash accounts with them, and are hereby interested to promote the trade of those companies by readily receiving their notes in all payments, and by encouraging all those with whom they have any influence to do the same. The banks, when their customers apply to them for money, generally advance it to them on their own promissory notes. These the merchants pay away to the manufacturers for goods; the manufacturers to the farmers, for materials and provisions; the farmers to their landlords for rent; the landlords repay them to the merchants for the conveniences and luxuries with which they supply them; and the merchants again return them to the banks, in order to balance their cash accounts, or to replace what they may have borrowed of them : and thus almost the whole money business of the country is transacted by means of them. Hence the great trade of those companies.

" By means of those cash accounts every merchant can, without imprudence, carry on a greater trade than he otherwise could do. If there are two merchants—one in London and the other in Edinburgh, who employ equal stocks in the same branch of trade, the Edinburgh merchant can, without imprudence, carry on a greater trade and give employment to a greater number of people than the London merchant. The London merchant must always keep by him a considerable sum of money, either in his own coffers, or in those of his banker, who gives him no interest for it, in order to answer the demands continually coming upon him for payment of the goods he purchases upon credit. Let the ordinary amount of this sum be supposed five hundred pounds. The value of the goods in his warehouse must always be less by five hundred pounds than it would have been had he not been obliged to keep such a sum unemployed. Let us suppose that he generally disposes of his whole stock upon hand, or of goods to the value of his whole stock upon hand, once in the year. By being obliged to keep so great a sum unemployed, he must sell in a year five hundred pounds' worth less goods than he might otherwise have done. His annual profits must be less by all that he could have made by the sale of five hundred pounds' worth more goods, and the number of people employed in preparing his goods for market must be less by all those that five hundred pounds more stock could have employed. The merchant in Edinburgh, on the other hand, keeps no money unemployed for answering such occasional demands. When they actually come upon him he satisfies them from his cash account with the bank, and gradually replaces the sum borrowed with the money or paper which comes in from the occasional sales of his goods. With the same stock, therefore, he can, without imprudence, have at all times in his warehouse a larger quantity of goods than the London merchant, and can thereby both make a greater profit himself and give constant employment to a greater number of industrious people who prepare those goods for the market. Hence, the greater benefit which the country has derived from this trade.

" The facility of discounting bills of exchange, it may be thought, indeed, gives the English merchants a convenience equivalent to the cash accounts of the Scotch merchants. But the Scotch merchants, it must be remembered, can discount their bills of exchange as easily as the English merchants, and have, besides, the additional conveniency of their cash account."*—*Wealth of Nations*, Book ii. chap. 2.

Query.—Is it better for a bank to make advances of money on cash credits, or by discounting bills of exchange?

Bills of Exchange versus *Cash Credits.*—1. Cash credits, when

---

* A fuller account of the system of cash credits will be found, further on, in The Practice of Banking.

once granted, cannot be called up, but bills of exchange soon fall due, and you can refuse to discount again.

2. If you discount bills of exchange they can be rediscounted to supply the bank with funds, if necessary, but advances on cash credits cannot be replaced.

3. In case of a panic or a run upon the bank, the persons having cash credits might have occasion to draw upon the bank, and the notes would immediately be returned upon the bank for payment in gold; but you could refuse to discount bills of exchange until the run was over.

Cash Credits versus *Bills of Exchange.*—1. A higher interest is charged upon cash credits than upon bills of exchange.

2. Cash credits, being of the nature of a permanent advance, are more beneficial to the parties; hence trade is more promoted, and the benefit to the bank must ultimately be greater.

3. Parties having cash credits are more closely connected with the bank, and hence would use their influence to prevent any run upon the bank, and to promote the prosperity of the bank.

4. The mode of recovering an advance upon a cash credit is more summary and certain, as the bond can be put into execution immediately, but an action for the recovery of an unpaid bill is very tedious, and may be frustrated by informality, &c.

A cash credit operates much in the same way as a discount account and a current account combined. It resembles a discount account inasmuch as a banker is usually in advance to his customer. It resembles a current account, as it is required that there be frequent operations upon it; that is, that there be perpetual payings in and drawings out of money. The bankers expect that a cash credit shall maintain a banking capital equal to its own amount. As the banker is usually in advance, a cash credit can create no banking capital by means of deposits; it can be done only by means of the notes. If then, the operations on a cash credit are sufficient to keep in circulalation an amount of notes equal to the amount of the credit, then it gives satisfaction to the banker; but not otherwise. Previous to granting a cash credit, the banks always make inquiries to ascertain if this is likely to be the case; and even after it is granted it is liable to be called up if it has not accomplished this object. Hence, cash credits are denied to persons who have no means of circulating the banker's notes, or who wish to employ the money as a dead loan. And in all cases they are limited to such an amount as the party is supposed to be capable of employing with advantage to the bank.

SECTION XIII.

LOAN BANKS.

LOAN banks are banks formed for the purpose of advancing loans upon articles of merchandize. Some are carried on for the purposes of gain, others from motives of charity.

The Bank of England was empowered by its charter to carry on the business of a loan bank. The following is the twenty-sixth section of the Act:—"Provided that nothing herein contained shall in anywise be construed to hinder the said corporation from dealing in bills of exchange, or in buying or selling of bullion, gold or silver, or in selling any goods, wares, or merchandize whatever, which shall really and *bonâ fide be left or deposited with the said corporation for money lent or advanced thereon*, and which shall not be redeemed at the time agreed on, or within three months after, or from selling such goods as shall or may be the produce of lands purchased by said corporation." In pursuance of the privilege granted by this clause, the directors gave public notice that they would lend money at four per cent., on "plate, lead, tin, copper, steel, and iron."

The Bank of Scotland was also authorized to act as a loan bank. The following is one clause of the Act by which it was established in 1795:—"And it is further hereby statute and ordained, that it shall be lawful for the said governor and company to lend, upon real or personal security, any sum or sums, and to receive annual rent for the same, at six per cent., as shall be ordinary for the time: as also that if the person borrowing, as said is, shall not make payment at the term agreed upon with the company, that it shall be lawful for the governor and company to sell and dispose of the security or pledge by a public roup, for the most that can be got, for payment to them of the principal annual rents and reasonable charges, and returning the overplus to the person who gave the said security or pledge."

The Royal Bank of Scotland were also empowered by their charter, " to lend to any person or persons, bodies politic or corporate, such sum and sums of money as they should think fit, at any interest not exceeding lawful interest, on real or personal security, *and particularly on pledges of any kind what-soever, of any goods, wares, merchandizes, or other effects whatso-ever,* in such way and manner as to the said company should seem proper and convenient."

" The Hibernian Joint-stock Loan Company," usually called the Hibernian Bank, was formed in 1825, " for the purpose of purchasing and selling annuities, and all public and other securities, real and personal, in Ireland, and to advance money and make loans thereof, on the security of such real and personal security, at legal interest, and on the security of merchandize and manufactured goods." This company, however, has never carried on the business of a loan bank, but has confined its transactions to the business of a commercial bank. It has not the power of issuing notes, but it is a bank of discount and of deposit.

Capital advanced, by way of loan, on the securities of mer-chandize, would produce the same effects as if advanced in the discounting of bills. If a party borrows 100*l.* on the security of his merchandize, it is the same as though he had sold his merchandize for a 100*l.* bill, and got it discounted with the banker. By obtaining this advance he is enabled to hold over this merchandize for a better market, and avoids a sacrifice which, otherwise, he might be induced to make, in order to raise the money for urgent purposes.

Every advance of money by a banker, let it be made in what way soever, is in fact a loan. To discount a 100*l.* bill that has three months to run, is much the same as to lend that amount for three months. The difference is, that the banker has two or more securities instead of one—the time of repayment is fixed ; and the interest on the whole sum is paid at the time it is advanced. But let one trader draw bills upon his customers, and take them to the bank for discount—let another trader give his customers three months' credit without drawing bills, and borrow of the banker the amount of the goods sold ; it is obvious that in each case the traders receive the same accommodation, and the effect on commerce will be the same. The bill is merely a transfer of the debt from the drawer to the banker, with the drawer's guarantee. Cash credits are loans—the amount of the loan varies every day, but the maximum is fixed. If a trader who has a cash credit for 500*l.* has always 300*l.* drawn out, it is nearly the same thing as though he had a loan for 300*l.* The advantage to him is, that he can draw exactly such a sum as he may need—that he can replace it whenever he pleases, and in such portions as he may find convenient; and he pays interest only for the sum drawn out. It is unnecessary to say that overdrawn accounts, mortgages, and all advances of money on pledges or securities of any kind are loans.

It is contrary to all sound principles of banking for a banker to advance money in the form of permanent loans, or as they are called, dead loans. In the first place, those dead loans do not create any banking capital—and, secondly, they cannot be suddenly called up. For a banker to lend out his banking capital in the way of permanent loan is obviously imprudent, as he knows not how soon that capital may be taken out of his hands; and it is almost equally imprudent to advance his real capital in that way, as the real capital ought to be kept in a disposable form, so that it may be rendered available in case of any sudden contraction of the banking capital. The investing of money in the public funds is not strictly an operation of banking. It does not increase the banking capital. Yet it is necessary that a banker should lay out some portion of his capital in this way, because he can so easily realize the money in case a run should be made upon his bank. The portion thus invested is probably less productive than any other part of his capital, except the sums kept in his till to meet occasional demands. Sometimes, however, a rise in the funds will be the means of affording him a considerable profit.

The second class of loan banks arose from motives of charity.

These institutions were first established in the fifteenth century, for the purpose of checking the extortions of usurers, by lending money to the poor upon pledges, and without charging interest.* They were originally supported by voluntary contributions; but as these were found insufficient to support the necessary expenses, it became necessary that the borrowers should be charged interest for the loans. These banks were at first distinguished by being called *montes pietatis*. It appears that the word mont, or mount, was at an early period applied

* See Beckmann's History of Ancient Institutions.

to any pecuniary fund, and it is probable that the promoters of this system added " pietatis " to give it an air of religion, and thus to procure larger subscriptions. A bank of this kind was formed at Perugia in the year 1464; another at Rome in 1539; one at Naples, which was considered the greatest in Europe, in the following year, and it took the name of *banco dei poveri*—the bank of the poor. These institutions were opposed in France. An attempt was made to introduce them under Louis XIII. in 1626, but the managers were threatened with punishment, and the undertaking was relinquished. The Mont de Piété, at Paris, was established in the year 1777; and so largely has the public taken advantage of the accommodation this afforded, that it has been known to have in its possession forty casks filled with gold watches.

These banks were not only called Mounts of Piety, but they were also called Lombards, from the name of the original bankers, or money-lenders. A loan-bank, or a Lombard, was established in Russia in 1772,* to prevent the usury and the oppression to which the poor were exposed, and the profit was given to the foundling hospital of St. Petersburg. The " Lombard " lent on gold and silver three fourths of the value, on other metals it lent one half the value, and on jewels as much as the circumstances of the times would allow, the estimate being made by sworn appraisers. The rate of interest was established throughout the empire, in 1786, at five per cent. At the Lombard, one year's interest is taken in advance. Pledges that are forfeited are publicly sold; and if they produce more than the loan, the interest, and the charges, the overplus is given to the owners.

In 1695, Sir Francis Brewster published his Essay on Trade and Navigation, "printed for T. Cockerell, at the Three Legs, in the Poultry, over against the Stocks-market." He has a section upon " Banks and Lumbers."† He recommends that in every shire a bank should be erected by Act of Parliament; and he states that it would be " the most effectual way for suppressing highwaymen; for that no man need travel with more than pocket-money for his expenses, when he may have bank tickets to any part of the kingdom where he goes." He afterwards observes, " that lumbers for poor artizans and others is an appendix to banks, and may by funds out of them in each

* Oddy, on European Commerce.　　† Lumbers, *i.e.*, Lombards.

county be supplied so as that the poor men have money to carry on their trade and employment on the pawns that may be so easy, and with the advantage of selling in public sales what they leave in pledge. And that what they borrow should be of more advantage and easy to them than if the money were lent them gratis, and may be of great use in the employment, and encouraging the manufactures of the nation, which are much discouraged by the necessities and hardships that are put upon the poor."

Loan banks, for charitable purposes, have, for a considerable time past, existed in Ireland. A voluntary association of this kind was established in the year 1756. This society was incorporated in 1780, under the title of " The Charitable Musical Society." They had their meetings at St. Ann's vestry-room, Dublin, on the first and second Tuesday in every month, for the purpose of lending money, interest free, to indigent tradesmen, in sums of not less than two pounds to any one person at one time, which sums are to be repaid at sixpence in the pound, weekly.

The Meath Charitable Loan Society was established in 1807. The committee of managers lent sums, not under five, and not exceeding twenty pounds, free of interest, to be repaid by weekly instalments of 1s. 6d. for 5l.; 3s. for 10l.; 6s. for 20l. Donations of 10l. and upwards being vested in government securities, the interest only to be applicable to the fund, or thrown into the floating capital, at the option of the donor.

It seems highly desirable that in England also charitable loan banks should be taken under the protection of the legislature. These institutions might be organized in the same manner as savings' banks. In most parts of England there are probably some persons of affluence who would become personally bound for the repayment of such sums as the government might be disposed to advance ; or, in other parts, the necessary funds might be raised by private donations. The funds might be employed in such a way as the committee might deem best adapted to promote the object of the institution. The loans might be made either in money, in raw produce, or in implements of labour. These might be recovered, if necessary by summary process. The state would thus become the Bank of the Poor. It would sustain the same relation to the humbler classes which ordinary banks sustain to the commercial classes.

It would be an intermediate party between the borrowers and the lenders. It could borrow, by means of savings' banks, from those who had money to lend; and lend, by means of loan banks, to those who wished to borrow.

SECTION XIV.

SAVINGS' BANKS.

SAVINGS' banks are banks formed to promote saving.—They are purely banks of deposit; they differ, however, from other banks of deposit in the following particulars :—First. Very small sums are received as deposits.—Secondly. All the money deposited is lent, upon interest, to the government.—Thirdly. The depositors are restricted as to the amount of their lodgments; these restrictions are designed to exclude from the bank all except the humbler classes of the community.

Loan banks, or institutions for lending money to the poor, are of ancient date; but savings' banks, or institutions for borrowing money of the poor, are entirely of modern invention. They were first urged upon the attention of the public and the legislature of this country, in the years 1815 and 1816, by the late Right Hon. George Rose. In his pamphlet upon the subject, he thus traces the origin of these establishments :—

" The idea was first suggested by the society for bettering the condition of the poor, of which I have long been a member, and it has been acted upon in Edinburgh and Bath with such a degree of talent, zeal, and perseverance, as to manifest the great advantage of it.

" In other parts of Great Britain, however, the principle has been acted upon on a small scale, especially in Scotland, where the *parochial* institutions for saving are called Maneges; so full an account of these is given by Mr. Duncan, the early promoter of them, as to render it quite unnecessary to enter on any particulars respecting them here. But however well intended they are, there are strong objections to them. In any event, extended establishments are infinitely more to be desired, on account of the preferable management of them, as well as for the safe custody of the money. By a large district being included, gentlemen of property are found to become trustees and managers; and a fund is easily furnished by small voluntary subscriptions at first, and by the surplus of the interest allowed to the depositors afterwards, to meet all the expenses of the institution.

" Since the first publication of these observations, a controversy has arisen by Mr. Duncan, the promoter of the parochial banks, insisting upon his having (by the establishment of the one at Ruthwell) been the first to bring the banks for savings into notice, in an address to Mr. Forbes, a gentleman of the highest respectability in Edinburgh, who was a zealous promoter of the banks there.   The truth is, that the two establishments are perfectly dissimilar, as above stated, which will appear more manifestly to whomsoever will take the trouble of reading the pamphlet of Mr. Duncan and the answer of Mr. Forbes to it.   As far as respects Scotland, it would seem that the Edinburgh plan has the merit of priority, *for general advantage*; but it may be hoped that in future there may be no contention, except how the public can be most benefited—it is of very little importance from whence the suggestion originated."

Mr. Rose proceeds to explain in detail the nature of these institutions, and points out the advantages they may be expected to confer upon different classes of the community :—

" Apprentices, on first coming out of their time, who now too frequently spend all their earnings, may be induced to lay by five shillings to ten shillings a week, and sometimes more, as in many trades they earn from twenty-four shillings to fifty and sixty shillings a week.

" The same observation applies, though somewhat less forcibly, to journeymen in most trades (whose earnings are very considerable) from not beginning so early, and to workmen in several branches.   With respect to these, it has been made evident to me, and to many members who attended the mendicity committee in a former session of parliament, that in numerous instances when the gains have been as large as above stated, the parties have been so improvident as to have nothing in hand for the support of themselves and families when visited with sickness, and have consequently with their families fallen immediately upon the parish. In some instances the tools and implements of their trade have been carried to the pawnbroker during illness, whereby difficulties were thrown in the way of their labour being resumed on the restoration of health.

" Domestic servants, whose wages are frequently more than sufficient for their necessary expenses.

" Carmen, porters, servants in lower conditions, and others may, very generally, be able to make small deposits, without finding the slightest inconvenience from the diminution of their income occasioned thereby.

" With respect to day labourers, the full advantage cannot be expected to be derived at first, as far as relates to married men with families : it too frequently happens that when there are two or three children, it is all that the father can do to support himself and those dependent upon him with his utmost earnings; but the single man, whose wages are the same as those of his married fellow-labourers, may certainly spare a small weekly sum, by doing which he would, in a reasonable time, have saved enough to enable him to marry with a hope of never allowing any one belonging to him to become a burthen to the parish.

" Nothing is so likely as a plan of this sort to prevent early and improvident marriages, which are the cause, more than any others, of the heavy burthen of the poor rates. When a young single man shall acquire the habit of saving, he will be likely to go on till he shall get together as much as will enable him to make some provision towards the support of a family, before he thinks of marrying.

" The welfare of the lower classes of society cannot be a matter of indifference to any, nor can it be doubted that their situation will be ameliorated by the adoption and promotion of these banks. The industry, sobriety, and economy among the lower orders of the people will thus be promoted by their being encouraged to make little savings for a provision against want and distress; and their moral improvement will be advanced, while their social comfort is augmented. By the plan which I here recommend, this beneficent and most important object will be obtained at no expense to the higher orders, or at so trifling a one as to be utterly unworthy of notice.

" This plan has in it the germ of valuable moral principles, and if it can be fairly brought into action, will tend more than anything to lessen the enormous and increasing burthen on the middle and higher classes, and at the same time to infuse into the minds of the lower order a legitimate spirit of independence. Its merits are so well expressed where its advantages were early experienced, that I cannot do so well as to quote a few words from one of the Edinburgh reports :—' It secures independence without inducing pride—it removes those painful misgivings which render the approaches of poverty so appalling, and often paralyze the exertions that might ward off the blow. It leads to temperance and the restraint of all disorderly passions, which a wasteful expenditure of money nourishes. It produces that sobriety of mind and steadiness of conduct which afford the best foundation for the domestic virtues in humble life. The effects of such an institution as this upon the character of the people, *were it to become universal, would be almost inappreciable.*' "

In the year 1817, Mr. Rose obtained an Act of Parliament, entitled, " An Act to encourage the establishment of Banks for Savings in England." About the same time an Act was passed, entitled, " An Act to encourage the establishment of banks for savings *in Ireland ;*" the provisions of which were similar to the preceding.

The establishment of Post-office Savings' Banks in 1861 (24 Vic. c. 14) has, by the greater facilities, and by the undoubted security which they afford, largely reduced the number of the (old) savings' banks, and still more largely the funds lodged in them. Government and the public are indebted to Mr. Sikes, manager of the Huddersfield Banking Company, for the suggestion, and for an outline of the plan, as well, of making the Money Order Offices contributory to the development of savings' banks.

Scotland has always had the advantage of savings' banks by

means of the deposit system, which is a regular branch of the business of the commercial banks. The deposit system of banking is universally considered to be one cause of the prudence and frugality by which the lower classes of the people of Scotland are distinguished.

In every point of view the savings' banks appear calculated to produce unmingled good. They extend to persons of small means all the benefits of banking. The industrious have thus a place where their small savings may be lodged with perfect security from loss, and with the certainty of increase. They tend to foster that disposition to accumulate which is usually associated with temperance and prudence in all the transactions of life. Upon the mercantile interests of society they have the same effect as commercial banking. The various small sums which were previously lying unproductive in the hands of many individuals, are collected into one sum and lodged in the public funds. The tendency of this, in the first place, is to raise the price of the funds. This advanced price may cause some of the holders to sell out and to employ their money in trade and commerce. Thus the savings' banks augment the productive capital of the nation.*

It is much to be regretted that the advocates for savings' banks should ever have proposed these institutions as substitutes for benefit societies. Cannot the interest of one excellent institution be promoted but at the expense of another? Savings' banks are a useful addition to benefit societies, but cannot supply their place. A labourer pays to a benefit club about thirty shillings per annum, and for that payment he receives about eight shillings per week during the time of illness. If this sum be lodged in a savings' bank, how soon will a few weeks' illness exhaust the whole. It is no doubt the revelling and excess that have too often attended the meeting of benefit societies at public houses that have given rise to objections against them. It may be expected, however, that as our labourers and mechanics become better instructed these excesses will be avoided.

---

* The funds lodged in savings' banks at the end of the year 1864 amounted to 39,417,995*l*; this being less by 1,840,373*l*. than in 1860, the last year before the institution of post-office savings' banks; but the funds lodged in these post-office banks amounted, at the end of 1864, to 4,993,124*l*.—*Annual Statistical Abstract of Progress of the United Kingdom.*

But while savings' banks do not supersede benefit societies, neither do benefit societies supersede the necessity for savings' banks. The benefit society is of use only in case of illness—in no other case has a member any claim upon its funds. He cannot draw out money to support his wife, to furnish his house, or to educate his children. The benefit societies are only to guard against calamity, not to increase enjoyment. By these, labourers may be saved from the parish workhouse, but they must also become depositors in a savings' bank if they wish to acquire independence.*

The last returns of savings' banks, which brings up their accounts to the end of 1869, shows that at this date the number of banks closed were, in England, 119 ; in Wales, 9 ; in Scotland, 6 ; in Ireland, 11 ; giving a total of 145 banks closed. The number of depositors' balances, on 20th of November, previous to date of notice to close, was, in England, 134,183 ; in Wales, 3,280 ; in Scotland, 2,034 ; in Ireland, 2,082. The amounts of the balances were, in England, 3,083,648*l.* 14*s.* 6*d.* ; in Wales, 72,147*l.* 18*s.* 2*d.* ; in Scotland, 19,944*l.* 4*s.* 4*d.* ; in Ireland, 52,527*l.* 17*s.* 8*d.* Thus the total number of depositors' balances throughout the United Kingdom, in the banks about to close, was 141,579, the total amount, 3,228,268*l.* 14*s.* 8*d.* The number of accounts thence transferred to post-office savings' banks was, in England, 73,911 ; in Wales, 782 ; in Scotland, 238 ; in Ireland, 360 : total number, 75,291. The amounts transferred were, in England, 1,785,552*l.* 13*s.* 6*d.* ; in Wales, 20,110*l.* 8*s.* ; in Scotland, 634*l.* 9*s.* 3*d.* ; in Ireland, 10,037*l.* 9*s.* 8*d.* : total amount 1,816,335*l.* 0*s.* 5*d.* These amounts were transferred by *transfer*

---

* By the Act of Parliament, 26 & 27 Vict., c. 87, the law relating to savings' banks is materially altered. The Act 27 & 28 Vict., c. 43, relates to Government Insurances and Annuities. It extends the limit of deferred annuities, previously fixed at 30*l.*, to 50*l.*; whilst the sum required to purchase such annuity is rendered payable in smaller instalments and at shorter periods. By the Act, 29 Vict. c. 5., power is given to the Treasury to substitute terminable annuities for capital stock, standing in savings' banks' accounts, to an amount not exceeding 2,500,000*l.*; the annuities to be terminable at a period not exceeding thirty years : the capital stock thus provided for to be cancelled, and the dividends to cease. The terminable annuities are to be provided for from the Consolidated Fund, and the Treasury may vary the periods at which payments are to be made. The Treasury have also power to cancel such further sums of capital stock as may be held by the Commissioners for the Reduction of the National Debt, substituting terminable annuities as they may from time to time deem expedient. Plain rules for the guidance of persons desiring to insure their lives, or to purchase government annuities, can be obtained at various post-offices, and without charge.

certificates only ; but in addition to them, it is estimated by the post-office authorities that 194,000*l.* were paid in cash by about 9,800 of the depositors in these closed savings' banks to the post-office savings' banks.

The total amount received from and paid to depositors in the *post-office* savings' banks throughout the United Kingdom, and of the computed capital of those savings' banks at the end of 1869, was :—received (including interest), 6,084,610*l.* ; paid, 4,227,056*l.* ; computed capital, 13,524,209*l.*

The total amount, according to official returns made up to the same date, received and paid by savings' banks *under trustees,* from and to depositors, was :—received, 7,667,735*l.* ; paid, 7,857,091*l.* ; and their computed capital, 37,500,522*l.*— which last amount, added to the computed capital of the Post Office savings' banks, exhibits the gratifying fact of no less a total than the immense sum of 51,024,731*l.* prudentially invested in these admirable banks of deposit by the humbler classes of the United Kingdom.

THE PRACTICE OF BANKING.

PART I.—OF PRACTICAL BANKING.

SECTION I.

THE NATURE OF BANKING.

"WHAT is it that we call a Banker? There is in this city a company or corporation, called goldsmiths, and most of those called bankers are of that corporation; but so far as I know, there is not a company or corporation in England called bankers, nor has the business any definition or description either by common law or by statute. By custom we call a man a banker who has an open shop, with proper counters, servants, and books, for receiving other people's money, in order to keep it safe, and return it upon demand; and when any man has opened such a shop we call him a banker, without inquiring whether any man has given him money to keep or no: for this is a trade where no apprenticeship is required, it having never yet been supposed that a man who sets up the trade of banking could be sued upon the statute of Queen Elizabeth, which enacts, that none shall use any art or mystery then used, but such as have served an apprenticeship in the same." *

A banker is a dealer in capital, or more properly a dealer in money. He is an intermediate party between the borrower and the lender. He borrows of one party, and lends to another; and the difference between the terms at which he borrows and those at which he lends, forms the source of his profit. By this means he draws into active operation those small sums of money which were previously unproductive in the hands of private

* Speech, delivered in the House of Commons, in 1746.—See the London Magazine for that year, page 120.

L

individuals; and at the same time furnishes accommodation to those who have need of additional capital to carry on their commercial transactions.

Banks have been divided into private and public. A private bank is that in which there are but few partners, and these attend personally to its management. A public bank is that in which there are numerous partners, and they elect from their own body a certain number, who are entrusted with its management. The latter are usually called Joint-stock banks.

The business of banking consists chiefly in receiving deposits of money, upon which interest may or may not be allowed;—in making advances of money, principally in the way of discounting bills;—and in effecting the transmission of money from one place to another. Private banks in metropolitan cities are usually the agents of the banks in the provinces, and charge a commission on their transactions. In making payments many country banks still issue their own notes.

The disposable means of a bank consist of—First, the capital paid down by the partners, or shareholders. Secondly, the amount of money lodged by their customers. Thirdly, the amount of notes they are able to keep out in circulation. Fourthly, the amount of money in the course of transmission—that is, money they have received, and are to repay, in some distant place, at a future time.

These disposable means are employed—First, in discounting bills. Secondly, in advances of money in the form of cash credits, loans, or overdrawn accounts. Thirdly, in the purchase of government or other securities. Fourthly, a part is kept in the banker's till, to meet the current demands. Of these four ways of employing the capital of a bank, three are productive, and one is unproductive. The discounting of bills yields interest—the loans, and the cash credits, and the overdrawn accounts, yield interest—the government securities yield interest—the money in the till yields no interest.

The expenses of a bank may be classified thus: rent, taxes, and repairs of the house in which the business is carried on; salaries of the officers; stationer's bill for books, paper, notes, stamps, &c.; incidental expenses, as postages, coals, &c.

The profits of a bank are that portion of its total receipts—including discount, interest, dividends, and commission—which exceeds the amount of the expenses.

SECTION II.

THE UTILITY OF BANKING.

In the first place, banks are useful as places of security for the deposit of money. The circumstance which gave rise to the business of banking in this country, was a desire on the part of the merchants of London to obtain a place where they might lodge their money in security. Every one who has had the care of large sums of money knows the anxiety which attends their custody. A person in this case must either take care of his money himself, or trust it to his servants. If he take care of it himself, he will often be put to inconvenience, and will have to deny himself holidays and comforts, of which a man who is possessed of much money would not like to be deprived. If he entrust it to others, he must depend upon their honesty and their ability. And, although in many important cases a master is compelled to do this, yet he does not feel the same satisfaction as if the money was actually under his own care. Some instances of neglect or of dishonesty will necessarily occur, and these will occasion suspicion in reference to other parties against whom no suspicion ought to be entertained. Besides, in both these cases, the money is lodged under the owner's own roof, and is subject to thieves, to fire, and to other contingencies, against which it is not always easy to guard.

All these evils are obviated by means of banking. The owner of money need neither take the charge of it himself, nor trust to his dependents. He can place it in the hands of his bankers. They are wealthy men, and are responsible to him for the amount. If they are robbed, it is no loss to him: they are pledged to restore to him the amount of his deposit when he shall require it. Whenever he wants money he has only to write an order, or draft, upon his banker, and the person to whom he is indebted takes the draft to the bank, and without any hesitation or delay receives the money.

2. The bankers allow interest for money placed in their hands.

By means of banking, the various small sums of money which would have remained unproductive in the hands of individuals, are collected into large amounts in the hands of the bankers, who employ it in granting facilities to trade and commerce.

Thus banking increases the productive capital of the nation. At the origin of banking, " the new-fashioned bankers," as they were called, allowed a certain rate of interest for money placed in their hands. The banks of Scotland carry this practice to the greatest extent, as they receive upon interest so low an amount as ten pounds, and also allow interest on the balance of a running account. Many of the country bankers in England allow interest on the balance of a running account, and charge commission on the amount of the money withdrawn. The London bankers generally do not allow interest on deposit, but neither do they charge commission. All their profits are derived from the use of their customers' money. The banks of Scotland do not charge commission, although they allow interest on deposits; but then those banks have a profit by the issue of their notes. The London bankers do not issue notes.

3. Another advantage conferred upon society by bankers is, that they make advances to persons who want to borrow money. These advances are made—by discounting bills—upon personal security—upon the joint security of the borrower and two or three of his friends—and sometimes upon mortgage. Persons engaged in trade and commerce are thus enabled to augment their capital, and consequently their wealth. The increase of money in circulation stimulates production. When bankers are compelled to withhold their usual accommodation, both the commercial and the agricultural interests are plunged in extreme distress. The great advantage arising to a neighbourhood from the establishment of a bank, is derived mainly from the additional supplies of money advanced in the form of loans, or discounts, to the inhabitants of the place. This principle is so well understood in Scotland, that branch banks are sometimes established in poor districts, with a view of obtaining a future profit from the prosperity which the bank will introduce.*

4. Another benefit derived from bankers is, that they transmit money from one part of the country to another.

There is scarcely a person in business who has not occasion sometimes to send money to a distant town. But how is this to be done? He cannot send a messenger with it on purpose—that would be too expensive. He cannot send it by post—that would be too hazardous. Besides, the sum may be some fraction

* Evidence before the Select Committee of the House of Commons, upon the Abolition of Small Notes, p. 43.   Report.

of a pound, and then it cannot go by post. The post, too, takes a considerable time, as three letters at least must pass on the transaction. If he live in London he may obtain a bank post bill, but he cannot obtain that in the country; and he may not be able to obtain it in London for the exact sum he wants. How, then, is the money to be sent? Every country banker opens an account with a London banker. If, then, a person lives at Penzance, and wants to send a sum of money to Aberdeen, he will pay the money into the Penzance bank, and his friend will receive it of the Aberdeen bank. The whole transaction is this: the Penzance bank will direct their agent in London to pay the money to the London agent of the Aberdeen bank, who will be duly advised of the payment. A small commission charged by the Penzance bank, and the postages, constitute all the expenses incurred, and there is not the least risk of loss.

Commercial travellers, who go collecting money, derive great advantage from the banks. Instead of carrying with them, throughout the whole of their journey, all the money they have received, when perhaps it may be wanted at home, they pay it into a bank, by whom it is remitted with the greatest security, and at little expense; and they are thus delivered from an incumbrance which would have occasioned great care and anxiety.

5. Wherever a bank is established, the public are able to obtain that denomination of currency which is best adapted for carrying on the commercial operations of the place. In a town which has no bank, a person may have occasion to use small notes, and have none but large ones; and at other times he may have need of large notes, and not be able to obtain them. But where a bank is established there can be no difficulty of this kind. The banks issue that description of notes which the receivers may require, and are always ready to exchange them for others of a different denomination. Banks, too, usually supply their customers and the neighbourhood with silver; and if, on the other hand, silver should be too abundant, the banks will receive it, either as a deposit, or in exchange for their notes. Hence, where banks are established, it is easy to obtain change. This is very convenient to those who have to pay large sums in wages, or who purchase in small amounts the commodities in which they trade.

6. By means of banking there is a great saving of time in making money transactions. How much longer time does it take to count out a sum of money in pounds, shillings, and pence, than it does to write a draft. And how much less trouble is it to receive a draft in payment of a debt, and then to pay it into the banker's, than it is to receive a sum of money in currency. What inconveniences would arise from the necessity of weighing sovereigns. What a loss of time from disputes as to the goodness or badness of particular pieces of money.

Besides the loss of time that must necessarily occur on every transaction, we must also reckon the loss which every merchant or tradesman, in an extensive line of business, would certainly sustain in the course · of a year from receiving counterfeit or deficient coin, or forged notes. From all this risk he is exempt by keeping a banker. If he receive payment of a debt, it is in the form of a draft upon his customer's banker. He pays it into his own banker's, and no coin or bank notes pass through his hands. If he draws bills, those bills are presented by his banker: and if his banker take bad money it is his own loss.

7. A merchant or tradesman who keeps a banker saves the trouble and expense of presenting those bills or drafts which he may draw upon his customers, or which he may receive in exchange for his goods. He pays these into the hands of his banker, and has no further trouble. He has now no care about the custody of his bills—no anxiety about their being stolen— no danger of forgetting them until they are over-due, and thus exonerating the indorsers—no trouble of sending to a distance in order to demand payment. He has nothing more to do than to see the amount entered to his credit in his banker's books. If a bill be not paid it is brought back to him on the day after it falls due, properly noted. The banker's clerk and the notary's clerk are witnesses ready to come forward to prove that the bill has been duly presented, and the notary's ticket attached to the bill assigns the reason why it is not paid. But if any indorser of the bill has given a reference in case of need—that is, if any indorser has written on the back of the bill that some other party will pay it in case the accepter does not, then the notary takes the bill to the referee, and procures the money from him.

This circumstance alone must cause an immense saving of expense to a mercantile house in the course of a year. Let us suppose that a merchant has only two bills due each day. These bills may be payable in distant parts of the town, so that it may take a clerk half a day to present them. And in large mercantile establishments it would take up the whole time of one or two clerks to present the due bills and the drafts. The salaries of these clerks are therefore saved by keeping an account at a banker's. Besides the saving of expense, it is also reasonable to suppose that losses upon bills would some-times occur from mistakes, or oversights—from miscalculation as to the time a bill would become due—from errors in marking it up—from forgetfulness to present it—or from presenting it at the wrong house. In these cases the indorsers and the drawers are exonerated; and if the accepter do not pay the bill the amount is lost. In a banking-house such mistakes are not so likely to occur, though they do occur sometimes; but the loss falls upon the banker, and not upon his customer.

8. Another advantage from keeping a banker in London is, that by this means you have a continual referee as to your respectability. If a mercantile house in the country write to their agent, to ascertain the respectability of a firm in London, the first inquiry is, Who is their banker? And when this is ascertained, the banker is applied to through the proper channel, and he gives his testimony as to the respectability of his cus-tomer. When a trader gives his bill, it circulates through the hands of many individuals to whom he is personally unknown; but if the bill is made payable at a banking-house, it bears on its face a reference to a party to whom the accepter is known, and who must have some knowledge of his character as a trades-man. This may be an immense advantage to a man in business, as a means of increasing his credit; and credit, Dr. Franklin says, is money.

9. The keeping an account at a banking-house enables a trader not only to give a constant reference as to his own respectability, but it also enables him to ascertain the re-spectability of other persons who keep bankers. There are numerous cases in which a trader may wish to know this. A stranger may bring him a bill, and want goods in exchange: or he may have drawn a bill upon a customer, and wishes to ascertain if this bill would be paid before he gave him any further credit. If this bill is not made payable at a banking-house he can obtain no information. But suppose the bill is

made payable at a banking-house; even then he can obtain no information unless he himself has a banker. If he take the bill to the banker's, at whose house it is made payable, and say, "Gentlemen, I will thank you to inform me if the accepter of this bill be a respectable man—May I safely give goods or money in exchange for it?" They will reply, "Sir, we never answer such questions to strangers." But if the holder of this bill keeps an account at a banker's, he has only to ask his banker to make the inquiry for him, and he will easily obtain the most ample information. Among nearly all the bankers in London the practice is established of giving information to each other as to the respectability of their customers. For as the bankers themselves are the greatest discounters of bills, it is their interest to follow this practice; and indeed the interest of their customers also, of those at least who are respectable.

10. By means of banking, people are able to preserve an authentic record of their annual expenditure.* If a person pays in to his banker all the money he receives in the course of a year, and makes all his payments by cheques—then by looking over his bank-book at the end of the year he will readily see the total amount of his receipts, and the various items of his expenditure. This is very useful to persons who have not habits of business, and who may therefore be in danger of living beyond their means. It is useless to advise such persons to keep an account of their expenses—they will do no such thing; but when short of money at Christmas to pay their tradesmen's bills, they may take the trouble of looking over their bank-book, and noticing how many cheques were drawn for the purchase of unnecessary articles. A bank account is useful also in case of disputed payments. People do not always take receipts for money they pay to their tradesmen, and when they do the receipts may be lost or mislaid. In case of death, or of omission to enter the amount in the creditor's books, the money may be demanded again. Should the payment have been made in bank notes or sovereigns, the payer can offer no legal proof of having settled the account; but if the account was discharged by a cheque on a banker, the cheque can be produced, and the payment proved

* In the year 1849 a committee of investigation into the affairs of a railway company reported that the company had kept no books for eighteen months, and knew their transactions only from their bankers' pass-book.

by the officers of the bank, who can be subpœnaed for that purpose.

11. Another advantage resulting from keeping a banker in London, is, that the party has a secure place of deposit for any deeds, papers, or other property that may require peculiar care.* Any customer who pleases may have a tin box, which he may leave with his banker in the evening, and call for it in the morning. In this box he might place his will, the lease of his house, policies of insurance, or any other documents he wished to preserve against fire. Stock-brokers and others who have offices in the city, and live out of town, have such boxes, which they leave overnight with their banker for the sake of security, in preference to leaving them in their own office. If a party were going to the country he might send his plate or jewellery to his banker, who will lock it up in his strong room, and thus it will be preserved from fire and thieves until his return. Solicitors and others, who have deeds or other writings of importance left in their custody, can send them to the bank during the night, and thus avoid the danger of fire.

12. By keeping a banker, people have a ready channel of obtaining much information that will be useful to them in the way of their business. They will know the way in which bankers keep their accounts; they will learn many of the laws and customs relating to bills of exchange. By asking the banker, or any of the clerks, they may know which is the readiest way of remitting any money they have to send to the country or to the Continent. If they have to buy or sell stock in the public funds, the banker can give them the name of a respectable broker who can manage the business; or should they be about to travel, and wish to know the best way of receiving money abroad; or be appointed executors to a will, and have to settle some money matters—the banker will in

* Secure to a certain extent. The reader is referred to the City Article in the *Times* of March 25th, 1869, for an elaborate notice of a then recent decision of the Privy Council, respecting the non-liability of bankers for securities held by them on behalf of their customers, and for a pertinent and forcible representation of the utter absence of redress in case of abstraction or loss. In the same article, and on subsequent occasions also, mention was made of a plan in successful operation at the Bank of France, and of similar means adopted in the United States, for the absolute security of such deeds, documents, and valuables. As yet, however, no action seems to have been taken in the matter.—Editor.

these, and many other cases, be able to give them the necessary information.

13. Banking also exercises a powerful influence upon the morals of society. It tends to produce honesty and punctuality in pecuniary engagements. Bankers, for their own interest, always have a regard to the moral character of the party with whom they deal; they inquire whether he be honest or tricky, industrious or idle, prudent or speculative, thrifty or prodigal, and they will more readily make advances to a man of moderate property and good morals, than to a man of large property but of inferior reputation. Thus the establishment of a bank in any place immediately advances the pecuniary value of a good moral character. There are numerous instances of persons having risen from obscurity to wealth only by means of their moral character, and the confidence which that character produced in the mind of their banker. It is not merely by way of loan or discount that a banker serves such a person. He also speaks well of him to those persons who may make inquiries respecting him, and the banker's good opinion will be the means of procuring him a higher degree of credit with the parties with whom he trades. These effects are easily perceivable in country towns; and even in London, if a house be known to have engaged in gambling or smuggling transactions, or in any other way to have acted discreditably, their bills will be taken by the bankers less readily than those of an honourable house of inferior property.

It is thus that bankers perform the functions of public conservators of the commercial virtues. From motives of private interest they encourage the industrious, the prudent, the punctual, and the honest—while they discountenance the spendthrift and the gambler, the liar and the knave. They hold out inducements to uprightness, which are not disregarded by even the most abandoned. There is many a man who would be deterred from dishonesty by the frown of a banker, though he might care but little for the admonitions of a bishop.

SECTION III.

BANKING TERMS.

Query I.—Is the word Bank a singular or a plural noun?

The word BANK, being a noun of multitude, may have verbs and pronouns agreeing with it in either the singular or the plural number, yet not without regard to the import of the term as conveying unity or plurality of idea. In the use of this term the following rules are usually observed:—

1. When any operation or feeling of the mind is ascribed to a bank, the verbs and pronouns are placed in the plural—as, "The bank *were anxious* to meet the wishes of the public." "The bank *have concurred* in the measure proposed." "Are you one of the persons who tried the question with the Bank of Ireland, whether *they conceived themselves* bound to pay in gold at *their* branches?" "The Bank of England petitioned against this bill, and *were* heard by *their* Counsel; but *their* representations produced no effect, and the bill having passed through both Houses, received the Royal assent." The following examples, wherein mental operations are ascribed to a neuter pronoun, are violations of this rule: "The bank *allows* the party having the cash credit to liquidate any portion of his debt to the bank at any time that may suit his convenience, and reserves to *itself* the power of cancelling, whenever *it shall think fit,* the credit granted." "It is usual for the bank when *it* gives a cash credit *to keep a watchful eye* over the person having that cash credit."

2. When a reference is made to a bank merely as an institution, the term is considered to belong to the singular—as, "The Bank of Scotland continued the only bank from the date of *its* establishment, in 1695, to the year 1727. In that year a charter of incorporation was granted to certain individuals named therein, for carrying on the business of banking, under the name of the Royal Bank; and subsequent charters were granted to this establishment, enlarging *its* capital, which now amounts to one million and a half." "The National Bank of Scotland *has* 1,238 partners." "If this measure be carried .into effect, the Provincial Bank must instantly be deprived of any sufficient means of reimbursing *itself* for the

heavy expense to which *it has* been subject." "*Has* your bank an establishment at Kirkcudbright?" "The Bank of England *has* the control of *its* issues entirely within *itself.*"

3. When we notice the rules or habitual acts of a bank, the word belongs to the singular—as, "The Provincial Bank *allows* interest at the rate of two per cent." "The bank *draws* bills upon London at twenty-one days after date." "The bank *discounts* bills at the rate of four per cent." "The bank *issues* notes payable in gold at the place of issue." "The London and Westminster *grants* interest upon deposits—*it does* not allow *its* officers to receive Christmas presents from *its* customers." In reference to cases that fall under this rule, there is, however, some contrariety of practice: "*Do* the Provincial Bank *issue* post bills? *They do* not." "Have the Bank of Ireland at *their* branch at Cork been in the habit of receiving gold to any amount in payments?" "*Have* the Bank of Ireland any deposits at the Cork branch? Do you know how *their* notes get into circulation? Do *they* pay any interest on *their* deposits? *They have* a great quantity of notes in circulation— *have they* not?"

4. When the word bank is connected with a past participle by means of the neuter verb *to be*, it usually belongs to the singular—as, "I am a director of the Bank of Scotland, which *is established* by Act of Parliament; *it does* not hold a charter from the Crown, but in common language *it is called* a chartered bank." "Suppose a bank *was enabled* to take 6 per cent. on a cash credit, instead of 4." "The Falkirk Union Banking Company *has been returned* to this house, as sequestrated in the month of October, 1816." "A new bank *was constituted* as a fund, upon which the sum of 2,564,000*l.* should be raised, and *it was called* the Land Bank, because established on land securities."

5. When the word bank is preceded by the indefinite article, *a, an*—by the demonstrative pronoun, *this, that*—or by the words *each, any, every, one*—it belongs to the singular; as, "Do you not think that *a* bank that *is* possessed of a capital of one million, may and will do more business than *a* bank that *is* only possessed of half a million?" "In a moment of pressure, an emergency like the present, *that* bank would get into great disrepute who called up any one of *its* cash credits." "What *is* the amount of the small note circulation in *that* bank, as

connected with *its* whole circulation?"   "*Each* bank *has* an interest to issue as much of the small note circulation as *it* can?—Certainly *it has,* provided the small notes can be kept out; but, as *every* bank *makes* an exchange at Glasgow twice every week, and the exchanges of *each* bank come back upon *itself,* and the balance is paid by a draft on Edinburgh at sight," &c.   "I believe almost *every* bank in Scotland *has* an agent in Glasgow." "Suppose *one* bank in Scotland made *its* notes payable in Scotland, at the place where the notes were issued."   "Is there *any* bank in Cork now that *issues* notes?"

6. When the word bank is introduced in either the singular or the plural number, the same number should be preserved throughout the sentence.   Hence, the following sentence of Smollett's is inaccurate: "By the same Acts the bank *was* required to advance a sum not exceeding 2,500,000*l.* towards discharging the national debt, if wanted, on condition that *they* should have 5*l.* per cent. for as much as *they* might advance, redeemed by Parliament."

7. When the word bank is used in the singular number, it is considered as a substantive of the neuter gender, and hence is associated with the relative pronoun, *which;* but when used in the plural number, it implies the idea of persons, and has accordingly the personal relative, *who;* as, "The bank with *which* he kept his account *has* stopped payment;" or, "The bank with *whom* he kept his account *have* stopped payment." "The bank, *whose* interests are affected by the proposed measure, *have* petitioned against it."   The bank upon *whom* the cheque was drawn *have* refused to honour it."   The following sentence is not in accordance with this rule: "In a moment of pressure, an emergency like the present, that bank would get into great disrepute *who* called up any of *its* cash credits."

I have not observ. d that any *English* writer, except Mr. McCulloch, considered a bank to be a lady; and this is only in the case of an Irish bank.   Under the article "Banking," in his Commercial Dictionary, he says, "The Bank of Ireland draws on London, at twenty days' date. *She* neither grants cash credits, nor allows any interest on deposits; *she* discounts at the rate of 5*l.* per cent."   This mode of expression is, however, very common with American writers.[*]

[*] It has now become more common with *English* writers, especially with reference to the Bank of England. 1849.

II. Should we write *accepter* or *acceptor* of a bill of exchange? The name of the agent to any verb is usually formed, in our language, by the addition of *r* or *er* to the verb; as, *indorser, talker, walker, speaker.* What reason, then, can be assigned why, in the present case, we should depart from the analogy of the language? We do not say, the drawor, the holdor, the payor of a bill; why then should we say the acceptor? When we speak of the accepter of a bill, why should we not spell the word in the same way as when we speak of the accepter of a present, or of a fee? Yet all our English legal authors write, acceptor: "A person who accepts for honour, is only liable if the original drawee do not pay; and to charge such *acceptor*, there must be a presentment for payment to such original drawee."—*Bayley.* "A foreign bill is binding in this country on the *acceptor*, though he accepted by parol, or by writing unconnected with the instrument."—*Chitty.* "Where the *acceptor* of a forged bill pays it, and is guilty of any negligence, or want of due caution in making such payment, he cannot recover the money so paid, from the innocent party to whom he paid it."—*Roscoe.* Scotch authors, however, write *accepter.* "An English inland bill has generally three parties to it—the drawer, *accepter, and* payee; whereas, in Scotland, most of the inland bills have, at first, but two parties, the drawer and the *accepter;* and they are made payable to the drawer or his order." *

III. Should we write *indorse* or *endorse?* Indorse is derived direct from the Latin, *in dorsum*, on the back. *Endorse* is derived from the Latin, through the French, *endosser.* In such cases, most writers adopt the Latin mode of spelling, in preference to the French, as *indorse, inquire, intire;* not *endorse, enquire, entire.* All legal authors write indorse. "A promise to *indorse*, though on sufficient consideration, cannot be treated as an actual *indorsement*."—*Bayley.* "The liability of the *indorser* is discharged by want of notice, as in the case of the drawer."—*Roscoe.* "A person who draws or *indorses* a bill, or *indorses* a note for the accommodation of the acceptor or maker, or payee, or prior *indorsers*, has on paying the instrument, a remedy over thereon against the acceptor or maker, or prior party."—*Chitty.* "A drawer or *indorser* cannot, in the character of *indorsee*, maintain an action against the

* See Glen on the Law of Bills of Exchange in Scotland.

accepter, where the indorsement is after the refusal of payment."—*Glen.*

IV. Should we say *indorsement* or *indorsation?* In England we always use the word indorsement. "No particular words are essential to an *indorsement;* the mere signature of the indorser is, in general, sufficient."—*Bayley.* "The *indorsement* may be upon the face, or at the back of the bill."—*Chitty.* "An attesting witness to an *indorsement* is necessary, when the bill is for a less sum than 5*l.*"—*Chitty.* In Scotland the term more generally used is indorsation. "If a bill or note be granted to a woman while single, and she afterwards marry, the right to transfer it by *indorsation* would vest in the husband." "After a bill has been paid no *indorsation* can take place, so as to affect the accepter, or any of the parties who would otherwise be discharged."—*Glen.* The word indorsement is also used in Scotland, though more rarely. Both words appear to have precisely the same meaning. "An *indorsation* is made, either by the indorser's writing, and subscribing an order to pay the contents of the bill to some particular person mentioned by name, which is styled a *full indorsement,* or by merely signing his name on the bill, and delivering it to the indorsee, or person to whom it is indorsed, which is termed *a blank indorsation.*"—*Glen.* "A fictitious *indorsement* to a bill is a forgery; such *indorsation* is clearly giving it a false credit."—*Glen.*

V. Should we say the *presentment* or the *presentation* of a bill of exchange? All writers agree in using presentment. "If upon the *presentment* of the bill for acceptance to the drawee, he refuse or neglect to accept it, the drawer is immediately responsible to the holder, although the bill has not become due according to its tenor."—*Chitty.* "If the bill be payable after sight, and the drawee detain it some days without declaring his intention to accept, and afterwards incline to do so, the acceptance must be from the date of the first *presentment.*"— *Glen.* "*Presentment* for payment must be made by the holder of the bill, or by an agent competent to give a legal receipt for the money."—*Glen.* "Upon a *presentment* for acceptance, the bill should be left with the drawee twenty-four hours, unless in the interim he either accept, or declare a resolution not to accept. But a bill or note must not be left (unless it be paid) on a *presentment* for payment; if it be, the *presentment*

is not considered as made, until the money is called for."—
Bayley.

VI. Should we write *draught* or *draft*? This word is derived
from the verb *to draw*, and probably was originally written and
pronounced *drawght*. But custom, which is the law of language, has changed both the pronunciation and the spelling to
draft. In the former editions of this work, I mentioned that
Mr. Justice Bayley had always spelled this word *draught ;* but in
a recent edition of his work, since published, I find that *draught*
has been changed to *draft*.

VII. Should we write *check* or *cheque*? This word is derived
from the French, *echecs, chess*. The chequers placed at the
doors of public-houses, are intended to represent chess-boards,
and originally denoted that the game of chess was played in
those houses. Similar tables were employed in reckoning
money, and hence came the expression—to check an account;
and the Government Office, where the public accounts were
kept, was called the Exchequer. It probably obtained this
name from the French *exchiquier*, a chess-board, though Blackstone states that this court was called the exchequer, from the
chequered cloth which covered the table. Of the two forms of
writing this word, *check* and *cheque*, the latter seems preferable,
as it is free from ambiguity, and is analogous to EX-CHEQUER,
the public treasury. It is also used by the Bank of England,
"CHEQUE-OFFICE." In *Bayley* both forms are employed. "A
cheque upon a banker was lost, and paid to a stranger the day
before *it bore date :* the banker was obliged to repay the money
to the loser." "By the usage of trade, a banker in London
will not render himself responsible by retaining a *check* drawn
on him, provided he return it at any time before five o'clock on
the evening of the day in which it was drawn."

SECTION IV.

THE GENERAL ADMINISTRATION OF A BANK.

To be a good banker requires some intellectual and some
moral qualifications. A banker need not be a man of talent,
but he should be a man of wisdom. Talent, in the sense in
which the word is ordinarily used, implies a strong develop-

ment of some one faculty of the mind. Wisdom implies the due proportion of all the faculties. A banker need not be a poet or a philosopher—a man of science or of literature—an orator or a statesman. He need not possess any one remarkable quality by which he may be distinguished from the rest of mankind. It is only necessary that he should possess a large portion of that practical quality which is called common sense. Banking talent (using the word *talent* here in the sense of adaptation of character to any particular pursuit) consists more in the union of a number of qualities, not in themselves individually of a striking character, but rare only in their combination in the same person. It is a mistake to suppose that banking is such a routine employment that it requires neither knowledge nor skill. The number of banks that have failed within the last fifty years are sufficient to show, that to be a good banker requires qualities as rare and as important as those which are necessary to attain eminence in any other pursuit. The dealer in money exercises intellectual faculties of a high order, and of great value to the community. His profession has a powerful bearing on the practical happiness of mankind.

" The philosophy which affects to teach us a contempt of money, does not run very deep; for, indeed, it ought to be still more clear to the philosopher than it is to the ordinary man, that there are few things in the world of greater importance. And so manifold are the bearings of money upon the lives and characters of mankind, that an insight which should search out the life of a man in his pecuniary relations, would penetrate into almost every cranny of his nature. He who knows, like St. Paul, both how to spare and how to abound, has a great knowledge: for if we take account of all the virtues with which money is mixed up —honesty, justice, generosity, charity, frugality, forethought, self-sacrifice,—and of their correlative vices—it is a knowledge which goes near to cover the length and breadth of humanity : and a right measure and manner in getting, saving, spending, giving, taking, lending, borrowing, and bequeathing, would almost argue a perfect man."*

But though wisdom—or, in other words, a high degree of common sense—does not imply the possession of any remarkable talent (the undue development of any one faculty), it always implies the absence of any remarkable defect. One great defect in a banker is a want of decision. A banker ought to know how to balance the evidence on each side of a question, and to arrive speedily at a just conclusion.

* Taylor's Notes on Life.

M

" Indecisiveness will be, *cæteris paribus*, most pernicious in affairs which require secrecy. 1st, Because the greatest aid to secrecy is celerity. 2nd, Because the undecided man, seeking after various counsel, necessarily multiplies confidences. The pretext for indecisiveness is commonly mature deliberation; but, in reality, indecisive men occupy themselves less in deliberation than others; for to him who fears to decide, deliberation (which has a foretaste of that fear) soon becomes intolerably irksome, and the mind escapes from the anxiety of it into alien themes. Or, if that seems too open a dereliction of its task, it gives itself to inventing reasons of postponement. And the man who has confirmed habits of indecisiveness, will come in time to look upon postponement as the first object in all cases, and wherever it seems to be practicable, will bend all his faculties to accomplish it."[*]

Another defect is a want of firmness. A banker having, after a mature consideration, made up his mind, should be capable of a strict adherence to his previous determination: he should know when to say, *No;* and having once said No, he should adhere to it. Another defect is a hasty or impetuous temper. Another is that of being swayed by any personal or constitutional prepossession. Almost every man has a sin by which he is most easily beset; a constitutional defect, against which it is necessary he should be upon his guard.

It is a great advantage to a banker, and indeed to every one else, to know himself. He should know wherein he excels, and wherein he is deficient. He ought to know whether he is disposed from his temperament to be excessively cautious, or excessively liberal—whether his manners are courteous or abrupt—whether he is apt to view matters on their gloomy or on their bright side—whether social intercourse renders him more or less fit for his official engagements—whether the presents and civilities he receives from his customers do, or do not, affect his transactions with them in matters of business. When he has made a loss, he should examine whether the loss was occasioned by the ordinary operation of events, or produced by any little weaknesses of his own character. He should record all those instances in which he has shown a want of firmness, of discretion, of discrimination, or of perseverance; and should guard in future against the exhibition of any similar defect:

" Man, know thyself ; all wisdom centres there."

But while a banker should make himself acquainted with his

---

[*] Taylor's Statesman.—I would advise all bankers, and all other persons at the head of large establishments, to read this little work.

own defects, he ought not to let his customers become acquainted with them. All wise men know their own defects; none but fools publish them. Crafty men, who often have occasion to borrow money, are quick in perceiving the weaknesses of their banker. And if they find that by coaxing, or flattering, or gossiping, or bribing, or threatening, they can influence his conduct, he will always be at their mercy. On this account it is, perhaps, advisable that a banker should not have too much social intercourse with those of his customers who have occasion to ask him for any large amount of accommodation.

Wisdom implies prudence and discretion, and these should regulate the whole conduct of a banker, not merely when engaged in banking transactions, but at all other times. We may apply to a banker the language we have elsewhere applied to a merchant :

" The amusements of a merchant should correspond with his character. He should never engage in those recreations which partake of the nature of gambling, and but seldom in those of a frivolous description. A judge is not always on the bench, a clergyman is not always in the pulpit, nor is a merchant always on 'Change ; but each is expected at all times to abstain from any amusements which are not consistent with his professional character. The credit of a merchant depends not merely on his wealth, but also upon the opinion generally entertained of his personal qualities; and he should cultivate a reputation for prudence and propriety of conduct, as part of his stock in trade."*

A banker should have a talent for selecting suitable instruments. He ought not only to know himself, he ought also to have a capacity for judging of others. He should know how to choose proper clerks for the discharge of the duties of the office. He should know also what parties to employ to procure him confidential information as to the character and circumstances of commercial houses, or of individuals. He should know how to choose his partners or coadjutors, and should endeavour to select those who possess qualifications in which he is himself deficient. In all cases when he has any object to effect he should know how to make use of other men. We may here, as in some other cases, apply to a banker the observations Mr. Taylor applies to a statesman :

" The most important qualification of one who is high in the service of the State, is his fitness for acting through others, since the operations

---

* Lectures on the History and Principles of Ancient Commerce. By J. W. Gilbart.

vicariously effected ought, if he knows how to make use of his power, to predominate greatly over the importance which can attach to any man's direct and individual activity."*

A neglect of this rule has occurred in the history of some joint-stock banks, where the manager has impaired his own health, and damaged his bank, by taking upon himself a vast variety of duties which should have been assigned to others; forgetful that in large establishments the chief officer should confine his personal attention to those duties which are intellectual, or which are of the chief importance; while the duties which are of a mere manual, or less important character, should be performed through the instrumentality of assistants.

A banker should know how to economize his own time. One mode of doing this will be, as we have intimated, to assign inferior duties to others. His accountant should keep his books, and make his calculations. His secretary should write his letters (except those of a private or confidential nature), and he should only sign them. His chief clerk should attend to the discipline of the office. A banker at the head of a large establishment should not only be acquainted with the art of banking —he ought also to be acquainted with the art of government. He ought to put a clever man at the head of each department, and reserve to himself only the duty of general superintendence. He should give these parties a pretty wide discretion, and not encourage them to ask his instructions about matters of comparatively trifling importance. If he does this, they will never learn to think for themselves,—never feel that wholesome anxiety which results from a sense of responsibility,—and never acquire that decision of mind which arises from the necessity of forming an independent judgment. Consequently, they will be less useful to him in their present position, and never become qualified for higher offices.

Another mode of economizing time is to observe a principle of order. A banker should come to the bank every day at the same hour; attend to his affairs, one by one, in the same order, and leave the bank at his usual time. By observing this routine, he will not only save much time, but he will avoid tumultuous feelings, and maintain a calmness of mind and of manner, that will be useful in all his affairs. He will also acquire from habit a coolness of investigation, and a promptness of decision; and he

* Taylor's Statesman.

will get through a great deal of work without ever appearing to be in a hurry.

Another mode of economizing time is, to make his interviews with his customers, or with other parties, as short as he can. He should not encourage conversation upon any other topic than that which is the occasion of the interview. He had better receive his customers standing; as in that case they will stand too, and are not likely to remain so long as if they were to sit down. And the furniture of the room should be so arranged that the customer, if he sit down, should sit near the door, so that he may depart whenever disposed. He is not likely to remain so long as if seated comfortably by the fire-side. It is also desirable that his room should be so placed, with reference to the other parts of the building, that while it has one door open to the public, it should have another door opening into the office; so that he may easily pass into the office, to ascertain the state of a customer's account, or to consult with himself or another person, in doubtful cases, as to the course to be adopted. It is not advisable that the customer who applies, for instance, to have a heavy bill discounted, should witness the hesitation or the deliberation of the banker. Hence it is better, when it can be done, to establish the practice of the customer giving the bills to a clerk, who shall bring them into the banker's room, and take back his reply.

A banker will take means for obtaining and recording information. He should not, as we have said, keep any books himself. But he ought always to have in his room, ready for immediate reference, if necessary, "the General Balance Book," containing the weekly balances of the general ledger, which will show the weekly progress of his business for several years past,—"the Daily Balance Book," showing the daily balance to the credit of each of his customers in the current-account ledger,—"the Weekly Discount Balance Book," showing the amount of discounts, loans, or other advances which each customer has every Saturday night,—"the Inspection Book," showing the amount of bills bearing the names of houses who do not keep an account with him,—"the Information Book," containing the character of all the houses about whom he has had occasion to make inquiries,—and, finally, "a Private Memorandum Book," in which is entered any special agreements that he has made with his customers. It is also useful to a banker to have a list of his customers, classified according to their trades or professions—such as corn merchants, leather factors, grocers, solicitors, &c., &c. The banker would thus see at a glance among what classes of society his connections lie. When any public event was likely to affect any class—such, for instance, as the corn merchants—he would see how many of his customers are likely to be affected. By thus, too, bearing in mind the trade or profession of his customers, he would be able to judge more readily whether the bills they brought him for discount had arisen out of their business transactions.

Of these books, one of the most important is the " Information Book." There is no doubt that a banker of great experience, and of a strong memory, may always bear in his mind a very correct estimate of the standing and character of all the houses that usually come under his notice. But this does not supersede the necessity for recording his information in a book. His memory may fail, and that too on important occasions; and certainly if he leave the bank for a short time, as he must sometimes have occasion to do, he will carry his memory with him. But if the " Information Book " be closely kept up, he will record his knowledge for the use of those who will have to take his place. It is no valid objection to the keeping of such a book to say that the position of houses is perpetually changing. Those changes should be recorded, so that their actual standing should always be readily referred to. If a banker is requested by a customer to make inquiry about a house, he should record the information he gets for his own guidance, in case any bills on that house should afterwards be offered him for discount.

A banker will get information about parties from inquiry at their bankers, as we have mentioned at page 151. This information may be defective in two ways. In the first place, their banker may judge of them from the account they keep—that is, from the balance to their credit—and thus he may give too good an account of them. Or, secondly, their banker may have an interest in keeping up their credit, and under this bias he may not give them so bad a character as they actually deserve. Another source of information is from parties in the same trade. Houses in the same trade know pretty well the standing of one another. Wholesale houses are well acquainted with the retail shopkeepers who buy of them. Most bankers have among their own customers some houses in almost every trade, who can give them any information respecting other houses which they may require. The bills that pass through his hands will also often give him some useful hints respecting the parties whose names are upon them.

It is of great importance to a banker to have an ample knowledge of the means and transactions of his customers. The customer, when he opens his account, will give him some information on this subject. The banker will afterwards get information from his own books. The amount of transactions that his customer passes through his current account will show the extent of his business. The amount of his daily balance will show if he has much ready cash. The extent and character of the bills he offers for discount, will show if he trusts large amounts to individual houses, and if these are respectable. On the other hand, the bills his customer may accept to other parties, and his payments, will show the class of people with whom he deals, or who are in the habit of giving him credit. But one main source of information is to see the man. This, like other means of information, will sometimes fail; but, generally speaking, the appearance and manners of a man will show his character. Some people always send their clerk to the banker with bills for discount, &c. This is all very well if they want no extraordinary accommodation; but if they ask for anything out of the usual way, the banker had better say that he wishes to see the principal. And if he had a doubt whether his customer was tricky or honest—speculative or prudent—let him be guided by his first impression—we mean the impression produced by the first interview. In nine cases out of ten the first impression will be found to be correct. It is not necessary to study physiognomy or phrenology to be able to judge of the character of men with whom we converse upon matters of business.

A country banker has greater facilities than a London banker of ascertaining the character and circumstances of other parties. In a country town everything is known about everybody.—A man's parentage and connexions—his family and associates—the property he has already received, and what he may expect to receive from his relations—and, above all, his personal habits and disposition. Upon the last point, we will make a short extract from an excellent series of " Letters to a

Branch Manager," published in the "Banker's Magazine," under the signature of "Thomas Bullion."

"Next in importance to a study of his accounts, the habits and character of a client are deserving of your attentive consideration. If a man's style of living, for example, becomes extravagant, and he gives himself over to excess, you cannot too promptly apply the curb, however regular the transactions upon his account may seem; because years may elapse before mere irregularity of living will make any impression on his banking account; whereas irregularity in business will exhibit itself immediately, and for this reason,—that whereas improvident habits of living involve a continuous waste in small sums, spreading over tolerably long periods, improvidence in business may involve in one fell swoop the loss perhaps of thousands. I hold, then, that you are not warranted in all cases in feeling satisfied of a man's perfect responsibility *until* his banking account exhibits indubitable evidence to the contrary."

A banker should always have general principles; that is, he should have fixed rules for the government of his bank. He should know beforehand whether he will or will not advance money on mortgage, or upon deeds, or upon bills of lading, or warrants; or whether he will discount bills based upon uncommercial transactions, or having more than three months to run. These are only a few of the cases in which a banker will find it useful to store his mind with general principles.

One advantage of this adoption of general principles is, that it saves time. If a banker can say, in reply to a customer, "It is contrary to the rules of our bank to advance money upon bills of lading," the reply is conclusive. But if he had not previously adopted any rule upon the subject, the reply would have taken up much more time. Another advantage is, that it gives decision of mind, and saves the banker from being "talked over" by any of his customers who may possess fluency of speech, or dexterity in debate. In this case, the banker whose mind is stored with general principles, though he may listen patiently to all his customer shall advance, will give the same reply which he would have given had the application been made in fewer words.

But although a banker ought to have a large stock of general principles—and this stock will increase as his experience increases—yet it may not be always wise to explain these principles to his customer. It is generally best, when a banker gives a refusal, to give no reasons for that refusal. Banking science is so little understood, that the public generally are unable to appreciate its principles. Besides, a man who wants to borrow money can never be convinced by reasoning that his banker is right in refusing to lend it to him; nor, in fact, did the banker himself acquire his knowledge of banking by reasoning. He acquired it not by reasoning, but by experience; and he must not expect that his customers, who have had no experience, will, by reasoning alone, readily acquiesce in the banking principles he may propound to them. In most cases, therefore, he had better keep his reasons to himself.

Nevertheless, while we contend that every banker should have general principles, we do not say that in no possible case should he depart from them. But he should not look for such cases; they are rare, and when they do occur they will force themselves upon his attention. If under shelter of the truism, "All rules have their exceptions," he departs from his general principles whenever he finds it convenient or profitable to do so, he may as well have no general principles at all.

It seems desirable that a banker in a large city should mark out for himself one or two main branches of business, rather than attempt to carry on banking in all its branches. . We see this line of conduct adopted by some of the most eminent London bankers. A west-end banker will not discount a bill :* a city banker will not lend money on mortgage. Different kinds of banking exist in different parts of the country, according to the character and circumstances of the district. And in London the classes of people are numerous, and it may be both, proper and advantageous for a banker to adapt his mode of business chiefly to the requirements of some one particular class. Different banks may thus pursue different courses, and all be equally successful.

A banker will exercise due caution in taking new accounts. He will expect the new customer to be introduced by some person to whom he is personally known. The more respectable the introducer, the higher opinion will the banker entertain of the party introduced. If a party apply to open an account without such an introduction, he is asked to give references to some well-known houses. He is expected to state to the banker the kind of business in which he is engaged, and the extent of accommodation, if any, that he is likely to

---

* Exceptions occasionally occur; but, as a general rule, the statement holds good.— EDITOR.

require. He will state the kind and character of the bills he will have to offer to discount, and mention any peculiarity in his business or circumstances that may occasionally require especial consideration. It is a great folly in a party opening an account to make any representation that will not afterwards turn out to be correct. Every banker is anxious to avoid taking .shabby accounts ; and especially such as are opened for the purposes of fraud, or to obtain a fictitious credit, or to get undue accommodation. It is considered to be not advisable to take the account of a party who has another banker, especially if he opens the account for the purpose of getting additional discount. The object of a party keeping two bankers is usually to get as much accommodation as he can from each. If an account is brought from another bank, the reason of the removal should be distinctly stated, and the banker will accept or reject it, according to circumstances. It is bad policy in a banker to attempt to draw away the connexions of another bank, by offering them greater accommodation. It is also usually bad policy to take the accounts of parties residing at a distance, as their transactions do not come under the notice of the banker ; and the fact of their passing by the banks in their neighbour-hood to go elsewhere, is one that should excite suspicion. It is not advisable for London bankers to take the accounts of private individuals who reside in the country. They should be referred to the bankers in their own districts.

A small banker should not attempt to take large accounts. Banks, otherwise well administered, have been ruined by one large account. If this account requires accommodation, it will absorb the banker's funds, so that he will be compelled to stint his other customers, or to have recourse to re-discount, or other modes of raising money. Even if it be only a deposit account, it may produce inconveniences. A small banker cannot so readily employ this large deposit profitably, and yet have it at command whenever required ; and the additional amount he must keep in his till will be proportionably greater than would be kept by a large banker. Thus, if 100,000*l.* be placed in a bank that has already 2,000,000*l.* of deposits, the additional sum kept in the till to meet daily demands may not be much increased ; but should it be lodged with a banker whose deposits are only 300,000*l.*, the increase of notes to be kept in his till will be very considerable. This shows that large deposits are not so profitable to small banks as to large ones. There is also a danger that a small banker will employ his large deposits in such a way as shall render him less ready to repay them punctually. Instances have occurred of small banks being greatly inconvenienced by the repayment of large deposits, which had been placed in their hands by railway companies. It is prudent, therefore, in a banker to apportion the amount of his transactions to the extent of his business.

A very important part of the business of a banker consists in the discounting of bills.*

In doubtful cases, the banker, before discounting a bill, will probably look through his books, and satisfy himself with regard to the following inquiries :—

What is the character of the customer ? This inquiry will be answered from the Information Book. What is the usual balance of his cash accounts? This will be answered by the Daily Balance Book. What amount has he now under discount ? This will be answered from the Discount Ledger, and will suggest other inquiries. Is that amount greater or less than usual ? What proportion does that amount bear to the average amount of his cash balance ? Is the amount chiefly upon few parties, or is it divided among a number? Have their bills been discounted chiefly upon the strength of the customer, or upon the strength of other parties? Are his bills generally paid? He will then proceed to inquire about the other parties to the bill. What is the character of the accepter in the Information Book? What is the nature of the transactions between the customer and the accepter, as far as can be ascertained? Has he had any bills upon him before, and have they been punctually paid? Are there any bills upon him now running, and how soon will they become due ?

In the discount of bills it is necessary to guard against forgeries. It has happened that parties carrying on a great business in London, have presented to their banker, for discount, bills drawn upon all parts of the country ; which bills, upon inquiry, have turned out to be purely fictitious. This is an additional reason for bankers making inquiry about the

---

* *Vide* pp. 115, 116, of The History and Principles of Banking, for an accurate classification and description of the bills presented to a bank for discount, together with remarks on the comparative advantages and disadvantages of long-dated and short-dated bills. —EDITOR.

accepters of the bills they discount, even when they think they have reason to be satisfied with the drawers. Even this is no protection against forgery. Sometimes the name of a most respectable house in a provincial town has been forged. Where the amount is large, therefore, it seems advisable to send the bill down to some banker in the town, and ask his opinion as to the genuineness of the signature. Of course in these, and many other cases in which a banker is liable to be cheated, much must depend upon personal discretion; no rules can be given for all cases.

To facilitate the detection of forged CHEQUES, it is advisable that the banker should have a printed number placed on every cheque, in every cheque-book, and keep a record of the name of the customer to whom each book is given. When a cheque with a forged signature appears, the banker can then turn to this registry, and see to which of his customers he had given out this cheque. This plan has been found useful in tracing forgeries that have been perpetrated by the clerks or servants of the party keeping the account. Some bankers, moreover, place on their cheque-books a printed label, requesting the customer will at all times keep the book under his own lock and key.

To guard against forgery in the case of DEEDS or BONDS, all these documents should be witnessed by an officer of the bank. And when a letter of guarantee is given by a third party, it should not be taken by the banker from the party in whose favour it is given, but the letter should be signed at the bank, and the signature witnessed by one of the clerks. A banker is also liable to loss from the alteration of cheques. The words six, seven, eight, and nine, can easily be changed, by the addition of y, or ty, into sixty, seventy, eighty, or ninety. Sometimes, too, when cheques are drawn for less than 10*l*., if a space be left open before the word, another word may be introduced. Thus, a short time ago a cheque was drawn on a banker for 3*l*., and the party who obtained it wrote the word sixty before the word three, and thus cheated the banker out of 60*l*. Letters of credit, as well as cheques, have heretofore been altered, by the original sum being taken out, and a larger sum being substituted. This is now prevented by staining the paper with a chemical preparation. Country banks also stamp upon their drafts the words " under ten pounds," " under twenty pounds," and so on, to prevent an alteration to any sum beyond those amounts.

The re-discounting of bills of exchange is an operation of much importance, and has a great influence on the monetary operations of the country. We quote from a former work of our own upon this subject :—

" Banks situated in agricultural districts have usually more money than they can employ. Independently of the paid-up capital of the bank, the sums raised by circulation and deposits are usually more than the amount of their loans and discounts. Banks, on the other hand, that are situated in manufacturing districts, can usually employ more money than they can raise. Hence, the bank that has a superabundance of money, sends it to London, to be employed by the bill-brokers, usually receiving, in return, bills of exchange. The bank that wants money sends its bills of exchange to London, to be re-discounted. These banks thus supply each other's wants, through the medium of the London bill-brokers."

But this principle of the re-discount of bills has been, in some cases, grossly abused, by being employed to give a sort of vitality to dead loans. A country banker lends upon mills and manufactories a larger amount of money than he can conveniently spare; then he asks the manufacturer to accept a bill for the amount, which the banker gets discounted in London or elsewhere. This bill, when due, is renewed, and the renewal is again replaced by another, and so the game goes on. As long as money is abundant all parties are pleased; the manufacturer gets his advance, the banker gets his commission, and the London bill-broker gets employment for his funds. But a pressure comes. The London bill-broker can discount no more, because the funds placed in his hands by his depositors have been withdrawn. The banker cannot get the new bills discounted elsewhere, and is unable to take up the old bills that are returned to him with his endorsement. The manufacturer, of course, cannot pay the money; the banker stops payment, and the manufacturer is ruined. The places at which this system has been chiefly carried on, are Manchester and Newcastle-upon-Tyne; and it is in these places that the greatest failures have taken place among the joint-stock banks. In fact, I believe it must be confessed, that the joint-stock banks have carried on this practice to a much greater extent than it was ever carried on by the private bankers. This has arisen from the greater credit which they possessed: it is one of the forms of the abuse of credit.

·A London banker is always anxious to avoid dead loans. Loans are usually specific advances for specified times, either with or without security. In London, advances are generally made by loans; in the country, by overdrafts. The difference arises from the different modes of conducting an account. In London, the banker is paid by the balance standing to the credit of the account. A customer who wants an advance, takes a loan of such an amount as shall not require him to keep less than his usual balance. The loan is placed to the credit of his current account, until the time arrives for its repayment, and then he is debited for the principal and the interest. The country banker is paid by a commission, and hence the advance to a customer is made by his overdrawing the account, and he is charged interest only on the amount overdrawn.

Loans are divided into short loans and dead loans. Short loans are usually the practice of the London bankers: a time is fixed for their repayment. Dead loans are those for the payment of which there is no specified time; or where the party has failed to make the repayment at the time agreed upon. In this case, too, the loan has usually been made upon *dead*—that is, upon inconvertible security. Without great caution on the part of the banker, *short* loans are very apt to become *dead* loans. A loan is first made for two or three months; the time arrives, and the customer cannot pay; then the loan is renewed, and renewed, and renewed, and ultimately the customer fails, and the banker has to fall back upon his securities. The difference between *short* loans and *dead* loans may be illustrated by a reference to Liverpool and Manchester. The Liverpool bankers make large advances by way of loan, but usually on the security of cotton. The cotton is sold in a few months, and the banker is paid. At Manchester, the banker advances his loans on the security of mills and manufactories; he cannot get repaid; and after a while the customer fails, and the mill or manufactory, when sold, may not produce half the amount of the loan.

Dead loans are sometimes produced by lending money to rich men. A man of moderate means will be anxious not to borrow of his banker a loan which he will not be able punctually to repay, as the good opinion of his banker is necessary to his credit. But a man of property has no scruples of the kind : he has to build a house, to improve his estate, or to extend his manufactory ; and he is unreasonable enough to expect that his banker will supply him with the necessary funds. He believes it will be only a temporary advance, as he will shortly be in possession of ample means. The banker lends the sum at first desired ; more money is wanted ; the expected supplies do not arrive ; and the advance becomes a dead lock-up of capital. The loan may be very safe, and yield a good rate of interest, but the banker would rather have the money under his own control.

Dead loans are sometimes produced by lending money to parties to buy shares in public companies. There was too much business of this kind transacted by some bankers a few years ago. The party did not at first, perchance, apply to his banker to enable him to purchase the shares ; but the calls were heavy, and his ready money was gone ; he felt assured, however, that in a short time he should be able to sell his shares at a high profit ; he persuaded his banker to pay the calls, taking the shares as security. Other calls were made, which the banker had to pay. The market fell ; and the shares, if sold, would not pay the banker's advances. The sale, too, would have caused an enormous loss to the customer. The advances became a dead loan, and the banker had to wait till a favourable opportunity occurred for realizing his security.

In this, and in other ways, a banker has often much difficulty with customers of a speculative character. If he refuses what they ask, they remove their account, and give him a bad name ; if he grants them their desires, they engage in speculations by which they are ruined, and probably the banker sustains loss. The point for the banker to decide is, whether he will lose them or ruin them. It is best in this case, for the banker to fix upon what advance he should make them, supposing they conduct their affairs prudently ; and if they are dissatisfied with this, he had better let them go ; after they have become bankrupts he will get credit for his sagacity.

The discounting of bills is an ordinary matter of business, and the banker has only to see that he has good names to his bill ; but in regard to loans, a banker would do

well to follow the advice which Mr. Taylor gives to individuals, and not to make a loan, unless he knows the purpose for which it is borrowed, and to form his own judgment
as to the wisdom of the party who borrows, and as to the
probability of his having the means of repayment at the time
agreed upon.*

Sometimes, when an advance of money is wanted for two
or three months, the party gives a note of hand. This is
better than a mere loan, as it fixes the time of payment, and
keeps the transaction fresh in the recollection of the borrower.
But care must be taken that the note, by repeated renewals,
does not in fact become a dead loan. Hence, when a renewal
cannot be avoided, attempts should be made to reduce the
amount. When public companies, of only a short standing,
and not fully constituted, wish to borrow money of their
banker, it is sometimes expedient to take the joint and several
promissory note of the directors. By this means the banker
avoids all knotty questions connected with the law of partnership; and the directors will, for their own sakes, see that the
funds of the company shall, in due time, be rendered available
for the repayment of the loan.

We have said that dead loans are usually advanced upon
inconvertible security. Sometimes that security consists of
a deposit of deeds relating to leasehold or freehold property.
In London, however, this kind of security is not considered
desirable, and the following rules are usually observed :—

No advances are made upon the security of deeds alone;
they are taken only as collateral security; and then only to
cover business transactions, and in cases where the parties are
supposed to be safe independently of deeds.

The value of the property should be much higher than the
sum it is intended to guarantee. When this is the case, and
the parties fail, their creditors may take the deeds, and pay the
debt due to the bank. The main use of taking deeds is to have
something to fall back upon in this way. A customer should
never receive more accommodation from having deposited his
deeds than that to which he is legitimately entitled. No
banker takes deeds if there is the slightest probability of his
being compelled to realize the property, as the legal difficulties
are very great.

* *Vide* Notes from Life, by Taylor.

In all cases in which deeds are taken, they are submitted to the inspection of the banker's solicitor, who makes a written report upon the value of the property, as far as it can be discovered by the deeds, and upon its legal validity as a security to the bank.

The rule of a banker is, never to make any advances, directly or indirectly, upon deeds, or any other *dead* security. But this rule, like all other general rules, must have exceptions, and when it is proper to make an exception is a matter that must be left to the discretion of the banker. He should, how-ever, exercise this discretion with caution and prudence, and not deviate from the rule without a special reason to justify such deviation.

Among country bankers, in agricultural districts, advances upon deeds are not considered so objectionable as in London. A landed proprietor, who wants a temporary advance, places his deeds in the hands of his banker, and takes what he requires. The banker thinks he can have no better security; but the loan is usually for only a moderate amount, and is paid off within a reasonable time. In the country the character and circumstances of every man are known. A landlord who wants an advance to meet immediate demands, until his rents come in, seems fairly entitled to assistance from his banker. But should a landlord who is living beyond his income, ask for an advance almost equal to the value of his deeds, he would not be likely to obtain it.

Another kind of security is bills of lading, and dock warrants. Advances upon securities such as these must be considered as beyond the rules which prudent bankers lay down for their own government; they can only be justified by the special circumstances of each case. In advancing upon bills of lading, the banker must see that he has *all the bills of the set*; for if he has not *all*, the holder of the absent bill may get possession of the property. It is also necessary that he have the policy of assurance, that, in case the ship be lost, he may claim the value from the insurers. In advances upon dock warrants, the banker should know that the value of the goods is equal to his advances, and will also give him a margin, as a security against any fall in the market price. But, in truth, no banker should readily make advances upon such securities. Now and then he may take them as collateral

N

security, for an advance to a customer who is otherwise respectable. But if a customer requires such advances frequently, not to say constantly, it shows that he is conducting his business in a way that will not ultimately be either for his own advantage, or that of his banker.

A banker should never make any advances upon life policies. They may become void, should the party commit suicide, or die by the hand of justice, or in a duel; or if he go without permission to certain foreign countries. The payment may be disputed, upon the ground that some deception or concealment was practised, when the policy was obtained. And, in all cases, they are dependent upon the continued payment of the premiums. The value of a policy, too, is also often overrated. The insured fancies that his policy increases in value in exact proportion to the number of premiums he has paid; but if he offers it to the company, he will find that he gets much less than he expected. The policy is valued in a way that remunerates the office for the risk they have run during the years that are past; and the valuation has a reference only to the future.

There are certain signs of approaching failure, which a banker must observe with reference to his customers. Thus—if he keeps a worse account than heretofore, and yet wants larger discounts—if the bills offered for discount are drawn upon an inferior class of people—if, when his bills are unpaid, he does not take them up promptly—if he pays his money late in the day, just in time to prevent his bills or cheques being returned through the clearing; but, above all, if he is found cross-firing: that is, drawing bills upon parties who at the same time draw bills upon him; as soon as a banker detects a customer in fair credit engaged in this practice, he should quietly give him reason for removing his account.

Sometimes two parties, who keep different bankers, will adopt a practice of exchanging cheques. Their cheques are paid into the banks too late to be cleared on the same day; and hence the parties' accounts appear better the next day than they otherwise would be. Some failing parties, too, have recourse to forged or fictitious bills, which they put into circulation to a large amount. The best way for a banker to guard against loss from this practice is, to inquire in all cases about the accepters of the bills that he discounts, not only when his customers are doubtful, but even when they are deemed respectable. Indeed, it is only people in good credit that can pass fictitious bills.

The banker's rule is, that they who have discounts must keep a proportionate balance: this is useful, as the amount of balance kept is an indication of the circumstances of the party. When a customer has heavy discounts, and keeps but a small balance, it may usually be inferred that he is either embarrassed in his affairs, or he is trading beyond his capital.

The operation which is called "nursing an account," sometimes requires considerable prudence, tact, and perseverance. A banker having made considerable advances to a customer, suddenly discovers that the party is not worthy of the confidence he has placed in him. If these advances should be called up, or discontinued, the customer will break, and the banker sustain loss. The banker must be governed by the circumstances of each case. It is sometimes best to continue to discount the good bills, and refuse those of a different character ; and thus gradually weed the account of all the inferior securities. Sometimes he may get the customer to stipulate that he will diminish his advances by certain fixed amounts, at certain periods ; and thus, by alternately refusing and complying, the banker may at length place himself in a state of security. At other times, the banker may offer to make still further advances, on condition of receiving good security also for what has been already advanced. This plan is advisable when the additional advance is not proportionably large, and the security is not inconvertible, otherwise the plan is sometimes a hazardous one. It requires some courage to look a loss in the face. And it has occurred that a banker, rather than sustain a small loss, will consent to make a further large advance upon inconvertible security ; and the locking up of this large advance for an indefinite period has proved the greater evil of the two. In fact, some of the largest losses of fallen banks have been made in this way. They have, in the first instance, made an imprudent advance ; rather than sustain this loss at once, they have made a further advance, with a view to prevent it. The advance has at last become so large, that if the customer falls, the bank must fall too ; for the sake of self-existence, further advances are then made ; these too are found ineffectual, and ultimately the customer and the bank fall together.

SECTION V.

THE ADMINISTRATION OF A BANK WITH REGARD TO PROCEEDINGS ON BILLS OF EXCHANGE.

WHEN a banker has discounted a bill, it is handed to the accountant, who will see that it is drawn on a right stamp. The accountant will read it through, and see that it is properly drawn, and will observe that the sum in writing corresponds with the sum expressed in figures, and that no alteration has taken place in the amount, the date, the term, or the place at which it is made payable; for these are *material* alterations, and would affect the validity of the bill. He will then calculate the time at which it falls due, and place this date upon the bill, or, if it was there before, he will check it, and see that it is right. He will then turn it over, and see that it is indorsed by the party in whose favour it is drawn, and also that the subsequent indorsements are regular and properly spelled; for if there be a variation of a single letter in the spelling of a name, the payment of the bill could not be legally enforced. He will also observe that the bill is indorsed by the party for whom it is discounted. He will then pass the bill through the books,* and at the close of the day deliver it with the others to the banker. The banker will, on the following morning, put these bills away in his bill-case according to the dates at which they fall due. This point should be recollected by persons who have to get bills from a banker before they are due; for, after they have given the amount and the names, the next question asked them will be, " When is it due ?" for among a multitude of bills, the only way of readily finding any individual bill is to turn to those that fall due on the same day. Every day the banker looks out the bills that fall due on the following day, and hands them to the chief clerk (or, in some cases, the chief clerk himself has the charge of the bills), who, after checking them against the books, distributes them among the clerks who are to collect them. If the bill be not paid, it is noted on the same evening, and on the following morning returned to the customer for whom it was discounted, and his account is debited

---

* These books are described in the Section on Banking Book-keeping.

for the amount. But if the party has not the sum to his credit, and the banker does not like to trust him, he merely receives notice of its dishonour; and notice is also given to every other party to the bill, with a demand for immediate payment. The bill has now become. that hated object, a "past due bill;" and after a while, if the parties are supposed to be "worth powder and shot," it is handed to the bank's solicitor.

I shall give a short description of Bills of Exchange, and notice a few of those points of law and of business which are of most importance to practical bankers.

A bill of exchange is a written order from one person to another, directing him to pay a sum of money either to the drawer or to a third person at a future time. This is usually a certain number of days, weeks, or months, either after the date of the bill, or after sight; that is, after the person on whom it is drawn shall have *seen* it, and shall have written on the bill his willingness to pay it. The party expresses this willingness by writing on the bill the word "*accepted,*" and his name. If the bill be drawn after sight, he also writes the date of the acceptance.

If the party in whose favour the bill is drawn wishes to transfer it, he writes his name on the back. This is called an *indorsement;* and may be either special or general. A special indorsement is made to a particular party; as, "Pay to Messrs. John Doe & Co. or order." A general, or blank indorsement, is when the person merely writes his name. It is held by the lawyers[*] that a special indorsement cannot *follow* a general indorsement, and that in such a case the holder may sustain an action for the amount though the bill be not indorsed by the party to whom it is thus specially assigned. In practice, however, this is very common; and bankers always refuse to pay bills not properly indorsed even though previous indorsements may be general. But, in regard to post bills, the Bank of England pays no regard to any special indorsement that may follow a general indorsement.

[*] If a bill be once indorsed in blank, though afterwards indorsed in full, it will still as against the drawer, the payee, the accepter, the blank indorser, and all indorsers before him, be payable to bearer, though as against the special indorser himself title must be made through his indorsee.—*Serjeant Byles on Bills of Exchange*, p. 115.

The following is the form of a Bill of Exchange :—

£1000.   *London, 1st of May, 1827.*
      Two months after date, pay to the order of Messrs. Quick,
Active, & Co. (or me or my order) the sum of One Thousand Pounds,
for value received.

      Hearty, Jolly, & Co.

      Accepted, payable at
To Messrs. John Careful & Co.   *Messrs. Steady & Co., Bankers.*
      Southwark.   *John Careful & Co.*

A Promissory Note is as follows :—

£1000.   *London, 1st of May, 1827.*
      Two months after date, we promise to pay Messrs. Hearty,
Jolly, & Co., or their order, the sum of One Thousand Pounds, for value
received.

      John Careful & Co.

At Messrs. Steady & Co.,
      Bankers,
   Lombard Street.

The acceptance is usually written across a bill, but should always be on the front, not on the back of the bill. An indorsement, as the name implies, should be placed on the back.

The person who draws a bill is called the drawer ; the person on whom it is drawn is called the drawee : after the bill is accepted the drawee is called the accepter. The person who indorses a bill is called the indorser ; the person to whom it is indorsed is the indorsee. The person who pays a bill is the payer ; the person to whom it is paid is the payee. These and similar terms may be illustrated by a circumstance said to have occurred on the cross-examination of a witness, on a trial respecting a mortgage.—*Counsellor.* " Now, sir, you are a witness in this case ; pray do you know the difference between the mortgager and the mortgagee ?"—*Witness.* " To be sure I do. For instance, now suppose I nod at you, I am the nod-er, and you are the nod-ee." The word discountee, denoting the person for whom a bill is discounted, is not used in England, but I observe in the parliamentary evidence that it was employed by some of the witnesses from Scotland.

All bills, except those payable on demand or at sight, are allowed three days' grace. Thus, a bill drawn at two months from the 1st of May, will fall due on the 4th of July ; but if that day be a Sunday, or a public holiday,* the bill will be due on the day before. Some bills, instead of being drawn after date or sight, state the time of payment, as " On the first of August pay, &c." These bills are allowed the usual three days of grace. Such a bill would fall due on the 4th of August.

Some parties, when they indorse a bill, write at bottom, " In case of need, apply to Messrs. C. D. & Co." That is, if the bill be not paid when due, Messrs. C. D. & Co. will on the day after it is due pay it for the honour of the indorsers. The notaries always observe the " cases of need " upon the bills that come into their hands, and apply to the proper parties. The advantage of placing a case of need upon a bill is, that the party endorsing it receives it back sooner in case of non-payment. It also makes the bill more respectable, and secures its circulation.

Were it not for the space it occupies, it would be very desirable that the indorser of a bill of exchange should be compelled to state also his address. This would prevent forged and fictitious indorsements, and give a banker who discounts a bill, a better opportunity of ascertaining the respectability of the parties. In case, too, the bill was unpaid, he might immediately apply to all the indorsers, whereas now he has to find them out in the best way he can. The indorsers and drawer of a bill would have earlier notice of its non-payment, and have a better opportunity of obtaining their money from the antecedent parties.

Bills are divided into Inland and Foreign. Inland bills are those in which both the drawer and the accepter reside in England. Bills drawn from Scotland, or Ireland, are considered as foreign bills. If a foreign bill be refused acceptance or payment, it should be immediately protested and returned. An

---

* To remove all doubts upon this subject, an Act of Parliament was passed (7th & 8th Geo. IV. chap. 5), which enacts " that from and after the tenth day of April, one thousand eight hundred and twenty-seven, Good Friday and Christmas-day, and every day of fast or thanksgiving appointed by his Majesty, is and shall for all purposes whatever, as regards bills of exchange and promissory notes, be treated and considered as the Lord's-day, commonly called Sunday." This Act does not extend to Scotland, but it has since been extended to Ireland. This Act does not vitiate a bill *dated* on a Sunday.

inland bill is only noted, and then only when refused payment. A foreign bill may be accepted verbally, or by letter ; but no acceptance of an inland bill is valid, unless written upon the bill itself.*

When a merchant in one country draws bills upon a merchant residing in another country, he usually draws them in sets : that is, he draws two, three, or more bills of the same tenor and date. These bills are sent to his correspondent by different ships. Thus he secures the swiftest conveyance, and his remittances will not be delayed by any accident that may happen to an individual ship. In drawing these bills, it is always expressly stated whether each bill be the first, second, or third of a set ; as, " Pay this my *first* of exchange (the second and third not being paid)." On the payment of any one bill, the others are of no value. If a merchant, say at Paris, has a set of bills drawn on a merchant at London, he will sometimes send over the first bill to his correspondent in London, to get it accepted, and to retain it until claimed by the holder of the second. The merchant at Paris will then write on the second bill, that the first lies accepted at such a house in London. He will then sell it or pay it away. By this means he is sure that the bill he negotiates will not be returned to him, and greater value is given to his bill, not only as it has the additional security of the accepter's name, but, if it be drawn after sight, it will become due so much the sooner. When the second bill arrives in London, the holder takes it to the house where the first is deposited, and it is immediately given up to him.

Foreign bills are often drawn at a '' usance '' after date. A usance from Amsterdam, Rotterdam, Hamburgh, or any place in Germany, is one month ; from France, thirty days ; from Spain and Portugal, two months ; from Sweden, seventy-five days ; from Italy, three months. Where it is necessary to divide a month upon a half usance, which is the case when the usance is either one month or three, the half month is always fifteen days. Bills drawn from Russia are dated according to the old style, and twelve days must be added to the date, in order to ascertain at what time they fall due.

A bill is sometimes accepted *for the honour* of the drawer, or of one of the indorsers. Thus, if a bill from Hamburgh be drawn upon a person in London, who refuses to accept it, another party,

* See 1 & 2 Geo. IV. cap. 78.

knowing the drawer or one of the indorsers to be a respectable man, may accept the bill himself, for the honour of the party with whom he is acquainted. By this means he prevents the bill being returned with expenses. This kind of acceptance renders him liable to pay the bill on the day after it is due, but he can afterwards recover the amount from the party for whose honour he had accepted it, and, of course, from all preceding parties. But, to secure himself, he must not accept the bill until after it has been protested for non-acceptance, and he must write, " Accepted for the honour of A. B. & Co.," upon the face of the bill. And when the bill is due, he must not pay it, until it has been presented for payment to the drawee.

Bills accepted, and made payable at a banking-house, in the usual manner, without the addition of the word ONLY, may be presented either at the banking-house, or at the residence of the accepter. In either case, it is a legal presentment,* as far as regards the accepter. In practice, however, bills are always presented at the place where they are made payable. If a bill be addressed to a banking-house or any other place ONLY, the payment cannot be enforced until it has been presented at that place. If any particular place of payment be mentioned in the body of a promissory note, it must be presented there.

When bankers receive any unaccepted bills, they send them out for acceptance, if they have four days to run. They are left at the house of the drawee, and are called for on the following day. On the day the bills are due, the tellers present them in the morning, at the place where they are made payable. If not paid when presented, they leave a printed notice or direction, of which the following is a copy :—

Bill for £
Drawn by Mr.
On Mr.
Lies due at Messrs. Steady & Co.,
       No.   *Lombard Street.*

Please call between Two and Four o'clock.

If not paid by five o'clock, the bill is sent to the notary's. It is brought to the banking-house the following morning, with

* 1 & 2 Geo. IV. cap. 78

the notary's ticket attached to it, stating the reason why it is not paid. The bill is then returned to the customer. If it be a foreign bill, that is, drawn from any foreign land, it must be protested. Foreign bills are also protested for non-acceptance; but inland bills are not. nor even noted*, but the party who remitted the bill to the banking-house is advised of the circumstance.

The following is the form of a Draft or Cheque :—

No. 457.   *London, May 1, 1827.*
          Messrs. Hope, Rich, & Co. Lombard Street.
    Pay John Doe, Esq., or bearer, the sum of One Hundred Pounds.
  £100.   *Peter Thrifty & Co.*

A bill given for an illegal consideration cannot be enforced by the drawer, but it may be enforced by an innocent holder who had no knowledge of the illegal consideration, and who received the bill before it was due. The principal illegal considerations are those arising from usury, gambling, and smuggling. But by the Act 17 and 18 Vic. c. 90, passed in the year 1854, the laws of usury are abolished.

The following are the Tables of Stamp Duties upon Bills of Exchange, corrected down to, and including 33 and 34 Vic. cap. 97, 1870.

	s.	*d.*
SECT. 47. *Bill of Exchange*, payable on demand . . .	0	.
Bill of Exchange of any other kind whatsoever (*except a Bank Note*) and *Promissory Note* of any kind whatsoever (*except a Bank Note*)—drawn, or expressed to be payable, or actually paid or indorsed, or in any manner negotiated *in* the United Kingdom :		
Where the amount or value of the money for which the bill or note is drawn or made does not exceed 5*l*. .	0	1
Exceeds 5*l*. and does not exceed 10*l*.	0	2
„ 10*l*. „ 25*l*.	0	3
„ 25*l*. „ 50*l*.	0	6
„ 50*l*. ., 75*l*.	0	9
„ 75*l*. „ 100*l*.	1	0
„ 100*l*.		
for every 100*l*., and also for any fractional part of 100*l*., of such amount or value	1	0

Exemptions.

Bill or note issued by the Governor and Company of the Bank of England or Bank of Ireland.

---

* Exceptions occur, though they are rare. Bankers never note their customers' bills.—EDITOR.

Draft or order drawn by any banker in the United Kingdom upon any other banker in the United Kingdom, not payable to bearer or to order, and used solely for the purpose of settling or clearing any account between such bankers.

Letter written by a banker in the United Kingdom to any other banker in the United Kingdom, directing the payment of any sum of money, the same not being payable to bearer or order, and such letter not being sent or delivered to the person to whom payment is to be made, or to any person on his behalf.

Letter of credit granted in the United Kingdom authorising drafts to be drawn out of the United Kingdom payable in the United Kingdom.

Government Drafts, Orders, and Bills.

Coupon or warrant for interest attached to and issued with any security.

SECT. 48. The term "bill of exchange" for the purposes of this Act includes also draft, order, cheque, and letter of credit, and any document or writing (*except a bank note*) entitling or purporting to entitle any person, whether named therein or not, to payment by any other person of or to draw upon any other person for, any sum of money therein mentioned.

An order for the payment of any sum of money by a bill of exchange or promissory note, or for the delivery of any bill of exchange or promissory note in satisfaction of any sum of money, or for the payment of any sum of money out of any particular fund which may or may not be available, or upon any condition or contingency which may or may not be performed or happen, is to be deemed for the purposes of this Act a bill of exchange for the payment of money on demand.

An order for the payment of any sum of money weekly, monthly, or at any other stated periods, and also any order for the payment by any person at any time after the date thereof of any sum of money, and sent or delivered by the person making the same to the person by whom the payment is to be made, and not to the person to whom the payment is to be made, or to any person on his behalf, is to be deemed for the purposes of this Act a bill of exchange for the payment of money on demand.

SECT. 49. The term "promissory note" means and includes any document or writing (*except a bank note*) containing a promise to pay any sum of money.

A note promising the payment of any sum of money out of any particular fund which may or may not be available, or upon any condition or contingency which may or may not be performed or happen, is to be deemed for the purposes of this Act a promissory note for the said sum of money.

SECT. 50. The fixed duty of one penny on a bill of exchange for the payment of money on demand may be denoted by an adhesive stamp, which is to be cancelled by the person by whom the bill is signed before he delivers it out of his hands, custody, or power.

SECT. 51. The *ad valorem* duties upon bills of exchange and promissory notes drawn or made *out* of the United Kingdom are to be denoted by adhesive stamps.

Every person into whose hands any such bill or note comes in the United Kingdom before it is stamped shall, before he presents for payment, or indorses, transfers, or in any manner negotiates, or pays such bill or note, affix thereto a proper adhesive stamp or proper adhesive stamps of sufficient amount, and cancel every stamp so affixed thereto.

Provided as follows:

> If at the time when any such bill or note comes into the hands of any *bonâ fide* holder thereof there is affixed thereunto an adhesive stamp effectually obliterated, and purporting and appearing to be duly cancelled, such stamp shall, so far as relates to such holder, be deemed to be duly cancelled, although it may not appear to have been so affixed or cancelled by the proper person.

> If at the time when any such bill or note comes into the hands of any *bonâ fide* holder whereof there is affixed thereto an adhesive stamp not duly cancelled, it shall be competent for such holder to cancel such stamp as if he were the person by whom it was affixed, and upon his so doing such bill or note shall be deemed duly stamped, and as valid and available as if the stamp had been duly cancelled by the person by whom it was affixed.

But neither of the foregoing provisoes is to relieve any person from any penalty incurred by him for not cancelling any adhesive stamp.

SECT. 52. A bill of exchange or promissory note purporting to be drawn or made *out* of the United Kingdom is, for the purposes of this Act, to be deemed to have been so drawn or made, although it may in fact have been drawn or made *within* the United Kingdom.

SECT. 53. Where a bill of exchange or promissory note has been written on material bearing an impressed stamp of sufficient amount but of improper denomination, it may be stamped with the proper stamp on payment of the duty, and a penalty of forty shillings if the bill or note be not then payable according to its tenor, and of ten pounds if the same be so payable.

Except as aforesaid, no bill of exchange or promissory note shall be stamped with an impressed stamp after the execution thereof.

SECT. 54. Every person who issues, indorses, transfers, negotiates, presents for payment, or pays any bill of exchange or promissory note liable to duty and not being duly stamped shall forfeit the sum of ten pounds, and the person who takes or receives from any other person any such bill or note not being duly stamped either in payment or as a security, or by purchase or otherwise, shall not be entitled to recover thereon, or to make the same available for any purpose whatever.

Provided that if any bill of exchange for the payment of money on demand, liable only to the duty of one penny, is presented for payment unstamped, the person to whom it is so presented may affix thereunto a proper adhesive stamp, and cancel the same, as if he had been the drawer of the bill, and may, upon so doing, pay the sum in the said bill mentioned, and charge the duty in account against the person by whom the bill was drawn, or deduct such duty from the said sum, and such bill is, so far as respects the duty, to be deemed good and valid.

But the foregoing proviso is not to relieve any person from any penalty he may have incurred in relation to such bill.

SECT. 55. When a bill of exchange is drawn in a set according to the custom of merchants, and one of the set is duly stamped, the other or others of the set shall, unless issued or in some manner negotiated apart from such duly stamped bill, be exempt from duty; and upon proof of the loss or destruction of a duly stamped bill forming one of a set, any other bill of the set which has not been issued or in any manner negotiated apart from such lost or destroyed bill may, although unstamped, be admitted in evidence to prove the contents of such lost or destroyed bill.

Prior to the passing of the 33 and 34 Vic. c. 93 (the Married Woman's Property Act, 1870), if a woman accepted a bill and married before it became due, her husband could be sued for the amount, but she could not; but by the above Act this is not so now, for that statute (sec. 12), enacts that " a husband shall not by reason of any marriage which shall take place after this Act has come into operation, be liable for the debts of his wife contracted before marriage, but the wife shall be liable to be sued, and any property belonging to her for her separate use, shall be liable to satisfy such debts as if she had continued unmarried." If a bill be indorsed to a woman, who afterwards marries, her husband must indorse the bill, unless she indorses it as the agent and by the authority of her husband. Should she have occasion to sue any of the antecedent parties to a bill, the action may be brought in the name of the husband, where the bill is drawn to " order," otherwise it must be brought in the joint names of the husband and the wife. If a woman who is actually married accepts a bill by and with the authority of her husband, the acceptance is binding on the husband; but if she accepts a bill without his authority, he cannot be legally compelled to pay it, unless it were given for articles necessary to her support.

A person under twenty-one years of age, whether accepter, drawer, or indorser of a bill of exchange, cannot be sued at law, except the bill be drawn upon him for necessaries; but if he draw a bill, and transfer it to a third person, the third party may sue the accepter. The term " necessaries " is generally considered to include not only those things which are essential to existence, but those also which are suitable to the rank of the party. Many articles are considered necessary to the son of a nobleman which would not be necessary to a man of an inferior station in society.

If the drawee refuse to accept a bill, the holder may immediately bring an action for the amount against all the other parties, without waiting until the bill becomes due. And should the word "at" be written before the name of the drawee, it makes no difference, especially if it be written in such a manner as if designed to escape observation. But it is the practice of the London bankers to hold bills refused acceptance, and merely give notice of the circumstance to the party who sent it to the bank. If, however, it be an inland bill, drawn after sight, the bill is noted for non-acceptance. If it be a foreign bill, it is protested, and the protest sent to the last indorser. If the bill be not paid when due, it is then protested for non-payment, and with the second protest returned to the last indorser. When a bill is drawn after sight, the day on which it is noted or protested for non-acceptance is regarded as the day on which the drawee has sent it, and the time on which it will become due is calculated accordingly.

If the accepter, drawer, and all the indorsers to a bill become bankrupts, the holder may prove for the full amount under each commission, and receive a dividend under each, provided he do not receive altogether more than 20s. in the pound. But if he receive a dividend under one commission before proving under the others, he can only prove for the balance.

If a bill be lost, immediate notice should be given to the accepter, and to the bankers or other parties at whose house it may be made payable. If, after such notice, they pay the bill to any person who has not given value for it, they are accountable to the loser. But a person who has given value for a lost or stolen bill, to a thief, or to a finder, can recover the amount from all the parties in the same way as though he had received it in the course of business from the last indorser, provided the bill was not specially indorsed. But if it was specially indorsed, and the thief or finder should have forged the indorsement, the holder cannot recover the amount, even though he may have given value for the bill, but he must sustain the loss.

If a lost bill should have been specially indorsed, or if the loser can prove that the bill has been destroyed, he can bring an action against the accepter for the amount. But if he cannot prove that the bill is actually destroyed, and it was indorsed in blank, he cannot recover from the accepter. For it is possible that a finder may pass it for a valuable consideration to another party, who would thus be a *boná fide* holder, and might compel the accepter to pay him the amount. In this case, therefore, the loser has no redress in *law*, but he may apply to a court of equity, and *might* obtain an order upon the accepter to pay the amount of the lost bill upon receiving a satisfactory indemnity. The loser of a bill should cause payment to be demanded from the accepter the day it falls due, and give notice of dishonour to the drawer and indorsers, in the same way as though he had the bill in his possession.

A country banker gave change for a Bank of England note for 100*l.* which had been stolen. It was done at the time of the races, and immediately on opening the bank. The party who brought it stated he had some bets to pay at the race-course, and gave a fictitious address, which was written on the note. The loser of the note brought an action against the banker, and recovered the amount. The judge who tried the cause stated that in his opinion there had been laches, *i.e.*, neglect on the part of the bankers in not making further inquiry, and under his direction the jury returned a verdict for the plaintiff.

Referring to the above decision, Serjeant Byles observes :—

"But it is now definitely settled that if a man takes *honestly* an instrument made or become payable to bearer, he has a good title to it, with whatever degree of negligence he may have acted, unless his gross negligence induce the jury to find fraud."[*]

The following case was tried in the Court of Queen's Bench :—

The question involved was the right of money-changers to take Bank of England notes in disregard of notices that they had been stolen. The action was brought by Messrs. Adam Spielmann and Co., of London, as correspondents of Messrs. Meyer Spielmann and Co., of Paris, to recover the amount of two Bank of England notes for 500*l.* each, which had formed portions of notes, for the value in all of 3,000*l.*, stolen from Messrs. Brown, Shipley and Co., of Liverpool. The notes were stolen in November, 1852, and it was proved that notices of the robbery were delivered at the places of business of both firms. One of the notes was alleged to have been received by Meyer Spielmann and Co., in Paris, from a person giving the name of G. F. Howard, and the other from A. Monteaux, a money-changer in Paris, which note also had the name of G. F. Howard upon it. Both notes were remitted by Messrs. Meyer Spielmann and Co. to Messrs. Adam Spielmann and Co., and received by them in London. On behalf of the plaintiff it was contended that,

[*] Byles on Bills of Exchange, page 126.

the notes having been taken in the ordinary course of business, he was entitled to recover upon them. Lord Campbell left to the jury the question whether Meyer Spielmann took the notes *bonâ fide* and for value; whether Adam Spielmann received them *bonâ fide* as a remitance; and whether the notices were left at the places of business of both parties. The jury found that Meyer Spielmann and Co. did not take the notes *bonâ fide* for value; that Adam Spielmann and Co. did take them *bonâ fide* as a remitance; and that the notices were duly received. Upon this finding, Lord Campbell directed a verdict to be entered for the Bank of England."

The Editor observes :—

" It is hoped that this decision will have the effect of preventing the practice, which has become too common, of taking stolen notes, which cannot be passed in England, to the chief cities of Europe, and there obtaining the amount through money-changers, who afterwards claim the value from the Bank, on the ground that the notes have been taken in due course of business, although, in fact, no sufficient inquiry has been made as to the *bona fides* of the transaction, or the respectability of the parties presenting them."*

But in a similar action brought by Messrs. Raphael and Co. on the part of Messrs. St. Paul and Co., of Paris, against the Bank of England, for the amount of another of these stolen notes, the verdict was for the plaintiff. The following were the points on which the jury were directed to decide :—

" 1. Was the money paid? 2. Were the notices served on St. Paul and Co.? 3. Did they know of, and had they the means of knowledge of the robbery at the time they discounted the note? The jury, after retiring for three quarters of an hour, found, in answer to these questions.— 1. That Messrs. St. Paul gave full value for the note. 2. That the notices were served. 3. That the notices were not taken proper care of, and that St. Paul had the means of knowledge if he had taken proper care of the notices, but that he did not know of the loss at the time; and, lastly, that the plaintiff took the note *bonâ fide*.

" Verdict for the plaintiff—534*l.* Execution to be stayed, but no points reserved."

Any material alteration of a bill of exchange vitiates the bill, and it cannot be legally enforced against any of the parties, unless the alteration be made before the bill be accepted, and also before it has passed out of the hands of the drawer.

Thus, if a bill be left for acceptance by the drawer, and the drawee alter the date, time, or amount of the bill, and then accept it, the alteration does not affect the validity of the bill: but if the bill be left for acceptance by a third party, and the

* Bankers' Magazine, March 1855.

drawee then alters and accepts the bill, the bill is vitiated. Any alteration in the date, sum, time, name of drawer or payee, or appointing a new place of payment, is a material alteration, and requires a new stamp. But any alteration made only with a view of correcting a mistake does not vitiate a bill, provided it be made with the concurrence of all the parties. If a drawee accepts a bill, and before he gives the bill out of his possession cancels his acceptance, he cannot be compelled to pay it.

A bill must be presented in *reasonable time*. But what is a *reasonable time* is a question of consideration for the jury, and the decision has varied according to circumstances. If a bill be presented at a banker's after the hour of business, the presentment is not in reasonable time. Nevertheless such a presentment is a legal presentment, if the banker or any person on his behalf should be there to give an answer to the party presenting it.

Cheques, and notes payable on demand, should also be presented for payment within a *reasonable time* after they are received. It has been held that a person who receives a cheque is not bound to present it at the banker's till the next morning; and if the bank was at a distance, he was not bound to put the cheque into the post-office until the next day. But, perhaps, it would not be safe to rely upon these decisions. No general rule can be given; for the time which may be *reasonable* in one case may be unreasonable in another.

If a banker receives a bill or note by post, he is not required to present it until the next day.

"A man taking a bill or note payable on demand, or a cheque, is not bound, laying aside all other business, to present or transmit it for payment the very first opportunity. It has long since been decided, in numerous cases, that, though the party by whom the bill or note is to be paid live in the same place, it is not necessary to present the instrument for payment till the morning next after the day on which it was received. And later cases have established, that the holder of a cheque has the whole of the banking hours of the next day within which to present it for payment."*

In the following case it was decided that the presentment of a bill of exchange at the Clearing-house is a legal presentment.

"On the 11th September, between one and two o'clock, the defendants gave the plaintiffs a cheque upon Bloxam and Co., the bankers, in payment for goods. The plaintiffs lodged the cheque with Messrs.

* Byles's Law of Bills of Exchange, page 123.

O

Harrison, the bankers, a few minutes after four; and they presented it between five and six to Bloxam and Co., who marked it as good. It was proved to be the usage among London bankers not to pay any cheque presented by or on behalf of another banker after four o'clock, but merely to mark it if good, and pay it next day at the clearing-house. On the 12th at noon Harrison's clerk took this cheque to the clearing-house, but no person attended for Bloxam and Co., who stopped payment at nine on that morning, and the cheque was therefore treated as dishonoured. The plaintiffs, in going with the cheque to Harrison's, passed Bloxam's house. On a case stating these facts, the court held that there had been no laches in the plaintiffs, in not presenting the cheque to Bloxam and Co. on the 11th for payment, or in his bankers in not presenting it at the banking-house, but merely at the clearing-house, and therefore gave judgment for the plaintiff."*

Bills may be negotiated after they are due, but the party receiving an over-due bill cannot acquire a claim which the party holding the bill did not possess. For instance, one party may draw an accommodation bill upon another. As in this case no value had been given, the drawer could not sue the accepter for the amount. But if the drawer had passed this bill *for value* to a third party *before it became due*, that party could sue the accepter. But if the drawer passed it to a third party even for value *after it became due*, the third party could not sue the accepter, but would stand in the same situation as the drawer.

If a party lodge bills with a banker for the purpose of being collected, and the amount when received to be placed to his credit, and the banker gets them discounted, and applies the money to his own use, the customer has no redress except against the banker. The party who has given value for the bills to the banker can enforce payment of them.

As the giving notice of the dishonour of a bill or cheque is of considerable practical importance, I shall make a few extracts upon the subject from Mr. Justice Bayley's Treatise on Bills of Exchange.

"Though no prescribed form be necessary for notice of the dishonour of a bill or note, it ought to import that the person to whom it is given is considered liable, and that payment from him is expected.

"And the notice ought to import that the bill or note has been dishonoured: a mere demand of payment and threat of law proceedings in case of non-payment is not sufficient.

"Especially if such demand be made on the day the bill or note becomes due.

* Bayley on Bills of Exchange.

" Notice must be given of a failure in the attempt to procure an acceptance, though the application for such acceptance might have been unnecessary ; otherwise the person guilty of the neglect may lose his remedy upon the bill.

" The notice must come from the holder, or from some party entitled to call for payment or reimbursement.

" A notice from the holder or any other party will insure to the benefit of every other party who stands between the person giving the notice, and the person to whom it is given. Therefore, a notice from the last indorsee to the drawer will operate as a notice from each indorsee.

" It is, nevertheless, prudent in each party who receives a notice, to give immediate notice to those parties against whom he may have right to claim ; for the holder may have omitted notice to some of them, and that will be no protection, or there may be difficulties in proving such notice.

" A notice the day the bill or note becomes due is not too soon ; for though payment may still be made within the day, non-payment on presentment is a dishonour.

" To such of the parties as reside in the place where the presentment was made, the notice must be given at the farthest by the expiration of the day following the refusal : to those who reside elsewhere, by the post of that or the next post day. Each party has a day for giving notice, and he is entitled to the whole day ; at least, eight or nine o'clock at night is not too late. He will be entitled to the whole day, though the post by which he is to send it goes out within the day.

" And though there be no post the succeeding day for the place to which he is to send. Therefore, where the notice is to be sent by the post, it will be sufficient if it be sent by the post of the following day. Or, if there be no post the following day, the day after.

" Where a party receives notice on a Sunday, he is in the same situation as if it did not reach him till the Monday ; he is not bound to pay it any attention till the Monday, and has the whole of Monday for the purpose. So, if the day on which notice ought thus to be given be a day of public rest, as Christmas-day or Good Friday, or any day appointed by proclamation for a solemn fast or thanksgiving, the notice need not be given until the following day.

" And it has been held that where a man is of a religion which gives to any other day of the week the sanctity of Sunday, as in the case of the Jews, he is entitled to the same indulgence as on that day.

" Where Christmas-day, or such day of fast or thanksgiving, shall be on a Monday, notice of the dishonour of bills or notes due or payable the Saturday preceding need not be given until the Tuesday.

" And Good Friday, Christmas-day, and any day of fast or thanksgiving, shall, from 10th April, 1827, as far as regards bills or notes, be treated and considered as Sunday.

" But these provisions do not apply to Scotland.

" If the holder of a bill or note place it in the hands of his banker, the banker is only bound to give notice of its dishonour to his customer, in like manner as if the banker were himself the holder, and his customer were the party next entitled to notice.

" And the customer has the like time to communicate such notice, as if he had received it from a holder.

" And therefore, by thus placing a bill or note in a banker's hands, the number of persons from whom notice must pass is increased by one.

" Thus notice sent by a London banker to a London customer, the day after the dishonour, is in time; and if the customer communicate that notice the day following, that will be in time also.

" It is no excuse for not giving notice the next day after a party receives one, that he received his notice earlier than the preceding parties were bound to give it ; and that he gave notice within what would have been proper time if each preceding party had taken all the time the law allowed him. The time is to be calculated according to the period when the party in fact received his notice. Nor is it any excuse that there are several intervening parties between him who gives the notice, and defendant to whom it is given; and that if the notice had been communicated through these intervening parties, and each bad taken the time the law allows, the defendant would not have had the notice sooner.

" Sending a verbal notice to a merchant's counting-house in the ordinary hours of business, at a time when he or some of his people might reasonably be expected to be there, is sufficient; it is not necessary to leave or to send a written notice, or to send to the house where ne lives. Sending notice by the post is sufficient, though it be not received; and where there is no post, it is sufficient to send by the ordinary mode of conveyance.

" And it is not essential the notice should be sent by the post where there is one ; sending to an agent by a private conveyance, that he may give the notice, is sufficient, if the agent give the notice, or take due steps for the purpose, without delay.

" Notice to one of several partners is notice to all : and when a bill has been drawn by a firm upon one of the partners, and by him accepted and dishonoured, it is unnecessary to give notice of such dishonour to the firm ; for this must necessarily be known to one of them, and the knowledge of one is the knowledge of all.

" Upon an acceptance payable at a banker's, notice of non-payment need not be given to the accepter, for he makes the bankers his agents; presentment to them is presentment to him.

" A person who has been once discharged by laches from his liability on a bill or note, is always discharged. And, therefore, where two or more parties to a bill or note have been so discharged, but one of them, not knowing of the laches, pays it; he pays it in his own wrong, and cannot recover the money from another of such parties."

As many bills drawn in foreign languages pass through the hands of a London banker, it may be useful to give a list of some of those words which express the amount and the time, the two main points in a bill of exchange :—

English . .	One	Two	Three	Sixty	Ninety.
German . .	Ein	Zwei	Drei	Sechzig	Neunzig.
Dutch . .	Een	Twee	Drie	Zestig	Negentig.
French . .	Un	Deux	Trois	Soixante	{ Quatre-vingt-dix, *or* Nonante.
Italian . .	Uno	Due	Tre	Sessanta	Nonanta, *or* Novanta.
Spanish . .	Uno	Dos	Tres	Sesenta	Noventa.
Portuguese .	Hum	Dous	Tres	Secenta	Noventa.
Swedish . .	En	Twa	Tre	Sexti	Nitti.
Danish . .	Een	To	Tre	Tredsindstyve	Halvfemtesindstyve.

English .	.	.	.	Two Months after date.
German .	.	.	.	Zwei Monate nach dato.
Dutch .	.	.	.	Twee Maanden na dato.
French .	.	.	.	A deux mois de date.
Italian .	.	.	.	A due mesi dopo data.
Spanish .	.	.	.	{ A dos meses de la fecha. { A dos meses data.
Portuguese .	.	.	.	A dous mezes de data.
Swedish .	.	.	.	Twa Manander ifran dato.
Danish .	.	.	.	To maaneder efter dato.

English .	.	.	.	Three days after sight.
German .	.	.	.	Drei tage nach sicht.
Dutch .	.	.	.	Drie dagen na zigt.
French .	.	.	.	A trois jours de vue.
Italian .	.	.	.	{ A tro giorni vista. { A tre giorni dopo vista.
Spanish .	.	.	.	A tres dias vista.
Portuguese .	.	.	.	A tres dias vista.
Swedish .	.	.	.	Tre dagar efter sigt.
Danish .	.	.	.	Tre dage efter sigt.*

In all the above languages, "at sight" is usually expressed by *a vista*, except the French, which expresses it by *à vue*. "At usance" is expressed by *a uso* or *ad uso*. The names of the months so nearly resemble the English, that a mistake can but rarely occur.

* These phrases are taken from a small pamphlet, called The Interpreter, compiled and translated by a Member of the Society of Public Notaries in London.

The following are forms of bills in each of the above-mentioned languages :—

FRENCH.

Lille, le 28 Septembre, 18 .   *Bon pour £158 9 Sterlings*
 Au vingt-cinq Décembre prochain, payez par ce mandat à l'ordre de nous-mêmes la somme de cent cinquante-huit livres sterlings 9 schellings valeur en nous-mêmes et que passerez suivant l'avis de

*A Messrs.*_____
 à Londres.

GERMAN.

Nürnberg, den 28 October, 18 .   *Pro £100 Sterling.*
 Zwei Monate nach dato zahlen Sie gegen diesen Prima Wechsel an die Ordre des Herrn_____Ein Hundert Pfund Sterling den Werth erhalten. Sie bringen solche auf Rechnung laut Bericht von der

Herren_____
 London.

DUTCH.

Grouw, den 1st November, 18 .   *Voor £59 17 6*
 Twee maanden na dato gelieve UEd te betalen voor dezen onzen prima Wisselbrief de secunda niet betaald zynde aan de ordre van de Heeren_____negen & vyftig Ponden zeventien schelling en zespences sterling, de waarde in rekening UEd stelle het op rekening met of zonder advys van.

de Heer_____
 te London.

ITALIAN.

Livorno, le 25 Settembre, 18 .   *Per £500 Sterlins.*
 A Tre mesi data pagate per questa prima de Cambio (una sol volta) all' ordine_____, la somma di Lire cinque cento sterline valuta cambiata, e ponete in conto M. S. secondo l'avviso Addio

Al_____
 Londra.

SPANISH.

Malaga, á 20 de Setb^{re} de 18 . *Son £300.*

A noventa dias fecha se serviran V^s mandar pagar por esta primera de cambio á la orden de loss S^{res}_____Tres cientas libras Esterlinas en oro o plata valor recibido de dhos S^{res} que anotaran valor en cuenta segun aviso de

A los S^{res}_____
    Londres.

PORTUGUESE.

£600 Esterlinas. *Lisbon, aos 8 de Dezembro de 18* .

A Sessenta dias de vista precizos pagará V_____por esta nossa unica via de Letra Segura, à nos ou à nossa Ordem a quantia acima de Seis Centas Livras Esterlinas valor de nos recebido em Fazendas, que passera em Comta segundo o aviso de

Ao Sen^r_____
    Londres.

SWEDISH.

Bjorneberg, den 23 September, 18 . *For £ Sterl. 100.*

Nittio Dagar efter duto behagade H. H. emot denna prima Wexel (secundo obetald) betala till Herr_____elle ordres Etthundra Pund Sterling som stalles i rakning enligt avis.

Herrar_____
    London.

DANISH.

Kjobenhavn, 9 December, 18 . *Rbae 4,000.*

Tre maaneder efter dato behager de at betale denne Prima Vexel, secunda ikke, til Herr_____eller ordre med Fire Tusinde Rigsbank Daler, Valutta modtaget og stilles i Regning ifölge advis.

Herrer_____
    London.

Formerly bills of exchange constituted a large proportion of the circulating medium of Lancashire, and supplied the place of country notes. The following account is given by J. Gladstone, Esq., M.P., before a Parliamentary Committee:—

" We sell our goods, not for payments in cash, such as are usual in other places, but generally at credits from ten days to three months, to be then paid for in bills on London at two or three months' date; those bills we pay to our bankers, and receive from them bills or cash when we have occasion for either, to make our payments. The bank notes or gold we require for our ordinary purposes and charges of merchandise of every description. The account is kept floating. The interest on both sides is calculated at the same rate, at present five per cent. Last year the rate was reduced to four; and the banker charges a commission of a quarter per cent. on the amount of one side of the account; that charge is his remuneration, and that of his bankers in London, for paying our acceptances there, both inland and foreign. The account fluctuates, depending on the confidence the banker may have in his customers; if that confidence is entire, the customer is occasionally in his banker's debt, but more frequently the balance is in his favour.

"Does that extend to the whole of Lancashire?—I believe the system at Manchester, Preston, and the other principal towns, is similar; I am not aware of any other. There are some small country bankers in the neighbourhood of Manchester, who issue promissory notes, but I do not know anything of their practice: none of the more respectable banks in Lancashire do issue them."*

"If I sell a thousand pounds' worth of goods to a wholesale grocer, or any other person who again distributes them to his customers in the country, when he comes to pay me the 1,000*l.* he will do so in bills, running from 10*l.* to any other sum; the 1,000*l.* may be paid in twenty or thirty bills of exchange, drawn on London, and generally at two and sometimes three months' date."†

Mr. Lewis Loyd, of the firm of Messrs. Jones, Loyd & Co., estimated in 1826 that the circulation of Manchester consists of nine parts bills of exchange, and the tenth part gold and Bank of England notes. Others think the proportion is as high as twenty to one, or even fifty to one.‡ Mr. Loyd stated he had seen bills of 10*l.* with 120 indorsements upon them; and when the stamp duties were lower, bills were drawn of a less amount. He gives the following *criteria* of accommodation bills. "Bills that are issued for speculation generally travel to London very rapidly, with very few indorsements upon them; they are wanted to be converted into bank notes immediately, and come quite clean, and without any marks of negotiation upon them; and besides that, we know the parties upon them pretty well." In Scotland an accommodation bill is called a wind bill.

It may be mentioned, that after the establishment of branches of the Bank of England at Manchester and Liverpool, the bill circulation of Lancashire was considerably diminished. Most

---

* Lords, 216, Gladstone.   † Lords, 227, Gladstone.
‡ See Evidence of Lewis Loyd, Esq., and of Mr. Henry Burgess, before the Committee of the House of Lords, pp. 294, 298.

of the banks made agreements with the branch bank, stipulating that, in consideration of having a certain amount of discount, at a reduced rate of interest, they would not issue for local circulation any bills they had discounted for their customers. These agreements have been modified since the Act of 1844; but still the main circulation of Lancashire consists of Bank of England notes. It would not now be possible to find a bill with 120 indorsements.

SECTION VI.

THE ADMINISTRATION OF A BANK WITH REGARD TO THE EMPLOYMENT OF ITS SURPLUS FUNDS.

THE means of a London banker consist mainly of his capital and his deposits. A certain portion of this sum is kept in the till, to meet daily demands; another portion is advanced in the way of discounts or loans to his customers. The remainder forms his surplus fund, of which a part will probably be invested in Government securities; loans to bill brokers, payable on demand; in short loans on the Stock Exchange, or in first-rate bills obtained through the bill brokers, and hence styled brokers' bills. The Government securities are the more permanent of these investments. The amount will seldom vary. It is not deemed creditable for a bank to speculate in the funds, or to buy and sell stock frequently, with a view of making a profit by the difference of price; hence a banker sells his Government securities only in a season of pressure, as a means of precaution, or in order to meet urgent demands. On other occasions, he will, when necessary, reduce his short loans or brokers' bills. These form his fluctuating investments. In seasons when money is abundant his deposits will increase, and perchance, at the same time, the demand of his customers for loans or discounts will diminish. His surplus funds will thus increase. But these temporary surplus funds he will on no account invest in Government securities, as his deposits will be certainly, and perhaps suddenly, reduced, and he might have to realize his Government securities at a loss. He will in this case increase his loans to brokers, and his brokers' bills. And though he will get as much interest as he can, he will take a very low interest rather than keep the money unproductive in his till, or invest it in a more permanent form. We will now take a short review of the different kinds of investment we have mentioned. The three grand points for consideration are, convertibility——exemption from loss—and a good rate of interest. But first we will notice those circumstances which regulate the amount of cash to be kept in the till.

The amount of money which a banker will keep in his till depends upon circumstances. First, the amount of his deposits. It is natural to suppose that when his deposits are large, he will keep more money to meet them than when his deposits are small.—Secondly, the amount of his daily payments. These will not at all times correspond with the amount of the deposits ; for some accounts are more *operative* than others. On commercial accounts, for instance, the payments will be much heavier in proportion to the average balance than on accounts which are not commercial. The City bankers pay much larger sums every day, in proportion to the amount of their deposits, than the bankers at the West-end.—Thirdly, if a banker issues notes, he will keep a less amount of other money in his till. The popular opinion is, that he keeps more, as he has to provide payment for his notes as well as his deposits. This is true in seasons of pressure. But in ordinary times he keeps less, as he pays the cheques drawn on account of his deposits with his notes, and these notes often get into the hands of another banker, with whom he settles by a draft on London. His reserve to meet his notes is kept, not in his own till, but in London, where it probably yields him interest. Indeed, when his deposits are withdrawn in large amounts, they are more usually withdrawn by a draft on London than in any other way.—Fourthly, the number of the branches. If a bank has many branches, the total amount of cash kept in the tills of the head office and all the branches put together will be considerably more than would be required if the whole of the business were collected into one place. In the case of a run the difference is considerable, as every point open to attack must be well fortified. The stoppage of one branch, even for a short time, would bring discredit upon the whole establishment. —Fifthly, in London the amount of notes to be kept in the till will be affected by the privilege of clearing. Those bankers that "clear," can pay bills and cheques upon them by the bills and cheques they have upon other bankers. Those banks that do not clear must pay all the bills and cheques upon them in bank notes before 'they receive payment of the bills and cheques they have upon other bankers. Hence they must lock up every night with a larger amount of cash in their vaults.

We need hardly say, that with every banker the amount in the till will fluctuate from day to day. Though a banker has a certain average amount in his own mind, below or above which he does not swerve very widely, yet the cash-book will seldom be exactly this amount. Sometimes he will strengthen his till, in the prospect of large payments that may come upon him suddenly. At other times he will run his till low for a day or two, in expectation of large sums that wil' shortly be due to him. During the day, too, either the receipts or the payments may be heavier than he expected; and hence, now and then, the cashier reports to the chief clerk or to the banker the state of the till, in order that, if necessary, it may be replenished. The temperament of a banker, too, has some effect in this case. Some bankers are so cautious that they will "lock up" with a large amount of cash; others are so anxious to make profit, that they will keep their cash very low. The state of the money market will also influence the tills of the bankers. When money is abundant, a banker will lock up with more money than he wants, because he cannot employ his funds. When money is so scarce as to betoken a pressure, he will also lock up strong, so as to be prepared for any emergency. In fact, there can be no general rule for regulating the amount of the till. Every banker must be guided by the experience of his own bank. The directors of the Bank of England consider that their reserve in bank notes and gold should be equal to about one-third of their deposits. From the accounts published by some of the London joint-stock banks, it would appear that the "cash in hand" is equal to about one-eighth or one-tenth of their liabilities. Even this, we conjecture, is a higher proportion than that which is generally kept by London bankers, especially by those who settle their accounts with each other at the Clearing-house.

To resume:—After a banker has furnished his till, and supplied his customers with such loans and discounts as they may require, he has a surplus of cash. This surplus may be considered as being divided into two parts—though it is never actually so divided—the permanent surplus, which the banker is not likely to require, except in seasons of extreme pressure, and the temporary surplus, arising from fluctuations in the deposits. We shall now notice those modes of investment to which we have referred.

With regard to Government securities, we have high authority from the testimony of practical bankers. The following are quotations given before the Joint-stock Bank Committee, in the year 1836, by the late Vincent Stuckey, Esq., the founder of Stuckey's Joint-stock Banking Company, in Somersetshire, and the late James Marshall, Esq., the Secretary of the Provincial Bank of Ireland.

Mr. V. Stuckey :- -

" What is your reason for keeping so large a sum in Government stock ?—I have always found from my experience, except two days in my life, that I could get money more easily upon those securities than any other.

" Is it easier, in times of emergency, to obtain money on Government stock than on good Mercantile bills ?—I have always found it so.

" You do not concur with any witnesses who state that they have found good negotiable bills more easy to obtain money upon than Government stock ?—No : I have never found that with a good bill, even of the house of Baring, I could get money more easily than on Government stock.

" Do you consider that, generally speaking, in London the rate of interest at which you borrow money on exchequer bills and stock is notoriously lower than that at which you borrow on bills of exchange ?—Yes, it is lower, and for that reason we generally adopt it."

Mr. James Marshall :—

" Will you inform the Committee whether it is the usage of the Provincial Bank to invest any portion of its funds in the public securities ?—It has been its uniform practice so to do.

" By public securities, what do you understand ?—The Consols, for instance : there are various kinds of Government stock ; exchequer bills, and Bank of England stock, are generally considered as a public sort of security.

" Do you hold stock in London only, or in Dublin as well as in London ?—In Dublin but to a limited amount, because it is not easily convertible there.

" On what ground is it that it is not easily convertible in Dublin ?—From the limited nature of the market as compared with London ; we could not sell even an immaterial sum without lowering considerably the price.

" Have there not been at various times, from various causes, runs on the Provincial Bank, which rendered it necessary to supply large amounts of specie to that country ?—There have, repeatedly.

" Do you consider, from your experience, that it would have been competent to the bank to have maintained its full security, with satisfaction to the directors, if they had not been possessed of very considerable funded property in this country?—Certainly not; speaking of the last run that happened, especially, I must say that that differed from any former run in this respect.

" You were conversant with the management of the Scotch banks prior to your connection with the Provincial Bank?—Yes.

" Is it not the usage of all the Scotch banks in like manner to maintain a very considerable portion of their funds as invested in the Government securities?—I believe the practice with all is generally so, but I can speak particularly to that of the three oldest banks—as they are commonly called, the three chartered banks,—the Bank of Scotland was erected by Act of Parliament, the Royal Bank of Scotland and the British Linen Company are erected by charter, but have been recognised in the same way, so that there are three public banks in distinction to any of the subsequently-formed banks. I can state, from personal knowledge, that these banks have had always a very large sum indeed invested in the funded property of the kingdom.

" Do you consider it would be a safe system of banking, if the capital of the bank was altogether invested in commercial bills?—Certainly not."

Of the various kinds of Government stock, consols are the best, as there is a more ready market for this kind of stock, and money can usually be borrowed on them until the next account day; so that, if a banker has only a temporary demand for money, he may thus obtain it at a moderate interest, when, by selling his stock at that time, he might sustain loss. The Bank of England has recourse, sometimes, to this mode of strengthening her reserve. Sometimes, too, a banker may make a profit by lending his consols. At the monthly settlings, among the brokers, stock is sometimes in demand and money may be obtained upon consols, until the next settling, without paying any interest; and the banker may employ the money in the mean time. As, however, the rate of interest is usually low in such seasons, his profit will rarely be great.

There are no time bargains in the reduced 3 per cents., or in the new 3 per cents.; but in ordinary times money can be borrowed upon them at the market rate of interest. In seasons of pressure these are not so saleable as consols. Bank stock, India stock, and long annuities, not being readily convertible, are not generally good investments for bankers.

Some bankers avoid all Government stock, and give a pre

ference to exchequer bills. They have some advantages. As the Government must pay the amount demanded in March or June, when they become due, there can be no loss beyond the amount of the premium at which they were purchased. A banker, too, can borrow money upon them quietly and secretly. A transfer of stock is always known, and, if for a large amount, will, when money is scarce, excite notice, and give the impression that the banker is compelled to realise some of his securities, to meet demands made upon him by his depositors. But a banker can hand his exchequer bills to a stock-broker, who will bring him the money, and the party who has granted the loan will know nothing about the party for whom it was required. On the other hand, there are some disadvantages. Almost every change in the market value of money affects the price of exchequer bills; and whenever money becomes abundant, the Government are very apt to reduce the rate of interest much below that which can be obtained from consols. But a greater objection is, that even in ordinary times, they are hardly saleable in large amounts. There are not now so many exchequer-bill jobbers as formerly, and hence these bills are not so readily saleable. On this account, the Bank of England, who were formerly large holders of exchequer bills, have changed their system, and are now holders of stock. The City bankers, too, prefer placing their money with the bill-brokers, to investing it in exchequer bills. But they are still a favourite mode of investment with bankers at the West-end.

East India bonds yield a higher interest than exchequer bills, and the interest cannot be reduced until after twelve months' notice from the Governor of India in Council. But they are by no means so saleable. Money, however, may generally be borrowed upon them; and the loans of the Bank of England are always announced to be granted on " exchequer bills, India bonds, and other approved securities."

Bonds of corporations, or of public companies, are by no means proper investments for a banker, except to a very moderate amount, and when they have a short time to run. They may, however, be taken as security for temporary advances to respectable customers.

Good commercial bills, of short dates, have this advantage over Government stock or exchequer bills, that a banker is sure to receive back the same amount of money which he advanced. He can calculate, too, upon the time the money will be received, and make his arrangements accordingly. And if unexpectedly he should want the money sooner, the bills can, in ordinary times, be rediscounted in the money market. Another advantage is, that he is able to avail himself of any advance in the current rate of interest. He will get no higher dividend from his investment in Government stock, should money afterwards become ever so valuable. But with regard to bills, as they fall due he will receive a higher rate of discount with the new bills he may take, and thus, as the market rate of interest advances, his profits will increase.

The bankers of Lancashire usually keep the whole of their reserves in bills of exchange. If they have a " good bill case," that is, a large amount of good bills in their case, they think themselves prepared to meet any emergency. Their objection to Government securities is founded, first, upon the low rate of interest which they yield; and, secondly, the possibility of loss, from fluctuations in price. They contend, too, that good bills of exchange are more convertible than even exchequer bills; and, even if not convertible, the money comes back as the bills fall due, and thus the reserve is constantly replenished.

The authority of Mr. Samuel Gurney, from his high standing in the City, is so constantly referred to upon this subject, that we copy his evidence. It was given before the Committee on Joint-stock Banks, in the year 1836; previous, of course, to the passing of the Act of 1844.

" Would not the result from that opinion be, that a properly-conducted establishment, whether a private or a joint-stock bank, should have some Government securities or exchequer bills on which always to rely as a resource in a moment of such emergency ?—Experience has shown that it is not needful; bills of exchange are quite as good a security to hold in time of difficulty as exchequer bills or stock; in most respects very much better.

" Cannot you conceive a state of things in the money market—a state of mercantile discredit, for instance—when it might be possible to procure money on Government securities when it could not be procured on private security in the shape of bills ?—Such difficulty may possibly exist under very peculiar circumstances; but I repeat my opinion, that bills of exchange have proved themselves to be a better investment for bankers than stock or exchequer bills.

" It is quite intelligible why, in ordinary times, bills of exchange should be a preferable investment for money, inasmuch as there is no risk of loss by variation of premium in the purchase and resale; but would you wish the committee to suppose that in the case supposed by the question, of a great degree of mercantile discredit and doubt, an amount of exchequer bills would not be a more certain security on which to raise money than the bills of private merchants?—That is a difficult question to answer; I doubt it.

"Supposing a period of difficulty to arise, and two country bankers came up to London, one who could exhibit Government stock to the extent of 25,000*l.* and 25,000*l.* in bills of exchange, and the other banker exhibiting 50,000*l.* in bills of exchange only, which do you think would have the best means of procuring accommodation in the London market to pay his engagements?—My apprehension is, that they would both get their supplies upon any particular emergency: it is my judgment, that to a banker a good supply of bills of exchange of first-rate character is a better investment for his funds, for which he is liable to be called upon on demand, than exchequer bills or any Government security."

A London banker never considers as a part of his reserve the bills he has discounted for his customers. Nothing could damage his credit more than any attempt to rediscount these bills. During the war, the London bankers had discount accounts with the Bank of England; and in the panic of 1825, it is well known they discounted largely with that establishment. But since that period they have not done so, and their indorsements are never seen in the money market. The practice is now more general of lodging money at call with the large money dealers. And it is in this way that the London bankers make provision for any sudden demand. It is rarely, however, that any large demand comes so suddenly as to occasion any inconvenience. And it may be observed that such bankers as are members of the Clearing-house have the whole day to make preparation—one of the circumstances which enables them to lock up at night with a smaller amount of cash.

In the morning the banker looks at his "Cash-book," and observes the amount with which he "locked up" the preceding night. He then looks at the "Diary," which contains his receipts and payments for that day, as far as he is then advised. He then opens the letters, and notices the remittances they contain, and the payments he is instructed to make. He will learn from these items whether he "wants money," or has "money to spare." If he wants money, he will "take in" any loans that may be falling due that day, or he may "call in" any loans he may have out on demand, or he may go farther, and borrow money for a few days on stock or exchequer bills. Should he have money to spare, he will, peradventure, discount brokers' bills, or lodge money on demand with the bill-brokers, or lend it for fixed periods upon stock or exchequer bills. There are some bill-brokers who usually make their rounds every morning, first calling on the parties who supply them with bills, and then calling on the bankers who supply them with money. The stock-brokers, too, will call after "the market is open," to inform the banker how "things are going" on the Stock Exchange, what operations are taking place, and whether money is abundant or scarce "in the house;" also what rumours are afloat that are likely to affect the price of the funds. It is thus that a banker regulates his investments, and finds employment for his surplus funds.

In our opinion, it is best for a banker not to adopt exclusively any one of the investments we have noticed, but to distribute his funds among them all. We have seen that practical bankers of high standing have been in favour of Government securities, as being at all times convertible. The objection on the part of others has been, that the value of these securities very much fluctuates, and as their realisation will be required only in seasons of pressure when the funds are low, it is sure to be attended with loss. On the other hand, it may be stated, with regard to "loans on demand," that the recent failures of bill-brokers have shown that the "demand" may not always be readily met. And with regard to "brokers' bills," the numerous failures among houses of the first standing have proved that great losses and most inconvenient "locks-up" may occasionally take place from such securities. Without condemning other modes of investment, we are strongly inclined to favour Government securities, though fully conscious of the losses they may occasionally produce. There is one consideration that must be taken into account: a bank that has large surplus funds, if it makes no investments in Government securities, will be strongly tempted to invest their funds elsewhere in other securities that may not be so convertible. It is true that more interest may for a time be obtained,* but ultimately the

* At the Meeting of the London and Westminster Bank, July 1855, the Chairman, J. L. Ricardo, Esq., M.P., made a comparison between the interest obtained on money invested in the funds and that employed with bill-brokers. Upon an average of twelve years the following is the result: On the 2nd January, 1843,

bank may, though in a state of perfect solvency, be compelled to stop payment from being unable to realise its investments.

Another advantage of a large investment in Government securities is, that the bank, by the publication of its balance sheet, has always the means of showing to its depositors that a large portion of its deposits is at all times amply secured. The Bank of England states the amount of their "Government securities" distinct from the "other securities." It may so be that the "other securities" are as good as the Government securities, and perhaps more profitable, but the public do not know that to be the case; and were all the investments in "other securities," they might not feel the same degree of confidence as to the prompt repayment of their deposits. The same principle applies to other banks. And it may reasonably be supposed that between two banks in similar circumstances as to other respects, depositors would rather lodge their money in a bank which had a large amount of Government securities than in one which had none.

As we have referred in this Section to some of the operations of the Stock Exchange, this may be a proper place to discuss the nature of these transactions, so far, at least, as concerns bankers.

The reader is of course aware that the "Stocks," or the "Funds," or by whatever other name they may be called, are debts due from the nation to those persons whose names are entered on the bank books. The man who holds 100*l.* consols is a creditor to the nation for 100*l.*, for which he receives 3*l.* per annum; and the price of consols is the amount of the money for which he is willing to transfer this debt from himself to another person. Now, if this man knows another who is willing to give him, say 90*l.* for this 100*l.* consols, they can go to the bank, and the seller being properly identified, will transfer this 100*l.* consols into the name of the person to whom he has sold it. His account is then closed in the bank books, and a new account is open in the name of the buyer; for every holder of

the price of consols was 94½, which yields an interest per annum of 3*l.* 3*s.* 6*d.* per cent. The interest allowed upon money at call by Messrs. Overend & Co. for twelve years, from January, 1843, to December, 1854, would average 2*l.* 10*s.* 10*d.* per cent. Upon bills, the rate allowed is usually half per cent. more, that is, 3*l.* 0*s.* 10*d.* per cent. 1,000,000*l.* invested at 3*l.* 3*s.* 6*d.* would produce annually the sum of 31,750*l.* At 3*l.* 0*s.* 10*d.* per cent. it would produce only 30,416*l.* 13*s.* 4*d.* This shows, that upon an *average of years* the funds are more productive than brokers' bills.

stock has an account in the bank ledger, in the same way as bankers and merchants open ledger accounts for their customers. The seller of the stock will also give a receipt to the buyer for the money on a printed form issued by the Bank of England.

But parties do not usually treat with each other in this way. A broker is employed either to buy or to sell, as the case may be. The members of the Stock Exchange are an association consisting of about 1200 persons, who meet together in a building in Capel Court, Bartholomew Lane, close to the Bank. Each member, before admission, must find three securities for 300*l.* each, which sum is applied to meet any claims the other members of the " House " may have upon him during the first two years. The suretyship then ceases.* The subscription paid by each member is ten guineas per annum. The House is governed by a Committee of thirty persons chosen from the members.

Although all the " members of the House " are called stock-brokers by the public, yet within the House they are divided into two classes, brokers and jobbers. A broker, as the name implies, is an agent who buys or sells for his customers out of the House, and he charges them a commission upon the amount of the stock. A stock-jobber is a stock dealer; but he does not deal with the public: he deals only with the brokers; and he is at all times ready either to buy or to sell. The price at which he sells is $\frac{1}{8}$ more than the price at which he buys. If one broker has an order from his customer to buy 100*l.* consols, and another broker has an order to sell 100*l.* consols, these two brokers do not deal together, but both go to a jobber, who will " make him a price." One will sell his consols to the jobber, say at 90, and the other will buy his consols from the jobber at 90$\frac{1}{8}$. Hence the difference between the buying and the selling price of consols is always $\frac{1}{8}$, and thus in the newspapers the price is quoted in this way, 90 to 90$\frac{1}{8}$.

A banker is, of course, one of the public, and when he wants to buy or to sell stock, he gives instructions to his broker, and the process is as we have now described.

Were there no jobbers, a broker would not easily find at all times another broker who had occasion to sell the same amount

* In addition to the above, every member must find two sureties, who become bound for him to the corporation of the City of London in the sum of 1000*l.* each.—EDITOR.

of stock which he wished to buy, and he would have a difficulty in buying or selling small amounts. But there is no difficulty with the jobbers. The jobbers will not only buy and sell stock on the same day, but they will buy stock on one day, and agree to sell it at a future day, or *vice versâ*. These future days are called the settling days, being the days on which the members of the House settle their accounts. They are fixed by the Committee of the Stock Exchange, and they now occur about once a month. Now, if a banker wants a sum of money for a short time, either to pay off a deposit, or to make an advance to a customer, he will direct his stock-broker to sell, say 50,000*l.* consols "for money," and buy them "for time;" that is, against the next "settling day," or, as it is sometimes called, the next "account day." On the other hand, if a banker has money he wishes to employ for a short time, he will reverse the operation, and desire his broker to buy consols for money and sell them for time. He thus gets interest for his money, according to the difference of price between consols for time and consols for money. Generally, the price for time is higher than the price for money; and the difference between these two prices is called the "Continuation." Supposing that the next settling day is a month distant, and the continuation is one-eighth per cent., that amounts to twelve-eighths, or one and a half per cent. per annum. The continuation will vary according to the near approach of the settling-day—according to the abundance of money, and the market rate of interest—and according to the abundance or scarcity of stock. The last cause is not so readily understood by the public, and we will therefore explain it. The stock-jobbers, as we have said, are stock dealers. Of course they are large holders of stock; it is their capital, on which they trade. But however large may be the sum they hold, they often agree to sell on the next settling day a much larger sum, expecting that in the mean time they shall buy a large sum, and thus be able to set off one against the other. But sometimes, as the settling day approaches, they find this is not the case, and they are consequently under an engagement to "deliver"—that is, sell—more stock than they hold. What can they do now? They will try to get stock from those who have it, by agreeing to buy it of them *now*, and selling it at the ensuing account day, a month hence, at the same price; thus abolishing "the continuation." When that is the case, a banker's broker will go to the banker and say, " If you like to lend your consols, you can get money for nothing till the next account day." The banker replies, " Well, I don't know that I can make much interest of the money just now ; but as I can lose nothing, you may lend them." Thus the jobbers get their stock, and complete their engagements. But sometimes the jobbers are obliged to go farther, and even to offer a premium to parties who will lend their consols. This premium is called "Backadation ;" it is just the reverse of " continuation," and implies that the time price of stock is less than the money price.

We have thus described the legitimate operations of the Stock Exchange, so far as it may be necessary to explain the transactions of bankers in the employment of their surplus funds. Those operations, called " Gambling in the Funds," and the mode in which the brokers and jobbers settle their accounts, we shall endeavour to describe when we come to speak of the Clearing-house.

SECTION VII.

THE ADMINISTRATION OF A BANK DURING SEASONS OF PRESSURE.

A PRESSURE on the money market may be defined a difficulty of getting money in the London market, either by way of discounting bills, or of loans upon Government securities. This difficulty is usually accompanied by an unfavourable course of exchange, a contraction of the circulation of the Bank of England, and a high rate of interest. These three circumstances have the relation to each other of cause and effect. The unfavourable course of exchange induces the Bank of England to contract her circulation ; and the contraction of the circulation, by rendering money more scarce, increases its value, and leads to an advanced rate of interest. The removal of the pressure is in the same order—the foreign exchanges become favourable—the Bank of England then extends her circulation—money becomes more abundant, and the rate of interest falls. The degree to which the exchanges are unfavourable is indicated by the stock of gold in the Bank of England ; and when this is at its lowest amount the pressure may be considered to have attained its extreme point; for as the amount of gold increases, the bank will extend her circulation, and the pressure will subside.

If we take a review of all the recent pressures on the money market, we shall find they have always been preceded by the following circumstances:—First, by abundance of money; secondly, by a low rate of interest; thirdly, by some species of speculative investments. The principal pressures that have occurred of late years, have been those of 1825, 1836, 1839, 1847, 1857, and 1866.

The following is Mr. Horsley Palmer's opinion of the causes of the pressure of 1825, as stated to the Bank Committee of 1832:—

" Will you state to the committee what, in your opinion, was the nature and the march of the crisis in 1825?—I have always considered that the first step towards the excitement was the reduction of the interest upon the Government securities; the first movement in that respect was, I think, upon 135,000,000*l.* of five per cents., which took place in 1823. In the subsequent year, 1824, followed the reduction of 80,000,000*l.* of four per cents. I have always considered that reduction of interests, one-fifth in one case, and one-eighth in the other, to have created the feverish feeling in the minds of the public at large, which prompted almost everybody to entertain any proposition for investment, however absurd, which was tendered. The excitement of that period was further promoted by the acknowledgment of South American republics by this country, and the inducements held out for engaging in mining operations, and loans to those governments, in which all classes of the community in England seem to have partaken almost simultaneously. With those speculations arose general speculation in commercial produce, which had an effect of disturbing the relative values between this and other countries, and creating an unfavourable foreign exchange, which continued from October, 1824, to November, 1825, causing a very considerable export of bullion from the bank—about seven millions and a half. Commercial speculations had induced some bankers, one particularly, to invest money in securities not strictly convertible, to a larger extent than was prudent; they were also largely connected with country bankers. I allude to the house of Messrs. Pole and Co.: a house originally possessed of very great property, in the persons of the partners, but which fell with the circumstances of the times. The failure of that banking-house was the first decisive check to commercial and banking credit, and brought at once a vast number of country bankers, which were in correspondence with it, into difficulties. That discredit was followed by a general discredit throughout London and the interior." —P. 47.

With regard to the pressure of 1836, there was in the beginning of that year no appearance of distress; but, on the contrary, every symptom of prosperity, attended by its usual concomitant, a readiness to engage in speculative undertakings.

The following description of this period is taken from the speech of Mr. Clay, on introducing his motion respecting Joint-stock Banks, May 12, 1836 :—

"To what extent the operations of the joint-stock banks may have contributed to create the present state of excitement in the commercial world, must, of course, be mere matter of conjecture. That they have had some considerable influence is probable, from the fact that the excitement and rage for speculation is greatest in those parts of the kingdom, where the operations of those establishments have been most active. London has been comparatively unmoved, but Liverpool and Manchester have witnessed a mushroom growth of schemes not exceeded by the memorable year 1825. I hold in my hand a list of seventy contemplated companies, for every species of undertaking, which have appeared in the Liverpool and Manchester papers within the last three months. This list was made a fortnight or three weeks since, and might probably now be considerably extended. It is impossible also, I think, not to suspect that the facility of credit, and consequent encouragement to speculation, to which I have alluded, cannot have been without its effect in producing the great increase of price in almost all the chief articles of consumption and raw materials of our manufactures. That increase has been enormous —not less than from twenty to fifty, and even one hundred per cent. in many of the chief articles of produce, of consumption, and materials of our manufactures."

These appearances continued with little alteration until the month of July, when the Bank of England raised the rate of discount to four-and-a-half per cent. It then became known that there had been a demand upon the bank for gold from the preceding April, and this measure was adopted by the bank as a means of rendering the foreign exchanges more favourable. This being found ineffectual, the bank in September raised the rate of discount to five per cent. Besides raising the rate of interest, the bank adopted other measures of increasing the value of money. A large amount of American bills upon first-rate houses had been offered for discount and rejected. A high degree of alarm was immediately spread throughout the community. The dread of a panic similar to that of 1825 almost universally prevailed. Those who had money were unwilling to part with it—trade became suddenly stagnant—the prices of all commodities fell considerably, and numbers of commercial houses, chiefly of the second class, suspended payment. Many railway and other projects now fell into oblivion.

The alarm that existed was kept up by the monthly accounts of the bullion in the Bank of England. The public returns showed a gradual decline from April, 1836, to February, 1837. It was therefore supposed that the Bank of England would be under the necessity, for her own safety, of still further contracting her issues, and thus increasing the existing pressure. This apprehension caused all persons who had money to retain it in their possession, and bankers and others withheld accommodation they would otherwise have been disposed to grant.

This state of alarm was considerably augmented by the publication of the Report of the Secret Committee of the House of Commons upon Joint-stock Banks. This committee had been appointed on the motion of Mr. Clay, the Member for the Tower Hamlets, whose speech on the occasion might be termed a bill of indictment. The joint-stock banks had rapidly increased; they had issued small shares; they had large nominal capitals; they had circulated an excessive amount of notes; they had promoted speculation. These were the charges brought against them; and they had greater weight from being advanced by a member who was known to be friendly to joint-stock banking. The report of the committee appeared to sustain all Mr. Clay's accusations. This report was highly creditable to the talents and industry of the committee, but marked by a decided hostility of tone. While it enumerated all the actual or possible imperfections of the joint-stock banks, it ascribed to them scarcely a single excellence. At the same time, the committee deferred to the succeeding session the proposal of any measures for their improvement; thus the public were led to suppose, that in the following session some stringent measures would be adopted with reference to joint-stock banks, but what they would be none could conjecture.

Had the report appeared at any other period it might possibly have done good; but as its appearance was contemporaneous with a pressure on the money market, and a high state of alarm, it unquestionably tended to weaken public confidence, at a time when it required to be strengthened. Persons who were unfriendly to joint-stock banks seized the opportunity of dispraising them, and believed, or pretended to believe, that the banks were unsound, and would certainly stop payment. Others, who were friendly, were apprehensive that the banks, being still in their infancy, would be found too weak to withstand the storm now raised against them. But though this alarm began with respect to joint-stock banks, it did not end there. It was soon foreseen that if a few joint-stock banks were to stop payment, the private banks in their neighbourhood would be put to a severe trial; and if the banks should even be compelled to withhold their usual advances to their customers, the credit of individuals must suffer. Hence the private bankers and the merchants, as well as the joint-stock banks, made preparations to meet any event that might occur, and by thus increasing the pressure on the London money market, occasioned still farther apprehensions.

The alarm was augmented by the stoppage of the Agricultural and Commercial Bank of Ireland, in the month of November, and the demand for gold which that stoppage occasioned in Ireland. The joint-stock banks of England now became subject to increased suspicion; the accommodation they had been accustomed to obtain by the re-discount of their bills in the London market was considerably restricted; and in the beginning of December, the Northern and Central Bank at Manchester, a bank having a paid-up capital of 800,000*l.*, with above 1,200 partners, and forty branches, applied for assistance to the Bank of England. This was afforded upon condition, in the first instance, that they should wind up all their branches, except that at Liverpool; and afterwards farther assistance was granted, upon condition they should discontinue business after February, 1837. Soon afterwards, the old and respectable London banking-house of Messrs. Esdaile & Co. received assistance upon similar terms.

The pressure which existed in England rapidly extended to America. A large amount of American securities, consisting chiefly of bonds of the respective States, had been remitted to the agency houses in England. This circumstance, in connexion with the exportation of gold to America, attracted the notice of the Bank of England. A large amount of bills drawn from America upon first-rate London houses was rejected. In America the pressure became severe—money was wanted to remit to England to meet the drafts that had been drawn upon England, either upon credit or against securities that could not now be sold. The rate of discount at New York rose to two, and even to three per cent. per month.

From the pressure upon the money market, and from the great fall in the price of American produce, the cotton and other commodities sent from America to meet drafts upon the English agents, could not be sold except at a ruinous loss. And other remittances not having arrived, several houses in the American trade, who were said to have given extensive credit to parties in America, applied for assistance to the Bank of England.

Such was the character of the pressure of 1836; we next proceed to the pressure of 1839. The pressure of 1836 may be said to have commenced from the month of May in that year. From that month the stock of gold in the bank gradually and uniformly declined until February, 1837, when it reached its lowest point of depression. From this point, it uniformly advanced: the lowest point of the circulation was in December, 1836, though even then it was not lower than it had been in the preceding January. The bank raised the rate of interest from 4 to 4½ per cent. in July, and to 5 per cent. in the following September. During the whole of the year 1837, the amount of gold in the Bank of England continued to increase; the bank extended her circulation, and after the payment of the July dividends, money became very abundant, and the market rate of interest experienced a considerable fall. The foreign exchanges continued to be favourable during the early part of 1838, and gold accumulated in the coffers of the Bank of England. In the spring of that year the directors of the Bank of England sent nearly a million of gold to America. Money became increasingly abundant, and the rate of interest fell. In February the bank reduced their rate of discount to 4 per cent., and the interest on the loans granted during the shutting of the funds was reduced in March to 3½ per cent. The low rate of interest caused large sums of money to be invested in American securities. Bonds of all kinds issued* by the Bank of the United States, by the various states in the Union, and by numerous private undertakings, were poured upon the English market, and found eager purchasers. Several of the directors of the Bank of England, in their individual character as merchants, became agents for the distribution of these securities. About July the exchanges became unfavourable, and in the latter part of the year some symptoms of uneasiness were apparent in the money market; but as the stock of bullion in the Bank of England was considerable, and the directors granted their usual loans in December at 3½ per cent., public confidence was not shaken. In the beginning of the year 1839 the exchanges became increasingly unfavourable, and the monthly returns of the bank showed a gradual diminution in the stock of gold. The price of corn rose so high as to admit of foreign wheat at the lowest rate of duty. This occasioned a further demand for gold to be exported. The stock of gold in the Bank of England rapidly declined, until, in the month of October, it was no more than 2,525,000*l.*, while the liabilities of the bank upon notes amounted to 17,612,000*l.*, and upon deposits to 6,734,000*l.* The bank directors were very anxious to stop this demand for gold. With this view, they raised the rate of interest on May 16th to 5 per cent., on June 20th to 5½ per cent., and on August 1st to 6 per cent.; and they charged the same rate upon their short loans. They are supposed to have sold large amounts of Government stock and exchequer bills, and on July 13th they announced that they were ready to receive proposals for the sale of the dead weight. None of the offers, however, met their approbation. Finding these measures not speedily effective, an arrangement was made with the Bank of France for a loan of 2,500,000*l.* Messrs. Baring & Co. drew bills on account of the Bank of England upon houses in Paris for this amount, which the bank of France undertook to discount. The directors also determined to refuse to discount any bills drawn or indorsed by any private or joint-stock bank of issue. Notwithstanding these measures, the stock of gold in the bank continued to decrease until the 18th October, when it reached the lowest point of depression. From this point it continued to advance, and the pressure began gradually, but slowly, to subside.

It may be useful to notice the differences between the pressure of 1836 and that of 1839. If we measure the intensity of the pressure by the difference between the largest and the lowest stock of gold in the Bank of England, the former pressure will range from 7,801,000*l.*, to 4,032,000*l.*, and the latter from 10,126,000*l.* to 2,525,000*l.* In the pressure of 1836, one joint-stock bank, a London private bank, two country private banks, three large American agency houses, and a great many respectable merchants, stopped payment. In the pressure of 1839, there was scarcely a failure until the month of December, and then only among the second class of traders. In the pressure of 1836, the prices of nearly all commodities fell considerably, and almost immediately. In the pressure of 1839, the prices of most commodities remained for a length of time nearly the same. In 1836, the Bank of England did not raise their rate of interest above 5 per cent. In 1839, the rate of interest upon both discounts and loans was raised to 6 per cent. In 1839, the bank gave notice that they were willing to sell the dead weight, and they made arrangements for borrowing 2,500,000*l*., sterling from the Bank of France. In 1836, the bank adopted neither of these measures. In 1836, the Bank of England rejected all bills drawn or indorsed by joint-stock banks of issue. In 1839, they rejected also all bills drawn and indorsed by private banks of issue.

It would appear that a season of pressure is always preceded by one of speculation ; and hence it follows that a banker who wishes to be easy in a time of pressure must act wisely in the previous season of speculation. It requires no ordinary firmness to do this. To act wisely in a season of speculation, is far more difficult than to act wisely in one of pressure. But unless a banker acts wisely in the previous time of speculation, his wisdom will probably be of little avail when the pressure arrives.

While, therefore, money is still abundant, the public funds high, and other bankers liberal in accommodation, he should be doubly cautious against taking bills of a doubtful character, or making advances upon irregular securities. He should not suffer the desire of employing his funds, or the fear of offending his customers, to induce him to deviate from sound banking principles. He should also take this opportunity of calling up all dead or doubtful loans, and of getting rid of all weak customers. He should also, under any circumstances, avoid making advances for any length of time, and investments in securities that are not at all times convertible, or the price of which is likely to sustain a great fall on the occurrence of a pressure. The discount of first-rate commercial bills having a short time to run, or short loans on stock or other undeniable security, however low the interest received, seem to be the most safe and advantageous transactions.

When the aspect of affairs seems to threaten that money will be in demand, and the failure of a number of merchants and traders may consequently be apprehended, it behoves him to prepare for approaching events by avoiding all discounts of bills of an inferior class, and by keeping his funds in an available state. With a view to these objects, he will review all his loan and discount accounts, call up his loans of long standing, where it can be done without injury to the interest or reputation of his bank, avoid all overdrawn accounts, and reduce the amount of discounts of the inferior class of accounts. In performing these operations, he will exercise due judgment and discretion, making proper distinctions between his customers, and reducing chiefly those bills which are of an unbusiness character, or which are drawn upon doubtful people, or upon parties that he knows nothing about; he will also mark particularly those accounts which require large discounts, but keep no corresponding balance to the credit of their current accounts.

As the pressure advances, he will find that there are three demands upon his funds. First, his customers will reduce their balances, and keep less money in his hands. Money lodged at interest will be taken away, because the parties can make higher interest elsewhere, or they will be tempted by the low price of stock to invest it in Government securities. Secondly, he will have a greater demand for loans and discounts, not merely from weak people whom he might not care about refusing, but from persons of known wealth, whom it is his interest and his inclination to oblige. Thirdly, he will think it prudent to guard against sudden demands by keeping a larger amount of bank notes in his till. To meet all these demands he will be compelled to realise some of his securities, and he will realise those first on which he will sustain no loss.

If a banker has money lying at demand with a bill-broker, he will now have occasion to call it in. If he has money lent at short periods at the Stock Exchange, he will, as he has occasion, take in the money as the loans fall due. If he has discounted brokers' bills, he will receive the amounts when due, and discount no more. Should these operations not be sufficient to meet the demands upon his funds, he will then sell his stock or exchequer bills, or borrow on them in the money market. A country banker who has kept his reserve in bills of exchange will be anxious to re-discount them, and will think himself lucky if he can do so readily and at a moderate rate of interest.

It will be useless for a banker to attempt to call up dead

loans, or to reduce his discounts, after the pressure has commenced. He should have thought of these matters in the previous season of abundance. As he cannot get in any outstanding advances, he had better not ask for them, but merely charge the parties an increased rate of interest. If he demand the money, he will not get it, and he may give rise to a surmise that he is short of funds. This season of pressure is, however, a good opportunity for calling up advances, or getting rid of connexions that he would, on other grounds, like to be without. The " scarcity of money," the " pressure on the money market," are capital reasons to assign for refusing applications which, even otherwise, he would refuse, and for calling up loans which, under any circumstances, he would like to see repaid.

During a pressure, a banker will have to give a great many refusals, and some discretion will be necessary in the form of giving these refusals. Let him refuse in what way he may at such a season, he will be sure to give offence. And the party refused will possibly publish the refusal, and, from motives of ignorance or malignity, represent the refusal as having arisen from want of means, and possibly may circulate a report that the banker is about to stop payment. Hence rumours about banks are always rife in seasons of pressure, and they add to the general want of confidence which then prevails.

During a pressure, a banker will have offers of new accounts to be transferred from other bankers, provided he will consent to make certain advances. Some caution must be exercised in this matter. It is quite possible that some perfectly safe parties, having large accounts, may be disposed to remove in consequence of their present bankers not being equal to the supply of their wants. In this case, the banker will be regulated by the value of the proposed account and the extent of his own means. On the other hand, it is equally possible that weak people, to whom their present bank might not, in any case, have given advances, may use the " scarcity of money " as a pretext for making application to a new banker, stating their belief that their old banker was unable to meet their requirements. It behoves a banker to use much discretion in such a case, especially if it be a large account. If he errs at all, he should err on the side of caution.

It will rarely be wise for a banker in a season of pressure to attempt to get away the customers of other bankers by offering them greater accommodation. The best way of getting new connexions is to treat well those that he has. It is better for a banker to employ his funds in supporting his old friends than in attempting to get new ones. If his funds are so ample that he can do both without inconvenience, very well. But caution is necessary in taking new accounts at this time, and he should be doubly cautious in making applications to parties. Unless he has the most ample and satisfactory information as to their circumstances, he had better wait until they apply to him. It would then devolve upon them to satisfy him that he would be justified in making the advances required.

During the pressure, a banker will find that some of his wealthier customers, who, when money was abundant, took their bills to be discounted by a bill-broker, because he would cash them at a lower rate, will come back, and expect to have discounts from their banker. This is no fault of the bill-brokers. People put money in their hands avowedly for temporary purposes. In seasons of abundance the bill-brokers are glutted with money. When the pressure commences this money is withdrawn. The consequence is, that in seasons of abundance the bill-brokers will discount at a lower rate than the bankers, and when money is scarce they discount at a higher rate, and in many cases will not discount at all. Sharp-sighted people, who are acquainted with the London money market, will, when money is abundant, take all their first-rate bills to a bill-broker, and send to their banker all their inferior bills, which a bill-broker would not take. Now, if a banker has occasion to curtail his advances in seasons of pressure, he should begin with people of this sort. But if he has ample means, and the parties are wealthy, he may deem it worth his while to take their bills, charging a high rate of interest, and gently reminding them of their former delinquencies. Exhortations to good behaviour have always a greater effect when administered in seasons of affliction. And reproof at this time to a party who has thus wandered, may induce him to pursue in future a more righteous line of conduct.

During a pressure, a banker will find that some of his customers will get into difficulties, and will apply to him for assistance. He will often be at a loss to decide whether he should or should not grant the assistance required. This hesitation will arise from his doubts as to the extent to which he can prudently rely upon the calculations and anticipations of his customer. The party states that he must immediately stop payment unless he has assistance; but he has abundance of property, and his difficulties arise only from not being able to realise it. If he has a certain sum he can then go on comfortably. The banker grants him this sum. After a while, he comes again, and states he must now stop unless he has a farther sum. The banker hesitates, but ultimately gives him this farther sum. He comes a third time, and states he has not yet got enough; and not being able to get more, he then stops, leaving the banker at best with a large lock-up, and probably with an ultimate loss.

During a pressure, those banks that allow interest on deposits will be asked for a higher rate of interest. It is quite right that those parties who have had deposits at the bank for some time, should receive a higher rate of interest, proportionate to the increased value of money. But it may be questioned whether it is worth while to receive farther lodgments, during a pressure, at a high rate of interest, unless they are lodged for a fixed period. For, should the pressure increase, these sums are sure to be withdrawn, or else applications will be made for a higher rate of interest than the banker can prudently give. Nor must it be forgotten that it is not wise for a banker to give, during a panic, an extravagant rate of interest. Should he do so, he will give rise to an opinion that he is short of funds, and this may cause more deposits to be withdrawn than he would obtain from his high rate of interest.

During a pressure, a banker will pay considerable attention to the published returns of the Bank of England. The increase or diminution of the gold and silver in the issuing department, will show the progress of the pressure. As these increase, money will become less scarce, the rate of interest will fall, and the pressure will subside. In this department, it is the progress of increase, or diminution, more than the actual amount, that should be the main object of attention. The banking department resembles any other bank. Its means are the paid-up capital—the real or surplus fund—the public deposits—the private deposits, and the seven-day bills. These means are employed in public securities, private securities, and cash in the till. Its ability to make advances, at any given time, depends on the amount of cash in the till. The diminution of this amount shows the increase of the pressure, and the banker will act accordingly.

As far as past experience goes, all panics or pressures have resulted in a subsequent abundance of money. It would be a grand thing for a banker if he could know beforehand at what precise point this change would take place. But this he cannot know, and he had better not speculate on the subject, but just follow the course of events as they occur. When, however, the point is fairly turned, he will act wisely in investing all his surplus funds in such convertible securities as are likely to advance in price, from the increasing low rate of interest. Exchequer bills are most likely to be the first affected, and then the public funds. He will, also, be more liberal in granting discounts, and other advances, and he will lower the rate of interest at which he takes deposits. At the same time, he will be cautious in the bills he discounts. For, though money may be abundant, yet trade may be depressed, and the effects of the previous panic may be the failure of a great number of persons in the middle class of society. The banker will therefore be cautious in extending his discounts, except on bills of an undoubted character.

We will observe, lastly, that, in a season of pressure, it is peculiarly necessary that a banker should pay regard to the state of his own health, and to the discipline of his own mind, so as to guard against any morbid or gloomy apprehensions with regard to the future. He should attempt to form a cool and dispassionate judgment as to the result of passing events ; endeavouring so to arrange his own affairs as to be prepared for whatever may occur, but taking care not to increase the present evil by predicting greater calamities. If he suffer a feeling of despondency to get the mastery of his mind, he will be less able to cope with the difficulties of his position. He will then, probably, refuse reasonable assistance to even first-rate customers, realise securities unnecessarily at a heavy sacrifice, and keep in his till an amount of unemployed treasure excessively disproportionate to the extent of his liabilities. This will increase the pressure. Fear, too, is always contagious. A banker of this melancholy temperament will impart his apprehensions to others, and thus the panic will become more widely extended.

Q

SECTION VIII.

THE ADMINISTRATION OF A BANK UNDER THE ACT OF 1844.

IT would not be consistent with the practical character of this work to discuss, at great length, any theory of the currency. But the Act of 1844, though founded on a theory, was a practical measure, and has so important a bearing on the administration of banking affairs, that our work would be regarded as incomplete were the subject altogether omitted.

" The Act of 1844 " is the 7 & 8 Vict. cap. 32, and is entitled, " An Act to regulate the Issue of Bank Notes, and for giving to the Governor and Company of the Bank of England certain privileges for a limited period." It enacts that from and after the 31st August, 1844, the Issue department of the Bank of England shall be separated from the Banking department——that the issuing department may issue notes to the extent of 14,000,000*l.* upon securities set apart for that purpose, of which the debt of 11,015,100*l.* due from the Government to the bank shall form a part—that no amount of notes above 14,000,000*l.* shall be issued, except against gold coin, or gold or silver bullion ; and that the silver bullion shall not exceed one-fourth the amount of gold coin and bullion. Any person is entitled to demand notes from the issuing department, in exchange for gold bullion, at the rate of 3*l.* 17*s.* 9*d.* per ounce. Should any banker discontinue his issue of notes, the Bank of England may, upon application, be empowered by an Order of Council to increase her issue upon securities to the extent of two-thirds of the issue thus withdrawn ; but all the profit of this increased issue must go to the Government.

The theory on which this Act was founded had, for several years previously, been brought before the public in pamphlets written by men of distinguished talent. Upon some of these pamphlets we wrote a critique, which appeared in the " Westminster Review " of January, 1841. That article was afterwards published separately, under the title of " Currency and Banking : a Review of some of the Principles and Plans that have recently engaged public attention, with reference to the administration of the Currency." In this review we made the following observations on the plan then proposed, and subsequently carried out in the Act of 1844 :—

" *The plan of making the amount of the circulation fluctuate in exact cor-*
respondence with the amount of gold in the Bank of England.

" This plan is open to the following objections :—

" Upon this plan there must be a perpetual increase and diminution in
the stock of gold ; consequently a perpetual increase and diminution in
the amount of the currency. The increase in the amount of the currency
would raise prices and stimulate speculation. The diminution in the
amount of the currency would reduce prices and produce distress. And
thus there must be a constant alteration from high prices to low prices,
and again from low prices to high prices—from speculation to distress,
and from distress to speculation.

" 2. But depression of prices, and their attendant miseries, may not be
experienced only when the foreign exchanges are unfavourable. Excessive
caution, an apprehension of war, or political feeling, may cause a domestic
demand for gold, and this would cause for a while a contraction of the
currency as severe as that which would arise from an unfavourable
exchange ; and, as the bank directors would have no discretionary power,
but would be required ' to adhere to principle,' by giving gold for notes, or
notes for gold, they could do nothing to assuage these calamities. According to Mr. Loyd, a drain, from whatever cause it may arise, must be
met by a contraction of the currency. Mr. Palmer, in laying down his
rule, put in a saving clause—' except under special circumstances,' but
Mr. Loyd* makes no exceptions.

" 3. To carry this system into operation, would require a separation of
the issuing department from the other departments of the business of the
bank, and this would cause still farther inconveniences. The management
of the issuing department would be exceedingly simple. The office of the
directors would be a complete sinecure, and, for anything they would
have to do, their places might be as well supplied by four-and-twenty
broomsticks. A few cashiers to exchange gold for notes, or notes for gold,
would be all the establishment required ; and could Mr. Babbage be
induced to construct a ' self-acting ' machine to perform these operations,
the whole business of the currency department might be carried
on without human agency. But the deposit department would require
more attention. ' It is in the nature of banking business,' says Mr. Loyd,
' that the amount of its deposits should vary with a variety of circumstances ;
and, as the amount of deposits varies, the amount of that in which those
deposits are invested (viz., the securities) must vary also. It is, therefore, quite absurd to talk of the bank, in its character of a banking
concern, keeping the amount of its securities invariable.' As, therefore,
the deposits might vary, the bank would be a buyer or a seller of
Government securities ; and as these variations are sometimes to a very

* I wish I could have made this quotation without introducing the names.
It would greatly assist our inquiries after truth, and lead to the formation of an
independent judgment, if we could engage in discussions of this kind without
any reference to those talented men who may have distinguished themselves as
either the advocates or the opponents of the doctrines we investigate.

large amount, the fluctuations in the price of the public funds, and of exchequer bills, would be very considerable. Thus the property of those who held these securities would be always changing in value. Again, the deposits would be withdrawn chiefly in seasons of pressure, and the bank would then be compelled to sell her securities. But suppose the scarcity of money should be so great that the securities would be unsaleable even at a reduced price, how then could the bank pay off her deposits?

" 4. If the currency were administered upon this principle, the bank would be unable to grant assistance to the commercial and manufacturing classes in seasons of calamity.

" Mr. Loyd exclaims, ' Let not the borrowers of money, Government and Commerce, approach, with their dangerous and seductive influences, the creator of money.' But, with all deference to Mr. Loyd, we contend that it is the province of a bank to afford assistance to trade and commerce in seasons of pressure. Mr. Loyd, as a practical banker, would no doubt afford assistance to his own customers in such seasons ; and if this be the province and duty of a private banker, the duty is more imperative on a public banking company, and more imperative still on a bank invested by the legislature with peculiar privileges for the public good. Mr. Loyd says, ' Let the bank afford this assistance out of her own funds.' But, under Mr. Loyd's system, she could grant assistance only by selling securities ; and what relief would she afford by selling securities with one hand, and lending out the money with the other ? Besides, is it certain that, under such a pressure as Mr. Loyd's system must occasionally produce, these securities would be saleable at even any price ? ' But,' says Mr. Loyd, ' individuals may afford this assistance.' In seasons of pressure few individuals have more ample funds than what are necessary for the supply of their own wants. . . . When the distress is caused by a contraction of the currency, it can only be removed by an increased issue of notes. And there are many cases, such for instance as that of the Northern and Central Bank, in which assistance can only be effectually rendered in this manner.

" We consider that any system of administering the currency, which prohibits the banking institutions of the country from granting relief to the commercial and manufacturing classes, must be unsound. We should condemn such a system at once, even if we could not detect the fallacies on which it was founded. In political economy we can judge of principles only by their practical effects—and any system which produces these effects must be unsound. When seasons of calamity occur, it is not for the national bank to exclaim, *Sauve qui peut.* They ought to co-operate with the Government in attempting to relieve the distress, and to preserve the tranquillity of the country."

These remarks, written in the year 1841, might, if put into the past tense, almost serve for a history of the year 1847. The Act of 1844 was formed upon the principle which is here condemned ; and the effects described have actually occurred.

There have been great fluctuations in the amount of the circulation, in the rate of interest, and in the prices of the public securities. There have been great speculations, followed by great distress. The Government funds have in large amounts been unsaleable; and the bank has been unable to afford relief to the commercial classes. A severe pressure has taken place; and, in consequence of this severe pressure, the Act was suspended. It has been denied that this pressure was produced or increased by the Act. But, how stand the facts? The Act was passed, and, as predicted, a pressure came : the Act was continued, and the pressure increased : the Act was suspended, and the pressure went away. These are not opinions—they are facts.

At the meeting of Parliament in the latter end of 1847, committees were appointed by both the House of Lords and the House of Commons, to " inquire into the causes of the distress which has for some time prevailed among the commercial classes; and how far it has been affected by the laws for regulating the issue of bank notes payable on demand." The following is an extract from the Report of the Lords' Committee as to the causes of the pressure :—

" A sudden and unexampled demand for foreign corn, produced by a failure in many descriptions of agricultural produce throughout the United Kingdom, coincided with the unprecedented extent of speculation produced by increased facilities of credit and a low rate of interest, and had for some time occasioned over-trading in many branches of commerce. This was more especially felt in railroads, for which calls to a large amount were daily becoming payable, without corresponding funds to meet them, except by the withdrawal of capital from other pursuits and investments. These causes account for much of the pressure under which many of the weaker commercial firms were doomed to sink, and which was felt even by the strongest. To these causes may be added a contemporaneous rise of price in cotton ; and, with respect to houses connected with the East and West India trade, a sudden and extensive fall in the price of sugar, by which the value of their most readily available assets underwent great depreciation.

" Some of these causes are obviously beyond the reach of legislative control. But upon those which are connected with the extension of commercial speculation, encouraged or checked by the facility or the difficulty of obtaining credit by the advance of capital and the discount of bills, the powers and position of the Bank of England must at all times enable that corporation to exercise an important influence. The committee have consequently felt it to be their duty to inquire into the course pursued by the bank acting under the provisions of the 7 & 8 Vict. c. 32, and they have come to the conclusion that the recent panic was materially aggravated by the operation of that statute, and by the proceedings of the bank itself. This effect may be traced, directly, to the Act of 1844, in the legislative restriction imposed on the means of accommodation, whilst a large amount of bullion was held in the coffers of the bank, and during a time of favourable exchanges; and it may be traced to the same cause, indirectly, as a consequence of great fluctuations in the rate of discount, and of capital previously advanced at an unusually low rate of interest. This course the bank would hardly have felt itself justified in taking, had not an impression existed that, by the separation of the issue and the banking departments, one inflexible rule for regulating the bank issues had been substituted by law in place of the discretion formerly vested in the bank."

The nature and extent of the pressure is thus described by the Governor and Deputy-Governor of the Bank of England:—

"The panic began by the failures in the corn trade. The price of wheat had risen to about 120s. Large arrivals of grain from the continent of Europe and from America, coupled with the prospect of an early and abundant harvest, caused a sudden fall in price to about 60s., with a corresponding decline in Indian corn. The failure of most of the corn speculators followed this great reduction in price, and their failure caused the stoppage of an eminent discount broker having a large country connexion. This latter failure, by closing one of the principal channels of discount between the country and London, caused distrust to extend into the country. Credit became affected by these failures, and several London firms of high standing also failed. Then followed in rapid succession the failure of the Royal Bank of Liverpool, the Liverpool Banking Company, the North and South Wales Banking Company, some private country banks, and the Union Bank of Newcastle, followed by a tremendous run upon the Northumberland and Durham District Bank. To these disasters succeeded alarm, and an almost total prostration of credit. The London bankers and discount brokers refused to grant the usual accommodation to their customers, and necessarily obliged every one requiring assistance to resort to the Bank of England. Money was hoarded to a considerable extent: so much so, that notwithstanding the notes and coin issued to the public in October, exceeded by 4,000,000l. or 5,000,000l. the amount with the public in August, still the general complaint was of a scarcity of money. Credit was so entirely destroyed, that houses trading to distant countries, carrying on their business through the means of credit by a renewal of their acceptances as they became due, were no longer able to meet their engagements, and were forced to stop payment. This was the state of things previous to the issuing of the Government letter in October." *

The Committee of the House of Commons delivered a Report in favour of the continuance of the bill without

* Lords, No. 12.

alteration—in opposition to the opinions of by far the majority of the witnesses who were examined.

Those witnesses who are friendly to the Act contend that it has secured the convertibility of the Bank of England note—that this convertibility was endangered in 1825, in 1837, and in 1839, and would have been endangered in 1847 but for this Act.[*]

By the phrase " securing the convertibility of the note," it is not meant that the issue department of the Bank of England held a sufficient amount of gold and silver to pay off all the notes it had issued. It is obvious that the gold and silver in hand must always be fourteen millions less than this amount, inasmuch as fourteen millions of notes are issued against securities. By " securing the convertibility of the note," is meant, that the issue department of the Bank of England were in a condition to pay off any amount of notes of which payment was likely to be demanded *for the purpose of exporting the gold*—the issue department was always in a condition to meet any *foreign* demand for gold. This is called, " securing the convertibility of the note."

It has been contended, that the Act has retained in the vaults of the Bank of England a larger amount of gold and silver than would otherwise have been retained. And as this amount is set apart for the express purpose of paying the notes, their payment is so far additionally secured. On the other hand, it has been maintained that, by thus reserving all the gold to pay the notes, we endangered the payment of the deposits. And had the banking department stopped payment, a domestic run would have taken place upon the issuing department, and thus the payment of the notes would still have been endangered.

The following is the evidence of a director of the Bank of Liverpool upon the subject :

" With regard to securing the convertibility of the notes, what is your opinion of the bill ?

" I do not think it has secured the convertibility of the notes at all. The notes remained convertible up to the suspension of the bill; but I believe that, if the bill had not been suspended then, or some similar measure adopted, notes would have ceased to be convertible. Looking to

---

[*] See the Evidence before the Committee of the House of Lords, Questions No. 1406 to 1409, and No. 3169.

the general state of things throughout the country, and to what I know
to have been the state of things in London, and the position of trade
generally—to the alarm that was spreading rapidly through the country,
and to the fact that the power of the bank had been reduced to such a
point, that if there had been any apprehension of the failure of the
country banks, it could not farther support them, and that very little
might have occasioned (I might perhaps go farther, and say, would have
occasioned) the failure of banks in large towns and in the country—
believing that if one or two country banks of any magnitude had failed,
alarm would have spread throughout the kingdom, or if one or two
London banks had failed, consternation would have been general—
seeing, also, the considerable amount of reserve in the hands of the
country bankers and joint-stock banks, and the necessity that there
would have been of having that reserve as early as possible converted
into gold if the bank was obliged to stop—seeing that a reserve of
20,000*l.* for each of 300 country banks would have taken six or seven
millions, or of 15,000*l.* each would have taken five millions—and that if
the run for gold had once begun, it would probably have gone on till
the treasury was drained—seeing all this, my firm opinion is, that the
bill of 1844 has not secured convertibility, and I state the grounds on
which that opinion is formed." *

It seems useless at present to speculate upon such a state
of things, as we NOW know that before the pressure arrived to
such a height as to cause the banking department to stop
payment, the Act would be suspended. But it seems fair to
ask, whether the precautions of the Act are not disproportionate to the danger? We ought to consider not merely
the greatness of the evil, but also the probability of its
occurrence; and is it wise to inflict upon ourselves a vast
number of serious evils merely to guard against a danger that
may never occur? It may farther be asked, whether the
stringent measures that were necessary to keep the banking
department from stopping payment, would not have been
equally effectual under the previous state of the law in
preserving the convertibility of the notes?

It should be recollected, too, that previous to the passing
of the Act of 1844, the bank had the power of rectifying the
exchanges by means of foreign credits, as they did in the
year 1839.† But the directors, being now relieved from all
responsibility with regard to the issue department, have no
inducement to engage in such an operation. Indeed, they

* Commons, No. 94.

† Several of the witnesses made suggestions for rectifying this exchange by
other means than the exportation of gold.—See Commons, 97, 2018, 2023, 2579,
2614, 2620.

might be censured for interfering with the principle of the Act, that the exchanges shall be rectified by a transmission of gold and silver.

It would appear from the evidence, that the SOLE advantage NOW claimed for the Act, is that it has secured the convertibility of the note. Other advantages, however, were expected to result. Those expectations are thus disposed of in the Report of the Lords' Committee :—

" It is true that to those who may have expected that the 7 & 8 Vict. c. 32, would effectually prevent a recurrence of cycles of commercial excitement and depression, the contract between the years 1845 and 1847 must produce a grievous disappointment. To those who anticipated that the Act would put a check on improvident speculation, the disappointment cannot be less, if reliance is to be placed (as the committee are confident it may) on the statement of the governor of the bank, and of other witnesses, that ' speculations were never carried to such an enormous extent as in 1846 and the beginning of 1847.' If the Act were relied on as a security against violent fluctuations in the value of money, the fallaciousness of such anticipation is conclusively proved by the fact, that whilst the difference between the highest and lowest rate of discount was in the calamitous years 1837 and 1839 but $2\frac{1}{4}$ to $2\frac{3}{4}$ per cent., the difference in 1847 rose to $6\frac{1}{2}$. If it was contemplated that the number and the extent of commercial failures would have been lessened, the deplorable narrative of the governor of the bank, recording the failure of thirty-three houses comparatively in large business, in London alone, to the amount of 8,129,000*l.*, is a conclusive reply. If the enormous extent to which railroad speculation has been carried be considered as an evil to which a sound system of banking could have applied a corrective, such a corrective has not been found in an Act, since the passing of which, during a period of three years, an increased railway capital of upwards of 221,000,000*l.* has been authorized to be raised by Parliament ; and when the enormous sum of 76,390,000*l.* is stated, on high financial authority, to have been actually expended on railways in two years and a half. If the power of obtaining banking accommodation on moderate terms were considered to be promoted by the Act of 1844, it cannot be said that this important object has been attained, since it appears in evidence that in 1847, in addition to an interest of 9 or 10 per cent., a commission was also frequently paid, raising the charge to 10, 20, or 30 per cent., according to the time which bills had to run."

The Report might have added, that if it was expected that the amount of notes in the hands of the public would fluctuate in exact correspondence with the fluctuations in the amount of gold in the Bank of England, that expectation has not been fulfilled. From the censure cast on the Bank of England before the Act was passed for not producing this correspondence, it may be inferred that such an expectation was entertained.*

Those who are opposed to the Act of 1844 bring against it the following accusations :—

First. The Act of 1844 is accused of having produced an abundance of money and a low rate of interest, and thus to have stimulated to excessive speculation. We showed, in the last Section, that these are always the precursors of a pressure.

According to this Act, all persons are entitled to demand from the issue department of the Bank of England, Bank of England notes in exchange for gold bullion at the rate of 3*l*. 17*s*. 9*d*. per ounce of standard gold. When, therefore, the foreign exchanges are favourable to the importation of gold, this gold, consisting of gold bars and foreign gold coin, which could not be used as money in this country, is taken to the issue department, and instantly converted into Bank of England notes. The amount of notes is thus increased beyond what the transactions of the country require. Money becomes plentiful, the rate of interest falls, and the low rate of interest gives facilities to speculative undertakings.

It must be acknowledged that, previous to the passing of this Act, the bank directors had adopted the principle of purchasing all foreign gold that might be offered them at 3*l*. 17*s*. 9*d*. an ounce ; and it formed a feature of their system of management, as explained before a committee of the House of Commons in the year 1832. When the advocates of the Act say that it is only during a season of pressure that the Act comes into operation,† they can mean only that it is during such a season that the system established by the Act differs from the system previously in existence. The Act is as much in operation when it gives out notes as when it gives out gold.

It must also be acknowledged that on the 31st August, 1844, when the Act came into operation, there was a large amount of gold in the bank, and a low rate of interest consequently prevailed. This gold had accumulated, not literally in consequence of the Act, but in consequence of the principle embodied in the Act. From the adoption of this principle, the gold in the

* See the Evidence taken before the Committee on Banks of Issue, No. 2677 —2713.

† Commons, 5121.

vaults of the bank still farther increased after the passing of the Act.

It must be farther acknowledged, that although the Act requires the issue department at all times to issue notes against gold, it does not require that the Bank of England shall at all times issue 14,000,000*l.* against securities. The Act merely requires that the amount *shall not exceed* 14,000,000*l.* And a London banker who was examined as a witness before the Lords' Committee, said he expected that when the Act came into operation the bank would not issue at first more than 11,000,000*l.* against securities, and that the remaining 3,000,000*l.* would not be issued until the rate of interest had advanced to 3¼ or 4 per cent. But the Act did not require the Bank of England to adopt this course; and its adoption would probably have been considered by some parties as a departure from its principle. For it is a fundamental principle of the Act, that the amount of circulation shall jerk up and down in exact conformity to the importations or exportations of gold. And hence during a favourable course of exchange money must be abundant, and interest must be low.

It is alleged that the Act still farther reduced the rate of interest, and promoted speculative undertakings, by placing the Bank of England in a position in which the directors were led to adopt a new system of management.

In September, 1844, soon after the Act was passed, the directors, whose rate of interest had never previously been lower than 4 per cent., reduced it to 2½ per cent. The object of this reduction was to invest a larger portion of their funds in the discount of bills. It is stated that, to effect this object, the directors not only reduced their rate of discount, but also canvassed for business, and thus gave a stimulus to new transactions. They had been told that the banking department of the Bank of England was to be managed "like any other banking concern using Bank of England notes." And it is not an unusual thing for bankers, when they cannot employ their funds at so high a rate of interest as they wish to obtain, to employ them at a lower rate. Nor is it unusual for a banker to offer his surplus cash to bill-brokers and others, who are known to be in the habit of supplying bankers with bills. But however consistent the conduct of the directors may have been with banking principles, the reduction of the bank rate of discount immediately caused a reduction in the market rate, and in the rates charged by bankers throughout the country. For it must be observed, that when the bank lowers her rate of interest upon money in seasons of abundance, it has the necessary effect of reducing the market rate of interest still lower than the bank rate. Suppose, for instance, the bank discounts at 5 per cent. and the market rate of discount is 4 per cent., of course no bills are offered for discount to the bank. Then the bank, to get discounts, lowers her rate of interest to 4 per cent. A portion of bills that were previously discounted by private bankers and bill-brokers will then be taken to the bank; but the notes thus drawn from the bank make money still more plentiful, and the market rate falls to $3\frac{1}{2}$ or 3 per cent. Now, should the bank reduce her rate to 3 per cent. the same effects would again follow. For the additional notes thus drawn out would make money so abundant as to reduce the market rate of interest to $2\frac{1}{2}$ or 2 per cent., and so on.

But in seasons of scarcity, precisely the opposite effect follows. For when the bank raises the rate of discount, it has the effect of raising the market rate still higher. Thus, if the bank should be discounting at 5 per cent. and the market rate should be $5\frac{1}{2}$ per cent., let the bank raise her rate to 6 per cent. and the market rate will immediately become 7 or perhaps 8 per cent., or even higher upon inferior bills. For the bank rate of discount will be the market rate for only the first class of bills—such bills as could be discounted at the bank; and all bills of the second class will have to pay an advanced rate, and those of a still more inferior character will not be discountable at all.

In 1844 the rate of discount was lower than in any previous season of abundance of money. This low rate of interest was produced, in the first place, by the principle of the Act of 1844, which caused the issue of a large amount of notes against gold and silver bullion; and, secondly, by that provision of the Act which separated the two departments, and thus brought the banking department of the Bank of England into competition with other bankers and money dealers, as discounters of bills.* The directors of the bank seem to think that the spirit of the Act of 1844 required that the bank should employ its reserve.

* Commons, 2275, 5189, 5347-5350.

" If we keep the notes in the reserve, instead of giving them out to the public, the effect that ought to be produced by gold coming into the country is counteracted; it induces a larger amount of capital to come into the country, because you do not allow that portion which has come in to be employed. If you do not put out the gold, or the representative of gold, you entirely prevent its having any effect upon the circulation. The exchange will be kept up, and gold will continue to come in." *

Thus it appears that, although there is no positive enactment in the Act respecting the management of the banking department, the directors so understand its spirit as to believe that when gold is going out of the country they ought to take measures to prevent its exit; and when gold is coming into the country, they ought to endeavour to drive it back again. The first object is attained by raising the rate of interest very high; the second, by reducing it very low. It must, however, be acknowledged that, apart from any efforts of the banking department, a large importation of gold will under the Act necessarily cause a low rate of interest.

Secondly. The next charge against the Act of 1844 is, that it does not admit of those occasional expansions of the amount of notes in circulation which are often required by the domestic transactions of the country.

It is alleged that one imperfection of the Act was strikingly manifested in the beginning of the year 1846. The Parliament required that all railway companies that intended to apply for an Act, should lodge 10 per cent. on their capital within fifteen days after the meeting of Parliament. It was impossible to say beforehand what amount of notes would be required to make these payments. It was variously estimated at from 12,000,000*l.* to 25,000,000*l.*, while all the notes in the hands of the public amounted to only about 20,000,000*l.* Ultimately the railway companies of Ireland and Scotland were allowed to make their payments in Dublin and Edinburgh, respectively; and the payments in London did not amount to more than 14,000,000*l.*† This large sum was paid by means of the banking department of the Bank of England lending out the money as fast as it was received. Had the Act of 1844 not been in existence, the Bank of England (as in the case of the West India loan, and of previous loans) might have lent out the money before the time of payment arrived, and no apprehensions would have been

* Commons, 3009.   † Lords, 1209, 1214.

entertained.   The notes in circulation would have been largely increased for a few days, and then again have subsided to the former amount.   As it was, the payment was not made through any virtue in the Act.   And had it been required under different circumstances, or when the banking department had a smaller reserve, it could not have been made at all.*

It is farther alleged, that the Act of 1844 requires an immediate contraction in the amount of the notes whenever gold is exported for merely a temporary or specific purpose.   Between March 13 and April 24, 1847, 2,237,200*l*. was exported in payments for corn.   An equal amount of notes was of course cancelled by the issue department.   The notes must have been taken out of the hands of the public, or from the banking department of the Bank of England.   About the same time, the Government had occasion to borrow of the banking department about 3,500,000*l*. to pay the April dividends.   The banking department, consequently, for a while limited their discounts, and even refused to grant loans on exchequer bills.   Great pressure was consequently felt, though it did not last for a long time.   Now it is alleged, that if the Act of 1844 had not existed, the directors would have allowed the gold to be exported without *immediately* contracting the notes in circulation.   They would have lent the money required by the Government, without refusing the loans and discounts to the public; and the contraction of the circulation, by being extended over one or two months, instead of a few weeks, might have produced no inconvenience.

By the Act of 1844, the circulation of the country banks was restricted to a certain amount.   The average of the twelve weeks ending the 27th of April, 1844, was fixed for the maximum.   During some months in the year the country requires more notes than this maximum ; and, as the banks can issue no more notes of their own, they obtain Bank of England notes from London.   In the year 1845 Acts of Parliament were passed for the regulation of the notes issued in Scotland and Ireland.   Beyond certain fixed amounts, the banks in these countries are required to hold gold equal to the amount of notes in circulation.   In both countries this circulation fluctuates. In Scotland, the highest amount is in November.   In Ireland, the highest amount is in January or February.   In these

* Lords, 1209.

months they require more gold, and this gold they obtain from the issue department in exchange for Bank of England notes. Before the Act of 1844, the circulation of the country parts of England, of Scotland, and of Ireland, expanded or contracted as required by the wants of the public, without affecting the London circulation of the Bank of England; but under this Act, the expansion of the circulation of the country banks, the banks of Scotland, and of Ireland, are attended by a contraction of the circulation of Bank of England notes in London. This may not be a matter of much consequence in ordinary times, when the banking department of the Bank of England has a large reserve; but in seasons of pressure, such as occurred in 1847, this drain on the London circulation may be more severely felt.

It may be farther stated, that the withdrawal or discontinuance of a certain amount of bills of exchange, through loss of credit or otherwise, would render a larger amount of bank notes necessary to fill up the space formerly occupied by those bills of exchange. But for such a circumstance no provision is made by the Act.*

Thirdly. It is alleged that the Act of 1844 tends to produce and to aggravate pressure, and at the same time deprives the Bank of England of the power of granting adequate assistance, even when the pressure is most urgent, and when assistance can be rendered without any danger of affecting the foreign exchanges.

This objection assumes that a pressure is an evil. It assumes, that to advance the rate of interest to a rate which no profit can afford to pay—to deprive solvent houses of the means of meeting their legitimate engagements—to cause a universal reduction of prices, and thus to baffle the calculations of even the most prudent—to reduce wealthy merchants to the condition of paupers—to deprive manufacturers of the means of executing their orders, and thus to throw thousands of industrious people out of employment—to sell to foreigners large amounts of goods and manufactures at less than the prime cost, thus causing a great national loss—to paralyse the national industry—to stop the progress of useful works—and to destroy confidence and credit—the objection assumes, that a pressure which produces effects like these is a national evil. And such must be the

* Lords, 232—235.

opinion of those who suspended the Act, and of those who approve of that suspension; for it was to prevent or to remove evils like these that the Act was suspended.

It is alleged that the Act tends to produce such pressures. By issuing notes against all the importations of gold, it causes abundance of money, lowers the rate of interest, and stimulates to speculative undertaking (thus the low rate of interest in 1844 and 1845 stimulated the railway speculations), and then, speculation is always succeeded by pressure. If, therefore, similar causes produce similar effects, and if the future shall resemble the past, the operation of the Act of 1844 will tend to produce pressure.

It is farther alleged, that when a pressure occurs without being produced by the Act, then the Act tends to aggravate the pressure. An unfavourable course of the exchange may be produced by a large importation of corn. The Act requires that the exchange shall be rectified by an exportation of gold, and that this exportation of gold shall be attended by a contraction of the domestic circulation (according to the present meaning of the word circulation) to an equal amount. It is hardly necessary to show that these regulations must aggravate a pressure.

It has been said, that the pressure of 1847 was produced by the railway speculations and the famine, and *therefore* it was not produced or increased by the Act of 1844. We do not perceive the soundness of this reasoning, and it seems to show a forgetfulness of the peculiar operation of the Act. The Act requires that the amount of notes in circulation shall fluctuate in exact accordance with the amount of bullion. Railway speculations, famine, foreign loans, or a hundred other things, may turn the foreign exchanges, and cause gold to be exported, but it is the Act which causes our circulation of notes to be contracted in proportion as the gold is withdrawn. So a hundred different circumstances may cause gold to be imported, but it is the Act which causes our circulation to be inflated in correspondence with this increased amount of gold. Herein, we think, is the injurious operation of the Act. When the exchanges are favourable, gold is imported. The gold is in bars and foreign coin, and could not pass as money. But the Act issues notes against this gold, thus increasing the circulation, lowering the rate of interest, and giving rise to speculations of all kinds. These speculations, co-operating possibly with other causes, turn the exchanges. Notes are then taken to the bank, and gold demanded, for the purpose of being exported. This contraction of the circulation of notes produces pressure, and the apprehension of farther pressure produces panic.

They who contend that the Act of 1844 has not "in the slightest degree tended either to create or to increase the pressure"* of 1847, seem to be inconsistent in contending, at the same time, that the Act has preserved the convertibility of the bank note. It was the pressure and the high rate of interest, and low prices consequent upon the pressure, that checked the efflux of gold, and turned the exchanges. Now, if the Act had no effect in producing or increasing that pressure, the convertibility of the note, by whatever causes it was secured, was not secured by the Act. If the Act did not in the slightest degree either create or increase the pressure, in what way, we ask, could it preserve the convertibility of the note? It appears to us that those who contend that the Act preserved the convertibility of the note, are bound by consistency to admit that the Act produced or increased the pressure.

It is farther alleged that the Act aggravates a pressure by the "panic" which it creates. It is stated that, during the pressure of 1847, notes to the amount of 4,000,000*l.* were hoarded under the influence of panic, and this hoarding was occasioned by the provisions of the Act. It must be acknowledged, however, that something of this kind has taken place in former pressures. We noticed this circumstance with reference to the pressure of 1836, and again with reference to the pressure of 1839.

A contraction of the circulation leads to a general apprehension of danger. Hence the bankers and others keep larger reserves of bank notes on hand, in order to be prepared for the worst, and thus the evils of the contraction are considerably increased. That portion of the notes of the Bank of England which is passing from hand to hand, may be called the active circulation. That portion which is hoarded, or kept in reserve to meet possible demands, may be called the dead circulation. Now, it is quite certain that the dead circulation, while it remains in that state, has no effect upon the prices of commodities—the spirit of speculation—or the foreign exchanges.

* Lords, 3106.

R

These are affected only by the active circulation. In seasons of pressure the dead circulation is increased at the expense of the active circulation, because people hoard their money to meet contingencies. Hence we find the pressure is often more severe than the reduction of the bank circulation would seem to warrant. But the fact is, that the pressure is in proportion to the reduction of the active circulation, and not in proportion to the reduction of the whole circulation. On the other hand, in seasons of abundance, the dead circulation is diminished, the active circulation proportionably increased, and hence the stimulus given to trade and speculation is much greater than the returns of the Bank of England would warrant us to expect.

If this disposition to hoard—or, more properly, to make provision for future or contingent demands—existed in 1837 and 1839, when the Bank of England had the unrestricted power of issuing notes; when there was the most unbounded confidence in her ability to render assistance—and when every solvent person expected, if necessary, to receive that assistance —it is natural to suppose that this disposition would be stronger in 1847, when the Bank of England had become divided into two departments—one of which could issue no notes except against gold, and the other had barely notes enough to meet its own obligations. For this alteration in the condition of the Bank of England, and the consequent feelings it inspired, the Act of 1844 is clearly responsible.

It is said that this desire of " hoarding " arose from PANIC; and that the sum thus " hoarded " amounted to 4,000,000*l.* of notes. It is difficult to state where prudence ends and panic begins. This hoarding was no doubt carried on by all the joint-stock and private bankers, who, having received from the public large sums of money payable on demand, deemed it prudent to put themselves in a condition to repay these sums in case they should be demanded. And, from the number of banking establishments that exist in London, and throughout the country, it is reasonable to suppose that the sums thus hoarded must have been considerable. Many private parties, too, from distrust of their bankers, probably kept their hoards in their own hands. No blame, however, can attach to the bankers; for, although this " hoarding " increases the pressure, yet, were they not to adopt this course, their banks might stop payment, and thus a heavier calamity would fall upon the public.

It is farther alleged that the Act of 1844 has deprived the Bank of England of the power of granting assistance by the issue of notes during a pressure, even when the pressure is most urgent, and the foreign exchanges are favourable. Before the passing of the Act, when there was no separation of departments, the bank directors restricted their issues when the exchanges were unfavourable, but extended them when the exchanges were favourable. Hence, during the pressure of 1837, they granted assistance by a farther issue of notes to the Northern and Central Bank, because the exchanges had become favourable. Between the periods of an efflux and an influx of gold there is always an interval of time. This interval is usually the highest point of the pressure; and heretofore the Bank of England would relieve the pressure by extending her issue of notes, in anticipation of the gold about to arrive. By this means solvent houses were prevented stopping. Confidence was restored, " hoarding " was diminished, and the pressure removed. But the Act of 1844 does not allow this. No additional notes can be issued until the gold has returned. The same course must be followed, whether the exchanges are favourable or unfavourable; and to anticipate the return of the gold, by a farther issue of notes, under any circumstances, however urgent, would be a departure from the principle of the Act. That such a departure, however, may be made with immense advantage to the public, is obvious from the effects which immediately followed the suspension of the Act in October, 1847.*

It is chiefly in this respect that the system established by the Act differs from the system previously in operation. And some of the witnesses, looking no farther than this, merely recommended that a power to suspend the Act in cases of severe pressure, should be lodged either with the Government or the Bank. We feel no regret that the Legislature did not comply with this recommendation. It is this inflexibility of the Act which makes the commercial classes *feel* the unsoundness of its whole principle. Had a dispensing power been granted, we should merely have fallen back upon the previous system, with the additional disadvantage that the bank would never be

* Commons, 5387—5389.

able to adopt a better system, even if so disposed. The directors had for several years professed to govern the issue of notes by the foreign exchanges, but departed from that principle according to their discretion. The Act of 1844, by its inflexible enactment, put this principle to the test of experiment. The principle could not bear that test, and hence the Act was suspended. There is now a chance, at least, that we shall, ultimately, get a better system. The following is the language we addressed to the joint-stock banks at the time the Act was passed :—

"It must be acknowledged that the principle of regulating the currency by the stock of bullion in the Bank of England, as proposed by Sir Robert Peel, is one which the joint-stock banks, as well as the private banks, have strongly condemned. But since we cannot obtain the adoption of our own views, the question for our consideration is, Whether the existing system or that now proposed will best promote the interests of our establishments? And we shall probably determine that it is better to have a uniform law, the operations of which may be subjected to some degree of calculation, than unknown laws, which are applied or suspended according to the impulse of caprice.

"The proposed measure is an experiment; and so excellent is the machinery, that the experiment interferes as little as possible with existing interests. And the old machinery being retained by the continuance of the country issues, the return is easy to the former system, if necessary, before any serious injury can be inflicted on the country.

"As practical bankers, we contend that experience is the only test of the soundness of a theory. Let, then, "the currency principle" be tried by this test. If it succeeds, the joint-stock bankers, in common with every other class of the community, will share the advantage. If it fails, then other principles will, perhaps, be tried; and, notwithstanding all the denunciations we have heard upon the subject, it may perhaps be ultimately found that the principle of 'competing issues,' as practised in Scotland, is the only effective principle by which the currency throughout the United Kingdom can be managed."

It is obvious that "the currency principle" has been tried and has failed. It seems now to be the proper time to try the antagonistic principle—that the amount of the domestic currency should be wholly unaffected by the importations or exportations of bullion. We doubt not that the talent and ingenuity which framed the Act of 1844 can construct a plan for bringing this principle also to the test of experiment. When this is done, we will judge of the soundness of the principle by its results. So far as it has hitherto been tried, it has never failed.

We have thus endeavoured to trace (impartially, as we believe,) the practical operation of the Act of 1844. It is reasonable to suppose, that under similar circumstances it will produce similar effects. What will be its effects under other circumstances we have yet to learn.

We may be reminded that, should the Act work unfavourably under any circumstances, there is one remedy always at hand—the remedy which has already been applied—to suspend it. And no doubt, under any Government, men will be found who will have the courage to apply this remedy. But this will not remove the previous evil. The suspension, too, may be long delayed, and in the meantime much mischief may arise. In the next pressure the nation will be like "a cat in a air-pump." The animal will not be allowed to die, but at what precise period of exhaustion relief will be afforded will depend upon the views and theories of the philosophic statesmen who may at the time be performing the experiment.

It will not be safe for practical bankers to calculate with too much confidence upon the suspension of the Act. They should make their arrangements on the supposition that it will not be suspended. And it behoves them to inquire what are the principles upon which, under such circumstances, their establishments ought to be administered. This we shall now proceed to do.

We pointed out at the passing of the Act the course which we thought prudent bankers ought to pursue.

In future, the amount of notes in circulation, we observed, will be regulated by the foreign exchanges. When the exchanges are favourable, money will be abundant; when they are unfavourable, it will be scarce. The evils arising from a scarcity of money can only be avoided by following a prudent line of conduct when money is abundant. We, then, as prudent bankers, ought at present to check our desires of making large profits and declaring high dividends, and be content to employ our funds at a low rate of interest, rather than lock them up in hazardous or inconvertible securities. We should call up our old overdrafts, and our dead loans, and, if necessary, increase our capital, so as to place ourselves in the position most favourable for meeting an adverse state of the foreign exchanges. In cases of pressure on the money market, arising from an unfavourable course of exchange, the Bank of England will not be able, as heretofore, to relieve that pressure by a farther issue of notes, and, so far from granting assistance to other banks, she may, from the extent of her transactions, be more in need of assistance herself. We must, therefore, conduct our banks, individually, on a principle of self-dependence ; we shall have to limit our overdrawn accounts, to avoid all advances on inconvertible securities, and to call up such an amount of capital as shall secure to us the means at all times of giving reasonable accommodation to our customers. On the recurrence of a pressure similar to that of 1839, the cry will be, *Sauve qui peut*—" Every one must take care of himself."

The knowledge we have acquired of the working of the Act will tend to give additional force to these recommendations. The attention of practical bankers will also be called to other points besides those which are here named.

It will become a question with them to what extent they should continue to allow interest on their deposits. Some of the joint-stock banks in London allow interest on the minimum balance of a current account. Others allow interest only on deposit receipts. But most London bankers, whether private or joint-stock, allow interest on the daily balance to their country connexions. In seasons of abundance, however, they usually limit the amount on which they allow interest, to prevent themselves being glutted with money from the country banks. But should the Act of 1844 produce those frequent alterations from abundance to pressure, and again from pressure to abundance, which we think it will produce, then it will become a matter of consideration how far the practice of allowing interest on deposits can be continued. It can never be worth a banker's while to allow interest on money which remains in his hands only so long as it cannot be employed, and is taken from him the moment it becomes valuable. During the year 1847 vast sums were withdrawn from both the London and the country bankers, not from any distrust of these bankers, but with a view to make more profitable investments. The rate of interest had been for some time previously very low. Consols had been at par ; and when consols fell so low as to yield 3½ per cent. interest, and the railway companies issued debentures bearing interest at 5 per cent., large sums were withdrawn from all the banks, as well as from the savings banks, for the purpose of being invested in these securities. The bankers had no right to complain of this, as they were called upon only to fulfil their engagements ; but they will probably be unwilling in future to allow interest on deposits of this description.

Another circumstance which the operation of the Act of 1844 will lead practical bankers to reconsider, will be the extent to which they should invest their surplus funds in Government securities. Many bankers have considered it as a sound principle to invest a certain portion of their funds in Government securities. We have laid before our readers extracts from evidence given before parliamentary committees, in favour of this principle, and we expressed our own convictions respecting the same doctrine. But we must acknowledge the operation of the Act is sufficient to show that this principle should be acted upon with caution, and should be limited in its application. The Act will cause money to be alternately abundant and scarce. When money is abundant, the funds are high ; and when money is scarce, the funds are low. In seasons of abundance the banker will be full of deposits ; in seasons of pressure his deposits will be withdrawn, and he will, moreover, be asked to assist his customers by farther advances. He will, therefore, always have occasion to sell out of the funds when the price is low, and thus he will sustain loss. It will, consequently, be his interest to employ his surplus funds in other investments, or even to keep his money unemployed in his till, rather than invest it in Government securities. His risk will be greater if the Act should be capriciously suspended. In October, 1847, several banks are said to have sold out of the funds only a few days before the appearance of the Government letter. After the issue of that letter the money was not wanted ; but, as the funds immediately rose, the money could not be replaced but at considerable loss. The reports and proceedings of the joint-stock banks brought to light some transactions of this kind, and it is probable that the private banks sustained heavy losses by similar transactions.

Another lesson that will be more deeply impressed upon the minds of practical bankers, will be to conduct their establishments in such a way as to be self-dependent in seasons of pressure.

The events of the year 1847 are sufficient to show to what extent dependence can be placed on the Bank of England. Several of the directors complained that everybody looked for assistance to the Bank of England. No expectation could be more complimentary to the bank, nor show more strongly the confidence she had inspired under her previous government. In no preceding pressure had she refused assistance upon the ground that she was unable to grant it. But in former pressures there was no separation between the issuing and the banking departments. Her great strength lay in the power she possessed of expanding the circulation. That power she surrendered to the Act of 1844. She then became like "any other banking concern issuing Bank of England notes." Her locks are now shorn.*

The Bank of Liverpool had been one of the oldest and most respectable of the connexions of the Bank of England. They had, from their commencement, never issued any but Bank of England notes, and had always a pretty large discount account with the branch at Liverpool. Yet, in the year 1847, their minute-book contains several entries similar to the following :— "The manager stated he had seen the agent of the branch bank this morning, and that he would not discount anything for us to-day." Even in the comparative light pressure of April, 1847, the bank suddenly restricted their discounts; and in October, 1847, they were quite unable to meet the public demand, although in some cases they lent consols instead of money. Indeed, it was because the means of the bank were unable to supply the demand for notes, that the Act of 1844 was suspended; yet the governor and all the other witnesses who supported the Act of 1844, stated their opinion that the pressure of 1847 was not so severe as some preceding pressures. How much sooner, then, would the means of the bank have been exhausted, if the pressure had equalled its predecessors in severity!

While bankers should not depend on the Bank of England, neither should they depend on the bill-brokers. A broker, as

* Commons, 769, 3223–4, 3941–2, 4566, 5389.

the name implies, is an intermediate party between the borrower and the lender.   When money is abundant the bill-broker has large funds at his disposal, with which he will discount at a lower rate of interest than the bankers.   When a pressure arrives, these funds are withdrawn, and his occupation is gone.   Some bill-brokers have large capitals of their own, and take in deposits, repayable on demand; and to this extent they may be regarded as bankers.   When money is abundant, sometimes cunning people, instead of going to their own bankers, will take their bills to the bill-brokers, who will discount them at a lower rate: and when the pressure arrives, and the brokers no longer discount, they think to return to their bankers.   It is said that some country banks have occasionally adopted the same system.   But it is clearly a bad system for any bank to adopt.   A bank that is dependent on re-discount will most likely feel some inconvenience in a season of pressure, even when the bills are all undoubtedly good.   But if the bank has, from a desire of making large profits, been induced in seasons of abundance to re-discount inferior bills, the results may be more serious.   For in a season of pressure, a large portion of those bills will not be paid, and the bank will have to provide payments for its own indorsements, while its former channels of re-discount will be closed.   All the joint-stock banks that stopped payment in 1847 had been accustomed to re-discount; and though some of them were unsound in other respects, yet the immediate cause of their stoppage was the inability to re-discount.   We again refer to the proceedings of the Bank of Liverpool.   " The manager stated that out of two small sums of 10,000*l.* sent to London to the brokers only one had been done." —" We had then 100,000*l.* at call with certain bill-brokers, who were unable, when applied to, to return us more than 25,000*l.*" The governor of the bank stated that the failure of the corn speculators caused the failure of an eminent discount-broker having a large country connexion; and this failure, by closing one of the principal channels of discount between the country and London, caused distrust to extend into the country.

Banks should not only avoid depending on the Bank of England, or on bill-brokers: they should also avoid depending on other banks.   Some banks in manufacturing districts are in the habit of discounting with banks in agricultural districts.   A very good practice, as we think.   But the banks requiring the discount should always recollect that when a pressure arrives, the discounting bank may have other ways of employing its funds. Country banks, too, should not rely too much on their London agents. Some London bankers have, no doubt, immense power. At the same time, in seasons of pressure, they have immense claims upon them.* If free from a run upon themselves, they will endeavour so to administer their funds as to afford reasonable assistance to all their connexions. And no one connexion should expect to receive more than this reasonable amount of assistance. But they may themselves be exposed to danger. The panic of 1847 was not a banking panic, but a commercial panic; and therefore the London bankers were comparatively free from molestation. The panic of 1825 commenced by the failure of a country bank. In such a case the London bankers could have rendered but little assistance to their country connexions. It must be recollected that the Act of 1844 was suspended upon the application of the London bankers. The governor of the bank stated to the Committee of the House of Lords—"The London bankers and discount-brokers refused to grant the usual accommodation to their customers, and necessarily obliged every one requiring assistance to resort to the Bank of England."

The most effectual way of acquiring this self-dependence that we have been recommending, is to call up an adequate amount of capital. During a pressure, as we have already said, a banker has three additional claims on his funds. In the first place, a large amount of his deposits may be withdrawn. Secondly, many of his customers, and some probably of the wealthiest, will require additional assistance, in the way of loans and discounts. And, thirdly, he will think it prudent to keep a larger sum in his till, to meet contingent demands. On the other hand, the bills he holds will not all of them be regularly paid; the temporary loans he has granted will have to be renewed; and should he call up any of his permanent or dead loans, it will resemble calling spirits from the deep. In this case he will find the benefit of a large capital; and it is only by means of a large capital that all these operations can be performed with comfort to himself and satisfaction to his customers. But if we increase our capitals to the full extent that may be required in seasons of pressure, we must not

* Commons, 2344–8.

expect to pay high dividends. It is obvious that with the same extent of business, a bank with a large capital must pay a lower dividend than a bank with a small capital. It seems therefore likely that the average rate of banking profits will be reduced.

The fluctuations in the value of money produced by attempting to regulate the currency by the foreign exchanges are injurious to both the London and the country bankers. In seasons when money is abundant, the bankers obtain but a low rate of interest on their loans and discounts—and they are tempted to make imprudent investments in order to employ their funds. And when, on the other hand, money is scarce, the amount of their lodgments is reduced—the rate of interest allowed on the permanent deposits is advanced— a larger sum is kept unemployed in the till—and there is more danger from losses, either by the failure of parties in debt to the bank, or by the necessity of realising Government securities. Those country bankers who are in the habit of re-discounting their bills in London are induced, when money is abundant, to carry this system to a great extent, because they can obtain money at 2 or 3 per cent. in London, and lend it in the country at 4 or 5 per cent. But when money becomes scarce they have to pay an exorbitant interest or are denied discounts altogether, and they are then compelled to refuse their customers their usual accommodation, and then great distress is occasioned in the provinces. Except under peculiar circumstances, both the extremes of abundance and scarcity of money are unfavourable to large banking profits. A state in which money is easy without being abundant, and valuable without being scarce, is the most conducive to the prosperity of both the banking and the commercial interests of the country.

While, however, the profits of a banker from the ordinary operations of his business may be diminished, it is possible he may have opportunities of making other profits by those fluctuations in the prices of public securities, which usually occur in the different periods of a circle of the currency. In the first period, immediately after a pressure, money is abundant without speculation; in the second period, money is abundant and speculations abound; in the third period, speculation begins to decline and money is in demand; in the fourth period, money is scarce and a pressure arrives. It is impossible to say how long each of these periods may last, as they will be influenced by political events—the abundance of the harvests—the direction which speculation may take—and the state of the public mind. Their approach or decline is generally indicated by the stock of gold in the Bank of England.

During the first period money will be abundant, because the importation of gold will cause an increased issue of bank notes; because, the import of commodities being diminished, there will be fewer bills drawn from abroad upon English houses, and offered for discount to the London bankers; and because trade will have become paralyzed at home, and prices will have fallen, so that less money will be required to carry it on. A banker at this period, will have more money than he can employ. But at this period, the prices of the public funds and of other securities are low. The Act of 1844, by causing great fluctuations in prices, gives great advantage to prudent capitalists, at the expense of the less prudent or less wealthy classes of the community. " All fluctuations in trade," says Mr. Gurney, " are advantageous to the knowing man." * To those who are not " knowing men," these fluctuations are injurious. The abundance of the circulation produces a multiplication of contracts, and then the contraction of the circulation produces an inability to fulfil them.† And those who have stock or any other kind of saleable property, are obliged to realise in order to fulfil their engagements. Bankers may during this period make advantageous investments; and as they may calculate that another pressure will not arrive for two or three years, they may purchase a limited amount of securities that have six or twelve months to run. During the second period, money will be in demand. though there may be no great advance in the rate of interest. The securities purchased by the banker in the first period, will now be falling due or advancing in price. But this will be the period of his greatest danger, and he must have a care not to let his desire of getting higher interest lead him to make undue advances upon the commodities or securities that may be the subject of speculation. The third period will be the most profitable for the banker in his direct business. Money will be in full demand at a good rate of interest, and his deposits will hardly have begun to decline. He should now sell out stock and exchequer bills, or

* Lords, 1324.   † Lords, 3845.

any other securities likely to be affected by the approaching pressure. He should make advances only by discounting short bills or making short loans. He should weed his accounts of such customers as have deeply engaged in the previous speculations—and put himself in a condition, to support liberally through the pressure, those who may be entitled to his assistance.

It seems, therefore, probable that bankers will, under the Act of 1844, endeavour to make up for diminished profits by investing more largely in securities. According to the evidence of Mr. Pease, the fluctuations in the currency have already produced similar effects in the departments of trade and commerce.

" I stated, as clearly as I was able to do, that the man who bought from hand to mouth, which is the common case, and did not watch those fluctuations of capital, so as to buy when things were unusually depressed, and to sell when things rose again, failed. The only man who succeeded in making money, succeeded in carrying on a speculative kind of business that has arisen from the want of regularity in the values of money and produce. The man who did not so speculate—buying largely at one time and selling very freely at another—did not succeed. It is of great importance that persons who do not desire to carry on a speculative business should have some assurance that it is moderately productive. That assurance they have lost, by being suddenly deprived by those fluctuations of that which they thought they had secured by their industry." *

Though we would not confound this kind of speculation with that which takes place by means of time bargains on the Stock Exchange, yet we do not think it desirable that banks should deal in the public securities merely with a view of making a profit from the fluctuations in price. Sometimes the banker will be out in his calculations, and, instead of selling at a profit, he will have to sell at a loss, or else submit to a lock-up of his funds. And at all times there is a danger that he will acquire a speculative feeling which will lead him to disregard the steady pursuit of his trade.

* Commons, 4700, 4702.

SECTION IX.

THE ADMINISTRATION OF THE BANKING DEPARTMENT OF THE BANK OF ENGLAND.

By the Act of 1844, the banking department of the Bank of England was separated from its issuing department; and was to be managed like "any other banking concern issuing Bank of England notes." Taking this view of the banking department, we propose to inquire on what principles it ought to be administered. We shall do this, however, not so much with the view of bringing forward any notions of our own, as to lay before the reader some account of those principles which the bank directors have adopted for their government. This will lead us, peradventure, to discuss some principles of practical banking to which we have not hitherto had occasion to refer. We shall then trace the operations of this department for some years subsequent to the passing of the Act of 1844.

The Act for separating the two departments came into operation on the 31st of August, 1844, and the following was the first return made under the Act, showing the condition of the banking department on the 7th of September, 1844:—

Account of the Liabilities and Assets of the Bank of England, for the week ending 7th September, 1844.

Dr.	ISSUE DEPARTMENT.		Cr.
Notes issued	£28,351,295	Government debt. . .	£11,015,100
		Other securities . . .	2,984,900
		Gold coin and bullion .	12,657,208
		Silver bullion	1,694,087
	£28,351,295		28,351,295

	BANKING DEPARTMENT.		
Proprietors' capital . .	£14,553,000	Government securities .	£14,554,834
Rest	3,564,729	Other securities . . .	7,835,616
Public deposits . . .	3,630,809	Notes	8,175,025
Other deposits . . .	8,644,348	Gold and silver coin . .	857,765
Seven-day and other bills	1,030,354		
	£31,423,240		£31,423,240

The following table will give a more detailed account of some of the items in the above return:—

7th September, 1844.

Dr.	£	£
Circulation—		
London	14,802,000	
Country	6,405,000	
		21,207,000
Deposits, Public, viz.—		
Exchequer Account	2,198,000	
For Payment of Dividends	315,000	
Savings Banks, &c.	501,000	
Other Public Accounts	617,000	
		3,631,000
Deposits, Private, viz.—		
Railways	30,000	
London Bankers	963,000	
East India Company	636,000	
Bank of Ireland, Royal Bank of Scotland, &c.	175,000	
Other Deposits	5,631,000	
Deposits at Branches	1,209,000	
		8,644,000
		£33,482,000

Cr.	£	£
Public Securities—		
Advances on Exchequer Bills Deficiency	870,000	
Other Exchequer Bills	311,000	
Exchequer Bills Purchased		
Stock and Annuities	12,821,000	
		14,002,000
Private Securities—		
Bills discounted:		
London	113,000	
Country	2,003,000	
		2,116,000
Exchequer Bills, Stock, &c	661,000	
East India Bonds	198,000	
City Bonds, &c.	3,357,000	
Mortgage	620,000	
Advances:—		
Bills of Exchange	883,000	
		5,719,000
		21,837,000
Bullion		15,209,000
		£37,046,000

It will be seen from the above, that the means or funds of the banking department for carrying on its business, consist of:—
1. The Paid-up Capital—2. The Rest or surplus fund—3. The Public Deposits—4. The other Deposits—5. The seven-day and other Bills. These funds are invested in "Government securities" and in "other securities," and the remainder is kept as a reserve in the till.

1. Viewing this as the condition of a private and independent bank, the first thing that would strike the mind of a practical banker, would be the large amount of the PAID-UP CAPITAL. The capital is 14,553,000*l.*; while the total deposits are only 12,275,157*l.* The object of a large capital is, in the first place, to secure the public confidence; then, to have the means of repaying the deposits whenever demanded; and also, of affording to the customers of the bank every reasonable accommodation in the way of loans or discounts. But after making due provision for these objects this amount of capital appears unnecessarily large. Were it only 7,000,000*l.*, that would be amply sufficient for carrying on the present extent of business, and the rate of dividends might then be increased. All above this amount could only be invested in Government securities, never likely to be required for banking purposes; and if required, could not be suddenly realised, or at least not within the period in which they are likely to be wanted.

2. The next thing that would appear remarkable for a private bank, is the large amount of the REST, or surplus fund.

The Rest, or surplus fund, or Guarantee Fund, as it is sometimes called, consists of the accumulation of surplus or remaining profits after the payment of the dividend. The amount of this fund should be regulated by the extent of the business, and the probable loss that might arise in conducting that business. If the fund is five or six times the amount of the deficiency that might possibly arise in making up the annual dividend, it would appear to be sufficient. For if, after making up this deficiency for one, two, or three years, it should appear that the profits of the bank had become permanently diminished, then the course would be to reduce the dividend, until the surplus fund had recovered its former amount.

Banks that have made large profits, have either increased the dividend, or distributed them among the shareholders in the form of bonuses, or have added them to the capital. The Bank of England have adopted all these plans. Yet, after all these distributions of increased dividends, bonuses, and additional capital, the bank had on the 7th of September, 1844, a rest, arising from surplus profits, of 3,564,729*l.* No other "banking concern carrying on business with Bank of England notes," would think it necessary to keep such a rest. Neither the kind nor the extent of business carried on is ever likely to require anything like this amount to meet any occasional losses. The amount is altogether excessively disproportionate to the purposes for which a surplus fund is usually applied, and at the same time it tends to give an erroneous view of the profits of the bank. This rest is employed in the business, and yields profits, but it pays no dividends. The profits go to swell the dividend on the capital, and hence the capital appears to yield a profit of 7 per cent. But the dividend of 7 per cent. is not made upon the capital alone, but on the capital and rest together, and hence upon the funds employed it amounts to only about 5¾ per cent.

3. THE DEPOSITS.

The Public Deposits are thus classified :—

	£
Exchequer account	2,198,000
For payment of Dividends	315,000
Savings Banks, &c.	501,000
Other public accounts	617,000
	£3,631,000

The "Exchequer account" is the current account with the Government, and this account is credited with the amount of the taxes as they are lodged in the bank. In the beginning of January, April, July, and October, this account is debited for the amount necessary to pay the quarterly dividends, and the amount is carried to the credit of the account "for payment of dividends." The balance here standing to the credit of this account is the amount of the dividends that had not then been claimed. The next account is called "Savings Banks, &c." The trustees of the savings banks throughout the country are required to lodge the deposits in the Bank of England to the credit of the Commissioners for the reduction of the National Debt, who afterwards invest it in the public funds. We do not know what is meant by "&c.," nor yet by the "other public

s

accounts." We believe there are certain accounts connected with the Court of Chancery that are required to be kept with the Bank of England; and by the last bankruptcy law, the effects of bankrupts' estates are required to be lodged in some one or other of the branches. These may form the "other public accounts."

The Private Deposits are thus classified :—

	£
Railways	30,000
London Bankers	963,000
East India Company	636,000
Bank of Ireland, Royal Bank of Scotland, &c.	175,000
Other Deposits.	5,631,000
Deposits at Branches	1,209,000
	£8,644,000

With regard to both the public and the private deposits, a banker would inquire whether they were fluctuating or permanent; whether repayable at fixed periods, or liable to be suddenly withdrawn. He would thus ascertain what proportion could be profitably employed, and what amount should be kept in the till, to meet constant or occasional demands. He would observe, on inspection, that the balance of the "exchequer account" increases gradually during the quarter, from the receipt of the taxes, until the commencement of the next quarter, when it is largely reduced by the payment of dividends. He will, therefore, provide for these quarterly payments; but his provision will be less ample when informed, that, as the public deposits decline, the private deposits will increase, and more especially those of the London bankers. This is partly in consequence of the bankers holding powers of attorney to receive the dividends due to parties who reside in the country, and partly because the abundance of money caused by the payment of dividends increases their own deposits, and thus enables them to keep for a time larger balances in the Bank of England. We have already said that no rule can be given as to the amount of notes which any banker should keep in his till—the proper amount can be ascertained only by experience. But we should imagine that in ordinary times the deposits in the Bank of England are sufficiently steady to prevent any perplexity on the subject. We may be asked what we mean by "ordinary times," since now every year differs from its predecessor, and the steadiness and uniformity which heretofore characterised banking and commercial affairs are no longer known. We reply, that by " ordinary times " we mean those times that are the least affected by the foreign exchanges. For some years past it has been the practice to regulate the issue of bank notes by the foreign exchanges. When the foreign exchanges bring gold into the country, bank notes are issued against it, money becomes abundant, and the bank deposits increase. When the exchanges take out gold, the bank notes are diminished, and the bank deposits decline. This system has, in a great measure, been acted upon by the bank directors since the year 1832, and it is now rigidly enforced by the Act of 1844. These extraordinary seasons of great influx or great efflux of gold appear to be subject at present to no general rules. But at other times there seems to be no reason why the Bank of England should not profitably employ a large portion of her deposits. We may observe, however, that as the bank allows no interest on any of her deposits, she sustains no loss even when they are not employed ; but were they to be employed her profits would be greater.

4. With regard to the INVESTMENTS, a banker would inquire first, Are they safe ? secondly, Are they convertible ?

There seems no ground to question their safety—their convertibility is not so obvious. The Government stock, Exchequer bills, and East India bonds, must be considered in ordinary times, and to a reasonable amount, as strictly convertible. But this is not the case with the Government annuities. They could not be sold in the market ; and even by private negotiation, few buyers would be found, except the insurance offices. Even with them the negotiations would probably occupy considerable time. As to the city bonds, railway bonds, and mortgages, they would in a season of pressure be altogether useless. It may be said, that the bank's capital being so large, a portion may, without inconvenience, be locked up in dead securities. This observation is valid to a certain extent, but not to an indefinite extent, and after giving it due weight, the amount thus invested seems too large.

The annuities form a large portion of the amount of the " Stock and annuities." The first is an annuity of 585,740*l.*, usually called the " Dead Weight," which commenced on the

5th of April, 1823, and is to continue for forty-four years from that time. Other annuities arose out of the Bank Charter Act of 1833. The Government were to pay to the bank one-fourth of the permanent debit of 14,686,830*l.*, amounting to 3,671,700*l.* At first it was arranged that the bank should receive in payment of this sum, 4,000,000*l.* 3 per cent. reduced annuities ; but it was afterwards changed to an annuity for twenty-six years, to expire in 1860, at the same time as the " Long Annuity."

The bills discounted, and the short loans called " Advances on bills of exchange, exchequer bills, stock, &c.," are most legitimate banking investments.

The plan of granting short loans was commenced in 1829, to obviate that tightness in the money market, which was felt for a month or six weeks before the payment of the dividends, through the gathering in of the taxes into the exchequer. The rate of interest charged was usually about one per cent. less than the discount charged on bills. The loans were repayable to the bank at about the time that the dividends were paid to the public. Notices were issued, stating the rate of interest, and the kind of securities on which loans would be made, and the time of repayment. The first notice was issued on the 3rd of December, 1829, and the practice continued until after the passing of the Act of 1844.

Advances on deficiency bills, are a kind of short loans made to the Government, whenever the taxes are less than sufficient to pay the public dividends. These advances seem to be very legitimate. The bank has one large customer. A customer who keeps large deposits will sometimes require large advances. These advances may peradventure be wanted at a time when it may not be exactly convenient for the banker to make them. All large accounts may at times be attended with some inconvenience. But if a banker takes such accounts, he must make his arrangements accordingly. In the present case, the bank has the advantage of knowing, by the progress of the lodgments on the " Exchequer account," whether such advance is likely to be required.

When the Government requires these advances, the bank must either make them out of her reserve in the till, or sell public securities to obtain bank notes, or restrict her advances to other parties. It is peculiarly unfortunate that the Govern-

ment is more likely to require these advances in seasons of
pressure, inasmuch as in those seasons the taxes are usually
less productive and are less punctually paid. Hence the bank
may be called upon to make advances to Government at
the same time that similar advances are required by the commercial classes. In some cases the bank might not have the
means of making advances to both parties. Had the Government required such advances in October, 1847, the commercial
distress must have been considerably increased.

5. THE RESERVE.—A practical banker would, at first sight,
consider this reserve as too large. From the amount and
character of the deposits it would not appear that so large a
reserve was necessary, and a portion might well be employed
in earning interest instead of lying unproductive in the till.
But, before we condemn the bank directors, we must give this
matter farther consideration. We have already stated that,
even before passing the Act of 1844, the directors had been
in the habit of issuing their notes against gold and silver bullion ;
and when a large amount of notes had been thus issued, the
deposits in the bank were increased. Now, when this Act came
into operation—August 31st, 1844—the bank had in this way
acquired a large amount of gold and silver bullion ; indeed, she
does not ever before appear to have had so large an amount in
the whole course of her history. If we look to those years
which preceded pressures (for in these years gold on hand is
usually large), we shall find that in 1824 the amount was
13,810,080*l.* ; in 1836, the highest quotation is 7,801,000*l.* ; and
in 1838, it is 10,126,000*l.* ; but on the 7th of September, 1844,
the amount returned in the issue department is, gold 12,657,208*l.*
and silver 1,694,087*l.*, while the sum of 9,032,790*l.* was retained in the banking department. Notes of course had
been issued against all this bullion, and the deposits in the
bank had consequently increased. " Well," it may be said,
" this will account for the increase of the deposits, but not for
the increase of the reserve. Why were not the deposits invested ?" We will explain this. There are some classes
of investments which the bank directors can make independently of other parties. For instance, they can purchase
Government stock, exchequer bills, and railway bonds, just as
they please. But, as we have stated, it is not prudent in a
banker to invest the temporary increase of his deposits in this

way, as, when the deposits are withdrawn, he may have to sell these securities at a lower price, and thus sustain loss. There are other classes of investments for which the bank is, to a certain extent, dependent on other parties; such, for example, as the discounting of bills and the granting of loans. The bank directors cannot invest their money in these ways unless there are parties willing to receive it. Now, while a portion of the notes issued against gold and silver bullion are lodged with the bank in the form of deposits, another portion, and sometimes the largest portion, do not go into the bank, but are circulated among the public, and soon find their way into the hands of bankers, bill-brokers, and money-dealers, who from the abundance of money, will discount bills and grant short loans at a lower rate of interest than the bank. The bank will, therefore, have no farther applications. When her bills and loans fall due, they will be paid, and the amount will go to increase her reserve. Thus it appears that the notes which, in a favourable course of the foreign exchanges, are issued against gold and silver bullion, will tend in two ways to increase the bank reserve; first, by increasing her deposits, and secondly, by diminishing her securities. This will account for the large amount of the reserve. The rule laid down by the directors is, that the reserve should be about one-third the amount of the deposits.

Having given these explanations, we shall now proceed to notice the operations of the banking department of the Bank of England after its separation from the issuing department by the Act of 1844:—

I. The operations of the Banking Department, from the passing of the Act in 1844, to September 5, 1845.

The Act came into operation on the 31st of August, 1844, and almost immediately some important changes were introduced. Up to that date the bank had never discounted at a lower rate than 4 per cent. This rate, in ordinary times, had seldom varied, and all bills discounted at the same time were charged the same rate. But, on the 5th of September, the rate of discount on bills was reduced from 4 to 2½ per cent., and on notes to 3 per cent. On the 18th of March, 1845, the bank introduced the principle of a *minimum* rate of discount; fixing 2½ per cent. as the rate on first-rate bills, and charging a higher rate on other bills. The object of these changes was to employ a portion of the reserve in the discount of bills.

This line of conduct was by no means unwarranted by the practice of "other banking concerns." It is an established principle in practical banking, that a banker, when he cannot employ his surplus funds at so high a rate of interest as he wishes to obtain, should employ those funds at a lower rate, rather than keep them unemployed in his till. And it is also an established practice to charge different rates of discount on different bills, according to the class or character of the bills —the respectability of the parties—the time they have to run— and a variety of other circumstances. In adopting these regulations, therefore, the directors were only performing the work assigned to them, of conducting the banking department " like any other banking concern issuing Bank of England notes."

These changes gave rise, in the parliamentary committees of 1847, to some discussion upon the question as to whether the Bank of England governed the market-rate of interest; or the market-rate of interest governed the bank-rate? There can be but little difference of opinion upon this subject. The " market-rate " of interest is the rate which bankers and bill-brokers charge for discounting first-class bills to the public. When the foreign exchanges are bringing gold into the country, and notes are issued against this gold, the abundance of money in the hands of the bankers and bill-brokers causes the market-rate of discount to fall below the bank-rate. If during this season the bank charges a high rate, she gets but few bills. On the other hand, when gold is going out of the country, and money becomes scarce, the market-rate is higher than the bank-rate. If during this period the bank charges a low rate, she must soon limit her discounts, or her reserve will be exhausted. But, though the bank cannot change the course of the current, she can give it increased strength. Though she cannot make money dear when it is cheap, nor cheap when it is dear, yet when it is cheap she can make it cheaper, and when it is dear she can make it dearer. Hence, every alteration in the bank-rate has always an immediate influence on the market-rate.

Such was the case in September, 1844. The large importations of gold had reduced the market-rate of discount to 2½ per cent. while the bank charged 4 per cent. But when the bank reduced her rate to 2½ per cent. the market-rate went down to 2, and even to 1½ per cent. To engage actively in discounting bills was a new feature in the bank management. In 1832 the then governor stated to the Committee of the House of Commons, that he thought the bank should be a bank of circulation and of deposit, and only *occasionally* a bank of discount. But the Act of 1844 placed the bank in a new position, and led to the adoption of new principles. Formerly the bank had invested her surplus funds in Government securities. But when she purchased, the price advanced; and when she sold, the price fell. This produced a fluctuation inconvenient to the public. Often, too, she purchased when the price was high, and sold when the price was low: and thus sustained loss. It was therefore deemed preferable to invest a portion of her reserve in the discount of bills. The sums thus invested would return as the bills fell due, and the reserve could at any time be strengthened by checking the discounts.

The directors having determined to invest a portion of their funds in discounts, it became necessary to reduce their rate of interest to nearly the market-rate, or they would have got no bills.

An eminent London banker, distinguished by his support of the Act of 1844, says—"If the bank is to continue as a large discounting body (of the expediency of which I entertain considerable doubts), I think it very desirable that its rate of interest should conform to the real market-value of money."* The directors seemed to think it necessary that they should in some way employ their reserve, in order to prevent the too great accumulation of bank notes in the issue department.† We here give no opinion as to the best way of employing the bank's reserve, but we are quite ready to admit, as the governor admits in reply to a question, that "the true principles of banking are, first, that a bank shall never place itself in such a position as that it shall be unable to meet its liabilities; and next, that it shall employ the whole of its resources at the greatest profit that it can with reference to prudence, looking to its reserve."‡

In thus coming into competition with the money dealers,

* Lords, 1632.　　　† Commons, 3009.　　　‡ Commons, 3722.

reducing the rate of interest, exciting a feverish state of feeling in the public mind, and giving facilities to the formation of companies for speculative purposes, the bank directors are accused of having violated their public duties as the bank of the Government, and thus sacrificed the interests of the nation to the interests of their proprietors. We shall not meddle with this question. We have here nothing to do with the PUBLIC duties of the bank directors. We are considering the banking department as " any other banking concern." Generally speaking, Providence has so constituted human society that all banking companies, and all individuals too, will most effectually promote the public interests when by honourable means they promote their own. If this is not the case with the Bank of England, it must have arisen from the acts of the Legislature ; and the fact—if it be a fact—is presumptive evidence against the wisdom and the justice of those laws by which she was placed in that position.

At the close of this period we find that the London discounts had increased from 113,000*l.* to 2,365,000*l.*, and the "City Bonds, &c." had increased from 3,357,000*l.* to 4,009,000*l.*, owing, it is presumed, to the purchase of railway debentures. The circulation of the issuing department had increased from 28,351,295*l.* to 28,953,300*l.*,* and the minimum rate of interest charged by the bank was 2½ per cent.

II. The Administration of the Banking Department from September 6, 1845, to September 5, 1846.

During this period there were three alterations in the minimum rate of interest. On October 16, 1845, it was raised from 2½ to 3 per cent.; on November 6th, to 3½ per cent.; and on August 17, 1846, it was again reduced to 3 per cent. In fixing the rate of discount, the directors took into account the amount of bullion in the issue department, the reserve in the banking department, and the amount of the discounts. The amount of bullion virtually regulated the other two; and thus the interest was governed by the foreign exchanges. At the same time, the directors, as practical bankers, would pay the greatest attention to their reserve, as it was only from this source that any advances could be made. Hence, sometimes one object of raising the rate of discount was to diminish the number of applications. It

---

* See the Returns at the end of this Section

was thought better to protect the reserve by raising the rate than by positively refusing to discount.

In the beginning of 1846 a circumstance occurred which increased both the deposits and the discounts of the bank, and added greatly to her profits. The railway companies who were desirous of obtaining Acts of Parliament to authorize the construction of their lines, were required to pay into the Bank of England, within fourteen days after the meeting of Parliament, 10 per cent. on the estimated amount of their capital—to be returned when the company had obtained the Act, or when the application had been rejected. Everybody wondered beforehand how so large a sum could be paid out of the amount of notes then in circulation. But the bank acted with the railway deposits as she had been accustomed to act with the public deposits previous to the payment of dividends. As fast as the money came in, it was lent out, and thus a transaction of large magnitude was effected without much difficulty. This shows the importance of a Government bank. Had the deposits been required to be lodged in the exchequer, and there to remain until reclaimed by the railway companies, the operation could not have been effected. The bank could have performed it with greater facility previous to the passing of the Act of 1844. She could then have lent out her notes *before* the lodgments were required to be made ; there would have been no previous apprehensions, nor any tightness during the operation.

III. The Administration of the Banking Department from September 5, 1846, to September 4, 1847.

In September, 1846, the minimum rate of discount was 3 per cent. On January the 14th, 1847, it was raised to 3½ per cent., and on the 20th of the same month to 4 per cent. On April the 8th to 5 per cent., and on the 5th of August to 5½ per cent.

During the whole of this period the foreign exchanges were unfavourable, and the circulation of the issuing department declined from 29,760,870l. to 22,396,845l.* This was attended by a decline in the reserve of the banking department, and an increase in the amount of loans and discounts.

The bank directors did not raise their rate of discount above 3 per cent. until the month of January, 1847. For this they

---

* By deducting 14,000,000l. from this sum, we see the amount of gold and silver bullion on hand in the issue department.

have been severely censured by parties who have had the advantage of not being compelled to form any opinion until after the result was known. The month of April was an important month. From the deficiency of the harvest, large importations of corn took place. These imports were paid for in gold, which was suddenly withdrawn from the issue department, for exportation.

Contemporaneous with this export of gold, the Government required to borrow 3,500,000*l.* upon deficiency bills in order to pay the dividends. Under the old system this might not have been a matter of much importance, but the case was different under the Act of 1844. The banking department was rather in danger of getting into what the Americans call " a fix." To avoid this " fix," the directors raised the rate of discount to 5 per cent. ; they refused to lend money even upon exchequer bills ; they limited their discounts ; and they borrowed 1,275,000*l.* on consols. These measures caused a severe pressure on the money market, but it soon subsided. From this period the foreign exchanges were favourable to this country.

The operations of this month of April, 1847, have given rise to much discussion.

The advocates of the Act of 1844 have pointed to the transactions of this month to prove that the management of the issue department cannot be safely entrusted to the bank directors. They say that if the bank had advanced its rate of interest they might have prevented the unfavourable course of exchange, and consequently have avoided the pressure which then occurred. On the other hand, it has been stated that the bank ought to be guided in its rates of interest by the amount of its reserve— that from November, 1846, to April, 1847, the reserve was above one-third of its deposits, a greater reserve than any other bank would think it necessary to keep—that the demand for gold was so sudden, and for so large an amount, that no ordinary rules could have prevented it ; and even had it been prevented, it might have been injurious to the country, as it would have checked the importation of corn, which was then required in consequence of the deficiency in the harvest. There can be no doubt that, under the Act of 1844, a sudden exportation of gold must cause a sudden contraction of the amount of notes in circulation. This " self-acting machine " acts by jerks, like a steam-engine without a fly-wheel ; and its advocates look to the banking department to supply the fly-wheel, and to cause the machine to move smoothly and equably. It may be doubted whether the banking department has the power of doing this. But when this is not done the advocates of the Act throw the blame upon that department. They resemble the court preceptor, who, when the royal pupil did anything wrong, inflicted the beating on his fellow-student. If on this occasion the bank did wrong, it may be feared that it was her court connexion which led her astray. The Government were then negotiating a loan of eight millions for the relief of Ireland. And "there was a feeling in the court that, in the face of the Government negotiating a loan, it would be an act of want of courtesy to put up the rate of interest immediately."* In the secret history of the Bank of England we may possibly find other instances of similar faults. But if on the present occasion she was influenced by such considerations, she did not act "like any other banking concern."

The events of April, 1847, also lead us to remark that the London bankers never vary their rate of discount with a view to regulate the foreign exchanges. If it behoves the banking department to do this, it has certainly to perform duties which are not considered to belong to "any other banking concern." Nor do the London bankers suddenly and abruptly stop discounting for those customers in whom they have confidence. The frequent occurrence of such suspension of loans and discounts as occurred in April, 1847, would form an insuperable barrier to the banking department ever acquiring that kind of business which is carried on by the London bankers. No merchant would like to depend on such a bank for the means of making his daily payments. We believe, however, that most mercantile firms that have a discount account with the Bank of England have another banking account elsewhere, and some have also accounts with the large bill-brokers.

The pressure that existed in April, 1847, has been attributed to the publication of the amount of the bank's reserve. It was said, and said truly, that the bank might very prudently reduce her reserve for a few days below the average amount, knowing that by bills falling due, or by other means, she would soon receive a sum that would replenish her coffers. But the public, seeing only the amount of the reserve, and knowing nothing of the sums about to be received, might become

* Commons, No. 3001.

unnecessarily alarmed, and hence, a panic might ensue. Upon this ground, some parties questioned the policy of publishing the bank accounts in their present form. But the remedy for this is not to suppress the returns, but to circulate throughout the community such an amount of knowledge as shall enable them to judge accurately respecting banking affairs. Other parties, of a higher class than those we denominate the public, have fallen into erroneous opinions by a literal adhesion to these returns. Almost up to the time of the suspension of the Act of 1844, it was contended by some who " sit in high places " that there could be no pressure on the commercial classes, since there were THEN more notes in the hands of the public than in former seasons when no pressure existed. And before the Parliamentary Committees of 1847 it was stated by the governor and deputy-governor, that it could make no difference to the public whether the bank advanced three millions, or any other sum, to the Government on deficiency bills, or advanced the same sum in loans and discounts to the commercial classes, inasmuch as the returns would show that the amount of notes in circulation would be the same. The events that followed the suspension of the Act showed the fallacy of these opinions. It was shown that the amount of notes in the hands of the public is not of itself a certain criterion by which to judge of the amount of banking facilities enjoyed by the commercial classes.

IV. The Administration of the Banking Department from September, 1847, to September, 1848.

During this period the minimum rate of interest was advanced from 5½ to 6 per cent. on the 23rd of September; to 8 per cent., by authority of the Government letter, on the 25th of October. It was reduced to 7 per cent. on the 22nd of November; to 6 per cent. on the 2nd of December; to 5 per cent. on the 23rd of December; to 4 per cent. on the 27th of January, 1848; and to 3½ per cent. on the 16th of June.

At the commencement of this period a great number of commercial houses failed, not only in London, but also in Liverpool and Glasgow, and other large places. The following is the account given by the Governor of the bank to the Committee of the House of Lords :—

" An unprecedented large importation of food, caused by a deficient harvest, required in payment the export of a large amount of bullion, to the extent of about 7,500,000*l.*, from the coffers of the bank, and probably not less than 1,500,000*l.* from other sources—together, 9,000,000*l.* From this great reduction in the available capital of the country, in addition to the still larger amount invested in railway expenditure, acting suddenly upon a previous high state of credit and excessive speculation, arose the pressure in the money market. There was an abstraction of 7,500,000*l.* from the bullion held by the bank, and consequently a diminution in the notes to that extent."*

During this period the bank acted with great liberality. The following is a list of the advances made between the 15th of September and the 15th of November :—

"1. The Bank of England being applied to by a very large firm in London, who had at that time liabilities to the extent of several millions sterling, advanced 150,000*l.* on the security of debentures to that amount of the Governor and Company of the Copper Miners in England, and thereby prevented them from stopping payment; it was distinctly understood that the operation was for that purpose. 2. The bank advanced 50,000*l.* to a country banker on the security of real property. 3. On the urgent representations of several parties of the first importance in the City of London, the bank advanced 120,000*l.* to the Governor and Company of the Copper Miners, on the guarantee of approved names, taking at the same time a mortgage on the Company's property for 270,000*l.* to cover this sum, and the amount of 150,000*l.* debentures before advanced upon; it was stated that the stoppage of this company would have thrown 10,000 people out of employment. 4. The bank advanced 300,000*l.* to the Royal Bank of Liverpool, on the security of bills of exchange, over and above their usual discounts to this bank; this advance unfortunately proved inadequate, and the Royal Bank, having no more security to offer, stopped payment. 5. The bank assisted another joint-stock bank in the country with 100,000*l.*, on the security of bills of exchange, over and above usual discounts. 6. The bank advanced 130,000*l.* on real property to a large mercantile house in London. 7. The bank advanced 50,000*l.* to another mercantile house on the guarantee of approved names. 8. The bank advanced 50,000*l.* to a joint-stock issuing bank on bills of exchange, and agreed to open a discount account with the said bank, on condition that it should withdraw its issues, but the joint-stock bank stopped payment before the arrangement could be completed. 9. The bank advanced 15,000*l.* on real property to a large establishment in London. 10. The bank assisted, and prevented from failing, a large establishment in Liverpool, by forbearing to enforce payment of upwards of 100,000*l.* of their acceptances, and engaging to give further aid if required. 11. The bank assisted a very large joint-stock bank in the country with advances on loans on bills of exchange to the extent of about 800,000*l.*, over and above usual discounts. 12. The bank advanced 100,000*l.* to a country banker on real property. 13. The bank advanced a joint-stock bank in the country 200,000*l.* on the security of local bills, besides discounting 60,000*l.* of London bills. 14. The bank assisted another joint-stock bank in the

* Lords, 12.

country with an advance of 100,000*l.* on local and London bills. 15. The bank advanced 100,000*l.* to a large mercantile house in London, on approved personal security. 16. The bank assisted a large house at Manchester to resume payment, by an advance of 40,000*l.* on approved personal security. 17. The bank advanced 30,000*l.* to a country bank on real property. 18. The bank assisted many other houses, both in town and country, by advances of smaller sums on securities, not admitted by the bank under ordinary circumstances; nor did the bank, during the period in question, reject at their London establishment any one bill offered for discount, except on the ground of insufficient security."[*]

Some of these advances were not made till after the appearance of the Government letter on the 25th of October. Up to that date the efforts of the bank were inadequate to allay the pressure, while they largely reduced the bank's reserve. On Saturday, the 23rd of October, a deputation from the London bankers waited on the Government, who then determined to suspend the Act of 1844; and on the same day gave intimation of their intention to the Bank of England. On Monday morning a letter appeared from Lord John Russell and the Chancellor of the Exchequer authorizing the directors of the Bank of England to enlarge their discounts and advances, and promising that if by so doing the existing law should be infringed, the Government would apply to the Legislature for a bill of indemnity. The letter suggested that these advances should not be made at a lower interest than 8 per cent. The effect of this letter was immediate. Confidence was restored, the hoarded notes were brought into circulation, and discounts were everywhere readily obtained. From these causes no infringement of the Act took place.

The state of the bank reserve at the date of the suspension of this Act occupied the attention of the Parliamentary Committees. On Saturday, the 23rd of October, the notes on hand amounted to 1,547,270*l.*, and the coin to 447,246*l.* This, it should be remembered, was the amount at the London office and at the thirteen branches put together. At the same time the public deposits were 4,766,000*l.*, and the private deposits 8,581,000*l.*, of which 1,615,000*l.* belonged to the London bankers. The questions put to the governor on this subject seemed designed to show that the bank, so far from being able to assist others, was not in a condition to meet her own engagements. But the governor contended that the amount of the

* Commons, 2645.

reserve should have been taken on the Friday night, before they were acquainted with the intention of the Government to issue their letter. The reserve then was 2,376,000*l.* The directors had from 2,000,000*l.* to 2,500,000*l.* of stock which they could have sold, and a large amount of the bills they held fell due in the following week. From these sources they would easily have increased their reserve. On the other hand, some of the witnesses declared that no large amount of stock could have been sold, and that, had a run taken place on the London bankers, such as that which had taken place on the banks at Newcastle, the bankers' deposits must have been withdrawn, and the Bank of England itself might have been placed in jeopardy.

As we have considered in a previous Section the operation of the Act of 1844, it is not necessary to pursue this subject any farther. After the Government letter was issued, the bank still continued to make advances with caution, and, with the view of not infringing the Act, they borrowed money on the Stock Exchange at 7 per cent., though they had the unlimited power of issuing notes.

Soon afterwards the gold began to return, and money became abundant. From the high rate of interest, the amount imported was large; and from trade having been paralyzed by the pressure, the demand for it was very small. As the gold increased, the bank rate of interest was reduced. By September 2nd, 1848, the circulation of the currency department amounted to 26,883,505*l.*, and the bank reserve to 9,410,952*l.*

To show the further progress of the bank since September, 1848, we have added the Returns for the week ending the 2nd of February, 1849, premising that since the year 1849 the Administration of the Bank of England has been influenced by the importations of gold from California and Australia. We shall here merely state the amounts of gold and silver on hand in the first week in September, in the years that have transpired since 1848, and the minimum rates of interest charged by the Bank of England at those respective periods.

Date.	Gold.	Silver.	Rate of Interest.
	£	£	
8 Sept. 1849	13,631,153	277,077	3
7 Sept. 1850	15,880,617	219,958	2½
6 Sept. 1851	13,674,190	33,375	3
4 Sept. 1852	21,334,921	19,154	2
10 Sept. 1853	15,866,770	nil.	3½
9 Sept. 1854	12,630,110	nil.	5
Sept. 1855	14,368,010	nil.	3½

The following are the dates of the changes in the rate of interest :—

Reduced, Nov. 1849, from 3 to 2½.

Advanced in December, 1850, from 2¼ to 3.

Reduced, Jan. 1852, from 3 to 2½.

Reduced in April 1852, from 2¼ to 2.

Advanced, Jan. 1853, from 2 to 2½.

Advanced again, in Jan. 1853, from 2½ to 3.

Advanced, June 1853, from 3 to 3½.

Advanced, Sept. 1853, from 3½ to 4.

Advanced again, in Sept. 1853, from 4 to 4½.

Advanced again, in Sept. 1853, from 4½ to 5.

Advanced, May 1854, from 5 to 5½.

Reduced, August 1854, from 5½ to 5.

Reduced, April 1855, from 5 to 4½.

Reduced, May 1855, from 4½ to 4.

Reduced, June 1855, from 4 to 3½.

Advanced, Sept. 1855, from 3½ to 4.

The following is a copy of the Official Returns for the four years that have passed under review :—

BANK OF ENGLAND WEEKLY RETURNS.

Account, pursuant to the Act 7th and 8th of Victoria, cap. 32, for the weeks ending as follows :—

ISSUE DEPARTMENT.

	1844. September 7th.	1845. September 6th.	1846. September 5th.	1847. September 4th.	1848. September 2nd.	1849. February 2nd.
	£	£	£	£	£	£
Notes issued . . .	28,351,295	28,953,300	29,760,870	22,396,845	26,883,505	28,330,845
Government Debt . .	11,015,100	11,015,100	11,015,100	11,015,100	11,015,100	11,015,100
Other Securities . . .	2,984,900	2,984,900	2,984,900	2,984,900	2,984,900	2,984,900
Gold Coin and Bullion . .	12,657,208	12,982,591	13,057,997	7,373,815	12,177,567	13,828,773
Silver Bullion . . .	1,694,087	1,970,709	2,702,873	1,023,030	705,938	502,072
	£28,351,295	£28,953,300	£29,760,870	£22,396,845	£26,883,505	£28,330,845

BANKING DEPARTMENT.

	1844. September 7th. £	1845. September 6th. £	1846. September 6th. £	1847. September 4th. £	1848. September 2nd. £	1849. February 2nd. £
Proprietors' Capital	14,553,000	14,553,000	14,553,000	14,553,000	14,553,000	14,553,000
Rest	3,564,729	3,608,180	3,864,479	3,986,593	3,826,382	3,576,625
Public Deposits (including Exchequer, Savings' Banks, Commissioners of National Debt, & Dividend Accounts)	3,630,809	6,474,705	7,318,919	7,722,704	5,021,591	3,922,307
Other Deposits	8,644,948	8,507,213	8,557,109	6,791,373	8,824,607	11,328,544
Seven-day and other Bills	1,030,354	1,921,689	935,830	842,711	1,016,921	1,144,824
	£31,423,240	£34,164,787	£35,229,337	£33,896,381	£33,242,501	£34,525,300
Government Securities (including Dead Weight Annuity)	14,554,834	13,468,643	12,961,735	11,696,840	12,462,735	13,882,267
Other Securities	7,835,616	11,967,081	12,528,550	17,508,119	11,368,814	10,314,654
Notes	8,175,025	8,255,505	9,231,095	4,189,880	8,784,795	9,553,460
Gold and Silver Coin.	857,765	473,558	512,957	562,092	626,157	774,919
	£31,423,240	£34,164,787	£35,229,337	£33,896,381	£33,242,501	£34,525,300

We have thus taken a review of the first four years of the proceedings of the Banking Department of the Bank of England. Whatever may be the future operations of that department, this portion of its history will always be interesting. This period is remarkable also as containing one of those monetary cycles to which we must always be liable as long as our currency is regulated by the Act of 1844. Each year has a peculiar character. The first commenced at a period of full currency—money was abundant and cheap, the minimum of the bank rate being $2\frac{1}{4}$ per cent. In the second year the exchanges fluctuated, and the rate of interest fluctuated also. During the whole of the third, the exchanges were unfavourable—gold was exported, and the rate of interest advanced. At the commencement of the fourth year came the pressure; then a favourable course of exchange brought back the gold, the rate of interest was reduced, and again money became abundant.

This period is moreover important as an indication of the principles on which the banking department will hereafter be governed. The governor and deputy-governor were examined before the parliamentary committees in March, 1848. They stated that they approved of the reduction of interest in September, 1844; but they expressed regret that the bank had not advanced the rate of interest in November, 1846, and that they suffered the reserve to fall so low in October, 1847. Should these sentiments be acted upon in future, we may expect that the " banking department " will reduce its rate of interest as heretofore; but when money becomes scarce, it will advance its rate at an earlier period, and be less liberal in making advances.

The following question was put to the governor by a member of the Committee of the House of Commons:—" You have described as part of the operation of the Act of 1844, that you were during the year 1847 obliged to lend consols instead of notes, on account of the limit prescribed by the Act,—that you borrowed on consols in April,—that you were obliged to raise the rate of interest to 9 per cent.,—that you refused loans on exchequer bills,—that there was a pressure in April, and a panic in October,—and that Government were obliged to interpose by a letter, in order to protect the public from the restrictive effects of the Act—Do you call that a satisfactory history of any system ?" *

* Commons, 3450.

We must, however, distinguish between "the system" as established by the Act of Parliament, and the administration of the banking department in consequence of the establishment of that system. We have given in the preceding section our opinion of the system. But the Administration of the Banking Department of the Bank of England under the system has, in our sober judgment, been distinguished by a high degree of both wisdom and liberality.

The administration of the banking department since September, 1848, does not call for any particular remark. We had the usual indications of the first stage after a panic. The bullion in the issue department increased from 12,883,505*l.* to 14,330,845*l.*; the notes in reserve from 8,784,795*l.* to 9,553,460*l.* Money had been abundant, and the rate of interest low. On the 2nd of November, 1848, the bank reduced the minimum rate of discount to 3 per cent. This would probably have been done at an earlier period but for the political aspect of the Continent. The same reason possibly induced the directors to maintain the same interest to February, 1849, although this appears to be an abandonment of the principle adopted in the year 1844.

SECTION X.

THE PANICS OF 1857 AND OF 1866.

MR. GILBART'S estimate, in the preceding section, of the effects of the Bank Charter Act of 1844, in producing that singularly similar sequence of variations in the rate of interest " to which we must always be liable as long as our currency is regulated by the Act," has been amply verified by subsequent experience. Nor are these fluctuations of rise and fall in the bank rate more marked in the regularity of their fitfulness, than is the recurrence of those far more momentous periodic changes in the money market which entail misery upon thousands of happy households, and even bring nations themselves to the verge of bankruptcy.

There is a general impression that panics recur at regular intervals of about ten years each; nor can this be wondered at, seeing that the years 1825, 1837, 1847, 1857, and 1866 have, from various causes, been marked by the catastrophes so named. Judging by this recurrence of disasters at an apparently fixed period, it certainly seems as if there were a cycle, and this of but short duration, fated to bring in its train ruin to the monetary world and to millions outside of it. Going further back than the earliest years named above, we find no such fatal sequences; and when we take into consideration that, together with the immense development within the last few years of trade and commerce, there has grown up along with it not alone a wholesome feeling of caution, the fruit of bitter experience, but a fuller and wider knowledge as well of the invariable. laws which prevail no less in the financial than in the physical world, one cannot but hope that the monetary whirlwinds called panics will eventually have their course defined as accurately, and the means of escape from their destructive force as distinctly known, as are those of the fiercest storm-winds. The dominant causes of the panics of the years specified, and their distinguishing characters, differ in some essential particulars. In one feature, indeed, they are all alike—the unreasoning fear which heralds, accompanies, follows, always accelerates, and sometimes produces these devastating tornadoes.

The presumed derivation of the word attests its significance. Causeless dread occasioned by the voices of mountain or of forest, which were ascribed to "the great god, Pan," became fossilized in the word "*Panic*;" or, according to another etymology, it originated in Pan, a general of Bacchus, putting to ignominious flight an army (which, outnumbering his own, was preparing to fall upon him in a rocky valley) by ordering his soldiers to awaken the surrounding echoes: their shouts reverberating on all sides, seemed to proceed from an innumerable host, and the enemy fled in fear. A stampede of horses or of buffaloes in the prairies of America, the panic which will indifferently seize a disorderly mob or veteran troops, and a monetary crisis, are "of imagination all compact"—they paralyse the reason. They also mournfully resemble each other in another sad particular; the misery they bring upon thousands of innocent persons. In these two points a picture and description of one would serve for a counterpart of all.

Like the awful panic of 1825, that of 1857 came suddenly upon the public. A general delusion had prevailed in the former year, countenanced by the speeches from the throne on the opening and on the prorogation of Parliament, as well as by the complacent remarks of members of both Houses, that the country was about to enjoy an era of unexampled prosperity. Peru and Mexico were to pour into her lap the fabled wealth of El Dorado, and the golden sands of Pactolus to be eclipsed by the treasures which every tide would bring up the Thames. By the end of the year those fairy visions had disappeared before stern realities. It was the same in 1857. Families that had been living in opulence, or revelling in fancied enjoyment of palaces like Aladdin's, were in a few brief agonising hours reduced to beggary and plunged in despair—their fortunes gone, their hopes dreams. Labour was driven from its accustomed fields; commerce laid prostrate; credit all but extinct; energy paralysed; fear and distrust in the ascendant; and enterprise a departed spirit. The gloom was universal, for thousands in every rank of life were ruined.

In sober truth, the crisis of 1857 fell upon the commercial world like a thunderbolt. Notwithstanding the extra expenditure entailed by the Crimean war, peace was concluded before the national resources had been strained beyond the limit their strength could bear.

" A period of nearly ten years," says an able writer, " uneventful as far as commercial disaster is concerned, may be passed over in silence, except to remark that in 1852 consols attained their maximum price since 1737, namely, 101⅜. The beginning of the memorable year, 1857, seemed to promise a long period of commercial ease, but the outbreak of the mutiny in India, the consequent suspension of remittances from that quarter, and the inverse demand for specie, the demand for capital to supply materials of war to the Government and the East India Company—all those causes tended to depress the funds. In January they reached 94⅜; in November, they fell to 87½—lower than at any time since January, 1856, during the pressure of the Russian war."*

Even so late in the year as the month of August, the public were unapprehensive of the storm soon to ensue, and few or none foresaw the severity with which it would rage. During the inquiry which followed, the Governor of the Bank stated :—

" Things were at this time pretty stationary; the prospects of harvest were very good; there was no apprehension that commerce was otherwise than sound. There were certain more far-seeing persons who considered that the great stimulus given by the war expenditure, which had created a very large consumption of goods imported from the East and other

* Commercial Panics, by Arthur Locker : *Companion to the British Almanac,* 1867.

places, must now occasion some collapse; and still more those who observed that the merchants, notwithstanding the enhanced prices of produce, were nevertheless importing as they had done successfully in the previous years. But the public generally viewed trade as sound, and were little aware that a crisis of any sort was impending, far less that it was so near at hand."

The crisis of 1847 had been owing chiefly to excessive railway speculations at home; this of 1857 was mainly due to over-trading abroad.

About the middle of September, the mails brought disastrous news from the United States. American railway securities had fallen nearly 20 per cent. The railway accounts had long been "cooked," and the too well-known results of the process followed—sudden and enormous depreciations of railway stock, widely-spread distrust, a drain upon the American banks, and failures shaking commercial credit to its centre. The proximate cause of this terrible crisis in America was the stoppage of the Ohio Life and Trust Company; an establishment which made advances on financial securities, and which, at the time it stopped payment, held deposits to the amount of 1,200,000*l.* Hereupon, a deliberately planned system of " bearing " operations was put in movement, which was described in the *Times* City article of September 10, 1857, as follows :—

" There is actually a powerful combination for the avowed purpose of bringing all the principal undertakings to ruin. A large body of active persons are known to be associated for the purpose: they influence the press to work out their views, and are alleged not merely to operate with a joint capital, but to hold regular meetings, and permanently retain legal advisers, whose chief vocation, it may be assumed, is to discover points that may enable the validity of each kind of security to be called in question, and thus to create universal distrust."

The downfall of the Ohio Land and Trust Company had been quickly followed by the failure of 150 banks in Pennsylvania, Maryland, Virginia, and Rhode Island ; and since no less than eighty millions of American railway stock were computed to be held in England, a large demand for bullion on American account set in here. The run for deposits in specie on the New York banks brought about by the villainous " bearing " organisation noticed above, swelled distrust in America into a panic, which soon reacted on England. By the middle of October failures began to be numerous here. Liverpool and Glasgow, ever necessarily the most sensitive to fluctuations in the

American markets, exhibited unmistakable indications of the probable severity of the coming storm. Rumours spread affecting the Borough Bank of Liverpool * and the Western Bank of Scotland ; and the alarm in London, where failures were following in quick succession, rose to its height when, on November 7th, the great firm of Dennistoun and Co., which had numerous agencies in America and Australia, stopped payment, with liabilities of about two millions; and when, on the morning of the 9th, news arrived of the failure of the Western Bank of Scotland for between six and seven millions. Together with this intelligence came a call for gold from Scotland, a most unexpected, because unusual and exceptional circumstance, the predilection of the Scotch for their one-pound note currency, and the confidence justly reposed in their tried, tested, and proven system of banking, inclining the Scotch banks to forego keeping any large metallic reserves. Three hundred thousand sovereigns were despatched to meet this demand ; and when, on the 11th of November, the city was excited by the suspension of Sanderson and Co., a great discount house, with liabilities to the amount of upwards of five millions, when further demands for gold came from Scotland, when large calls followed from Ireland as well, when tremendous failure succeeded tremendous failure, and the utter rottenness which had pervaded the commercial world became apparent, and general bankruptcy seemed imminent—recourse was had, for the second time, to the panacea—suspension of the Bank Act of 1844. Government authorized the Bank of England to exceed the prescribed limit of its issues by discounts and advances upon approved securities.

This authorization, which was given on the 12th, at once quieted the public mind ; but there was this notable difference between the effects of the first suspension of the Act in 1847 and of the present, that whereas in that year the mere notice of suspension had operated as a charm, and notes to the amount only of 400,000*l.* were actually issued in excess of the statutory limit,—in 1857 the bank issued, from November 13th to the end of the month, no less than 6,776,000*l.* of notes beyond the limit (14,475,000*l.*) fixed by the Act.† Nor did the reverses consequent upon fraudulent financial management and reckless overtrading end with the allaying of the general panic. Trade with America had acquired such development here and on the

---

* Not long afterwards it stopped payment.   † Now raised to 15,000,000*l.*

continent, in Germany especially, that failures in the Hanse Towns and other centres of commerce brought about the downfall of many English houses in this connexion, and, superadded, were stoppages of large firms connected with the Baltic trade; among them the Northumberland and Durham Bank for three millions—so that it was hardly before the close of 1858 that the collapse of dishonest trading and fictitious credit was complete, and commercial affairs resumed their legitimate course.

We have said that the crisis came upon the world without a note of warning, and remarked that the consequences of the financial earthquake which shook the moneyed institutions of America to their base, were severely felt on the continent, as well as in the United Kingdom. In the autumn of 1857 (August 17) the Bank of England entered into a negotiation with the East India Company to supply a million in specie for transmission to the East. At this date the bullion was 10,606,000*l.*, the reserve 6,296,000*l.*, and the rate of discount 5½. By the 8th of October, the bullion had fallen to 9,751,000*l.*, the reserve to 4,931,000*l.*, and discount was raised to 6 per cent. On the 12th, the rate was raised to 7 per cent., and on the 19th to 8 per cent. By this time the bullion had sunk to 8,991,000*l.*, and the reserve to 4,115,000*l.* At Paris, discount had risen to 7½, and at Hamburgh to 9 per cent. On the 5th of November the Bank of England raised its rate to the latter figure, and on the 9th, to 10 per cent.; whilst the Bank of France raised its rates to 8, 9, and 10 per cent. for one, two, and three months. By the 11th, the bullion in the bank was reduced to 6,666,000*l.*, and the reserve to 1,462,000*l.* So that at this date there was a decrease, since the middle of August, of about four millions in the bullion, and of close upon five millions in the reserve. As soon as the pressure had begun to be felt, a great demand for gold on American account had set in; and in the interval between this period and the rise of the crisis to panic height, large amounts of specie had to be sent to Scotland and Ireland, whilst the discounts meantime were in proportion to the magnitude of the calls for assistance; on the 12th, they amounted to 2,373,000*l.* The state to which the bank was reduced on the evening of this eventful Thursday, when the Act was suspended, is shown by the startling fact that its total reserve in London was but 384,144*l.*, and at its branches, only 196,607*l.* more. The bankers' balances alone against it on this very evening were 5,458,000*l*.   It is clear, therefore, that but for the suspension of the Act the bank must have stopped.

We present the views taken at the time, by the more influential organs of public opinion, of the operation of the Bank Charter Act, premising that they concurred in approval of its suspension.   The *Times* observed :—

" On the merits of this step" (the suspension) "we will say but little. It may be consistent with the maxims of political economy to regulate the issue of notes in ordinary times, and thus to check rash speculation and the embarkation in business of men destitute of capital, while when an actual dearth of money prevails, the chief banking institution of the country may be allowed to extend its issue of notes under a public guarantee.   But if such is to be the principle of our monetary system, the sooner it is embodied into a law the better.   If the bank is to extend its legal issue of notes as often as its rate of discount is necessarily raised above a certain point, then an Act of Parliament should establish the practice on sound and intelligible principles.   The commercial interests of the country should not be subjected to a system by which a law is obeyed as long as obedience is easy, and temporarily swept away as often as pressure or panic supervenes.   The houses which, in 1847 and 1857 have stopped payment before the relaxation of the law, may well complain that, while they have been crushed by the operation of the Bank Charter Act, others not more solvent or of higher standing than themselves have been saved by the suspension of it."

The *Daily News* remarked :—

" This is not the first time that England has awoke to find that she has been slumbering upon an incipient earthquake.   We are too sincerely grateful for the escape of the country from a great danger to entertain any feeling of animosity towards the party who, whilst acting doubtless to the best of their judgment, have laboured hard to close the safety-valve; but we must tell the supporters of the Bank Charter Act that they brought the nation, even so recently as yesterday, to the verge of an explosion which might have shattered the entire financial edifice, and carried deep distress into thousands of households."

The comments of the City article writer in the *Morning Herald* are of a more hesitating and deliberative character :—

" Whether, by any alteration in the law, commerce might be benefited, is of course a matter for future consideration.   The committee appointed to investigate this question have not yet brought their labours to a conclusion.   Under the circumstances, therefore, it would be impossible for ministers to rush into the other extreme, and attempt, or even appear to sanction, a permanent alteration of the law."

The *Morning Chronicle* is more outspoken :—

" Even a fortnight since, the appearance of the ministerial letter we publish to-day would have averted many catastrophes, and spared the mercantile community a long series of calamities. . . . . But the question is everywhere asked, why was the remedy withheld so long? It might have been applied in time to save the Western Bank of Scotland, the City of Glasgow Bank, Messrs. Sanderson, and many other firms of less note, but whose suspension will involve thousands in ruin. The delay has proved most disastrous to all the commercial interests of the country. . . . By the bigoted partisans of the Act of 1844, the violation of its restrictive enactments now authorized will be regarded as something like a mortal sin. . . . The only peril which the partisans of convertibility anticipate from any relaxation in the Bank issues is that of a 'run for gold. This was the bugbear of financial theorists during the early decades of the present century. In truth, the public mind in this country has outgrown any such suicidal tendency."

The commercial atmosphere having been cleared by the monetary hurricane of 1857, a period of comparative tranquillity ensued. The bank rate of discount was not reduced below 5 per cent. until the bullion in its vaults exceeded 15,000,000*l.*; but, generally speaking, its rate was moderate throughout 1859 and 1860, and, with the exception of a rise to 8 per cent. in 1861, which was but of brief duration, the same may be observed of that year and of 1862. Owing to the large issues of paper money by the belligerent governments of the North and South, bullion soon disappeared from circulation in the warring States, and floated hither. Hence money was plentiful and its price easy. But the advantage was soon more than counterbalanced by the monetary derangement ensuing from the absence of the supply of cotton from the Southern States—itself a consequence of the civil war then and there raging. The price of this great staple of British manufacture rapidly rose. Supplies had to be sought from new sources, and had to be paid for in cash. The drain which then set in, and the apprehension of over speculation excited by the number of new companies forming under the Limited Liability Act, which came into operation at this conjuncture, caused a general uneasiness. This state of feeling commenced in the fall of 1863. Between this date and the summer of 1864 the fluctuations in the bank rate of discount evidenced the feverish condition of the country. On one occasion the Bank of England raised its rate twice in one week, from 5 to 6, and then to 7 per cent. This was in the winter of 1863; and again in May, 1864, it raised its rate, twice in one week, to 9. In fact, the rate of discount during this period was continually oscillating. Similar disturbance of the money market was manifested in France; occasioned, primarily, by the American civil war, and the failure in the supply of cotton. Large amounts of specie were drawn from the Bank of France, which raised its rate of discount several times, concurrently with the Bank of England, and to the same figure.

"Already in March, 1864," writes Mr. Macleod, "the number of new companies formed under the Limited Liability principle gave great uneasiness. Up to that time it appeared there were 263 companies formed, with a nominal capital of 78,135,000*l.*, out of which 27 were banks, and 15 discount companies. In August, 1864, the long-dated acceptances of the new financial companies began to press on the market, and lay the foundation of the crisis of 1866."

On the 20th of June, 1865, the rate of discount reached its minimum, 3 per cent. From the 3rd of August to the 28th of September, the minimum rate of discount was 4 per cent.; on the 28th of the same month it was raised to $4\frac{1}{2}$, on the 2nd of October to 5, on the 5th to 6, and on the 7th to 7 per cent.—a rise of 3 per cent. in nine days. In November a drain set in of gold to Paris, and of silver to the East. The bank raised its rate in January from 7 to 8. At the same time, the Bank of France raised its rate from 4 to 5 per cent.; and this simultaneous rise seems to have exercised a healthy influence upon jobbers and speculators. February was a period of intense perturbation among the holders of miscellaneous securities. Some large firms engaged in railway contracts suspended payment. Investments became unmarketable which a few months before had been eagerly sought after, and the public scouted concerns which had "floated" readily during the Limited Liability mania. Suspicion everywhere prevailed, and all kinds of securities were thrown upon the market at once. The editor of the *Bankers' Magazine*, reviewing the events of the previous month, pertinently remarked in April, 1866:—

"Company winding-up seems likely to become one of our national institutions. By the mere force of circumstances it has, for nearly all practical purposes, established a court of its own. . . . . Many weeks ago, Lord Romilly was complaining of the degree to which this particular kind of business was stopping the way for everything else; keeping ordinary suitors waiting, and rendering his court almost unavailable for its proper purpose of a court of original jurisdiction in Chancery. If this complaint were well founded in the beginning of January, it applies with infinitely greater force in the middle of March. The process of winnowing company wheat from company chaff has, during that period, been going on with a regularity and rapidity entirely unexampled. . . . The number of cases in which once promising concerns are now going through the Chancery mill is quite sufficient to show that for many months past there has been something very rotten in the state of Denmark. Several general companies for pottery manufacture, ship-building, mining, cork-cutting, and hotel-keeping have figured in the official list; and last, but not least, that gigantic example of directorial mismanagement, the Joint-Stock Discount Company. . . Only a very slight acquaintance with the requirements of the money market was needed to satisfy any one that the creation of companies demanding a hundred millions of money a year could not be kept up for ever. Yet there were those who, in the flush of a financial fever, were ready to maintain this or any other equally absurd proposition."

. It was the break-up of the Joint-Stock Discount Company, mentioned in the above extract, which first sounded the tocsin; and the alarm-bell pealed more loudly upon the stoppage in April of Barned's Bank, at Liverpool, with liabilities of three and a half millions. The sounds became "deeper and deeper still," and more and more ominous of fright culminating into universal panic. On the 3rd of May, the bank raised its discount from 6 per cent., the quotation for the previous month, to 7; on the 8th, to 8; on the 9th, to 9; and on the 10th (which brought with it the most disastrous failure that ever filled the City with panic and dread, the stoppage of the great house of Overend, Gurney, and Co., for upwards of ten millions sterling) the rate was raised to 10 per cent. This momentous news was only known after banking hours; but when made public by the papers the next morning, that of Friday, the 11th, the scene of excitement which then took place is said to have thrown all previous wild terrors of the kind into the background; it was, said the Chancellor of the Exchequer, next evening in the House, declared by the oldest inhabitants of the City to have been without a parallel.

"At midday," writes Mr. Patterson, "the panic was at its height. Lombard Street was actually blocked up by crowds of respectable persons who thronged the doors of the banks and other establishments. Lothbury, Bartholomew Lane, and the adjoining streets, were also thronged with excited knots of people. While depositors rushed to withdraw their money, a body of onlookers gathered before each bank or financial establishment, expecting to see it close its doors. Every one was on the alert for bad news, and discussed only too freely the dangers which threatened the various establishments. A list of the shareholders of the fallen firm of Overend, Gurney, and Co., published at the high price of one shilling, was eagerly bought up at 2s. 6d. The penny papers, in like manner, were bought at threepence—so great was the eagerness to learn the latest news or rumours. Consols were unsaleable: no one mistrusted their value, but there was no currency wherewith to purchase them. The Bank of England itself would not give loans upon them."*

The following was the account given by the *Times*, in its impression of May 12, 1866, of this bewildering scene of unreasoning fear, immeasurably idle, irreflective curiosity, and bitterly painful anxiety :—

" The doors of the most respectable banking houses were besieged, more, perhaps, by a mob actuated by the strange sympathy which makes and keeps a mob together, than by creditors of the banks; and throngs, heaving and tumbling about Lombard Street, made that narrow thoroughfare impassable. The excitement on all sides was such as has not been witnessed since the great crisis of 1825, if indeed the memory of the few survivors who shared that panic can be trusted when they compare it with the madness of yesterday. Nothing had happened since the day before to justify such a fear as was everywhere shown. Rumour, however, like the false woman in the Laureate's legend, 'ran riot amongst the noblest names,' and left no reputation unassailed. Each man exaggerated the suspicions of his neighbour; and until a report, at that time unfounded, was circulated in the afternoon, that the Government had authorized the bank directors to issue notes to the extent of five millions beyond the limit imposed by the Bank Charter Act, it seemed as if the fears and distrust of the commercial world had become boundless."

This ominous day, known in the city annals as "Black Friday," is thus described in the *Revue des Deux Mondes* by M. Wolowski, an eminent writer on banking and finance :—

" The 11th of May will be long remembered in London; it was a day of distress and terror, and seemed to be the signal of general ruin. No one was sure of any one else, or of himself, the moment it became known that the great house had closed its doors. It was by hundreds of millions that the engagements of that gigantic financial firm, whose fall made the very ground tremble, were counted. The settlement of a great portion of the commerce of the world is concentrated in England; the settlement of the commerce of England was concentrated in the City; and the house of Overend, Gurney, and Co., held one of the foremost places among the small number of establishments in whose houses is the settlement of the commerce of the City. For a long time it enjoyed immense credit; it disposed of enormous securities; a renown more than European had multiplied the number of its customers, and augmented the amount of deposits confided to it. Thus, the fatal Friday which witnessed the disaster continues to be popularly known as the 'Overend Friday.'"

Sensational writing has invaded every province of our literature, and no wonder that the swelling hyperboles of romance should be used to typify the magnitude of disasters which have been occasioned by carrying imagination and the *ignis fatuus*

* Patterson's Science of Finance, p. 233.

spirit of speculation into the domain which ought by right to belong to sober calculation alone. Homelier language, however, even of a familiar and every-day character, is often more suggestive, more pregnant with meaning, and presents the true consequences of a momentous event more fully and vividly to the mind than rounded periods or ornate phrases; and when we find it stated in a monthly publication, already quoted, that " the only word that can give an adequate idea of the extent of the collapse is the significant word 'Crash,'" we feel the truth of the assertion, and the thorough comprehensiveness of the idiomatic word. The writer goes on to say: "A greater crash has never taken place in any one week in any country in the world. Looking at the list of suspensions, it will be seen that their business ramifications are more than European. More or less they embrace all the four quarters of the world, and we have yet to feel the reaction from the effect which the news will produce as it extends from point to point."

The fever was at its height, the crisis had set in, and, for the third time, suspension of the Bank Charter Act wrought the cure. In reply to the questions certain to be asked in the House of Commons on emergencies of the kind, the Chancellor of the Exchequer said :—

"I stated in the commencement of the evening that representations had been made to me from quarters of the greatest influence and credit with respect to the extraordinary state of the market, and the distress prevailing in the City to-day. I stated that those representations had come to me from gentlemen representing in particular the private banks of London, and I expected that I should shortly have received similar representations from those connected with the joint-stock banks. Those representations I have received accordingly, and they were pressed even more earnestly and urgently than I anticipated. I stated also, at the time when I had the honour of addressing the House, that the effects of the day's proceedings through the Bank of England had not been fully given to us. Since then we have become acquainted with them, and we find that the bank, through a desire to extend relief, has raised its loans and discounts to-day to a sum of something more than 4,000,000*l.* The effect of that large accommodation was to reduce the reserves of the bank to a sum not very far short of 3,000,000*l.* of money. Under these circumstances, as far as the facts are known, and there being no reason to believe that any great change has occurred in the state of things, the estimate is sufficiently accurate for all practical purposes, we find the bank reserves reduced in a single day from a sum approaching 6,000,000*l.* to a little exceeding 3,000,000*l.* The Government have felt that this is a state of things which, combined with the public feeling, calls for intervention on their part. We have taken the opportunity during the evening of considering the state of the facts, and the result has been that we have addressed a letter to the governor and deputy-governor of the bank, substantially the same as was addressed to those high officers in 1847 and 1857. That is to say, if the bank, proceeding upon its usual prudent rules of administration, shall find occasion to make such advances from the issue department as shall exceed the limits allowed by law, we recommend that they should not hesitate to make that issue, and we undertake to make immediate application to parliament for its sanction. (Cheers.) There are other points of detail, but that is the substance of the letter which shall be in the hands of the governor and deputy-governor of the bank to-morrow, and which I earnestly hope may have the effect of allaying the feeling of uneasiness which prevails in the country, especially as it does not arise from any general unsoundness in the condition of our commercial relations, but only from causes of a peculiar and specific character. In that respect we are able to draw a favourable distinction between the present crisis and others in former times; but there is also another distinction, and that is the extraordinary rapidity with which the crisis has come upon us, and which has prevented the adoption of measures which otherwise would have been taken for its relief. We have not, however, hesitated to act, to address ourselves to the subject with all the means in our power, and we trust that our proceedings will meet with the approbation of Parliament." (Cheers.)

The foregoing took place on the evening of the 11th ; and on the 17th the Chancellor was again interrogated as follows :—

Captain Gridley asked the Chancellor of the Exchequer—

" Whether he was aware that the Directors of the Bank of England had declined to make advances upon the lodgment of Government securities, on the ground that they ought to be realised; and whether he considered the directors had complied with the expressed understanding that they, on getting permission to increase the issue of bank notes, were to afford accommodation to bankers and merchants."

Mr. Wyld asked the Chancellor of the Exchequer

" If it were true that the Bank of England had refused to make advances on consols, and had otherwise neglected to give to merchants, bankers, and others, the accommodation not only implied, but expressed, when they obtained power to increase their issue of notes."

The Chancellor of the Exchequer :

" It may be convenient that, in answering the questions of the hon. members, I should combine them together, as they are so nearly akin. In the first place, I may say that I have not received complaints from any persons who consider themselves aggrieved by the conduct of the Bank of England. At the same time, certain rumours have gone abroad, and it is in respect of those rumours, as embodied in the questions of the hon. members, that I give my reply. The two points principally raised are these. First, whether I am aware that the directors of the Bank of England have declined to make advances upon the lodgment of Government securities, on the ground that they ought to be realised; and, secondly, whether I am

U

of opinion that the directors have complied with the express understanding that they, on getting permission to increase the issue of bank notes, were to afford accommodation to bankers and merchants. I think these questions have been very opportunely put, because they enable me to remove a misapprehension that has got abroad, and which appears, from all that I can see, to have taken possession to a certain extent of the public mind. The misapprehension refers equally to the subject of advances upon bills and discounting of bills, and to advances upon Government securities. The best account that can be given of the operations of the Bank of England with regard to these two great branches of banking, is to state the figures relating to them, and I think it will be found on referring to them that the Bank of England has not refused to make advances on Government securities. These figures are as follows:—The advances made by the Bank of England on Government securities on Friday, the day of the panic, amounted to 919,000*l.*, on Saturday to 747,000*l.*, and on three subsequent days various amounts, making up the total amount advanced on these securities, in five days, to 2,874,000*l.* (Hear, hear.) Then with regard to the accommodation of commerce in general, the best measure that can be given of the manner in which the Bank has exercised its functions is shown in this—that it has made advances upon bills and has discounted bills to the extent of 9,350,000*l.*, making a total of advances and discounts in five days of 12,225,000*l.* (Hear, hear). Looking at these figures, I do not think that a very strong *primâ facie* case has been made out of the bank having declined to afford to commerce the accommodation it should have given, but it is only due to the bank that I should point out certain words in the letter of Government which were expressly intended to serve as a notice to the world that the Bank of England was not to be expected, in the then circumstances of difficulty, to depart from all rules of caution. The conditional promise made in the letter, signed by the First Minister and myself, was a promise to apply to Parliament for its sanction, in case it should happen that necessity should require the bank, for the purpose of making advances and discounting bills, to issue notes beyond the limit fixed by law, subject to the restriction that the bank was not to give to everybody everything that was asked, but that it should be governed by those prudent rules of caution by which it was generally guided. That was a very important limitation, and it reserved, I think, entirely, as it was meant to do, the discretion of the gentlemen of the Bank of England, in whom we have every reason to place confidence. With regard to the Government securities and other points, the foundation upon which the rumours rest is of the slightest possible nature. I cannot find that there is any possible ground for supposing that any limit was placed by the bank on its advances on securities, either upon Friday, the day of the severest pressure, or upon Saturday, which was also a critical day; but on Monday, when the panic began to subside, and when Government securities were brought to the bank for advances, the bank directors suggested, in various instances, to the holders of those securities, that it would be better for them to try the open market and to realise for themselves. (Hear, hear.) In consequence of that view—in my opinion, not an unreasonable one on the part of the directors of the bank—certain sales of securities were effected. These sales, I believe, were effected by one, two, or three persons only; and whenever representations were made to the bank that sales could not be made—meaning, I presume thereby, without serious loss—the bank met all the reasonable demands of the parties. With respect to other kinds of accommodation, commercial accommodation strictly so called, I have not been able to discover, nor are the authorities at the bank aware of any other ground for the rumours existing than the circumstance that applications did arise from one or two quarters, not for an amount of discount to a given limit, but for an unlimited amount of discount to be made use of in case necessity should arise. The directors of the Bank of England did not consider that their duty compelled them to accede to such demands, and as far as I am able to judge, I think that, under the circumstances of the times, they acted wisely in giving no engagement to meet an unlimited amount of discount. That, I believe, to be the sole foundation for the rumours which are abroad. I think the explanation I have given is one which the House will be glad to receive, and I believe that the authentic figures which I have stated to the House will do more than any mere verbal statement to explain the liberal, yet judicious manner in which the operations of the Bank of England are conducted at critical periods. I hope the effect of such communications will be that all that hereafter transpires with respect to the state of the bank will tend not to disturb, but further to compose the public mind. (Cheers.)

Annexed is the correspondence which passed between the Government and the bank on this momentous occasion:—

" Sir, " Bank of England, May 11, 1866.
" We consider it to be our duty to lay before the Government the facts relating to the extraordinary demands for assistance which have been made upon the Bank of England to-day, in consequence of the failure of Messrs. Overend, Gurney, & Co.
" We have advanced to the bankers, bill brokers, and merchants, in London, during the day, upwards of four millions sterling, upon the security of Government stock and bills of exchange—an unprecedented sum to lend in one day, and which, therefore, we supposed would be sufficient to meet all their requirements, although the proportion of this sum which may have been sent to the country must materially affect the question.
" We commenced this morning with a reserve of 5,727,000'., which has been drawn upon so largely that we cannot calculate upon having so much as 3,000,000l. this evening, making a fair allowance for what may be remaining at the branches.
" We have not refused any legitimate application for assistance, and unless the money taken from the bank is entirely withdrawn from circulation, there is no reason to suppose that this reserve is insufficient
" We have the honour to be, Sir,
" Your obedient Servants,
" (Signed) H. L. HOLLAND, *Governor.*
" (Signed) THOS. NEWMAN HUNT, *Deputy-Governor.*
" The Right Hon. the Chancellor of the Exchequer, M.P.
&c. &c. &c."

U 2

" *To the Governor and Deputy-Governor of the Bank of England.*

" Downing Street, 11th May, 1866.

" Gentlemen,

" We have the honour to acknowledge the receipt of your letter of this day to the Chancellor of the Exchequer, in which you state the course of action at the Bank of England, under the circumstances of sudden anxiety which have arisen since the stoppage of Messrs. Overend, Gurney, & Co., Limited, yesterday.

" We learn with regret that the Bank reserve, which stood so recently as last night at a sum of about five millions and three quarters, has been reduced in a single day by the liberal answer of the bank to the demands of commerce during the hours of business, and by its great anxiety to avert disaster, to little more than half that amount, or a sum (actual for London and estimated for the branches) not greatly exceeding three millions.

" The accounts and representations which have reached her Majesty's Government during the day exhibit the state of things in the city as one of extraordinary distress and apprehension. Indeed, deputations composed of persons of the greatest weight and influence, and representing alike the private and joint-stock banks of London, have presented themselves in Downing Street, and have urged, with unanimity, and with earnestness, the necessity of some intervention on the part of the State, to allay the anxiety which prevails, and which appears to have amounted, through great part of the day, to absolute panic.

" There are some important points in which the present crisis differs from those of 1847 and 1857. Those periods were periods of mercantile distress, but the vital consideration of banking credit does not appear to have been involved in them, as it is in the present crisis.

" Again, the course of affairs was comparatively slow and measured, whereas the shock has in this instance arrived with an intense rapidity, and the opportunity for deliberation is narrowed in proportion. Lastly, the reserve of the Bank of England has suffered a diminution without precedent relatively to the time in which it has been brought about, and in view especially of this circumstance her Majesty's Government cannot doubt that it is their duty to adopt, without delay, the measures which seem to them best calculated to compose the public mind, and to arrest the calamities which may threaten trade and industry. If, then, the directors of the Bank of England, proceeding upon the prudent rules of action by which their administration is usually governed, shall find that, in order to meet the wants of legitimate commerce, it be requisite to extend their discounts and advances upon approved securities, so as to require issues of notes beyond the limits fixed by law, her Majesty's Government recommend that this necessity should be met immediately upon its occurrence, and in that event they will not fail to make application to Parliament for its sanction.

" No such discount or advance, however, should be granted at a rate of interest less than 10 per cent., and her Majesty's Government reserve it to themselves to recommend, if they should see fit, the imposition of a higher rate. After deduction by the bank of whatever it may consider to be a fair charge for its risk, expense, and trouble, the profits of these advances will accrue to the public.

"We have the honour to be, gentlemen,

"Your obedient Servants,

"(Signed)   Russell.

"(Signed)   W. E. Gladstone."

The official correspondence is completed by the following letter and accompanying resolutions:—

"*To the Right Hon. Earl Russell and the Right Hon. W. E. Gladstone, M.P.*

"Bank of England, May 12.

"My Lord and Sir,

"Having laid before the court of directors the letter received from you yesterday with respect to a further issue of notes, if necessary, beyond the limit affixed by the Act of 1844, we have now the honour to enclose a copy of the resolutions of the court thereupon.

"We have the honour to be, my Lord and Sir,

"Your most obedient servants,

"H. L. Holland, *Governor*.

"Thos. N. Hunt, *Deputy-Governor*."

"*(Copy of Resolutions Enclosed.)*

"At a court of Directors of the bank, on Saturday the 12th of May, 1866.

"*Resolved,*—That the governors be requested to inform the First Lord of the Treasury and the Chancellor of the Exchequer that the court is prepared to act in conformity with the letter addressed to them yesterday.

"*Resolved,*—That the *minimum* rate of discount on bills not having more than ninety-five days to run be raised from 9 to 10 per cent.

"Hammond Chubb, *Secretary*."

The announcement of the third Suspension of the Bank Charter Act of 1844, for the third time operated like a charm. Mr. Macleod winds up his account of the crisis as follows:—

"The bank raised its rate to 10 per cent., and everything was calmed down; and subsequently to this some other stoppages took place, yet the knowledge that the bank had power to make advances on good securities abated the panic. . . . The sum that was paid away during the panic can probably never be known, but it was something perfectly fabulous. It has been said, though, of course we know not on what authority, that *one* great bank alone paid away 2,000,000*l.* in six hours."

Mr. Patterson observes:—

"It was midnight before the announcement was made. In the

interview which the deputation from the banks had with the Chancellor of the Exchequer, the necessity of suspending the Act was urged upon the Government by all present, except the representative of the Bank of England. This was mere bravado on the part of the Bank. The other banks could have shut it up at once, simply by withdrawing the reserves which they keep at the Bank. Indeed, one of the representatives of the joint-stock banks is reported to have said plainly, addressing the Bank's representative, ' I can draw a couple of cheques to-morrow morning which will shut you up at once.' The Bank Directors knew this quite well; but they knew also that they could indulge in bravado safely, as it was perfectly certain that the Bank Act must be suspended. . . . The effect of the announcement of the suspension of the Bank Act was so salutary that next day (Saturday) it was generally thought that the crisis was at an end. But, as became visible in a day or two, the crisis was not at an end —the panic revived. Large commercial failures began, imperilling the banks which held the bills of the fallen merchants; the ' bearing' operations went on; a run for deposits was kept up on several of the banks. It was impossible for these establishments to convert their securities into bank-notes in sufficient amount to meet the run upon them. After paying out 50 per cent. of its deposits in cash, the Bank of London (a substantially solvent establishment) had to stop; as almost every bank in like circumstances must do. When the Bank of London stopped, the Consolidated Bank came to the rescue. . . . But as the Consolidated Bank did not engage to take over the ' acceptances' of the Bank of London, the legality of the arrangements between the two banks was challenged, and the Consolidated Bank was threatened with a suit in Chancery. . . . In these circumstances, the Consolidated Bank was unable to meet the run upon it; and after paying out a large sum to the depositors of the Bank of London as well as its own during a struggle of three days, it closed its doors. After a still longer struggle—and mainly in consequence of a lying telegram sent from this country to Bombay, announcing its failure—the Agra and Masterman's Bank was likewise compelled to suspend payment.

"Contemplate the magnitude of the disaster. Overend, Gurney, and Co., the oldest and most powerful discount-house in the kingdom—the English Joint-Stock Bank, which fell because a large portion of its deposits was locked up in the stoppage of Overend and Co.—the Imperial Mercantile Credit Company, the European Bank, the Bank of London, the Consolidated Bank, and the Agra and Masterman's, with its wide-spread connections, were wrecked during that terrible season of panic. All three —the Bank of London, the Consolidated Bank, and the Agra and Masterman's—were perfectly solvent establishments; and the two latter subsequently resumed business. Their suspension (which was only momentary in the case of the Consolidated Bank) was caused not by a want of assets, but from the impossibility of converting their assets into currency (Bank of England notes), in order to meet the unusual demand upon them." *

* Patterson's Science of Finance, pp. 237–239.

The several panics that have occurred have originated, or are supposed to have originated, in as many distinct causes.   Thus, the panic of 1825 has been ascribed to anticipated profits on working foreign mines ; that of 1836 chiefly to the rapid extension of joint-stock banks; that of 1847 to excessive railway undertakings ; that of 1857 to reckless over-trading ; and the last, that of 1866 (mainly due to a mistaken estimate of the advantages of the Limited Liability Act, which led to the too rapid formation of financial companies), has been styled a " banking panic."   But, although it be true that each crisis of the kind is in large part produced by a distinct proximate cause, yet the primary cause of each and all is inordinate speculation begotten of the lust of gold.   Men are in haste to be rich.   This is no new thing.   It has been observable in all times, and in all countries.   But the fact is more patent now than ever.   Men live, as they journey, at railroad pace.   So long as appearances can be kept up, they " lay the flattering unction to their souls " that some lucky hit will make all right. Honesty gives place to expediency.   Shifts, evasions, trickery, undermine the moral sense, and grow into confirmed habits. The shams of private life are transported into men's public business.   To seem is to be.   Existence is undervalued unless men can " grow to what they seem " as respects wealth, that is ; or, at least, can manage to make their " Brummagem lacquer " look like gold.   Hence petty frauds develope into gigantic swindles.   Covetousness—a maddening desire to bound at once, say, from competence to riches—hurries the flies into the meshes cunningly woven for them, and the weak become the victims.

The disclosures elicited by the Select Committee of the House of Commons (appointed, after the panic of 1857, to inquire into the operation of the Bank Act of 1844), and published in their Report issued the succeeding year, show, so instructively, the mechanism of the " bubble-blowing," whose brilliant but evanescent colours dazzle and bewilder the public eye so as to cheat the multitude into a belief of the airy nothings being globes of solid metal, that we quote largely from its warning pages.   It is to be regretted that a like inquiry was not instituted after the panic of 1866.   Revelations of even more startling character would, most probably, have been the result.   The exposure of the machinery of commercial fraud, of banking incapacity, and of general gullibility which we proceed to extract, will, however, apply, *mutatis mutandis*, to every monetary crisis yet recorded; and affords far too valuable a lesson to be omitted.   The Committee, then, report as follows :—

"The first occurrence in this country which caused alarm, was the failure of the House of Macdonald and Co., of Glasgow and London, which took place in October, and was accompanied by the failures of Monteith and Co., and Wallace and Co., of Glasgow.   The house of Macdonald employed a great many work-people in sewing muslin goods for the home trade, and for the American market, and this they carried on to a very large extent.   They had been in fair credit till very nearly the time of their failure, but shortly before that period, they are described as having given out that they had changed their mode of doing business, for the purpose of embracing a wider field.   This, however, is represented as having been a deception, intended to cover *a system to which they had recourse of drawing fictitious bills,* and to give to those bills the appearance of genuine business transactions.

" From the records of the public tribunals, it appears that a very considerable number of persons (one of the partners is said to have admitted as many as seventy-five) in London, and other places, were employed by this firm, *for a small commission,* to put their names to fictitious bills, which were then discounted, a large proportion of them in Glasgow; and when the house of Macdonald failed, it was found to be indebted to the Western Bank £422,000*l.*"

" For a general review of the failures which occurred in England your Committee have been indebted to Mr. Coleman and to Mr. Ball, of the firm of Messrs. Quilter and Ball, both eminent accountants in London. These gentlemen do not profess to have studied abstruse questions of currency; they do not represent themselves as particularly conversant with the operation of the Act of 1844.   They, however, assign what appears to your committee an adequate cause for the recent commercial crisis.   Availing themselves of their experience in 1847, the affairs of which have now been finally closed, to illustrate the transactions of 1857, which still appear in estimate, and are therefore liable to correction, they ascribe the calamities of both periods to the same principal cause, viz., the great abuse of credit, and consequent over-trading.   They notice also this difference between the two periods : many of the houses which fell in 1847, they say, had once been wealthy, but had long ceased to be so.   Those of 1857 had, with few exceptions, never possessed adequate capital, but carried on extensive transactions by fictitious credit.   In 1847, for example, one house, which had been originally wealthy, failed, with liabilities amounting, in the whole, to upwards of 1,800,000*l.*, of which not quite 1,000,000*l.* were to be paid by other parties, leaving more than 800,000*l.* the direct liabilities of the house.   The capital, as represented in their books at the time of suspension, was 215,000*l.*, and the assets, according to their own valuation, 800,000*l.*, or nearly sufficient to meet the whole of their liabilities. Very different, however, was the valuation of the accountant, who estimated their assets at 185,000*l*., and even that was materially diminished in the result. *The dividend ultimately paid was only ninepence in the pound!* This firm, originally merchants, insensibly advanced their capital to planters in the East Indies, until it became necessary for them to be planters themselves. They then were compelled to obtain advances from others, which they accomplished by the sale and circulation of bills in the East Indies upon the house, to a great extent. Obtaining credit in that manner they postponed their fall many years, and ultimately fell, paying only ninepence in the pound. In this case, advances had been made on the credit of the next year's crop. This was an extreme case, and was connected with peculiar considerations at that time affecting the price of colonial produce, the principal property of the house. But Mr. Coleman, from whose evidence these particulars have been taken, says, that the estates which came under his notice as insolvent in that year, paid generally very small dividends, not averaging more than 4*s*.

" Another example of the same period is described by Mr. Ball as follows : It was that of a house which failed in 1847 ; they were engaged very largely as merchants in this country, and they were a house of very old standing. In the course of their business, they came under advances to a house in one of the colonies, on the security of the crops to be sent forward from time to time. The parties to whom those advances were so made failed to repay them ; that is to say, to recoup the London house for them ; and eventually the London house was obliged to take upon themselves the business which was originally conducted by those whom they accommodated with advances ; in other words, the merchant in London did practically become the planter and the owner of estates. After he had so become the planter, his position was changed from that of being a person who made advances, and he himself found it necessary to obtain advances. Most likely the course would be this, that the house on the other side, perhaps the correspondents themselves of the London house, would draw upon the London house, or draw upon some third party, and remit to the London house ; which bill the London house would take to its banker and get discounted, and by that process would be placed in funds to provide from time to time for its own engagements. The result of which would be to sustain for some time the credit of the house, after the capital of the house had been exhausted. The effect would be to enable them to hold produce in expectation of better prices ; the longer it was continued, the heavier would be the ultimate loss. After an interval of ten years, this house has, within the last few months, paid a final dividend, *making a total of* 1*s*. 10*d. in the pound.*

" Mr. Ball is asked,—

"' Looking back to the experience of the year 1847, were the dividends that were paid by the insolvent houses generally very small?'—' The average dividend would be small, so far as I recollect. Here and there would be a house which would pay in full, or would pay a very large dividend ; but the general result was, that a small dividend upon the whole was received by the creditors.'

"' Looking back now, with your experience, to the results of 1847, is it your opinion that if the law had afforded greater facilities for obtaining credit at that time for the purpose of sustaining these houses longer, the result would have been more advantageous to the houses themselves, or to the community at large ?' 'Knowing what I do of the internal state of those houses when they did stop, I should say that had they been able to obtain further credit for a continued period of time, it would only have had a temporary effect upon their position, and that most of them (of course I have a reserve of some good cases in my mind), from their internal condition being worn out, and from the want of real capital in their concerns, must have failed ultimately, and that the *longer the assistance was continued simply upon their credit, the greater the ultimate loss would be.*'

" ' Such is your view of the failures that took place in 1847, speaking generally ?'—' That is my view.'

" Your Committee have thought it not irrelevant to place on record these instances, which it was not in the power of their predecessors in 1848 to give, because they furnish an instructive example how readily misfortunes are at the time attributed by the sufferers, and others sympathising with them, to the operation of statutory enactments, which misfortunes, upon a full review of all the circumstances attending them, it is obvious *that no wisdom of the legislature, no regulation of the currency could have prevented.*

" Your Committee have before them the particulars of thirty houses which failed in 1857. The aggregate liability of these houses is 9,080,000*l.* of this sum the liabilities which other parties ought to provide for amount to 5,215,000*l.*, and the estimated assets, 2,317,000*l.* Besides the failures which arose from the suspension of American remittances, another class of failures is disclosed. The nature of these transactions was the system of open credits which were granted ; that is, by granting to persons abroad liberty to draw upon the house in England to such extent as had been agreed upon between them ; those drafts were then negotiated upon the foreign exchanges, and found their way to England, with the understanding that they were to be provided for at maturity. They were principally provided for, not by staple commodities, but by other bills that were sent to take them up. There was no real basis to the transaction, but the whole affair was a means of raising a temporary command of capital for the convenience of the individuals concerned, merely a bare commission hanging upon it ; a banker's commission was all that the houses in England got upon those transactions, with the exception of receiving the consignments probably of goods from certain parties, which brought them a merchant's commission upon them ; but they formed a very small amount in comparison with the amount of credits which were granted. One house, at the time of its suspension, was under obligation to the world *to the extent of about* 900,000*l. Its capital at the last time of taking stock was under* 10,000*l.* Its business was chiefly the granting of open credits, *i.e.*, the house permitted itself to be drawn upon by foreign houses without any remittance previously or contemporaneously made, but with an engagement that it should be made before the acceptance arrived at maturity. In these cases, the inducement to give the acceptance is a commission varying from ½ to 1½ per cent. The acceptances are rendered available by being discounted, as will appear hereafter, when the affairs of the banks which failed come under our notice.

" The obvious effect of such a system is first, unduly to enhance, and then, whilst it continues, to sustain the price of commodities. In 1857, that fall of prices which, according to Mr. Neave, ' far-seeing people had anticipated,' actually occurred.   Tables have been put in by more than one of the witnesses, exhibiting an average fall of 20 or 30 per cent., in many instances much more, upon the comparison of July, 1857, with January, 1858. It needs no argument to prove what effect such a fall must have upon houses which had accepted bills, on the security of produce consigned, *to the extent of one hundred times the amount of their own capital.*

" The witness is asked,—

" ' In the case which you are now describing to the Committee, these transactions had gone on to the extent of 900,000*l.*   The real guarantee was partly produce and partly bills of exchange; to whatever extent that produce was depreciated, of course the liability of the firm to failure would arise, and the capital of that firm, to meet such depreciation of produce, was about one-hundredth part of the whole of their liabilities ?' —' That is so.'

" ' Do you consider that case to be a fair illustration of the recent commercial disasters which have occurred ?'—' I think it is, though I should mention that in some cases the proportion of capital possessed was larger than that which I have mentioned. . . . . .'

" The commercial crisis was very little felt in Ireland until the failure of some of the banks in England and Scotland.   The trade of Ireland, with the exception of that of Belfast, being little connected with the United States, did not feel directly the effect of the failures there, but when failures began to take place at home there was an internal pressure consequent upon them, which, about the early part of the month of November, manifested itself severely in a demand for gold by depositors and holders of notes, and there was a run on the savings banks.   The Bank of Ireland advanced to the banks in Ireland requiring gold to the extent of about 250,000*l.*; and they were obliged to draw from the Bank of England from 1,000,0000*l.* to 1,200,000*l.* besides.   Belfast has a large trade with the United States, as well as a constant intercourse with Scotland, but there was no alarm until the time of the Scotch Bank failures.   *There was then, what had never been known before in Belfast since the institution of the joint-stock banks, a considerable run for gold in exchange for their notes.*   But the amount of gold which they held under the Act of 1845 was a source of strength.   The banks appear to be well constituted, and no serious results ensued. . . . . .

" Your Committee have examined Mr. Joshua Dixon, who in August, 1857, first assumed the post of managing director of the Borough Bank; Mr. Fleming, who has been, since July, 1857, assistant manager, manager or liquidator of the Western Bank of Scotland; and Mr. Kirkman Hodgson, a member of the House, and director of the Bank of England, who, being well acquainted with the trade of Newcastle, went to that town in November, for the purpose of ascertaining how far it was right that the Bank of England should give assistance to the Northumberland Bank.

"The state of these three banks at the time of their failure may be collected from the following summary, viz. :

"Mr. Joshua Dixon, for many years resident in the United States, and once a private banker at New Orleans, settled at Liverpool in 1852, and soon afterwards became a shareholder and director of the Borough Bank. This institution was originally a private bank, that of Messrs. Hope, in whose hands it was prosperous, and they retired as wealthy men about the year 1834. In 1847, however, the Borough Bank was under the necessity of obtaining assistance from the Bank of England. When Mr. Dixon became connected with it, he found that the board, which consisted of twelve directors, chose two managing directors and a chairman. The entire management of the bank was amongst the managing directors and the manager. On the 1st August, 1857, Mr. Dixon himself became a managing director, and thus describes the state in which he found the affairs of the bank :—Its position, he says, was that of its available means being very much reduced, being far smaller than was at all consistent with the sound and safe position of the bank. Speaking irrespectively of any general commercial pressure, he tells your Committee that, from the 1st of August, when his attendance at the bank was daily, as he became more and more thoroughly acquainted with the position of individual accounts, and with the whole circumstances of the bank in proportion as time lapsed, he became more and more convinced that the position of the bank was one of exceeding danger. When the commercial crisis showed itself, of course the danger to the Borough Bank became imminent, and they made an application to the Bank of England for assistance, some time between the 20th and the 23rd of October. The position, in general terms, of the bank was, that its assets were all locked up and unavailable, and that some 600,000*l.* or 700,000*l.* of its assets or claims on its debtors, which had until a short time previously been considered good, could not be relied upon, even for ultimate realization. About 3,500,000*l.* bills were at that time in London under the indorsment of the Borough Bank of Liverpool; of which from 700,000*l.* to 1,000,000*l. had no negotiable validity at all,* except the indorsement of the Borough Bank of Liverpool.

" Pending the negotiations with the Bank of England, there appeared in the *Times,* of October 27th, an article stating that arrangements had been made for giving assistance to the Borough Bank; in consequence of which a run took place, and the doors of the bank were closed. That run lasted only two or three hours, but the cash at their command was reduced to between 15,000*l.* and 20,000*l.*; while their liabilities on deposit were in all 1,200,000*l.* of which 800,000*l.* were at call, and the remainder at periods varying from two to six months. The dividend of this bank, which had previously been seven per cent., had, at the last meeting, held on 10th July, 1857, been reduced to five; and the sum of 165,000*l.* was, on the face of the report, acknowledged to have been lost. *The total loss,* so far as the witness could estimate it, amounted to 940,000*l., being the total capital of the bank.* It is ascribed, not to advances improperly made to favoured persons, but to want of discretion in the management.

" The Western Bank of Scotland was founded in 1832. In 1834 it was already in difficulties, and their correspondents in London dishonoured their bills. They applied to the other banks for assistance, and received it upon certain conditions. In the year 1838 they applied to the Board of Trade for letters patent, which were refused. At this time the Bank of Scotland and other banks addressed a memorial to Mr. Poulett Thomson, alleging the breach of the conditions referred to.

"In 1847 the Western Bank was again in difficulties, and was assisted by the Bank of England, receiving an advance of 300,000*l.* The then manager, Mr. Donald Smith, appears to have taken alarm from the occurrences of 1847; and in 1852, when he retired, the bank, though not in a satisfactory position, stood better than it had stood before since 1847. When it failed on 9th November, 1857, it appeared that the four insolvent houses of Macdonald, Monteith, Wallace, and Pattison, *were indebted to it in the sum of* 1,603,000*l.*; *the whole capital of the bank being only* 1,500,000*l.* One of the conditions of the co-partnery was, 'that if it shall at any time appear, on balancing the company's books, that a sum equal to 25*l.* per centum on the advanced capital stock of the company has been lost in prosecution of the business of the company, such loss shall, *ipso facto*, and without the necessity of any further procedure, dissolve and put an end to the company.'

"Mr. Fleming became assistant manager in July, 1857, and at once examined the affairs. He estimated that even supposing the debts of these four houses (which had not yet become insolvent) were assumed to be good, there appeared on the face of the books as good assets 573,000*l.* of bad debts; and deducting the rest and guarantee fund, which then amounted to 246,000*l.*, there remained an apparent deficiency or encroachment on the capital of the bank of 327,000*l.* This of itself nearly approached the limit which dissolved the partnership and put an end to the existence of the board; and of this state of affairs Mr. Fleming believes that up to that time the directors were in a state of almost entire ignorance. In 1853, previously to the first meeting of the shareholders after Mr. Smith's departure, an examination was instituted preparatory to the annual balance. From a confidential paper, having marks upon it in the handwriting of the then manager, it appears that a sum of 260,000*l.* was reported to him as irrecoverable on one branch of the assets, *which nevertheless appeared as good assets in the published balance sheet.* The modes in which this kind of disguise can be accomplished will perhaps be best understood by stating the manner in which a debt called 'Scarth's debt,' comprised in a different branch of the assets, was disposed of. That debt amounted to 120,000*l.*, and it ought to have appeared among the protested bills. It was, however, divided into four or five open credit accounts, bearing the names of the acceptors of Scarth's bills. These accounts were debited with the amount of their respective acceptances, and insurances were effected on the lives of the debtors to the extent of 75,000*l.* On these insurances 33,000*l.* have since been paid as premiums by the bank itself. These all now stand as assets in the books. Though this substitution took place in 1848, yet down to the time when Mr. Fleming's examinations began to bring to light the true state of affairs, the six directors appear to have regarded these sums as part of the available property of the shareholders. This being the actual state of the accounts, the dividend was raised in 1854 from 7 to 8 per cent., and in 1856 to 9 per cent. *Nine per cent. was the dividend declared in June*, 1857, at which date a very slight acquaintance with the books must have led to the strongest suspicion, not to say to the clear conviction, *that for some time a considerable portion of the capital had been lost.*

" This bank had 101 branches throughout Scotland. It had connections in America, who were allowed to draw upon it for the mere sake of the commission. At home it made advances upon ' indents ;' or, in other words, provided the manufacturer with the capital with which yet unmade cloth was thereafter to be produced. Its discounts, which in 1853 were 14,987,000*l.*, had been increased in 1857 (till 9th November) to 20,691,000*l.* With what care this business was conducted may appear from the circumstances *that Macdonald's bills were accepted by* 124 *different parties ; that only* 37 *had been inquired about, and in the case of* 21 *the reports received from the correspondents of the bank were unsatisfactory, or positively bad.* Yet the credit given to Macdonald continued undiminished. The rediscounts of the bank in London, which in 1852 had been 407,000*l.*, rose in 1856 to 5,407,000*l.* The exchanges of notes in Edinburgh have been always against the Western Bank, and for an average of the last six years to an extent of not less than 3,000,000*l.* a year. This circumstance is accounted for by Mr. Fleming chiefly by reference to the nature of the transactions with Macdonald's and other houses in accommodation bills ; 988,000*l.* were due to the bank from its own shareholders.

" About the end of October the Northumberland and Durham Bank applied for assistance to the Bank of England. It was declined, as they could not give any satisfactory explanation of their real position. They applied a second time, urging the great peril in which they were placed by the continued discredit, and by the constant drain of small deposits ; they urged also the fear of disturbances and breach of the peace which might ensue if they were to fail, they being so largely connected with collieries and ironworks. Accordingly on Tuesday, 24th November, Mr. Hodgson went down to Newcastle, and told the directors that he had been sent down by the Bank of England to examine into their books, and see whether it was possible to render them such assistance as would enable them to go on ; but that the first condition of the Bank doing anything was that they should prove themselves solvent. The result was that Mr. Hodgson found the liabilities, as then stated, amounting to 2,600,000*l.*, of which there were 1,350,000*l.* of deposits, 1,150,000*l.* accounts current, and they had rediscounted 1,500,000*l.*, of which they expected that 100,000*l.* would come back upon them, and for which they would ultimately be liable, making altogether 2,600,000*l.* Their assets were of a very peculiar nature indeed, the early realization of which would be almost impossible. They held about 1,000,000*l.* in securities of different kinds. They held in trade bills, that is to say, small bills on shopkeepers of Newcastle, about 250,000*l.*, bills which were probably good in themselves, but which were not available anywhere out of Newcastle ; they were not bills which could have been discounted in any other part of the money market. They had in overdrawn accounts 1,664,000*l.*, without any specific securities attached to them. Of these 1,664,000*l.*, there were 400,000*l.* which one of the directors very candidly confessed must be considered as totally bad, *and which ought to have been written off long before, but which still remained in the account as good debts.* The capital of the concern was 656,000*l.* nominally, but in reality it was considerably less than that; because in 1847 they had been in trouble, and in order to get out of that trouble they had made a call of 5*l.* or 10*l.* a share, which was not paid upon some of the shares, which shares were forfeited, and taken by them into the stock of their bank, to be reissued should occasion warrant their doing so. The consequence was that the subscribed capital of the bank was about 600,000*l.* This statement at once showed that any attempt to help them, short of taking up the whole concern and liquidating it for them, would be perfectly useless. It was evident that the whole capital was gone; and, looking at the character of the securities, Mr. Hodgson came to the conclusion, not only that the capital was gone, *but that the bank was totally insolvent.* Being very much struck with the extraordinary loss which had taken place in the bank, which, when a private bank, he knew to have been a very flourishing one, he inquired whether there was not some old sore of which nothing had as yet been said. He was told that there was one; there was rather a disinclination to mention what it was, but he felt it his duty to press it, and they told him they had a very large debt with the Derwent Iron Company. He inquired the amount of this debt, and found, much to his astonishment, that it amounted to 750,000*l.*, the capital of the bank being 600,000*l* For that debt there was a kind of security, which consisted of 250,000*l* of what were called Derwent Iron Company's debentures, which were, however, in reality, *nothing but the promissory notes of the directors,* there being very few persons in this Derwent Iron Company. The bank had also 100,000*l.* mortgage on the plant, and the remaining 400,000*l.* was totally unsecured. In addition to this original debt then mentioned of 750,000*l.*, there is now another charge upon it of 197,000*l.*, resulting from bills which have not been paid, and which, in order that the Derwent Iron Company might get them discounted, the bank had endorsed or otherwise guaranteed. These have now come back, so that the total liability for which the Derwent Iron Company is indebted to the bank is about 947,000*l.* ; very nearly 1,000,000*l.* The Derwent Iron Company appears to have been, almost from the time of the conversion of the bank into a joint-stock bank, very intimately connected with it. Mr. Jonathan Richardson, who was the moving spring of the whole bank, in fact the person who managed everything, was, *though not a partner in the Derwent Iron Company, very largely interested in it* as holding the royalties upon the minerals which they worked. It appears that the concern has been worked extremely badly; that it has never made any profits at all, even in the very finest years, for the ironmasters, *and it has gone on absorbing the money of the bank unchecked by the directors.*

"Mr. Hodgson says that 1,000,000*l.* of securities were taken of the most extraordinary nature for any bank to hold that he ever saw; that 1,000,000*l.* of securities, which was the only tangible asset which they had against the 2,600,000*l.* of liabilities, consisted of 350,000*l.* of the Derwent Iron Company's obligations, 250,000*l.* being debentures, and 100,000*l.* mortgage on the plant. They had besides these, 100,000*l.* on a building speculation at Elswick, near Newcastle, which however was not a primary mortgage.

there being a mortgage of 20,000*l.* on that land belonging to Mr. Hodgson Hinde. They had also another 100,000*l.* on other building land and houses in the neighbourhood of Newcastle. They had about 350,000*l.* in securities of works and manufactures of different sorts, and they had about 50,000*l.* in navigation bonds guaranteed by the railway, but which railway was the only security to which they could look in any given time to realise any sum of money; that made about 1,000,000*l.* altogether. The other securities were absolutely unmarketable. This bank had derived assistance from the Bank of England in the former crisis, that of 1847. Almost exactly the same circumstances arose then which arose in 1857, and almost from the same cause. The bank, however, applied at that time to the agent of the Bank of England at Newcastle, and he, on his own responsibility, made them a very large advance, which carried them through; he taking at the same time a very considerable security from them in various mortgages, pretty much of the character which has been above mentioned, but better in quality, although not any more banking securities than these; between 700,000*l.* and 800,000*l.* altogether.

"'The whole of the advance made in 1847 was repaid to the Bank of England, was it not?'—'Yes. With regard to the late occasion I represented at the same time that, though the bank could not be assisted, yet the fact of its failing, which it would do the moment it was known that the Bank of England would not help it, would be at that moment a very serious thing for the district, because it was so much connected with the collieries and ironworks that it paid every week, either for persons who had balances with it, or for persons whose bills it discounted, and thus gave them the money, about 35,000*l.*, on which the wages of 30,000 people were dependent; and as their pay-day was on the Friday, and the bank would stop on the Thursday, it was very desirable that something should be done to prevent the confusion which would arise if there was no preparation made for that conjuncture. In consequence of that the Bank of England requested me to go down again that night, with full powers to make arrangements with all persons who might have any tangible and good security, though, perhaps, not perfectly regular security, so as to provide them with the means of making their pays on the Friday. I went down accordingly, and arranged with almost everybody, or with everybody, I may say, to make such advances as would enable them to meet the pays for that week and for the next, should it be necessary. I also advised the manager of the savings bank to open his bank on Saturday for payments, though it was not the usual day, and authorised him to draw upon the Bank of England for any sum of money which he might require for the purpose of making any payment; but owing to the fact of the Bank of England thus enabling the proprietors, the coal mines, and the works, to make their weekly payments, there was no run whatever upon the savings bank, and everything passed off quite quietly.'

"'Was there any limit to the authority which you had from the Bank of England to give assistance in Newcastle?'—'No, there was no limit, it was left to my discretion to do what might be necessary. We knew very well that it could not amount to a sum, under any circumstances, of much more than from 50,000*l.* to 70,000*l.*'

"'Are there any other particulars connected with the Newcastle Bank which you are able to lay before the committee ?'—I will, if the committee wish, give them the actual result of the accounts of the bank when it was finally wound up in January this year, as compared with those in November, 1857 : it will show a little difference. In November, 1857, the liabilities of the bank were 2,600,000*l.*; these consisted of deposits, 1,350,000*l.*; accounts current, 1,150,000*l.*; and estimated liabilities on re-discounts, 100,000*l.* In January, when the bank was positively wound up and the thing ascertained, it appeared that there were of deposits 1,256,000*l.*, in accounts current, 766,000*l.*, and in liabilities on rediscounts, 231,000*l.* The only great difference was in the accounts current, which were diminished about 400,000*l.* This was principally, I believe, from the fact that many persons who had accounts current had deposit accounts also ; they kept two accounts, one of which had a balance in its favour, and the other was overdrawn ; therefore, one account being set against the other, it diminished it by so much, and at the same time diminished the amount of overdrawn accounts ; the assets which were estimated in November at 2,500,000*l.* had fallen in January to 2,000,000*l.*; and there was one peculiarity which was, that while the debt of the Derwent Iron Company was taken as an asset in November at 750,000*l.*, in January it was taken as an asset at 947,000*l.*, and that it is an asset of a very doubtful nature ; *the position of the bank is much worse in reality than is shown by the statement of the figures.*

"This disclosure was the result of an examination which lasted about two hours; *yet the bank had declared, at the last half-yearly meeting, a dividend of seven per cent., making to the shareholders a statement the substance of which showed a very prosperous state of things.* Mr. Hodgson mentions that he remarked on the fact of their having declared a dividend in June, when it was admitted that half the capital was lost, and he asked how they could have done so ; it was stated, in reply, that there were so many persons who depended entirely for their livelihood on the dividends received, that they really could not bear to face them without paying any dividend.

" Each of these three banks had been in peril in 1847, and though by the assistance of the Bank of England they were enabled to surmount it, they fell on the next occasion of severe commercial pressure, under circumstances still more injurious both to their own proprietors and to the public. Two bill-broking houses in London suspended payment in 1847, both afterwards resumed business. In 1857 both suspended again. The liabilities of one house in 1847 were, in round numbers, 2,683,000*l.*, with a capital of 180,000*l.*; the liabilities of the same house in 1857 were 5,300,000*l.*, the capital much smaller, probably not more than one-fourth of what it was in 1847. The liabilities of the other firm were between 3,000,000*l.* and 4,000,000*l.* at each period of stoppage, with a capital not exceeding 45,000*l.*

" These five houses contributed more than any others to the commercial disaster and discredit of 1857. It is impossible for your committee to attribute the failure of such establishments to any other cause than *to their own inherent unsoundness, the natural, the inevitable result of their own misconduct.*

x

" Thus we have traced a system under which extensive fictitious credits have been created by means of accommodation bills and open credits, great facilities for which have been afforded by the practice of joint stock country banks discounting such bills, and rediscounting them with the bill brokers in the London market, upon the credit of the bank alone, without reference to the quality of the bills otherwise. The rediscounter relies on the belief that if the bank suspend and the bills are not met at maturity, he will obtain from the Bank of England such immediate assistance as will save him from the consequences. Thus, Mr. Dixon states, ' In incidental conversation about the whole affair, one of the bill brokers made the remark that if it had not been for Sir Robert Peel's Act the Borough Bank need not have suspended. In reply to that, I said, that whatever might be the merits of Sir Robert Peel's Act, for my own part, I would not have been willing to lift a finger to assist the Borough Bank through its difficulties, if the so doing had involved the continuance of such a wretched system of business as had been practised ; and I said, if I had only known half as much of the proceedings of the Borough Bank while I was a director (referring to the time previous to the 1st of August, when I became a managing director) as you must have known, by seeing a great many of the bills of the Borough Bank discounted, you would never have caught me being a shareholder ;' the rejoinder to which was, ' Nor would you have caught me being a shareholder ; it was very well for me to discount the bills, but I would not have been a shareholder either.' "

The subjoined illustrative table supplies its own commentary :—

ABSTRACT STATEMENT of the (Estimated) Position of Sixteen Firms who suspended Payment during the Monetary Crisis of 1857–58.

—	Estimated Capital.	Total liabilities on Acceptances, Endorsements, and Open Balances at Date of Suspension.	Estimated amount of General Assets.
	£	£	£
1	None.	107,000	14,000
2	None.	54,000	5,000
3	None.	56,000	3,000
4	9,000	900,000	80,000
5	400	41,000	3,000
6	3,000	180,000	12,000
7	7,000	320,000	37,000
8	16,500	440,000	40,000
9	23,000	580,000	90,000
10	70,000	905,000	140,000
11	40,000	460,000	80,000
12	14,000	162,000	22,000
13	11,500	120,000	14,000
14	7,000	50,000	2,500
15	18,000	105,000	36,000
16	2,000	16,000	2,000
	221,400	4,496,000	580,500

The foregoing disclosures are as beacon lights to warn against the dangers of the rocks and shoals and quicksands which beset the track of modern adventurers in search of the Golden Fleece. Disclosures of the kind could be multiplied almost *ad infinitum*. But, once the gold-fever sets in, it rages until the moment of the crisis. And what follows then? We cannot answer the query better than by quoting from her " History of the Thirty Years' Peace," Miss Martineau's description of the consequences resulting from the terrible panic of 1825 :—

"There are many now living," wrote that talented lady in 1846, " who remember that year with bitter pain. They saw parents grow white-haired in a week's time; lovers parted on the eve of marriage; light-hearted girls sent forth from home as governesses or sempstresses; governesses, too old for new situations, going actually into the workhouse; rural gentry quitting their lands; and whole families relinquishing every prospect in life, and standing as bare under the storm as Lear and his strange comrades upon the heath !"

Must these vicissitudes continue? A recent writer on the subject* remarks—

" If crises must work their will when they arise, how are they to be prevented in the future? The problem is difficult, yet not absolutely insoluble. The difficulty lies more in moral than in physical or trade forces: it is the want of knowledge, and still more of observation and reflection, which generates real crises. . . . . . Crisis is not merely another word for poverty. If the diminution of wealth is met by wise curtailment of speculation even in its legitimate form, property may dwindle, but the convulsions peculiar to a crisis will not be developed. Then, again, if farmers never drained except with the surplus of a good harvest, if manufacturers never built new mills except out of realised profits, if goods were not produced except under a very strong presumption that they were in demand, if bankers never lent except upon solid and realisable security, no crisis would ever desolate the world. Traders and bankers, like sailors, have a difficult task in predicting the coming weather; and, like sailors, they must try to acquire the sailor's eye—the faculty of discerning small signs and judging their significance accordingly. The vital point is that they should notice the right things, the causes which are at work in brewing mischief. They must be studied at their origin. The difference between the intelligent merchant or banker, and the unintelligent, lies in the ability to understand the forces which make deposits and their withdrawals great or small—in the skill *rerum cognoscere causas*. This is a wide study beyond doubt. It is easier, no doubt, to float down the stream as it runs in the present, to make profits and to let to-morrow take its chance, or to set up some empirical rule, some high-sounding jargon,

* Mr Bonamy Price, in No. cvi. of the ' North British Review.'

without stopping to inquire whether it possesses the reality as well as the look of knowledge. But if men choose to let their actions be guided by such methods, they must look out for crises—sharp, sudden, and overwhelming crises. The responsibility weighs heaviest upon banks, not upon the Bank of England only, as some proclaim, but upon all bankers collectively. Everything depends on the sagacity and prudence they bring to bear on the loans they grant. The periodical recurrence of these convulsions seems to indicate that prudence lasts a year or two after disaster ·has punished folly; care and caution are developed in all commercial classes; and the energy and industry of the people restore the losses incurred. Prosperity follows; prudence gradually disappears; then heedlessness encourages every kind of enterprise; and again the thunder and lightning avenge forgotten virtue."

In other words, a cynic may remark on the above, when men shall become strictly moral and profoundly wise, the financial cataclysms, called panics, will be things of the past.

Although not expecting mankind to advance to that pitch of perfection which the writer just quoted seems to consider not only possible, but essential for the prevention of these catastrophes, our faith, as we intimated early in the present chapter, inclines to the hopeful. The panic of 1866 seems to have sunk deep into the public mind. Its effects on the rash spirit of eager speculation are still felt: indeed, undertakings which may fairly be called legitimate are looked upon coldly, and are with difficulty launched. The secrets of the manufacture of companies by promoters and directors, who, as soon as the market is "rigged," and shares at a premium, make their fortunes upon the ruin of the victimised purchasers, are now patent to most; and there are few, comparatively speaking, who do not understand that the holding out the inducement of exorbitant interest means certain risk to the capital invested, if not its sure loss. Yet, at this very moment of writing, an event is about to take place which, whilst it will rejoice every feeling heart, and gladden the whole civilised world, is already marking a change in the aspect of monetary affairs, so that what was true of their state but a few seconds ago, as it were, is quickly becoming a misrepresentation of the present, and of most questionable accuracy as respects the future. Peace will, too probably ban as well as bless. Speculation is already watching its opportunities with open eyes; and the prophet is not yet born who can foretell whether the next decennial cycle will, like the past, be black with doom, or inaugurate a new, a brighter, and a more auspicious era.

SECTION XI.

THE ADMINISTRATION OF JOINT-STOCK BANKS, WITH AN INQUIRY INTO THE CAUSES OF THEIR FAILURES.

THE chief points in which a joint-stock bank differs from a private bank are,—the number of its partners—the permanency of its capital—and the form of its government. A private bank formerly could not have more than six partners; a joint-stock bank may have a thousand partners. If a partner in a private bank die, or become insolvent, his capital is withdrawn from the bank; in the case of a partner in a joint-stock bank, his shares are transferred, and the capital of the bank remains the same. In a private bank all the partners may attend to its administration: a joint-stock bank is governed by a board of directors. The business principles on which these two kinds of banks are administered are the same, and the observations of the preceding sections will equally apply to both. The topics, therefore, to which we shall in this section more particularly direct our attention will be those that have a special reference to the constitution of joint-stock banks. We shall first consider the principles which should regulate their formation and management, and then notice the modifications imposed on new banks by the " Act to regulate Joint-stock Banks," * passed in 1844. After the 6th of May, 1844, it was not lawful for any new company of more than six persons to carry on the trade or business of bankers *in England,* unless by virtue of letters patent to be granted by her Majesty according to the provisions of that Act.

I. All joint-stock banks have a certain amount of paid-up capital.

The payment of a certain portion of the capital before the commencement of business, is a pledge that the project is not a mere bubble, and this is especially necessary when the proprietors have no further liability. But even with unlimited liability a certain amount appears to be necessary. The employment of capital judiciously is sometimes a means of acquiring business; and in case of loss there should always be a sufficient capital to fall back upon without recurring to the shareholders.

There is an evil in a bank having too small a capital. In this

* 7 & 8 Vict. cap. 113.

case, the bank will be but a small bank; the number of proprietors will be few, and the number of persons eligible to be chosen directors will be few; hence there will not be the same guarantee for good management. If a bank with a small capital have also a very small business, it had much better cease as an independent establishment, and become the branch of a larger bank. If, on the other hand, it has a large business, with a large circulation, large deposits, and large loans or discounts, its losses will sometimes be large, and hence the whole capital may be swept away. It is true, that while it avoids losses the shareholders will receive large dividends; but these large profits had much better be left in the bank as an addition to its capital than shared among the proprietors in the form of dividends. There is danger too that the high premium on those shares may induce many shareholders to sell out and form other, and perhaps rival establishments.

On the other hand, there is an evil in a bank having too large a capital. In this case, as the capital cannot be employed in the business, the directors are under the temptation of investing it in dead or hazardous securities for the sake of obtaining a higher rate of interest; perhaps too they may speculate in the funds, and sustain loss. Hence it is much better that a bank should commence business with a small capital, and increase the amount as the business may require.

It is difficult to state in all cases what proportion a capital ought to bear to the liabilities of a bank. Perhaps the best criterion we can have is the rate of dividend, provided that dividend be paid out of the business profits of the company. When we hear of a bank paying from 15 to 20 per cent. dividend, we may be assured that the capital is too small for the business. The liabilities of the bank, either in notes or deposits, must far exceed the amount of its capital. As a general maxim, the greater the capital the less the dividend. Let the whole capital be employed at any given rate of interest, say 3 per cent., then the capital raised by notes or deposit, produces. after paying all expenses, a certain sum as profit. Now, it is evident that if this amount of profit be distributed over a large capital, it will yield a less rate per cent. than when distributed over a small capital. Sometimes, however, a large capital may have increased the rate of dividend, in consequence of having been the means of acquiring a large increase of business. It may have done this in consequence of inspiring the public with confidence in the bank, and thus inducing them to make lodgments or circulate its notes; or it may have enabled the bank to make large advances, and thus gained the support of wealthy and influential customers.

Although the proportion which the capital of a bank should bear to its liabilities may vary with different banks, perhaps we should not go far astray in saying it should never be less than one-third of its liabilities.* I would exclude, however, from this comparison all liabilities except those arising from notes and deposits. If the notes and deposits together amount to more than three times the amount of the paid-up capital, the bank should call up more capital. It may be said, that the bank is liable also for its drafts upon its London agents, and for the payment of those bills which it has endorsed and re-issued: admitted; but in both these cases, the public have other securities besides that of the bank.

Presuming that banks are to commence with a moderate amount of capital, and to increase that amount as the business increases, the question is suggested, what is the best way of increasing the capital? . The English banks have followed two ways of doing this; one, by a further issue of shares; and the other, by further calls upon the existing shareholders. The capital of all the joint-stock banks in England is divided into certain portions, called shares; each proprietor holds a certain number of these shares, and pays a certain sum upon them. If he wishes to transfer a portion of his capital he cannot transfer a half share or a quarter share, but must transfer a whole share, or a certain number of shares. Thus, if the capital of a bank be 500,000*l.* it may be divided into 5,000 shares of 100*l.* each, or 50,000 shares of 10*l.* each, and a certain proportion of the amount of each share will be paid up; and this proportion is called the real or the paid-up capital. Thus, if one tenth of the above capital is paid up then, 50,000*l.* will be the real or paid-up capital, and 500,000*l.* will be called the nominal capital. In the chartered banks, on the other hand, there is usually no nominal capital, and the real capital is not divided into shares or portions, but any fractional sum may be transferred. The

---

* This is about the proportion in Scotland; but in England, or at least in London, the capitals of the Joint-stock Banks bear a much less proportion to their liabilities.

capital is then called stock. When there is no nominal capital, nor any way of increasing the amount of the real capital, this is the best way. But, in the other case, it is more convenient to have the capital divided into shares.

Some persons have objected altogether to a nominal capital ; but their objections have been directed more to the misrepresentations that may attend it, than to the thing itself. They say, " a bank announces that it has a capital of 500,000*l.*, whereas few shares are issued, and but a small sum is paid on each share; hence people are misled, and the bank acquires a confidence which it does not deserve." The objection here is against representing the nominal capital to be paid-up capital; it does not bear upon the principle of a nominal capital. In fact, we are misled by words. What is called nominal capital is nothing more than a further sum, which the directors have the power of calling up. If this sum had not been called capital, it would not be objected to, as it could lead to no misapprehension. But the inquiry simply is, ought the directors to have the power of calling upon the shareholders for a further amount of capital beyond that already paid up ? Were they not to have the power, the bank would at its commencement probably have too large a capital, and after its business had advanced would have too small a capital. And if the bank by any unforeseen occurrence became involved, and should have occasion for further sums to extricate itself from its difficulties, it could not make any further call upon its shareholders, although a very small advance might prevent its utter ruin. In case of a very large capital, such as two or three millions, a nominal capital may not be necessary, as so large a sum is likely to be in all cases amply sufficient. But in banks of a second class, it will always be best to give the directors the power of making further calls upon the shareholders.

The second way of increasing the capital of a bank, is by the issue of new shares. The whole amount of shares to be issued is fixed in the first instance, and the bank commences as soon as a certain proportion has been issued. If the bank was not allowed to commence business until the whole of the shares were taken, a small amount would be fixed upon, and the bank would be proportionably weaker. But by beginning with a small number of shares you have capital enough for your business, and you acquire more as you proceed. Many persons will join a bank after it is established who would not take shares at the commencement. Some shares are therefore reserved for persons of this description; and as the shares are more valuable when the success of the undertaking is no longer doubtful, they are often given out at a premium, and always a greater degree of caution is exercised as to the persons to whom they are distributed.

Some members of the parliamentary committee of 1836 appear to have an objection to shares of a small amount; they apprehend that these shares are taken by an inferior class of persons; and hence the body of proprietors are less respectable. But it would appear from the returns, that the general effect of small shares is, that each shareholder takes a greater number. Thus in the banks of 100*l.* shares each proprietor has taken upon an average twenty-eight shares, on which he has paid the sum of 444*l.* In the banks of 20*l.* shares, each proprietor has taken forty-three shares, and paid 359*l.* In the banks of 10*l.* shares, each proprietor has taken fifty-two shares, and paid 400*l.* While in the only bank of 5*l.* shares, each proprietor has taken 117 shares, and paid 585*l.* It appears to me that the chief objection to which small shares are liable is, that they do not admit of a large amount of nominal capital. The banks of 5*l.* and 10*l.* shares have usually the whole capital paid up, and hence in case of necessity the directors have no power to call for a further amount.

II. Joint-stock banks are governed by a board of directors.

" The directors are chosen from among the shareholders at a general meeting—the pecuniary qualification being that they hold a stipulated number of shares in the company.

" There are several points of view in which a man becomes eligible as a director of a bank, independent of his qualification as the holder of the required number of shares. Indeed, his qualification as a shareholder, merely, must not be taken into the account.

" 1. He ought, in the first place, to be a man enjoying public confidence. Unless he is a man whom the community contemplate as deserving of their confidence and esteem, it is not presumable he can be of much service to the bank, either by his influence or character. The public are not likely to deposit their money in an establishment where they cannot place the fullest reliance upon the directors; and, for the same reason, parties of respectability will not readily be induced to open accounts with the bank.

" 2. He ought to be a man possessing a knowledge of commercial business. It is a matter of great importance to the satisfactory and efficient management of a bank, that those to whom is entrusted the direction of its affairs, be in some measure conversant with the ordinary affairs of trade. Men who are retired from business are unquestionably the most eligible, not merely from their business knowledge, but because they are not apt to be contemplated with that suspicion, jealousy, and distrust, which tradesmen will sometimes exercise towards such directors of a bank as are likewise engaged in trade. But retired men of business are not readily to be had as directors of a bank, nor are they in most cases disposed to accept of such an office. Where such is the case, men of high standing and character, engaged in trade, should be sought for.

" 3. A bank director should be a man of strict integrity and uprightness. This is a qualification perfectly indispensable to the welfare of the bank. He must be above all trafficking in the stock of the company, or taking any undue advantage over the other shareholders through his intimate knowledge of the state of their affairs as regards the bank. He must never for a moment forget, that while he is a partner in the concern, and as an honest man, is bound to conduct it in as faithful and diligent a manner as he would his own private affairs, that he is at the same time appointed to a solemn trust, in having the interests of numerous others, equally interested with himself, under his management and control. In fact, unless the director of a bank is a man of strict integrity, he is placed in a position calculated to be productive of great mischief. He is invested with power to ruin the fortunes of others, and to inflict much commercial evil upon the community. Where there is a want of integrity, there is a want of principle, and the bank must necessarily be mismanaged.

" 4. A bank director should be a man of influence and respectability. He ought to be a man well known and respected in the district. Such a man is desirable in a variety of ways. He adds his own personal respectability to the establishment, and he influences the favour and support of his friends and acquaintances. His standing in society gives the public confidence in the establishment with which he is connected—and they bring their money and business to its support; the paper of the bank becomes more readily current in the district, and the weight of his influence destroys any suspicion of its stability.

" 5. A bank director should be in good pecuniary circumstances. It would be a most wholesome regulation, were it stipulated in all deeds of settlement that no bank director should be privileged to overdraw his account. The great facilities which directors enjoyed of raising money from overdrawing their bank accounts, have, in some instances, resulted in extensive commercial disasters, and in the total wreck of large establishments. The temptation to speculations of all descriptions which such facilities hold out, necessarily increases the risk of the bank, and induces a less rigid inspection of the accommodation afforded to other customers. Where those who are entrusted with the management of the bank forget the extent and importance of the trust reposed in them, and begin to enter into unwarrantable speculations with the funds committed to their care, it is not supposable that they will be particularly scrupulous as to the general management of the affairs of others.

" 6. A bank director should be one who can bestow some attention upon the affairs of the establishment. It has appeared in evidence that gentlemen have been appointed, and have accepted the office of directors of banks, who gave little or no attention to the affairs : who, in fact, appear to have considered that the office of director was conferred on and accepted by them more for the purpose of complying with the letter of the deed of settlement, which enjoined the appointment of a certain number of directors, than from any idea of their being expected, or of its being necessary for them to know anything regarding the management. The consequence of this has been, that the duties which devolved upon the directors, perhaps six individuals, were confined to two, or possibly only one, and the others approving, without suitable knowledge or proper inquiry, of all their acts, the mass of shareholders, as well as an extensive commercial circle, have been involved in the disastrous results of mismanagement. It is altogether an anomaly that any man, or body of men, should have the credit, honour, and distinction of being managers and directors of a bank, and yet not exercise any of the active functions and important duties that relate thereto. Upon what principle can they undertake, as by accepting the office they unquestionably do, to discharge a solemn trust, in faithfully administering the affairs of a bank, into which they make it no part of their business to look? Were the fact not very well known, it would seem absurd; yet it is not the less absurd that it is known." *

Mr. Taylor, in his "Statesman," makes the following observations upon the *age* of members of public boards:—

" Boards, or other co-operative bodies, should be so formed that youthfulness and elderliness may meet in due proportion in their counsels. If any such body be wholly composed of elderly men, it will commonly be found to be ineffective, so far as invention of new courses, and intrepidity of purpose is required; and perhaps, also, unequal to any unusual amount of spontaneous activity. If, on the other hand, it be composed wholly of young men, its operations will probably be wanting in circumspection; and the foresight by which it will be guided will be too keenly directed to the objects of a sanguine expectation—too dully to prospects of evil and counteraction. The respective positions in life of the young and the old operate to these results not less than their temperaments; for the young have their way to make—a reputation to earn—and it is for their interest to be enterprising, as well as in their nature; the old have ascertained their place in life, and they have, perhaps, a reputation to lose."

The Act of 1844 requires that provision shall be made in the deed of partnership " for the retirement of at least one-fourth of the directors yearly, and for preventing the re-election of the retiring directors for at least twelve months."

III. Joint-stock banks have a principal officer, called a manager.

" The prudent and satisfactory management of a Joint-stock bank very materially depends upon the upright and consistent discharge of those social duties and reciprocal interchanges of confidence which ought to characterise the directors and manager.

" The manager, from his experience, and the importance of the office he fills, is entitled to the kind consideration and entire confidence of the directors. He is selected by them to occupy an arduous and highly responsible situation, and ought to be rewarded not merely with an adequate pecuniary re-

* These observations are taken from the ' Philosophy of Joint-Stock Banking,' by G. M. Bell (Longman). I recommend the perusal of this little work to all directors and managers of joint-stock banks.

muneration, but with the respect and friendship of the directors, by whom he should be considered in every respect, so far as regards the bank, at least upon an equally elevated footing. Without the confidence and friendship of the directors, he can neither take his place at their meetings free from restraint, discuss with them matters relating to the welfare of the establishment with composure, nor appear before the customers with that satisfaction and independence which is required to the proper discharge of his duties. Having placed him in the position of manager of the bank, it is their duty always to contemplate him in that light, to respect and confide in his opinions and conduct, which in many cases have been formed by long years of active and arduous employment in the profession; and to speak well of him among their friends and acquaintances. In the degree in which the manager is respected, and well spoken of by the directors, will respect and confidence be extended to him, and consequently to the establishment, by the public, and a good opinion entertained of their judgment and discernment in his selection.

" The conduct of the manager ought to be characterised by great circumspection and uprightness. He ought, unquestionably, in every instance, to be chosen for his business qualifications, and not because he is a rich man, a gentleman, a man of fashion, or a man with an extensive circle of friends. To choose him on account of any one of these qualifications, and not principally from his practical experience of banking, would be similar to appointing a man to the care and management of a steam-engine, who knew nothing of its mechanism, nor the nature of its operation, but was recommended solely because he had a taste for travelling; or it would be like placing a man at the helm to pilot a vessel over quicksands, and through a reef of rocks, who knew nothing of a seafaring life, but was fond of contemplating the grandeur of the elements. The manager of a joint-stock bank ought to be chosen exclusively for his experience in banking; other qualifications are well enough in their own place, but ought never to be taken into consideration in choosing a person to act as manager of a bank. In this way a stimulus is given to persons of talent, who may be looking forward to the reward of a life of toil and drudgery; and thus merit is patronised and protected. In a well-regulated office no one will be promoted over the head of another, but a prudent selection being made at the outset, a system of regular promotion should be uniformly practised.

"The manager of a bank may be contemplated in three important points—in his intercourse with the customers and the public; with the directors; and with the subordinate officers of a bank. In each of these departments he has important duties to perform. He must be scrupulously diligent in his attention to the affairs of the bank, courteous in his interviews with the public, affable and unreserved in his communications with the directors, and kind and conciliating towards the subordinates of the bank, treating them as those who may be one day placed in a similar situation with himself. The days are now gone past when a man of business was considered in the light of a machine—a mere automaton for the purpose of forming figures and casting up accounts; but it is still necessary, enlarged as our views of the powers and capabilities of the human mind are, in order to the proper management of any business, that it be carefully attended to. The manager of a joint-stock bank, being allowed a competent salary, cannot be justified in occupying his time with any other employment which may occasion his absence from the duties of the bank. But it is not intended to insinuate that he must be a man of one idea, and restrained from turning his mental acquirements to his own amusement or profit. This would be as absurd as it would be unreasonable. Nor is it meant that a man of business may not be also a man of great erudition, and it may happen, of literary and scientific eminence. On the contrary, it cannot be denied that, in the present day, this is often the case. What is contended for is, that the bank is entitled to, and ought to have, his close and chief attention.

"As it is obvious that he cannot manage any other trade or profession, without sacrificing or delegating more or less the duties he owes to the bank; it seems also very doubtful whether he can be justified in taking a prominent part in public or political affairs. There are two arguments against his being a public character: the first is, that he may be drawn away during the hours of business; the second, that, by becoming a partisan, he is certain of being more or less obnoxious to a portion of the inhabitants, and, it may be, of the bank's customers. A man whose mind is occupied in framing political speeches, in promoting political schemes, and whose time is partially given to political, magisterial, or other meetings, cannot possibly, from the exciting nature of such subjects, give that cool, deliberate, and uniform attention to the duties of the bank which they necessarily require.

" The customers ought always to be treated with civility and kindness, their business transacted promptly and cheerfully, and every inquiry regarding their accounts, or any matter of business, readily and satisfactorily explained. When an accommodation is to be declined, it ought to be done in as polite and inoffensive a manner as possible—the manner of a refusal being of paramount moment to the character of a manager.

" The shareholders, being, in other words, the proprietors of the bank, are to be received with that freedom and confidence which is due to their character as such, but without compromising or revealing to them either the business and accounts of each other, or of the customers of the bank.

"Next to being secret and cautious, a manager ought to be prompt and decided in all his measures, free from party influence, and firm in his purpose. A habit of promptitude and decision is very essential to the proper regulation of the business of a bank, and acquired by forethought and circumspection. It is, perhaps, a constitutional virtue which cannot be enjoyed by every one in the same degree, but it is nevertheless a virtue which every one may acquire by proper attention. Nothing makes a manager look more silly and contemptible than a hesitating, dubious, and capricious manner. His answer ought to be prompt and satisfactory; he should be sufficiently acquainted with business to say, at once, whether an act can be done or not, and should appear free from restraint, and not disposed to alter an opinion when once formed." *

IV. In joint-stock banks the administrative functions are usually distributed between the directors and the manager.

With reference to both private and joint-stock banks, the distribution of the administrative functions is a most important topic of inquiry. By what parties ought these functions to be exercised?—We have spoken of " the banker," as though a bank consisted of only one person, and this one person administered all the powers and functions of the bank. But few banks consist of only one person. One class of banks consists of two,

* Bell's ' Philosophy of Joint-stock Banking.'

three, four, five, six, or more persons, some or all of whom attend to the practical administration of the bank. Another class of banks consists of a great many, it may be of several hundred persons, who appoint some dozen or score of their own number to administer the bank on their behalf.

But how many soever the number of partners may be in a bank, the administrative functions are in fact practically exercised by a small number of persons. A private bank may consist of as many as six or more partners, but it is rarely, we believe, that so many as six are actually engaged in the business. When more than one are thus employed their duties may be distributed according to their seniority or other circumstances. In ordinary matters there may be a division of labour, and each partner may preside over a distinct department of the business. But in all important cases there is usually one leading partner who practically guides the others. When a bank has risen speedily to eminence, it has generally been through the talents of some one man. It does not follow that this one man did not receive great assistance from the advice or suggestions of his partners. It is the part of a wise man to avail himself of the knowledge and wisdom of others; and he will often gather much useful information from men far below himself in general talents. There is, perhaps, more uniformity, consistency, and energy in the proceedings of a bank managed by a few partners than by many. On the other hand, banks have sometimes been ruined by placing too much power in the hands of one or two of the partners.

In a joint-stock bank, though the number of directors may be large, the daily exercise of the administrative power is practically in the hands of a few persons. In some banks this power is vested solely in the manager; sometimes in one or two managing directors; sometimes in a permanent committee of two directors and the manager; and in other cases, in a changeable committee, on which each member of the board takes his rota of service for two or three weeks in succession. In all cases, however, the board of directors lay down the general principles on which the bank is to be administered; reports are made to them at their weekly meeting of the actual condition of the bank in all its departments, and all very important matters are reserved for their special consideration.

V. Some joint-stock banks have many branches.

When the law existed in England that no bank should have more than six partners, the branch system scarcely existed. In some cases, a bank had a branch or two a few miles distant, but no instance occurred of a bank extending itself throughout a county or a district. But with joint-stock banking arose the branch system—the head office was placed in the county town, and branches were opened in the principal towns and villages around. The credit of the bank being firmly established, its notes circulated freely throughout the whole district. The chief advantages of this system are the following :—

There is greater security to the public. The security of the whole bank is attached to the transactions of every branch ; hence there is greater safety to the public than could be afforded by a number of separate private banks, or even so many independent joint-stock banks. These banks could have but a small number of partners—the paid-up capital and the private property of the partners must be comparatively small ; hence the holder of a note issued by one of the independent joint-stock banks could have a claim only on that bank : but if that bank, instead of being independent, were a branch of a large establishment, the holder of a note would have the security of that large establishment ; hence the branch system unites together a greater number of persons, and affords a more ample guarantee.

The branch system provides greater facilities for the transmission of money. The sending of money from one town to another is greatly facilitated if a branch of the same bank be established in each of those towns, for all the branches grant letters of credit upon each other. Otherwise you have to ask the banker in the town from which the money is sent to give you a bill upon London, which is transmitted by post ; or you request him to advise his London agent to pay the money to the London agent of the banker who resides in the town to which the money is remitted. This takes up more time, and is attended with more expense. A facility of transmitting money between two places usually facilitates the trade between those places.

The branch system extends the benefits of banking to small places where independent banks could not be supported. An independent bank must have an independent board of directors, who in most cases will be better paid—the manager must have

Y

a higher salary, because he has a heavier responsibility, and a large amount of cash must be kept unemployed in the till, because there is no neighbouring resource in case of a run. There must be a paid-up capital, upon which good dividends are expected ; a large proportion of the funds must be invested in exchequer bills, or other Government securities, at a low interest, in order that the bank may be prepared to meet sudden calls ; and the charge for agencies will also be more. On the other hand, a branch has seldom need of a board of directors, one or two being quite sufficient—the manager is not so well paid : there is no necessity for a large sum in the till, because in case of necessity the branch has recourse to the head office, or to the neighbouring branches ; nor is a large portion of its funds invested in Government securities that yield but little interest, as the head office takes charge of this, and can manage it at a less proportional expense. Besides, at some branches, the manager attends only on market days, or once or twice a week. The business done on those days would not bear the expense of an independent establishment.

The branch system provides the means of a due distribution of capital. Some banks raise more capital than they can employ, that is, their notes and deposits amount to more than their loans and discounts. Others employ more capital than they raise, that is, their loans and discounts amount to more than their notes and deposits. Banks that have a surplus capital usually send it to London to be employed by the bill-brokers. The banks that want capital must either restrict their business, or send their bills to London to be rediscounted. Now, if two banks, one having too much, and the other too little capital, be situated in the same county, they will have no direct intercourse, and will consequently be of no assistance to each other ; but if a district bank be established, and these two banks become branches, then the surplus capital of one branch will be sent to be employed at the other—thus the whole wealth of the district is employed within the district, and the practice of rediscounting bills in London.will be proportionately diminished.

The branch system secures a better system of management. The only way to secure good management is to prevent the formation of small banks. When banks are large, the directors are men of more wealth and respectability—they can give large salaries to their officers, and hence can command first-rate talent

—there will be a more numerous proprietary ; and in a large number there will be always some active spirits who will be watchful of the conduct of the directors and the manager; besides, in a numerous proprietary there is a greater number of persons eligible to be directors, and consequently there is a wider choice.   In populous cities, such as London or Manchester, a large bank may be formed without branches ; but in smaller places there is no way of forming a large bank but by giving it branches throughout the district.   A branch bank in a small town will probably be better managed than an independent bank in the same place.   The directors and manager of the branch will be appointed by the directors at the head office, assisted by the general manager, who are very competent to judge what qualifications are necessary for these offices, and who would not be biassed by local partialities.   But the directors of the independent bank would most likely be self-appointed, or chosen by the proprietors, because no others could be obtained, and these directors would appoint some friend of their own to be manager.   The manager of the branch, besides the super-intendence of the directors, which he has in common with the manager of the independent bank, will be subject to visits from the general manager or the inspector ; and he must send weekly statements of his accounts to the head office.   The consciousness of responsibility will thus secure a more anxious attention to his duties; and, besides, he will probably be looking forward for promotion to a higher branch as a reward for his successful management.   These circumstances seem to insure a higher degree of good management to the branch.

At the same time, it must be admitted that banks with numerous branches require a proportionate paid-up capital, and that the capital be kept in a disposable form ; it also requires vigilant and constant inspection, and a rigid system of discipline.

A proportionate paid-up capital is necessary, because, in case of a run, there are a greater number of points of attack : hence the funds must be divided to meet all these possible attacks ; for if one branch be overpowered, the whole bank is immediately exposed to suspicion.

Another danger arises from the incompetency or negligence of the managers of branches.   Among a number of men, it is not likely that all are clever, and all prudent ; and one case of neglect on the part of one manager may, in times of alarm, throw discredit on the whole establishment. Besides, there is sometimes danger even from the zeal of the branch managers. Each manager is naturally anxious to increase the business of his own branch ; and he will perhaps find that the most easy way of doing this is to extend his loans and discounts. Hence each manager tries to employ as much capital as he can ; and the urgent remonstrances he receives from head-quarters, requiring him to restrict his discounts, are either evaded or delayed. Thus the bank proceeds until some heavy demand for money arises at head-quarters, and it is then found that all the capital of the bank has been absorbed by the branches. These advances cannot be suddenly recalled, and thus the bank is ruined.

What number of branches a bank ought to have, and what distance they ought to be from the head office, have been the subject of much discussion. No general rules can be given. The subject may very safely be left to the discretion of the banks themselves. The banks in Scotland have from seventeen up to one hundred and fifteen branches. The Provincial Bank of Ireland, and the National Bank, whose head offices are in London, have branches spread all over Ireland. I am not aware that in these cases any danger or inconvenience has been experienced. When branches are found troublesome or un-profitable, they will very soon be discontinued. In some instances, even in Scotland, the branches of the larger banks have been withdrawn, in consequence of being unable to sustain a competition with the local banks of the district.

Had the Act of 1826 permitted joint-stock banks of issue to be established in London, we should probably by this time have had ten or a dozen banks having their head-quarters in London, and extending their branches throughout the country. But as the law prohibited joint-stock banks being established within sixty-five miles of London, it necessarily gave rise to banks occupying particular districts in the country. The advantages which are alleged to belong to the district system are the following :—That the bank will be better adapted to the wants and habits of the people—that a local feeling will be excited in its favour : hence the inhabitants of the district will take shares, and the occurrence of runs upon the bank will be less probable—that a better system of management may be expected, as it can more easily be governed, and will be more under control—that a panic in the district will not affect the other parts of the country, and hence supplies may be more easily obtained—that banks will be of a moderate size, and hence will be attended with the advantages arising from numerous banks acting as checks upon each other, instead of a few large banks who may combine for objects injurious to the nation ; and that as each bank will have an agent in London, the bills they draw will thus have two parties as securities, and the public will have a pledge that there is no excessive issue in the form of kites or accommodation bills. On the other hand, it may be contended, that in Scotland the large metropolitan banks, which have branches extended throughout the country, have generally been more successful than the provincial or district banks—that there is a greater security to the public for the notes or deposits—that advances are not so likely to be made to speculative parties merely on account of their local influence—that the capital raised in one part of the country can be employed in another—that the transmission of money from one part of the country to another is more rapid and direct— that the establishment of the bank being on a larger scale, you have a superior class of directors, and can demand the services of higher talents in those who are employed as officers.

It does not appear that these two systems are necessarily at variance with each other. County or district banks have no doubt many advantages, but they do not seem to supersede banks on a larger scale.

VI. Joint-stock banks have half-yearly meetings of shareholders, to whom is usually exhibited a balance-sheet showing the assets and liabilities of the bank.

All banks do not exhibit a balance-sheet.* The practice is said to be open to the following objections :—

1. That it is not a fair criterion by which you can form any judgment of the real condition of the bank. You might see that the bank had a certain amount of securities, or had advanced a certain sum upon loans ; but whether those securities were available, or whether those loans could suddenly be called up, are points upon which the balance-sheet could give no information. The Agricultural and Commercial Bank of

---

* All the Joint-Stock Banks in London do, but it is not the practice generally in the country.

Ireland published a very satisfactory balance-sheet a few weeks only before they stopped payment.

2. It lays the bank open to attacks from its rivals or opponents. The balance-sheet will show in what way the funds of the bank are employed, but it will not state the reasons why they are so employed. The opponents of the bank may attack every item of the balance-sheet, and the directors may not be able to repel those attacks without a breach of confidence that would be injurious to the establishment. Suppose, for instance, the balance-sheet should show that the bank had advanced a few thousand pounds upon mortgage. This might be justly considered as a departure from the sound principles of banking ; yet it might in this case be justified by some peculiar circumstances, which, nevertheless, the directors could not publish without serious injury to the parties concerned. The production of a balance-sheet is advocated upon the ground that it would enable the shareholders to judge of the ability and prudence of the directors. But how can they do this without knowing the reasons by which the directors are influenced in their decisions ?

3. It causes a great deal of speculation in the shares. The shareholders and the public would form their opinions of the bank from the statements in the balance-sheet ; and according to these opinions the price of the shares would fluctuate in the market. Suppose it were seen that the bank had invested a large portion of its funds in Government securities, and it was known that during the year the price of those securities had experienced a considerable fall, would not the bank shares immediately fall too ? Again, suppose at the end of a year like 1836, it should appear that the bank held a considerable amount of overdue bills, the apprehension of loss would cause the bank shares to fall ; soon afterwards these bills might be paid, and then the shares would rise again.—Thus, the publication of balance-sheets would keep the prices of shares in perpetual fluctuation, and furnish a most fruitful source of speculation and gambling.

4. It is perfectly inefficient as a protection against fraud. The balance-sheet, it seems, is to be a check upon the directors, and yet the directors themselves are to prepare the balance-sheet. They must be stupid knaves indeed, if they produce such a balance-sheet as shall expose their own knavery.

Besides, the balance-sheet merely shows the state of the bank on one day in the year. Would it not be easy to put the bank on that day in such a condition as would give satisfaction to the shareholders?

VII. At the annual, or the half-yearly meeting, the directors announce the amount of the profits and the mode of their distribution.

The first appropriation of the profits is to pay to the shareholders a dividend on the capital. But all the profits are not usually thus appropriated; a certain portion is generally retained as a rest, or surplus fund, or, as it is sometimes called, a guarantee fund. This last title has led to an erroneous impression with regard to the nature and purposes of this fund. It is not designed as a guarantee to the depositors for the amount of their deposits—these are guaranteed by the paid-up capital and the liability of the shareholders—but as a guarantee to the shareholders for the uniformity of their dividends, Should the profits in any one year fall below the sum necessary to pay the usual dividend, the deficiency may then be taken from the surplus or guarantee fund. The amount of this fund, therefore, will be regulated by the amount of the transactions, and the consequent danger of loss. But it sometimes happens that, after paying a liberal dividend, the surplus fund accumulates far beyond the sum necessary for the above purpose. In this case a portion of the fund may be employed either in still farther increasing the dividend, or it may be distributed to the shareholders in the form of bonuses, or it may be added to the capital. The course to be adopted must depend upon circumstances. When the capital is small, it will probably be best to make an addition from the surplus fund; but when the capital is sufficiently large, the best way will be to give an occasional bonus to the proprietors. This is usually better than increasing the dividend. For if the dividend be once increased, the same rate of dividend will always be expected. And it is better not to make any advance, unless there is good reason to believe that the same rate will always be maintained.

Those persons are under a mistake who object to a reserved or surplus fund on the ground that it takes away the profits from the existing shareholders, and gives them to the future shareholders. This is not the fact. An existing shareholder who keeps his shares until the fund is in some way distributed, receives or course his portion of the fund. But an existing shareholder who sells out his shares before the fund is distributed receives the value of his portion of the fund in the price of his shares. The amount of the surplus fund will influence the market value of the shares. In proof of this, we may observe that after a bank has declared a bonus, the market-price of the shares usually falls, as in fact, *cæteris paribus*, it ought to do.

We consider it of high importance that a bank should maintain an ample surplus fund. Without such a fund the dividends will fluctuate very widely, and sometimes there may be no dividend at all, even though upon a series of years the bank may have been very successful. Even if it is known that a bank has met with losses, its credit is not so much affected when it has an ample reserved fund to fall back upon. And besides the ordinary losses in the way of business, a bank will sometimes, in a season of pressure, be called upon to sustain loss by the realisation of securities; and it is very convenient to have a surplus fund sufficiently ample to bear all these contingencies. Such a fund too has a moral effect in strengthening the reputation of the bank in public estimation. It is regarded as an indication that its affairs are governed by a wise and prudent administration.

It will assist us in forming a correct judgment as to the principles on which joint-stock banks ought to be administered, if we take a view of those banks that have fallen, and notice the causes to which their failure may be assigned. In investigating these causes, we shall find that the disasters which have befallen joint-stock banks have arisen not from any unsoundness in the principles of joint-stock banking, but purely from mal-administration. It was predicted by their opponents that they would be ruined by the excessive issue of their notes; but the banks that have failed have been chiefly those that did not issue notes. It was stated they would be ruined by carrying on an extensive business with a small capital; but among the banks that have stopped have been some of the largest capital. It was supposed they would be ruined by unprincipled men getting to be directors, who, having no property of their own, would care little about squandering the property of others. But the fallen banks are chiefly those which were governed by honourable men; and the greatest sufferers have been the directors. Nor can it be said that the joint-stock banks have made their losses by engaging in speculations unconnected with banking. Private bankers have done so. But joint-stock banks are confined by their deeds of settlement to the business of banking. Nor has it appeared—except, perhaps, in the Isle of Man Bank—that they have violated their deeds in this respect. To what, then, must we ascribe the failure of so many joint-stock banks? We reply, To mal-administration; or, in other words, to bad management. And this leads us to inquire, In what way has this mal-administration been exemplified? What are those erroneous principles that have led to these fatal results? Without attempting to enumerate them all, we will endeavour to specify a few of the most prominent.

L. Taking the unsound business of other banks.

One cause of the rapid extension of joint-stock banks in 1836, was the " merging " of numerous private banks. It apppears that 138 private banking establishments merged in joint-stock banks. Some of the private banks sold their business after the joint-stock banks had come into operation. Others formed a joint-stock bank upon the private bank, the senior partner often becoming a director, and the junior partner the manager, of the new bank.

In by far the majority of cases, these unions, or " merges," were advantageous to both parties. The private bankers obtained the value of the business they had surrendered, and an interest in the future prosperity of the bank they had joined. On the other hand, the new joint-stock bank acquired a business already formed, and also obtained the advantage of the practical knowledge and superintendence of experienced bankers.

But in some instances the bargain was a disastrous one for the joint-stock bank. The bad and overdrawn accounts were taken without due examination, and soon afterwards occasioned considerable loss. The loss of the purchase-money was generally by far the smaller loss of the two. A joint-stock bank in the west of England purchased a private bank in a country town for a large sum, and took the overdrawn accounts without a guarantee. These accounts were considered good at the time, but a few years afterwards the parties failed, and the joint-stock bank lost considerably. A joint-stock bank gave to the Northern and Central Bank the sum of 6,500*l.* for their business at Leeds, after they had stopped. The accounts they took over were afterwards the occasion of great loss. The Isle of Wight Joint-stock Bank was formed upon a private bank, but a few months only had elapsed when they found they were insolvent from the losses that would arise from the bad accounts they had accepted. They immediately determined to wind up, and transfer their business to the National Provincial Bank of England. Other instances might be adduced of joint-stock banks having been founded on private banks which are now supposed to have been, at the time, in a state of insolvency.

II. Some banks have sustained losses by making advances on dead security.

Instead of the word "some," we think we might use the word "all." For among the banks that have failed we doubt if we could find one that had not sinned in this respect. But the greatest sinners were those banks that were established in places of the greatest trade. All the banks at Newcastle advanced money on collieries, and also on other public works. The banks of Manchester made advances on mills and manufactories, as did also some of the banks at Leeds. These advances were attended with several evil effects. In the first place, there was a lock-up of capital, which restrained the operations of the bank. To relieve themselves from this restriction, they took bills for their loans, and rediscounted them in the London money market. The facilities thus obtained induced them to extend this system of advance. Bills were perpetually renewed, and perpetually rediscounted. At last a pressure came, and the renewed bills could not be rediscounted. The bank could not take up the old bills that were returned, and consequently stopped payment. Sometimes, too, the bank tried to relieve itself from this pressure by increasing its drafts on its London agent. It has for a long time been the practice in Lancashire to pay for cotton with a three months' banker's bill. Banks in difficulties avail themselves of this practice to make all their advances by drafts on London, instead of cash. The Bank of Manchester had at one time an enormous circulation of this kind.

Another effect was that, however good the security might be at the time the advance was made, when a change took place in the state of trade, its value fell much below the amount of the advance, and in some cases it could not be sold at any price. But the evil did not stop here. As the property given us security would have been worth nothing if not worked, the bank was induced to make farther advances, to carry on the works on their own account. A colliery, if not kept in operation, soon gets out of order; and it will then require a considerable sum to set it at work again. Hence some of the collieries at Newcastle were worked by the banks; and mills in the neighbourhood of Manchester were carried on in the same way. The plan, however, does not often succeed. It is generally throwing good money after bad. The ultimate loss is usually increased. We may just observe in passing, that the banks in the East Indies get involved in the same way, through making advances on indigo works. These works are of no value except when kept in operation; and hence it has occurred that a bank which has made an advance, is compelled to carry on the works to keep up the value of its security. To show that a bank governed by the strictest rules may sometimes be drawn into transactions of this kind, it may be observed that an iron concern in Wales was said to have been carried on by the Bank of England. It belonged to the Governor and Company of the Mines Royal. The bank made an advance on mortgage to this corporation during the pressure of 1847, and took the profits of the works. Some joint-stock banks have made advances upon buildings. This has occurred chiefly in places where there has been an increasing population. A few years ago a joint-stock bank in a town of fashionable resort advanced large sums to builders upon the security of the houses they were erecting. The houses did not let—they could not be sold for anything like the cost price —the builders were ruined—and the loss fell upon the bank. The bank had recourse to the expedient of rediscounting the builders' bills; but after a while it was compelled to stop payment. In agricultural districts banks have sometimes made considerable advances to farmers and graziers. Indeed, it is almost a universal practice to do so at some seasons of the year. These advances are not individually of large amount, and are not usually attended with much loss—not with anything like the losses incurred by advances on collieries, mills, and houses. But it is a lock-up of capital until the year comes round.

III. Some banks have lost large amounts through advances made by way of loan or discounts to men engaged in speculative undertakings.

Two of the banks that stopped at Newcastle-upon-Tyne sustained great losses through advances to corn-merchants. Speculations in corn are usually carried on more by bills than by loan. A merchant buys a quantity of corn, and places it in the hands of a factor, and draws bills for something under the market value, leaving the factor a margin to guard against loss. He gets these bills discounted, buys more corn, which he also places in the hands of his factor, and then draws fresh bills. This second batch of bills he also gets discounted, and buys more corn; and thus he goes on in the same course. Now if he thinks the market will rise (as all speculators do), he will not allow his factor to sell the corn; but when the first bills fall due he will renew them, and with the produce of the new bills, when discounted, he will pay the old ones. It is thus that a large speculation may be carried on with a small amount of capital (and that may be borrowed from the bank), and all the specu- lation is kept afloat by bills. These bills are always for large amounts, and when the parties fail the losses are usually heavy. The failures in the corn-trade in 1847 fell heavily on the banking and monied interests. It was the stoppage of Messrs. Lesley, Alexander, & Co., the corn-factors, that caused the stoppage of Messrs. Sanderson & Co., the bill-brokers.

Wool is another " heavy article," as it is called; that is, it costs a great deal of money, and the bills are usually for large amounts. Occasionally there is much speculation in this article.

Builders are generally a speculative class. Banks that advance money to parties engaged in this trade have usually to take possession of the buildings. We have already noticed an instance of this in the conduct of a joint-stock bank.

People who speculate in railway and other companies are dangerous customers to a bank.

It may be remarked, that it is generally bad policy in a bank to make a very large permanent advance to any one customer. The word " large" is a relative term, and must be understood with reference to the extent of business that the customer is carrying on, and to the means of the bank. It is not the business of bankers to supply their customers with capital to carry on their trade. But it is their business to make temporary advances, and these advances may sometimes be large. In such cases, the banker should have a kind of security, that shall not only secure the debt, but shall prevent its becoming permanent. Almost every bank that has failed can point to some one, two, or three large accounts, to which it mainly ascribes its failure.

But the worst form of illegitimate advance is that which is made by a bank to one of its own directors.

A bank that is known to act imprudently in making large advances will occasion a suspicion that its smaller advances are made with, at least, equal imprudence. A large number of imprudent small transactions may be as fatal to a bank as a smaller number of a larger amount. A sum which appears small as a loan will appear large as a loss. A manager who accustoms himself to examine all the circumstances connected with the small bills he discounts, will acquire a habit of investigation that will guide him with safety in dealing with large transactions. But if he get into a laxity of manner in regard to small amounts, he will ultimately deal less carefully with large sums, and be in danger of making great losses. In every case the rules of sound banking should be strictly applied.

IV. Some banks have become involved in difficulties through a general want of system and discipline in conducting its affairs. This laxity usually shows itself in two ways—the absence of a good system of book-keeping, and the want of a proper control over its branches.

We could not adduce a more striking illustration of this observation than has been furnished in the history of the Agricultural and Commercial Bank of Ireland, as related before a Committee of the House of Commons in the year 1837. The following are extracts from this evidence. The books at the head office had not been posted for four months. There were no stock books, showing the amount each shareholder had paid on his share. There were no books showing the amount of the circulation. An auditor states: " They showed us no general account—their books were in a perfect chaos." They had no account at the head office by which they could check any transaction at the branches. Bills were sent away to be re-discounted without any entry of them being made in the bank books. At the branches there was no regular system of accounts. At no one branch was there a system of accounts that formed an adequate check upon the amount of notes in circulation; " and from one branch we were told that returns had not been made to the head office for fourteen months, and from another for six weeks, and there was no question about it from the head office."

We will not intimate that anything like this has ever existed in a joint-stock bank in England. We never heard that any one has had any difficulty in making out a statement of its affairs. With some banks, however, there has been a laxity in regard to the government of their branches. The system of inspection was not well understood—the returns from the branch were not so ample as they should have been—and the orders of the head office were not rigorously enforced. We could mention the names of several fallen banks that lost very considerably by their branches. In some cases the banks had opened branches in towns that required an amount of capital disproportionate to the means of the bank, and their administration had been entrusted to parties who had neither banking nor local knowledge.

A good system of book-keeping cannot be too highly valued. Its object is not merely to secure accuracy of accounts between the bank and its customers. A farther object is to classify and arrange all the transactions in such a way as easily to produce a weekly balance-sheet, showing the actual condition of the bank. Nor must it be supposed that such abstracts or balance-sheets are intended merely for the use of the directors. They are of the utmost use to the manager, and should be the subject of his constant study. A manager who, day after day, attends only to individual transactions, and that, too, possibly in a state of mental excitement, may involve his bank in difficulty, even though each transaction may, upon its own ground, be perfectly justifiable, unless he attends to those summaries and classifications of his transactions which are presented in the weekly balance-sheet. He will there see on one side the means of the bank, and on the other the way in which his funds are employed. He will notice if his loans, or overdrawn accounts, or past-due bills, are unduly increased. If a good system of book-keeping does not prevent a manager from going wrong, it will prevent his going wrong without knowing it. If he act unwisely, his balance-sheet will stare him in the face and remind him of his faults.

It is a great defect not to take an accurate estimate of the losses every half-year before striking the balance of profit and loss. It is clear that common sense and common honesty require that the loss should be taken into account as well as the profit. Yet some of the banks that failed went on, year after year, exhibiting a balance-sheet to their shareholders showing a respectable profit, which enabled the directors to declare a fair dividend, and to make an addition to the reserved fund. While the annual balance-sheets thus showed a steady increase of profit, the bad debts had actually eaten up the whole of the capital.

Another defect is, not to have an account in the general ledger showing the amount of bills reissued or rediscounted. The amount of these bills not due should appear on both sides of the account—on one side as a liability, and on the other as an asset. For want of doing so, some banks have not been able to ascertain easily what amount of bills they have under re-discount. But it is important to know this. For it may be expected that, during a season of pressure, no small portion of these bills will be returned unpaid, and the bank must find funds to take up its endorsements. If they fail to do this, it amounts to a stoppage of payment. In fact, the amount of such bills suddenly returned has in some cases been the *immediate* cause of a bank stopping payment.

We have no horror of numerous branches. When we see that the largest and most prosperous banks have each a large number of branches, we are led to believe that branches are not attended with any dangers which cannot be overcome by wise administration. At the same time, we are ready to admit that numerous branches require a peculiar mode of government, and a rigid system of discipline. The chief officer of such a bank should be a good banker, and something more. He must be a good administrator; that is, skilled in the administrative department of good government.

In the first place, each branch must have a good system of book-keeping, and the system must be uniform at every branch. Secondly, Care should be taken to appoint efficient officers. Thirdly, A code of laws should be drawn up, and the branch manager should be distinctly informed as to the extent to which he may exercise his discretion, and what cases must be referred for the consideration of the directors. Fourthly, Weekly returns must be made to the head office of all the transactions, and a half-yearly balance-sheet, attended with full supplementary details. Fifthly, Special reports should be occasionally required, as special circumstances may occur, either with reference to the branches generally, or with reference to a branch individually.

Sixthly, An inspector should be appointed for the purpose of visiting the branches. His duties will be to explain the instructions of the directors, and to see that they are properly observed —to maintain a uniform system of transacting business at all the branches—to instruct the officers of the branch in their duties when necessary, and to communicate the knowledge he has acquired in visiting the other branches—to answer any difficult or knotty questions that may be proposed to him by the manager, and to consult with the manager as to the best means of promoting the interests of the branch—to observe the talents and capabilities of the several officers, and to recommend for promotion any who seem to have qualities that might be usefully employed in a higher department in the bank. In large banks there are usually several inspectors.

Branches should always be kept in strict subordination to the head office. Prompt obedience to orders is a duty that must be rigidly enforced. The chairman of the Northern and Central Bank stated to the Parliamentary Committee, that at some of the branches where the heaviest losses had occurred, the managers had not obeyed the orders they had received from the directors. Similar accusations were made against some of the branch managers of the Commercial Bank of England. It is quite impossible for any bank to be well administered as a whole, if every branch is allowed to exercise an independent authority. Upon this ground some parties object altogether to the appointment of local directors at the branches. A local board, consisting of the branch directors and the manager, are more likely than the manager alone to assume independent authority—to postpone carrying out the directions they may receive from head-quarters—and to take upon themselves the responsibility of acting somewhat at variance with the strict letter of their instructions. And although local directors may sometimes be useful in extending the connexions of the bank, or in aiding the managers with information or advice, yet, for the above or other reasons, they are now in England but very seldom appointed. The branch is under the sole care of a manager. The general manager of the bank is not merely the manager of the head office, but has authority also over all the branches. Whenever necessary or expedient, he issues circular letters of instruction to the branch managers, and these instructions the branch managers are expected to obey.

V. Some banks have been unfortunate in consequence of having made no provision to meet contingencies.

This class of banks has not fallen into any of the practices that we have enumerated. They have not, on the whole, been badly managed, but they have traded to the full amount of their means, and have kept no reserve, either in Government stock, exchequer bills, or bills of exchange, to meet those contingencies to which all banks are liable. One bank of this class had, during the railway speculation, received from some of these companies a large amount of deposits. A portion of these deposits was lodged, as its agent, with another bank. That bank stopped. This bank was, consequently, unable to pay back the deposits to the railway companies. From this circumstance, and the known connexion between the two banks having damaged its credit, it also was compelled to stop payment. Another bank had but a small capital, but for a number of years it was exceedingly well managed. In 1847 it had discounted, and again re-discounted, a large amount of bills on a first-rate London house that failed. The London house afterwards paid 20s. in the pound. But the directors concluded from this circumstance, that a bank with a small capital was not in a condition to bear a large loss, and they resolved to wind up the concern. After sustaining the losses and expenses of winding up (and in such a case some losses necessarily occur), the bank realized nearly the whole of its paid-up capital. We doubt not that some of the other banks that have wound up their affairs have done so from causes similar to those we have described.

We consider that this head of our inquiry is not less instructive than the four by which it was preceded. *They* will teach us the vices we ought to avoid—*this* will teach us the virtues we ought to cultivate. The lessons we here gather are, that we ought not only to avoid all mismanagement, but we ought also to provide for those contingencies to which, even with good management, we are exposed. We ought to raise our capital in proportion to our business, or else keep down our business to a level with our capital—we ought to have a surplus fund adequate to meet any unforeseen loss—we ought to have a reserve of convertible securities ready to meet contingent evils ; and, finally, we ought always to keep our bank in such a condition that, even if not successful, we shall still be in a condition to wind up our affairs without inconvenience to the public.

VI. We may observe, that these erroneous principles of administration have sometimes been the result of a defect in the constitution of the bank—of the appointment of incompetent persons—or of an unwise distribution of the administrative functions.

Joint-stock banking did not grow up gradually in England as in Scotland. On the introduction of this system into England, the directors were necessarily unacquainted with the practical operations of banking.* For all the practice and experience were confined to the private bankers, whom the new system was intended to subvert. In some places there was a prejudice against directors who were in business. Hence officers in the army, barristers, solicitors, medical men, retired tradesmen, and country gentlemen, were considered as the most eligible directors. These boards of directors, all of whom were unacquainted with banking, and some of whom were destitute of business habits, had to encounter difficulties which would have tried the most experienced bankers.

The want of experience in a board of directors did not, however, produce any dangerous consequences when they appointed an efficient manager. He prudently advised and instructed them. They gradually increased their knowledge, adopted his principles, and were guided by his counsels. By their daily intercourse with him, by their own reflections, by the direction given to their thoughts, and by the experience they acquired, they became in a few years as conversant with their duties as the manager himself. We believe this was almost uniformly the case with those joint-stock banks that were formed within five or six years after they were allowed to be established in England. As a proof that such was the case, it may be stated that the greater portion of the banks formed during that period have, at the present moment, the same managers they had at their commencement.

But, after joint-stock banks were started as matters of speculation, they increased more rapidly than efficient managers could be found. The new banks naturally enough looked to

---

* The Chairman of the Northern and Central Bank gave the following answers to a Committee of the House of Commons :—

" Is there any one of your colleagues in the direction of the bank that had previous experience in banking business ?—I do not think there was one.

" Had any of the directors of the joint-stock banks about you previous banking experience ?—I do not recollect one. '—*Committee on Joint-Stock Banks,* 1837.

Scotland. But the Scotch banks had the sagacity to raise the salaries of their principal officers, to prevent their emigration to England. In some cases, those Scotchmen who were appointed managers of English banks had never held office in a bank before, or else it was an office so inferior that all they knew about banking was merely the routine of the office. Wherever efficient managers were appointed, whether English or Scotch, the same effects were produced as in the former cases The inexperienced directors acquired the knowledge and experience necessary to the discharge of their duties, and the banks prospered. But sometimes the case was reversed. The manager was inefficient, and the directors inexperienced, and then the effects were disastrous.

In some cases the manager laboured under an inconvenience from being taken from a lower social position. Not a few of the managers were previously bankers' clerks ; and the appointment to the office of bank manager did not, in England (as it does in Scotland and in Ireland), raise him to the same social position as a banker. This was injurious to the bank in several ways. It lessened his influence with his directors. From the days of Solomon to the present time, the degree of deference paid to even good advice has depended upon the social rank of the party who offered it : "Wisdom is better than strength ; nevertheless the poor man's wisdom is despised, and his words are not heard." * The public, too, had been so long accustomed to private banking, that, seeing the manager paid by a salary, they could not bring their minds to view him as *the* banker, but considered him as holding an office analogous to that of chief clerk in a private bank. It may be feared, that in some banks the directors took the same view, and thought that the influence and the salaries of the two offices ought to correspond. These impressions have now passed away.

In some cases the manager was superseded in his functions by the appointment of managing directors. The manager was a man of banking knowledge and experience, but he had placed over him a couple of managing directors, who had neither knowledge nor experience. Consequently, his voice was never heard in the board-room, and, with the name of manager, he acted only in the capacity of a chief clerk. The manager was thus deprived of the opportunity of discharging the most important

* Eccles. viii. 16.

of his functions—that of giving advice to the directors—and was required to confine his attention to the more easy duty of obedience.

In other cases the managing directors and the manager formed a secret committee, who alone were acquainted with the actual condition of the bank.   The directors of the Bank of Manchester stated, in their first report, that "two of their body, who are out of business, alone have access to the accounts, and are authorized to advise with the manager, when requisite, on the current transactions of the bank.   At the same time, each of the other directors engaged, individually, to refrain entirely from inspecting any of the customers' bills or accounts; thus combining all the secrecy of a private bank with the advantages of a public institution."   The Bank of Manchester had at that time the largest paid-up capital of any joint-stock bank in England. Three of its directors were examined before the Bank Charter Committee, in the year 1832.   They presented to the Committee a list of twenty-three joint-stock banks then formed, and strongly urged that measures should be adopted to require from them an adequate amount of paid-up capital.   It is somewhat remarkable that, out of these twenty three banks, the only one that has stopped payment is the Bank of Manchester.   Another has ceased to exist, but it was by a transfer of its business.

In some cases a bank has been ruined by its manager; in others, by the manager and the managing directors conjointly; in others, by the managing directors without the manager; and in others, by one, two, or three directors, who, though not formally appointed managing directors, have, by their influence with the board, virtually monopolized that office, and discharged its functions.   It may be questioned whether any case has occurred in England of a bank being ruined by the acts of its whole board, where all the directors were honest and intelligent men, and each was accustomed to think and judge for himself.

VII. We may observe, that sometimes joint-stock banks have been led into erroneous principles of administration by the proceedings of the proprietors.

The constitution of joint-stock banks appears theoretically absurd.   The manager—the banker—who is presumed to have some knowledge and experience in banking, is placed under the command of a board of directors, whose knowledge and experience are supposed to be inferior to his own. These directors are again placed under the control and instruction of a body of proprietors, whose knowledge of banking is much less than that of the directors. Practically, however, the system works well. But when an attempt is made to carry out the theory, the effects are injurious ; and some joint-stock banks have fallen into danger through the operations being too much regulated by the proceedings of the proprietors.

Sometimes the directors have been influenced by the applauses of the shareholders.

It is natural to all shareholders to wish for large dividends upon the capital they have invested. Hence they applaud most loudly those directors who contrive to declare the highest dividends, to make the largest bonuses, to keep up the shares at the highest premiums in the market, and then to distribute more shares at par. The directors, knowing these to be the feelings of the shareholders, very naturally attempt to gratify them. But those transactions that yield a large immediate profit are either attended with a risk of loss, or a lock-up of capital. But the profit is immediate : the danger is remote. With the applauses of the shareholders ringing in their ears, the directors become too giddy for reflection, and recklessly engage in a course of action that ends in ruin. This evil is increased when there are two joint-stock banks of about equal strength in the same place. The spirit of rivalry is natural to man. The competition between the two boards of directors is not which bank shall be governed with the greatest prudence, and with the strictest regard to sound banking principles, but which shall produce the most glowing reports—which shall declare the largest dividends—and which shall keep up its shares at the highest price in the market. A strong competition is carried on, which ends in the destruction of one or both of the rival banks. Such feelings are said to have prevailed at Manchester ; and at that place several boards of directors were presented with services of plate, by their respective shareholders, within a short time of the stoppage of their banks.

Sometimes directors are induced to act unwisely from the censures of their shareholders.

Every one who knows anything of banking must know that it cannot be carried on without occasional losses. A bank that is so conducted as never to make a loss, will seldom make much profit. And sometimes these losses will be so great as to absorb a large portion of the profits of the year. The object of having a surplus fund is to provide for these contingencies, so that the usual dividend may be maintained. But when an occasion arises for making use of a portion of this fund, there is often what is called "a stormy meeting," and the shareholders walk away sulky and dissatisfied. This produces a bad effect on the minds of the directors. It is a great mistake to suppose that boards of directors are indifferent to the applauses or censures of their shareholders. As a general rule, the fact is lamentably the reverse. In some cases they have had so much dread of "the general meeting" that they could not muster courage enough to make honest reports. Had they done so in the first instance, their banks might have been saved from destruction.

Sometimes directors are in danger of being led astray by the admonitions and instructions of their shareholders.

A very prudent class of proprietors exhort the directors to practise the strictest economy. When rightly understood, this exhortation is worthy of the rounds of applause with which it is usually attended. But it is liable to be misunderstood. In banking, as in housewifery, the lowest priced article is not always the cheapest. The largest portion of the expenditure of a bank consists of salaries. Hence an exhortation to economy amounts to—"Keep down the salaries of your officers;" and as the manager has the largest salary, he will most likely be the heaviest sufferer.

A more mischievous recommendation, when thus understood, can hardly be conceived. Next to having a dishonest manager, the greatest evil is to have one that is badly paid. If he is known to be poor, his advice will have less weight in the board-room ; the directors individually will treat him with less respect ; his·wealthy customers will not disclose to him their private affairs; the needy class, when refused discount, will insult him by threatening to complain to the directors, and his inferior officers will be less prompt in their obedience. But worse than all this will be the effect produced upon his own mind. He will not be, and he cannot be, so efficient a manager when badly paid, as he would be if he received a liberal remuneration. It is the besetting sin of men of business, that they never pay attention to MIND, though among no class are mental phenomena more strikingly exhibited.   The amount of his salary is the only tangible means by which a manager can judge how far his character and his services are appreciated.   It is not the money alone, but the feelings, of which the money is an indication, that produces an effect on the mind.   It is a law of our nature, that the kindness, liberality, and generosity of others will produce corresponding feelings in ourselves.   And it is another law of our nature, that when the mind is under the influence of such feelings, it is capable of intellectual efforts of a higher order. But we forget;—we were writing about pounds, shillings, and pence, and our pen has darted off into philosophy.   We will now return.

Sometimes the shareholders fly at higher game, and canvass the salaries of the directors.   Such discussions are always unpleasant, as they are carried on in the presence of the parties interested.   Among all the charges brought against the directors and managers of banks that have failed, we have never met with the accusation that they received excessive salaries.   We are tempted to fancy that, had their salaries been higher, the banks might not have failed.   As far as salary is concerned, they certainly would have had a greater interest in preventing the failure.   In some banks, however, directors have paid themselves for their services in ways far more costly to the bank.   Take the following instance :—

" The qualification for directors of the Northern and Central Bank was 100 shares.   It was, however, ascertained that each of the original directors took 1,000 shares, and that besides these, other shares were, at later dates, distributed among the directors and their near connexions. Instead of paying the calls to the bank, the directors and their nominees were severally debited with the amount in a private ledger, locked up, and the key deposited with the chief accountant.   In addition to this, each director had a current account with the bank, and many of them had overdrawn their accounts to a very large amount.   Nor was this all, for it further appeared that many of them were also indebted in large sums of money on notes of hand, which being placed to the account of securities, did not appear in the books as a debit against the directors.   Upon combining these several items of debt, it was ascertained that there was no less than 290,000*l.* due by the directors, and that there was near 14,000*l.* due by the managers and clerks."

It is not creditable to any bank to receive the services of its directors as a matter of charity.   Nor is it wise.   A director who is paid for his services may justly be called to account for neglect of duty. In this case, too, he cannot expect payment in any other way. In his transactions with the bank he is then on the same footing as any other customer. It has been said, that the directors are such honourable men that they will attend to their duty as strictly if badly paid as if liberally paid. If so they ought to be liberally paid, as it is very desirable that such honourable men should be most closely attached to the bank. But we doubt the fact. In matters of almsgiving, men will give only what they can conveniently spare. If a director is to give his time for nothing, he will give only that portion of his time which he cannot more profitably or more agreeably employ elsewhere. In matters of business, men will apportion their services according to the return they receive for them. There is no way of securing constant punctuality of attendance on the part of directors, but by paying them liberally for that attendance. In some cases where payment has not been given, or given only to the managing directors, it is said that the government of the bank has fallen into the hands of a few persons, whose punctuality of attendance has been almost their only banking virtue. But the main advantage of liberal payment is its effect upon the *minds* of the directors. Every honourable man will attend to his duty with alacrity and energy, and will even make extra exertions for the benefit of the bank, when he finds that his services are handsomely and liberally appreciated.

We need hardly say, that the faults we have pointed out in the administration or constitution of joint-stock banks are by no means inherent in the system. They are accidental circumstances, arising from its establishment in a new country, by parties who had no previous opportunity of understanding its principles. The system is no longer new—its principles are now well understood—and it may reasonably be expected that the calamities of the past will never recur.

SECTION XII.

THE ADMINISTRATION OF THE OFFICE.

IN this Section we shall consider the following topics :—
    I. The Arrangement of the Office.
    II. The Selection and Appointment of the Clerks.
    III. The proper Distribution of their Duties.
    IV. The Amount of their Salaries.
    V. The System of Promotion.
    VI. The Rules of Discipline.
    VII. The Training of Clerks for higher Offices.

I. The arrangement of the Office.

The proper situation of a bank is a matter of some importance. It should be situated in what is deemed the most respectable part of the town. If it be placed in an inferior locality, approachable only by narrow and disagreeable streets, and surrounded by buildings the seats of smoky and dirty trades, it is not likely to be so much frequented, nor to acquire so large a business, as though it were more pleasantly situated. Another point to be observed is, that the bank itself should be a handsome building. The necessary expenditure for this purpose is no sin against economy. It is an outlay of capital to be repaid by the profits of the business that will thus be acquired. A portion of the building will probably be set apart for the private residence of the manager, or of some other officer of the establishment. It is desirable that this portion should be entirely separated from the office. The communication should be only by a single door, of which the manager should keep the key. The building should be so constructed that what is going on in the private house, whether in the kitchen, or the nursery, or the drawing-room, should not be heard in the bank. The office being thus isolated, must then be fitted up in the way that will most effectually promote the end in view. And here are three points to be considered—*space, light,* and *ventilation.*

A chief consideration is *space.* A banker should take care that his clerks have room enough to do their work comfortably. Every accountant knows that he can often work faster if he can have two or more books open at the same time; but if his space is so confined that he must shut up one book, and put it away, before he can use another, he will get on more slowly. The cashiers, too, will be much impeded if they are obliged to stand too close to each other; and the public will be huddled together, and will often count incorrectly the money given to them, and thus take up the cashiers' time to put them right. Want of space will necessarily occasion errors, from the confusion it produces, and from one clerk being liable to interruption from the noise or vicinity of the others. A banker should therefore take care that his office is large enough for his business; and that it will admit of being enlarged in case his business should increase. Ample space is also conducive to the health of the clerks, as there will be more air to breathe, and the atmosphere is less likely to become polluted by the burning of lamps and candles.

Another consideration is *light*. It is well known in every London bank, that fewer mistakes are made by the clerks in summer than in winter. Abundance of light prevents mistakes, and saves all the time that would be employed in the discovery of errors. Light is also of great importance to the cashiers in detecting forged signatures and bad or counterfeit money. Thieves are also less likely to attempt their robberies in a light office than in a dark one. Faint or illegible handwriting can be more easily read, and hence mistakes are less likely to occur. The clerks, too, perform their duties with more quickness and cheerfulness. The gloominess of an office throws a gloom over the mind; but "light is sweet, and a pleasant thing it is for the eyes to behold the sun."

The lightest part of the office should be devoted to the clerks. We have observed sometimes a violation of this principle. The entrance door has been placed in the middle of the front, with a window on each side, and the counter thrown across the room, so that the lightest part of the office has been given to the public. It is better that the entrance be placed at the right or the left corner, and the counter be made to run from the window to the opposite wall. The light will thus fall lengthwise on the counter, and the space behind the counter will be occupied by the clerks.

Ventilation.—Volumes have been written by medical men upon the advantages of fresh air, and on the unwholesome atmosphere of crowded cities. If the air that circulates in the streets of towns and cities is impure, what must be the state of those offices or rooms where twenty or thirty persons are breathing close together during the whole of the day, and gas lights are burning during the evening. In such cases we are told that a person afflicted with consumption of the lungs may communicate the complaint to others, as they must inhale a portion of the atmosphere which he has breathed out. The air in a close office is not only rendered impure by the number of people that breathe it, and by the burning of gas, but it also contains very frequently particles of dust arising from the floor, through the number of people constantly walking in and out. It is almost impossible for persons so circumstanced to enjoy for a length of time even moderate health. A portion of this evil may be mitigated by a good system of ventilation. To obtain this should be regarded as an object of the first importance. If a banker does not insist upon the architect performing this in the most effectual manner, he must be content to be often put to inconvenience through the illness and consequent absence of his clerks.

Having made due provision for space, light, and ventilation, it will now become necessary to arrange the counter, desks, and other furniture, so as to enable any given number of clerks to discharge their duties with the greatest efficiency, and so as best to promote the public convenience. It is not necessary, or possible, to give very minute instructions on this head, as much will depend upon the form of the building, the extent of the business, and other circumstances. We will notice only a few general objects to be kept in view.

It is desirable at all times to make those arrangements that shall best promote the convenience of the public.

The counter should be readily accessible, and of sufficient length to meet the requirements of the business ; and the cashiers' desks sufficiently wide apart for the public to be promptly served, and to stand without jostling one another. Some banks have two counters, one for paying, and the other for receiving. At other banks the cashier does not enter the credits, but merely agrees the amount with the customer, and then passes them to a clerk, who enters them in the Waste-Book. In the same way, when a cheque is presented for payment, he gives it to a clerk behind him, who enters it, and hands the notes to the cashier, who pays out the gold and silver. When the business is large, extra or supernumerary cashiers are appointed, who take the place of the regular cashiers when they are absent at dinner or otherwise, so that during the whole of the day all the cashiers' desks are occupied. To relieve the counter, the payment of bills that have been presented in the morning and not paid, is usually received at a separate desk or office. All these are expedients that should be adopted when necessary, to save the time of the public. There are few things that try a man's temper more than to be kept waiting a long time at a banker's counter; and he will be very apt to give vent to his impatience by quarrelling with the clerks, or reproaching the establishment.

Another object is, to place near together those clerks whose duties will require them to have frequent communication with each other. If this rule be not observed, the clerks will lose much time in the course of the day in passing from one part of the office to the other; and the work will not be so expeditiously performed. It is especially desirable that the ledger keepers should be placed close behind the cashiers; so that if a doubtful cheque be presented for payment, the cashier may be able to show it to the ledger keeper, and be informed if he may pay it, without being observed by the party presenting it.

Another point is, to place the desk of the chief or head clerk in such a position that he can see all over the office. "A master's eye will do more work than both his hands." In this case, if the counter is crowded, the chief clerk will perceive it, and appoint additional clerks to assist the cashiers. If disputes take place between the clerks, or between the cashiers and the public, he will come forward and settle the matter before the dispute is carried to high words. He will observe, too, the customers who come frequently to the counter, and from their transactions he will often draw conclusions respecting their circumstances which will be serviceable to the bank. It is generally best that many of the clerks should be so placed as to look towards the counter. It has been said that this draws off their attention from their work; but we do not think this is generally the case, although it may occasionally relieve the irksomeness of their duties. A dishonest person standing at the counter, and watching an opportunity of committing a robbery when the cashier is engaged, will be more likely to abstain from making the attempt when the eyes of other clerks have a command of the counter. This arrangement will depend in some measure on the direction of the light. The clerks should not have their faces or their backs towards the window, but the light should fall on them sideways. These matters may appear trifling, but they will not be deemed unimportant to those who are entrusted with the practical administration of an office. It is only by attention to minute things that the business of an office can be well conducted.

II. The Selection and Appointment of Clerks.

When a bank is first formed, they sometimes advertise for clerks; but this is usually for clerks of a higher rank, who have had some experience in the business of banking. When a bank is established, it has seldom occasion for new clerks of this class. A vacancy in one of the higher departments is filled up by the next clerk in rank, and so on in order, and the new clerk comes in as a junior. Applications for this post are usually so numerous that the only difficulty is in making the selection. Those recommended by parties known to the bank, as customers or shareholders, usually have the first claim. In some banks the nomination of the junior clerks is regarded as a portion of the patronage of the directors, upon the understanding, however, that they nominate none but such as are properly qualified, and who shall prove their fitness to the satisfaction of a committee of directors.

In making inquiries into the qualifications of applicants, it is necessary to ascertain in the first place their age. In London the age at which clerks are admitted into a bank is usually about nineteen. As their first duty is to collect payment of bills, it is necessary they should have arrived at a sufficient degree of strength to be able to make some resistance were an attempt to be made to rob them of their bill-case; and also that they should have arrived at an age to be conscious of the responsibility of their office. In the country parts of England, and in Scotland, clerks are taken at an earlier age; but the duties are different from those discharged by the same class in London.

Another consideration is the class of society from which clerks are taken. Candidates for the office of bank clerks are usually the sons of the middle class of tradesmen, or of professional men, as clergymen, officers in the army or navy, or persons in the service of Government. During the last war, bankers' clerks were generally the sons of tradesmen, as the sons of gentlemen could easily find employment under Government. But now that places under the Government are not so easily obtained, members of what are called respectable families are found among the candidates for admission into the service of banks. Each class has some advantages. The sons of gentlemen have generally a better literary education, and have usually a more courteous address. On the other hand, they have no notion of business, and no business habits. They have been accustomed to go a-hunting and a-fishing with the sons of men of large property, and they look upon banking business as a drudgery to which they submit from necessity, but which is much beneath the destiny to which they think they are entitled. On the other hand, the sons of tradesmen have been accustomed to notions of business from the ordinary conversation of their fathers' fireside; they know they must get their own living; they look upon their admission into a bank as a lucky event, and, consequently, apply themselves to their duties with heartiness and cordiality.

Another inquiry of those who are candidates for admission into a bank is, How they have been employed? Lads just come from school of course know nothing of the business of a bank, and, if taken at all, they should be taken upon trial for three or six months, so that their qualifications may be discovered before they are permanently appointed. Those who have been two or three years in a merchant's counting-house are generally found to be the most efficient. But to have been in the office of a stock-broker or a solicitor, or to have studied for one of the learned professions, is no recommendation. Clerks from country banks, and especially those from the banks of Scotland, when introduced into London banks, are at first usually considered to be slow.

It is also proper to inquire into the parentage of the candidate. For although honesty and dishonesty do not run in the blood, yet it is probable that religious and virtuous parents have given their children a religious and virtuous education; and a youth who has been accustomed to see examples of excellence at home, will be the most likely to exhibit those excellences in his own conduct. A high degree of moral principle is in itself a necessary qualification in a post of trust and responsibility, and it is usually associated with a cultivated and improved state of the intellectual faculties.—" If there be in the character not only sense and soundness, but virtue of a high order, then, however little appearance there may be of talent, a certain portion of wisdom may be relied upon almost implicitly. For the correspondences of wisdom and goodness are manifold, and that they will accompany each other may be inferred, not only because men's wisdom makes them good, but also because their goodness makes them wise. Although, therefore, simple goodness does not imply every sort of wisdom, it unerringly implies some essential conditions of wisdom ; it implies a negative on folly, and an exercised judgment, within such limits as Nature shall have prescribed to the capacity." *

Testimonials are to be received with caution. Young men who come to London in search of a place, often bring with them a host of testimonials, which they expect will place them at the head of any list of candidates. When upon other grounds there is an intention of engaging the applicant, these letters of recommendation may sometimes be read. It may be useful to observe by whom the testimonials are given, and whether those persons have had opportunities of judging of the adaptation of the party for the office he seeks. It may also be noticed what qualities are, and more particularly what qualities are *not*, ascribed to the applicant. It has been said that when a lady is praised for being " amiable and accomplished," it may be inferred that she is neither young nor handsome. So if a testimonial speaks highly of a young man's " industry and integrity," it may generally be inferred that he does not possess much talent. It is true that these qualities are of more importance than talent. But while they are more important, they are also more common. And if a young man possesses any kind of intellectual superiority, the fact will certainly not be omitted in his testimonial.

III. The distribution of the duties of the various clerks is a matter of no small importance. Experience is the only efficient guide in making such arrangements. We may, nevertheless, lay down a few general principles. The great division of the business of a bank office is into the cashiers' department and the accountants' department. In London banks there is a third—the tellers', or out-door department. In the distribution

* Taylor's 'Statesman.'

of duties, it is desirable that the accountants' department should be a check upon the other departments. The cashiers must not have the control of the books, nor the accountants the care of the cash. The accountants' books should show what amount of cash is in the hands of the cashiers; and it is the business of the cashiers to show that they have that amount of cash which corresponds with the accountants' books. If the same officer has the care of the cash and the command of the books, he may abstract a portion of the cash, and alter the books to make them correspond. It is further desirable, in large establishments, that two books which act as a check upon one another, should not be kept by the same clerk. While it is not proper to indulge a spirit of suspicion in regard to individuals, it is advisable that the duties of a bank office should be so distributed that the intromissions of any one clerk, either by the abstraction of cash or the falsification of the books, should be liable to immediate detection by the entries in some book kept by another clerk. For the same reason, it is proper that any document issued to the public (such as deposit receipts, drafts on London, &c.) should be signed by two officers, of whom one should belong to the cash, and the other to the accountants' department. There ought to be a complete division of labour in a bank. Every clerk should have fixed duties to perform, and every duty, however unimportant, should be assigned to some particular clerk. If anything is neglected, there should be no doubt as to who is to blame. No one should be able to say, " It was not my business; it was yours." Nor ought any duties to be assigned in common to two or three clerks, to be performed by them as each may find time. In this case, each will do as little as he can, and nothing will be done well. If any dispute arises among the clerks as to the due division of their labours, a reference should be made to the chief clerk, who will give to each man his work, and hold him responsible for its proper performance.

IV. The Amount of their Salaries.

According to Adam Smith, the wages of labour are regulated by the following circumstances:—1. The agreeableness or disagreeableness of the employments themselves. 2. The easiness and cheapness, or the difficulty and expense of learning them. 3. The constancy or inconstancy of employment in them. 4. The small or great trust which must be reposed in those who exercise them. 5. The probability or improbability of success in them.

Mr. Mill makes the following observations with regard to the salaries of clerks :—

" A clerk from whom nothing is required but the mechanical labour of copying, gains more than an equivalent for his mere exertion if he receives the wages of a bricklayer's labourer. His work is not a tenth part as hard, it is quite as easy to learn, and his condition is less precarious, a clerk's place being generally a place for life. The higher rate of his remuneration, therefore, must be partly ascribed to monopoly, the small degree of education required being not even yet so generally diffused as to call forth the natural number of competitors, and partly to the remaining influences of an ancient custom, which requires that clerks should maintain the dress and appearance of a more highly paid class.

" It is usual to pay greatly beyond the market price of their labour all persons in whom the employer wishes to place peculiar trust, or from whom he requires something besides their mere services. For example, most persons who can afford it pay to their domestic servants higher wages than would purchase in the market the labour of persons fully as competent to the work required. They do this, not from mere ostentation, but from reasonable motives—because they desire that those they employ should serve them cheerfully, and be anxious to remain in their service—because they do not like to drive a hard bargain with people whom they are in constant intercourse with—and because they dislike to have near their persons, and continually in their sight, people with the appearance and habits which are the usual accompaniments of a mean remuneration. Similar feelings operate in the minds of men in business with respect to their clerks."*

There would be considerable difficulty in applying the rules laid down by political economists with regard to the wages of labour to the case of bank clerks. A banker does not hire a clerk because he is the cheapest man he can get, nor does he dismiss him as soon as he can get another man to do the same work at a lower price. He would not find it his interest to do this ; for his work is of a peculiar kind. His clerks must have a certain degree of education and of manner, and be taken from a certain class in society. They are not allowed to engage in any other employment. They have to maintain a respectable appearance. They must be qualified not merely for the lowest post in the bank, but must be prepared to take higher posts should vacancies occur. And in every post they are entrusted with a large amount of property, and upon their integrity and prudence much reliance must at all times be placed. All these

* Principles of Political Economy, by John Stuart Mill, vol. i. pp. 461–475.

circumstances serve to show that, in fixing the amount of their salaries, the banker should be anxious to err (if he errs at all) on the side of liberality.

He ought also to take into consideration the effect which the amount of salary produces on the mind and condition of the party receiving it. If an advance of salary quickens the attention or the zeal, or strengthens the fidelity of a party, or induces him to cultivate those talents which add to his efficiency—or if it enables him to move in a higher class of society, and gives him a station and an influence which enable him to be useful to the bank—then is such advance of salary—though entered in the books under the item of expenditure—an outlay of capital which is repaid to the banker with interest in the effect it produces—an outlay that becomes probably one of the most profitable of his investments.*

In all banks the junior clerks have lower salaries than the senior clerks. In Scotland, a clerk usually serves an apprenticeship of three years, during which he receives but a small salary. This plan has been introduced into some of our country banks. In London it does not exist. In the private banks, a junior clerk usually commences with 60*l.* a-year, and a portion of the Christmas money. In the joint-stock banks, where no Christmas money is allowed, the commencing salary is usually 80*l.* But the rules of advance are various, and, indeed, must be so,

* We have great pleasure in transcribing the following letter from Mr. Samuel Jones Loyd.[1] It was addressed to the chief clerk of his London bank. We abstain from all eulogium, as the letter will speak for itself:—

"DEAR MR. KIRBY,

"The enclosed draft for 1000*l.* I request you will place to the credit of the 'Clerks' Christmas Fund.' At the close of the first year since my accession to the head of this concern, I am desirous of offering to those through whose assistance I have been enabled to bring it to a satisfactory conclusion some substantial proof of my sense of their services, and of the interest which I feel in all that concerns their comfort and happiness. The year now closing has been marked by some circumstances of an accidental and temporary character, which have tended to throw an unusual degree of labour and trouble on the clerical department of the office. Of the readiness with which this difficulty has been met and overcome I am very sensible, and for this, as well as for the uniform zeal and integrity with which the general duties of the office are discharged, I beg that the clerks will accept my grateful acknowledgment, and that you and they will believe me to be the faithful friend of you all.

(Signed) "S. J. LOYD.

"*Lothbury, Dec. 24th*, 1845."

[1] Now Lord Overstone.

depending as they do upon the prosperity of the banks, and other contingent circumstances. One bank may assign a certain fixed annual increase to each clerk, whether he advance in rank or not. In this case, his salary will be regulated entirely by the number of his years of service. Another bank may have a fixed salary for each post, and a clerk has no increase of salary except when he takes a step in rank. Another bank may adopt a scale of salaries combining the principles of the other two. For instance, every post in the bank may have a fixed *minimum* salary. But each clerk holding a post for a certain period (say for five years) has an annual advance for that period. Then he stops, and receives no further advance until he is promoted to the next post, where again he becomes entitled to the annual advances belonging to that post. We give no opinion as to the respective merit of these plans. But there is one principle we would enforce—that the salaries of the clerks should be regulated by the prosperity of the bank. If the bank is prosperous, the clerks ought to share in its prosperity ; and if the bank is unfortunate, the clerks must consent to share in its ill fortune. But, under any circumstances, a scale of salaries is desirable. It prevents caprice on the part of the bank, and jealousy on the part of the clerks. The amount of salary in each case should be fixed by rule, and not by favour.

With reference to this subject we quote from Mr. Taylor's work, entitled ‘The Statesman’—a work which he states to have been the result of twelve years' official experience :—

" It is often said, that in order to get efficient service good pay must be offered. But this is not true, as applied to first appointments of young men. On the contrary, it will often happen that the largeness of the temptation, by bringing into activity the most powerful interests through which abuses of patronage are engendered, will lead to the appointment of a worse man than would have been obtained by a smaller offer. On the other hand, though men of promise are to be *had* cheap, whilst they are young and their value is little known to themselves or others, they cannot, when this is no longer their condition, be kept for a small consideration, or at least kept contented. But a reasonable degree of contentment is of essential importance where the understanding is the workman. There is no position so strong as that of a man who stands upon his head ; and if he be not induced to the activity of just thinking and clear reasoning, he will hardly be coerced to it. Upon the whole, therefore, I would say, that what is most conducive to good appointments in the first instance, and thenceforward to deriving benefit from them, is to offer small remuneration to the beginner, with successive expectancies proportioned to the merits which he shall manifest, and of such increasing amount as shall be calculated to keep easy, through the progressive wants of single and married life, the mind of a prudent man. Upon such a system, if unfit men belonging to influential families shall make good an entrance into the service, they will be more easily got rid of; since, finding that they have got but little in hand, and have but little more to look to, they will hardly be desirous to continue in a career in which they must expect to see their competitors shoot ahead of them."

Securities.—In all banks the clerks give sureties for their integrity—usually two, of 500*l.* each; and in some banks these amounts are increased on accession to higher offices. Of late years societies have been formed, both in England and Scotland, for the purpose of giving, on the part of clerks and others, the amount of security required.

The Lords of the Treasury, indeed, all Government Departments which require securities, and most of the great banking companies and private banks, accept the guarantee of these societies in preference to private suretyship.

In the year 1841 the Bank of England took measures for discontinuing the system of requiring sureties from the clerks. Every clerk subscribed annually two shillings per cent. upon the amount of his surety-bond. When he had subscribed in the course of five years (or immediately if he chose), ten shillings per cent., the liability of his sureties ceased. Every new clerk subscribes, when admitted, ten shillings per cent. on the amount of the bond he would otherwise give. These contributions are invested in the Three per Cent. Reduced, or Consols. This fund is fixed at 6,000*l.* stock. When at this amount, the interest is given to the "Clerks' Widows' Fund," a fund established by the clerks, with the assistance and support of the bank. When the claims have reduced the guarantee fund below 6,000*l.* the interest goes to this fund until it has increased to this amount. If the claims reduce the fund so low as 4,700*l.* then the clerks are required to make a further contribution until the fund is again raised to 6,000*l.* But this contribution is never more than two shillings per cent. per annum on the amount of their respective bonds. Nor can any claim be brought against the fund greater than the amount of the bond that would have been required from the defaulter. The clerks still give their personal bonds, which are for the full amount of their deficiencies. This is an admirable plan for a large establishment. In adopting it the directors have shown a sound discretion, as it makes all the clerks interested in watching over one another. At the same time, they have manifested that kindness and goodwill which have, we believe, at all times distinguished the Directors of the Bank of England in their conduct towards their clerks.

Mr. Thomson Hankey, when Governor, delivered to the Banking Institute the following account of the working of this system :—

" With regard to the guarantee system, it appeared to him that the principle adopted in the Bank of England in 1841, by his predecessor, was capable of extension, with great benefit to the clerks, to many of the other banking institutions of the country. The principle of that plan was, that a compulsory payment of 1*l.* a-year for five years, or 5*l.* in one sum, was required from each clerk, on entering the establishment. These payments accumulated until they amounted to a sum of 6,000*l.*, the interest of which was then to be applied to another purpose, for the benefit of the clerk; but in the meanwhile the fund was applicable to all losses at the bank, which, under ordinary circumstances, would fall upon the private sureties. Every clerk, on entering the establishment, was bound to give security to the amount of 1,000*l.* Well, he believed the lowest premium the guarantee societies would take was 10*s.* per cent., or 5*l.* for the 1,000*l.*, and this 5*l.* premium had to be renewed every year. Now, the amount of this 5*l.* premium from each of the 700 clerks of the Bank of England would be 3,500*l.* a-year. Well, since the guarantee fund to which he had alluded had been established in 1841, the total defalcations in the Bank of England had only amounted to about 1,500*l.* Now, if the 700 clerks had paid the 5*l.* a-year each to the guarantee societies for the whole of that period, it would have raised nearly as much as 40,000*l.*, the whole of which would have gone into the pockets of the guarantee societies, with the exception of the 1,500*l.* which would have been necessary to make good the defalcations. Now, if 40,000*l.* had been paid in premiums, and 1,500*l.* had been the loss, it would require very little argument from him to show that the guarantee societies would have been very great gainers, at the expense of the clerks."

V. The System of Promotion.

It need hardly be observed that some posts in a bank are more important than others, and it is always desirable that the most clever men should occupy the most important posts. This object is desirable, but how is it to be attained?

The three main divisions of employment in a London bank are—the cashiers' department—the accountants' department—and the tellers', or out-door department. All the clerks enter in the first instance in the tellers' department, and their first duties comprise the collection of the payment of bills. The senior tellers are occupied within doors in various duties connected with the out-door operations.   From this department, as vacancies occur, the clerks are promoted to higher posts in either the cashiers' or the accountants' department.*

The Cashiers' Department.—The cashiers of a bank stand at the counter, and attend to the public.   These officers, in Scotland, are called tellers; but in Scotland their duties are less important, as tellers pay no cheques until they have been marked by the accountant, who is their superior officer.   We should form a very inadequate idea of a cashier in a London bank if we considered him only as a mere counter of money. Quickness in counting money is indeed one very necessary qualification.   But besides this he should have such a mental organization that he can recollect the general average of each customer's balance, so as to be able to pay their cheques without a too frequent reference to the ledger-keeper.   He should also possess a quickness of eye in detecting forged signatures—a self-possession, so as to be cool and collected when the counter is thronged with people—a command of temper, so as not to be irritated by undeserved reproach—and not only a general courtesy of manner towards the public, but a peculiar urbanity towards the customers of the bank, with a readiness and an anxiety to promote their convenience in any matter on which they may require information or advice. In fact, it may justly be said, that there is no class of clerks on which the reputation of a bank with the public so much depends as on the cashiers.   And hence, in London banks, those clerks who are deemed the quickest, the most able, and the most gentlemanly, are usually promoted to this office.

The *Accountants' Department* refers to the keeping of the books and the accounts.   The main qualifications for the clerks in this department are—good handwriting, accuracy in figures, and method in the arrangement of their work.   Slowness is no positive disqualification, provided it be associated, as it often is, with application and perseverance.   An accountant is not compelled to do any given quantity of work within a given time. By a proper arrangement of his duties he can usually contrive to keep himself pretty equally employed during the whole of

---

* It is of course in large banks, where there is necessarily a great subdivision of labour, that these three departments exist in a separate form.   In smaller banks, though the duties are the same, yet one clerk may, in one day, perform duties belonging to each of the three departments.

the day, and on busy occasions he can perform what remains in the evening, after the hours of public business. A steady perseverance is of the first importance. But we must distinguish between those qualities required in the clerks of the accountants' department, and those required in the accountant himself.

The chief accountant in a bank is not a mere book-keeper. It is one thing to keep a set of books previously prepared and arranged, and another to frame a set of books, or a new system of book-keeping, adapted for any operation that is proposed to be carried on. In the latter case, mental powers are required that are by no means common. And even where a system is established, the chief accountant of a bank will often have occasion to consider the best way of passing certain transactions through the books—of framing abstracts of operations which the books may not immediately supply—of making difficult calculations, and of examining lengthy and complicated accounts, and exhibiting them with clearness and brevity. A good system of book-keeping, and a clear-headed accountant, would have prevented many a bank from stopping payment.

From this statement of the qualifications of cashiers and accountants, it will appear that most clerks will be more fitted for one office than the other, and it is desirable that each clerk should be placed in the department for which he is best adapted. Where there is no peculiar adaptation, and where there is no marked difference among the clerks, the promotion should go according to seniority—not seniority in regard to age, but seniority according to the time they have been in the bank. But it will often happen, not only in the first, but also in subsequent steps of advancement, that the clerk who is entitled to a vacant post by length of service, is not so well qualified for it as some of his juniors. But even in this case, the individual should not be passed over, if he can perform the duties with an average degree of efficiency. Should he, however, be wholly unqualified, or fall below mediocrity in his qualifications for the office, there should be no hesitation in promoting over him some other clerk better adapted for the office. As, however, all such cases will give rise to some suspicion of favouritism, and as the party who is passed over is sure to think himself unfairly treated, it is desirable that the clerk thus promoted should possess such a marked superiority over the other, that no doubt can exist of the justice and propriety of the arrangement.

VI. The Rules of Discipline.

As the discipline of the office must depend very much upon the chief clerk, a description of his duties will describe many of the duties of the other clerks.

The office of chief clerk requires qualifications of no ordinary kind. It need hardly be said that he should possess a thorough knowledge of the business of the office. He ought also to possess certain moral qualifications, such as a command of temper, a love of order and regularity, a rigid adherence to discipline, accompanied by kindness of disposition and of manners towards his colleagues, a gentlemanly and courteous demeanour, and, above all, he will be expected to exemplify in his own conduct those precepts it may become his duty to inculcate upon others.

The following are the principal duties of a chief clerk :—

To see that the clerks come at proper time in the morning, are not absent unnecessarily during the day, and that they do not leave the bank at night until they have finished their work.—To see, by occasional inspection, that all the books of the office are kept in a proper manner, and where he finds this not to be the case, to give such instructions and admonitions as the circumstances may require.—To see that during the day the counter is properly appointed, and that no delay takes place in attending to the wants of the public. For this purpose it is desirable that his desk should be so placed as to command a view of the counter.—To see, by occasional inspection, that the customers' books are written up in a proper manner, and in case of complaint he will personally investigate the matter, and explain it to the customer.—To see, early in the morning, that the balance was correct on the preceding night, and when otherwise, he will himself attend on the second or third evening, and direct that proper means be employed to discover the difference.—To count, at such times as may be deemed proper, the money of the several cashiers, and when necessary to report thereon to the Banker.—To see that all the officers of the bank conduct themselves towards each other and the public in a courteous and gentlemanly manner, and to maintain throughout the office a proper state of discipline and subordination.—To take charge of the stationery and other matters used in the office, and to prevent any loss or waste of any portion of the property of the bank.

Besides the points of discipline hinted at in the above description, there are others that may require more particular notice, as

Punctuality of Attendance.—To insure punctuality of attendance in the morning, some banks adopt the practice of keeping a book, in which every clerk writes his name on his arrival, and when the time has expired, a line is drawn, which shows who has arrived in time and who has arrived late.

Punctuality of attendance is an index of character. It may fairly be inferred that those who are the most punctual in the morning will be most attentive to their duties during the day, that they have formed the most regular habits, and are, consequently, the most deserving of promotion. Those, too, who are the most punctual are the most deserving of occasional holidays. They who are habitually late must be regarded as having chosen to take their holidays by piece-meal each day, and they can, therefore, have no claim to other holidays besides. In all applications for promotion or leave of absence, it is deserving of inquiry, whether the party is usually punctual in his attendance. With regard to absence from illness, it cannot be supposed for a moment that any clerk would pretend to be ill when he is not so, in order to have an excuse for absenting himself from the bank. An act of this kind would show such a want of personal honour as should be a disqualification for holding any office in a bank.

" Few things occasion more dissatisfaction and annoyance to the superiors in a bank than the absence of clerks on every slight attack of illness. Unless a clerk feels himself quite unable to perform his duties, it is very injudicious for him to absent himself. It interferes with his promotion, for his superiors will be reluctant to advance him to any post where his absence would be more inconvenient than while he is engaged in an inferior situation. In addition to this, the superior in the office may attribute the attack of ' bile ' or ' indigestion ' to the indulgence of a convivial taste, which it will be well for a clerk to avoid obtaining a character for. And, under any circumstances, a man who continues at his post as long as he is able, will stand much higher in the estimation of those with whom he is engaged than he who forsakes his duties on every trivial occasion." *

A clerk should take care of his own health. We think it it is better for him to stand than to sit at his work. His desk should be raised to such a height that he can do this without stooping. He should at all times avoid pressing his chest against the edge of the desk, as that may produce serious complaints. The post most friendly to health is that of cashier. He is generally standing; his attention and mental faculties are in more constant activity, and he is obliged to talk, which is useful to the lungs. It may be doubted whether the exercise of the intellectual faculties, when not carried to excess nor attended with anxiety, is ever injurious to health. Those mental operations which are connected with the office of a bank clerk are in themselves beneficial. It is the confinement, the impure air, and the keeping of the body too long in one posture, that affects the health. Hence clerks should live at a distance from the bank, and *walk* to and fro. If they reside at the bank, they should take exercise in the open air, either in the morning or the evening. When the weather is bad, they can walk up and down the room, with the windows open. Any kind of amuse-ment that should throw the body into a variety of attitudes, would be useful. Singing is friendly to health, if not carried to excess, nor practised in confined or crowded apartments. Boating, in moderation, is serviceable. Gardening is highly beneficial. A clerk who wishes to enjoy good health should never keep late hours, nor get into debt, nor gamble in the funds. He should also have a hobby, that is, some kind of fixed amusement to employ his time when absent from the bank, in order to change the current of his thoughts, and to counteract those evils that sometimes arise from a monotony of occupation. If this hobby should be of a kind to be useful or instructive as well as recreative, all the better. The great disease against which he should guard is con-sumption. He will be more subject to this in youth than in more advanced age. And it has been remarked that healthy young men, fresh from the country, when appointed clerks, have become more susceptible of consumption than less

* The Banker's Clerk, p. 151, an excellent little work, published as one of the series in the Guide to Service, by Mr. Charles Knight.

robust persons who have been seasoned by a residence in London.

The Bank of England have a medical gentleman who attends at the bank one hour every day. He is employed by the directors upon matters connected with the health of their clerks. Every clerk, when appointed, is examined, to ascertain that he is in good health. If he applies for leave of absence on the ground of ill-health, he undergoes a medical examination. If absent from illness, he is visited by the bank surgeon, who reports to the directors upon the nature of his complaint, and its probable duration. If a clerk complains that his employment is injurious to his health, he is examined, and in some cases his employment is changed. If he applies for a pension on account of age or illness, he is also examined. In each of these cases a formal medical report is drawn up, and laid before the directors. It is not the duty of the surgeon to prescribe for the clerks; but in the case of the porters or messengers, he acts as their medical attendant, and is paid by the bank.

It is worthy of inquiry, whether this excellent arrangement might not be extended, and adopted by other banking institutions. Why should not every large company give a fixed salary to a medical man to attend to the health of all their clerks? This would often be useful in preventing illness, or in checking its first approaches. It would thus preclude, in some cases, those inconveniences which are now felt through the absence of sick clerks; while it would be a boon to the establishment, and save them what, in some instances, must be a heavy item of expense.

Holidays.—It is desirable, on several accounts, that all the officers of a bank, and especially those who are entrusted with cash or other property, should once a year have leave of absence for at least a week or a fortnight. This should not even be optional—it ought to be a fixed rule with which they should be expected to comply. These absences should be arranged to take place at those seasons of the year when they will be of the least inconvenience to the business of the bank. These holidays ought to be readily granted on the ground of kindness and humanity; but where these feelings do not exist, motives of self-interest alone would prompt a ready acquiescence in such applications. In the first place, a great inconvenience

is often experienced in large establishments from the illness of
the clerks when they are denied proper seasons of relaxation.
In this case, the loss of time from ill-health is greater than that
which would be occasioned by holidays. A sick clerk, even
when he attends to his duties, is neither so quick, nor so correct,
nor can he get through so much work, as a clerk who, by proper
recreation, has been kept in perfect health. These occasional
holidays tend very much to improve the efficiency of an office.
When a clerk is absent, the next in seniority takes his place ;
and when all the clerks have been absent in turn, every duty
in the bank becomes perfectly familiar to at least two persons,
so that in the case of those absences which arise from unavoidable causes, little inconvenience comparatively is felt.
But while the bank is thus rendered independent of any one
individual, it must not be supposed that the absence of a clerk
lessens the importance attached to his services. When a clerk
is really efficient, an occasional absence renders his value more
apparent, and increases the estimate formed of his character ;
while the indulgence he has received will stimulate his energies
and increase his desire to render himself more than ever useful
to his principals.

Another advantage to a banking establishment from the
absence of their clerks is, that it furnishes an additional
guarantee for their honesty. We have known instances of
frauds being carried on for several years by clerks who were
constant in their attendance, while a single day's absence would
necessarily have led to a detection of their dishonesty. When
a clerk takes his holidays, all the property under his care is
given over into other hands ; and the knowledge that he will be
called upon to do this periodically, may deter him in the first
instance from commencing a career which must be thus
necessarily exposed.

The following is stated in a City Article of the *Times* to be
the arrangement of the Bank of England on this subject :—

" It is not generally known that the Bank of England have recently
entered into an arrangement by which all the persons on the establishment
are allowed leave of absence once every year, the holiday varying in
length according to the length of service. To carry out this plan, the
whole number of persons is divided into four portions, and each of these
four portions takes the vacation in one of the four periods of the year
that follow the payment of the dividends, and precede the shutting, these
being the periods in which the least business is done. So complete is the

system, that the parties who take their holiday in the spring quarter one year, take it in the summer quarter in the year following, and so on through all the four, that one may not have an unfair advantage over the other. The shortest holiday, we understand, is about nine days, and the longest about three weeks."

Customers' Books.—It should be a great object with the chief clerk to see that the customers' books are written up correctly and neatly, in a good handwriting, and free from blots or erasures. These are the only books that go out of the bank, and therefore they are the chief means by which the customers can judge as to the manner in which the business of the office is conducted. It is not advisable that the writing up of these books should be left to the junior clerks. They should be placed in the hands of clerks of some standing. The same book should always be written up by the same clerk; and when it can be so managed, the credit and debit side should both be in the same handwriting. One of the best writers in the office should be appointed to this post, and his salary should be proportionate to its importance.

It is the practice of all bankers to let the customers' book be a copy of the ledger with the sides reversed. Thus the credit side of the ledger is the debit side of the customers' book. The reason assigned for this is, that the ledger is the banker's account against his customer, and the book is the customer's account against the banker. Hence the customer, when he looks at his book, has at his left hand the sums with which he has debited his banker, and at his right the sums which are to the banker's credit.

Cashiers' Deficiencies.—It cannot be expected that a cashier can receive and pay away money for a whole year, and yet never make any mistakes. Some deficiencies will be sure to arise. Each cashier is considered liable to make good his own loss. But, to meet these deficiencies, some banks allow to each cashier a certain sum—say 20*l.* or 30*l.* per annum—which is called risk-money. Others pay such deficiencies as may arise during the year, giving an admonition to any cashier whose deficiencies are usually large. Superior accuracy in this respect is also considered as one test of superior merit, and therefore as forming one claim to promotion. When a cashier takes his holidays, he delivers up his cash to the chief clerk, who counts it, and sees that it is correct, and then delivers it to the clerk who is to act for the cashier, who signs an acknowledgment in the money-book that he has received the right amount. The cashier, on his return, will make a similar entry. It is said to be the practice in some establishments for the chief clerk to count the cash of all the cashiers every Saturday night. But when, from the extent of the business, this cannot be done, he counts the cash of each cashier individually, at such times as may be most convenient to himself, giving the cashier no previous notice of his intention to do so. He immediately reports to the banker any deficiency he may discover. In all banks it is understood that the cashier is not allowed to apply any part of the bank money, even temporarily, to his private use, nor to lend any sum, however small, to the other clerks, upon their I.O.U.s, or other engagement. Any violation of this rule, though with no fraudulent intention, is considered a sufficient ground for instant dismissal.

Gambling in the Funds, or in Shares.—Some banks make it a rule to dismiss any clerk that is found to be engaged in transactions of this kind. The evil effects of such practices are very great. Speculative engagements will necessarily distract their minds, and draw their attention from their official duties. If unfortunate, their personal comforts may be diminished: they may incur debts that will require years of saving to liquidate, or they may be tempted to actions which would ruin themselves and disgrace their families.

VII. The Training of Clerks for higher Offices.

Whatever natural talents a young man may have when he enters a bank, he cannot be expected to perform his duties well until he has been instructed. There is a good way and a bad way, a quick way and a slow way, of performing even the most simple operation. Incorrect or slovenly habits, when once acquired, are not easily abandoned. When, therefore, a young man enters a bank, he should be placed under the tuition of another clerk, well qualified to instruct him with regard to all his immediate duties. It is also desirable that the chief clerk should not have much manual labour, but should have leisure to walk round the office—stand for a while at the elbow of each clerk—observe his peculiar defects—and give such instructions as he may deem necessary or useful. The senior clerks, generally, should also be ready at all times cheerfully and courteously to give instruction to their juniors.

There are many ways of ascertaining the relative merits of a clerk. There is one obvious way; that is, to inspect the books which he keeps. It can readily be seen if they are kept in a good and neat hand—if there are any blots or erasures—and if they indicate any great degree of carelessness or otherwise. Quickness is generally an evidence of cleverness. A clerk who can count notes very fast, or who can cast up a long column of figures very quickly, and yet accurately, is generally a clever man. Quickness of hand denotes quickness of head, and it will generally be found that these two kinds of quickness go together. We do not say that this mechanical quickness of head proves soundness of judgment, but neither does it prove the reverse. In a clerk it is a decided recommendation.

Another test of the cleverness of a clerk is, the opinion formed of him by his fellow-clerks. When men associate together day after day for a number of years, both their excellencies and their defects become known to each other, and each man falls into the position to which his qualities entitle him. The opinion which any one clerk expresses of the relative merits of the other clerks will generally be correct, when his own interest is not concerned. The opinion he may express will, in fact, be the opinion of the office, formed not only on his own experience, but also on the experience of all the other clerks.

The report of the chief clerk will generally express this united opinion of the office. But it is well for a banker to keep himself well acquainted, at all times, with the sentiments generally entertained by the chief clerk respecting the other clerks, and not ask his opinion merely when there is an opening for promotion. On these occasions, feelings of kindness, or the reverse, may induce a chief clerk to speak of the party in a somewhat different tone from that which he would employ at ordinary times.

With a view to the proper training of clerks, it is desirable that there should not be too many in proportion to the work. If the clerks are unemployed for any considerable portion of the day, their habits of attention, of industry, and of quickness, are impaired, so that they do less work even in those hours in which they are occupied. The duties of each clerk should be sufficiently heavy to require a continuous application of the mind during the whole of the working hours. If a banker find that the clerks have time to read books or newspapers, or to carry on either gambols or quarrels among themselves, during the hours of business, he may safely infer that he has too many hands. By reducing the number he will make each clerk more efficient, and the work will be better done. He will also be able to increase their salaries individually. It is better that the same amount of money should be distributed among a smaller number of effective men than among a larger number who are less effective. The amount of Christmas money received by each will also be greater.

For the purpose of training the clerks, it is desirable that their labours should be so subdivided as that the duties of one office should be a training for the office immediately above it. The clerk, on his entrance into the bank, will thus have to perform those operations that require the least degree of professional knowledge—of knowledge peculiar to the business of a bank—and will advance step by step (each step requiring but a small addition to his previous knowledge) to the higher posts. When it is ascertained for which department—the cashier's or the accountant's—the teller is best adapted, he should be put into that post the operations of which will form the best training for those duties which, when promoted, he will have to discharge.

The occasional absences of the clerks are conducive to their improvement. The juniors thus learn to perform the duties of their superiors. New arrangements are formed temporarily for a different division of labour, and, the hands being fewer, an additional stimulus is given to exertion. It is also useful, when it can be done, for the clerks to change occasionally, and do each other's work. Every clerk should be encouraged to suggest any improvements for abridging or facilitating his own labour. When a bank has several branches, it is often advisable that an occasional absence at one branch should be supplied by a clerk brought from another branch. A good inspector of branches will inspect the cashier's and the accountant's department, as well as the manager's; and when he finds any improvement at one branch, he will introduce it into all the other branches.

But the greatest stimulus to improvement in the clerks is an impartial system of promotion. It is, perhaps, desirable that instances should occur sometimes, of a clerk, who is entitled to a higher post from seniority, being unfit to take it, in order to show that superior merit is regarded. But it should always be obvious that the clerk who is promoted has superior merit. If a clerk is put over the head of another from favouritism, or caprice, on the part of the banker—or from the influence of friends, customers, or shareholders—or even for qualities good in themselves, but not increasing his efficiency as a clerk—then will great evils arise from his appointment, even though he should be as well qualified as the man who was entitled to the post from seniority.

Another effectual means of training clerks is the daily balance. The books are balanced every night, before the clerks leave the bank. But mistakes will necessarily occur during the day, and to discover these will occupy a little time. The total amount of error is called "the difference;" and to endeavour to discover the error is called "searching for the difference." Those clerks who are thus employed in the evening are said to be "upon the balance." In large establishments it is usual to divide the whole body of clerks into classes, who take it in turn to be "upon the balance." By this arrangement, all those who are not "upon the balance" can leave the bank as soon as their own work is done. The smaller the number of clerks on the balance, the better. Thus, in a bank of forty-two clerks, six would be sufficient to be on the balance. If a larger number—say twelve—were retained, the juniors would do nothing, or else they would be employed on the inferior books, from which they would learn nothing. But when only six are retained they must all work, and, what is better still, they must all think. They will all acquire a thorough knowledge of the whole system of book-keeping, and be able to ascertain in what way errors in one book may counteract errors in another book, and how the errors discovered will bear upon "the difference." In large establishments, almost the only way in which a junior clerk can learn the whole system of book-keeping, is from being "upon the balance." But this is an effectual one. It also gives him an opportunity of showing his talents. Some clerks are far more quick in discovering the difference than others are; and this quickness is generally a fair criterion of the general talent of the party. The clerk who "skulks" the balance avoids the best means of improvement, and the best opportunity of showing his talents. But such persons have usually no

2 B

talents to show. A clerk who acts in this way betrays a consciousness of being a fool.

We have here spoken of that kind of training which is adopted to the making of clever clerks. But as in the joint-stock banks a clerk may become a manager, it is desirable that those clerks who are deemed the most clever should be put under a course of training that will, with experience, qualify them for that office. It is, in some respects, more difficult to do this in a large establishment than in a small one. In a bank that has forty clerks, one clerk sees only a fortieth part of its operations. In a bank where there are only ten clerks, one clerk sees a tenth part, and may easily acquire a tolerable knowledge of the whole. A bank that has many branches has a great facility for training clerks to become managers. When a branch manager is absent from illness, or any other cause, one of the senior clerks of that or some other branch will take his place, and thus gradually become accustomed to the duties of the office.

The clerks thus selected for this kind of training should be young men who are quick and efficient in the discharge of all their official duties, and, moreover, possess a good temper, gentlemanly appearance and manners, a degree of literary information, with a desire of improving their knowledge and their talents. They should not be young men who have entered the bank until they can get something better, but those who look to banking as their profession, and are ambitious of attaining to the highest posts in the establishment. But beyond the qualities we have enumerated, it is necessary, above all things, that they should have habits of business.

" Habits of business is a phrase which includes a variety of qualities—industry, arrangement, calculation, prudence, punctuality, and perseverance. And these virtues are exercised, not from the impulse of particular motives, but from habit. If you hear a man boast of being industrious, you may safely infer that he does not possess the habit of industry; for what a man does from habit, he does mechanically, without thinking of the merit of his actions, though they may be highly meritorious. Habits of business are essential to a merchant. But though essential to a merchant, they are not peculiar to him. They are as necessary to a professional man as to a merchant—as necessary to ladies as to gentlemen—as necessary for the government of a family as for the government of a commercial establishment. The greater the intellectual talents of the individual, the more necessary are habits of business to keep him steady in his course. The more canvas he spreads, the more ballast he requires. If we examine the history of those illustrious characters who have risen to eminence as the masters, the legislators, or the instructors of mankind, we shall find they have been as much distinguished by their habits of business as by the superiority of their intellect ; while, on the other hand, we could easily point out, in every science and in every path of life, some young men who, though of towering genius, have become lost to themselves, and have disappointed the hopes of all their friends, through a want of habits of business. They have burst upon the world with more than noon-tide splendour, they have attracted universal notice, they have excited big expectations, and suddenly they have darted into an oblique course, and passed into oblivion."[*]

If a clerk be intended to be trained for a manager, it may be questioned whether he will be improved by remaining a long time as a clerk. The two offices are very distinct, and they call into operation distinct qualities and operations of mind. A very old banker's clerk (unless he has been a chief clerk) is, generally, from the very length of his service, disqualified for being a manager. Seven to ten years' experience as a clerk is quite long enough, and after that period the sooner he becomes a manager the better, provided he has the necessary qualifications. Even during that time he should have been occasionally employed in those operations that require the exercise of his faculties as a man of business. It has often been said, that good servants make bad masters. If this be true, it is probably the result of an intellectual more than a moral deficiency. A lengthened service causes the mental faculties to move in a routine from which they cannot be suddenly aroused into an attitude of independence, so as to be able to trace causes and effects, to balance opposing considerations, and to engage in those reasoning processes which are required by the exercise of authority. Hence it is, that before a clerk is appointed a manager, he should undergo some kind of training. The best training for being a manager is that of being chief clerk, or of holding an equivalent post next to the manager. It will necessarily follow that the holder of such a post will have occasionally to take the place of the manager, and the manner in which he may then act will be a fair criterion by which to judge of his qualifications for that or a similar situation.

Among the means of training clerks for superior offices, we should give a high rank to the formation of a library of banking books, to which the whole of the establishment should at all times have access. The remarks we made in a letter, addressed

* Lectures on Ancient Commerce, by J. W. Gilbart.

2 B 2

to the manager of a country bank, in the year 1846, and which was afterwards published in the sixth volume of the *Bankers' Magazine,* are, we think, not inapplicable to this subject :—

"I wish you would advise your directors to celebrate their success by sending to each of their branches monthly a copy of the *Bankers' Magazine.* I am sure this would be a profitable investment of some portion of your surplus funds, and would yield an ample return in the results arising from the increased knowledge and skill of your managers. Here they will learn points of *law* and of *practice,* with which they were previously unacquainted, and be better prepared to deal with such cases when they occur in their own experience. It seems peculiarly necessary that managers of branches, who have not the opportunity of immediately consulting with any of the directors, should be supplied by the bank with the means of obtaining this kind of information. Losses are sometimes incurred by joint-stock banks through the want of knowledge of a little banking law on the part of their principal officers. The managers would not be the only gainers. The other officers of the branches would have the opportunity of self-improvement, and thus routine clerks might become intelligent bankers, and you would train in your own establishment a constant supply of able men to take the places, when necessary, of the existing managers. It is one of the excellences of our system, that the junior clerks may look forward to being placed at the head of the establishment; but this can only take place in those instances wherein the clerks endeavour to acquire that professional and general knowledge which is necessary in the present day, in order to discharge the duties and maintain the position of a manager. Unless they do this, those who are now clerks will remain clerks as long as they live, and the next generation of managers will be taken from the more instructed classes of society."

The manager of a joint-stock bank in the midland counties informs us that his directors recently voted 100*l.* towards the formation of a bank library. To the directors of other banks we would say, "Go and do likewise." *

* In the year 1850 a Literary Association was formed by the clerks of the Bank of England. The directors assigned three rooms within the Bank for a Library, a Reading-room, and a Lecture-room, and gave 500*l.* towards the funds. Several of the directors individually presented also handsome donations of both money and books.

In training clerks for intellectual offices, it is advisable not to give them too many instructions with regard to minute details. They should be taught to think for themselves. A man's talents are never brought out until he is thrown, to some extent, upon his own resources. If, in every difficulty, he has only to run to his principal, and then implicitly obey the directions he may receive, he will never acquire that aptitude of perception, and that promptness of decision, and that firmness of purpose, which are essentially necessary to those who hold important and responsible offices. Young men who are backward in this respect should be entrusted at first with some inferior matters, with permission to act according to their discretion. If they act rightly, they should be commended; if otherwise, they should not be censured, but instructed. A fear of incurring censure—a dread of responsibilty—has a very depressing effect upon the exercise of the mental faculties. A certain degree of independent feeling is essential to the full development of the intellectual character. It should be the object of a banker to encourage this feeling in his superior officers. Those bankers who extend their commands to the minutest details of the office, exacting the most rigid obedience in matters the most trivial, harshly censuring their clerks when they do wrong, and never commending them when they do right, may themselves be very clever men, but they do not go the way to get clever assistants. At the same time, they exhaust their own physical and mental powers by attending to matters which could be managed equally well by men of inferior talent.

After a clerk has become a manager, his education has yet to be completed. Lord Bacon observes, that reading makes a wise man; writing an exact man; and conversation a ready man. Whatever knowledge he may have acquired by reading or otherwise—however exact he may have been in the discipline of the office—the young manager has yet to become a ready man. He has to apply his knowledge promptly and independently, and, at the same time, wisely. This habit he will acquire by time. The exercise of authority over other men produces an independence of mind which is friendly to the maturing of the understanding; while the necessity for giving immediate decisions in conversation with his customers will have a tendency to produce promptness of judgment. There is no profession in which experience is more useful than in banking. But it is useful, not so much in the amount of knowledge that is acquired (though that is important), as in the improvement it imparts to those intellectual faculties which are called into exercise. It is by constant practice that these faculties gather strength. Habits are formed by repeated acts, and they can be formed in no other way.

Before closing this section on the administration of the office, we may observe, that although the duties of a chief clerk are quite distinct from those of a banker, yet in small establishments they are often performed by the same person. In branch banks, generally, the manager is both the banker and the chief clerk. But as the branch increases, the manager will gradually transfer to the second officer the duties of the chief clerk, and confine his own attention to those of a banker. It is too much the practice in England to view a bank manager as holding the same relative position in a joint-stock bank which a chief clerk does in a private bank. This is an error. A manager is not a banker's clerk—he is a banker. And although he may reserve some important cases for the consideration of his directors, yet they are usually such cases as a private banker would reserve for consultation with his partners, or on which, had he no partners, he would take time to form his own determination.

It may also be observed, that although the government of the office will generally be left entirely to the chief clerk, and it is not necessary that the banker should be made acquainted with all the trivial delinquencies of the clerks, yet there are certain acts of misconduct that must always be reported, and when reported must be dealt with by the banker himself. In a well-disciplined establishment these cases will be rare, but they will occur sometimes, and then the mode of reproof or punishment will be regulated by the kind of offence and the character of the party. Every act of dishonesty, however trifling the amount purloined, must be followed by instant dismissal. Acts of deliberate disobedience to orders, gross disrespect to superior officers, or acts of immorality that would bring discredit on the bank, will generally be visited with the same punishment. But extreme punishment should be inflicted only in extreme cases. Mere accidental errors, though they may sometimes occasion great loss, must not be treated in the same way as those faults which arise from gross neglect, or which imply a deficiency in personal honour. It is generally a good rule that a banker should not reprove a clerk in the presence of the other clerks. By following this rule, he can adapt his reproofs to the character and position of the party ; for a valuable clerk, even when really culpable, is not to be treated in precisely the same way as another whose services are of less importance. Nor is it any violation of justice, that those faults which arise from inadvertence should be viewed differently from those that arise from bad habits. Nor will it tend to impair the discipline of the office should it be known that a good character will sometimes get a young man out of a scrape, while he who had not that good character would be punished more severely for a less important offence. Another rule to be observed in administering reproof is,—in reminding a clerk of his defects, to commence with telling him of his *good* qualities. There is a credit as well as a debit side in every man's character; and it seems hardly fair to run over all the debit items, and say nothing of the other side of the account. This plan, too, increases, instead of diminishing, the pungency of the reproof, while it removes from the mind of the party any impression that the banker is influenced by motives of personal dislike.

SECTION XIII.

BANKING BOOK-KEEPING.

" ALTHOUGH the business of keeping books is extremely easy when once the accounts are properly arranged, yet the adaptation of the principle of Double-entry to extensive and complicated transactions, so as to receive the full benefit of the system, is a process which requires the most complete knowledge, not only of the *practice*, but also of the *science*, of book-keeping."

" Book-keeping, like all other arts, can only be mastered by industry, perseverance, and attention. The learner must think for himself, and endeavour to understand the *why* and *wherefore* of all that he does, instead of resting satisfied with vague notions and words devoid of sense."

" The study of book-keeping affords an excellent means of intellectual discipline; that is, when its principles are exhibited as well as their application. When the reasoning powers are called into exercise as well as the memory, the student who has carefully attended to the instructions, and who is the *master*

and not the *slave* of rules, will experience no difficulty in un-
ravelling or adjusting any set of accounts, however complicated
or diversified."*

We have commenced this section with these quotations in
order to quicken the attention of the reader to a subject which
by those who do not understand it is considered complicated, and
by those who do understand it is considered dull. It is, in fact,
neither the one nor the other. But still it is a subject on which
it is difficult to write in such a way as to avoid the possibility
of being misunderstood. We purpose in this section—

    I. To notice those Preliminary Operations with which a
       young Book-keeper should become acquainted.
    II. To describe the system of Banking-book-keeping as pub-
       lished in the former editions of this work.
    III. To state those Improvements of which this system has
       been found to be susceptible.
    IV. To trace the Resemblance between Banking Book-keeping
and Mercantile Book-keeping.

I. Preliminary Operations.

When a young man enters a bank as a clerk, he should be
instructed to be careful with regard to his handwriting, or, in
his anxiety to write fast, he may forget to write well. If he
write a bad hand, he should not be above taking a few lessons
from a professor of penmanship, who will teach him to write
fast and well at the same time. But, however badly he may
write, he should try to write plainly. Plainness is of more consequence than neatness or elegance. He should be very careful
in writing the names of the customers of the bank. If he write
them illegibly, there will be a loss of time in making them out,
or they may be misunderstood, so that money may be posted to
the wrong account, and thereby loss arise to the bank. On this
account also, when two or more customers have the same sur-
name, he should be very careful to write the Christian names
fully and distinctly.

The necessity for writing quickly, and the want of carefulness
at first, are the causes why so few bankers' clerks comparatively
write a good hand. But they should remember, that this is a
most important qualification, and a deficiency in this respect
may be an insuperable bar to promotion. Without this attain-

* Double-Entry Elucidated, by B. F. Foster.

ment a clerk cannot be put to write up the customers' books, nor to make out the country accounts, nor to write the letters, nor to fill the office of secretary. " You ought to be careful to write a plain hand. You impose upon your correspondents a very unnecessary and a very unpleasant tax if you require them to go over your letters two or three times in order to decipher your writing. A business hand is equally opposed to a very fine hand. A letter written in fine elegant writing, adorned with a variety of flourishes, will give your correspondent no very high opinion of you as a man of business."*

The plan of writing-masters who advertise to teach good and expeditious writing in a few lessons is as follows :—The pupil rests his hand upon the paper without touching it with his little finger. All the motion is then made from the wrist. Those who have to write their names many times in succession, such as in signing bank notes or in accepting bills, will find that on this plan they can get through their work in much less time than if they bend their fingers with every stroke of the pen.

The young clerk should also be taught to make his figures clear and plain, so that a 2 cannot be mistaken for a 3, nor a 3 for a 5. He should also take care that the tail of his 7 or his 9 does not run into the line below, and thus turn a 0 into a 6, and and also that the top of his 4 does not reach so high as to turn a 0 in the line above it into a 9. He should be careful, too, in putting his figures under one another, so that the units shall be under the units, the tens under the tens, the hundreds under the hundreds, and the thousands under the thousands. Otherwise, when he adds up the columns together, he will be in danger of making a " wrong cast."

He will also learn to use both hands at the same time. In counting gold or silver coin, he will count with two hands instead of one, and thus do double the work. In *entering* a number of cheques or bills, while he holds the pen in one hand he will hold a cheque in the other, and then turn over the cheques as quickly as he enters them. He will always turn them over one on the back of the other, so that they will be in the same order after he has entered them as before, and when they are "called over" they will come in the same order in which they are entered.

* Lectures on the History and Principles of Ancient Commerce, by J. W. Gilbart.

He must also learn to "cast" quickly and accurately. The two main qualifications in this operation are accuracy and quickness. To insure accuracy a clerk will *cast* everything twice over. The first time he will begin at the bottom of the column, and the second time at the top. If he begin both times at the bottom of the column, the association of figures will be the same; and if he has fallen into an error the first time, he will be apt to fall into the same error the second time: but if he changes the order, the association of the figures will be different, and he will not be likely to fall into the same error. Quickness can be acquired only by practice. But he will accelerate his speed by making his figures plain, and placing them strictly in a line under one another. He should also learn to cast without speaking, for the eye and the head will go faster than the lips.

He must also be taught to "call over." When he first comes into the bank he will call this sum, 315*l.* 10*s.* 6*d.*, three *hundred and* fifteen *pounds* ten *shillings and* six *pence;* but he will soon learn that more than half these words may be suppressed, and he will say, three, fifteen, ten, six. And so in the larger amount, 4,785*l.* 13*s.* 4*d.*, instead of saying, four *thousand* seven *hundred and* eighty-five *pounds* thirteen *shillings and* four *pence,* he will call, forty-seven, eighty-five, thirteen, four. By proceeding in this way, and speaking quickly and yet distinctly, a column of figures may be called over and checked in a very short space of time. He will, however, take care to avoid ambiguity. Thus, if the sum be 40*l.* 5*s.* 6*d.*, he will not say forty, five, six, as that would mean forty-five pounds six shillings; but he will say, in this case, forty *pounds,* five, and six. In cases where the pounds consist of five figures, the two first denoting the thousands are expressed separately; thus, 25,347*l.* 8*s.* 6*d.* is called over twenty-five, three, forty-seven, eight, six; and six figures, say 468,379*l.* 8*s.* 6*d.*, is called over, forty-six, eight, three seventy-nine, eight, six.

He will also be taught to *balance;* that is, to find the difference between two sums by *addition,* instead of subtraction. Thus, if the two sums be 1,347*l.* 16*s.* 3*d.* and 4,834*l.* 19*s.* 8*d.*, he will be apt at first to put one under the other and subtract, in this way :—

$$
\begin{array}{r}
\text{£4,834} \quad 19 \quad 8 \\
\text{1,347} \quad 16 \quad 3 \\
\hline
\end{array}
$$

Difference . . . £3,487 3 5

But he must be taught to proceed by a mental process, and will add the difference to the smaller number, thus :—

	£1,347	16	3	—	£4,834	19	8
Difference . . .	3,487	3	5				
	£4,834	19	8				

He performs this operation by beginning with the pence, saying, or rather *thinking*, " three and five make eight," and so on. And thus the two sides of an account are made to balance ; that is, both sides are of the same amount.

The principle of balancing pervades the whole system of book-keeping. For example, we know that if to the amount of cash in the bank last night we add the amount received to-day, and deduct the amount paid to-day, the remainder will show the amount on hand to-night ; and a novice would very naturally put it down in this form :—

	£
Cash on hand last night	100,000
Received to-day	60,000
	160,000
Paid to-day	80,000
Cash on hand to-night	£80,000

But an accountant would arrange these four items in such a way as to form a balance, thus :—

	£			£
Cash paid away to-day . .	80,000	Cash on hand last night .	100,000
Cash on hand to-night . .	80,000	Cash received to-day . .	60,000
	£160,000	Balance .	£160,000

In keeping the Progressive Ledger, the principle of balancing is of constant occurrence. The ledger-keeper brings out a new balance every time he turns to an account. But he never deducts—always adds. And if he post several articles at the same time, the method is the same, thus :—

If the credit balance is			£1214	3	7
And he posts the following sums to the *debit* of the account .	£141	2	4		
	8	7	6		
	49	3	11		
	305	4	2		
			£710	5	8

he will add up these items, and mentally add a sum that will make the whole equal to 1,214*l*. 3*s*. 7*d*., bringing out this sum as a new balance, and placing it under the former one as he goes on. Thus he will say, or rather think,—" 4 and 6 are 10, and 11 are 21, and 2 are 23, and (here he must supply the figure) 8 are 31 = 7 and carry 2 ;" and he puts down the 8 in the pence division of the balance column ; and goes on in the same way to the shillings, and afterwards to the pounds. When he has placed this sum, 710*l*. 5*s*. 8*d*., he adds up the whole, including this sum, in order to check the operation, and to be sure that he is right.

He will then acquire a knowledge of the names and functions of the different books, and of the terms and phraseology used in book-keeping. The same book is sometimes called by different names in different banks, and different terms are employed to describe the same operations. But every clerk should use the language of the office in which he is placed. He should call every book by its proper name, and employ the phrases which are used by others. For instance, if the word " money " is used to denote coin, he must always use it in that sense ; and not say " money " when he means bank notes.

It will be of great advantage to a sensible youngster, if one of the senior clerks should take the trouble to give him a general notion of the system of book-keeping, and show him the connexion that exists between the books that he keeps and the other books of the office.

II. We shall now describe the system of Banking Book-keeping, as published in the former editions of this work.

Every person, on opening an account with a London banking-house, enters his name in a book called the Signature-Book, and this book is referred to whenever a draft is presented having a doubtful signature. The person is supplied free of cost—stamps excepted—with a book of printed drafts and a cash-book, called in some houses a Pass-Book, in which is entered an account of his debts and credits, as often as he thinks proper to leave it for that purpose.

London bankers do not usually give receipts for money paid into their hands, but they enter the amount into the customer's book. A person paying money on account of a country bank, will sometimes require a receipt, and he is then given what is called a shop-receipt, in the following form :—

> *London, May* 1, 18   .
> *Received of* [*the country bank*] *the sum of one thousand pounds.*
> *To account for on demand.*
> *For Hope, Rich, and Co.*
> £1000. *A Cashier.*

The name of the party paying the money is not inserted in the receipt, as that would require a stamp.

The payment of a draft or a bill is always made either in Bank of England notes, or sovereigns, as the party receiving it may desire. The London bankers never reissue any country notes or bills of exchange that may come into their hands. When a cheque is paid, it is cancelled by drawing the pen four times in different directions across the name of the drawer. In Scotland a paid note or cheque is said to be "*retired.*" It is retired or withdrawn from circulation.

Before explaining the banking system of book-keeping, I will define a few terms which are often used in connexion with the subject. By the word *bill* is always meant a bill of exchange not yet due. The word *cash* denotes the various items included in a credit or cash entry, and may denote *due* bills, cheques, bank notes, country notes, or coin. The terms *cheque* and *draft* are used synonymously, and denote an order on a banker, payable on demand. The word draft is never used in London to denote a bill of exchange, though this use of the term is very common in the country. Both bills and drafts are often called *articles;* and if they are cash, they are styled *cash articles.* An *addressed bill* is a bill made payable at a banking-house. A discounted bill is usually called a *discount.* By *money* is always meant coin. To *post* an article is to *place* or *enter* it in the ledger. One book is said to *mark against* another when the same entry is made in both books. One book is *checked by* another, when any error in one book would be detected by some operation in another. To *check* a book, or an account, is to examine it, and prove it correct, or make it so. To *cast,* or *cast up,* means to add together. The *balance* of an account is the difference between the credit and the debit side. An account is said to *balance* when the credit and the debit side are of the same amount. To *balance* an account is to enter the balance, and to add up both sides, and then to bring down the balance as a new amount. The *credit* side of an account, or that on which the cash received is placed to the credit of a customer, is the right-hand side as you face the ledger ; the *debit* side is the left-hand side. In London, the establishments of bankers are usually called *banking-houses*, not banks. A person who has an account at a banking-house, is said to *keep a banker*.

I shall now describe the various books in the order of the different departments to which they belong.

I.—*The Cash Department.*

The principal books in this department are the following :—

1. Two Waste-Books.—One is called the Received-Waste-Book, and the other the Paid-Waste-Book. In the former is entered an account of all the cash *received*, and in the latter is entered an account of all the cheques and bills *paid*. The Received-Waste-Book is ruled with a double cash column on the right-hand side of the page. In making an entry into this book, you will proceed as follows :—First, enter the name of the party who lodges the money ; then enter in the first cash column the particulars of which the credit consists, specifying each particular in the space at the left-hand. In receiving Bank of England notes, the number and date of each note must be mentioned ; but if the notes are numerous, make them up in a parcel, and write on the outside the total amount, and the name of the party of whom they were received. Call this parcel "Sundries" in your entry. These parcels of sundries will be marked, and sent to the Bank of England for other notes on the following day. Cheques on your own bank are to be entered by the name of the drawer and the amount. Country notes are to be entered by the name of the London banker at whose house they are made payable. These are distinguished from cheques upon bankers, by stating short the number and denomination of the notes—thus, $\frac{1}{10}$, $\frac{5}{1}$. All gold and silver are to be called money. After entering all the particulars of a credit, add them together, and carry out the amount into the farther cash column. At the close of the day add up this outer column, and see that the total agrees with the amount in the Day-Book.

If a customer brings his book with him when he lodges cash, the cashier enters the credit, and returns the book to him, unless it be left at the bank for the purpose of having the debit side also written up.

In receiving money for a deposit receipt, the entry is made in the same way as when the money is placed to a current account; but the words Deposit Receipt, or the letters D. R., are written against the name of the depositor.

In the Paid-Waste-Book is entered an account of all the bills and cheques paid by the bank. This book is ruled on each page with a cash column on the right hand, and another on the left hand, leaving a space between. When a cheque is paid, the amount is placed in the left-hand cash column—then the name of the drawer in the open space—and in the right-hand cash column are entered the particulars of the payment. Bank of England notes are entered by their number. It is not necessary to enter the date, as that can be found if necessary either in the Cash-Book of the preceding evening, or in the Received-Waste-Book, or the Lists of the same day. When a deposit receipt is paid, the same order is observed, but the letters D. R. are added. All gold, silver, and copper are called money. At the close of the day, all the payments are added together, and should agree with the amount in the Day-Book.

Each cashier has a Received-Waste-Book, a Paid-Waste-Book, and a Money-Book.

2. MONEY-BOOK.—This is a small book ruled with a cash column on the right-hand side of each page, and it contains an account of all the coin, that is, the gold, silver, and copper in the bank. Each cashier will enter in his own Money-Book the money he receives and pays in the course of the day. On the left-hand page of the book he will copy from his Paid-Waste-Book the various sums of money he has paid, and on the right-hand page he will copy from his Received-Waste-Book the various sums of money he has received. In each case he will enter against the respective sums the totals in which they are included. Thus, if in paying a cheque of 175*l*. 2*s*. 6*d*., he pay 5-2-6 money, he will enter it thus—" £175 2. 6. £5-2-6." The money is counted up at night, and must agree with the balance of the Money-Book; and this balance is then entered in the Cash-Book.

3. CASH-BOOK.—In this book is entered every night a specification of all the cash in the bank. The items will consist chiefly of Bank of England notes, parcels of sundries, country notes, cheques on other banks, and the balance of the money. The Bank of England notes are entered by their number, date,

and amount. The parcels of Bank of England notes, called sundries, are entered by the word "Sundries," then the name of the parties of whom they were received, and the amounts: country notes by the name of the country bank, and the London agent at whose house they are made payable ; cheques on other banks by the name of the drawer of the cheque, the name of the banker, and the amount. In this book generally the cash articles are more fully described than in the Received-Waste-Book. In some banking-houses the Cash-Book is called the STOCK-BOOK, and in others the MAKE-UP-BOOK.

4. DAY-BOOK.—This book is ruled with a double cash column at the right-hand side of each page. The accountant enters in the Day-Book an account of all cash paid and received during the day, placing each transaction under the class of operations or accounts to which it belongs. On the left-hand page of the book he enters the cash which is paid, and on the right-hand side the cash which is received. He commences by writing the day of the week and of the month : then on the left-hand side he writes a heading, "CURRENT ACCOUNTS." Under this head he enters all the cheques paid, copying from the cheques the name of the drawer and the amount, which are placed in the first cash column. The sum of all the cheques is brought forward into the second cash column. The second heading is "DEPOSIT RECEIPTS ;" under which head the individual receipts paid are entered, mentioning the number, the name of the depositor, and the sum; and bringing out the total amount, as before, into the second cash column.

The accountant may, if he please, make these headings in the morning, leaving such a space for the transactions under each head as his experience may show him to be necessary. Thus he may keep up his Day-Book throughout the day, and merely have to add it up and balance it when the bank closes. The other headings may be, " Bills Discounted this day," " Interest paid on Deposit Receipts," " Bank Premises," " Incidental Expenses," " Branch Accounts," &c. &c., answering to the accounts in the General Ledger.

On the right-hand page, or credit side of the Day-Book, the cash received is entered under corresponding headings, as "CURRENT ACCOUNTS," "DEPOSIT RECEIPTS," "BILLS DISCOUNTED PAID THIS DAY," &c. &c. The entries under the heads of Current Accounts, and Deposit Receipts, are copied from the

Received-Waste-Books: the entry expresses only the name and the amount.

After all the entries have been made, add up the debit and the credit sides. To the credit side add the amount of the Cash-Book on the preceding evening; to the debit side add the amount of the Cash-Book on the same evening; and, if the totals agree, the "bank is right," that is, the transactions of the day have been correctly entered; but if not, then the bank is wrong, and the error must be discovered by "marking off" the various books.

In large establishments the Day-Book is divided into two books; the debit side forming one book, and the credit side the other book. One is called the "Paid-Day-Book," and the other the "Received-Day-Book." The advantage of this division is, that two persons can be employed at the Day-Book at the same time. In some banks the Day-Book has three cash columns, the third being used for transfer entries. These are entries in which no cash is actually paid or received by the bank, but an amount is transferred from one account to another. In other banks, all the transfers are passed through the Received-Waste-Book. By some London houses the Day-Book is called the Cash-Book, and its two divisions are called the "RECEIVED-CASH-BOOK," and the "PAID-CASH-BOOK."

5. CURRENT-ACCOUNT-LEDGER.—In this book every customer has a separate account. The sums received to his credit are posted from the credit side of the Day-Book, and the Ledger folio is placed in the Day-Book, in a column ruled for that purpose. The debit side is posted from the cheques themselves, and the Ledger folio placed in the debit side of the Day-Book on the following morning, when the Day-Book is marked against the Ledger. The entry of a cheque in the Ledger includes the date of payment, the name of the party to whom it is payable, and the amount. The entry of a credit includes the date, the word "Cash," and the amount. When the cash is paid into the bank by a third party, it is usual to enter it in the Ledger as "Cash per A. B." When a credit arises from a bill lodged for collection having become due, the *name of the accepter* is substituted for the word cash.

Some banks follow what is called the *progressive* plan of keeping the Ledger. By this plan the balance is brought out every day, and thus we see the *progress* of the account. In the

2 c

ordinary way, each page of the Ledger is divided into the debit and the credit side, and each side has ruled columns for the date, the transaction, and the amount. But in the progressive Ledger there is only one column for the date of both the credits and the debits—one space for a description of the transaction, whether credit or debit—and then three cash columns. The first column is the debit column; the second is the credit column; and the third is the column into which the daily balance is brought out. The advantage of this plan is, that you can see at once what sum a party has on his account, without the delay of adding up the debit and the credit columns. Most banks that allow interest on the balance of the current accounts keep their Ledger on the progressive plan; and, besides the columns I have mentioned, there are, on the right side of the balance column, a space for inserting the number of days the balance may remain stationary, and two interest columns—one for the interest of a credit balance, and the other for the interest of a balance overdrawn. Most banks divide the Current-Account-Ledger into two or more parts, and the names of the depositors are placed in alphabetical order, from the beginning of the first Ledger to the end of the last.

6. DEPOSIT-RECEIPT-BOOK.—Deposit Receipts are receipts granted for sums of money that are likely to remain a considerable time, and upon which interest is allowed. These receipts are distinguished from current accounts. Cheques cannot be drawn against any sum lodged as a deposit receipt; but when the amount, or any part thereof, is withdrawn, the receipt itself must be produced at the bank, and delivered up. The Deposit-Receipt-Book is not kept *ledger-wise;* that is, each person has not a separate account opened for him in a distinct part of the book, but the receipts are entered chronologically, according to the date of the lodgment. The entry includes date of lodgment, name of depositor, profession, residence, amount, interest paid, principal and interest. The last two particulars are of course not entered until the receipt is cancelled. If a party is desirous of withdrawing only a part of the lodgment, the whole receipt is entered as paid, and a new receipt made out for the sum which remains.

II.—*The Bill Department.*

Bills are divided into two classes—bills deposited, and bills discounted. Bills deposited are bills lodged in the bank for collection, to be placed, when due, to the credit of the depositors. Bills discounted are those for which the money has been advanced, and which are, therefore, the property of the bank. These two classes of bills are entered in separate sets of books; but, as the books are kept in nearly the same manner, I shall describe them together.

1. BILL-REGISTER. } These books are kept, as the word DISCOUNT-REGISTER. } register seems to imply, chronologically—the bills being entered immediately after each other, in the order in which they come into the bank. The entry includes date when deposited or discounted, name of ingiver, drawer, accepter, date, term, when due, amount, daily amount. The bills are numbered, and the register-number placed upon each bill. The daily amount of the Discount-Register is entered in the debit side of the Day-Book, under the head, "Bills Discounted this day." I advise that the headings of the columns of this, and of all the other books, be printed. This saves time and prevents mistakes.

2. BILL-LEDGER. } In these books a separate account DISCOUNT-LEDGER. } is opened for each party; and the same bills which have previously been entered in the Registers are entered in these Ledgers; but the entry is much shorter. A full description of a bill is given in the Register only, and the register-number is placed as a reference in every book in which the bill may subsequently be entered. The entry in the Bill, or Discount-Ledger, includes date when deposited or discounted, name of accepter, when due, and amount. In some banks the Discount-Ledger is kept upon the progressive plan, which is very useful, as it shows at once to what amount any party may be under discount. In addition to this, some banks place in the Discount-Ledger an account of all bills they may have discounted, to which the party is an accepter. These bills are distinguished from those which have been discounted for the party himself, by being placed on the left-hand side of the page. This account is also kept on the progressive plan. A Discount-Ledger, kept in this way, will have three cash columns ruled on each side of the page: the three on the left

2 c 2

hand will be headed, " Where Accepter ;" and the three on the right-hand will be headed, " Where last Indorser." Between the two sets of columns will be entered—date when discounted—register-number—name of accepter or drawer—when due. The advantage of this plan is, that on turning to any party's account, you see at once the whole of his engagements to the bank, whether arising from bills that have been discounted for himself, or bills to which he is only the accepter.

3. BILL–JOURNAL. ⎱ In these Journals the bills are
DISCOUNT–JOURNAL. ⎰ entered under the respective days on which they fall due. For this purpose the day of the week, and of the month, is placed at the top of each page. This book may be made to last exactly a year, by having headings for every day, from the 1st of January to the 31st of December, omitting Sundays. The entry includes the register-number, name of depositor, or for whom it was discounted, accepter, and amount. The Discount-Journal has three cash columns; one for the amount of each bill, another for the bills paid, and another for those unpaid. The entry is made in the first column, on the day the bill is discounted, and in the other two on the day the bills fall due. The total amount of bills paid each day is copied from the Journal into the received side of the Day-Book. Those unpaid are entered into the transfer column of the Day-Book, and in the Past-Due-Bill-Book. The Bill-Journal need only have one cash column, as most banks find it more convenient to credit their customers' accounts with all the bills on the day they fall due, and debit them on the following day for those that remain unpaid. Those banks, however, that prefer it, may have separate columns in the Bill-Journal for the paid and the unpaid bills; and, in that case, the unpaid bills are returned on the following day to the depositor, without being passed through his cash account. This is sometimes called being " entered short." Some banks make one book serve the purpose of both a Bill-Journal and a Discount-Journal; one page of the book being used as a Discount-Journal, and the opposite page being used as a Bill-Journal.

4. THE LISTS.—Each banking-house divides London into a certain number of districts, according to the extent of its business. Each district is called a Walk, and usually takes its name from the direction in which it lies; as the East Walk, the West Walk, and so on. To each walk is assigned a book.

in which is entered every day a *list* of the bills due in the walk, and hence the book is called a List.   Each List takes its name from the walk to which it belongs, as the East List, the West List, &c.   The page is divided into four columns, the first and third of which are cash columns.   In the first column is entered the amount of the bill, in the second, the name of the accepter and the register-number.   This is done the day before·the bills are due.   After the teller has returned from presenting these bills for payment in his walk, he "answers" each bill; that is, he places against it an account of the cash he has received for it, whether cheques, bank notes, or money.   The amount is entered in the third column, and in the fourth the description of each kind of cash.   If the bill be not paid, he writes L. D. for "left direction," and then enters the bill in the "Unpaid-List."

In the UNPAID-LIST are entered all the bills not paid when presented for payment.   In the course of that day or the following these bills are "answered," either by being paid, or by being passed to the debit of a customer's account, or by being transferred to the Past-Due-Bill-Book.   In some banks the Unpaid-List is called the "TAKE-UP-BOOK."

Cheques upon other banks are entered in the Lists in the same way as bills, unless the bank sends a clerk to the Clearing-house, and then they are entered in the "Clearing-out-Book."

From this description it will be seen, that when a sum is received to the credit of a current-account, it is entered in the Received-Waste-Book, copied from thence into the Day-Book, and from thence into the Current-Account-Ledger.   When a cheque is paid to the debit of a current account it is entered from the cheque itself into the Paid-Waste-Book, the Day-Book, and the Current-Account-Ledger.

When a sum is received for a deposit receipt, the sum is entered before the receipt is granted in the Deposit-Receipt-Book, and afterwards in the Receipt-Waste-Book and Day-Book.   When a deposit receipt is paid, it must be discharged in the Deposit-Receipt-Book, then entered in the Paid-Waste-Book, and afterwards in the Day-Book.

When a bill is discounted, the discount is calculated by the accountant, who at the same time observes if it is drawn on a proper stamp, and is in every respect a regular and negotiable instrument.   If the party for whom it is discounted have a current account, the full amount of the bill is placed to his credit, and he is debited for the interest. If he have no account, he is paid the amount minus the discount, and the entry is made in the Paid-Waste-Book. The bills discounted each day are entered individually in the Discount-Register, and the total amount copied into the Day-Book. The bills are also entered individually in the respective accounts in the Discount-Ledger, and under the days they fall due in the Discount-Journal. When these bills are due, the amount paid each day is entered in the Day-Book in the cash column, and the amount unpaid is transferred to the Past-Due-Bill account, and is entered in the Day-Book in the transfer column.

When a bill is deposited, it is entered in the Bill-Register, the Bill-Ledger, and the Journal. When due, it is placed to the credit of the party by whom it was lodged, and is copied from the Journal into the Day-Book, thence into the Current-Account-Ledger. If unpaid, the account is debited on the following day, and the bill is returned to the depositor.

At the commencement of each day, all the entries made the preceding day in the Day-Book, are marked against the respective books by the accountant, or under his superintendence. He also marks the Cash-Book, and checks the adding-up. The Customer's Books are then compared with the Current-Account-Ledger. The debit side of these books is usually written up the preceding evening from the vouchers by the tellers, or out-door clerks. The accountant writes up the credit side, and sees that both sides agree with the Current-Account-Ledger.

III.—*The Country Department.*

In this department is managed the business of the country banks, and of those customers who live in the country. When the letters are delivered in the morning by the postman, one clerk takes them and enters in the Waste-Book the *cash* enclosed in the letter to the credit of the respective parties. Another clerk takes the letters and enters the *bills* in the Country-Bill-Register, the Bill-Ledger, and the Bill-Journal. The letters are then handed to a third clerk, who copies off into a book all the *payments*, which are to be made immediately in cash. This book is usually called the Draft-Book, as the party receiving the money signs a draft for the amount, which is as good as signing a receipt. If the payment is to be made to a banker, he receives notice in a printed form called a memorandum; but if the payment is ordered to be made to a private individual, he must call for it and claim the exact amount. The following is the form sent to a banking-house. The right-hand side is filled up by the house to whom it is sent, and the memorandum is paid through the clearing.

<table>
<tr><td>

London, December 1, 18 .

Messrs. Steady & Co.

  Receive of [the country bank]
per Messrs. Hope, Rich, & Co.,
the sum of £100.

     On account of [E. F. Esq.]

</td><td>

London, December 1, 18 .

Messrs. Hope, Rich, & Co.

  Pay E. F. Esq., or bearer, the
sum of one hundred pounds, on
account of [the country bank].

     For Messrs. Steady & Co.

£100.   *A Clerk.*

</td></tr>
</table>

A fourth clerk now takes the letters, and enters all the *advices* (that is, bills *advised* to be paid when due) in the Advice-Book and in the Advice-Journal. The corresponding clerk who answers the letters usually manages the stock department. Hence he observes the orders to purchase or sell stock, to procure powers of attorney, and other business of that kind. When writing a reply to the letters received, he notices if all the items in the letters are marked by the proper clerks. If anything is wrong he is informed of it. Bankers' letters are usually short and plain, comprising only two or three lines. The following example includes all the ordinary topics.

Messrs. HOPE, RICH, & Co., *Bankers, London.*

Country Town, May 1, 18 .

  GENTLEMEN,—Enclosed we remit you sixteen bills, value 1,750*l.*, and cash 250*l.*, making together 2,000*l.* to our credit; and we subjoin a list of payments and advices, to be made to our debit. We will thank you to purchase 10,000*l.* new fours, in the name of James Wealthy, gentleman, of Stately House, near Prince Town, and forward us a power of attorney for sale, and dividends of 200*l.* Consols, now standing in the name of Susan Thrifty, spinster, of this place. Please inform us of the respectability of Messrs. John Careful & Co., of Southwark—they bank at Messrs. Steady & Co., Lombard Street. The bill you sent us to present here for payment has been paid, and we credit you 50*l.*, the amount. We herewith send you the signature of our relative, Mr. John Keen, who is going to London, and whose drafts to the extent of 3,000*l.* we wish you to honour to our debit. On Mr. Keen's return, which will be in about a week or ten days, he will bring with him our paid notes.

          We are, Gentlemen,

            Your obedient Servants,

              KEEN, BUSY, & Co.

Messrs. KEEN, BUSY, & Co., *Bankers, Country Town.*

London, May 2, 18 .

GENTLEMEN,—We have received your favour of yesterday's date, enclosing sundries, value 2,000*l.*, which we have passed to your credit, and note your lists of payments and advices. We also credit you 1,476*l.* 16*s.* 6*d.*, per Messrs. Good & Co., on account of John Green. We have inquired of Messrs. Steady & Co. as to the respectability of Messrs. John Careful & Co., and are informed they are highly respectable. We now enclose a stock receipt for Mr. James Wealthy's 10,000*l.* new fours, 10,012*l.* 10*s.* to your debit; and also Susan Thrifty's power of attorney, for which we debit you 1*l.* 1*s.* 6*d.*; also a dishonoured bill on Badluck, noted 100*l.* 1*s.* 6*d.* to your debit; and your weekly cash account and monthly account current, which we trust will be found correct. We debit you 50*l.* for the bill you had the goodness to present for us, and we now enclose another on White, 120*l.*, which we will thank you to get accepted and return. We have opened a credit in favour of Mr. John Keen for 3,000*l.*, and will forward your paid notes by him as requested.

> We are, Gentlemen,
> Your obedient Servants,
> HOPE, RICH, & Co.

Those London bankers who act as agents to banks, or to other parties in the country, will have occasion for the following books. The first seven are kept in the same manner as the corresponding books in the Town Department. All the entries in the Country-Ledger, as well as those in the Town-Ledger, must first pass through the Waste and Day-Books. The *credit* side of the Ledger is posted from the Bill-Journal and the Day-Book. The *debit* side is posted from the vouchers themselves, and, like the debit side of the Town-Ledger, will mark against the Paid-Day-Book and the " Clearing-in-Book."

1. A Country-Ledger.
2. Country-Bill-Register.
3. Country-Discount-Register.
4. Country-Bill-Ledger.
5. Country-Discount-Ledger.
6. Country-Bill-Journal.
7. Country-Discount-Journal.
8. Advice-Book.—In this book are entered an account of bills *advised* to be paid on account of the Country Banks. This book is kept ledger-wise, each bank having a separate account.

9. Advice-Journal.—This book is similar to the Bill-Journal, and it contains the *advices* under the heading of the days on which they are to be paid.

10. Credit-Book.—This book contains an account of the credit granted by a country bank in favour of any party. Each party has an account open for him in this book, and the amount of his credit is placed to this account. He is debited for such cheques as he may draw, and the cheques are then passed to the debit of the country bank in the Country-Ledger.

11. Acceptance-Book.—In this book are entered those bills which have been received from the country, and which require the acceptance of the party on whom they are drawn. The entry includes the date when taken out, the name and residence of the drawee, the register-number, and the amount. There are also two vacant columns, in one of which the clerk who takes the bill for acceptance enters his initials when he brings it back; in the second column are entered the initials of another clerk to whom the bills when "brought in from acceptance" are delivered. Though this book is connected with the country department, it is usually kept in the town office.

12. Stock-Book.—London bankers have usually powers of attorney from their correspondents in the country, authorizing them to receive dividends on the Government funds. All these are entered in a book called the Stock-Book. The book is divided into several parts for the different kinds of stock, as 3 per cent. Consols, 3 per cent. Reduced, &c. &c. In each division are entered the powers of attorney held by the bank. The entry includes date of the powers, names of the attorneys, names of the holders of the stock, and the amount. These entries should be made a tolerable distance apart from each other, to leave room to notice any alteration that may take place in the amount of the stock either by sales or new purchases.

Every country bank keeps an account with a London bank. The country banker receives from London a weekly statement of his cash accounts, and a monthly account current. The cash account is a copy of the London banker's ledger. But as the London banker does not consider as cash anything which may not be immediately turned into Bank of England notes, the cash account does not exhibit a statement of the *undue* bills which the country banker may have remitted, nor of the bills which he may have advised to be paid. By means of a monthly account current he has a full view of all these transactions. On the credit side of the account current is entered the total amount of each remittance, whether it consists of bills or cash. These are followed by entries of " extra " sums of cash that have been lodged to the credit of the country bank by parties resident in London. On the debit side of the account current is placed the total amount of the " advices ;" that is, of bills advised to be paid, and also any " extra " payments of " drafts " to persons in London. Then the account is balanced, and we have an easy check by which any error that may have crept into either the cash account or the account current is detected. For if both accounts be correct, the amount of advices not yet due, added to the balance of the account current, will be equal to the amount of bills not due, added to the balance of the cash account.

IV.—*The Note Department.*

Those banks that issue notes will have occasion for

A NOTE-REGISTER, in which the denomination, number, and date of the notes will be entered when prepared for circulation. The total amount of notes, as soon as they are received from the stamp office, or at least as soon as they are signed by the banker or manager, are entered to the credit of " note account," and are afterwards taken down daily as part of the " cash " in the possession of the bank. If the notes on hand be deducted from the balance of the note account, the remainder will show the amount of notes in circulation. Another way is to open an account for " Notes in Circulation," and to credit this account for the notes on hand every morning, and debit it for the notes on hand every night : the balance will show the amount of notes in circulation. There should also be a book for the " Register of Cancelled Notes," in order to keep an account of those notes which, having become unfit for further use, have been cancelled and destroyed. The notes when cancelled are placed to the debit of the " Note Account."

V.—*The Branch Department.*

In those banks that have branches, the head-office keeps an account with each branch, in the same way as a London banker keeps an account with a country bank. There is usually an additional "Bill-Register" for the bills payable at branches. Each branch has also two Bill-Registers, for bills payable at the head-office, and the bills payable at branches, and frequently another for the bills sent for collection to agents, where the branch does not remit all its bills to the head-office, but direct to agents in other places in order to be collected. Every country banker has also similar Bill-Registers for "Bills payable in London," "Bills payable at Bristol, Manchester," &c., as the case may be ; and of course corresponding accounts must be opened in the General-Ledger.

There must also be a book for entering "Branch Notes paid." These notes may either be placed as the debit of the branch on the day they are paid, or they may be carried daily or weekly to the debit of an account to be called "Branch Note Account," and may be placed to the debit of the branch on the day they are sent home.

VI.—*The General-Ledger.*

Into this Ledger, under the various accounts, will be entered the totals of the corresponding headings or accounts specified in the Day-Book. The accounts in this Ledger denote the various classes of operations, and the balances show at all times the exact state of the bank. Every Saturday night the totals and balances of these accounts should be taken off on a balance-sheet. When all the debits are added together, and all the credits are added together, the two sides will agree ; that is, they will be of the same amount. These balance-sheets may be printed and bound together in a book, to be called "the General-Balance-Book." I cannot better explain the General-Ledger than by giving the form of the weekly balance-sheet, with the names of those accounts which most banks have occasion to introduce. I have distributed these accounts into five classes :—1. Lodgments. 2. Investments. 3. Expenditure. 4. Cash Account, with Branches ; and 5. Proprietors' Accounts. Each bank, however, will open such accounts as are adapted to its transactions. Whatever books the business may render necessary will require to have corresponding accounts. The General-Ledger contains the summaries of all the other books. Thus, the account called "Current-Accounts" contains the summary of the Current-Account-Ledger. The account called

"Deposit Receipts" is a summary of the Deposit-Receipt-Book. The account called "Bills discounted" is a summary of the Discount-Register and the Discount Journal. In this way every book in the office has a corresponding summary in the General Ledger. Hence, this book is a check upon all the other books ; and by means of these summaries, the partners or directors of a bank can see at once the actual state of their affairs, and can trace the progress or decline of different branches of their business.

Every branch of a Joint-Stock Bank has a "General-Balance-Book," and sends to the head-office every week a balance-sheet of its affairs as they stood on the previous Saturday night. At the head-office these various balance-sheets are consolidated, and form a general statement of the affairs of the whole bank. This statement comprises the balance of the General-Ledger at the head-office, and that of each branch. These statements are printed and bound together beforehand, so as to form a book—it is called the Statement-Book, and is laid before the directors at their weekly meetings. The balances of the General-Ledger are given in the form on the opposite page (397), and those of the Statement-Book in the form at page 405.

It will be observed that the accounts introduced into the balance-sheet on page 397 are such as would be necessary to a London bank that had country agencies and branches, and issued notes. No such bank exists. But I have introduced all these accounts, that each bank may take those which are adapted to its transactions. It will also be observed that I have kept the country business distinct from the town business, so that the comparative extent of each may be immediately perceived. I have introduced cash columns for the AMOUNT as well as the BALANCES ; for although the balances are sufficient to show the actual state of the bank, yet the amounts are necessary to show the business that has been done since the previous half-yearly balance.

1. The first class of accounts, under the head of LODGMENTS, are all credit accounts ; that is, the balance is on the credit side.

CURRENT ACCOUNTS are those which are usually kept by the London bankers, and are called by the Bank of England " Drawing Accounts." DEPOSIT RECEIPTS are more permanent lodgments, upon which the joint-stock banks allow interest.

THE_____ BANKING COMPANY.

Amounts and Balances of the GENERAL-LEDGER *on* _____

Amounts. Dr.	Balances. Dr.	Titles of Accounts.	Ledger Folio.	Balances. Cr.	Amounts. Cr.
		I. LODGMENTS.			
		London Current Accounts.			
		Country ditto.			
		Deposit Receipts.			
		Bills Deposited (in London).			
		Ditto (from the Country).			
		Notes in Circulation.			
		Credits on Agents.			
		II. INVESTMENTS.			
		Bills Discounted (in London).			
		Ditto (from the Country).			
		Past-Due Bills.			
		Government Stock.			
		East India Bonds.			
		Exchequer Bills.			
		Loans to Customers.			
		Ditto to Brokers.			
		Interest Account.			
		III. EXPENDITURE.			
		Bank Premises.			
		Rent.			
		Taxes.			
		Salaries.			
		Stationery.			
		Incidental Expenses.			
		Law Expenses.			
		IV. CASH ACCOUNT WITH BRANCHES.			
		Branch A.			
		Branch B.			
		Branch C.			
		Branch D.			
		V. PROPRIETORS' ACCOUNTS.			
		Paid-up Capital.			
		Preliminary Expenses.			
		Dividend Account.			
		Unclaimed Dividends.			
		Surplus Fund.			
		Profit and Loss.			
		Fund for Bad Debts.			
		General Account of Cash.			

The account " BILLS DEPOSITED," not being a cash account, might be omitted without deranging the balance of the General-Ledger. If introduced, its balance must be placed on both sides the balance-sheet, or the totals will not agree. The General-Ledger is no check upon the accuracy of this account. It should, therefore, be checked periodically, by taking off the daily amounts current from the Journal, and comparing the total with the balance of " Bills Deposited in the General-Ledger."

Some banks distribute their bills deposited into several accounts, as " Bills Deposited by Agents," " Bills Deposited by Branches," " Bills Deposited by Private Parties," &c. &c. On the debit side of the General-Ledger these " bills deposited" are mixed with the bills discounted in different accounts, according to the places where the bills are payable, as " London Bills," " Manchester Bills," " Branch Bills," &c. Those deposited bills that are payable in the place where the bank is established, are usually distinguished from the discounted bills; one account being called " Local Bills Discounted," and the other " Local Bills Deposited."

NOTES IN CIRCULATION.—When the notes are made payable at any other place beside the place of issue, this account will only show the " apparent circulation," as the notes that have been paid by the agents, or at the other branches of the bank, cannot be brought into the account until they have been returned for reissue. 1 have classed this account under the head of Lodgments, because it denotes a portion of the debt due from the bank to the public.

CREDITS ON AGENTS.—When a bank grants a Bill, or Letter of Credit, upon their agents, the money received is placed to the credit of this account. When the bill is due, or the credit paid, it is placed to the debit of this account, and to the credit of the agent's cash account. The business of some banks requires a subdivision of their credits, as " Credits on London Agents," " Credits on Bristol Agents," &c. Some banks have also an account for " Credits on Branches;" but where all the credits granted are payable on demand, they are usually placed at once to the credit of the cash account of the branch on which they are drawn.

2. INVESTMENTS.—The accounts belonging to this class are

all debit accounts; that is, the balance (if any) is always on the debit side.

In the foregoing balance-sheet it is presumed that all the bills are payable in London, as the London bankers do not discount bills payable elsewhere. The division into two accounts is merely to show the comparative extent of the town and the country business. The first account includes the bills discounted for parties resident in London, and the second includes the bills discounted for parties resident in the country. Where the bills are payable at different places, they are referred, as I have already intimated, to different accounts, as "London Bills," "Bristol Bills," "Manchester Bills," &c. It is not usual, in these cases, to distinguish between the bills discounted and the bills deposited, but to place them together on the same account; for instance, the account "London Bills" would include all bills payable in London, whether discounted or deposited. If thought proper, however, they may be easily divided into separate accounts, as "London Bills Discounted," and "London Bills Deposited."

PAST-DUE-BILLS.—When a discounted bill is not paid, it is transferred to the debit of this account. "Bills deposited" never pass into this account, but if unpaid, are returned to the parties by whom they were deposited.

When the bank purchases "Government Stock," "Exchequer Bills," "India Bonds," &c., the purchase money is passed to the debit of an account raised for the purpose. Upon re-sale the account is credited for the money received, and the difference between the money invested and the money received is passed, at the end of the year, to the debit or the credit of profit and loss account.

LOANS.—This account is debited for the amount of any loan granted to a customer, or to any other party, on security. When a customer wants a temporary advance, the usual way, in London banks, is not to let him overdraw his account, but to place to his credit the sum he may require, and debit the loan account. The interest is charged upon the full amount of the loan. When the loan is repaid, this account is credited.

3. EXPENDITURE.—The accounts under this head require little explanation. "Bank Premises" is debited for the expense of altering, painting, &c., the buildings and offices connected with the bank. The other accounts are debited for the different

classes of expenditure as they occur. At the end of the year these accounts are credited, and the several amounts are placed to the debit of profit and loss account.

4. Cash Account with Branches.—The title of this class of accounts is sufficiently explanatory. I will only observe, that in some banks each branch keeps a distinct cash account with every other branch, and with the several agents of the bank with whom it may have transactions. But, in other banks, each branch passes all its transactions through its cash account with the head-office. It debits the head-office for whatever it may remit to either a branch or an agent, and it credits the head-office for whatever sums it may receive from a branch or an agent.

5. Proprietors' Accounts.—This class of accounts refers to the internal operations of the bank.

Paid-up Capital.—If the capital has been paid up at different times, this account may be divided into " First Instalment," " Second Instalment, " Third Instalment," &c.

Preliminary Expenses.—Several joint-stock banks have passed to an account of this sort the expense of forming the company; and these expenses are discharged out of the profits, by equal portions, in the course of five or ten years. This is considered a more equitable mode than to pay these expenses out of the profits of the first two or three years.

Surplus Fund.—When the whole of the annual profits are not divided among the partners or proprietors, the surplus is transferred to an account called " Surplus Fund," where it remains for the purpose of being applied to meet any losses or contingencies that may occur in after years.

Profit and Loss.—To the credit of this account is placed all interest and commission received; and to the debit is placed all interest paid. These entries are made at the time the transactions occur. At the end of the year this account is credited for all the profits that have been made during the year upon Government Stock, Exchequer Bills, &c., and is debited with the several items of expenditure. The Profit and Loss Account may be subdivided into several accounts, as " Interest Received on Bills Discounted," " Commission Received," " Interest Paid on Deposit Receipts," " Charge for Agency," &c. &c. When it is not thus divided, a complete abstract of the account should be made out at the end of the year.

GENERAL ACCOUNT OF CASH.—The introduction of this account makes the General-Ledger a perfect check upon the other books. For by this means the total of all the balances of the debit side of the General-Ledger are equal to the total of all the balances of the credit side. To the *debit* of this account is passed, every day, the total amount of the *credit* side of the Day-Book ; and the account is *credited* for the amount of the *debit* side of the Day-Book ; consequently the balance of this account will be always on the debit side, and will be equal to the difference between the sum of all the other debit balances, and the sum of the credit balances ; that is, it will show the amount of cash in the bank. The General-Ledger is usually kept on the progressive plan,* so that the balance of any account can be seen upon inspection, and its progress from any past period can be distinctly and readily traced.

VII.—*Periodical Balances.*

DAILY BALANCE.—It is well known that bankers try their balance at the close of their business every night, with a view of correcting any errors that may have occurred during the day. The process is very easy. If to the amount of the Cash-Book last night, we add the amount of the cash received to-day, and deduct the amount of the cash we have paid, the remainder will be the amount of the Cash-Book to-night. If, on trial, we find this is not the case, there must be some error. Suppose, for instance, the Cash-Book last night amounted to 100,000*l.*, and we have received 40,000*l.* and paid 50,000*l.* to-day, then will the Cash-Book to-night amount to 90,000*l.* The trial stands thus :—

Cash-Book last night . . £100,000	Paid-Day-Book £50,000
Received-Day-Book . . 40,000	Cash-Book to-night . . . 90,000
£140,000	£140,000

The daily balance, therefore, is nothing more than the balance of the Day-Book ; and the only books employed are the Day-Book and the Cash-Book. But as these books, when finally closed, include the amount of several other books, the trial is usually made (for the purpose of avoiding alterations) on a half-sheet of paper, called the trial paper, previous to those

* See page 385.

2 D

entries being made, and then the amounts of these several books are stated separately, in the following manner :—

Dr.	BANKING HOUSE.	*Cr.*
Amount of Cash-Book last night . . . . . . [This is usually called the Rest.] Ditto of Received-Day-Book . . . . Ditto of Bill-Journal . . Ditto of Discount-Journal .		Amount of Paid-Day-Book . Ditto of Clearing-in-Book* Ditto of Balance* of the Clearing . . . . . Do. of Cash-Book to-night . Ditto of Balance of Money-Book . . . . . . Ditto of Discount-Register

The balance of the clearing † is always to the credit of the house ; for, if the clearing " takes out," then the bank notes paid away at the Clearing-house are entered in continuation of the clearing-out ; so that, in this case, the balance is usually thrown a small sum on the other side. When the clearing is finally closed, the notes forming this balance are entered in continuation of the clearing-in, and subsequently in the Cash-Book. The notes entered in the clearing-out are, of course, not entered in the Cash-book.

WEEKLY BALANCES.—The daily balance checks the Waste-Books, the Discount-Register, the Journals, the Day-Books, the Lists, and the Money-Books. If any errors occur in any of these books throughout the day the balance will be wrong. But the daily balance does not check the Current-Account-Ledger, though this is the most important book of all. The Ledger is therefore " marked off " every morning against the Day-Book, the Bill-Journal, and the Clearing-in-Book: but this is not a sufficient check. Hence the balances of all the accounts in the Current-Account-Ledger should be taken off weekly in a book called the Current-Account-Balance-Book, and added together, and the amount made to agree with the balance of " current accounts " in the General-Ledger. This is usually done by the London bankers quarterly or half-yearly. When the Ledger is kept on the progressive plan, it may be done weekly without much trouble. The " Current-Account-Balance-Book " should be ruled so that the names of the parties having accounts may

---

* When a bank does not " clear " these items are of course omitted.
† The present clearing-house system is described in a subsequent section.

be placed under one another at the left hand, and all the rest of the left-hand page, and the whole of the right-hand page, divided into double cash columns—one column for the balances of the accounts when in cash, and the other for the balances over-drawn. On this plan it will not be necessary to write the names more than once in seven weeks.

In the same way the balances of the Discount-Ledger should be taken off weekly in the " Discount-Balance-Book." The balances of the General-Ledger are also taken off weekly in the " General-Balance-Book " in the way I have already described.

HALF-YEARLY BALANCE.—The weekly balancing of the Ledger does not preclude the necessity for a half-yearly balance. The usual days for balancing are the last days of June and December. Some banks, however, balance on the *last Saturday* in June and December, and others on the 30th of June and on Christmas-eve. On the balancing day the following operations are passed through the books :—1. The current accounts will be debited for any interest or commission that may be due from the party to the bank.—2. The Current-Account-Ledger will be balanced, and the balance will be brought down as the com-mencement of the transactions of the ensuing half-year.—3. The customers' books must be balanced, and made to agree with the Current-Account-Ledger.—4. The interest due upon the out-standing deposit receipts must be calculated, and the sums added together.—5. The General-Ledger must be balanced, and at the December balance the amount standing to the debit of the several classes of expenditure must be passed to the credit of those accounts, and to the debit of profit and loss account, and the several sums of profit that have been realized upon Govern-ment Stock, India bonds, &c., are transferred to the credit of profit and loss account.

For each half-year a book must be provided to be called the Half-Yearly-Balance-Book. This Book will contain the follow-ing entries :—

1. A balance-sheet showing the balances of the respective accounts in the General-Ledger in the same way as the weekly balance-sheet.—2. A debtor and creditor balance sheet, showing the exact condition of the bank.—3. An abstract of the profit and loss account.—4. A list of all the balances of the current accounts.—5. A list of all the outstanding deposit receipts, and the interest due upon each.—6. A list of all discounted bills,

2 D 2

current, i.e., bills not yet due.—7. A list of all deposited bills current.—8. A list of all other securities, distinguishing those that belong to the bank from those that are lodged by its customers.

The debtor and creditor balance-sheet will contain the same amounts as the balance sheet of the General-Ledger (see page 397), but differently arranged. They may be disposed according to the form exhibited on the opposite page.

The abstract of the profit and loss account may be made out in the following form :—

Abstract of Profit and Loss Account, from Jan. 1 to Dec. 31.				
Dr.				*Cr.*
To Bank Premises . . . . Furniture . . . . . Rent . . . . . . Salaries . . . . . Stationery . . . . . Incidental Expenses .		By Interest on Bills dis- counted . . . . . . By Interest on Loans . . By Commission on Cur- rent Accounts . . . . By Profit on Exchequer Bills, &c.		
Total Expenses . . . . Loss on bad Bills, &c.. . Balance in favour of the Bank				

At the end of the year the final balance of the profit and loss account is transferred to other accounts according to the purposes to which it is to be applied. If intended to be held as a "surplus fund," it is transferred to that account. If intended to be divided among the proprietors, it is transferred to a "dividend account," which is raised for that purpose. If the balance of the profit and loss account should be against the bank, then it must remain "on the wrong side," until further profits shall turn the balance the other way.

Besides the books connected with the business of banking, every joint-stock bank will require,

1. A SHAREHOLDERS' REGISTER.—In this book the names of the shareholders are entered chronologically in the order in which they become shareholders. The entry includes the date, the name, residence, number of shares, and sum paid.

2. TRANSFER-REGISTER.—In this book are entered the transfer

Statement of the Affairs of the Bank, on

| Dr. | THE | BANKING COMPANY. | Cr. |

Dr.		BANKING COMPANY	Cr.
DUE TO THE PUBLIC ON CURRENT ACCOUNTS.		DUE TO THE BANK ON OVERDRAWN ACCOUNTS.	
Head Office, Town		Head Office, Town	
Ditto, Country . . .		Ditto, Country	
Branch A		Branch A	
Branch B		Branch B	
Branch C		Branch C	
Total Current Accounts . . .		Total Overdrawn Accounts	
		BILLS DISCOUNTED.	
DEPOSIT RECEIPTS.		Head Office, Town	
		Ditto, Country . . .	
Head Office		Branch A	
Branch A		Branch B	
Branch B		Branch C	
Branch C		Total Amount of Bills Discounted	
Total Deposit Receipts . .		LOANS.	
		Head Office	
Notes in Circulation . . .		Branch A	
Credits on Agents		Branch B	
		Branch C	
Total Lodgments		Total Amount of Loans	
		INVESTMENTS.	
		Government Stock . . .	
		Exchequer Bills	
INTEREST ACCOUNT		India Bonds	
		Other Investments . . .	
Head Office		Total Investments . . .	
Branch A		Total Available Assets .	
Branch B		EXPENDITURE.	
Branch C		Head Office	
Total Amount of Interest		Branch A	
		Branch B	
		Branch C	
		Total Expenditure . . .	
FUND FOR BAD DEBTS.		PAST-DUE-BILLS.	
		Head Office	
Head Office		Branch A	
Branch A		Branch B	
Branch B		Branch C	
Branch C		Total Amount of Past-Due-Bills	
Total Amount of Fund for Bad Debts . . .		SUNDRY ACCOUNTS.	
		Stamp Account	
PAID-UP CAPITAL . . .		House Account	
		Ditto Branch A . . .	
		Ditto Branch B . . .	
SUNDRY ACCOUNTS.		Ditto Branch C . . .	
		Total . . .	
Forfeited Shares		GENERAL ACCOUNT OF CASH.	
Dividends		Head Office	
Unclaimed ditto		Branch A	
Surplus Fund		Branch B	
Profit and Loss		Branch C	
Total Sundry Accounts		Total Amount of Cash .	
Total . . .		Total . . .	

of shares from one proprietor to another. The entry includes date of transfer, from whom transferred, residence, ledger-folio, to whom transferred, residence, purchase-money, transfer stamp.

3. PROPRIETORS'-LEDGER. — In this ledger each proprietor has an account open, in the same way as in a cash-ledger. He is credited for the number of shares, and an entry is made of the different instalments he may pay. When he sells or transfers his shares, he is debited the shares, and they are placed to the credit of the party who may have purchased them. The entry includes the date, number of register, calls and transfers, number of shares, and amount.

III. We shall now consider those Improvements of which the above system is capable, so as to render it more efficient in large establishments.

As a bank increases its business, it becomes of importance to improve its system of book-keeping, and to adopt means of increasing the efficiency of its clerks. A large establishment can generally be conducted with a less *proportionate* number of hands than a small one. It admits of a more extensive application of the principle of a division of labour. In a small bank, one clerk may keep two or three books of various kinds, or perhaps act as both cashier and accountant. But in a large bank, each clerk is in general kept wholly to one employment. The effects of this separation of occupations are the same in banks as in manufactories ; and the description of these effects given by Adam Smith will equally apply to both cases.

" The great increase in the quantity of work which, in consequence of the division of labour, the same number of people are capable of performing, is owing to three different circumstances: first, to the increase of dexterity in every particular workman ; secondly, to the saving of time which is commonly lost in passing from one species of work to another ; and lastly, to the invention of a great number of machines which facilitate and abridge labour, and enable one man to do the work of many."

The increase of dexterity by constant practice is very observable in the practice of " casting up." A clerk who is much accustomed to this operation will cast up a long column of figures with singular quickness and accuracy. It is also very observable in " calling over." Besides, owing to the abbreviations we have mentioned in page 378, a clerk in calling over will speak so rapidly that an unpractised ear will hardly be able to

follow him. Mr. Babbage gives the following instance of great
dexterity acquired by practice :—

"Upon an occasion when a large amount of bank notes was required, a
clerk in the Bank of England signed his name, consisting of seven letters,
including the initial of his christian name, five thousand three hundred
times during eleven working hours, and he also arranged the notes he had
signed in parcels of fifty each."*

The loss of time in passing from one operation to another is
as obvious in mental processes as in those which are purely
mechanical.

"When the human hand or the human head has been for some time
occupied in any kind of work, it cannot instantly change its employment
with full effect. The muscles of the limbs employed have acquired a
flexibility during their exertion, and those to be put into action a stiffness
during rest, which renders every change slow and unequal in the commencement. A similar result seems to take place in any change of mental
exertion; the attention bestowed on the new subject is not so perfect at the
first commencement as it becomes after some exercise."†

The invention of expedients for facilitating and abridging
labour is also as common in a bank as in a manufactory.

Mr. Francis has recorded, in his 'History of the Bank of
England,' a variety of improvements introduced into that establishment by Mr. William Rae Smee, son of a former chief
accountant.

He proposed an alteration in the cheque office, by which he
stated that the work which employed three principals and
twenty-one clerks would be done more effectually by two principals and seven clerks. In the circulation department, the
posting, which previously took fifty, occupied only eight clerks ;
whereas the whole of that department, conducted upon the old
system, would probably have required before now a hundred
additional assistants. In the National Debt Office Mr. Smee
introduced such measures that "the directors were enabled so far
to consult the accommodation of the public as to enable the
transfers in the various offices to be made eight or nine days later
than usual, the business which formerly occupied about thirty-
two days being accomplished in about twenty-three." ‡

Similar improvements have been introduced into commercial
book-keeping.

* The Economy of Machinery and Manufactures. By Charles Babbage.
† Ibid.
‡ History of the Bank of England: its Times and Traditions. By John
Francis. Vol. ii. p. 141.

" The old method of journalizing and posting each transaction separately unnecessarily swells the accounts in the ledger with a multiplicity of figures, which greatly increases the difficulty of balancing, and, to say nothing of extra labour and loss of time, the liability to error is always in proportion to the number of entries, and *vice versâ*. If a hundred sums are posted when one would answer, then a hundred chances of error are incurred where only one was necessary; and in the event of an error in adjusting the accounts, a hundred entries must be called over and examined instead of one."[*]

The expedients introduced to improve any system of book-keeping have for their object either the saving of time *directly* by abbreviating the entries, or to save time *indirectly* by new modes of preventing or detecting errors. And it may be observed, that a minute alteration, hardly worthy of being adopted in a small bank, where it would save but a few minutes a day, may be very properly adopted in a large establishment, where the time saved would be in proportion to the greater extent of business. Sometimes an entry may be shortened by omitting some of the particulars. Thus, where we have been accustomed to enter with every bill—the name of the last indorser—the drawer and his residence—the accepter and his residence—the date, term when due, and the amount—we may properly perhaps omit some of these items. Or where we have repeated the same entry in several books, we may enter it in fewer books— or perhaps make the individual entries in only one book, and enter the total amount in the others—or, at other times, the whole form of a book may be changed, and we may by a new arrangement obtain the same results more clearly and in less time. Almost every bank will occasionally make some alteration of this kind as its business may require. And even each accountant has usually some little expedients of his own for facilitating his daily operations. We will notice a few of those amendments that have been adopted with the view of saving time and labour in some of our banking establishments.

Some large banks have adopted the " horizontal system of book-keeping," which is in some respects an improvement on the system described in the former editions of this work. The chief difference is in the mode of ruling the Received and the Paid-Waste-Books.

The Received-Waste-Book, instead of being ruled as described on page 382, has *four* cash columns, three at the left hand as you face the book, and the fourth at the right hand, with a space

* Doubly Entry Elucidated. By B. F. Foster. p. 18.

between the third and the fourth. The different items of a credit entry, instead of being placed under one another, as in the former system, will be placed separately in the first three columns, and the total in the fourth column. Thus, if a sum of 543*l*. 10*s*. 7*d*. be received from Mr. Smith, and this sum consists of 3*l*. 10*s*. 7*d*. in coin or money, 100*l*. in a Bank of England note, and 440*l*. in a cheque on Jones, Loyd, & Co., the entry will stand thus:—

Money.			Bank Notes.	Sundries.			Name.	Total.		
£	*s.*	*d.*	£	£	*s.*	*d.*	Smith.	£	*s.*	*d.*
3	10	7	100	440	0	0	Jones, Loyd & Co.	543	10	7

Thus it is seen that the first column is for money, the second column for bank notes, and the third column for " sundries ;" that is, for all other articles ; and these three columns are added together " horizontally," and the total brought out into the fourth cash column at the right hand. It will be observed, that the cashier has to add the items together, not longways, but crossways—not longitudinally, but " horizontally." After a little practice one way is just as easy as the other.

Some cashiers prefer having two columns only at the left hand, and two at the right hand, with the space between the second and third column, as the numbers of the bank notes, and the names of the bankers on whom the cheques are drawn, can then be placed on the same line, but this is not a matter of much consequence.

Now, if you " cast up " the first left-hand column, you will have at the close of the day the total amount of money, *i. e.*, coin, received during the day. If you cast up the second column, you will have the total amount of bank notes. The third column will give the total amount of " sundries." And the amount of these three columns together will be equal to the fourth column, containing the total amount of the credits. If this should not be the case, there must be some error, which must be discovered forthwith. Thus the Horizontal-Received-Waste-Book is a check upon itself. As soon as the cashier gets to the bottom of a page he casts up his book, and sees that the three columns are exactly equal to the fourth. Thus he keeps his book right as he goes on. Whereas, in the former system, any error in the Received-Waste-Book would not be discovered till the General Balance was tried at the close of business, and not then, perhaps, until after a long course of " marking off."

To simplify my explanation, I have described the Received-Waste-Book as having only four cash columns, and these are perhaps enough for a small bank. But large establishments have sometimes seven or eight, perchance in the following order :—1. Money, *i. e.*, coin. 2. Bank notes. 3. Parcels of bank notes, called sundries. 4. Country notes. 5. Cheques on clearing bankers. 6. Cheques on bankers who do not clear. 7. Cheques on our own bank. —— a space. 8. The total amount of the credit.

The Horizontal-Paid-Waste book is ruled with three cash columns. One to the left for the amount of the cheque paid ; then an open space for the name ; then a column for the bank notes, and another for the money, *i. e.*, coin. The London bankers do not pay away any bills or country notes in exchange for cheques, but only Bank of England notes and coin. The entry stands thus :—

Amount of Cheque.			Name and No. of Bank Note.	Bank Notes.	Money.		
£	s.	d.		£	£	s.	d.
101	4	3	White.　　1473.	100	1	4	3

The amount of the columns containing the bank notes and the money will of course be equal to the column containing the amount of the cheques. And thus this Paid-Waste-Book contains a check upon itself.

The Horizontal-Paid-Waste-Book may have at the left hand two cash columns, one for the town and the other for the country departments, and also a separate column for the country notes ; thus :—

Town.		Country.		Country Notes.	Name.	Bank Notes Paid.	Money.

This prevents the necessity for having both a Town and a Country Paid-Waste-Book, while the two departments are still kept distinct. The country notes are also separated, and can be checked by themselves. When all are added together, the total of the three columns at the left must be equal in amount to the total of the two columns at the right hand. The articles paid must be equal to the bank notes and money which were issued in payment.

We shall now point out some of the advantages of the horizontal system of keeping the Waste-Books.

First. As all the receipts and payments of money, *i. e.*, coin, are entered individually in the Received and Paid-Waste-Books, and the amounts added together, it will not be necessary that these sums be copied individually into the Money-Book. The total amount only of each column is entered in the Money-Book at the close of the day's business, and the Money-Book is balanced. Thus, all the time employed in making the entries individually in the Money-Book is saved.

Secondly. As all the credits to current accounts are added together in the received-Waste-Book, it is not necessary they should be entered individually in the Day-Book. They can be individually posted direct into the Ledger, and the total only be entered in the Day-Book. The same remark will apply to the Paid-Waste-Book. This is another saving of time and labour.

Thirdly. Every Waste-Book, as we have already intimated, is a check upon itself. We have spoken of a Received-Waste-Book, and a Paid-Waste-Book, as though a bank had but one—and in small banks this is the case. But in large banks, there are seven or eight cashiers or more, each having a Received-Waste-Book and a Paid-Waste-Book for the town department, and another Received-Waste-Book and Paid-Waste-Book for the country department, with a Supplementary-Received-Waste-Book, and a Supplementary-Paid-Waste-Book, and a Money-Book besides. Now, it is a great advantage to have the means of keeping all these books free from errors during the day, and to know at night that they are all correct. If the "Balance" be wrong, the field of inquiry is thus very much limited, and the time that would otherwise be employed in checking the Waste-Books is devoted to the examination of the other books of the bank.

Fourthly. This plan gives the means of checking separately

those items that have a column appropriated to them. Take, for example, the column of bank notes. If we add to the amount of bank notes on hand last night the amount received to-day, and deduct the amount paid away, the remainder should be the amount on hand to-night. When this is the case the bank notes are right. In the same way we may check the money columns, the clearing columns, &c. Thus, when the trial balance is wrong, we can check these items separately, and thus more readily discover the error. Without this expedient we should have to "mark off" the whole business of the day.

It will be observed that the above Waste-Books refer only to receipts and payments on current accounts. All other receipts and payments are entered in a Supplementary-Receipt-Book and a Supplementary-Paid-Book. These books are ruled in the same way as the other Waste-Books, and they embody entries in connexion with deposit receipts, received or paid, credits or debits to interest accounts, debits to salaries, taxes, incidental accounts, &c. &c. All these items are then entered in the Day-Book, from whence they are posted into the General-Ledger. A book is also provided, usually called a Transfer-Book, in which are entered all the cheques on the bank paid in by other customers, as these merely cause a *transfer* of the amount from one customer to another.

Books which are designed chiefly as registries or summaries should be kept on the horizontal system. Thus, a London bank which keeps an account with the Bank of England, will have to lodge to its credit notes, gold, silver, post-bills, cheques, dividend warrants, &c.

To keep a registry of this, a book may be opened horizontally —the first column at the left hand being the date; then the articles entered over separate columns, at the top of the page; afterwards a column for the total amount of all these items—then a credit column for the cheques drawn each day— and then the daily balance. If this book be made of such a size as to contain about thirty lines, then each page will contain the transactions of a month. And, by adding up the columns, the figures at the bottom of the page will show the separate amounts of notes, gold, silver, &c., paid into the Bank of England in the course of a month. By comparing the different pages, it will be seen on what months the largest or the smallest sums are paid into the bank.

In constructing Tables it is also best to follow the horizontal system. Thus, to keep a record of the weekly returns of the Bank of England, it is best to arrange the items into columns, with the heading at the top of each column—the first column containing the dates of the several returns. It will then be easy to trace the fluctuations in any one item ; such, for instance, as the "Public Deposits," "the Private Deposits," "the Rest," &c. &c. Some of the Returns published in the Appendix to the Parliamentary Evidence of 1847 have been arranged on this principle.

We will now notice some further improvements that have sometimes been adopted by large banks in their system of book-keeping. The great object of all these improvements is, as we have already mentioned, either to save time directly, in making the entries, or indirectly, by preventing or discovering errors. These are—

1. The abolition of the Discount-Register. Here the bills are entered at once in the Discount-Ledger, under the names of the respective parties for whom they are discounted ; and the total amount of bills discounted each day is entered in the Day-Book from the Interest-Book, which contains the calculations of discount. The only objection to this plan is, that the space in the Discount-Ledger does not admit of so full a description of the bill as is usually given in the Discount-Register. The Bill-Register is also abolished in the same way.

2. The adoption of a Check-Ledger facilitates the discovery of errors, and thus diminishes the time employed in searching for them. Though this book is called a Check-Ledger, it is not kept ledger-wise. It is ruled with a cash column on each side the page. In the column opposite your left hand you enter, from the cheques themselves, all the cheques paid during the day. In the right-hand column you enter, from the Received-Waste-Books, all the credits of the day. When you add up these two columns, they will of course agree with the amounts of the Paid-Waste-Book and the Received-Waste-Book. Thus the accuracy of the Check-Ledger is insured. Now, where the balances of the Current-Account-Ledger are checked every week, you employ the Check-Ledger to test their accuracy in this way. If to the amount of the balances of the Current-Account-Ledger last week, you add the total credits entered in the Check-Ledger during the week, and deduct the total debits

entered in the Check-Ledger during the week, the remainder
will show the total amount of the balances of the Current-
Account-Ledger for the present week.   Each Current-Account-
Ledger will have a Check-Ledger, and thus each Ledger will be
checked separately, so that when the total balance is wrong, it
will at once be seen in which Ledger the error has occurred.

Time is sometimes lost by a clerk taking up the wrong
book—opening it, putting it down, and then taking up the
right one.   A cashier, for instance, will sometimes take up the
Paid-Waste-Book instead of the Received-Waste-Book.   To prevent this, the two books may have covers of different colours—
one white, the other green.   Time may be lost by two clerks
wanting the same book at the same time.   The ledger-keeper
may want to post from the Received-Waste-Book when the
cashier is using it.   To prevent this, there may be two sets of
Waste-Books—one for Mondays, Wednesdays, and Fridays, and
the other for Tuesdays, Thursdays, and Saturdays; and, to prevent mistakes, the names of the days should be written in large
letters on the covers of the books.

IV. We will now make a comparison between the system of
Book-keeping practised by Merchants and that practised by
Bankers.

The merchants have their Waste-Book, Journal, Ledger.   The
bankers have their Waste-Book, Day-book, Ledger.

In both cases the Waste-Book is the book in which transactions are first entered.   But this book is capable of subdivision: it contains a record of various transactions, some of
which may be entered in separate books.   Bankers have their
Received, Paid, and Supplementary Waste-Books; also their
Deposit-Receipt-Book, Discount-Registers, and other books sub-
sidiary to the Waste-Book.   So merchants have their Waste-
Books subdivided into various books, according to the nature
of the transactions.   There is the Invoice-Book, containing an
account of all goods purchased; the Sales-Book, containing an
account of all goods sold; a book for "Bills Receivable," containing a list of all bills in the merchant's hands, which when
due he will *receive;* another for bills payable, containing a list of
all bills he has accepted, and which when due he will have to
pay; a Cash-Book, containing an account of all cash he receives
or pays away; and several others, varying according to the cha-

racter and extent of the business. Now all these subdivisions of the merchant's Waste-Book resemble those of the banker's in two things:—first, they are all kept *chronologically*—they contain a record of the transactions in the order of time in which they occurred; and, secondly, all the transactions thus recorded must afterwards, upon the system of double entry, pass, either individually or in totals, through the book which merchants call a Journal, and bankers call a Day-Book.

The words "Journal" and "Day-Book" have the same meaning, and in this instance the use of the two books is similar. But in the merchant's Journal individual transactions may be entered, while in the banker's Day-Book they are always entered in totals. Thus the total amount of " Bills Discounted," and the total amount of credits and payments on current accounts, are entered in the Day-Book, but not the individual items. Another difference is, that over each entry in the merchant's Journal you state to what account it is to be posted; for every entry is posted to two accounts—to the debit of one account, and to the credit of the other. And this is denoted by Dr. being placed before the name of the account to be debited. Thus, if a merchant buys some goods for ready money, the Journal entry is preceded by—

Goods Dr. to Cash;

implying that the account "Goods" is to be debited, and the account "Cash" to be credited. On the other hand, if he sells goods for ready money, the transaction will be journalized thus :—

Cash Dr. to Goods.

If he sells goods upon credit to John Brown, it will be—

John Brown Dr. to Goods.

If he sells goods for a bill of exchange, it will be—

Bills receivable Dr. to Goods.

If he sends goods abroad, as a speculation, in the ship *Adven ture,* he may raise an account for the ship, and say—

Ship Adventure Dr. to Goods.

The entries in the banker's Day-Book are made daily, but

the entries in the merchant's Journal are generally made once a month.

THE LEDGER.—We have stated that in the merchant's Ledger every entry is made twice—one account being debited, and another credited—and these two accounts are indicated in the Journal. This is what is called book-keeping by double entry. If it be asked, whether bankers keep their books by double entry?—the answer is, that those bankers who have no General-Ledger (and this is the case with not a few of the private bankers) do not keep their books by double entry. The Current-Account-Ledger is not kept by double entry. It contains none but personal accounts, and its accuracy is tested only by the periodical balancings. The banker's Ledger which corresponds in this respect with the merchant's Ledger, is not the Current-Account-Ledger, but the General-Ledger. This is kept by double entry. In a ledger kept by double entry, the sum of all the debit balances will be equal to the sum of all the credit balances; and the sum of all the debit amounts will be equal to the sum of all the credit amounts. When this is not the case there is an error in some of the accounts. This is the case with the banker's General-Ledger. But, as the transactions are not posted individually, but only in totals, the double entry does not appear on the face of the accounts. Thus, if a bill be discounted for a customer, and the amount placed to the credit of his current account, the Journal entry, on the principle of mercantile book-keeping, would stand thus:—

Bills Discounted Dr. to Current Accounts.

But the bill discounted is placed to the debit of the account of "Bills Discounted," in a total of all the bills discounted on that day. And the amount is placed to the credit of Current Accounts, in the total of all the sums received to the credit of Current Accounts on that day. Thus, the "double entry," though equally real, is not so apparent as though the transactions were posted individually.

So, again, if a country banker should discount a bill, and the customer ask for a draft on his agent in London, the Journal entry, on the commercial system, would stand thus:—

Bills Discounted Dr. to Drafts on London.

It would go to the debit of "Bills Discounted," in the total of all the bills discounted that day, and it would go to the credit of " Drafts on London," in the total of all the drafts on London issued on that day.

The accounts in a merchant's Ledger are usually classified into Personal Accounts, Real Accounts, and Profit and Loss Accounts. The Personal Accounts are the accounts of persons who may owe the merchant money, or to whom he may owe money. The Real Accounts are accounts denoting property, such as cash, bills receivable, bills payable, merchandize, ship adventure, &c. The Profit and Loss Accounts are rent, commissions, expenses, and all other accounts which are ultimately transferred to the debit or the credit of the Profit and Loss Account.

The banker's General-Ledger has no Personal Accounts, as these are all kept in the Current-Account-Ledger. The usual accounts are those I have enumerated in page 253, and are all either Real Accounts or Profit and Loss Accounts.

It would be possible (but not desirable) to introduce all the Personal Accounts into the banker's General-Ledger, and thus to form the Current-Account-Ledger and the General-Ledger into one, and keep the whole by double entry. In this case we should omit the totals of Current Accounts, now introduced into the General-Ledger, and insert every transaction individually. If John Brown drew a cheque on the bank, the Journal entry would stand thus :—

John Brown Dr. to Cash.

And if he paid in money to his credit, the Journal entry would stand thus :—

Cash Dr. to John Brown.

All the entries passed to the Dr. and Cr. of these Personal Accounts would of course pass to the Cr. and Dr. of Cash. Indeed, all the entries to the Dr. and Cr. of Cash would be the same as are now made in the Check-Ledger, except that the debtor column would be called creditor, and the creditor column would be called debtor. By the use of such a Check-Ledger as we have described, page 272 (for there are various kinds of Check-Ledgers), the Current Accounts are virtually kept by double entry ; and we have the additional advantage that, when there are more than one Ledger, we are enabled to check each Ledger separately.

2 **E**

To accountants in banks where a General-Ledger is not kept, it appears strange that "Cash" should be *credited* for money which is *paid away*, and *debited* for money which is received. But this strangeness will vanish, if for the word "Cash" they would fix in their mind the word "Cashier." If they had an account with a cashier, they would of course *debit* him, as they do their banker, for all moneys they paid into his hands, and credit him for all moneys they drew out. And the difference between the amounts of these debits and credits would be the balance either in their favour or against them.

In thus comparing the commercial and the banking systems of book-keeping, I have hitherto supposed that all merchants keep their books by double entry. But this is not always the case with the smaller houses. And then their system more nearly resembles the system of those bankers who do not keep a General-Ledger.

"In keeping books by single entry, the *Daily-Books* are kept in the same manner as in double entry, with the exception of a column of reference to the Ledger in each book, which takes the place of a column of reference in the Journal—this book being dispensed with. The entries are posted directly from the Daily-Books into the Ledger. In the Ledger, by single entry, strictly speaking, there ought to be only one kind of accounts; namely, Personal Accounts, including all persons to whom a merchant becomes indebted, and all persons who become indebted to him."*

It will be seen from this account, that, in mercantile book-keeping by single entry, the merchant's Ledger resembles the Current-Account-Ledger of the banker. In single entry the merchant dispenses altogether with his Journal; but the banker usually retains his Day-Book, even when he does not keep a General-Ledger. But, in this case, the Day-Book contains only the debits and credits, individually, of the Current Accounts, which are posted afterwards into the Current-Account-Ledger. In the horizontal system, as we have stated, the debits and credits of the current accounts are not entered individually in the Day-Book, but the total amounts are taken from the Paid and Received Waste-Books.

* Wallace's Pocket Guide to Commercial Book-Keeping.

SECTION XIII.

BANKING CALCULATIONS. ·

WHEN a bill is discounted, the party is credited for the full amount, and debited for the interest. The interest is calculated from the day on which the bill is discounted to the time it falls due. The shortest way is to make use of an interest book.

There is often a difference in the amount of interest according to the method of calculation, either by months or by days. A month from the 10th of February to the 10th of March, is only 28 days; but from the 10th of March to the 10th of April, a month is 31 days. The half year from the 1st of January to the 30th of June, is 181 days; but from the 1st of July to the 31st of December, the half year is 184 days. The interest of 10,000*l.* for six months is 250*l.*; for 181 days it is only 247*l.* 18*s.* 11*d.*; for 184 days it is 252*l.* 1*s.* 1*d.* Time Tables are published, showing the number of days from every day in the year to any other day in the year.

Interest tables, calculated at any rate of interest, give the means of readily ascertaining the interest on any sum at a different rate. This is done by taking that proportion of the principal, or of the time, which the given rate of interest bears to the rate of the interest tables. For example, if it be necessary to ascertain the discount on a bill of 100*l.* for 50 days at 4 per cent., and you have interest tables calculated at 5 per cent.; you may take either four-fifths of the time or four-fifths of the amount. For, the interest of 100*l.* for 40 days, or the interest of 80*l.* for 50 days, at 5 per cent., is equal to the interest of 100*l.* for 50 days at 4 per cent.

When a bill is discounted, bankers charge interest on the full amount of the bill, and take it at the time. Thus, if a bill be discounted at 5 per cent., they will obtain more than 5 per cent. on the money actually advanced. This is allowed by law, and is not liable to be set aside on the ground of usury.

Bankers differ in their mode of calculating the interest upon current accounts. Some have an Interest-Ledger, or cash columns ruled in the Current-Account-Ledger, in which they state the interest upon every individual item in the account. Thus, for instance, the general balance takes place the 30th of

June, and the 31st of December.   If a sum of money is paid in
on the 1st of May, the interest is calculated on that amount
from the 1st of May to the 30th of June, and is then carried to
the *credit* of the party's interest account.   On the other hand
if a cheque be drawn on the 1st of May, the interest is calculated
and carried to the *debit* of the interest account.   On the 30th of
June, the interest account is balanced, and the balance is carried
to the debit or credit of the party's current account.   Other
bankers take off the balance of the current account into a
separate book (or have columns ruled in the ledger for bringing
out the balances*) for every day, from the 1st of January to the
30th of June ; add all these amounts together, and then take
the interest of the total for one day.   To take the interest for
one day is a very easy operation.   The interest of any sum for
one year at 5 per cent. is one-twentieth part of the principal,
and the interest for one day is the 365th part of the interest for
a year.   Now 365 multiplied by 20 gives 7,300.   You have then
only to divide any sum by 7,300, and you have the interest of
that sum for one day at 5 per cent. per annum.   The interest
of any sum for one day at any other rate than 5 per cent. may
be found by multiplying the principal by twice the rate of
interest and dividing the product by 73,000.   But the best way
is to make use of Gilmer's Interest Tables, published by Sims
and M'Intyre, of Belfast.   Similar Tables have also been
published by Mr. Coulthart, manager of the Ashton-under-Lyne
Joint-Stock Bank.

Banks who compound for the stamp duty on their notes and
fourteen-day bills on London calculate the sum to be paid by
ascertaining the amount in actual circulation every Saturday
night.   The amounts for all the Saturdays in the half-year being
added together, and divided by 26, the number of weeks, the
quotient shows the average amount in circulation during that
period, and the duty paid is at the rate of 3s. 6d. per cent. upon
this average amount.   This is at the rate of 7s. per cent. upon
the average annual amount.

To ascertain what denomination of notes remains the longest
in circulation, let the total average circulation for any given
period be represented by the number 1000 ; and let the amount
of each particular denomination be represented by a proportionate part of 1000.   Then let the total amount of notes paid

* See page 386.

during the same period be represented by 1000, and the amount of each denomination of notes be proportionally ascertained; then place these two series of numbers in juxtaposition, and it will immediately be seen what denomination of notes remain out the longest. For instance, if the average amount of a banker's circulation consist of 20,000*l.* in 5*l.* notes; 15,000*l.* in 10*l.* notes; 10,000*l.* in 20*l.* notes; and 5000*l*, in 50*l.* notes; then the proportionate numbers will stand thus:—

Total Circulation	£5.	£10.	£20.	£50.
1,000	400	300	200	100

Then if during the same period the amount of notes paid of different denominations have been—15,000*l.* in 5*l.* notes; 15,000*l.* in 10*l.* notes; 12,000*l.* in 20*l.* notes; and 8000*l.* in 50*l.* notes, the proportional numbers will stand thus:—

Total Paid.	£5.	£10.	£20.	£50.
1,000	300	300	240	160

By placing these numbers under the preceding ones, it will be perceived that the amount of 5*l.* notes paid is less than the proportional amount in circulation; and consequently, notes of this denomination remain out the longest; the 10*l.* notes remain out a less time; the 20*l.* a still shorter term; and the 50*l.* notes the shortest term of all.

To ascertain how long a banker's notes remain out, take the average amount in circulation for any given period, say three months; ascertain the amount of notes paid during that period. If the amount paid during the three months is twice the average amount in circulation, then the notes have remained out six weeks. If the amount paid is three times the amount in circulation, then the notes have remained out one month. The term which any particular denomination of notes remains in circulation can of course be ascertained in the way I have already described. These calculations are easily made by a table of logarithms.

In passing through the books a purchase of Annuities, debit the account of Annuities for the purchase money. Then calculate how much per annum the annuity will yield upon the capital invested, recollecting that the annuity will expire on the first quarter in the year 1860. Supposing this rate to be 4 per cent., you will, when the annuity is received in July or January, debit Annuity account 4 per cent. interest on the purchase money, and credit the same account the amount of the annuity received. The first entry will be passed to the credit of Profit and Loss Account. The second entry will be passed to the debit of Cash Account, as a return of capital. The balance of the Annuity Account after each entry is made, will show the amount of capital that then remains invested in Annuities.

The stock brokers charge one-eighth commission on all purchases and sales of stock; one shilling per cent. on Exchequer Bills and India Bonds. The charges are made on the amount of stock, not on the amount of money invested.

If the stock stands in the name of several persons, any one may receive the dividends, but they must unite to execute a sale. If one or more of the parties die, the stock is transferred by the survivors, without the concurrence of the executors or representatives of the deceased party. Hence, if a father wished to give his son a certain amount of stock at his death, he might place the stock in their joint names, and upon his death his son would become the actual possessor of the property. Powers of attorney made and executed for the sale or transfer of stock must be deposited at the bank, for examination, before two o'clock, the day previous to being acted upon; if only for receiving dividends upon stock, it is sufficient to present the power of attorney at the time when the first dividend thereon becomes payable. A power of attorney for receiving dividends costs 5s. ; and for sale of stock, 11s. 6d.

The stamp duties for conveyance or transfer, whether on sale or otherwise, are :—

	£	s.	d.
(1.) Of any stock of the governor and company of the Bank of England	0	7	9
(2.) Of any stock of the East India Company	1	10	0
(3.) Of any debenture stock or funded debt of any company or corporation : For every 100*l*., and also for any fractional part of 100*l*., of the nominal amount transferred ..	0	2	6

The dividends on the 3 per cent. Consols are paid in January and July. The dividends on the 3 per cent. Reduced, and on the New 3 per cent., are paid in April and October. This last stock bore interest at 3¼ per cent. until October, 1854; it was then reduced to 3 per cent.; but the interest cannot be farther reduced until October, 1874.

The following quotations from Waterston's 'Commercial

Dictionary,* will serve to explain the operations connected with foreign bills of exchange :—

" A foreign bill of exchange is an order addressed to a person residing abroad, directing him to pay a determinate sum of foreign money to the person in whose favour it is drawn, or to his order. The amount of foreign money, therefore, to be paid is fixed by the bill; but the amount of British money (or money of the country in which the drawer resides), to be given for the purchase of the bill, is by no means fixed, but is continually varying."

" Of the two terms of comparison between the money of one place and that of another, one is fixed, the other is variable. The place whose money is reckoned at the fixed price is, in commercial language, said to *receive* the variable price : the other is said to *give* the variable price. Hence the higher the exchange between any two places, the more it is in favour of that which receives the variable price; the lower, the more in favour of that which gives the variable price;— the exchange being said to be favourable or unfavourable to any place, according as a smaller or larger amount of the currency of that place is required for discharging a given amount of foreign payments. Thus London receives from Paris a variable number of francs and centimes for 1*l.* sterling; and taking the par at 25 francs 34 centimes for 1*l.*, exchange will be 5 per cent. in favour of London when it rises to 26 francs 62 centimes, and about 5 per cent. against London when it falls to 24 francs 7 centimes."

" Bill merchants study the exchanges, not only between the place at which they reside and all other places, but also between all those other places themselves, by which means they are generally enabled to realize a profit by buying bills in one place and selling them in another ;—in this way preventing any great fall in the price of bills in those countries in which the supply exceeds the demand, and any great rise in those countries in which the supply happens to be deficient. Sometimes exchange operations are conducted with little outlay of capital. Thus, if a bill merchant in London can sell a bill on Amsterdam at half per cent. premium, and buy one at Paris at half per cent. discount, and with the latter buy one at Paris on Amsterdam at par, he will have gained 1 per cent. by the transaction, without the employment of any capital;—the bill remitted from Paris to Amsterdam arriving in time to meet the bill drawn there upon his correspondent. Again, a bill merchant, in order to take advantage of a premium on the exchange, may obtain a credit abroad upon which he may draw bills, under the calculation that at some future and not very distant period he will be able to replace the funds at a lower rate of exchange, and thereby realize a profit by the operation. The central points for such transactions are Hamburgh, Amsterdam, Vienna, Paris, New York, and above all, London, the great money change of the world."

" In this country the buying and selling of bills on foreign countries is conducted by brokers, all such transactions centring in the metropolis. In London the days for the negotiation of foreign bills are Tuesdays and

* A Cyclopædia of Commerce, Mercantile Laws, Finance, Commercial Geography, and Navigation, by William Waterston, Esq.

Fridays, the *foreign post days*, as they are still called. The brokers go round to the principal merchants, and discover whether they are buyers or sellers; and a few of the more influential, after ascertaining the state of the market, suggest a price at which the greater part of the transactions are settled, with such deviations as particular bills may be subject to from their high or low credit. For the bills they buy on one post-day, houses of established credit pay on the following post-day, when they receive the second and third bills of the set; foreign bills being usually drawn in sets of three. The brokerage charged on bills is 1 per mille, or one-tenth per cent.

" On the evenings of Tuesdays and Fridays, the market rates for bills on all the principal foreign cities, with the current prices of bullion, are published in Wetenhall's ' Course of the Exchange.' "

All bills are drawn in the money of the country in which they are to be paid.

We often find in the City Article of the *Times*, the *Economist*, and other journals, paragraphs like the following :—

" The premium on gold at Paris is 7 per mille, which, at the English mint price of 3*l.* 17*s.* 10½*d.* per ounce for standard gold, gives an exchange of 25·32½ ; and the exchange at Paris on London, at short, being 25·25, it follows that gold is 0·30 per cent. dearer in Paris than in London."

" By advices from Hamburgh, the price of gold is 435½ per marc, which, at the English mint price of 3*l.* 17*s* 10½*d.* per ounce for standard gold, gives an exchange of 13·10¼ ; and the exchange at Hamburgh on London, at short, being 13·10⅝, it follows that gold is 0·17 per cent. dearer in London than in Hamburgh."

" The course of exchange at New York on London is 108½ per cent. ; and the par of exchange between England and America being 109⅔⅔ per cent., it follows that the exchange is 1·08 per cent. against England ; but the quoted exchange at New York being for bills at 60 days' sight, the interest must be deducted from the above difference."

The real par of exchange between two countries is that by which an ounce of gold in one country can be replaced by an ounce of gold of equal fineness in the other country. In England gold is the legal tender, and its price is fixed at 3*l.* 17*s.* 10½*d.* per ounce. In France, silver is the currency, and gold, like other commodities, fluctuates in price according to supply and demand. Usually, it bears a premium or agio. In the above quotation, this premium is stated to be 7 per mille ; that is, it would require 1,007 francs in silver to purchase 1,000 francs in gold. At this price the natural exchange, or that at which an ounce of gold in England would purchase an ounce of gold in France, is 25·32½. But the commercial exchange—that is, the price at which bills on London would sell on the Paris Exchange—is 25 francs 25 cents., showing that gold is 0·30 per cent. dearer in Paris than in London. Tables have been constructed to show the results of each fluctuation in the premium of gold in Paris, Amsterdam, &c. &c.

It is useful sometimes to know how many persons enter a bank in the course of a day, and during what hours the greater number arrive. To do this, set a person in the hall, with a paper marked 9 to 10, 10 to 11, and so on. Then, when a person enters a bank between the hours of 9 and 10 o'clock, he will make a mark like a figure 1. This mark he will repeat as every additional person enters. He will go on in this way all through the day. When the bank closes, he will ascertain by counting the marks how many persons have entered the bank during each hour, and how many altogether. The cashiers should go to dinner during the hour in which the fewest people come to the counter. And if a clerk wants a day's holiday he should fix on the day in which the fewest people enter the bank. It is in this way that a man standing in the street is able to keep a register of the number of omnibuses that may pass him during the day.

"If you are a clerk in a public office, and are behind your time a quarter of an hour every morning, in three hundred days that will amount to seventy-five hours; more than equal at six hours a-day to a holiday of twelve days in the course of the year. A large number of small parts will make a great whole.

"The following anecdote *proves*, by multiplication, the importance of punctuality :—

'A member of the Committee being a quarter of an hour behind the time, made an apology, saying, the time passed away without his being aware of it. A Quaker present said—"Friend, I am not sure that we should admit thy apology. It were matter of deep regret that thou shouldest have wasted thine own quarter of an hour; but there are seven besides thyself, whose time thou hast also consumed, amounting in the whole to two hours—and one-eighth of it only was thine own property.'"

Banking Documents.—By banking documents, I mean reports, bonds, deeds, letters, or other writings, used in connexion with banking—such as prospectuses, applications for shares, deeds of settlement, bonds of security by managers and clerks, declarations of secrecy by the same, agreements with reference to lodgment of deeds as securities, cash credit, bonds, certificates of shareholders, deeds of transfers, notices of calls for further payment on shares, &c. &c. The forms in which these and the like documents may be drawn up are as easily procurable as forms of wills, indentures, and bonds; but vary at the discretion of directors, secretaries, managers, and solicitors.

When any persons propose to form a joint-stock bank in any district, they procure the statistical returns of the district; such as the tables of the population—the exports and imports —the duties paid—the returns of the sales in the various markets—and every other information respecting the trade and wealth of the district. If these prove satisfactory, they take notice of the banks already established there, and observe whether they are joint-stock banks, or private banks—whether strong or weak—and whether likely to oppose or to join any new establishment. If the existing banks be joint-stock banks, the projectors procure from the stamp-office a list of the shareholders, in order to observe the strength of their proprietary, and whether they reside chiefly in the district.

Having satisfied themselves that a new bank would be successful, the first document drawn up is a prospectus. This document usually sets forth the great advantage of joint-stock banking to both the public and the shareholders, and then points out the facilities of the district in which the bank is proposed to be established.

Previous to issuing the prospectus, some leading persons in the district are requested to become members of a provisional committee for the formation of the bank, and they obtain the assistance of an influential solicitor, to whose office the applications for shares are usually addressed. The committee then appoint a secretary, or sometimes the office of secretary is filled by the solicitor.

Attached to the prospectus is the form of an application for shares.

As the applications come in, they are entered in a book prepared for the purpose. In the first column is entered the date of the application; then follow the name, profession, and residence of the applicant; then the number of shares applied for, and in a farther column the number of shares granted. After the committee have determined what number of shares to allot to each applicant, letters are addressed to the respective parties.

After the sums to be paid up have been received, a general

meeting of the shareholders is called, when the provisional committee make a report of their proceedings. Resolutions are then passed—1. That the report be received and printed;—2. That certain shareholders then named be appointed directors;—3. That the thanks of the meeting be given to the provisional committee. The bank is now formed, and the government is assumed by the directors. They appoint the manager and other officers; they prepare the deed of settlement; and they adopt the measures necessary for the commencement of business.

THE PRACTICE OF BANKING.

PART II.—OF BANKING INSTITUTIONS.

SECTION I.

THE BANK OF ENGLAND.

THE history, constitution, and administration of the Bank of England up to the year 1828 have been traced in an early chapter of the present edition,* and, later on, are continued to several years† after the passing of the all-important Bank Charter Act of 1844 (7 & 8 Vict. c. 32), the principal provisions of which are as follows:—

"That from and after the 31st of August, 1844, the issue of promissory notes of the Governor and Company of the Bank of England, payable on demand, shall be kept wholly distinct from the general banking business of the said governor and company; and the business of such issue shall be thenceforth conducted and carried on by the said governor and company in a separate department, to be called "the issue department of the Bank of England;" and it shall be lawful for the court of directors to appoint a committee or committees of directors for the conduct and management of such issue department.

"II. That upon the same day there shall be transferred, appropriated, and set apart by the said governor and company to the issue department securities to the value of fourteen million pounds, whereof the debt due by the public to the said governor and company shall be a part; and at the same time so much of the gold coin and gold and silver bullion as shall not be required by the banking department; and thereupon there shall be delivered out of the issue department into the banking department such an amount of notes as, together with the notes then in circulation, shall be equal to the aggregate amount of the securities, coin, and bullion so transferred to the issue department; and it shall not be lawful for the governor and company to increase the amount of securities for the time being in the issue department, save as hereinafter is mentioned, but it

* Section III.—History and Principles of Banking.
† Pages 226 to 227.

shall be lawful for them to diminish the amount of such securities, and again to increase the same to any sum not exceeding in the whole the sum of fourteen million pounds, and so from time to time as they shall see occasion ; and from and after such transfer and appropriation to the issue department it shall not be lawful for the governor and company to issue bank notes, either into the banking department, or to any persons or person whatsoever, save in exchange for other Bank of England notes, or for gold coin or for gold or silver bullion received or purchased for the issue department under the provisions of this Act, or in exchange for securities acquired and taken in the issue department under its provisions : Provided always, that it shall be lawful for them in their banking department to issue all such notes as they shall at any time receive from the issue department.

" III. That it shall not be lawful for the bank to retain in the issue department at any one time an amount of silver bullion exceeding one-fourth part of the gold coin and bullion at such time held in the issue department.

" IV. That all persons shall be entitled to demand from the issue department bank notes in exchange for gold bullion, at the rate of three pounds seventeen shillings and ninepence per ounce of standard gold.

" V. That if any banker who on the 6th of May, 1844, was issuing his own bank notes shall cease such issue, it shall be lawful for Her Majesty in Council to authorize the governor and company to increase the amount of securities in the issue department to an amount not exceeding two-thirds the amount of bank notes which the banker so ceasing to issue may have been authorized to issue; and every such Order in Council shall be published in the next succeeding ' London Gazette.'

" VI. That an account of the amount of notes issued by the issue department, and of gold coin and of gold and silver bullion respectively, and of securities in the issue department, and also an account of the capital stock, and the deposits, and of the money and securities belonging to the said governor and company in the banking department, on some day in every week to be fixed by the commissioners of stamps and taxes, shall be transmitted weekly to the said commissioners, and shall be published by them in the ' London Gazette.'

" VII. That from the same date the bank shall be released from payment of any stamp duty upon their notes.

" VIII. That from the same date the payment of the annual sum of 120,000*l.* made by the bank under the provisions of the Act passed in the fourth year of the reign of his late Majesty King William the Fourth, out of the sums payable to them for the charges of management of the public unredeemed debt, shall cease, and in lieu thereof, in consideration of the privileges of exclusive banking, and the exemption from stamp duties, given to them by this Act, they shall, during the continuance of such privileges and such exemption, allow to the public the annual sum of 180,000*l.*

" IX. That all profits derived by the bank from the increase of their issues beyond the 14,000,000*l.* prescribed by the Act shall go to the public.

" X. That from and after the passing of this Act no person other than a banker who on the 6th of May, 1844, was lawfully issuing his own notes shall issue notes in any part of the United Kingdom.

" XI. That after the passing of this Act it shall not be lawful for any banker to draw, accept, make, or issue, in England or Wales, any bill of exchange or promissory note or engagement for the payment of money payable to bearer on demand, or to borrow, owe, or take up, in England or Wales, any sums or sum of money on the bills or notes of such banker payable to bearer on demand, save and except that it shall be lawful for any banker who was on the 6th of May, 1844, carrying on the business of a banker in England or Wales, and was then lawfully issuing, in England or Wales, his own bank notes, under the authority of a licence to that effect, to continue to issue such notes under the conditions hereinafter mentioned ; and the right of any company or partnership to continue to issue such notes shall not be prejudiced by any change which may take place in the personal composition of such company or partnership : Provided always, that it shall not be lawful for any company or partnership now consisting of only six or less than six persons to issue notes after the number of partners therein shall exceed six.

" XII. That if any banker in any part of the United Kingdom who after the passing of this Act shall be entitled to issue notes shall become bankrupt, or shall discontinue the issue of notes, it shall not be lawful for him to resume such issues.

" XIII. That every banker claiming under this Act to continue to issue notes in England or Wales shall, within one month after the passing of this Act, give notice in writing to the commissioners of stamps and taxes of such claim, and of the place and name and firm at and under which such banker has issued such notes during the twelve weeks next preceding the 27th of April, 1844 ; and thereupon the commissioners shall ascertain the average amount of those twelve weeks' issues ; and it shall be lawful for every such banker to continue to issue his own notes : Provided, nevertheless, that such banker shall not have in circulation upon the average of a period of four weeks, to be ascertained as hereinafter mentioned, a greater amount of notes than the amount so certified.

" XIV. That if it shall be made to appear to the commissioners of stamps and taxes that any two or more banks have become united within the twelve weeks, it shall be lawful for the commissioners to certify the average amount of the notes of the two or more banks so united as the amount which the united bank shall thereafter be authorized to issue, subject to the regulations of this Act.

" XV. That the said commissioners shall, at the time of certifying, publish a duplicate of their certificate in the ' London Gazette,' and the gazette shall be conclusive evidence in all courts whatsoever of the amount of notes which the banker named in such certificate or duplicate is by law authorized to issue.

" XVI. That it shall be lawful in case banks become united, for the commissioners to certify the amount of bank notes which each bank was authorized to issue, and the amount stated shall be the limit of the amount of notes which such united bank may have in circulation : Provided always, that it shall not be lawful for any such united bank to issue notes at any time after the number of partners therein shall exceed six.

" XVII. That if the monthly average circulation of notes of any banker shall at any time exceed the amount which such banker is authorized to issue, he shall in every such case forfeit a sum equal to the amount by which the average monthly circulation shall have exceeded the amount which such banker was authorized to issue.

" XVIII. That every banker in England and Wales authorized, under the provisions of this Act, to issue notes, shall transmit to the Commissioners of Stamps and Taxes a weekly account of his issues, for them to publish in the 'Gazette;' and if such banker shall neglect or refuse to render such account as required by this Act, or shall render a false account, he shall forfeit the sum of 100*l.* for every such offence.

" XIX. In this clause the mode of ascertaining the average amount of notes of each issuing bank was set forth.

" XX. The commissioners were empowered to cause the books of bankers, containing accounts of their notes in circulation, to be inspected, and, if it were thought fit, copied; and a penalty, in case of refusal, of 100*l.* for every such offence, imposed on the refusing banker.

" XXI. All bankers to return their names once a year to the Stamp Office.

" XXII. Bankers to take out a separate licence for every place at which they issue notes or bills; with a proviso in favour of bankers having four such licences in force on the 6th of May, 1844.

" XXIV. The Bank of England are authorised to compound with banks desirous of withdrawing their own notes and issuing those of the Bank of England; the amount of composition not to exceed 1 per cent. per annum, and payment thereof to cease on the 1st of August, 1866.

" XXVI. Any society or company, though exceeding six in number, carrying on the business of banking in London, or within sixty-five miles thereof, may draw, accept, or indorse bills of exchange, not being payable to bearer on demand.

" XXVII. The bank are to enjoy the privileges secured by this Act, subject to redemption upon twelve months' notice, to be given after the 1st of August, 1855, and upon repayment of the public debt, and of all sums and arrears whatsoever owing to them by government.

A searching inquiry will be found in Part I. of this work* into the design, import, and effects of this much-debated Act; of which it has been said by a high authority, alike in questions of banking and of political economy, Mr. H. D. Macleod, that " of all the Acts in the Statute-Book, there is none which comes home to every man—which so nearly affects every man's interest —as this Act."

We proceed to give a summary of the business operations of the bank, and of the changes which have taken place in its relations to government and the public, since Mr. Gilbart wrote the masterly disquisition referred to above.

* Sections VIII. and IX.

The Bank of England can now issue to the extent of 15,000,000*l*. against that amount of securities set apart for this purpose. She can issue to any farther amount against lodgments of gold and silver, as regulated by the above Act. This amount of 15,000,000*l*. may be issued either at the office in London or at the branches. Were she to reduce the number of her branches she would not be required to issue less than this 15,000,000*l*.; and were she to increase her branches, she could issue no more. If other banks discontinue their circulation, she may upon application receive permission to extend her issues to two-thirds the sum thus withdrawn; but all the profit of this increase must go to the Government. She cannot issue any note for a less amount than five pounds. All the notes are payable in gold on demand. The payment of those issued in London can be demanded only at the London office. But the payment of those issued at the branches may be demanded either at the London office or at the branches where they were respectively issued. Bank of England notes are a legal tender in all cases, except when tendered by the bank herself.

The Bank of England is a bank of deposit, of loan, and of discount as well as of issue. She allows no interest on any portion of her deposits, nor permits any account to be overdrawn. She charges various rates on the bills she discounts, but does not go below the rate she announces to be her minimum. She does not act as the London agent of country banks; but is the agent of the Bank of Ireland, and the Royal Bank of Scotland. She does not accept any bills that may be drawn by those banks, or by her own branches—they are all drawn without acceptance. She does not issue any circular notes on foreign countries, nor grant letters of credit on foreign banks. She remits money to and from her branches, and from one branch to another, and issues at the London office bank-post bills, drawn at seven, fourteen, and any greater number of days after sight.

The Bank of England is also the banker of the Government. She has always a large amount of public deposits, on which she allows no interest. She receives the public revenue, and pays the dividends on the National Debt.[*]

The profits of the bank are derived from her capital, her rest,

---

[*] Thus the bank are at the same time bankers for the State, and bankers on their own account, transacting the ordinary business of London bankers.—EDITOR.

public and private deposits, bank-post bills, her agencies, and her circulation. From these funds she makes investments in public securities and private securities. These bring dividends and interest. She also has a profit on the 15,000,000*l.* of notes in circulation. This profit is the difference between the expense of maintaining the circulation, and the interest received on the securities set apart to meet this circulation. The bank has an annual payment from the Government for managing the National Debt. She also receives a commission from those banks to which she is the London agent. A profit is also supposed to be obtained on bullion transactions. Against these profits the bank has to place the expense of conducting the establishment, and the losses incurred by bad debts, forgeries, and unfortunate investments.

The Bank of England established branches in the year 1826, at the suggestion of Lord Liverpool, in order to extend to the provinces the advantage of a *secure* circulation. This was considered the grand desideratum at that time, in consequence of the numerous failures that had recently taken place among the country bankers; and was effected with the greater facility, in consequence of the establishment of joint-stock banks, who made arrangements for issuing Bank of England notes.

The branches being not merely banks of circulation, but of deposit, of discount, and of remittance, they came into competition with the country bankers. This, in some cases, reduced the charges previously made on banking transactions. As banks of discount, they charged the same rate which was charged at the London office—a charge usually below that of the country banks. As banks of remittance, they granted letters of credit at a shorter term. As banks of deposit, they charged no commission. But, on the other hand, they allowed no interest on the balance, and they allowed no account to be overdrawn; and they would not receive from their depositors any country notes unless the banks had previously opened an account with them, and made a lodgment to meet their notes.

While, therefore, the branches have obtained a large circulation, and have transacted a good business as banks of discount and of remittance, they have not made much progress as banks of deposit.

The branches are all subordinate to the parent establishment. They carry on the ordinary business of local banking,

2 F

and of London banking as well, in addition to issuing bank notes and bills. Cash for their notes can be demanded only at the particular branch which has issued them, or in London. The accounts are balanced every night, and the balance transmitted to town daily, together with particulars of all the transactions of the day. One of the most important public services performed by the branches is the remittance of the revenue, which is paid into them by the collectors, and credit is then at once given to the exchequer account in London.

The bank has branches at Birmingham, Bristol, Hull, Leeds, Leicester, Liverpool, Manchester, Newcastle, Plymouth, Portsmouth, and one in London, called the West-end Branch.

It had originally branches at Exeter, Gloucester, and Norwich.

The branch at Exeter was closed May 1, 1834; the Gloucester branch on the 28th February, 1849, and the Norwich branch May 31, 1852. The reasons assigned for withdrawing these branches do not appear very satisfactory. The Exeter branch was closed because another branch was opened on the same day at Plymouth, and the branch was said *to be removed* to Plymouth. The opening of a new branch at Plymouth seems to have no necessary connexion with the closing of that at Exeter. The Gloucester branch was closed because a railway had been opened to Bristol, and the people of Gloucester might, if so disposed, transact their business with the Bristol branch. The distance between Gloucester and Bristol is about the same as that between Manchester and Liverpool; but the directors have never announced any intention of closing their branch at Manchester, upon the ground that there is a railway to Liverpool. The true reason, we believe, to be that the business at these branches had not realised the anticipations of the directors. The active opposition of the private bank of Messrs. Sparkes & Co. (afterwards merged in the Devon and Cornwall Bank), prevented the Exeter branch obtaining much business. At one time the Gloucestershire Banking Company issued only the notes of the Gloucester branch, but afterwards they resumed the issue of their own notes, and hence, in 1843 and subsequent years, the circulation of this branch declined. The Norwich branch not only obtained but small business, but made large losses. It appears from parliamentary returns that so early as the year 1831, the bad debts at this branch amounted to

£32,000. It may be remarked that the three branches withdrawn were located in the centre of agricultural districts, and the most prosperous branches have been located in manufacturing and commercial towns, as Manchester, Liverpool, Birmingham, and Newcastle.

Here is another anomaly of the Act of 1844. The Bank of England is placed in a position in which it is her interest to withdraw some of her branches. At the same time, the banks of issue in the neighbourhood of those branches are not allowed to extend their issues so as to fill up the vacuum which is thus occasioned in the amount of the local circulation.

[In addition to the management of the Government Funded Debt, which has always been conducted by the Bank of England, that corporation has of late years undertaken the management of the Government Unfunded Debt, formerly managed by the Exchequer Office; of the Indian Debt,* and of the Funded Debt of the Metropolitan Board of Works.

Pari passu with this increase of business, additional facilities have been afforded to the recipients of dividends of the various stocks by giving them the option of receiving their dividend warrants, by post, or at any of the branches of the Bank of England. The bank has also waived the charge of 1*s*. 6*d*. which it formerly made for preparing Powers of Attorney for the receipt of dividends.

In the Bullion Office an important modification has been made in the assay by which gold is bought and sold. Formerly, what was called the Trade Report was used, and the fineness of the gold was quoted to the $\frac{1}{8}$ of a carat grain, equal to $7\frac{1}{4}$ grains Troy, or the 768th part of the whole. This left a small profit to the bank on gold bullion imported by them into the Mint for the purposes of the coinage, since the Mint assayed much closer; whereas the assay now used at the bank determines to the $\frac{1}{5}$ of a millième, equivalent to the $\frac{1}{3000}$ part of the whole, and leaves no appreciable difference between the bank and the Mint assay.

The price at which light gold coin is bought by the bank has also been raised from 3*l*. 17*s*. 6½*d*. per ounce to 3*l*. 17*s*. 9*d*., the authorities of the Mint receiving this coin from the bank at 3*l*. 17*s*. 10½*d*., instead of requiring it to be remelted and reassayed,

---

* Namely :—India 5*l*. per cent. stock. India 4*l*. per cent. stock. East India 4*l*. per cent. transfer stock. Rupee Promissory Note Loan.

2 F 2

as was the practice previously. It is to be hoped that this change, which decreases the loss on light coins, will tend to induce bankers to withdraw them from circulation, and thus lend their aid to purge the gold currency, which is at present in a very unsatisfactory condition.

Under the Stock Certificates Act, 1863 (26 Vict. c. 28), the bank issues stock certificates for consols, new 3 per cents., and reduced 3 per cent. annuities. These certificates are transferable by delivery; but the transfer may be restricted by the holder filling in his name, address, and quality, in a space provided for the purpose. These certificates are of the denominations of 50*l*., 100*l*., 200*l*., 500*l*., and 1000*l*., and coupons are attached, payable to bearer, for the two half-yearly dividends due next after the date of issue.

The stockholder, when he desires to obtain certificates, transfers the stock in the Transfer Office in which the business of that particular stock is transacted, where he receives a certificate of the transfer, and this he exchanges in the Chief Cashier's Office for the stock certificate he requires.

When a holder of stock certificates wishes to have the stock they represent reinscribed, he delivers them up in the Chief Cashier's Office, and receives a certificate entitling him to have a corresponding amount of stock inscribed in his name in the Transfer Office of the stock.

The Government makes a charge of 2*s*. per cent. for the issue of certificates, and 1*s*. per certificate for reinscription.

Stock certificates for Metropolitan Consolidated 3½. per cent. stock are issued in exactly the same terms as certificates for the Government Funds, and for corresponding amounts, with the exception that there are no certificates of 200*l*.

Stock certificates for India 4 per cent. and 5 per cent. stock are issued for 100*l*., 500*l*., and 1000*l*.; but the transfer of these certificates cannot be restricted, and the charges are slightly different from those for the Government Funds.

The occasions and reasons for the increase of the bank note issue have been lucidly set forth as follows, in the *Bankers' Magazine* :—

" The authorized issue of Bank of England notes based on Government securities, which was fixed at 14,000,000*l*. by the Act of 1844, and which having been increased in 1855 and 1861 respectively, by the sums of 475,000*l*. and 175,000*l*., now stands at 14,650,000*l*., is to be further augmented by 350,000*l.*, which will raise the total to 15,000,000*l.* The process is in conformity with the provisions of the law, and is perfectly simple. The basis on which the amount of purely paper circulation was fixed at the date of Sir Robert Peel's measure was as follows:—Long experience has shown that whenever the note circulation of the country declined to a point approaching 22,000,000*l.*, through the contraction forced upon bankers by an adverse state of the foreign exchanges, the scarcity of currency was so felt in its action upon prices as to cause invariably a strong turn of the tide. That total of 22,000,000*l.* was, therefore, fixed as the safe amount at which paper, secured only by the credit of the Government, might be allowed to pass as a legal tender, and was made up by 14,000,000*l.* issued by the Bank of England, and 8,000,000*l.* of issues of private and joint-stock banks in the provinces. At the same time a provision was made, that if any of the latter establishments should fail or withdraw from business, then in each such case the right of issuing notes should be forfeited; and that it should be competent for the Government, by an order in council, to authorise the Bank of England to supply the deficiency thus created.

" To effect that purpose, it would not be necessary for the bank to issue more than two-thirds of the amount of the circulation that had been forfeited, because it was taken for granted that every issuing bank would keep at least a reserve of gold, equal to one-third of the notes it had issued payable on demand, and which might therefore be presented at any time ; and that, consequently, the actual currency which each had put out was practically only two-thirds of its nominal amount, since to the extent of the remaining third, other currency—that is to say gold—was withdrawn from use and locked up in their tills. Accordingly, the new issues of the Bank of England, in supplying the deficiencies from any such failures or withdrawals, were to be limited to two-thirds.

" Gradually, after the passing of the Act in 1844, individual country banks broke down or died out, but it was not till 1855 that the vacuum thus occasioned attracted much public attention. At that date it was found that issues had during the preceding eleven years been extinguished to the extent of 710,000*l.*, and an order in council was then put forth for an increase of 475,000*l.* in the notes of the Bank of England. Between 1855 and 1861 further lapses occurred to the amount of 262,500*l.*, and these were made up by a new order in council for an additional issue of 175,000*l.* Thus the total paper circulation of the bank was increased from its original sum of 14,000,000*l.* to 14,650,000*l.*, the amount at which it stood up to Thursday last.

The process by which the new issue is effected merely consists in the purchase of Government securities to the required amount. Stocks may be bought in the open market, or an advance made to Government on Exchequer bills. The gain from this investment in the present, as in the previous instances, after deducting the annual expense for the manufacture of the notes, &c., will be placed to the credit of the Government, the bank being only an agent in the business. The actual amount of the country circulation that has lapsed since the last filling up took place in 1861, is 739,965*l.*, of which 442,000*l.* was from a voluntary surrender on the part of the National Provincial Bank, when it determined to change its character from that of a country to a London bank. Two-thirds of this amount of 739,965*l.* would be 493,310*l.*, but the present order is limited to 350,000*l.*, a circumstance for which no other reason can be conjectured than a desire to take the opportunity of fixing the Bank of England circulation at the symmetrical figure of 15,000,000*l.* The amount was included in the account published for the week ending 21st February.*]

The Laws of the Currency with Reference to the Bank of England.—In March, 1841, I was, at the request of the joint-stock banks, examined as a witness before a Select Committee of the House of Commons, "appointed to inquire into the effects produced on the circulation of the country by the various banking establishments issuing notes payable on demand." The charge advanced at the time against the issuing joint-stock banks, and generally against all banks of issue, was, that they did not make the amount of their circulation correspond with the amount of the circulation of the Bank of England. With reference to this accusation, I laid before the committee a variety of tables, designed to show the laws which regulated the circulation of the Bank of England, of the country banks, and of the banks of Ireland and of Scotland, respectively. The inference was designed to show that no correspondence could exist between the circulation of these several banks. These tables cannot be introduced here. But the following is a summary of my evidence on this subject, taken from an article on "The Laws of the Currency," which I published in the "Foreign and Colonial Review" of April, 1844:—

"We have before us two reports from the Committee on Banks of Issue, laid before the House of Commons in the years 1840 and 1841. The committee report the evidence, and abstain from giving any opinion upon the great questions involved in the inquiry. They, however, recommended the passing of the Act 4 & 5 Vict. c. 50, requiring a monthly registry of the circulation of the Bank of England, and of the other banks of issue, with the amount of bullion, to be published in the *Royal Gazette.* It may therefore be expected that, in a course of years, a sufficient number of facts will be recorded to enable future generations to form 'well-grounded opinions' on this important subject.

"In the mean time we will make use of the information we already possess. We will take the monthly returns of the cir-

* Bankers' Magazine for March, 1865.

culation for the period that is past, that is, from September 1833 to the end of 1843, and endeavour, by observing their various revolutions, to discover if they are governed by any fixed causes or principles—to ascertain if those principles are uniform in their operation; and if we should discover that the revolutions of the currency are regulated by any uniform principles, we shall call those principles the Laws of the Currency.

"We shall begin with that portion of the currency which consists of notes issued by the Bank of England. On looking over the monthly circulation of the Bank of England, given in the Table, No. 34, in the Appendix to the Report of 1840, we observe, that the circulation of the months in which the public dividends are paid is higher than in the subsequent months. Thus, the average circulation of January is higher than that of February or March. The circulation of April is higher than that of May or June. The circulation of July is higher than that of August or September. And the circulation of October is higher than that of November or December. This, then, we may consider as one law of the circulation of the Bank of England—that it ebbs and flows four times in the year, in consequence of the payment of the quarterly dividends. This law does not apply to any other bank, as all the Government dividends are paid by the Bank of England.

"Again, the purchase and sale of Government stock and exchequer bills by the Bank of England affect the amount of her circulation. If the bank purchase Government stock or exchequer bills, she pays for them in her own notes, and thus increases her circulation. If, on the other hand, she sell Government stock or exchequer bills, she receives payment in her own notes, and thus her circulation is diminished. Another law, then, and one peculiar to the Bank of England, is, that her circulation is affected by the purchases and sales of Government securities.

"As the payment of the public dividends puts into circulation the notes of the bank, the receipt of the public revenue will of course withdraw her notes from circulation. A large amount of the public revenue is paid at the latter part of the year, and this probably is the main cause why the amount of the Bank of England circulation is always the lowest in the month of December. Although the circulation ebbs and flows four times in the year, yet the December* point is always the lowest point throughout the year; and this is the case in every year, although the Bank of England is always open in December for short loans, the granting of which increases her circulation. This, then, is another law of the circulation.

"If the bank purchase bullion with her notes, that will of course increase her circulation; if she sell bullion, that will diminish her circulation: and, as the bank is always open for the purchase of bullion at a fixed price, and as gold may at all times be withdrawn from her in payment of her notes, her circulation is subject to considerable fluctuation from this cause. There is not, however, any uniform correspondence between the amount of her circulation† and the amount of her bullion; for when she pays the public dividends, she increases her notes, but diminishes her bullion; and when she receives the public revenue, as in December, her circulation is diminished, but the bullion is increased. These contrary fluctuations are occasioned by that portion of our currency which is under 5*l.* consisting of the precious metals; but they do not impugn the law which states that the purchase of gold increases, and the sale of gold diminishes, the amount of her circulation.

"We have thus traced those peculiar laws which regulate the monthly revolutions of the circulation of the Bank of England. We shall now proceed to its annual revolutions.

"Any of the causes of the monthly fluctuations of the circulation of the Bank of England, if called into operation more in one year than in another, may become causes of annual fluctuations. But the most uniform and permanent cause of annual fluctuation appears to be made by the purchases and sales of bullion. The word 'bullion' in the bank returns, means gold and silver, whether coined or uncoined, and whether lying at the head office or at the branches. When the foreign exchanges are in favour of this country, bullion is imported and sold to the Bank of England; and when the exchanges are unfavourable, gold is exported, and the exporters obtain the gold from the Bank of England, either by purchase or by demanding payment

* There was an exception to this law in December, 1843, in consequence of the calling in of the light sovereigns.

† The word "circulation" means of course the amount of notes in the hands of the public. Since the passing of the Act of 1844 the word has been sometimes used in a more extended sense, so as to include also the notes in the banking department of the Bank of England.

of her notes. In most cases, however, the circulation does not fluctuate so much as the bullion. For when notes are issued against a large importation of bullion, money becomes abundant and cannot be employed, and hence it is lodged by bankers and others in the Bank of England, on deposit. But so long as the bank keeps her securities of the same amount, the increase of the bullion will always be about equal to the increase of the circulation and the deposits added together. And on the other hand, when an adverse exchange draws bullion from the bank, the deposits decrease as well as the circulation ; and the decrease in both together will be equal to the amount of gold withdrawn ; that is, supposing the securities to remain the same.

" By ' securities ' is meant Government stock, exchequer bills, loans, discounted bills, or anything else on which the bank may have advanced money. It is a principle of management by the bank to keep the total amount of their securities equal, or nearly so ; and so long as this rule is acted upon, the tendency of exportations or importations of bullion to produce the variations we have described, must be considered as one of the laws of the circulation."

One Bank of Issue.—Mr. Cotton, who was the Governor of the Bank of England when the Act of 1844 was passed, stated in the evidence before a Committee of the House of Commons, in 1848, that the ultimate object of that Act was the establishment of one bank of issue.* I was examined on this subject before the committee on banks of issue, in the year 1841. The following is a summary of my evidence :—

1. *If we had only one bank of issue we should have sometimes too much money and sometimes too little for the wants of trade.*— " I think it is one of the inconveniences of a metallic currency, and would, in fact, be one of the inconveniences of a sole bank of issue, that at one part of the year we should have too much money, and at another part too little ; because, as money would not fluctuate in amount, and the demands of trade would fluctuate, the amount of money would not be proportionate throughout the year to the demands of trade." . . . . " I have shown, from Appendix 34, that even taking the whole circulation together, there is a difference varying from two to four millions in the total amount of the circulation ; and, therefore, after supposing all these transfers to have taken place, if they

---

* Commons, 4561.

could have taken place at all, and that the surplus of one district was to supply the wants of another, still there would be a very great inequality in the amount of money, as compared with the demands of trade."

" It appears, from Appendix 34, that the total amount of notes in England, Scotland, and Ireland, varies very considerably in different months of the year. Supposing, then, that you had one bank, and that all the notes in circulation were the notes of that one bank, which did nothing but issue notes against gold, and gold against notes, how would you employ those notes which were not wanted in the slack periods of the season?" . . . . " It is evident, from Appendix 34, that during some part of the year there is not employment for the entire amount of money that is required in another season of the year; and if you had one bank of issue, as you could not contract the circulation, you would have a surplus circulation, which would have the effect of lowering the rate of interest, and promoting speculation."

2. *One bank of issue would reduce the means of the country bankers to afford assistance to their customers, and hence cause great distress, especially in the agricultural districts.*—" What would be the effect which you think it would produce upon country bankers?" . . . . " I think the banks, in the first place, having to pay off their notes, it would reduce their funds, from which they now give accommodation to their customers; and in order to find funds to pay off those notes, they would have to recall loans, and to reduce discounts to such a degree as to cause considerable distress throughout the country, and more especially in the agricultural districts."

3. *The bankers would be compelled to increase their charges.*— " What effects do you imagine would ensue when the measure had once been carried into effect?" . . . . " After the measure had once been carried into effect, the charges which the country bankers would be compelled to make upon that accommodation which they would still have the power of affording must be considerably increased."

" Why?" . . . . " Because they would then get no profit upon the notes; at present they can afford to advance money at a low rate of interest when issued in their own notes, because of the profit upon those notes. When I was in Ireland, I discounted bills at the same rate which was charged by the Bank of

England here, and for the same reason, because I issued my own notes; but if the country bankers had to bring the money from a distance and lend it to their customers, they must get a greater interest from their customers than they could get by employing it in London or elsewhere, and hence they must make, either in the form of interest, or in the form of commission, heavier charges than they made before."

4. *One bank of issue would cause some of the smaller banking establishments to be discontinued.*—"The profit on the circulation being thus reduced, there would be a further effect by the limitation of banking establishments; for some of those establishments are so small, and established in places so remote, that they would scarcely pay the expense of conducting them, unless for the profits of the circulation; and yet the withdrawal of those establishments, though connected with no great profit to the bank, would be attended with very considerable loss and inconvenience to the inhabitants of those places, because those banks act as receivers of the surplus capital, and hence they are useful to persons who have money to place in those banks; they act as discounters and granters of loans, and hence they are useful to the productive industry of the country; they are also useful as banks of remittance, for the purpose of making payments from those places elsewhere, and hence they are useful to traders; and those useful purposes, as far as many small banks are concerned, would be altogether annihilated if those establishments did not issue their own notes."

"In your opinion, the suppression of their circulation would render it necessary for them to charge a higher commission upon their operations, or a higher interest upon the loans which they make?" . . . . "With regard to those small establishments, I do not think any rate of commission could pay the expense: with regard to the larger establishments, you might make up for the deficiency of profit upon the circulation by an increased charge of commission; but with regard to small establishments, in remote places, the business is not sufficient, even with the charge of commission, to pay the expense without the profits of the circulation; annihilation of the circulation would lead to annihilation of the bank."

5. *One bank of issue would lead to the substitution of bills of exchange, or some other form of credit currency.*—"Do you conceive that it would have any effect upon what you have called

the amount of the circulation, which in your opinion is required at different times of the year ?". . . . . "I think it would have a considerable effect generally in the reduction of the circulation ; because, if the circulation was issued by one single bank, the local bankers in the respective districts would have no interest in increasing the amount of that circulation, and hence, in places where it could be done, the bankers would most likely have recourse to a bill circulation, and they would substitute bills for the circulation of this one bank of issue. We know that at Manchester and Liverpool, and in other places in that district, a bill circulation a short time ago was almost the entire circulation ; and it was not till the Bank of England established branches in those places, that the bill circulation became considerably reduced ; and even then the bank obtained a circulation in those places only by offering their notes to country bankers at a reduced rate of interest. Now, if you had only one bank of issue, it is not to be supposed that the country bankers would obtain those notes at a reduced rate of interest, and consequently they would have no advantage in getting them into circulation ; they would fall back upon their bill circulation, upon which they got a profit, and the amount of note circulation would, I think, be considerably reduced."

6. *With one bank of issue the reactions of the Foreign Exchanges would produce great and universal distress, and yet not accomplish that constant conformity between the London and country circulation which is sought to be attained.*—"Do you conceive that such a change as has been contemplated, namely, the abolition of country bank notes, would produce any effect upon the foreign exchanges ?" . . . . "The effect upon the foreign exchanges would depend upon the principle upon which the single bank of issue was conducted. If conducted merely by issuing gold for notes and notes for gold, I consider that when the foreign exchanges were favourable, and brought in a large amount of gold, then there would be a large amount of notes put into circulation. I think that was the case in 1837 and 1838, although the Bank of England did not issue to such an extent as, upon the principle assumed, this one bank of issue would be compelled to do. I consider that thus this large amount of notes put into circulation against the importation of gold would reduce the rate of interest, would excite speculation, and lead to foreign investments ; that a reaction would then take place, and

the amount of contraction would be very considerable, so as to produce very great distress."

" Now, whether you have different banks, or whether you have only one bank, if there is a certain amount of circulation in the country, and a certain amount in London, and the Bank of England, or the central bank, purchase a large amount of bullion in London, that immediately disturbs the proportion that existed between the London circulation and the country circulation ; and, on the other hand, if there is a demand for bullion to go abroad, and bullion is sold at the central office, that will contract the circulation, and contract it much more than it could be immediately contracted in the country. If, therefore, the liability to a disproportion in amount between the country and the London circulation is a defect in the existing system, it is a defect which the establishment of only one bank of issue will not remedy."

7. *The establishment of one bank of issue would embarrass the fiscal operations of the Government.*—" I may now state, with reference to the payment of the public dividends, that the Bank of England advances loans in December, before the dividends are paid, which loans are discharged after the dividends are paid, and thus the fluctuation in the currency is very considerably diminished from what it otherwise would be. Now, if we had a bank that could not do this, if the currency were issued upon what have been called currency principles, then the Chancellor of the Exchequer must have the whole amount of the January dividends in his strong room before he could pay those dividends. Out of the circulation of England and Wales, consisting of about 28,000,000*l.*, you must collect eight millions and a half, and lock them up in the custody of the Government previously to the payment of the dividends ; then you pay out in a mass these eight millions and a half, and that in a state of contracted currency ; and thus you go on, four times in the year, producing the most violent and most extravagant fluctuations : whereas now, by the excellent plan adopted by the Bank of England, in issuing her notes before the payment of the dividends, by means of loans, which are discharged after the payment of the dividends, notwithstanding you pay eight millions and a half of dividends, you produce a fluctuation in the currency of only two millions and a half."

8. *The principle of one bank of issue cannot be applied to the*

various currencies of the United Kingdom.—" What is the general conclusion which you propose to draw from the tables you have put in?" . . . . " The general conclusion I would draw is, that the Bank of England is governed by certain laws which do not apply to the country circulation ; that the country circulation of England is also governed by laws peculiar to itself ; that the circulation of Ireland is also governed by laws peculiar to itself ; that the circulation of Scotland is also governed by laws peculiar to itself ; that those respective circulations are all governed by uniform laws, as is shown by their arriving at nearly the same point at the same period of the year ; and, therefore, that you cannot introduce any system by which all those various circulations, governed by different laws, can be amalgamated into one system ; that such a system would be at variance with itself, and would tend to destroy that beautiful system of country banking which now exists in this country—a system which has tended very much to the prosperity of this country, which, by receiving the surplus capital of different districts, and giving out the capital for the encouragement of trade, calls forth all the natural resources of the country, and puts into motion the industry of the nation, and at the same time supplies a circulation which expands and contracts in each district according as it is required by the trade or agriculture of the district. Those expansions or contractions take place at different periods of the year in different districts ; the circulation expands when the wants of trade require it, and when no longer wanted it again returns ; and I think this beautiful system, in the language of the resolutions passed by the deputies from the joint-stock banks, ' has greatly promoted the agriculture, trade, mining, and general industry of the nation, and that equal advantages cannot be produced by one bank of issue.' "

SECTION II.

THE LONDON PRIVATE BANKERS.

By the Bank Charter Act of 1844 (7 & 8 Vict. c. 32, s. 21), it was enacted " that every banker in England and Wales, who is now carrying on, or shall hereafter carry on business as such, shall, on the first day of January in each year, or within fifteen days thereafter, make a return to the Commissioners of Stamps and Taxes at their head office in London, of his name, residence, and occupation, or in the case of a company or partnership, of the name, residence, and occupation of every person composing or being a member of such company or partnership, and also the name of the firm under which such banking company or partnership carry on the business of banking, and of every place where such business is carried on ; and if any such banker, company, or partnership, shall omit or refuse to make such return within fifteen days after the said first day of January, or shall wilfully make other than a true return of the persons as herein required, every banker, company, or partnership so offending, shall forfeit and pay the sum of 50*l.* ; and the said Commissioners of Stamps and Taxes shall, on or before the first day of March in every year, publish in some newspaper circulating within each town or county respectively, a copy of the return so made by every banker, company, or partnership carrying on the business of bankers within such town, or respectively, as the case may be."

This was the first time that any of the banking companies in London were required to make returns to Government of the number or names of their partners. All banks that issued notes were required, when they applied for a licence, to name their partners ; but as none of the London bankers issued notes, they required no licence, and made no return. Nor did the joint-stock banks established in London make any returns to the Government of their partners. For as they did not possess, until 1844, the power of suing and being sued in the name of their public officers, they did not register, at any Government office, the names of their partners, though, in some cases, these names were appended to the Annual Reports of the directors. This Act came into operation in January, 1845, and we have now, therefore, the means of obtaining the names of all the partners in all the banking establishments throughout England and Wales.*

The Act not only requires that the bankers shall make these returns between the first and fifteenth of January in each year, it requires also, that the Commissioners of Stamps and Taxes shall publish them before the first of March following, in some newspaper that circulates within the town or county in which the bankers making the return carry on their business. The

* These are inserted every year in the Banking Almanac.

returns from the London banks are published in supplements to the *London Gazette*, which we presume is considered to be a newspaper within the meaning of the Act.

The particulars required to be returned by the Act, and stated in the *Gazette*, are, the name of the firm or company; the name, residence, and occupation of the persons of whom the company or partnership consists ; and the name of the place or places where the business is carried on.

The London banking establishments, each not having more than ten partners, may be divided into three classes :—

I. Those who are members of the Clearing-house.

II. Those located east of Temple-bar, but not members of the Clearing-house.

III. Those located west of Temple-bar.

The Clearing Banks are banks of deposit and of discount, and they act as agents to the country banks. The banks in Fleet-street and in Westminster do not usually discount bills for their customers, nor act as agents to country banks. Their connexions embrace chiefly the clergy, the gentry, and the nobility. Their loans to their customers are chiefly upon landed security, and they are supposed to hold a large amount of exchequer bills and other Government securities. Few of the London bankers allow interest on deposits, or charge commission on town accounts. Those who act as agents to country banks charge a commission on the debit side of the account, and some of them allow interest on the daily balance. Instead of a *pro ratá* commission, some country banks pay their agent by a fixed annual payment, or by keeping in his hands a certain balance without interest. None of the present London bankers have ever issued notes, though, until the year 1844, they had legally* the power of doing so. Most of them issue " Circular Notes," for the use of travellers on the Continent.

The following is a summary of part of the evidence delivered before the Bank Committee of 1832, by George Carr Glyn, Esq., respecting the London bankers :—

" There are sixty two private banks in the metropolis, none of which for the last fifty years have issued notes of their own, though it would seem that such of them as consist of fewer than six† partners might lawfully circulate their own paper if they pleased. As they act entirely with the Bank of England paper, it is doubtful whether there be any limit to the

* By common law, through oversight of the legislature.—EDITOR.

† The number to which they were then restricted by the law.

number of partners of which London private banks may consist. They receive deposits, upon which they pay no interest. The system of allowing interest on deposits was formerly tried in London, but the houses that attempted it invariably failed. The deposits held by the London bankers are generally composed of very large sums, which are necessarily payable on demand; and hence they cannot be made use of to the same extent as those which are entrusted to country bankers, and which, whenever interest is allowed, are usually left with them for a stipulated period. On the other hand, in all ordinary transactions, the London banks charge no commission to their customers.

"The London banks, in order to be able to meet their engagements, usually keep a large deposit, nearly equal, perhaps, to half of what they hold in reserve, in the Bank of England; a portion of their current funds they necessarily hold at home in bank paper, and a small amount in gold. Their deposit in the bank they consider as so many notes in their drawer, liable to be called out by the daily fluctuations in the accounts of their customers. The balances in their hands, often very large, are frequently withdrawn without notice; hence their intercourse is almost hourly with the Bank of England, from which they receive every facility.

"In order to turn their funds to profit, the London bankers employ as much money as they can amongst their customers. They invest a considerably larger proportion of their deposits in bills of exchange and promissory notes than in public securities. The city banker is, however, under a disadvantage in this respect, which is not felt by the banker at the west end of the town. The latter may, to a certain extent, depend upon the use of the money deposited with him, as his accounts are usually those of country gentlemen, and individuals out of trade; whereas the former, whose accounts are principally those of persons actively engaged in commercial or money operations, can hardly know three days beforehand what the amount of his deposits may be at any given period. The London bankers are obliged to employ their money occasionally at a very low rate of interest. In some cases, it may have been within the last twelve months, 2½ per cent.; but the average has been from 3 to 3½, and it has fairly kept at that rate. The highest rate has been 4 for short bills, but 5 has been charged for bills of twelve or eighteen months."

The circumstances that attended the failure of Messrs. Strahan & Co. have called attention to the following section respecting bankers inserted in the Act 7 & 8 Geo. IV. c. 49.

" *Agents embezzling Money entrusted to them to be applied to any special Purpose; or embezzling any Goods or valuable Security entrusted to them for safe custody, or for any special Purpose, guilty of a Misdemeanour.*

"And, for the Punishment of Embezzlements committed by Agents entrusted with Property, be it enacted, That if any Money, or Security for the Payment of Money, shall be entrusted to any Banker, Merchant, Broker, Attorney, or other Agent, with any Direction in Writing to apply such Money, or any Part thereof, or the Proceeds or any part of the Proceeds of such Security, for any Purpose specified in such Direction, and he shall, in violation of good Faith, and contrary to the Purpose so specified, in

2 G

anywise convert to his own Use or Benefit such Money, Security, or Proceeds, or any Part thereof respectively, every such Offender shall be guilty of a Misdemeanour, and being convicted thereof, shall be liable, at the Discretion of the Court, to be transported beyond the Seas for any Term not exceeding Fourteen Years nor less than Seven Years, or to suffer such other Punishment by Fine or Imprisonment, or by both, as the Court shall award ; and if any Chattel or valuable Security, or any Power of Attorney for the Sale or Transfer of any Share or Interest in any Public Stock or Fund, whether of this Kingdom, or of *Great Britain* or of *Ireland*, or of any Foreign State, or in any Fund of any Body Corporate, Company, or Society, shall be entrusted to any Banker, Merchant, Broker, Attorney, or other Agent, for safe Custody, or for any special Purpose, without any Authority to sell, negotiate, transfer, or pledge, and he shall, in violation of good Faith and contrary to the Object or Purpose for which such Chattel, Security, or Power of Attorney shall have been entrusted to him, sell, negotiate, transfer, pledge, or in any Manner convert to his own Use for Benefit such Chattel or Security, or the Proceeds of the same, or any Part thereof, or the Share or Interest in the Stock or Fund to which such Power of Attorney shall relate, or any Part thereof, every such Offender shall be guilty of a Misdemeanour, and, being convicted thereof, shall be liable, at the Discretion of the Court, to any of the Punishments which the Court may award, as hereinbefore last mentioned."

But it was said that the parties could escape punishment if they complied with the 52nd Section of the Act.

" Provided always, and be it enacted, That nothing in this Act contained, nor any Proceeding, Conviction, or Judgment to be had or taken thereupon, against any Banker, Merchant, Broker, Factor, Attorney, or other Agent as aforesaid, shall prevent, lessen, or impeach any Remedy at Law or in Equity which any Party aggrieved by any such Offence might or would have had if this Act had not been passed ; but nevertheless the Conviction of any such Offender shall not be received in Evidence in any action at Law or Suit in Equity against him; *and no Banker, Merchant, Broker, Factor, Attorney, or other Agent as aforesaid, shall be liable to be convicted by any Evidence whatever as an offender against this Act, in respect of any Act done by him, if he shall at any Time previously to his being indicted for such Offence have disclosed such Act, on Oath, in consequence of any compulsory Process of any Court of Law or Equity in any Action, Suit, or Proceeding which shall have been bonâ-fide instituted by any Party aggrieved, or if he shall have disclosed the same in any Examination or Deposition before any Commissioners of Bankruptcy.*"

Messrs. Strahan, Paul, and Bates stopped payment the 11th June, 1855. They were made bankrupts, and on the 25th June they voluntarily declared, in the Court of Bankruptcy, that securities amounting to 113,000*l.*, lodged with them by their customers for safe custody, had been sold or otherwise parted with, and the proceeds applied to their own use. They were committed for trial, and it was presumed they intended to plead the above clause in the Act, in the hope that it would save them from punishment.*

We shall now describe the mode of conducting the clearing, or the way in which many of the London bankers make their exchanges with each other. These exchanges are made at the Clearing-house, which is situated in Lombard-street, in a part of the old Post-office.

[*The London Clearing House.*—The Clearing House was established in 1775, by several of the London bankers, for the purpose of facilitating their exchanges with one another. Every London banker having claims against others, and they against him, it used to be their practice to send out clerks daily to collect the debts due to them, which were settled in cash or notes. The inconvenience of this clumsy method of transacting business, and the necessity it involved of keeping cash in their tills to meet demands made upon them for settlement of these exchanges, led to the formation of this establishment, the example of which had been previously set by the Edinburgh banks; indeed, a similar plan seems to have been adopted as early as the sixteenth century, by the merchants who met at the great annual fair held in the city of Lyons. They made their bills payable at this fair only. By this means they were relieved from the necessity of keeping coin or bullion to discharge them, had the bills been drawn at

* Strahan, Paul, and Bates were tried at the October 1855 session of the Central Criminal Court. They pleaded not guilty, and Sir F. Thesiger applied, on their behalf, to plead in addition 52nd sect. of 7 & 8 Geo. IV. c. 29. They were not allowed to plead it in addition; but the point, among others, was raised by Serjeant Byles in his address to the jury for Paul. It appeared that the statement made by the prisoners in the Bankruptcy Court (coupled with the account to which it referred) merely disclosed a dealing in April, 1855, with certain Danish Bonds which had been purchased by the prisoners in substitution for certain other similar bonds deposited with them by the prosecutor, and which they had previously converted, for which conversion of the original (not the substituted) bonds they were indicted, but that the statement also referred the assignees to certain of the firm's books, in which the conversion of the original bonds appeared. The presiding judge (Alderson), in summing up, ruled that the statement was an insufficient disclosure, in not relating to the original bonds, which were the subject matter of the indictment; and then continued :—" It never could have been intended that a person by voluntarily disclosing any act could evade the penalties of the misdemeanour to which such act had rendered him liable. People cannot thus be allowed to play fast and loose with the criminal law; now rendering themselves liable to be transported for fourteen years, and then, by a mere process got up for the purpose, voluntarily absolving themselves from the consequence of their acts." Baron Martin and Justice Willes concurred.

the usual dates ; meanwhile their bills went into circulation, got covered with indorsements, and were yearly set off against each other when adjusting their mutual accounts—so that, as we learn from Boisguillebert,* by this means transactions to the amount of 80,000,000*l.* were settled without the need of a single *sou* in coin.

Originally the Clearing House was an assemblage of bankers who met daily to settle their claims upon each other, paying the difference of their balances in cash or notes, and admission to it was jealously restricted. The joint stock banks were not admitted until 1854, nor the Bank of England till ten years later.

The admission of these important establishments has enlarged to an immense extent the business of the Clearing House, which is performed with a simplicity, exactitude, and regularity, as astonishing as the great development of its transactions.

The following is an accurate, if somewhat technical account of the system now pursued at the Clearing House :—

The delivery of bills due on the day, and all bills due on the city banks, are presented daily (Saturdays excepted) at 10·30 A.M.

The parcels of drafts then brought in by the clerks of these banks are entered up in charges on the city banks, and are entered before the clearers leave—which is at noon.

The West-end bankers clear through their agents in the city.

On the 4th of the month (the great pay-day of commerce) and on Saturdays, the Clearing House opens at 9 A.M.; thus forwarding the operations an hour and a half, and responding to the general call for earlier closing hours on Saturdays.

The country clearing commences at noon. The delivery of this has to be made up by 12·30, and the charges of country cheques are then agreed : the payment of these takes place after an interval of two days, required for the receipt of advices from the country.

The ordinary clearing is carried out at 2·30. This comprises all cheques paid in, country remittances of bills and cheques, and *tickets* for country notes—the notes themselves not being brought in, nor indeed any notes or cash.

In this, the afternoon clearing, the charges are endorsed with amounts, so that a system of agreeing between the houses delivering and the houses crediting is carried out without the clerks

* *Dissertation sur la nature des Richesses.*

meeting : by this means facilitating the settlement of the account at 4 P.M.—at which hour the house closes for the delivery.

In the interval between 4 and 5, the delivery of returns or unpaid articles takes place. The final hour for receipt of those is 5. They are given credit for after the balances are struck, and come into the general balance.

The Clearing House then *tries*. A difference of 1500*l.* over, or of 1000*l.* short, is allowed to stand over to the following day ; but so large a difference is rarely carried over.

The Clearing House is under the control of Sir John Lubbock, Bart., who represents the committee of bankers, of which Lord Wolverton is chairman, and Mr. C. L. Bevan deputy chairman. The House is managed by Mr. George Derbyshire, Chief Inspector, and Mr. J. C. Pocock, Deputy Inspector—the clerks who enter the charges being the representatives of the banks.

The country clearing (all country bankers now clear) was introduced in 1858 by Sir John Lubbock, and has effected an economy of some five millions of gold, which is thus added to the general circulation. The statistical returns of the daily amounts passed through the Clearing House, and which are published weekly, are due to the same gentleman.

With reference to those returns, it is to be regretted that the amount of bills and of drafts is not shown separately. Distinct returns of the two, during the recent continental war, would have been highly valuable, by displaying the changes in the course of trade, and the commercial losses produced by the lamentable conflict.

As bearing on this subject, we quote the following excellent remarks from the *Echo,* January 19th, 1871 :—

" There are two settlements in the Stock Exchange each month, and on those days the cheques and bills passed through the London Clearing House swell to an amount never reached on other occasions. The " 4th of the month " will not compare with it. In the first column we give the total clearing on each of these days in the year, and in the second we give an approximation of the " clearing " arising from the Stock Exchange. The following are the figures :—

	Total clearing on Settling Days.	Probable Stock Exchange Clearing.
January	£26,473,000 26,849,000	£14,473,000 16,349,000
February	25,845,000 28,736,000	11,845,000 18,736,000

	Total clearing on Settling Days.	Probable Stock Exchange Clearing.
March	£29,658,000	£16,658,000
	28,484,000	17,484,000
April	32,702,000	20,702,000
	27,712,000	17,712,000
May	27,384,000	16,384,000
	27,975,000	16,975,000
June	33,952,000	22,952,000
	30,366,000	18,366,000
July	32,461,000	22,461,000
	30,300,000	19,300,000
August	22,500,000	11,000,000
	20,512,000	9,512,000
September	18,741,000	7,741,000
	22,992,000	12,992,000
October	21,243,000	10,243,000
	23,005,000	13,000,000
November	26,596,000	16,596,000
	25,018,000	15,018,000
December	22,380,000	12,380,000
	23,030,000	13,030,000

" Any one who will look carefully down the second column will see the commercial and political history of the year. Little as, in many respects, the war has interfered with business generally, there is a very marked contrast between the first and second six months of the year. The declaration of war was made known to the French Chambers on the 15th July, and up to that date Stock Exchange, as well as other business, had been enlarging month after month, under the encouraging influences of cheap money and political quietude. At the first settlement in April the Stock Exchange cleared cheques to the amount of 20,702,000*l*., and at the first settlement in June the clearing was nearly 23,000,000*l*., probably the largest amount ever recorded in the history of the Stock Exchange. From the beginning of the year to that date the lowest clearing had been 11,845,000*l*. Quite a different aspect is presented by the clearings subsequent to that date. Instead of uniform progress there is fluctuation. The first settlement in July included the war panic, and the forced closing of accounts ran the total of paid moneys up to 22,461,000*l*., or the second highest of the year; notwithstanding that literally dozens of members and outside speculators utterly succumbed, very few of whom have since retrieved their position. So great was the liability unexpectedly incurred, that by common consent, though contrary to the rules of the Stock Exchange, many accounts stood over for settlement to the end of the month. Then the clearing exceeded 19,000,000*l*. From then till the first settlement in September business became more and more confined, until the clearing had receded to 7,741,000*l*., or not much more than a third of what it was in the hey-day of peace! From that date to the end of the year the tendency was to regain some of the lost activity, the Germans having obtained unlimited success, and the prospect of other powers being drawn in having become very remote. The first settlement in October amounted to 16,596,000*l*., the highest since the collapse of July, though below every clearing, excepting in the first six months of the year. The denunciation of the Treaty of 1856 caused some consternation, but the former panic had cleared out the weak holders, and very little, if any, durable effect was produced.   The tendency now is to wait the final result of the war.   This will be followed by a rebound upwards, but a reaction must, we think, set in when the full extent of the destruction is realised. Not only will money leave this country in large quantities in payment of temporary loans placed here for security, but the sums required for the restoration of railways and other indispensable works and buildings will long form a constant drain upon our resources."

Up to 1854, settlement at the Clearing House was completed by the payment of bank notes, when a further economy was effected through settlement by transfer from one banker's account to another at the Bank of England, where all London bankers keep their balances.   Previously to this improvement the bankers had to keep a stock of cash in their tills to meet their clearings, which now augments the circulation to the advantage of the country generally, and no less to the profit of the Threadneedle establishment.

As one instance, out of many that could be cited, of the perfection of the system which regulates the operations of the Clearing House, we may mention that on Wednesday, the 15th March of the current year, 30,000,000*l*. were passed through it, and the house tried right.*]

All the articles in the clearing are entered at home in a book called the Clearing-Book.   On the left hand are entered the bills and drafts upon other bankers.   These are called the " clearing-out."   On the right hand are entered the drafts which are drawn upon the house, and which have *come in* from the clearing.   These are called the " clearing-in."   If the " clearing-out " is a greater sum than the " clearing-in," the clerks say, " the clearing brings in ;" that is, the clearing clerk will bring in money from the Clearing House.   In the other case, they say, " the clearing takes out ;" that is, he will have to draw from the Banking-house to settle at the Clearing House.   The balance of this book should agree with the clearer's balance-sheet, except the differences of the preceding night, which he may have settled.   When this is the case, the clearer is right ; if not, he is wrong, and he must discover the error.   The clearer may be wrong through errors made either in his own book at the Clearing House, or in the Clearing-Book at home.   The error at home may be either in the " clearing-in " or in the

* There are 105 *sittings*, or counters in the Clearing House, with an average daily attendance from the clearing banks of about 90 clerks.—EDITOR.

" clearing-out." If the error be in the clearing-out, it will make the Banking-house wrong; if in the clearing-in it will not. Suppose, for instance, the clearing-out is wrong cast 1000*l.* too much, the house will be 1000*l.* over, and the clearer will be 1000*l.* short. But if the clearing-in be wrong cast 1000*l.* too much, it will not affect the balance of the house, because the Cash-Book will, consequently, be 1000*l.* less; and these two amounts, those of the Cash-Book and the Paid-Day-Book (into which the amount of the Clearing-In-Book is entered), are placed on the same side of the trial paper. But this error will make the clearer wrong. The way in which the clearer discovers his errors is, by marking off his book against the Clearing-Book, and by recasting both the books. An error may have occurred at the Clearing House. If the clearer has placed a wrong balance on his sheet, or has wrong cast his balance-sheet, the Clearing House will be wrong, and the inspectors will make it their business to discover the error. But if the clearer has entered an article wrong in his book, and the clerk of the house upon whom the draft is drawn has entered it wrong also, then the Clearing House will be right, and both these clearers will be wrong; one being as much over as the other is short.

All the articles in the clearing-out must mark against either the Journals, the Received-Waste-Books, or the Lists. To secure greater accuracy, the clearing-in is entered not only in the regular Clearing-Book, but also in another book by itself, which for distinction is called the Clearing-In-Book. The amount of the clearing-in is entered in the Paid-Day-Book previous to the daily balance. On the following morning, the Clearing-In-Book is marked against the debit side of the Ledger, and the Ledger-Folio placed against each entry.

Country notes are not paid at the Clearing House, but are taken round to the banking-houses, and exchanged for tickets called memorandums, which are passed through the afternoon clearing. The following is the form of these memorandums:—

London, 1*st May*, 18 .

Due to Messrs. Steady & Co.

One Thousand Pounds
for Country Notes, to be paid in the clearing of this day.

For Messrs. Hope, Rich, & Co.

£1,000.   *A Clerk.*

Drafts that are paid into the Banking-house after four o'clock are taken to the houses upon whom they are drawn "to be marked;" that is, it is asked if these drafts will be paid in the clearing of the next day. If so, one of the clerks *marks* the cheque by placing his initials upon it. If the cheque is refused to be marked, it is returned as dishonoured, on the following day, to the person who has paid it in. Had it not been sent to be marked, the draft would not have been refused payment until the next day, and it could not be returned to the customer till the day afterwards.

The operations on the Stock Exchange cause a great number of cheques to be drawn on bankers, and thus increase the operations at the Clearing House.

A person who wants to buy 100*l.* consols, gives his order to a broker, and pays him possibly by a cheque on his banker, which the broker takes and pays to his own banker. He then buys the 100*l.* consols from a jobber, and pays him by a cheque. The jobber possibly replaces this stock by buying 100*l.* consols from another broker who is ordered by his principal to sell that amount of stock. The jobber gives the broker his cheque upon his banker, and the broker probably will give his principal the produce of the stock by a cheque. No money has passed between the parties, and the result of the whole is, that the buyer of the stock has 90*l.* less in the hands of his banker, and the seller has 90*l.* more. Four cheques have been drawn, and these have caused transactions with five different bankers. The total number of credit and debit operations in all the banks is eight.

1. The banker of the buyer of the stock pays his cheque through the clearing, and debits his customer.

2. The banker of the broker who buys the stock credits him with the purchaser's cheque, and debits him for the cheque he gives to the jobber.

3. The banker of the jobber credits him for the cheque he has received from the buying broker, and debits him for the cheque he gives to the selling broker.

4. The banker of the broker who sells the stock credits him for the jobber's cheque, and debits him for the cheque he gives to his customer who is the seller.

5. The banker of the seller credits him for the cheque of the broker who has sold the stock, and will debit him for any cheques he may draw against it.

Should neither the buyer nor the seller of the stock keep a banker, then only three cheques would be drawn.

Besides these daily transactions arising out of real business, the brokers have large transactions in what are called " time bargains." This is what is usually meant by "gambling in the funds." The parties buy or sell consols against the next settling day. No real purchase or sale is ever intended. When the settling day arrives, the losing party has to pay the difference that has arisen from the fluctuations in the price. A settlement takes place among the brokers in a way somewhat resembling the settling between the bankers at the Clearing House. All the differences are paid by cheques. A broker may give twenty, thirty, or forty cheques to as many different brokers, and he may receive an equal number from other brokers. All these cheques are paid by the respective bankers through the Clearing House. Besides settling days for consols, there are also settling days for foreign funds, and for shares in railway companies. The differences in these cases are also settled by cheques upon the clearing bankers.

Those West-end bankers who keep an account with a city bank do not in all cases pass the whole of their transactions through the Clearing House. They pay and receive with the Clearing bankers individually, and sometimes leave their unpaid bills with their City agent. They occasionally pay into the City bank the cheques they may have on the Clearing bankers, and on the other bankers too.

The stock-brokers usually write across every cheque they draw the name of the banker of the party in whose favour it is drawn; and if they do not know the name of the banker, they write " _____ & Co." The banker on whom it is drawn will then pay it only in the clearing.

If a broker intends a cheque to be paid in bank notes across the counter, he writes on it the word "cash." Such cheques are given only to persons who do not keep bankers.

Many persons now cross the cheques they draw with the name of a banker, to guard against fraud in case the cheques should be lost or stolen. The cheque can then only be paid to the banker whose name is on the cheque. If it be crossed with the names of two bankers, it will be refused payment to either, unless the matter be satisfactorily explained.

Clearing bankers never make payments to each other except through the clearing.

[The following letter, addressed last year by Sir John Lubbock to the leading papers, shows in a striking manner the marvellous effects, economic and other, resulting from the machinery of the Clearing House :—

" SIR,

" The third year during which the Clearing House statistics have been published has now elapsed, and Messrs. Derbyshire and Pocock, the inspectors, have prepared for us certain statistics, from which the following will, I think, be interesting to many of your readers,

" The total amount of cheques and bills paid at the Clearing House, during the year ending 30th April, 1870, have amounted to 3,720,623,000*l.*, being an increase of 186,584,000*l.* over 1869, and of 463,212,000*l.* over 1868.

" The amounts passing through on the 4th of the month form the best indication as to the state of the internal trade of the country ; and it is, therefore, satisfactory to find that the total for 1870 has been 168,523,000*l.*, showing an increase of 6,662,000*l.* over 1869, and of 150,320,000*l.* over 1868.

" The payments on the 24 Stock Exchange settling days for 1870 have amounted to 594,763,000*l.*, showing an increase of 44,141,000*l.* over 1869, and of 150,320,000*l.* over 1868.

" The payments on the 12 Consol settling days for the same period have amounted to 148,822,000*l.*, showing an increase of 6,552,000*l.* over 1869, and an increase of 16,529,000*l.* over 1868.

" I am sir,
" Your obedient servant,
" JOHN LUBBOCK,
" Hon. Sec. London Bankers.

" 15 *Lombard Street, 5th May,* 1870."

If a bank owes money to the Clearing House, the settlement is made by a cheque in the following form on the Bank of England :—

(No. 1.)

Settlement at the Clearing House.

London,＿＿＿＿＿＿ 18

To the Cashiers of the BANK of ENGLAND,

Be pleased to TRANSFER from our Account the sum of ＿ ＿＿＿＿＿

and place it to the credit of the Account of the Clearing Bankers, and allow it to be drawn for, by any of them (with the knowledge of either of the Inspectors, signified by his countersigning the Drafts).

£＿＿＿＿＿

For which the bank signs the following certificate :—

(No. 2.)

Settlement at the Clearing House.

BANK OF ENGLAND,

_____ 18

  A TRANSFER for the sum of _____

has this evening been made at the Bank, from the account of Messrs.
_____ _____ to the Account of the Clearing
Bankers.

					For the Bank of England,

£ _____

This Certificate has been seen by me,			_____

_____*Inspector.*

If a bank has to receive money from the Clearing House, the
settlement is made in the following form, addressed to the Bank
of England :—

(No. 3.)

Settlement at the Clearing House.

					London, _____ 18

To the Cashiers of the BANK of ENGLAND,

  Be pleased to CREDIT our Account the sum of _____

_____

out of the money at the credit of the account of the Clearing Bankers.

£ _____				_____

Seen by me,

_____*Inspector at the Clearing House.*

For which the Bank gives the following certificate :—

(No. 4.)

Settlement at the Clearing House.

BANK OF ENGLAND,

_____ 18

  The account of Messrs. _____ _____

has this evening been CREDITED with the sum of _____

_____

out of the money at the credit of the account of the Clearing Bankers.

					For the Bank of England,

£ _____				_____

  To distinguish readily these forms from each other, Nos. 1
and 2 are on white paper, Nos. 3 and 4 on green.

The Clearing Balance Sheet.
THE ALLIANCE BANK.

Debtors.   Creditors.

			*					
			Barclay					
			Barnett					
			Bosanquet					
			Brown					
			City					
			Consolidated					
			County					
			Dimsdale					
			Fuller					
			Glyn					
			Imperial					
			Joint					
			Bank					
			London & West^r					
			Martin					
			Metropolitan					
			National					
			Nat^l Provincial					
			Prescott					
			Robarts					
			Southwark †					
			Smith					
			Union					
			Williams					
			Willis					
			Country Clearing					
			C. H.					

* There are sheets for each Clearing Bank, *headed* with its name, which is of course omitted from the *list*, as that of the Alliance is from its place here : thus in the sheet *headed* Barclay's, or Glyn's, or Union Bank, &c., the name would not appear in the alphabetical list.

† This is the Southwark branch of the London and Westminster Bank, which was admitted into the Clearing House in 1855—a singular instance, not only from the circumstance of a branch bank being treated as an independent bank, but from the fact of its being outside of the City.]

SECTION III.

JOINT-STOCK AND BANKING COMPANIES.

The London and Westminster Bank, the London Joint-Stock Bank, and the Union Bank, being the three oldest of the joint-stock banks established in London, we may briefly revert to their formation.

I.—*The London and Westminster Bank.*

In the Act for renewing the Bank of England Charter, passed in 1833, it was declared to be the law that companies or partnerships consisting of more than six persons might carry on the business of banking in London. Immediately after the passing of this Act, a prospectus was issued, proposing to form the London and Westminster Bank. The shares, however, were taken up but tardily, and the bank did not commence business until March 10th, 1834, and then only with a paid-up capital of 50,000*l.*, and of this capital a large portion is said to have been subscribed by shareholders who resided in the country.

As the Bank Charter Act did not prescribe the way in which companies of more than six persons were to sue or be sued, the directors of the London and Westminster Bank brought a bill into Parliament, in the session of 1834, to authorise them to sue and be sued in the names of their public officers, in the same manner as those banking companies that were located beyond sixty-five miles from London. This bill was carried by large majorities through the house of Commons, although opposed by the influence of the Bank of England and by Lord Althorp, then Chancellor of the Exchequer. The bill, however, was lost in the Lords. In consequence of this failure, the bank followed the plan of suing and being sued through the medium of trustees.

Previous to the commencement of business, the directors applied to the Committee of Private Bankers for admission to the Clearing House. This was refused. The directors also applied for permission to have a drawing account at the Bank of England. This, too, was refused.

At the commencement of the year 1835, the Bank of England instituted legal proceedings to prevent the London and Westminster Bank accepting bills drawn at less than six months after date. Supported, however, by the legal opinions of Sir John Campbell, Sir William Follett, and Mr. Pemberton, the trustees continued to accept such bills, and resisted the proceedings of the Bank of England.

In the beginning of the year 1837, the suit brought by the Bank of England was terminated, by the Master of the Rolls granting an injunction to restrain the London and Westminster Bank from accepting bills at less than six months after date. The country joint-stock banks then adopted the practice of drawing upon the London and Westminster Bank " without acceptance," in the same way as the Bank of Ireland draws upon the Bank of England. No practical difficulty was experienced, and the London and Westminster Bank lost none of its connexions in consequence of this adverse decision. At the end of the year the directors declared the usual dividend of 5 per cent.

In the year 1841, Mr. Gilbart, the general manager, was examined for four days before a Select Committee of the House of Commons, at the request of a meeting of deputies from the joint-stock banks. In the report of March, 1844, we read— " As the speech from the throne has called the attention of Parliament to ' the state of the law with regard to the privileges of the Bank of England and to other banking establishments, the directors have co-operated with the representatives of other joint-stock banks in bringing under the consideration of the Government the defects of the laws relating to banking companies, which they feel confident the Legislature will not refuse to remedy." In this year the bank obtained the power to draw, accept, or endorse any bills of exchange not payable to bearer on demand, and immediately commenced accepting the bills drawn by its country connexions, and issuing circular letters of credit for the use of travellers and residents on the Continent. In the same year the bank obtained the power of suing and being sued in the names of its public officers, and accordingly registered the names of its trustees for that purpose.

II.—*The London Joint-Stock Bank.*

The Joint-Stock Bank was formed in the year 1836. That year was one of great excitement in favour of the principle of joint-stock banking both in London and in the country. The shares of the new bank were readily taken by a very respectable proprietary, most of whom were resident in London. The bank had also from its commencement the advantage of an influential commercial directory. A new feature in London banking was announced. The bank agreed to allow interest at 2 per cent. on the minimum balance of a current account, and at the end of each month interest was allowed on the lowest balance that had appeared to the party's credit at the close of any day during the month.

The capital of the bank was fixed at 3,000,000*l.*, divided into 60,000 shares of 50*l.* each.

III.—*The Union Bank of London.*

The Union Bank of London was formed in 1839, chiefly by gentlemen who were, by birth or otherwise, connected with Scotland. The capital was fixed at 3,000,000*l.*, in 60,000 shares of 50*l.* each.

The bank adopted the principle of allowing 2 per cent. interest on the minimum balance of a current account :—" Parties keeping current or drawing accounts will be credited on the first day of every month, on the smallest balance at the credit of their account at the close of business on any day during the past month, provided that such balance shall not be less than 100*l.* The total amount of interest will be passed to account every six months."

[We gladly borrow from Mr. Macleod's elaborate and learned work, the following sketch of the history of Joint-Stock banking, and, with the greater satisfaction, on account of the testimony it bears, by implication, to the merits of the late Mr. Gilbart, and the " enormous difficulties " talent and energy such as his alone could have surmounted :—

An attempt in 1823 to gain the consent of the Bank of England to give up the privileges of their Charter, so far as to permit joint-stock banks to be formed in the country, having failed, even though a bribe was offered, nothing further took place till 1826, when the disasters of the preceding year being very generally attributed to the improper management of the country banks, the Ministry were powerful enough to compel the Bank to give up its unjustifiable monopoly, and at length agreed to permit joint-stock banks to be formed beyond sixty-five miles from the metropolis. The Statute 1826, c. 46, was passed for this purpose.

This Act made no provisions regarding the constitution or capital of these companies. Each one was allowed to devise a constitution for itself, to name its own capital, and to make any public announcement regarding it that it pleased. The formation of joint-stock banks under this Act proceeded very slowly at first, not more than four or five being formed in as many years. In fact, such banks could only be successfully formed by influential persons, and, of course, each of these had already his own bank, which he would naturally be unwilling to injure by the formation of so powerful a rival. The first joint-stock bank was formed at Lancaster, the next at Bradford, and another at Norwich, before any one was formed at one of the great manufacturing towns. It was not till the prosperous years of 1833-34-35-36, that any very remarkable increase took place in their numbers. In these years, however, they multiplied rapidly, more especially in 1836, when upwards of forty were established in the spring.

On the renewal of the Bank Charter in 1833, it was determined to take off the vexatious restriction of preventing banking companies making their bills and notes for less than 50*l.*, payable on demand by their agents in London. And they were required to keep weekly accounts, to be verified on oath, of the amount of their notes in circulation, and make a return to the Commissioners of Stamps of the average amount in circulation every quarter.

It was at this time that the discovery made in 1822 by Mr. Joplin, that the Bank Charter did not prohibit joint-stock banks being formed in London, and carrying on their business on the method then adopted by the London Bankers, attracted attention, and, on the case being submitted to the law officers of the Crown, they confirmed this view. The flank of the monopoly of the Bank of England, as we may say, being turned in this extraordinary and unexpected manner, excited much consternation and alarm in that body, and they requested to have this omission rectified, but Lord Althorp decidedly refused anything of the sort, and told them that the bargain was that their privileges should remain as they were, and he would not consent to any extension of them. To remove all possible doubts on the subject, a declaratory clause was inserted in the Bank Charter Act, expressly permitting joint-stock banks to be formed, provided they did not borrow, or take up in England, any sum or sums of money, on their bills or notes payable on demand, or at any less time than six months from the borrowing thereof. This declaratory clause was not long in being acted upon; and soon after the Act was passed, measures were taken to constitute a joint-stock bank in London. This was the London and Westminster Bank, which has since been managed with such distinguished success.

The enormous difficulties which must have attended the successful organisation of this great establishment may be conceived when we remember that it was not formed under the Joint-Stock Banking Act at all, which had no force within sixty-five miles of London, but that it was nothing but an ordinary partnership at common law. One of the least of the inconveniences of this was that it could not maintain an action at law for the most trivial debt, without enumerating all and each of the partners, and the slightest mistake in the spelling of a single name would at that time have vitiated any proceeding. This bank was the largest common law partnership which has existed in England; and all the London joint-stock banks which were formed before the Act, Statute 1844, c. 113, are nothing but common law partnerships. The excessive inconvenience

2 H

attending this state of things led to a bill being brought into Parliament to enable the London and Westminster Bank to sue and be sued in the name of its chairman. This was warmly opposed by the Bank of England, and by Lord Althorp. Nothing could be more paltry than the reasons alleged by him in opposition to it, but he was beaten by a majority of 141 to 35. The Government, however, had influence enough to have the bill thrown out in the Lords. The Bank being thus defeated, adopted the plan of making all contracts through the medium of trustees, and all the London joint-stock banks had to adopt this plan, till the Joint-Stock Banking Act of 1844. The other banks formed on a similar plan to the London and Westminster, are, the London Joint-Stock Bank, founded in 1836; the Union Bank, in 1839; the London and County Bank, in 1839; and the Commercial Bank, in 1840, which afterwards wound up its business.

A question, however, of very great importance soon arose. It was a settled question that no partnership or corporation consisting of more than six persons could accept bills, at any less date than six months, no matter whether they were a banking partnership or any other. It was clear, therefore, that the bank could not itself directly accept bills. But it did not appear that the words of the Act prohibited *trustees* accepting bills for a less date, on behalf of the company. Nor, if trustees could accept, was there anything to prevent them accepting by procuration. Consequently, there appeared to be this method open, of circumventing the monopoly of the Bank of England. On the 21st of February, 1835, the Bank of St. Albans drew a bill for 25*l.* upon the London and Westminster Bank, payable 21 days after date; which, on the 23rd, was presented for acceptance at the London and Westminster Bank, and was accepted in the following form :—

Accepted,

At 36, Throgmorton-st., per procuration of
the trustees of the London and Westminster Bank,

J. W. GILBART, *Manager.*

The Bank of England moved for an injunction to restrain the bank from accepting bills in this form, and the case having been argued, the Court of Common Pleas held that it was an infraction of the Bank Charter Act of 1833, and the other Acts then in force respecting the Bank of England. Accordingly, the Master of the Rolls granted an injunction, restraining them from accepting bills at less than six months' date. The only result was, that the bank paid the bills drawn upon it without acceptance. The London and Westminster Bank being defeated in this manner, the London Joint-Stock entered the lists against the Bank of England in another form. It agreed with a bank in Canada, that the latter might draw upon Mr. George Pollard, who might accept in his own name, and the London Bank agreed to find the funds to meet Mr. Pollard's acceptances, and such transactions were to be matters of account between the two banks. Mr. Pollard was not a shareholder in the London Bank; but he was their manager, and the transaction was substantially an acceptance by the bank. The House of Lords, however, declared this ingenious device to be illegal, as it was merely doing indirectly what they were forbidden to do directly. Thus ended the attempts of the London joint-stock banks to free themselves from this monstrous oppression, from which they were not relieved till the Act of 1844.

It was always held at common law, that a man could not sue himself. Consequently, if the same individual was member of two partnerships, they could not go to law against each other. The consequence of this was, that no partnership could sue one of its members, or *vice versâ*, and if the same person had shares in two different banks, they could not have sued each other for any demands or debts. The Statute 1838, c. 96, was passed to remedy this anomalous state of matters. It enacted that a banking company might sue, or be sued, by any of its members, exactly as if they were separate individuals; and by the Statute 1840, c. 111, this was extended to criminal cases, so that if a member of such a banking partnership steals or embezzles any property belonging to it, of any description, or shall commit any offence against it, he may be indicted, and convicted exactly as if he were a stranger.

It being unlawful for spiritual persons to engage in any trading concerns, and such partnerships, of which any of its members were spiritual persons, being held to be void and illegal, it was suddenly found that most of the banking companies in England were illegal, and all their contracts void, because some of their shareholders were clergymen. The Act, Statute 1841, c. 14, was passed to remedy this, and declared that such partnerships should not be illegal and void; and that their contracts should not be illegal and void, although some of their shareholders were clergymen.

When the impediments to the formation of joint-stock banks beyond sixty-five miles from London were removed in 1826, they were left perfectly free as to the provisions of their deeds of constitution, their nominal and their paid-up capital, and all the details of management, nor were they obliged to publish any accounts. The public, consequently, were perfectly in the dark as to the magnitude and position of the bank, because they might advertise that their nominal capital was 1,000,000*l.*, divided into any number of shares. But no one had any means of knowing how many of the shares were taken and paid upon. Consequently, although the capital of the bank might be advertised in the papers as 1,000,000*l.*, no one could tell whether it had *bonâ fide* 500*l.* paid up.

The first few joint-stock banks having been apparently successful, naturally turned speculation into that channel. Numbers of new banks were started in all parts of the country, and many private bankers, fearing that the competition would be too powerful for them, united and formed themselves into joint-stock banks. The rapid growth of these establishments led to much mismanagement, and many disasters, as might have been expected, and Committees of the House of Commons were appointed to inquire into the subject in 1836–7 and 1840–1.

The great abuses which were revealed in the course of these inquiries determined Sir Robert Peel, who was supposed to be the minister who *par excellence* understood banking, to bring in a bill to regulate the future constitution of these establishments. An Act, containing many elaborate provisions for this purpose, was accordingly passed, statute 1844, c. 113. Fully admitting the enormous evils which this Act was intended to remedy, we will only say that a more unfortunate specimen of legislation, or one more entirely unsuitable to the nature of the business it related to, has not emanated from Parliament in recent times; and, being found to be an unmitigated nuisance, without any counterbalancing advantages, it was wholly repealed in 1857.

We have already said that Sir Robert Peel's Joint-Stock Banking Act, Statute 1844, c. 113, was found to be wholly unsuitable for the purposes it was intended, and totally repealed. This was done by the Act, Statute 1857, c. 49. The principal provisions of this Act are as follows :—

I. Every company formed under the Acts, Statute 1844, c. 113, or the Statute 1845, c. 75, were to register themselves before the 1st January, 1858, under the said Act, under severe penalties.

II. Any banking company, consisting of seven or more persons, having a capital of a fixed amount, divided into shares also of a fixed amount, and legally carrying on the business of banking before the passing of the Act, may register itself under this Act, and then all provisions of any Act, letters patent, or deed of settlement constituting or regulating the company, as are inconsistent with the Joint-Stock Companies' Acts, 1856, 1857, or with the said Act, are thereby repealed in regard to that Company.

III. The above Banking Acts were then repealed as to any future companies, and as to existing companies, as soon as they were registered under this Act.

IV. Seven or more persons might register themselves as a company, other than a limited company, under this Act, provided the shares into which the capital of the company is divided are not less than 100*l*. each.

V. The number of partners permitted in a private bank is extended to ten.

The question of admitting the principle of limited liability into commercial partnerships in this country has long been debated with much acrimony. The old theory of the law was expressed by Lord Eldon, who said that a man who entered into a commercial partnership, rendered himself liable ' to his last shilling and his last acre ' for the debts of the company. And this, no doubt, was true, as far as regards ordinary private partnerships. But many great companies had been formed and incorporated, in which the privilege of limited liability was specially conferred upon them. A principle may be good when applied to ordinary traders, who are supposed all to take an active part in the business, and to be each and all parties to every transaction. But in the case of great companies it is rather different. In them the great majority of the partners are specially debarred from all knowledge of the real nature of the transactions, which are expressly left in the hands of a small committee. Now, as there are many great objects in commerce which can only be carried by means of a great company, and it was obviously desirable that they should be carried out, it has long been the practice in granting Acts to these companies to limit the liability of the shareholders.

This was done in the case of the Bank of England itself; in railway and other companies; also, almost universally, in the charters granted to Colonial banks. But for a very long time the application of this principle to private partnerships in England was vehemently resisted. However, this resistance was overcome in 1855, and in that year an Act was passed, Statute 1855, c. 133, to permit the formation of joint-stock companies with limited liability. However, although the principle was conceded as to other companies, joint-stock banks were still most jealously excluded, on account of some unintelligible distinction between their trading and other trading. In the Joint-Stock Banking Act of 1857 this exclusion was still strictly maintained. But the terrible examples of the failures of joint-stock banks in 1857, at last compelled the Legislature to yield, and in 1858 an Act was passed to extend limited liability to banks.

The chief provisions of this Act, Statute 1858, c. 91, are:—

I. So much of the last mentioned Statute of 1857, as prevented banks being formed on the principle of limited liability, was repealed.

II. All banks which issue promissory notes are subject to unlimited liability, as far as regards their notes, for which they are to be liable, in addition to the sum for which they are to be liable to the general creditors.

III. Every existing banking company may register itself under this Act, upon giving thirty days' notice to each and all of its customers. Any customer to whom it may fail to send notice retaining his full rights as before.

IV. All companies formed, or registering themselves, under this Act, must, on the 1st February and 1st August in each year, post up in a conspicuous place in its head office, and each branch, a statement of its liabilities and assets, made up in a form prescribed by the Act."]

We are indebted to the *Echo* of the 19th of January, 1871, for the following pithy remarks, which form an apt conclusion to the present section :—

" The proportion of ' acceptances ' to ' deposits ' in the joint-stock bank accounts, now being almost daily laid before the public, affords as usual food for interesting reflection. The bank that puts its name to other people's bills is incurring a risk inevitably, but the risk may be measured and security can be obtained equivalent to the risk. In spite of this consideration, however, the bank that has few acceptances is looked upon as doing the least risky business. The few subjoined figures which we have put together will show that the most esteemed Companies evidently avoid ' accepting ' as much as possible, and that one, the National Discount, may be said never ' to accept :'—

	Deposits. £	Acceptances. £
Alliance	1,351,165	252,527
City	2,436,187	1,837,730
Consolidated	2,341,817	154,915
Imperial	1,529,172	189,622

	Deposits. £	Acceptances. £
London and Westminster . .	21,986,196	883,173
Metropolitan	543,000	70,955
Midland	1,035,111	nil
Union of London	11,207,634	4,205,591
National Discount	9,152,375	1,263

There are two banks—the London Joint-Stock and the Central of London—who do not divide their deposits from acceptances. That the London Joint-Stock Bank should persist in lumping these two totally dissimilar items, astonishes the advocates of joint-stock banking. Compliance with so obvious a requirement is the least that could be expected of a bank holding the position occupied by the London Joint-Stock."

SECTION IV.

THE COUNTRY PRIVATE BANKS.

THESE banks cannot have more than ten partners. They are banks of deposit, of loan, and of discount. As banks of deposit they usually allow interest on both deposits and balances of current accounts, and charge a commission on the amount of the transactions. In commercial or manufacturing districts, their advances are usually made by way of discount ; in agricultural districts, frequently by loans. They remit money by issuing bills or letters of credit on London, or they direct their agents to make payments to bankers or other parties resident in London. As banks of circulation, they have at various times occupied a large portion of public attention, and have been the subject of much legislation.

Those bankers who wish to issue notes, or unstamped bills of exchange, must take out a licence, which will cost 30*l.*, and must be renewed every year. They may reissue any notes not above the value of 100*l.* as often as they think proper. And should any of the firm die or remove from the business, the notes may be issued by the remaining partners. But they cannot be reissued by a new firm which does not include any member belonging to the firm by whom the notes were first issued.

If the half of a note be lost or stolen, a banker cannot be compelled to give a new note in exchange for the remaining half. But if it can be proved that one half of a note is burnt, or otherwise destroyed, then the holder may perhaps recover the note from the banker.

In such cases, the bankers always pay the value of the note on receiving a respectable indemnity.

Bankers may be compelled to pay whole notes that have been lost or stolen, provided the holder has given actual value for them.

The stamp duty on country notes is as follows:—

	£	s.				£	s.		s.	d.	
Notes not exceeding	1	0	..	..	..		..	..	0	5	each.
Exceeding ..	1	0	and not exceeding			2	0	..	0	10	„
Ditto	2	0	,,	,,		5	0	..	1	3	„
Ditto	5	0	,,	,,		10	0	..	1	9	„
Ditto	10	0	,,	,,		20	0	..	2	0	„
Ditto	20	0	,,	,,		30	0	..	3	0	„
Ditto	30	0	,,	,,		50	0	..	5	0	„
Ditto	50	0	,,	,,		100	0	..	8	6	„

Country banks are allowed to compound for the stamp duties on their notes, at the rate of three shillings and sixpence per cent. upon the half-yearly amount in circulation, and to include, on the same terms, their bills drawn on London at twenty-one days after date. But whether a country banker compounds for the stamp duties or not, he must make a return to the Government of the amount of his notes in circulation every Saturday night. These returns are consolidated, and the result published in the *London Gazette.*

I am not aware that we have any authentic details of the rise and progress of country banking in England. It is generally understood that very few country banks existed previous to the American war—that they rapidly increased after the termination of that war—that they received a severe check in the year 1793, when twenty-two became bankrupt, and that they increased with wonderful rapidity after the passing of the Bank Restriction Act. Since the year 1808 every bank that issues notes has been compelled to take out an annual licence—and since 1804, the notes have been subject to a stamp duty. This duty was increased in 1808, and again in 1815.

In the year 1775 bankers were prohibited by Act of Parliament to issue notes of a less amount than 20s. And in 1777 they were prohibited to issue notes of a less amount than 5l. But after the passing of the Bank Restriction Act in 1797, the last restriction was removed, and the country banks commenced issuing notes of 1l. and 2l. And in 1822 the permission to issue such notes was continued until the expiration of the Bank

Charter in 1833. But after the memorable panic of 1825, the Government refused to issue any more stamps for notes under 5*l*., and it was enacted that all such notes already stamped should cease to be issued by the bankers after the year 1829.

The speculations that preceded the panic of 1825 were attributed by the Government of the day to a wild spirit of speculation fostered by the country banks. To guard against the recurrence of similar evils, not only were notes under 5*l*. abolished, but two other measures were introduced. Banks of issue, consisting of more than six partners, were permitted to be formed at a greater distance than sixty-five miles from London; and the Bank of England was induced to open branches in the provinces.

And here it will be proper to notice a peculiarity in the county of Lancaster, and particularly in Manchester and Liverpool. In these places there were no country notes, and but a small proportion of Bank of England notes. The circulation consisted mainly of bills of exchange, which passed from hand to hand like bank notes, having the endorsement of all the parties through whose hands they had passed. In Liverpool large notes were required to pay the duties at the Custom House; and in Manchester small notes were required to pay wages. These were obtained from the Bank of England in London: but the transactions between manufacturers and dealers were transacted by bills of exchange; and as these bills were all made payable in London, bank notes were not required in Manchester and Liverpool, even for the payment of these bills.

The measures adopted by the Legislature in the year 1826 led to the establishment of branches of the Bank of England in Manchester and Liverpool. From this period the circulation of bills of exchange declined, and was superseded by Bank of England notes. This was accelerated by the circumstance that the joint-stock banks formed in these places did not issue their own notes, but those of the Bank of England. This establishment had offered to discount for the joint-stock banks at 1 per cent. less than they charged to the public, and the joint-stock banks thought it more for their interest to obtain the notes of the Bank of England on these terms than to issue notes of their own. The circulation of the country now consisted of notes of the branches of the Bank of England, notes of the joint-stock banks, and notes of the private bankers; and as many of the weak private banks had ceased to exist, and as others had merged into joint-stock banks, and as all notes under 5*l.* were abolished, it was supposed that the country had now obtained the advantage of a secure circulation.

But in the latter end of the year 1836 another panic arrived, when it was discovered that the country circulation was again at fault. But the charge now was, not that it was unsafe, but that it was excessive; and this charge of having issued to excess was more especially directed against the joint-stock banks.

Here it may be observed, that in the panic of 1825 the amount of country notes in circulation was unknown. No returns at that time were made to the Government, and the amount of notes in circulation could only be calculated, and that very imperfectly, from the number of stamps, of different denominations, issued from the Stamp Office. But in the year 1833, the Chancellor of the Exchequer, Lord Althorp, obtained an Act (3 & 4 William IV. c. 83) which required all banks issuing promissory notes to make returns to the Stamp Office of the average amounts of notes in circulation in the quarters ending the first day of January, April, July, and October in each year. The quarterly average was to be formed from the amount in circulation at the end of each week. These quarterly returns were afterwards published in the *London Gazette.*

From these returns it was evident that the country circulation had increased by the beginning of the year 1836; and as a general spirit of speculation prevailed at the same time, it was inferred that the country circulation was the cause of this speculation; and as by the end of the year the speculations had ended in panic, the country circulation was the cause of this panic.

Another panic occurred at the end of the year 1839, and here, again, blame was cast on the country notes. But the complaint now was not that the country circulation was unsafe or excessive, but that it was ill-regulated. An opinion had been adopted by some distinguished political economists that the country circulation, as well as that of the Bank of England, ought to correspond at all times with the amount of gold in the Bank of England. It is true that the circulation of the Bank of England did not fluctuate in exact accordance with this amount of gold; but the country circulation did not correspond even with that of the Bank of England. And as the fluctuations in the country circulation did not correspond with the fluctuations either of the gold of the Bank of England or with the notes of the Bank of England, it was assumed that the country circulation was ill-regulated; and, being ill-regulated, it was assumed to be the cause, or at least one cause, of the panic that occurred at the end of the year 1839.

To examine into the truth of these opinions, a Committee of the House of Commons was appointed in the year 1840, to consider the state of the law with reference to Banks of Issue. The Committee examined witnesses during the sessions of 1840 and 1841; but the only practical result was that an Act was passed requiring weekly returns of their circulation from every bank of issue.*

Before proceeding farther, it may be fair to state the replies which the country bankers at various times gave to these severe accusations.

In reply to the charge that the currency was unsafe, from the number of failures which occurred among the country banks of issue, they state in their memorial to Earl Grey, in the year 1833, " the number of London bankers that have failed is believed to be relatively greater, and the amount of their debts relatively larger, than that of country banks."

In reply to the charge that they had by an excessive issue of their notes promoted speculation, they state :—

" All experience shows that great fluctuations have originated in the speculations of influential merchants, and never originated in the channels to which the issues of country bankers are confined; their source is in great mercantile cities, and they are promoted by the issues of the Bank of England. That this is the invariable course which fluctuations resulting in excess and derangement take, is proved by the evidence of Mr. Ward and others, before the Bank Charter Committee, and is fully explained by the speeches of the King's Ministers in the year 1826. The debts of a few speculative merchants who failed in a single year in the town of Liverpool, where country bankers' notes never circulated, amounted to between seven and eight millions sterling, and their bills were either lodged in the Bank of England for loans, or were current in all parts of the country, stimulating circulation and promoting excess."

* 4 & 5 Victoria, c. 50.

In reply to the charge that they had turned the foreign exchanges against this country, they reply :—

" Your memorialists are prepared to prove that the issues of country bankers have less tendency to promote fluctuations in the country than those of the Bank of England ; and that their effect in throwing the exchanges against the country is comparatively insignificant. The slightest attention to facts would indicate the truth of these positions. It has been established by parliamentary evidence that the issues of country bankers fluctuated much less between the years 1817 and 1826 than those of the Bank of England ; and it is indisputable that adverse exchanges, which endanger the bank, always succeed great importations of foreign produce, and that they never can be occasioned by large exportations of domestic productions. Now, it is notorious that the circulation of country bankers acts almost exclusively in promoting these productions : and that, when it is in an extended state, the direct and proper influence, even of an alleged excess of that circulation, would be to provide the means of paying for the importations of foreign produce, without causing so great an export of gold as to derange and endanger the monetary system of the country."

In reply to the charge that they had not governed their issues of notes by the foreign exchanges, they reply that such system is not applicable to the nature of a local circulation.

" Then with respect to miners and manufacturers, any system which would bring them into immediate contact with the operation of the bank for regulating the foreign exchanges, without that protection and defence from those convulsive changes which the local circulation afford, would be a system pregnant with indescribable hazard."

The Laws of the Currency with reference to the Country Banks.—These are thus stated in the article previously quoted (p. 438), in the ' Foreign and Colonial Review : '—

" It will readily occur to every reader, that the laws which regulate the circulation of these country banks must be different from those which regulate the London circulation of the Bank of England. They do not pay the public dividends ; they cannot issue their notes in purchasing bullion, or Government stock, or Exchequer bills, as all these operations take place in London, where their notes do not circulate. They are also subject to certain restrictive laws to which the notes of the Bank of England are not subject. Their notes are not only legally payable on demand, but payment is constantly demanded; while no one demands payment of a Bank of England note, unless he has occasion to export the gold. There is also a system of exchanges between country bankers, by which all notes that are paid into any of the banks are immediately brought back for payment to the banks that issued them. It is the practice, too, throughout the country, to allow interest on deposits; and thus all notes not required for the actual wants of the community are promptly withdrawn from circulation, and lodged with a bank upon interest.

" On inspecting the monthly returns of the country circulation for the last ten years, we find that the highest amount is in the month of April; thence it descends, and arrives at the lowest point by the end of August, which is the lowest point in the year. It gradually increases to November; a slight reaction takes place in December; but it then advances, until it reaches the highest point in April. The general law is, that the country circulation always makes one circuit in the year—being at its lowest point in August, and advancing to December, and continuing to advance to its highest point to the month of April, and then again descending to its lowest point in August.

" The laws which regulate the circulation of the country banks are derived from the state of trade in the respective districts in which the banks are established. As these banks are chiefly located in agricultural districts, the operations of agriculture have a very considerable influence in their regulation. Hence the advance in the spring, and the advance again after August, in consequence of the harvest. It is clear that the laws must be uniform in their operation, because the fluctuations of circulation in each year are uniform, and constantly recur with the return of the season. The slight reaction in December is probably occasioned by the collection of the public revenues and of landlords' rents in the country districts, and the general dulness of trade in that month.

" It may also be observed, that the issues of the joint-stock banks, and of the private banks, are subject to the same laws. The issues of both classes of banks rise together and fall together, and they have maintained nearly the same *relative* amount during the last seven years.

" The laws which regulate the annual fluctuations of the country circulation, that is, which determine the variations in the amounts of the country circulation, not within the year, but taking corresponding periods of different years, are also dependent on the state of trade in those years. If there be an increase of trade without an increase of prices, more notes will be required to circulate the increased quantity of commodities. If there be an increase of commodities, and also an advance of prices, a still larger amount of notes would be required. There are also other circumstances that may permanently affect the amount of the country circulation.

Principles of the Country Circulation.—I cannot better state my own views of the principles of the country circulation, than by transcribing a portion of my evidence given before the Committee on Banks of Issue, in March, 1841, when examined by Sir Robert Peel :—

" *Sir Robert Peel.*—Would you recommend that the paper thus issued should be convertible into gold at the will of the holder ?—Yes.

" You think that is an absolutely necessary check against excessive issues ?—I think it is a necessary check.

" What reference is made in the issue of paper to the quantity of gold in the country, and to the ultimate ability of the parties to discharge their paper engagements in gold ?—The bankers in issuing their notes do not make any reference to the quantity of gold in the country, but they make reference to their ability to discharge those notes when returned to them for payment.

" What is the nature of the reference which they make ?—By keeping securities available for the purpose of being sold, in order to discharge those notes whenever presented to them for payment.

" They have no reference whatever to the state of the exchanges?—No : when I say no, I mean not with the view of regulating the amount of notes by the exchanges; but bankers, whether banks of issue or not, notice the exchanges as naturally as they would notice the prices of the funds, in order that they may be able to judge as to the future value of money, so as to exercise their discretion with reference to their investments.

" They do not notice the state of the exchanges with a view to determine the policy of contracting or increasing their issues ?

—No; not with a view of making the amount of their issues correspond. If they see that the exchange is likely to become unfavourable, bankers will naturally be more cautious in making advances, and more cautious of coming under engagements, than they would be when they found that the exchanges were favourable; but there is no intention on the part of the country banks to make their notes correspond with the amount of the bullion in the Bank of England.

" A country banker would rely upon the sale of his securities, and that only in case of a demand for gold ?—In case of a general run, he would depend upon the stock he had in hand, and the further stock he might realize by a sale of securities.

" If all parties continued to issue, none of them having reference to the state of the exchanges, but relying upon the available resources which a sale of securities might supply, do not you think that there might be a danger of a sudden demand for gold, and of an inability on the part of those issuers to discharge their engagements in gold ?—I do not think there would be any danger of that at all, because each bank would take care of itself. If you suppose that the whole circulation of the country comes in at once and demands gold, it is quite clear that gold cannot be found to pay it off, and that is equally the case with the Bank of England and any other bank, and it is equally the case with us who are banks of deposits. If all the depositors were to come together at the same time and require their deposits, we should be unable to pay them, but we could realize our securities, and pay them off, if they were to come gradually.

" Suppose there was one bank which had the charge of the paper circulation of the country, and had the means, therefore, by constant reference to the state of the exchanges, of determining the amount of the paper circulation, do not you think that there would be a greater security against a sudden demand for gold, and an inability to pay that gold, than there is when there are a great many issuers, none of whom, according to your own statement, pay the slighest regard to the state of the exchanges ?—No, I think not.

" What then supplies the check ?—The check upon the private bankers is, that their circulation cannot be issued to excess; whereas if you had a bank which should issue notes for so much gold, then every time there was a favourable course of exchange, there would be a large issue of notes, which notes would necessarily reduce the rate of interest, lead to speculation, and turn the exchanges again by causing investments to be made in foreign countries. Now, as issues are at present conducted, bankers are under several checks which would not apply to such a bank. For instance, the check of the interchange with each other of their different notes once or twice a week, and the check of having their notes payable on demand; whereas the notes of such a bank as you suppose would not be diminished except when gold was wanted to be sent abroad. Another check is the practice of giving interest upon deposits, by which all the surplus circulation is called in and lodged with the banks. Now, such a bank as you have supposed would not be under the control of those checks, and it would be under the necessity of increasing the circulation whenever the exchange became favourable; and we know by experience, that the most sure way of making the exchanges unfavourable is a previous excessive issue; that previous excessive issue would necessarily arise, on the principle you have supposed, every time the exchange was favourable.

" You think that there is some cause in operation which applies equally to all issuers of paper, and prevents any undue issue of paper, and dispenses with the necessity of any reference on the part of each issuer to the state of the exchanges?—That is the case with all country issuers of paper. With regard to the Bank of England, who have the power of issuing their notes in exchange against bullion, in the purchase of Exchequer bills and Government stock, it is quite clear that notes put into operation in that way, being thrown in a mass upon the previously existing state of trade, will have the effect of raising prices and reducing interest, and turn the exchanges; but if notes are issued merely to pay for transactions that have previously taken place, and are drawn out by the operations of trade, those notes will have no such effect.

" Supposing, at present, the Bank of England observed that the exchanges continued unfavourable for a long period, and that there was a progressive diminution in the amount of their bullion, and supposing that they saw that in the course of two years their bullion was reduced from ten millions to four millions; do you think it would be desirable that the Bank of England should take any step whatever to guard against the ultimate consequences of that state of things by restricting the paper circulation?—I think such a case may occur, but I think in ordinary times the Bank of England might hold foreign securities, by which they would bring back gold to this country, and thus prevent any necessity for a contraction of the circulation. At the same time, I do not at all question the possibility of such a case occurring as may render a contraction necessary; nor do I at all question the influence of a contraction to have some effect upon the exchanges; but I contend that, as an ordinary principle of action, the bank ought not to expand their circulation, so as to cause the exchanges to be unfavourable, nor calculate upon a contraction of the circulation for the purpose of remedying the exchanges.

"Then you do think that the expansion of the circulation of the Bank of England may cause unfavourable exchanges?—Yes.

"Why should not the expansion of the circulation on the part of the country issuers produce the same effect?—Because the country circulation is under checks, whereas the Bank of England circulation is not; the country circulation can be issued only in consequence of transactions which have taken place, and to the extent only required by the wants of the district; whereas it is obvious that the Bank of England has the power of increasing the circulation by the purchase of Exchequer bills or stock, or by purchasing bullion, and throwing a mass of notes on the market when the state of trade does not require them."

"*Chairman.*—Have you any further observations to make to the committee?—When the first question was asked of me, at the commencement of my examination, I stated that I appeared before the committee as the representative of the joint-stock banks, and that, therefore, in expressing any opinions consistently with the resolutions which they had passed, I wished to be considered as speaking the sentiments of the joint-stock banks; but, should the committee ask me any question not connected with the circumstances of country issues, that I wished to be considered as speaking my own individual opinions. The points upon which I wished to be considered as speaking the sentiments of the joint-stock banks are as follows: I speak the opinions of the joint-stock banks in saying that their circulation cannot be made to fluctuate in exact conformity with the circulation of the Bank of England, or with the stock of gold in the Bank of England; that the country issue is drawn out by the demands of trade, and is subject to checks to which the circulation of the Bank of England is not liable; that the country bankers have not the power of issuing their notes to excess; that they cannot contract their circulation or expand it as they please; and also, that the country circulation does not influence the prices of commodities, and that it cannot be regulated by the principles of the foreign exchanges. I speak the opinions of the joint-stock banks when I say, that the abolition of the country circulation would cause very considerable distress; would limit the power of the country banks to grant the same accommodation to their customers; would compel many of their customers to sell their property, thus lessening the value of real property; that country bankers would be compelled to increase their charges to their customers; and, in some cases, that those banking establishments would be altogether abolished, in consequence of not being able to supply sufficient profit for carrying them on; that, in some other cases, however the country circulation might be substituted or superseded by a bill circulation, nevertheless considerable distress would exist throughout the country, and that not only country banks themselves, but their customers and the public in general, would be subject to very considerable loss and inconvenience. In other opinions which I have expressed with regard to the regulation of the currency, and the principles upon which the Bank of England ought to be managed, also, as regards the extracts which have been made from my own works, and other matters I need not particularly specify, I wish to be understood as giving my own opinions, without saying whether those opinions do or do not meet the concurrence of the joint-stock bankers. I take the responsibility of these entirely upon myself."

Notes under Five Pounds.—The most important circumstance in which the banks of Scotland and Ireland differ from those of England, is in their power to issue notes under 5*l*. That portion of our currency in England which is under 5*l*. consists of gold and silver coin. And it may, under present circumstances, be worth while to inquire—suppose we should have a protracted war, and be compelled to export our gold, either to subsidize foreign powers, or to maintain our fleets and armies abroad, what additional supply of gold could we obtain by means of issuing 1*l*. notes? I do not think we can get any certain reply to this question; but there are some inquiries that may assist our reasonings on the subject. First, we may inquire, when the Bank of England issued small notes, what proportion did the notes under 5*l*. bear to the amount of the whole circulation? That establishment issued such notes from the year 1797 to the year 1821. We find that the highest proportion was in the years 1815 and 1816. On the last day of February in those years the circulation stood thus—

	Notes under £5. £	Notes of £5 and upward. £	Total Circulation. £
1815 . . .	9,035,250	18,226,400	27,261,650
1816 . . .	9,001,400	18,012,220	27,013,620

Here we find that the notes under 5*l*. were about half the amount of those of 5*l*. and upwards. This was in 1815 and 1816, nearly forty years ago, and when the notes were issued only in London. Supposing, therefore, in round numbers, that the Bank of England circulation is now 20,000,000*l*., then in the same proportion she might maintain a circulation of 10,000,000*l*. of small notes. But we must remember that during the last forty years the population, the trade, and the wealth of the nation has vastly increased. And if pecuniary transactions were conducted in the same way, the notes in circulation must have increased in proportion. But, in consequence of the more general use of bills of exchange, the extension of banking accounts, the more frequent exchanges between country bankers, and the operations of the Clearing House in London, a smaller amount of bank notes is now necessary. All large transactions are now settled, not by notes, but by bills and cheques and transfers. But these banking facilities which diminish the demand for large notes do not in the same proportion diminish the use of small notes. On the contrary, from the great increase in the labouring population, and the consequent increased extent of retail trade, the demand for small notes to pay wages and to settle small transactions must, during the last forty years, have greatly increased. Seeing, then, that the demand for large notes has diminished, and the demand for small currency has increased, it seems reasonable to suppose, that were the Bank of England now to issue small notes, the amount in circulation would bear a higher proportion to the large notes than was the case forty years ago.

I have already stated that we have no returns of the amount of the country circulation previous to the year 1833. But we have the number of notes stamped of different denominations, and we find that in the years 1820 to 1825, the amount of notes stamped under 5*l*. varied from 37 to 50 per cent., making an average of 44 per cent. of the whole circulation. This makes the small notes nearly equal in amount to the large ones. But here again it is probable that the small notes remained out longer than the large ones. A greater proportion of the large notes were probably in the banker's till, and a larger proportion of the small notes in the hands of the public. It seems probable, therefore, that the amount of small notes in active circulation was usually higher than the amount of large notes. And if the Bank of England, whose issues were made only in London, and whose circulation was chiefly in London and Lancashire, maintained one-third of her circulation in small notes, it seems likely that the country banks, whose notes were issued in almost every town and village in the country, would maintain a much higher proportion than even one-half.

If we look to the present state of the circulation in Ireland and Scotland, we shall find that the small notes form the larger proportion, and the amount furnishes no confirmation of the doctrine that small notes diminish in wealthy countries. Scotland is a wealthier country than Ireland, yet has a larger proportion of small notes. And the north of Ireland is wealthier than the south, yet the banks of Belfast have a larger proportion of small notes than the banks of the south.

From the former circulation of the Bank of England, the stamps issued to the country bankers, and the present circulation of Scotland and Ireland, we have then materials for forming an opinion as to the amount of small notes that might be maintained in circulation in England ; and though we cannot fix the amount with that precision which the science of statistics requires, yet after putting the facts and reasonings together, we seem warranted in drawing the conclusion that the amount would not be less than thirty millions; and, consequently, we have the power, when necessary, of releasing from their present duties thirty millions of sovereigns, and employing them for national purposes elsewhere.

Suggestions on the Country Circulation.—It is not my object to examine here any of the enactments of the Act of 1844 that

2 I 2

have a reference to the Bank of England; but when the subject is brought under consideration, means should be employed to obtain some modification of those clauses that have a reference to the country banks. The country circulation should be preserved in its integrity—should be rendered capable of expansion, so as to meet the demands of a more numerous population, extended commerce, higher prices, and increased taxation—its issues should be allowed to be regulated by the demands of trade and agriculture in the respective districts in which the banks are established, and should be rendered as much as possible free from the operation of the foreign exchanges.

We find that in 1844, when the country circulation had greatly declined, we took the actual circulation of the then existing country notes, and made it a maximum circulation—an arrangement which, necessarily, from the fear of incurring penalties, reduced the amount of the actual circulation below the maximum. We apply this maximum to a circulation that fluctuates very much in different parts of the year. If, then, we keep below the maximum in April, we necessarily fall much lower in August. We divided this maximum among 277 banks, and imposed heavy penalties upon every one that shall exceed his portion of the maximum,—a circumstance that tends to reduce still farther the actual circulation. No one is forbidden to reduce his issue as low as he pleases; and if he abandons it altogether, only two-thirds can be supplied, and that by permission of the government; and then only upon the application of a bank whose head-quarters are in London, who is to get nothing by the operation, and whose issues are governed by laws which have been declared by the country bankers to be inapplicable to the operations of a local currency, and unsuitable to the requirements of domestic industry. This maximum must never be exceeded, while those banks that previously issued Bank of England notes are not allowed to resume their own circulation, and no new bank of issue is allowed to be established. The result of this arrangement has been, that an authorized issue in 1844 of 8,648,853l. is now reduced to an authorized issue of 7,942,466l., and that the actual circulation is generally below 7,000,000l., and has been below 6,000,000l.; while every banker, in certain seasons of the year, has been compelled to watch the issue of his notes, lest he incur those enormous penalties which attend even the accidental violation of the Act.

In endeavouring to remove those inconveniences, we would be governed by a regard to the spirit of the Act of 1844, and attempt only to correct its practical defects.   Among the modifications that may be suggested, perhaps the following may deserve a special consideration :—That the present maximum which applies to an average of four weeks should apply to an average of twelve months ;—that all the banks who had formed agreements with the Bank of England, and whose compensation will cease in 1856, should then be allowed to circulate their own notes to the amount to which they had circulated Bank of England notes ;—that the country circulation should not be less than the amount fixed by the Act of 1844, and that the deficiency of 706,387*l.*, which has since taken place, should be redistributed among the country banks (whether at present issuing or non-issuing), in the district in which the deficiency has taken place ;—that we adopt the enactments of Scotland and Ireland, by allowing the existing banks of issue to extend their issues beyond their fixed amount, provided they have gold, either at the head office or at any of the branches,* equal to the amount of the excess ; and as Bank of England notes are a legal tender in England, and can be converted into gold upon demand, they might in this instance be placed upon an equality with gold ;—that banks of issue be permitted to continue their fixed issue in the same locality, even should they increase their partners to a greater number than six ; and that this regulation be made retrospective, so as to include all unions of banks of issue with other banks that have taken place since the year 1844 ; and further, that we adopt the law of Scotland and Ireland, by allowing two or more banks of issue, whatever may be the number of their partners, to unite and to retain the united amount of issue of all the united banks.   With reference to the issue of notes under 5*l.*, we think that is a question for the consideration of statesmen, and its adoption must depend upon the political circumstances of the country.   As long as Australia can supply us with gold sufficient to meet our foreign

---

* The Act of 1845, in reference to Ireland, is imperfect in this respect.   The Provincial Bank of Ireland, for instance, can issue notes against gold held in Dublin, Belfast, Limerick, and Cork, but not against gold held at any of the other branches.   There seems to be no reason for this distinction.

requirements and to maintain our domestic currency, probably we had better remain as we are. At the same time it may be useful to know, that in case of necessity, we have here a magazine from which we may draw a large supply of the sinews of war.

Country Bank Exchanges.—The country bankers residing in the same neighbourhood usually make their exchanges once a-week, and pay the difference in London on the following day. This arrangement is of considerable advantage to all parties. Suppose I, as a country banker, receive in the course of a week the sum of 10,000*l.* in the notes of a neighbouring bank, and that bank receives the same amount of my notes ; if we exchange notes, there is an end of the transaction. I pay the notes that bank has upon me by the notes I have upon that bank, and each of us has 10,000*l.* less in circulation. But suppose we refuse to exchange notes with each other, then I take his notes and demand Bank of England notes and sovereigns, and he does the same with me. Hence each of us must keep a balance of 10,000*l.* more in gold or Bank of England notes, and also an additional sum to answer any sudden emergency that may arise at any time from that banker having more than the usual amount of notes, and to meet any run that he may be disposed to make upon me. Thus it is that country banks, by exchanging notes, and receiving payment of the difference in London, are enabled to carry on their business with a less amount of ready cash, and to prevent the danger that might arise from being run upon by each other. Those banks only exchange which are in the same neighbourhood. Were I to receive the notes of a bank at some distance off, I should send these notes to London, and that banker would send my notes to London, and they would be paid by our London agents. We should not exchange with each other, because it would cost more to send a messenger with the notes to be exchanged than it would cost postage to London. Here I have to pay the postage of these notes to London, and I have also to pay the expense of having my notes which have been paid in London sent down to me.

The exchange between any two banks established in the same place will be regulated by the character and extent of the business they may respectively carry on. The balance may for a considerable length of time be uniformly in favour of one of these banks, and then for a considerable period in favour of the other ; or it may fluctuate weekly, and at the year's end be found to be neither favourable nor unfavourable. I shall endeavour to investigate the causes which govern these changes. In the first place, I shall presume that each bank is a bank of deposit, of discount, of remittance, of agency, and of circulation. The claims upon each bank will then consist of—1. Cheques drawn against deposit accounts. 2. Its own notes. 3. Notes issued by its agents or other branches. 4. Letters of credit granted by agents or branches. These claims or obligations will get into the possession of the rival bank by some of the following ways :—1. As lodgments on deposit accounts. 2. In payment of local bills. 3. For bills or letters of credit on agents or branches. 4. Received for collection by post from some agents or branches. The exchanges will now be more or less favourable, according to the following circumstances :—

1. The discounting of bills not payable in the place where the banks are established has a tendency to render the exchanges unfavourable.

If, for example, a country banker discounts bills payable in London, he issues his own notes for the amount at the time the bill is discounted, and some of these notes will get into the rival bank, and render the exchanges unfavourable. When the bills are due, the London agent receives the amount from the accepters, but this has no effect on the local exchange. Hence a bank that discounts a large amount of London bills must expect to have large sums to pay in the exchanges. There are some cases, however, in which the discounting of London bills will not affect the local exchange : these are—1. When the amount of the bill is not taken in notes, but in a draft on the London or some other agents. 2. When the amount of the bill is placed to the party's current account, the exchanges will not be affected so long as it remains on that account. 3. The exchanges will not be affected, if the notes issued for the London bill should be retired either by the bank that issued them, or by any of its agents.

2. If a bank has to pay a large amount, or letters of credit issued upon it by its agents or branches, the exchanges may become unfavourable.

The exchanges between any two banks may be affected by

other circumstances than local connections. If one bank is *drawn upon* by agents or branches, or has to pay notes issued by agents or branches, and the other has no such connections, then the exchange will be unfavourable to the former bank and favourable to the latter. Some of these notes or letters of credit, and some of the notes issued for the letters of credit, will probably get into the possession of the rival bank, and appear in the exchange.

3. If a bank issues a large amount of bills, or letters of credit upon its agents or branches, the tendency is to render the exchange favourable.

The bank receives the money for these bills or letters at the time it issues them. This money will often be composed of the notes chiefly in circulation, and a part of them will consist of the notes or obligations of the rival bank, and will be paid in the exchange : or if the bank receive from its agents or branches any claims upon the rival bank, or even any bills to be collected, the effect will be to render the exchange favourable in the same way as the granting letters of credit upon those agents or branches.

4. The increase of lodgments on current accounts has a tendency to render the exchanges favourable.

On these accounts money is received and money is paid out daily. The receipts of money tend to throw the exchange in favour of a bank, because some portion of these receipts will consist of the obligations of the rival bank. The payment of money tends to render the exchange unfavourable, because some of the notes issued in payment will find their way into the other bank. When, therefore, the receipts are more in amount than the payments, the exchanges are likely to be favourable. When the total deposits lodged in a bank continue to increase, the exchange will probably be favourable *during the progress of* such increase; but after the deposits have ceased to increase, the exchange will not be more favourable than before the increase began. As long as the amounts of the deposits in the respective banks remain stationary, the operations on those accounts will not affect the exchanges, although the deposits in one bank may be twice the amount of those in the other. But if, from a transfer of accounts or from other causes, the deposits increase in one bank and diminish in the other, the exchanges during these operations will be in favour of the bank whose deposits are on the increase. But let the progress of increase be over, and the amounts of the respective lodgments become permanently fixed, then, as far as the operations on the current accounts are concerned, the exchanges will again be equal.

5. An increase in the amount of local bills under discount has a tendency to render the exchanges unfavourable. Local bills are bills payable in the place where the bank is established. The operations on the local bill account are similar to those on the deposit account. When these bills are discounted, notes are issued—when the bills are paid, notes are received. When the amount of local bills paid is greater than that discounted, the tendency is to render the exchanges favourable. Thus, to reduce the amount of local bills under discount is to render the exchanges favourable; and to increase the amount, is to render them the reverse. But though the operations on the local bill account are similar in their nature to those on the current accounts, yet the effect is different as to their influence on the exchanges. For as the amount of the local bills under discount increases, the exchanges become unfavourable; but as the deposits increase, the exchanges become advantageous. In the increase of local bills, the issue of notes will be more than the receipts; but in the increase of the deposits, the receipts will be more than the issues.

As the laws of the country circulation are the same, whether the notes are issued by private or by joint-stock banks, I have introduced the subject into this section.

SECTION V.

THE SCOTCH BANKS.

In this Section we shall consider the following topics :—

   I. The Law of Scotland with reference to Banking.

   II. A Comparison between the Banks of Scotland and those of England.

   III. The Laws of the Currency with reference to Scotland.

   IV. Those operations of the Scotch Banks that refer to the system of Cash Credits, Interest on Deposits, Remittances to India, and the settlement of the Exchanges.

I.—*The Law of Scotland with reference to Banking.*

The general provisions of the law of Scotland bearing upon this subject are calculated to promote the solidity of banking establishments.

1. There is no limitation to the *number* of partners.
2. The *private fortune* of every partner is answerable for the debts of the bank.
3. *Land*, as well as other property, *may be attached* for debt.
4. In Scotland *all Land is registered;* so it is easy for any individual, by referring to the records, to ascertain what landed property is possessed by the partners of the bank, and also whether or not it be mortgaged. The following is the language of the Report of the Committee of the House of Commons, appointed in 1826 to consider the expediency of abolishing all notes under 5*l.* :—

" There is no limitation upon the number of partners of which a banking company may consist; and, excepting in the case of the Bank of Scotland, and the two chartered banks, which have very considerable capitals, the partners of all banking companies are bound jointly and severally, so that each partner is liable to the whole extent of his fortune for the whole debts of the company.

" A creditor in Scotland is empowered to attach the real and portable, as well as the personal estate of his debtor, for payment of personal debts, among which may be classed debts due by bills and promissory notes; and recourse may be had for the procuring payment to each description of property at the same time. Execution is not confined to the real property of a debtor merely during his life, but proceeds with equal effect upon that property after his decease.

" The law relating to the establishment of records gives ready means of procuring information with respect to the real and heritable estate of which any person in Scotland may be possessed. No purchase of an estate in that country is secure until the seisine (that is, the instrument certifying that actual delivery has been given) is put on record; nor is any mortgage effectual until the deed is in like manner recorded.

" In the case of conflicting pecuniary claims upon real property, the preference is not regulated by the date of the transaction, but by the date of its record. These records are accessible to all persons; and thus the public can with ease ascertain the effective means which a banking company possesses of discharging its obligations, and the partners in that company are enabled to determine with tolerable accuracy the degree of risk and responsibility to which the private property of each is exposed.

" There are other provisions of the law of Scotland which it is not necessary minutely to detail, the general tendency of which is the same with those above mentioned."

The following Acts of Parliament have been passed in reference to banking in Scotland :—

" The first notice of banking in Scotland which occurs in the statute-book, is an Act of King William the Third, passed in the year 1695, under which the Bank of Scotland was established. By this Act an exclusive privilege of banking was conferred upon that bank, it being provided, ' that for the period of twenty years from the 17th July, 1695, it should not be lawful for any other person to set up a distinct company or bank within the kingdom of Scotland, besides those persons in whose favour this Act was granted.' No renewal of the exclusive privilege took place after the expiration of the twenty-one years.

" The Bank of Scotland first issued notes of 20*s.* in the year 1704; but the amount of notes in circulation previous to the Union was very limited.

" The Bank of Scotland continued the only bank from the date of its establishment in 1695, to the year 1727.

" In that year a charter of incorporation was granted to certain individuals named therein, for carrying on the business of banking under the name of the Royal Bank; and subsequent charters were granted to this establishment, enlarging the capital, which now amounts to one million and a half.

" An Act passed in the year 1765, is the first and most important Act of the Legislature which regulates the issue of promissory notes in Scotland.

" It appears from its preamble, that a practice had prevailed in Scotland of issuing notes which circulated as specie, and which were made payable to the bearer on demand, or payable at the option of the issuer at the end of six months, with a sum equal to the legal interest from the demand to that time.

" The Act of 1765 prohibits the issue of notes in which such an option as that beforementioned is reserved to the issuer. It requires that all notes of the nature of a bank note, and circulating like specie, should be paid on demand; and prohibits the issue of any promissory note of a sum less than 20*s.*

" With respect to the issue of promissory notes in England, an Act was passed in 1775, prohibiting the issue of any such notes under the sum of 20*s.* And in the year 1777, restraints were imposed by law on the issue of notes between the sum of 20*s.* and 5*l.*, which were equivalent to the prohibition of such notes circulating as specie.

" In the year 1797, when the restrictions as to payments in cash were imposed upon the Bank of England, the provisions of the Act of 1777, with regard to the issue of notes between 20*s.* and 5*l.*, were suspended. By an Act passed in the third year of his present Majesty, the suspension was continued until the 5th of January, 1833; but now stands limited, by an Act of the present session, to April 5, 1829."

" The general result of the laws regulating the paper currency in the two countries is this :—

" That in Scotland, the issue of promissory notes payable to bearer on demand for a sum of not less than 20*s.* has been at all times permitted by law, nor has any Act been passed limiting the period for which such issue shall continue legal in that country. In England, the issue of promissory notes for a less sum than 5*l.* was prohibited by law from the year 1772 to the period of the bank restriction in 1797. It has been permitted since 1797; and the permission will cease, as the law at present stands, in April, 1829."

The Act which now regulates the issue of bank notes in Scotland is 8 & 9 Vict. c. 38, passed in the year 1845.

By this Act, the power of issuing notes is confined to those banks that issued notes in the year preceding the 1st day of May, 1845. And the amount to which each bank may issue is not to exceed the average amount of notes it had in circulation during the year ending the 1st of May, 1845, and the amount of gold or silver coin it may at the time have in possession at the head office or principal place of issue, in the proportion that the silver shall not be more than one-fourth the amount of the gold.

This Act was to come into operation on the 6th day of December, 1845. After which day each banker is to make weekly returns to the Stamp Office of his notes in circulation, and of the gold and silver coin on hand; and the averages of four weeks are to be published in the *London Gazette*, with a certificate from the commissioner as to whether the bank has held the amount of coin required by this Act.

All banks, except the Bank of Scotland, the Royal Bank of Scotland, and the British Linen Company, are required to send to the Stamp Office, between the 1st and 15th days of January, inclusive, the names of all their partners, which shall be published by the 1st day of March following, in some newspaper circulating within each town or county respectively in which the head office or principal place of issue of such bank is situated.

Bank of England notes are not to be a legal tender in Scotland.

In the Acts of Parliament passed in 1844 and 1845 for Regulating Banks of Issue in England and in Scotland, we may observe the following differences :—

1. The maximum of the circulation in England is the average of the twelve weeks ending the 27th of April, 1844. The maximum in Scotland is the average of the year ending the 1st day of May, 1845.

2. The English banks are not, under any circumstances,

allowed to exceed the fixed limit. The Scotch banks are allowed to exceed their limit, provided they hold in their coffers at the head office an amount of gold and silver equal to such excess.

3. In England, should two joint-stock banks of issue effect a junction, the circulation of one of them would be forfeited,* and the united bank could issue only to the amount which the other bank had previously issued. In Scotland, the united bank is allowed to issue to the amount of the two circulations added together.

4. In Scotland, notes under 5*l.* are still permitted. In England, notes under 5*l.* are still prohibited.

II.—*A Comparison between the Banks of Scotland and those of England.*

The differences between the English and the Scotch banks are the following :—

1. The Scotch banks are all joint-stock banks. In England there is a mixture of joint-stock and private banks.

2. The Scotch banks are nearly all banks of issue. In England there are many, both private and joint-stock banks, that are not banks of issue.

3. The Scotch banks generally have branches. · In England most of the private banks, and some of the joint-stock banks, have no branches.

4. The Scotch banks universally grant interest on the balance of current accounts—a practice not universally adopted in England, especially in London.

5. The mode of making advances by way of " cash credit " is general in Scotland, but exceptional in England.

We may also observe some other differences, chiefly of a business character, which have an important bearing on the interest of the community.

---

* There is no express provision in the English Act with reference to the junction of two joint-stock banks. We consider that only one of the banks would lose its issue, *provided* the continuing bank retained its original title, so as not to create a new bank. But if by the union a new bank should be formed, then both the banks would lose their issues. In the same way, we think that the union of an issuing and a non-issuing bank would cause no change in the issue. But then the new bank must retain the title of the old issuing bank. Its right of issue would not be affected by taking new directors or new shareholders.

1. The banks of Scotland have generally a large paid-up capital.

"Two great errors appear to have been committed in the formation of joint-stock banks in England, and, until these are remedied, such establishments can hardly expect to reach a higher degree of importance or credit than is attainable by a wealthy private bank. These evils are, in the first place, too small a capital relatively to the extent of business undertaken; and, in the next place, the circumstance of the issues of the joint-stock banks being left uncontrolled by any effective system of *exchange*.

"The advantage of a small capital in banking is, that it enables the establishment, if at all successful in business, to pay a large dividend. The profits of banking depend, in a great measure, on the amount of deposits and circulation, and, according as these are great or small compared with the extent of the capital, will the company be enabled to divide a larger or smaller dividend. It therefore becomes the obvious policy of those establishments, the managers of which conceive that the success of a bank is proved by the early payment of a high dividend, to keep the capital of the company within the narrowest possible limits. This system has been carried to the utmost extreme in England; and hence, although large dividends have been paid to the shareholders, there has been no corresponding increase of confidence on the part of the public.

"The Scotch banks, on the other hand, have pursued a directly opposite course. Their object has been to secure public confidence by the extent of their capital, and they have continued to pay moderate dividends to their shareholders, until justified in augmenting them by years of success, and a large accumulated sinking-fund. So well, indeed, is this system understood, and so completely has it attained its purposes, that the slightest appearance of improvidence displayed by a Scotch joint-stock bank, in fixing the amount of its dividend, has been invariably attended with a decrease of the public confidence in the stock of the establishment. In this manner public confidence has been secured, the value of Scotch bank stock has risen in the market, and the shareholders have received their extra profits as a *bonus*, or in the increased value of their own shares. Thus, instead of being looked upon as establishments aiming at the ephemeral advantage of making a large dividend, for stock-jobbing or temporary purposes, our banks have almost invariably assumed the character of permanent national establishments, identified with the prosperity of the country, and, by means of their small-note circulation, conferring benefit on, as well as obtaining the confidence of, every class in the community."*

2. In operating on his current account, it is not the general

* Letter to James William Gilbart, Esq., on the Relative Merits of the English and Scotch Banking Systems; with Practical Suggestions for the Consolidation of the English Joint-stock Banking Interest. By Robert Bell. Mr. Bell, the manager of the City of Glasgow Bank, at Edinburgh, was examined in 1848, as a witness before the Committee of the House of Commons on Commercial Distress. He died in 1854.

practice in Scotland for a customer to draw cheques * on the bank for his individual payments, nor to accept bills payable at the bank. If he has to make twenty payments in the course of the day, he will go to the bank in the morning, and draw out in one sum a sufficient amount of notes to make all these payments. On the other hand, if a customer should receive money from twenty different people in the course of the day, he will not receive cheques, as there are none in circulation, but bank notes, which at the close of the day he will pay in one sum into the bank. In England, all these receipts and payments would be made in cheques, each having probably odd shillings and pence. From this cause, the trouble and expense to a bank of conducting a current account is much greater in England than in Scotland.

3. The system of numerous branches leads to uniformity all over Scotland in the terms on which business is transacted in the banks.

From the small number of banks that existed for many years in Scotland, and from the circumstance that the head offices of most of these banks were fixed at Edinburgh, it was easy for them to form arrangements among themselves for the regulation of their business. Hence arose a uniformity of practice among all the banks, and throughout the whole of Scotland.

This uniformity does not exist in England. The system of London banking is different from that in the country. And the banking of one district differs from that of another district. It would be difficult to produce any general union in England, even among the joint-stock banks. There is a difference in the character of their localities. Their head offices are too wide apart to admit of frequent personal communication. And it may be feared that among the joint-stock banks of England there is not enough of that *esprit du corps* which is essential to the existence of a general confederation.

There is, however, considerable competition among the banks of Scotland. This rivalry, however, does not lead to transacting business on lower terms.† Indeed, these terms are always very

* This custom is very much modified now-a-days—the English system of cheques being more common, and a daily clearing instituted.—EDITOR.

† The banks have entered upon an agreement to maintain a uniform scale of charges for commission, exchange, &c., and meet from time to time to settle the rates of discount and interest—these being regulated by the rise and fall in the Bank of England rates.—EDITOR.

moderate. The difference between the rate of interest allowed and charged is rarely more than one per cent. No commission is charged on current accounts; and it is only recently, we believe, that commission has been charged on the amount (not the operations) of cash credits. Sometimes the banks at Glasgow, when there is a great demand for capital, have been disposed to grant a higher rate of interest than the banks of Edinburgh; but this difference has soon been arranged. The provincial banks, too, have carried on a strong opposition against the branches of the Edinburgh banks. The late Thomas Kinnear, Esq., when asked what had led to the discontinuing of some branches of the Bank of Scotland, replied:—

"With respect to those that are beyond my memory, I cannot say what was the cause; but those that have been given up within my recollection, in point of fact were given up in consequence of the town in which that branch had originally been established having accumulated wealth to such a degree that it could afford a banking capital of its own, and that it had in point of fact established a local bank; then the connection of that local bank went so strongly against us by fair competition, that we found we could employ our capital to better purpose elsewhere, and gave up the branch." *

4. The system of numerous branches enables the banks of Scotland to transfer the surplus capital of the agricultural districts to the manufacturing and commercial districts, without going through the process of rediscounting their bills.

Some Scotch writers have considered it a reproach to the English banks that they rediscount their bills, and have boasted that, with rare exceptions, the practice of rediscount is unknown in Scotland. The accusation is made without due consideration. The system of branches makes a difference in all banking arrangements. A bank in an agricultural district, say at Norwich, has a superabundance of money. A manufacturing town, say Manchester, has a demand for money. The bank at Norwich will send its money to a bill-broker in London. The bank at Manchester will send its bills to the same broker. A rediscount takes place. But let us suppose that the bill-brokering establishment should become the head office of a large bank, having one branch at Norwich and another at Manchester. Then no rediscount will occur. The bills discounted at Manchester will never pass out of the possession of the bank. Nevertheless, the surplus funds at Norwich will be transferred to meet the wants

* Commons, 132, Kinnear.

of Manchester as effectually as before. This is an illustration of the branch system in Scotland. A bank at Edinburgh will have branches in both the agricultural and the manufacturing districts. Or a bank whose head office is in a manufacturing town, will have branches in the agricultural districts. Thus the surplus funds of Perth, Ayr, and Dumfries are speedily transferred to be employed at Glasgow, Paisley, and Dundee. Were a bank to be established at Glasgow without branches, it would probably have occasion for discount at certain times, as well as the banks at Manchester or Leeds.

At the same time, we think this transfer of capital by means of branches is better than by means of rediscount. There is no occasion for the intermediate party, the bill-broker. The bills do not go out of the bank, so that men's transactions do not become known. The abuses connected with rediscount by fictitious bills are effectually prevented, and the bank can more readily regulate its advances in accordance with its means. To recur to our illustration:—The bank at Norwich may lose a large amount of its deposits; the bank at Manchester, knowing nothing of this, may continue its advances in dependence upon receiving its usual rediscount. The check may at length come so suddenly that the Manchester bank may be placed in difficulty. Under the branch system, should any large amount of deposits be withdrawn from one branch, the bank would immediately limit its advances at the others. The advantage of this system on the approach of a pressure is obvious.

5. The system of numerous branches leads to more regularity and uniformity in the mode of making their exchanges.

The Scotch bankers are loud in their praises of the system of exchanges.* And justly so. But they are in error when they suppose that nothing like it exists in England. We have shown that the country banks make their exchanges with each other, and pay the difference by a draft on London. These operations· have the same effect as the exchanges in Scotland of withdrawing from circulation all the superfluous notes; that is to say, all the notes that come into the hands of the bankers. If it be true that notes remain out longer in circulation in England than in Scotland, it arises not from any difference in the system of exchanges, but from a difference in the habits of the people with

* The rules have been remodelled since Mr. Gilbart's time : they will be found at the end of this section.—EDITOR.

2 K

regard to " keeping a banker." If a Scotch banker issue 1,000*l.* of notes in the morning, he feels assured that these notes will be paid into some other bank in the course of the day. An English banker is not so sure. The party may not " keep a banker," and he may then lock up the notes in a strong box for a week or ten days, until he have occasion to make a payment. We think it desirable that every man who has money should lodge it in a bank, not merely for interest, but for security, and therefore we approve of the Scotch practice. But it is this universal practice of having a banker, and not merely the system of exchanges, that withdraws notes so rapidly from circulation.

At the same time, it should be stated that the Scotch bankers are of opinion that our system of banking in England is chargeable with some portion of the blame. They say that as the English banks do not universally allow interest on deposits and current accounts, the people have not the same inducement as in Scotland for placing their money in a bank. And as many banks charge commission on the operations of a current account, it is the interest even of those who keep bankers to pay away the notes they receive to other parties, rather than to lodge them to their credit with their banker. On this subject I may quote the following extract from a second letter addressed to me by Mr. Bell :*—

" In Scotland we have adopted every means to concentrate the resources of the country in the hands of the banker. We allow a liberal rate of interest on deposits, while we not only encourage small capitalists and traders to open accounts with us, but we induce our customers to make frequent operations on their accounts, and the result is that every superfluous bank note is rapidly returned upon the issuer. The very opposite course is pursued in England. You allow no interest on deposits, you give no encouragement to small depositors, while you put a barrier in the way of your customers making frequent operations, by the charging a commission on the debit side of their accounts; the consequence of which is, that not only your paper, but your gold currency, stagnates in the hands of the public during times of prosperity, leaving the paper issues to be poured back upon the issuers in seasons of adversity, thus aggravating in no slight degree the severity of monetary pressures."

Even were the keeping of a banker as general in England as in Scotland, the same system of exchanges could not be adopted. The Scotch system requires,—an equality, or an approach to it,

---

* A Letter to J. W. Gilbart, Esq., on the Regulation of the Currency by the Foreign Exchanges, and on the Appointment of the Bank of England to be the sole Bank of Issue throughout Great Britain. By Robert Bell.

among the several banks—that the head offices of these banks, generally, should be in the capital,—and that the banks should have numerous branches throughout the country. These circumstances do not exist in England. And, moreover, we have the Bank of England, whose notes are a legal tender. It is obvious there can be no exchange of notes in places where, as in London, there is only one bank of issue. But the exchanges between English country banks are precisely upon the same principle as those in Scotland, and have similar effects. The differences are paid by drafts on London, payable on demand, and these drafts again pass through the clearing.

Another advantage ascribed to the Scotch system of exchanges is, the surveillance which, by this means, the large banks at Edinburgh are able to exercise over the smaller banks in the provinces. That this surveillance exists in Scotland, and that it has been exercised beneficially, we entertain no doubt. It is equally true that such a surveillance does not exist in England. But the system of exchanges is not the cause of this surveillance, it is merely the instrument. In Scotland, the banks being few, and all their head offices being at Edinburgh, they are able to confer together, and to fix on rules for their general government. With any inferior bank that refuses to comply with these rules they can refuse to exchange notes, and thus force it to compliance. In England, where the banks are numerous, and where their head offices are distant from each other, such a system cannot well be formed; and hence each bank is free from the control of other banks, and may pursue any course it pleases, however injurious to itself or to others, so long as it is able to make good its payments to the public. The banks at Edinburgh, too, by means of their numerous branches, have the earliest information of any irregular practice that may have been adopted by a local bank in the provinces;—but the large banks in London have comparatively but a very imperfect knowledge of the operations of either the private or the joint-stock banks that are scattered over the country.

From a want of this surveillance, banks in England have carried on business for years after they have been supposed to be insolvent. Hence they have gone on until their losses have not only absorbed the whole of their capital, but have required to replace them further demands to a large amount from their shareholders. In Scotland, these banks, if they could not be kept in the right path, would probably have been compelled to stop before they had wandered so widely.   Banks, as we have seen, do sometimes fail in Scotland, but never under circumstances that shake the public confidence in the general banking institutions of the country.

6. The confidence placed in the banks of Scotland by the public renders them less exposed to inconvenience during a season of pressure.

When a pressure takes place in England, the first objects of suspicion are the banks.   People that have money in their banker's hands draw it out, and hoard it.   The bankers, knowing that they are liable to these demands, draw in their funds, and make provision accordingly.   Hence the capital of the country is rendered dormant at the time when it is most required to be in a state of activity.   Banks that issue notes are more liable than others to these sudden demands.   But no such feeling exists at present in Scotland.   And should the Act of 1845 have the effect of inoculating the people with the love of gold, and by this means place the banks in the same position during a pressure as the banks of England, it must be regarded as a national calamity.

On this subject we again quote from the letter of Mr. Bell :—

" Nor are these benefits, great as they are, the only advantages which we have derived from our system of banking.   Our one-pound notes connect and familiarize every artizan and labourer in the country with our banking establishments; and the implicit confidence in our paper currency thus created, and perpetuated by the general experience of the sufficiency of our banks, has on many occasions been remarkably illustrated. It is no exaggeration to say, that at this moment nine-tenths of the labouring classes of Scotland, if they had their choice, would *prefer* a one-pound note to a sovereign; and, as a consequence of this feeling of security, combined with a sense of the other advantages of the system, no one in Scotland can have forgotten the truly national stand, on behalf of our currency, which was made by rich and poor in the year 1825, when your English economists proposed to visit us with an injury similar to that which was in that year inflicted on England.

" With banking establishments thus pre-eminently possessed of national confidence, no mercantile convulsion has hitherto created any general run on our great joint-stock banks.   It has been otherwise in England, where, in consequence of legislative enactments, the public have been taught to regard *gold and silver* as the only representatives of value.   The bond of union between the banks and the mass of the people has thus been severed; and when a monetary crisis occurs, its consequences are incalculably more injurious.   With us (though very rarely), runs have been occasionally made on particular banks; but it has been merely to withdraw a deposit from one bank to place it in another; or to exchange the notes of a suspected bank for the *notes* of one of our national joint-stock banks, the prevailing confidence in our paper currency remaining unshaken. In this way the disposable banking capital or resources remain in the aggregate unchanged; whereas with you the run is for *gold*; and the coin thus withdrawn from one bank is not redeposited in another, but hoarded till the panic is over, by which means the entire banking resources of the country are involved in the consequences of the temporary disaster; and this, too, at the very time when these resources are most needed."

III.—*Laws of the Currency in Scotland.*

In Scotland the lowest point of the circulation is in March, and the highest in November. The advance, however, between these two points is not uniform—for the highest of the intervening months is May, after which there is a slight reaction; but it increases again until November, and falls off in December. The reason of the great increase in May and November is, that these are the seasons for making payments. The interest due on mortgages is then settled, annuities are then paid, the country people usually take the interest on their deposit receipts, and the servants receive their wages. There are frequently large sums transferred by way of mortgage. It is the custom of Scotland to settle all transactions, large as well as small, by bank notes—not by cheques on bankers as in London. It is remarkable that these monthly variations occur uniformly every year, while the amount of the circulation in the corresponding months of different years undergoes comparatively little change.

The circulation of Scotland is at its lowest point in the mouth of March, is higher in July, and reaches its highest point in November. In the corresponding months of different years there is but little deviation in the amount of the circulation. These facts prove that the circulation of Scotland does not produce any effect upon prices, nor, consequently, upon the foreign exchanges. It is hardly necessary to adduce evidence in proof of the fact, that the prices of commodities do not go on increasing from March to November in every year; and if they do not, they cannot be regulated by the currency. This regularity in the circulation shows that it must be governed by some uniform laws, arising from the local circumstances or habits of the country; and this, we think, will always be the case where the banks are passive, and permit themselves to be operated upon by the wants of the trade and commerce carried on in their respective districts.

Though the Act of 1845 does not appear to have had much effect on the laws of the currency, it has had an effect in other ways. It has required the Scotch banks to keep a larger amount of gold in their vaults.

It has also had the effect of inducing the banks to increase their charges, and to decline granting cash credits. The banks are required to keep in their coffers a larger amount of gold. This increased amount yields no interest, and hence to that extent the Act diminishes their profits. To make up the same amount of profit as heretofore, the charges for discounts and advances are increased. This illustrates a principle that we think will always be found correct, that *restrictions upon banks are taxes upon the public.* This principle is not sufficiently obvious to statesmen, nor even to the public, in England; the mercantile classes have been pleased, rather than otherwise, when laws have been passed injurious to bankers. In Scotland such matters are better understood. The commercial classes have always rallied round the banks; they have had the sagacity to perceive the truth of the principle we have advanced; they know that capital employed in banking must be made to produce an average profit; and if the Legislature causes one branch of business to be less productive, the bankers must make other branches more productive, in order to render capital employed in banking as profitable as it would be if employed in other occupations. But the Act of 1845 not only increased the charge; it led to a limitation of accommodation. There is no one point on which Scotchmen, of all classes, are more unanimous in opinion, than on the advantages that have arisen to their country from the system of cash credits. This system can exist only with a note circulation. One of its objects on the part of the banker is to increase his circulation. But he has no profit by increasing his circulation of notes, if he must keep in his coffers an additional amount of gold equal to that increase. But gold is the idol of our currency theory. The cash credit system, therefore, with all the virtues it produced, has been offered up in sacrifice to this "golden calf."

The Act has, however, not been successful in imparting to the people of Scotland a taste for gold. The bankers are too wise to issue the gold, unless when it is demanded; and the public

are too wise to make such a demand. Hence, when the increase
of the currency requires a further importation, the gold is quietly
brought from London to Edinburgh, is quietly locked up in the
vaults of the bank, and, when no longer required, as quietly
sent back again. Of course this is a loss to the banks of issue,
but in this way it is less injurious than if put into circulation.
Disastrous for Scotland will be the day when the people shall
become inoculated with the love of a gold currency. The effect
of such a desire in England is strikingly exhibited in seasons of
pressure. When such pressures occur in Scotland, the banks,
unlike those of England, can employ their whole resources to
assist their customers, and to support public credit.

Among the theories on the currency was a notion of establishing one bank of issue for the United Kingdom. The following evidence on this subject was given by Mr. Kennedy, the
manager of the Ayrshire Bank, before the Committee on Banks
of Issue, in 1841 :—

" Do you think the establishment of a single bank of issue for the United
Kingdom would be advantageous or otherwise to Scotland ? . . . . " I
conceive that it must be very destructive to Scotland."

" In what way ?" . . . . " It is perfectly clear that it would overturn
the present system of banking in Scotland. Our system of banking is
based upon the power that our currency gives us to allow a high rate of
deposit interest. If you take from us the profit that our currency yields,
we must make our profit from some other source ; we must increase the
charges to the community, and allow less interest, or probably no interest
at all, and our system will be totally changed."

Another favourite notion has been the abolition of all notes
under 5*l.* A Committee of the House of Lords and a Committee of the House of Commons made reports on this subject
in the year 1826. The evidence produced by the Scotch
bankers was so overwhelming, that both the committees
recommended the postponement of the measure. Robert Paul,
Esq., secretary to the Commercial Bank of Scotland, stated
to the Committee of the House of Lords that the following would
be the effects of the abolition of the small notes : *—

" We should diminish the number of our branches, because we should
be involved in an expense in the transmission of gold, which the profits
arising out of our branches could never compensate ; they are not the
most profitable part of our business ; they are attended with a great many
hazards and disadvantages.

" We should withdraw our cash accounts, because they could no longer

* Lords' Report, p. 204.

accomplish the end for which they were granted, which was the maintaining our circulation, especially of our small notes.

" We should diminish the interest of our deposit accounts, because we should then be required to keep a very large amount of dead stock of gold in our coffers, to meet the constant variations that would arise, and to keep it wholly unproductive. I imagine that if a gold currency were substituted for a small-note currency, there would be a much greater amount of gold required than there is at present of notes. We have at present, in order to meet the constant variations, a large amount of notes constantly on hand, and in the same way we should require a stock of gold, and that would be proportionably larger as the general circulation would be greater."*

The following letter, written by an agent at Inverary, to Roger Aytoun, Esq., manager of the Renfrewshire Bank at Greenock, states the inconveniences which the writer apprehends would result from the introduction of a metallic currency into that part of Scotland :—

" With regard to the proposed measure of suppressing bank notes in Scotland for less than 5*l.*, I think it would be ruinous to this country; for I cannot see how, if it takes place, the business of the country can be carried on. Confining myself to some of the most prominent instances in which the Highlands will be affected, I shall state the difficulties that occur to me. Our produce chiefly consists of cattle and sheep, grain, wood, kelp, and the production of the fisheries. Cattle are brought to the country markets by the breeders, chiefly small farmers, every man attending his own, and having generally from one to three young animals for sale. There they are met by the dealers and graziers, who purchase such of the beasts as suit them; and it is seldom that a single animal, at the age of one or two years, being the ages at which they sell them to the dealers and graziers, comes to the price of 5*l.*; the price is more frequently from 2*l.* to 4*l.* Of these a dealer often purchases two or three hundreds in single beasts, so that he has more than 1*l.* and less than 5*l.* to pay to each of as many sellers; but he has no notes under 5*l.*, and the sellers are not able to return balance in any coin. This will occur to many dealers at every market; and how is the difficulty to be removed? The dealers must all come loaded with gold and silver, and this they cannot carry to the necessary amount; and besides, they will not be supplied by banks with gold and silver for their bills, by which there would be no profit. The means of paying being wanting the seller will not deliver, and the object of the parties is frustrated; and thus a difficulty is cast in the way of disposing of this material article of Highland produce, which must discourage the sales, and occasion a reduction of price, and consequently of the rent and value of land.

" It is the same in the case of grain, of which bear or barley is what is chiefly sold by small farmers to the distilleries. In settling for some bolls, bought in small quantities of two or three bolls, 5*l.* notes will be

* Lords' Report, p. 132.

found most inconvenient ; and the purchasers and manufacturers of wood and bark, and of seaweed for kelp, who require many hands, and pay off their workers generally once in the month, none of whom will draw so small a sum as 1*l*., nor so large a sum as 5*l*., will experience the same difficulty.

" The herring fishery on our coasts employs several thousand men, and is of very great importance. Instances have occurred of herrings being taken in Lochfine alone to the value of 40,000*l*. in one season, and a thousand boats are generally employed there in the fishing. The fishermen every morning sell their fish to the curers on shore, receive their money, and set out in quest of more. The value of each boat's fishing for a night sometimes exceeds 5*l*., but generally is under it; and there are, in this fishing station alone, a thousand boats to be paid off every morning, of whom most probably two-thirds have to receive less than 5*l*. each. It will be impossible to provide gold and silver sufficient for such a purpose ; and in the remote parts of the North Highlands, where the fishery is much more extensive, and banks at a greater distance, the difficulty is insuperable.

"At present the business of the Highlands is transacted by means of bank notes of 1*l*. and 1*l*. 1*s*., with some larger notes on occasions, and that with the greatest facility. Cattle dealers, and all others having to pay away money to any amount in small sums to a number of people, as in the instances mentioned, prepare themselves by a mixture of notes, some large and some small, accompanied by a few pounds of silver, and everything goes on well. These notes are preferred by the country people before gold, both because they are unable to distinguish between the genuine and base metal, and because these coins are more liable to be lost from their pockets than notes; and they have no reason to repent their confidence in the stability of these banks, whose notes they have been accustomed to receive for so many years in their transactions. But if small notes are superseded, and gold substituted, it is not easy to see how the supply of gold is to be kept up to carry on the business and transactions of this country. Should a quantity of it be received into the circulation, it would not remain long, but find its way into the banks, who will not again give it out in bills as they do their notes, and it will immediately become a scarce article in the country. A person, then, having to pay in small sums, will on every such occasion be obliged to send his large notes to the bank that issued them, perhaps a hundred miles off, to receive gold and silver in their place, to answer his purpose. The conveyance of it to him is next to be provided for. The weight may be too much for the post. There are no mail coaches ; and he must either employ a carrier, moving too slowly for his occasions, or be at the expense of sending a trusty person for the treasure.

" In transmitting money from one part of the country to another, the same difficulty will often present itself. Suppose a person in the Western Isles has to pay 19*l*. to one on the Continent. At present this may be conveniently done by three notes of 5*l*. and four of 1*l*. enclosed by post; but when there shall be no 1*l*. notes, the odd 4*l*. must be sent in gold or silver, not conveniently carried in a post letter, and requiring that a person be employed for the purpose, and at some expense.

"Many other such difficulties and inconveniences will occur. These presented themselves to me, and I stated them hastily, without regard to order. If you find anything in them useful for the purpose, I shall be pleased. But it appears extremely hard that the Scotch system should be disturbed, and that we should be obliged to adopt one not only unsuitable to our purposes, but ruinous to the business of our country."

IV. *Those Operations of the Scotch Banks that refer to Cash Credits, Deposits, Remittances to India, and the Settlement of the Exchanges.*

Cash Credits.—A cash credit is an undertaking on the part of the bank to advance to an individual such sums of money as he may from time to time require, not exceeding in the whole a certain definite amount ; the individual to whom the credit is given entering into a bond with securities, generally two in number, for the repayment on demand of the sums actually advanced, with interest upon each issue from the day upon which it is made.

Cash credits are rarely given for sums below 100*l.* ; they generally range from 200*l.* to 500*l.*, sometimes reaching 1,000*l.*, and occasionally a larger sum.

A cash credit is, in fact, the same thing as an overdrawn current account, except that in a current account the party overdraws on his own individual security, and in the cash credit he finds two sureties who are responsible for him. Another difference is, that a person cannot overdraw his current account, without requesting permission each time from the bank ; whereas the overdrawing of a cash credit is a regular matter of business,—it is, in fact, the very thing for which the cash credit has been granted. The following advantages have been ascribed to the cash credit system :—

1. Cash credits enable young men of good character to acquire wealth and respectability.

"I have known many instances of young men who were starting in the world from low situations—of servants, who have conducted themselves well during the time they were apprentices—of farm-servants even, who were able to procure an account from a bank by means of some friends or acquaintances becoming their securities—that in the course of their business have raised themselves by becoming farmers of considerable extent, or manufacturers in a way highly creditable to themselves and beneficial to their country.*

* This and the following quotations are taken from the evidence given by the witnesses from Scotland, before the Committees of Lords and Commons, appointed to consider the expediency of abolishing the notes under 5*l.* in 1826.

" Without cash credits, sober, attentive, and industrious people would not have the means at all of following up what they very deservedly might be encouraged to follow up. They begin the world, in all probability, with a mere trifle, which trifle they have been known to make by their own industry. Having made that, it recommends their character to persons of, perhaps, a little more fortune, who, to encourage them, become sureties for their cash accounts.

" The classes of persons who have cash credits are very various; but they are generally the industrious classes of persons—merchants, and traders, and farmers.

" The accommodation is more readily given to a small than to a large amount—the bank preferring to grant ten credits for 100*l.*, than one for 1,000*l.*, thereby demonstrating that their accounts are quite as much for the assistance of the poor as for the accommodation of the rich."

2. Cash credits furnish great facility to tradesmen and others in carrying on their business, either in the way of raising money, in making purchases, or in employing at particular seasons their surplus capital.

" Is the advantage to the party borrowing greater under the system of cash credit than under the system of lending in the ordinary mode ?— Infinitely.

" Why ?—As to the question of actual pounds, shillings, or pence, paid in the shape of interest, there is, in the first place, this difference, that when he discounts a bill, he pays the interest on the sum for three months, if that be the currency of it. Should any accidental mercantile transactions throw into this individual's hands, on the next day, the same amount which he had received thus from the banker, he has lost the benefit of the transaction, because he must keep this : if he has a deposit account with the banker he must keep it at banker's interest, while he is anticipated by having paid to the banker three months' discount interest on his bill. If a trader were to take his money systematically by discounts instead of by cash accounts, a disadvantage to him would arise. The same principle applies to small sums : if half or a quarter, or any part of the advance which he may have received upon the cash account comes into him, he immediately lessens the advance by paying it into the bank, and the interest being calculated at the close of the account, there is a progressive account of interest diminishing with the principal sum till it is extinguished. So far as to actual benefit of interest; but the convenience of getting money when wanted affords a very material advantage, independent of the actual benefit.

" What are the facilities that exist in obtaining this sort of advantage, compared with those of obtaining an ordinary loan ?—When a person applies for a cash account, which is not an immediate advance of money on the part of the bank, but a conferring of the power or privilege of drawing upon the bank to the extent specified, the person proposes two or more personal securities : a bond is made out, and he draws as occasion requires. In this way, he has never more from the bank than is absolutely necessary for the purposes of his business. The account is never recalled, unless it has ceased to be beneficial to the bank, by having been but little operated upon, and thus not having promoted the circulation of the bank's notes. Whenever it becomes a dead advance, the bank calls it up. In the case of a person obtaining a loan, he would probably, in the first place, have to pay the interest down at once; he would have to pay it upon the whole sum, whether he should require it ultimately or not, and it would be liable to be recalled by the lender at his pleasure.

" The person who procures a cash credit, does so upon the security of two or three substantial individuals. He may be a man of little property, but upon that security he gets a credit, perhaps of 500*l.* : his bill to anything like that amount, without those securities, would not be discounted.

" After the permanent credit is given, the option of using it lies solely with the borrower, not with the bank, as does also the option of the period of repayment.

" If a small trader borrow of an individual (not a banker) 100*l.*, that individual would not be disposed to receive back his money in 5*l.*, or 10*l.*, or 15*l.*—he would wait till the term expired, when he would receive the whole. When a credit is granted, the individual, perhaps, draws out 50*l.* to-day and pays in 40*l.* to-morrow, and goes on in that way, always having credit with the bank to the extent originally stipulated.

" The repayment as well as the overdraught is permitted by the bank to be made in small sums piecemeal: so that by attention in his repayment, the borrower saves himself from paying interest on more than the precise advance for which he has occasion at the moment, and can constantly convert to a safe and profitable purpose the money which he may receive in the course of his trade, however small the amount.

" These advantages are steadily and uniformly afforded at all times to the industrious tradesman, or farmer, the merchant, the professional man, and the landlord."

3. **Cash credits supply capital for carrying on extensive branches of trade, employing the population, and constructing public works.**

" Cash credits for small sums enable the poor to be as instrumental, as far as their means go, in increasing the capital of the country, as the rich are. For the produce of that industry which cash account credits enable to operate, and of that capital which they leave at liberty to be employed in trade, goes to increase the real wealth and capital of the country ; and a great proportion of the transactions, carried on through the instrumentality of cash accounts, consists of those of the poorer classes.

" I apprehend that those cash credits have enabled a large number of manufacturers to carry on business, and to employ the population of the country, who, if they had not such credits, could not have carried on such business, nor employed such population.

" Cash credits are granted to almost all descriptions of persons throughout the country. Every young man who has a prospect of success on entering life, applies for a cash credit. A great many gentlemen have cash credits, and a great many farmers. There is hardly any public work undertaken in Scotland that the first object is not to apply for a cash credit, to carry it on to advantage. All the roads in Scotland are managed by Parliamentary trustees; and I believe there is hardly any one of those sets of trustees which have not cash accounts for the purpose of carrying on their operations. I am sure many of the most important public works in Scotland would not have been carried on, or certainly not with the same advantage, but for the credits they obtain from the banks."

4. **Cash credits prevent large manufacturers setting up as bankers, and thus they exclude those evils which in other countries have resulted from the failure of private banks.**

" When the system is applied to the case of large manufacturers, employing hundreds or thousands of workmen, and possessing a cash credit to a proportionate amount, upon sufficient security, one obvious effect is, that the temptation is removed from the manufacturer of attempting to issue notes, and becoming himself a banker—an error or temptation which, if what is said is true, has been the main cause of the institution of many insufficient English bankers, whose partners, from being good traders, became bad bankers, and brought upon their own district the distress which bad banking sooner or later always produces."

5. **Cash credits have a considerable moral influence upon the habits and character of the people.**

" The security afforded to a bank by its debtor, or rather its customer, on a cash credit, is by bond, with two sureties at the least : occasionally there are not two sureties, but frequently many more; the practical effect of which is, that the sureties do, in a greater or less degree, keep an attentive eye upon the future transactions and character of the person for whom they have thus pledged themselves. And it is, perhaps, difficult for those who are not intimately acquainted with it to conceive the moral check which is afforded upon the conduct of the members of a great trading community, who are thus directly interested in the integrity, prudence, and success of each other. It rarely, indeed, if ever, happens, that banks suffer loss by small cash credits.

" This system has a great effect upon the moral habits of the people, because those who are securities feel an interest in watching over their conduct; and if they find they are misconducting themselves, they become apprehensive of being brought into risk and loss from having become their securities; and if they find they are so misconducting themselves, they withdraw the security.

" Sometimes cash credits are recalled from the interference of the securities. They have the power of knowing from the bank at any time the state of the account, and the operations upon it; and if from that, or from other circumstances, they have been led to think less favourably of the person for whom they gave the security, they can immediately cease to allow that account to be farther operated upon."

The Report of the Committee of the House of Lords contains the following observations upon the effects of cash credits :—

"There is also one part of their system which is stated by all the witnesses (and in the opinion of the committee very justly stated) to have had the best effects upon the people of Scotland, and particularly upon the middling and poorer classes of society, in producing and encouraging habits of frugality and industry. The practice referred to is that of cash credits. Any person who applies to a bank for a cash credit, is called upon to produce two or more competent securities, who are jointly bound; and after a full inquiry into the character of the applicant, the nature of his business, and the sufficiency of his securities, he is allowed to open a credit, and to draw upon the bank for the whole of its amount, or for such part as his daily transactions may require. To the credit of this account he pays in such sums as he may not have occasion to use, and interest is charged or credited upon the daily balance as the case may be. From the facility which these cash credits give to all the small transactions of the country, and from the opportunities which they afford to persons who begin business with little or no capital but their character, to employ profitably the minutest products of their industry, it cannot be doubted that the most important advantages are derived from the whole community."

As by cash credits the banks render themselves liable to be called upon at a moment's notice for the amount of the credit granted, it is natural to suppose that they contemplate some advantage in return. The advantage contemplated is the circulation of their notes. It is not intended that the cash credit shall be a dead loan of capital. It is expected that there shall be a perpetual paying in and drawing out of money; and the smaller the denomination of the notes drawn out, the more advantageous is the account to the bank. Manufacturers who pay away large sums every week in wages, linen buyers and cattle dealers, millers and provision merchants, who make their purchases in small sums, and generally all those who have quick returns of money passing through their hands, have the means of making a cash credit profitable to the bank. On this subject I again quote the evidence :—

"To secure to the bank the advantages of circulation, which is to make it worth while to afford these facilities at so little expense to a customer, he, on his part, is to lose no opportunity of bringing to the bank, and thus withdrawing from circulation, the notes of every rival bank which comes into his hands in the course of his transactions; or of paying away, and thus introducing into circulation, as many of the notes of the bank as his transactions admit of, always 1*l.* notes if possible. The payments and receipts must be frequent, for in this consists the banker's profit, inasmuch as the payments are uniformly made by him in his own notes, and the receipts are generally, in a very great degree, in the notes of other banks. Thus, supposing a shopkeeper to have a credit for 50*l.* or 100*l.*, if his receipts and payments average 5*l.* per day, he may, in six months, or 150 days, have placed 750 of his banker's 1*l.* notes in circulation.

"It is quite necessary, in order to render a cash account beneficial, that there should be repeated and continued operations upon it; that the transactions should be numerous; that there should be a continual drawing out and paying in of money; and that, by these means, a circulation of the bank notes may be promoted; otherwise the account is withdrawn, and the great reason of this is, that these accounts are not intended to form dead loans, but to be productive of circulation to the bank.

"The explanation of the cash credit system is this:—The bank who first opened a cash credit opened it with an individual shopkeeper. He received payment of his goods in the currency of the country. Previous to that system, he used to put his currency into his drawer, 8*l.* or 10*l.*, or whatever it was. If people brought him larger money to pay for his goods, he returned those people change; or if he did not, he kept it until he wanted to purchase for himself. But after the banker had explained to him what he wished him to do, when the shopkeeper received the currency of the country, instead of putting it into his till, he looked to the banker's shop as his till, and handed it over to the banker, and left his own till with only the change which he could not do without. Then, when he required sums to pay away, instead of taking them from his till, he sent to the bank, and took from it what he required, the banker giving him his own notes. So much of the previous currency was thus removed, and the banker's notes taken in its place. That was the effect of the first operation, when the thing was only in so simple a state that there was only the notes of one bank and a metallic circulation. If you apply the same principle where there are thirty banks, the result would be the same. The amount of the circulation of the country continues the same, but the proportions between its parts vary."

Deposits.—A sum of money deposited or placed in a bank is called a deposit. Some banks grant interest on these deposits, others do not. Few London bankers allow interest on deposits, but the English country bankers usually do. The Scotch banks have carried this practice to the greatest extent, and the deposit system forms a very important branch of the banking system in Scotland.

Those regulations which the banks have established as the rule of the transactions between themselves and the depositors are the following:—

The depositor may place in the bank any amount of money he pleases above 10*l.*

The whole or any part of the deposit may be withdrawn at the pleasure of the depositor without previous notice.

Interest is allowed on the deposit from the day it is lodged in the bank until the day it is drawn out. Provided, that is, it has been allowed to lie a month, no interest being paid upon a sum deposited for a shorter period.

The balance of a current account is allowed interest at the rate of ½ per cent. less than if it were a permanent deposit when calculated on the minimum for the month, or one per cent. less when calculated daily.

The following are the advantages ascribed to the deposit system :—

1. The system of deposits is advantageous to the lower classes—in providing a place of safety for their deposits—in granting them interest on their savings—in encouraging habits of frugality—and thus often enabling them to advance in society.

"The deposit branch divides itself into two parts:—There is, first, what is called a running account, where the party pays in from day to day the whole surplus funds in his hands, and on which he receives interest. These depositors are, in general, shopkeepers, and merchants, and traders, more particularly in large towns; and in these deposit accounts there is found at their credit, at the close of every day, the whole amount of the money for which they have not immediate employment in their trade. The second branch of deposits consists of small sums placed in the hands of the bank at interest, which have been in general the savings of their industry, and which are put into the hands of the bank to accumulate, and on which they may operate not in the way of a running account. They may receive a partial payment whenever they please; but in general these deposits are very seldom removed, excepting when an individual has occasion to build a house or begin business. This class of deposits is distinguished from running accounts by the name of deposit receipts.*

" What class of the community is it that makes the smaller deposits? —They are generally the labouring classes in towns like Glasgow. In country places, like Perth and Aberdeen, it is from servants and fishermen, and just that class of the community who save from their earnings in mere trifles small sums till they come to be a bank deposit. There is now a facility for their placing money in the provident banks, who receive money till the deposit amounts to 10*l.* When it amounts to 10*l.* it is equal to the minimum of a bank deposit. The system of banking in Scotland is just an extension of the provident bank system. Half-yearly or yearly these depositors come to the bank, and add the savings of their labour, with the interest that has accrued from the previous half-year or year, to the principal. And in this way it goes on, without being at all reduced, accumulating, till the depositor is able either to buy or build a house, when it comes to be one, two, or three hundred

* Lords' Report, p. 80.

pounds, or till he is able to commence business as a master in the line in which he has hitherto been a servant. A great part of the depositors of the-bank are of that description; and a great part of the most thriving of our farmers and manufacturers have arisen from such beginnings. And in regard to the deposit receipts, I may just mention what is generally the way in which they are granted. To-day a person from the country appears at the bank, it may be with 20*l*. or 30*l*. or 50*l*. We probably never see him again till that day twelvemonth, but we are sure of seeing him about that very day. If he has 20*l*. in the bank, he may come and say, 'There are four guineas; you will give me a receipt for 25*l*.' He knows well that the 20*l*. has earned 16*s*. interest; and I do consider that the four guineas are just the savings of the year. He goes away with his new receipt, and returns on that day twelvemonth; then again it is added to, and thus accumulated—and so in many instances throughout the country."*

2. The system of deposits is advantageous to capitalists in furnishing them with a secure mode of employment of capital, either for a longer or a shorter period, at their pleasure.

"What class of persons form the large and steady depositors in the Scotch banks?—The middling and the lower order of society, industrious poor people, who are saving their money, and small capitalists who have raised a moderate sum of money, upon the interest of which they live.

"Do many persons live upon the interest of their deposits, as far as you know?—Yes, a great many."†

"Do you know whether it is the practice of persons who have small capitals in Scotland, to invest them in the public securities in London, or to deposit them with the banks in Edinburgh?—I believe, almost universally, to deposit them with a Scotch bank.

"And they live upon the interest of what they so deposit, in the manner as persons here live upon their interest on stock?—Yes; they often look to the permanent capital with a view of leaving it at their death, taking the interest during their lives."‡

"The deposit accounts are of two kinds: one kind from the commercial people, who have large sums that they wish to keep in a disposable form, waiting an opportunity of any investment which may occur. Of the operating deposits, there are others who keep the money until a favourable turn in the Stock Exchange enables them to invest it there. And there are others, respectable householders, who keep it for the purposes of their family expenditure. I reckon that these and the sums due upon them average one-half of the aggregate amount of a bank's deposits."§

"Have you formed any estimate of the amount of deposits in all the banks in Scotland?—I certainly have been at very great pains to

---

* Commons' Report, p. 159.   † Lords' Report, p. 165.
‡ Commons' Report, p. 124.   § Lords' Report, p. 183.

get information upon the subject; and I am satisfied that the amount is considerably above twenty millions—I should say, twenty-five millions.*

"From what class of persons are those deposits chiefly?—Generally from industrious tradesmen, small shopkeepers, varying from 10*l.* to 500*l.* The greatest number of deposits, and the greatest in their aggregate amount, are in small sums.

"Are there not, however, deposits from richer classes, and each of them to a much larger amount?—Certainly, there are deposits from 1,000*l.* to 20,000*l.* and 30,000*l*"†

"In the spring of 1824, the banks in Scotland began, in some instances, to decline accepting deposits at all. In the autumn of 1824, the great banks made an express rule that they would not accept more than 5,000*l.* from any one depositor. They allowed 2½ per cent. on the first 3,000*l.*, and 2 per cent. upon the remainder of the 5,000*l.*, and above that they would not allow any interest. That was the general rule with the great banks at that period. There were many people who preferred leaving their money, though they received little or no interest, to taking it away. That commenced in 1825."‡

3. The system of deposits is advantageous to the country —by augmenting the amount of national capital—by increasing the demand for labour—by granting facilities to trade and commerce—and by removing the temptations to engage in hazardous speculations and foreign investments.

"This system was adopted before the middle of the last century. The rate of interest allowed since then has been regulated by the value of money, and has, of course, fluctuated considerably; but it has ever been such as to afford as high a return to the depositor as has been consistent with the reasonable profit, and of course the security of the bank. The effect of this system has been to encourage and to afford the means of the accumulation of capital among the lower, as well as the higher orders, by placing within the reach of all, a convenient, safe, and moderately profitable investment of money, and to offer an inducement to capitalists to retain their accumulations in Scotland, notwithstanding the opportunities or temptations which foreign investments might hold out."§

"The system of deposit accounts, I think, is a very great stimulus to the habits of industry and economy and frugality in Scotland. The whole surplus capital of the individual is thus rendered productive.

"Under the system on which you conduct your business, is not the money arising from those deposits issued out, to encourage the farther consumption of labour in the country?—Yes.

"It would be a loss, then, to the country, if it was to be removed from the channel in which it is now placed, into this country, on Government debentures?—It certainly would.

---

* The amount at present deposited with the banks in Scotland, in permanent deposit and current accounts, is upwards of sixty millions.—*February*, 1871.
† Lords' Report, p. 231.   ‡ Ibid. p. 158.   § Ibid. p. 175.

" Under this system, does not the poor workman gain immediate interest for his saving, whilst the saving is immediately employed through the bank in putting a farther portion of labour into motion ?—Precisely so. It is in this way that the wealth of those individuals is concentrated, and through the agency of the bank is brought to bear in carrying on the business of the country."*

" Is there not an advantage to the public from the gathering of those small capitals together, forming part of the deposits of the bank, and so being sent out again in large sums, like other capitals, for the purpose of being applied to increase the powers of productive industry ?—The Scotch banks form a sort of reservoir for receiving the small sums of capital scattered throughout the community, and then sending them forth into channels of trade, so as to promote the commerce, manufactures, and agriculture of the country."†

" Are you of opinion, that if the deposits with the banks of Scotland were considerably lessened, the banks could afford the same accommodation by discounts which they do at present ?—I should think that is impossible, because it forms part of their capital. It would diminish the capital which is at present employed in that business, of which discounting forms a great part.

" Would not any such diminution of discount operate injuriously to the general trade of the country ?—The want of those discounts must diminish the trade of the country, inasmuch as the manufacturer or merchant receives his money at least three months sooner by discounting his bills, than he could possibly get payment of his account."‡

" The system of deposits forms a great part of the funds arising from our banking system. It is a great deposit of money which is given out to the trade of the country, for the profit of one per cent. for which the bank runs the risk of its business. If that great deposit were withdrawn, and could not be issued with the same degree of safety, I conceive the consequences would be a total derangement of the whole system, and ruin of our country."§

" If the banks are under the necessity of reducing the interest on deposit accounts, the depositors must look about them and find out on what security they can lend their money so as to obtain a higher rate of interest. It would certainly diminish the capital of the trading part of Scotland, inasmuch as the banks would not have it in their power to assist them in trading by discounting; but it might be lent on Government securities or landed property, and the temptation of a higher interest from individuals would, undoubtedly, be a temptation to many—and a temptation that could scarcely be resisted by those whose income depends entirely upon the interest of that lent money—to lend it on personal and doubtful security.

" When the banks reduced their interest some time ago, a great part of the deposits was drawn out, to be invested in various different ways. And as the depositors did not get from the banks the interest on which they were depending, and did not choose to take a less interest, many

* Lords' Report, p. 283. † Commons' Report, p. 203.
‡ Lords' Report, p. 266. § Lords' Report, p. 235.

of them went into schemes, which have turned out very ruinous to them. It has been one great cause of over-speculation, that the people did not get the interest they had been accustomed to from the banks. They, therefore, drew it out to invest it in joint-stock companies, lent it to builders, or other inferior securities, or became builders themselves."*

4. The system of deposits is advantageous to the banks —by inducing every person to deposit his money in a bank —by furnishing the banks with capital to carry on their business—and by putting in circulation a large amount of their notes.

"The universal practice at Glasgow is, to pay into the bank with which the individual transacts his business, the whole of the notes he has in his possession, or nearly the whole, every day."†

"Unquestionably, the giving of interest upon deposits is an inducement to every person that has any surplus money in his hands, to place it in the hands of his banker. And in the same way in the case of cash accounts, every payment by the holder of a cash account into the bank, either diminishes the interest he has to pay to the bank, or if the account should turn in his favour, enables him to get interest from the bank, and that is a great inducement for every person to pay in daily into his banker's hands all the money which he does not require for the purposes of his business."‡

"The means of a bank I conceive to consist of three things—first, capital paid in its own stock—secondly, the notes which the bank is able to keep afloat in the circle—thirdly, the amount of the deposits."§

"And if the amount of deposits were lessened, in that case their means of issuing money upon discount would be proportionably lessened?—Yes."‖

"Every bank constituted as the banks of Scotland are, makes advances in two ways.—They make them upon cash credits, and they make them upon the discount of bills. They also borrow in two ways.—They borrow upon deposit receipts, and they borrow also upon accounts current. That is, if a gentleman opens an account, and puts 100*l.* to his credit, and operates upon it, drawing out a part of it, leaving a balance in the hands of the bank, then there is a borrowing to the extent of the balance that is so left. Those accounts we do not allow to be overdrawn, so that the advance is in two ways, and the borrowing in two ways—that is, in two different forms."¶

"In the case of small depositors, a considerable part of the profit arising from the deposit of that money is the circulation of the notes. When a depositor withdraws his money from the bank he receives it in the notes of the bank, and, of course, they go into circulation. As long as they remain out they are a source of profit."**

* Lords' Report, p. 250.   † Commons' Report, p. 50.
‡ Commons' Report, p. 201.   § Lords' Report, p. 195.
‖ Commons' Report, p. 150.   ¶ Commons' Report, p. 180.
** Commons' Report, p. 45.

" The banks issue their notes two ways; they make advances upon cash accounts, and they make advances upon discounts. They also issue their notes in payments upon accounts current, and also in the repayment of deposit receipts."*

" The deposit and cash accounts are the instruments for supporting our circulation, and without the continued operations upon the deposits and cash accounts our circulation cannot be maintained."†

Remittances to India.‡—Although this branch of banking business is not peculiar to Scotland, yet I believe the banks of Glasgow have carried it on to a greater extent than any other banks. This has arisen partly from the more intimate connexion that exists between Glasgow and India, and partly from the character of Scotch banking. We refer to the practice of granting bills of exchange to be sent out to India, accompanied by an undertaking to accept them when presented.

To enable our readers to understand distinctly this branch of business, we must give a short description of the banking and commercial operations of India. The business transacted at each of the Presidencies consists of importing British manufactured goods, and exporting the produce of the country, such as cotton, indigo, &c., &c. Some of the merchants who are engaged in these operations act also as bankers. They receive deposits, and allow interest on them, receive dividends on India stock, and make remittances to England. Their business in this way was formerly very extensive, but has recently been much reduced by the establishment of banks all over the country. One part of the business of these mercantile bankers is to advance money on shipments of goods either to England or to China, taking as security the bill of lading and the policy of insurance. Here they often find a powerful competitor in the East India Company; and the mercantile interests, in both India and Glasgow, are desirous of excluding the Company from this kind of business.§

I cannot better describe the kind of business carried on in India, than by the following extract from a letter I received in reply to some inquiries I made on the subject:—

---

* Lords' Report, p. 236. † Ibid. p. 135.
‡ The following account is retained as being of historical interest.—EDITOR.
§ See the Evidence taken before the Committee of the House of Commons on Commercial Distress, 1848.

" One part of business which the houses used to do largely was advancing on shipments of goods to England and China, and it is still done by Messrs. _____ and _____ . The system is :— *A.* ships 10,000*l.* worth of goods for England, and takes the bills of lading and policies of insurance to *B.*, who agrees to advance three-fourths of the value ; the shipping documents are indorsed by *A.* to *B.*, and *A.* draws bills on the consignee of the goods in London for the value, in favour of *B.*, payable at six months' sight, and directs him to accept the bills when presented by *B.'s* London correspondent. As the goods will most probably arrive in London before the bills fall due, the consignee will take them up before the due date, and with the bills receive the shipping documents from *B.'s* correspondent. Sometimes, however, it may be that *A.* has no agent in London, and the goods are therefore consigned to *B.'s* correspondent, who is instructed to sell and remit the proceeds by bills, or with the purchase-money of the Indian goods to buy British manufactured goods, and ship them consigned to *B.* You will easily perceive what large profits could be realized in this way, as commission is charged on the sale of the Indian goods and purchase of British, and a high rate of interest on the advance until it is paid off.

" The East India Company usually get a portion of the money required for the home expenditure, from India, in this manner. Last month the Government here gave notice, that in pursuance of instructions from the Court of Directors, it was proposed to provide a sum of 800,000*l.* in India during the remainder of the official year 1846-7, for the service of the East India Company in London, by the purchase of bills of exchange to be secured by the hypothecation of goods. Advances in cash are accordingly made for the purpose by the governments of Bengal, Madras, and Bombay, at the rate of exchange of 2*s.* per Company's rupee ; the operation is exactly the same as I have stated in the former case. *A.* ships goods, and on the security of the bills of lading, policies of insurance, and his bills on consignees in London, at six months' sight, receives from the Government an advance equal to three-fourths of the value of the goods ; the bills, with the shipping documents attached, are sent to the India House, and in due course accepted by the drawee ; on the arrival of the goods, the bills are paid, and the goods given up. In the event of the ship arriving, and the bills not being taken up, the goods are then lodged in one of the Dock Company's bonded warehouses. If the bills are dishonoured at the due date, the goods are sold, to reimburse the East India Company for the advance ; this, however, is an extreme case, and could only occur in the event of the bankruptcy of the acceptor.

" With reference to the bills drawn from India, with an engagement on the part of the drawee to accept, in the margin, these bills are obtained from a respectable London house, and sent out to this country for negotiation ; but I must have recourse again to my favourite plan of illustrating by an example. *A.* having credit with a London house, or if not, lodges security, and obtains bills, with an engagement in the margin to accept, and remits them to *B.*, his correspondent in India, for the purchase of produce ; the drawee being well known, the bills obtain a favourable rate in the market, and *B.* is enabled to purchase produce, which he ships, consigned to *A*. in London, who, before the bills fall due, pays them; on paying the London house commission on the amount, the transaction is concluded.

" There is another system, and you very probably may have seen some of the bills in the London market. *A*. a merchant in New York, proposes to send a ship to China for goods, but unwilling to have his money locked up on board ship for so many months, with the additional risk of loss, he obtains, either on personal or other security, from say Messrs.   's agent in New York, a letter of credit on the house in London, to honour the bills of the captain or supercargo of the ship. On the arrival of the ship in China, the cargo is purchased and paid for by the bills on Messrs.   , London; the bills are negotiated in China, with the indorsement of   's agent there; and as soon as *A*. in New York receives advice of the same, he remits the amount to London, to meet the bills when they fall due. I enclose you a form of one of these American bills. Sometimes money is sent to India by means of London bankers' bills, and I have seen Messrs.   's bills offered for sale, but being drawn at short dates, they do not obtain such good rates of exchange as might be expected; they are seldom used for commercial purposes, but are taken by officers of the civil and military services, wishing to make remittances to their families at home. I understand that the Western Bank of Scotland issues bills with an engagement to accept.

" This operation, as far as an exchange operation, of the banks issuing the bills, would not realise a profit sufficient to cover the risk. Suppose the London and Westminster Bank sent out to an agent here its bills at six months' sight, for 20,000*l*., and that the bills are sold at 2*s*. per rupee; the agent must then remit the rupees (200,000) which he has received, and even admitting that he could obtain good commercial bills at 2 per cent. under that rate, it would scarcely pay his commission on the transaction.

" The usual way in which merchants settle their exchange operations in Bombay, and I believe it is the same all over the East, is by sending a notice to each house, intimating that *A. & Co.* have 10,000*l*. to draw for on England; *A. & Co.* are called *sellers*. *B. & Co.* want to remit 5000*l*. to England, are called *buyers*, and offer for that amount of *A. & Co.* bills; *C. & Co.* are also buyers, and offer for 5000*l*. more, so that the whole transaction is completed; and unless a bank is prepared to buy up all the bills offered for sale, at the same or a more favourable rate than a merchant can offer, it cannot carry on its exchange operations profitably. The merchants buying and selling among themselves, save all the bankers' charges. This, I imagine, has been the case in all countries before the system of banking operations was clearly understood; and I have 'no doubt, but that in a short time we shall see all exchange business done by the banks."

The Bank of England had their attention called to this subject, and consequently issued expressly for remittance to India bank post bills drawn at sixty days' sight. The following account of this arrangement is taken from a City Article of the *Times* :—

"About the year 1836, the bills of the East India firms had been brought into temporary discredit by some failures which happened at the time, so that these bills did not find ready purchasers in the Bombay market. It was conceived, therefore, that a new sort of paper of unquestionable credit might be introduced into India with advantage, and nothing seemed more fitted for this purpose than bills made by the Bank of England, and payable by themselves. A resolution, passed in April, 1836, authorized the issue of the required paper, and since that time it has been in use.

"The bills so obtained are remitted to India, and have a peculiar advantage, which is expressed by the condition in the form that the 'firsts' are to be accepted, and held by the Bank of England. The paper, which is drawn by a firm in India on London, is generally made payable at 60 days after sight, but the 60 days do not begin to run till after their acceptance in London. The bank paper, on the contrary, being accepted at once, and held for the purpose of being delivered to the holders of the 'seconds' and 'thirds,' the 60 days begin to run from the date, and the bills are payable immediately on their return to London from India. This advantage, and the unquestionable credit of the paper, often enable the holder to dispose of them at a good premium in the India market in certain states of the exchanges, and thus they become, as it were, an article of commerce."

[*Rules to be observed at the Exchanges of Notes and General Settlements of Balances between the Banks in Edinburgh.*

I. There shall be every Tuesday morning an exchange of the notes collected on the previous Saturday and Monday, and every Thursday morning an exchange of the notes collected on the previous Tuesday and Wednesday, and every Saturday morning an exchange of notes collected on the previous Thursday and Friday.

In addition to the regular Saturday morning exchanges, there shall be others on the afternoons of the three Saturdays immediately following each of the Term days of Whitsunday and Martinmas ; and also, when the Term day falls upon a Sunday or Monday, on the afternoon of the immediately preceding Saturday ; and when it falls upon a Saturday, on the afternoon of that day. On any other Saturday, any bank, provided it gives due notice to the other banks before half-past eleven o'clock on that day, shall be entitled to receive from them its notes in their hands at the close of that day's business, in exchange for vouchers to be included in the next general settlement. This rule shall extend to Glasgow, Paisley, Greenock, and Dundee.

II. Every Tuesday, Thursday, and Monday, there shall be a general settlement of the balances of the Edinburgh exchanges of Monday, Thursday, and Saturday respectively, which settlements shall include also the balances of the Edinburgh clearings up to the time of settling. The clearings shall include exchange vouchers issued in Edinburgh, and drafts on

Edinburgh, received there from other towns (whether granted for the balances of the regular exchanges, or otherwise), up to the time of clearing.

III. When Tuesday or Thursday is a holiday, the exchange and general settlement shall be made on Wednesday or Friday. When Saturday is a holiday, the exchange shall be made on Friday afternoon. When Monday is a holiday, the general settlement shall be made on Tuesday.

IV. The meetings for the exchanges and general settlements shall take place in the Clearing-House at the following hours :—

> On Tuesday at 10 A.M. for exchange, and again at 1·45 P.M. (after the clearing has been completed) for the general settlement.
> On Thursday at 10 A.M. for the exchange, and again at 1·45 P.M. (after the clearing has been completed) for the general settlement.
> On Saturday at 10 A.M. for the exchange.
> On Monday at 1·45 P.M. (after the clearing has been completed) for the general settlement.
> The Saturday afternoon " Term exchanges " shall take place in the Clearing-House at 2 P.M. When the Term day falls on a Saturday, the afternoon exchange shall take place at such an hour as may be agreed upon.

The clerks shall be in attendance punctually at the hours stated, *ten minutes* after which the doors are to be closed, and the notes or documents of the banks not represented excluded until next exchange. Such banks shall, however, retire by granting bills on London in accordance with Rule VII., the notes or documents brought into the Clearing-House against them by other banks.

V. The clerks from each bank shall all remain in the Exchange Room until the whole of the notes received by them have been counted, and at least one clerk from each bank shall remain until the whole of the notes delivered by that Bank have been counted. In case of a dispute arising on any occasion as to the amount contained in any parcel of notes received or delivered by a bank which has infringed this rule, such bank shall, in the absence of conclusive evidence in its favour, be held to be in the wrong.

To prevent any undue delay in counting the notes, each of the banks shall provide a competent staff for that purpose, to the satisfaction of the settling bank of the day.

VI. The settlements shall be undertaken on Thursdays by the exchange clerk of the Bank of Scotland, and on Mondays by the exchange clerk of the Royal Bank of Scotland ; but neither bank shall be held to incur any responsibility in respect of these transactions.

VII. When the balances of the general settlement have been struck, the settling clerk of the day shall at once enter the particulars in a Record provided for that purpose, and the banks who are debtors in the settlement shall, on the same day before the close of business, send to the banks who are creditors, a bill or bills on London for the respective amounts due. These bills shall be drawn at 5/8 days' date. The banks drawing them shall bear the expense of the stamp-duty, and shall, on delivering them, pay in cash to the respective banks in whose favour they are drawn, eight days' interest on the amounts, at the rate of 3 per cent. per annum.

VIII. In the event of any exchange draft being dishonoured, without prompt and satisfactory explanation of the cause, the bank issuing such draft shall be immediately excluded from the Clearing-House, and their notes shall be refused in future transactions with the public.

IX. When Exchanges are established in provincial towns, the exchangeable notes received at the agencies there must wait for the return of the next local exchange day ; and must, under no pretext, be forwarded to meet the exchanges in Edinburgh, or at the other agencies.

X. It is further understood and agreed, in consideration of the circulation of each bank (other than what may be issued against gold and silver coin) being fixed and limited by the Act 8 and 9 Vict., cap. 38, that the banks shall bring to the Exchange room regularly, at their head offices and agencies, all the exchangeable notes which they receive ; and that under no circumstances shall any of the subscribing banks issue the notes of another bank of issue in Scotland, without permission first asked and obtained.

XI. The vouchers of the Glasgow and Leith Exchanges shall be conveyed by special messengers from the different branches there, in rotation ; and the letters containing the vouchers shall be delivered by the messengers personally at the banks to which they are addressed in Edinburgh.

XII. The record of the general settlements shall be open for the inspection of any of the subscribing banks, at such times as may be convenient.

XIII. Any of the parties to this agreement shall be entitled to withdraw from it on giving three months' notice.

For the BANK OF SCOTLAND, D. DAVIDSON, Treasurer.
For the ROYAL BANK OF SCOTLAND, LAUR. ROBERTSON, Cashier.
For the BRITISH LINEN COMPANY, PATRICK BRODIE, Manager.
For the COMMERCIAL BANK OF SCOTLAND, A. K. MACKENZIE, Manager.
For the NATIONAL BANK OF SCOTLAND, W. J. DUNCAN, Manager.
For the UNION BANK OF SCOTLAND, SAML. HAY, Manager.
For the CLYDESDALE BANKING COMPANY, JA. GREENHILL, Manager, Edinburgh.
For the CITY OF GLASGOW BANK, W. BAIN, Manager, Edinburgh.
  EDINBURGH, January, 1867.

NOTE.—A Clearing House was established in Edinburgh, Glasgow, and Dundee, some years ago, for the daily exchange of cheques and vouchers, the balances of which are treated in the same manner as the balances of the exchange of notes, and are carried forward and settled at the *same time* by means of drafts on London at 5/8 days' date.]

SECTION VI.

THE IRISH BANKS.

THE last Act of Parliament for regulating banks in Ireland is the 8 & 9 Vict. cap. 37, passed in the year 1845.

This Act recites that by the Act 21 & 22 Geo. III. an Act was passed for establishing a bank by the name of the Governor and Company of the Bank of Ireland ; and which prohibited any other company consisting of more than six persons to issue notes payable on demand or within any time less than six months.   That by the Act 1 & 2 Geo. IV. cap. 72, other companies consisting of more than six partners might issue notes payable on demand, at a greater distance than fifty miles (Irish) from London.   And that by 6 Geo. IV. cap. 42, and 1 Wm. IV. cap. 32, such co-partnerships of bankers might transact certain matters of business by agents in Dublin, including the payment though not the issue of notes.

The Act farther recites that the Bank of Ireland had at various times advanced for the public service the several sums of 600,000*l.*, 500,000*l.*, and 1,250,000*l.*, late Irish currency ; and that by the 48 Geo. III. cap. 103, the charter of the Bank of Ireland was extended to the 1st day of January, 1837—upon twelve months' notice to be published in the *Dublin Gazette,* and after the repayment of the above-mentioned sums.   And that by the Act 1 & 2 Geo. IV. cap. 72, the Bank of Ireland had agreed to advance a farther sum of 500,000*l.*, and the bank was empowered to enlarge their capital to 3,000,000*l.* ; making the total advances 2,850,000*l.*, late Irish currency, equal to 2,630,769*l.* 4*s.* 8*d.* sterling money of the United Kingdom of Great Britain and Ireland ; on which by the Act 3 & 4 Vict. c. 75, the bank received an annuity from the Government of 115,384*l.* 12*s.* 4*d.* sterling, payable on the 5th of January and 5th of July in each year, redeemable upon six months' notice, to be given after January 1st, 1841, and after payment of the abovementioned sums.

The Act farther recites, that the above annuity of 115,384*l.* 12*s.* 4*d.* has, with the consent of the said governor and company, been reduced to 92,076*l.* 18*s.* 5*d.*, being at the rate of $3\frac{1}{2}$ per cent. per annum on the capital sum of 2,630,769*l.* 4*s.* 8*d.*, which capital sum shall not be repaid until the expiration of six months' notice, to be given after January 1st, 1855; and that, during such term, the said governor and company shall manage the public debt free of all charge. The company is to continue a corporation, for the purpose of carrying on the business of banking, but not to have any exclusive privileges. The charter to continue until the expiration of twelve months' notice to be given and published in the *Dublin Gazette*, after January 1st, 1855, and upon repayment of the sums due from the Government to the bank.

The Act removes, from the 6th day of December, 1845, all restrictions upon banks having more than six partners issuing notes and carrying on business in Dublin and within fifty miles thereof. But no banker shall issue any larger amount of notes than the average amount he had in circulation during the year ending the 1st day of May, 1845 (which amount shall be certified by the Commissioners of Stamps), and the amount of gold and silver coin he may have in his hands, in the proportion of not more than one-fourth of silver to that of gold.

In case two banks should unite, the new bank to have the power of issue to the amount of both the united banks. Any bank may arrange with the Bank of Ireland to give up its issue, and in that case the Bank of Ireland may increase its issue to that amount. But the bank that thus contracts shall not afterwards resume its issue. All notes for a fractional part of a pound are prohibited. Each bank issuing notes is required to send to the Stamp Office weekly returns, stating the amount of notes in circulation on each Saturday, distinguishing those below 5*l.*; and also the amount of gold and silver coin held at each of the head offices or four principal places of issue in Ireland. And from these returns the Commissioners of Stamps and Taxes shall make a monthly return, which shall be published in the *Dublin Gazette*. This monthly average must not exceed the amount certified by the commissioners and the amount of gold and silver on hand.

All banks are required to send a list of their shareholders to the Stamp Office every year, between the 1st and the 15th of January, to be published in the *Dublin Gazette* before the 1st day of the succeeding March. All banks, whether they issue notes or not, are entitled to sue and be sued in the name of their public registered officer.

Upon the Act of 1845, for the regulation of Banks in Ireland, we may observe :—

1. The authorized issue is like that of the banks of Scotland, the average amount of the year ending on the 1st day of May, 1845.

2. If any two banks unite, the new bank may issue to the amount of the circulation of both the united banks. Here the law is the same as that of Scotland, but different from that of England.

3. If any bank gives up its issue, and agrees to issue Bank of Ireland notes, the Bank of Ireland may increase her authorized issue to the full amount of the issue of the bank whose notes are withdrawn. In England, the Bank of England can, in a similar case, issue only to the extent of two-thirds of the issue of the bank whose notes are withdrawn. There is no similar provision in the Act referring to Scotland.

4. Another difference may be noticed between Ireland and Scotland. All the notes issued at the branch banks in Scotland are payable only at the head office of the bank that issued them. In Ireland, by the Act 9 Geo. IV. c. 81, all notes must bear to be payable at the place or places where they have been issued or reissued. Hence the banks in Ireland must keep some gold at every branch, while the banks in Scotland need not have any gold except at the head office. In both countries, the banks must hold a stock of gold equal to the amount of notes in circulation beyond the authorized issue; and, according to the Act, this gold must be at the head office, or chief places of issue. The gold held at the branches, however necessary for business purposes, is not taken into account in the returns to the Stamp Office. The banks, indeed, return the whole amount of the gold in their possession; and it is this which is published in the newspapers. But the amount held against the excess of authorized issue must be held at the chief office, or at four chief places of issue. In the Provincial Bank of Ireland these places are Cork, Limerick, Dublin, and Belfast.

The banking institutions of Ireland are the Bank of Ireland, which is a chartered bank, like the Bank of England. It is the Government bank. It issues notes, and has branches in the principal towns throughout Ireland. It has now no exclusive privileges.

The Provincial Bank of Ireland, and the National Bank.

These are joint-stock banks that issue notes, and have numerous branches. These two banks are governed by boards of directors, who meet in London.

The Hibernian Bank, and the Royal Bank of Ireland. These are joint-stock banks, that do not issue notes. The former has fifteen Country Branches and the latter a Branch at Kingstown.

The private banks of Messrs. Ball & Co., and Messrs. Boyle, Low, Murray, & Co.

There are three joint-stock banks at Belfast, all of which issue notes and have branches. They are the Northern Bank, the Belfast Bank, and the Ulster Bank.

At Cork the Munster Bank, Limited, was established in 1865, and has now numerous branches chiefly in the South. Its Paid-up Capital is £175,000.

The Bank of Ireland.—In tracing the history of banking we may observe that most public banks have been formed, in the first instance, under the protection of the Government of the state in which they were established. Such was the case with the Banks of Venice, Genoa, and Amsterdam; and such, too, was the case with the Banks of England, of Scotland, and of Ireland. The former were closely connected with the state, and may properly be called "State Banks;" the latter had peculiar privileges bestowed by charter, and are usually called " Chartered Banks." These privileges may be divided into two classes, those which refer to the proprietors themselves, and those which refer to other parties. The privileges of the first class relate to the amount of capital, the form of Government, the number of the directors, and the mode of their nomination, the meeting of the proprietors, and the specification of the branches of business the bank are allowed to carry on. The privileges of the second class refer to the restricted liability of the shareholders, and the prohibition of other parties carrying on the same business.

If the charters granted to banking companies conferred only the first class of privileges, they would be liable to but little objection. In the infancy of commerce and of banking, the assistance of the Government may with propriety be granted to encourage the formation of institutions so eminently calculated to promote the public advantage. But of what avail are prohibitory clauses? If no other persons are disposed to form similar institutions, then those prohibitions are a nullity. But if other parties are disposed to form similar companies, without the assistance of the Government, then why should the Government interfere at all? Why should they grant a charter to effect an object which can be effected without their assistance?

In the charter first granted to the Bank of England in 1694, there was no prohibitory clause. But when the charter was renewed in 1708, it was enacted that no other company formed of more than six persons should carry on the business of banking in England. The charter granted to the Bank of Scotland, in 1695, contained the following prohibition:—"That for the period of twenty-one years from the 17th of July, 1695, it should not be lawful for any other persons to set up a distinct company or bank within the kingdom of Scotland." This privilege was not renewed after the expiration of the twenty-one years; and in the year 1727 a charter, without any prohibitions, was also granted to the Royal Bank of Scotland. In the year 1746 the British Linen Company was formed, and carried on the business of banking as a joint-stock company. Subsequently this bank also obtained a charter, but without any exclusive privilege. Hence Scotland has had the advantage of chartered banks, and joint-stock banks, and private banks, all working well together, without producing those effects which in this country have followed the prohibitory clauses of the charter of the Bank of England.

Both in its constitution and government the Bank of Ireland closely imitated the Bank of England; and it has produced in Ireland most of the advantages and evils which that establishment has produced in this country. It has supplied the country with a currency of undoubted solidity; it has supported public credit, it has granted facilities to trade, and it has assisted the financial operations of the Government. On the other hand, its prohibitory clauses necessarily led to the formation of many private banks, whose failure was the cause of immense wretchedness to all classes of the population.

The charter of the Bank of Ireland contained a clause which prevented more than six persons forming themselves into a company to carry on the business of banking in Ireland. In the year 1824, they surrendered this exclusive privilege, as far as regards those places which are situated at a greater distance than fifty Irish miles from Dublin; and in 1826, the Bank of

England made a similar surrender, with regard to places at a greater distance than sixty-five miles from London. As eleven Irish miles are equal to fourteen English miles, fifty Irish miles are equal to about sixty-five English miles. But it must be observed, that Dublin is situated on the sea-coast, therefore, the Bank of Ireland had only the monopoly of a semicircle, whose radius is fifty Irish miles. But London being situated inland, the Bank of England had the monopoly of a whole circle of 130 English miles in diameter.

The Bank of Ireland was established by an Act of Parliament passed in 1782, 21 and 22 Geo. III. cap. 16. The following are the provisions of this Act :—

The capital was 600,000*l.*, which was lent to Government at 4 per cent. No one person was permitted to subscribe more than 10,000*l.* If the bank incurred debts to a greater amount than their capital, the subscribers were answerable in their private capacity to the creditors in proportion to their subscriptions. The bank were not either to borrow or to lend money at a higher interest than 5 per cent., nor to engage in any business but banking. The stock to be transferable and deemed personal estate, and as such to go to the executors of the holders, and not to their heirs. No transfer of bank stock to be valid, unless registered in the bank books in seven days from the contract, and actually transferred in fourteen days ; the charter to expire at twelve months' notice after the 1st day of January, 1794, and repayment of all sums due by the Government to the bank.

The charter is dated May 15, 1783, and contains as follows : —Such persons as should subscribe before January 1, 1784, the sum of 600,000*l.*, were to be formed into a corporation, to be styled the Governor and Company of the Bank of Ireland. The corporation were to have a governor, deputy-governor, and fifteen directors ; which governor, deputy-governor, and directors, or any eight or more of them, shall be called a Court of Directors, for the management of the affairs of the corporation.

Fifteen directors shall be chosen annually, between March 25 and April 25 in each year, and not above two-thirds of the directors of the preceding year to be re-elected.

The notice for the meeting of general courts of proprietors to be affixed upon the Royal Exchange in Dublin at least two days before the time of meeting. The qualification for a voter at a general court shall be 500*l.* stock, to be held for six months preceding, unless it came by will, marriage, &c. The qualification for governor shall be 4,000*l.* stock, and for deputy-governor 3,000*l.*, and for director 2,000*l.*

No dividend shall at any time be made by the said governor and company, save only out of the interest, profit, or produce, arising by or out of the said capital, stock, or fund, or by such dealing, buying, or selling, as is allowed by the said Act of Parliament; nor without the consent of the members of the said corporation, in a general court qualified to vote as aforesaid.

The governor, or deputy-governor, shall summon four general courts at least in every year. One in the month of September, one in December, one in April, and another in July.

The governor or deputy-governor shall also summon a general court, whenever requested to do so by nine members, each holding 500*l.* stock.

If governor and deputy-governor be absent one hour after the usual time of proceeding, at any general court or court of directors, a chairman shall be chosen for that time only, who shall have like privileges as the governor or deputy-governor.

Governor, deputy-governor, or chairman, not to vote in general courts, or court of directors, save when there shall happen to be an equal number of votes on each side.

The Bank of Ireland commenced business at St. Mary's Abbey, June 25, 1783. After the Union, its office was removed to the Parliament House.

In the year 1821, the capital of the Bank of Ireland was increased from 2,500,000*l.* to 3,000,000*l.* Irish currency. The additional sum of 500,000*l.* was taken from the bank's surplus fund and lent to the Government at 4 per cent., to be repaid by the 1st January, 1838. The increased capital was divided among the proprietors, at the rate of 20*l.* for every 100*l.* they possessed. In consideration of this increase of capital, the bank consented to a clause in this Act, whereby persons in partnership, residing fifty miles from Dublin, might carry on the business of banking, although such partnership might consist of more than six partners; but that such partnership should possess no other privilege than being allowed to sue and be sued in the name of a public officer, should Parliament hereafter think fit to grant such a power. This privilege was of little

2 M

practical use, for, according to the construction put upon the Act, it required that all the partners in these banks should reside in Ireland.

In this year an Act was passed (5 Geo. IV. cap. 73), " to relieve bankers in Ireland from certain restraints imposed by the provisions of the 29 Geo II., and to render all and each of the members of certain co-partnerships of bankers, which may be established, liable to the engagements of such co-partnerships, and to enable such co-partnerships to sue and be sued in the name of their public officer."

Those clauses in the former Act that required the names of all the partners to be subscribed to the notes, and which prohibited bankers being traders, are by this Act repealed. Banking partnerships exceeding six persons, and carrying on business at any place beyond fifty miles from Dublin, shall be registered at the Stamp Office, Dublin; and also the names of the public officers in whose names such partnerships sue and are sued. The names of those public officers were also required to be subscribed to all notes and receipts issued by the company. Judgments against the public officers to operate as judgment against the partnership, and execution upon judgment may be issued against any member of the society, and the public officer to be saved harmless.

In the year 1825 was passed the " Act for the better regulation of co-partnerships of certain bankers in Ireland." It was obtained by the directors of the Provincial Bank of Ireland, as the Acts previously granted did not furnish the facilities which the Provincial Bank required for the beneficial exercise of its operations. It confirmed the permission granted by former Acts to establish joint-stock banks at a greater distance than fifty miles from Dublin, and permitted persons resident in Great Britain to become shareholders in such banks. The banks were required to register at the Stamp Office in Dublin an account of the names of the firms, the several partners therein, and the public officers thereof. The partnerships shall sue and be sued in the name of their public officers. Parties obtaining judgments in Ireland may authorize the acknowledgment of like judgment in Great Britain; and, in like manner, parties obtaining judgment in Great Britain, may proceed thereon in Ireland. Judgments against public officer shall operate against the society, and execution upon judgment may be issued against any member of the co-partnership. All transfer of shares must be registered at the Stamp Office.

In this year, too, an Act of Parliament was passed to assimilate the currency of Ireland to that of England. It is entitled, " An Act to provide for the assimilation of the currency and monies of account throughout the United Kingdom of Great Britain and Ireland." (6 Geo. IV. cap. 79.) The Act recites, that the pound sterling in Great Britain and Ireland respectively is divided into twenty shillings, and the shillings into twelve pence ; but the silver coin which represents a shilling in Great Britain is paid and accepted in Ireland for thirteen pence, and the pound sterling of Great Britain is, at the par of exchange, paid and accepted for one pound one shilling and eightpence of the currency of Ireland ; and that great complexity of accounts, and other inconveniences, arise from the said difference of currencies. It then enacts, that the currency of Great Britain shall be the currency of the United Kingdom, and all receipts, payments, contracts, and dealings, shall be made in such currency. And all contracts, debts, &c., made or contracted previous to the commencement of this Act, shall be carried into effect, and satisfied by payment in British currency of 12-13ths of the amount according to Irish currency. All duties and public revenues, and all funds and public debts shall be estimated in British currency, and the accounts thereof kept accordingly. After a day to be named by proclamation, British silver and gold coins shall be current in Ireland at the same rate of pence as in Great Britain. On the like proclamation, Irish copper coin shall be brought into the Bank of Ireland, and exchanged there for British copper coin, at the rate of twelve pence British for thirteen pence Irish, and the Irish copper coin shall cease to circulate. Bankers' notes shall be made payable in British currency. No notes payable in Irish currency shall be reissued after the commencement of this Act, under a penalty of 50*l.* for each offence. Bankers may deliver into the Stamp Office reissuable notes, payable in Irish currency, and receive in lieu thereof new stamps to the whole amount of the stamps delivered up, if dated within one year previous, or three-fourths if within two years, and one-half if within three years. This Act came into operation on the 5th day of January, 1826.

2 M 2

Very ample returns* of the state of the Bank of Ireland are published in the Appendix attached to the Reports of the Parliamentary Committees.

The Provincial Bank of Ireland.—Public banks may be divided into three classes :—first, Chartered Banks, those which have received a charter from the crown; secondly, Joint-stock Banks, formed under the common law ; and thirdly, Joint-stock Banks, formed under the statute law.

The common law of England allowed any number of persons to form themselves into a partnership to carry on banking. At the same time it presented this inconvenience in the formation of such partnerships—in all actions at law it was necessary to state the names of all the individuals who composed the company. Another inconvenience of partnerships formed under the common law was, that all the partners were answerable for the debts of the company to the full extent of their property, not only while they were partners, but after they had ceased to be partners, as far as regards any transactions that took place during the continuance of their partnership. The banks avoided these inconveniences, in the first place, by conducting their business in the names of trustees, in the same way as some of the insurance companies ; and in the second place, by inserting a clause in the deed of settlement, that in case the bank should lose one-third or one-fourth the amount of its paid-up capital, it should immediately be dissolved.

The statutes of 6 Geo. IV. c. 42, with reference to Ireland, and 7 Geo. IV. c. 46, with reference to England, not only repealed those Acts of Parliament which prohibited the formation of banking companies having more than six partners, but they also removed the inconveniences of the common law. It was enacted, that it should no longer be necessary, in legal actions, that the names of all the partners should be placed upon the record ; but that the company should register at the Stamp Office the name of some one person in whose name they wished to sue and be sued. Any party who had a disputed claim upon the company must sue this public officer, and when he had obtained a verdict in his favour, he might issue judgment against all the partners, in the same way as though he

* The Bank of Ireland, like the other banks of issue in Ireland, has since the year 1845 made weekly returns of its issues, and the average amount is published in the monthly *Dublin Gazette.*

had obtained a verdict against them all. And that he might have no difficulty in ascertaining who were or were not partners, it was required that the names of all the partners should be annually registered at the Stamp Office. The statute law also obviated the second inconvenience of the common law, by enacting that every partner, as soon as he had transferred his share, should be released from all liability as to the subsequent acts of the company, and at the end of three years he was no longer liable for any acts that took place even at the time he was a partner.

The Provincial Bank of Ireland was formed under the statute 6 Geo. IV. c. 42. Few banks have, in so short a time, advanced to so high a degree of prosperity. The circumstances of Ireland at that period were friendly to the growth of such an establishment. The recent abolition of the union duties, and the introduction of steamboats, had given a stimulus to the trade between the two countries, while nearly all the banks in the south of Ireland had been swept as by a whirlwind from the face of the land. The operations of the bank were also facilitated by the assimilation of the currency, and the measures taken by the Government and the Bank of Ireland to prevent those fluctuations in the exchanges which had previously existed. But the prosperity of this bank must be attributed chiefly to the wisdom and prudence manifested in its constitution and in its subsequent government. The capital was raised chiefly in England, and London was, consequently, made the seat of government. The board of directors was composed of merchants and statesmen, and the latter were taken from the leading men of the two parties into which Ireland was then divided. The local government of the respective branches in Ireland was composed of directors possessing local knowledge and influence, and of managers selected for their experience in banking, and the manager had a veto upon the decision of the board. An inspector was appointed to visit the branches, and to report to the London office.

At the same time, the bank had considerable difficulties to contend against. Property in Ireland was considered insecure; political and religious feelings often interfered with matters of business; the habits of the people were not commercial; and the country had suffered so severely from private banking, that confidence was not easily acquired for a new company, the members and constitution of which were but imperfectly known. Before these difficulties had been completely overcome, the bank became involved in a competition with branches of the Bank of Ireland, and exposed to sudden demands for gold arising out of political events.

The object of the bank was thus stated :—

" The bank to have a capital of 2,000,000*l.*, if necessary, subscribed in shares of 100*l.* each.   To have a board of directors in London, and establishments for business in the principal towns of Ireland which are distant above fifty miles from Dublin.   At each of these places, a part of its stock to be subscribed, and from the stockholders a local board of directors to be chosen.   The establishments to be managed by steady experienced persons sent from England, with the advice and under the inspection of the local directors, but subject to the entire control of the London board, to whom accounts shall be regularly transmitted."

The 11th Annual Report (May, 1836), in allusion to Banking in Ireland at the period of its formation, says :—

" To show the progress of competition, it may be sufficient to state, that prior to 1825, when the Act 6 Geo. IV. c. 42 was passed, under which the Provincial Bank was established, the Bank of Ireland had no establishment out of Dublin.

" That in Dublin itself there were only four more, and these private banks ; and that in all Ireland besides there were no other than private banks, and these only in Belfast, Cork, Wexford, and Mallow.

" From 1825 to 1834 banking offices in the chief cities and towns of Ireland had been gradually established by the Provincial Bank, the Bank of Ireland, the Northern and the Belfast Banks, to the number of about fifty ; while, within the short space of the last two years, the offices of joint-stock banks having resident managers or agents beyond fifty miles from Dublin, added to the branches of the Bank of Ireland, have increased to upwards of 120, and appear to be daily augmenting in number. Besides which, there are a great variety of stations attended on market-days by non-resident agents, on behalf of one or other of such banks ; and, in addition to all these, several establishments on a large scale have been lately announced in Dublin as in connexion with some of the joint-stock banks most recently formed in the provinces.

" The directors cannot, however, regard this unexampled rapidity of increase in the number of banks as a certain indication of prosperity. Amidst the excitement arising out of this state of things, they have considered it to be their duty to impress upon all their local directors and managers the necessity of increased caution and vigilance, and to warn them of the extreme danger of entering upon a race of competition, in which those who engage in it are too apt to overlook what is essential to their own safety."

There is no joint-stock bank of whose rise and progress we

have a more detailed account than the Provincial Bank of Ireland. This account is furnished to us in the evidence given to a Committee of the House of Commons by the late secretary, Mr. James Marshall.* We recommend the following quotations to the especial consideration of students in practical banking, as showing most minutely the various steps by which prosperity is obtained by banking institutions.

1.—*The Constitution of the Provincial Bank of Ireland.*

" Can you explain to the committee the constitution of the Provincial Bank ?—I can. I may make reference to the annual reports of the institution, of which, I understand, that copies were furnished to this committee. A report is made to the proprietors on the third Thursday of May in each year.

" By whom is that report prepared?—By a special committee.

" A committee of the board of directors ?—A committee of the board of directors, whom it is my duty to attend on such occasions, and to be their organ in acting as the clerk of that committee.

" When that sub-committee has prepared the report, what further step is then taken ?—It is submitted then to the general court of directors.

" Is it examined by them?—By the general court; it is laid before them, and every part of it is explained to them; and they have it in their power to examine any part, to refer instantly to the books, or the source from which it is drawn. The committee in making it up go very minutely to work, and examine very particularly.

" Then are the committee to understand, that before the report is laid before the proprietors, that report is first submitted to a select committee, reported by them to the general court, and approved of by the general court ?—It is ; it is, in the first instance, signed by the chairman of the committee when presented to the general court.

" When laid before the proprietors, is it laid before the proprietors on the responsibility of the court of directors ?—Completely so.

" Just confine yourself at present to the constitution of the bank.— It may be here proper to state, for the information of the proprietors, the regulations which have been adopted, in the first place, for conducting business in a proper manner at the branches ; and, secondly, for the control

* Mr. James Marshall was the accountant of the Provincial Bank of Ireland at its commencement, and in the year 1826 succeeded Mr. Thomas Joplin in the office of secretary. He retired in 1845, upon a pension of 1,000*l.* a-year. The chairman stated to the General Meeting in 1846, that Mr. Marshall's salary was 1,200*l.* a-year, but as 200*l.* a-year was regarded as an equivalent for a house, the Directors considered he had retired upon full pay. The officers of the Bank subscribed to have his likeness taken, and an engraving was presented to each subscriber. After his retirement he became an auditor of an insurance office, and a director of the Oriental Bank. In the latter capacity he paid a visit to Bombay in the year 1847. He died in London on the 14th day of January, 1852.

and superintendence which are exercised over them by the directors in London. First, as to the branches. For the due management of the business at each a suitable house has been obtained, and the following officers have been provided; viz., manager, accountant, teller, clerk, porter, all of whom find security for their fidelity. Where the scale of business requires it, the number of the inferior officers is increased, but there are only two principal officers at any branch, viz., manager and accountant; and for securing more effectually the proper discharge of the duties of all, and assisting the manager with advice and information, there has been appointed at each station a board of local directors, consisting, according to circumstances, of three, four, or five gentlemen of the first respectability in the place, who, in order to be eligible, must themselves have an interest in the establishment, by holding ten shares each of its stock. The duty of these gentlemen is to meet daily at a given hour at the bank's office, and, along with the manager, to judge of bills presented for discount, and of all applications for credits. For every act of business of this nature it is necessary that two local directors and the manager be present; and it is provided, that where applications for discounts or credits exceed, in individual cases, a certain fixed amount, or when the manager differs in opinion from the majority of the local board, the matter must be submitted to the decision of the court of directors in London. It is further the duty of the local directors to compare daily the vouchers with the entries in the cash-book, to count, at stated intervals, the cash in charge of the manager, and to certify the returns made periodically from the branch to London.

"Are the committee then to understand distinctly that the local directors, in the case in which the manager, who is the head officer of the society, differs with them, although he may differ singly, are bound to refer those cases to the London board before any decision is come to?—In every case.

"In another contingency it would appear, that where the pecuniary transactions in question exceeded a given amount, that, too, although the board might be unanimous, is brought under the consideration of the London board of directors?—It is.

"What does that sum generally amount to? Is it a fixed sum, or does it vary according to the circumstances of the different branches?—It has varied according to circumstances; but, generally speaking, from 300*l.* to 500*l.* is considered the extent to which anything in the shape of a credit, other than the discount of a mercantile bill, would go."

2.—*The Selection of Officers.*

"Be so good as to explain to the committee what steps were taken by the Provincial Bank of Ireland in the selection of their various paid officers at the branches?—I believe that is detailed in this said report. The selection of officers in particular was a matter of paramount importance, both on account of the great number required to fill the intended situations in Ireland, and the necessity there was to scrutinize their qualifications as to character and ability. Communications were made on this subject with various gentlemen in different parts of the country, from whom it was expected the best information could be obtained. The prospectus of the society having set out with the resolution that the business should be conducted on the principles which had been so long and so successfully acted upon in Scotland, it seemed desirable to obtain from that country persons trained up in banks there, provided their qualifications in other respects were such as to recommend them. With this view, the secretary (that was not myself at the time) was sent down to Edinburgh in February, for the purpose of making inquiries; and notice having been given in the public papers that persons were wanted to fill situations in the projected establishments in Ireland, a gentleman in the above city was employed to receive applications and to institute the most minute and scrupulous inquiries regarding the character and qualification of those who should apply. Another gentleman from the same city was also engaged to proceed to London, to assist the directors in the formation and prosecution of a plan for conducting the business, when they should be ready to commence it in Ireland (that alludes to myself). The extensive correspondence which the applications and inquiries, produced by the measures above mentioned, necessarily occasioned, occupied the attention of the directors very closely, and for a considerable length of time, and the result has been that the services of a number of most valuable officers have been secured to the society.

"But at that period was there a greater facility in procuring the services of gentlemen more particularly who had experience in the Scotch banking than there would be subsequently, when there was a more active competition in the establishment of banks?—No doubt of it.

"What description of security were these officers required to give?— Unexceptionable personal security; two persons, at least, generally were joined in a bond for the fidelity of the officer.

"Was there any fixed proportion between the amount of the security required and of the salary paid, or the duties to be performed?—The amount had respect to the duties to be performed rather than to the salary.

"What was the general security that was taken by bond for the fidelity of these officers?—The lowest clerk was 1,000*l.*; the highest 10,000*l.*, for a manager at the largest branch.

"And that has been enforced by the Provincial Bank with respect to its officers?—The amount of 10,000*l.* has not been required, as we have practically found 5,000*l.* to be a more commandable sum; I would say, within the reach of the description of parties who are aspirants to these offices.

"Now, with respect to the local directors, how were they selected?— It is mentioned here that there should be selected three, four, or five gentlemen of the first respectability in the place, of commercial knowledge, whenever those could be obtained; if having had that commercial knowledge, and being disengaged from business, they were considered as so much the more eligible.

"But in the selection of local directors, so far from excluding persons by reason of their having commercial or banking knowledge, are the committee to understand that such parties were preferred?—Where they had it, and were not understood to be in a situation to require banking accommodation for themselves.

" You have stated that the local directors were required to take ten shares each, at the least ? — Yes.

" Will you have the goodness to state what the reason was that they were required to take those shares ?—In order that they might have a greater interest in the establishment ; feel a personal interest. I must say we have not, in every instance, been able to get gentlemen of that description. We have, in some instances, appointed gentlemen who, from various causes, declined to become shareholders ; at least, we have elected gentlemen to be local directors without requiring the fulfilment of that condition. There are some instances at present of gentlemen who are so ; but no doubts regarding the solvency of the bank ever deterred any of them."

3.—*The Choice of Directors.*

" Now tell us how they are appointed ?—The directors in London were, of course, originally appointed by the gentlemen who associated together for the purpose of forming this establishment ; and they continued, with the approbation of the meeting, until a certain time, when, by the deed of settlement which was afterwards prepared, four were to go out every year.

" In the vacancy of the four, who appoints their successors ?—The proprietors generally ; the general meeting of proprietors.

" Are they re-eligible ?—They are declared by the deed of settlement to be re-eligible.

" Are they recommended to the court of proprietors by the court of directors ?—They are ; they have been virtually so : and I beg to refer to one of the annual reports, which gives an explanation upon that point. It is in the report made the 17th of May, 1827, in which it is stated : ' The directors have now to advert to a circumstance of some importance as connected with the constitution of the society. By the deed of settlement, the number of directors was limited to twenty. Since the completion of the deed, that number has been reduced by death or resignations to sixteen ; and the directors having found by experience that the latter number is quite sufficient to insure a due attendance for the efficient management of the business of the establishment, have not thought it necessary to enforce the terms of the deed by proposing the election of new members ; and they think themselves now justified, by past experience, in unanimously recommending to the court of proprietors to limit the number of directors for the ensuing year to sixteen. The directors may add, that this arrangement will be attended with a considerable saving of expense ; and, in conclusion, they beg to state to the proprietors an opinion in which they also unanimously concur, viz., that in future elections, it will greatly conduce to the harmony and cordiality which it is so desirable should prevail amongst the directors themselves, as well as to the good management of the bank's affairs, if a recommendation shall be made by them to the proprietors in favour of those candidates whom, after due inquiry, they shall find to be the best qualified to fill the situation.'

" Have those recommendations been generally complied with by the proprietors ?— Always.

" Uniformly, without exception?—Uniformly; it has uniformly been acquiesced in. Two or three candidates had upon more than one occasion started, but when the matter was explained to them, they have uniformly acquiesced in it. It is necessary to state, to complete this, that the recommendation to limit the number of directors to sixteen was afterwards the subject of a special provision by an additional deed of the proprietors; therefore the number cannot be extended beyond sixteen without altering the deed.

" Are the directors paid for their attendance?—They are.

" What is the amount of payment which they receive?—It is so regulated that no director can receive above 250*l.* a year, the director in London, I mean, were he attending at every possible meeting that he could.

" Is the payment an annual payment, or proportionate to the attendances?—Proportionate to the attendances, ascertained every quarter.

" According to the number of attendances, so the parties are paid?—Yes, according to the attendances.

" Was that sanctioned by the proprietors and by the society?— The deed of settlement contains a provision allowing the directors to take the sum of 5,000*l.* as remuneration."

4.—*The Daily Committee.*

" Will you state how they transact their business?—By meeting daily in committee (a general committee), which is open to all to attend; but in order to be a quorum there must be three present; and by a weekly court, held each Friday, at which all ought to be present.

" Is there a record in writing of all the directions and the acts of that special committee?—There is.

" Are each of those acts brought under the examination and review of the general court on Friday?—At the weekly court they are; the minutes are read over.

" Is the question put upon the confirmation of those minutes, or is it open to the general court to vary or alter them?—The question is specially put by the chairman of the weekly court, whether it is the pleasure of that court to confirm the minutes of the past week which have been read.

" Have you known instances in the management of the bank in which there have been any variations upon the proceedings of the committee proposed by the general court, so as to show that it is an active as well as a theoretical superintendence?—I have seen instances where the subject has been brought under revision, and which has produced an alteration of the resolution of the committee.

" Having now explained to the committee the formation of your local administration at the branches, and your general administration in London, will you state what the course of proceeding is, to insure to the court in London a knowledge of that which takes place at the different branches?—I read from the report already referred to: ' Regular advices of the proceedings at the branches are transmitted by the managers to London by post every second or third day, according to circumstances;

and at the end of each week a complete statement of the whole trans-actions is made up, and forwarded by the mail-coach. These returns are first examined by the officers of the London establishment, and then submitted to the directors. For giving the necessary orders arising out of these communications, for judging of all matters referred to them from the branches, for disposing of the bank's funds in London and Dublin, and for the discharge of all other duties implied in the exercise of a superintendence over the whole establishment, whether in Ireland or in London, the directors hold regular and daily meetings.'

" Are the accounts which are sent from the branches accounts in detail of the whole of the operations of the bank ?—They are.

" Are they, in fact, transcripts of the accounts of the bank from period to period ?—They are so ; with this explanation regarding the current accounts of parties holding accounts with the bank, every particular draft or receipt is not sent to London, or rather the entries of these, I mean, are not copied or sent to London ; but there is this check on the operations of the branches, the exact balance of every man's account at the end of each week is given, and forms part of an abstract of the balance-sheet which is sent forward, and which must agree ; therefore, if it were wrong, it would at once detect itself.

" Then no variation can take place in the actual balance without the attention of the court being at once called to it ?—None can.

" And is the name of each individual to whom these advances are made from time to time brought under the special notice of the court of directors in London ?—Yes; by the following process. The branches are divided amongst the directors, so many allotted to such a sub-committee, who take up the affairs of these branches each week in succession, and examine all the bills that have been discounted, the advances that have been made of any description, and the balance of each man's account, whether in his favour or against him."

5.—*The Inspection of Branches.*

" Have you any system of inspection by which you are enabled from time to time to verify the correctness of the proceedings of the branches? —We have. Besides having a half-yearly balance-sheet made out with all the details of the affairs of each branch at the time, and which is scrupulously examined at London, there is an inspector (two at present) whose duty it is to go through the branches and to examine personally and verify every voucher and every particular, and to remain at the branch until they are fully satisfied that all is right.

" Are the visits of your inspectors at stated and known intervals, or is any branch at any one moment liable to the visit of an inspector, and to an immediate examination and verification of their accounts and bills and balances ?—Every branch is so liable to be visited; there is no pre-vious intimation given, except the visit be for some particular purpose which, by a representation from the branch, calls on the inspector to go.

" As an additional security, have you yourself, or any of the directors, been accustomed to visit the branches, and to report thereon ?—I have myself every year, and sometimes oftener than once a year, even twice or three times in a year, gone to Ireland, and have gone through the whole branches, in fact, more than once, at different times; and on all occasions have made examinations which appear to me to be necessary; and besides that, the directors have in person repeatedly visited the branches; deputations of the London directors, I mean, have so done."

6.— *The Declaration of a Dividend.*

" Will you explain to the committee what steps you take before you declare a dividend ?—We have regularly a balance every half-year; the dividend has only been declared once a year, at the termination of the year, which is in March; our year ends in March. Prior to that period, each manager is directed to send up a special report of every obligation which is outstanding, or of any which is doubtful, describing particularly in the report every party to such obligation; that is preparatory to going further into the matter; then when the balance at the end of March is completed, a complete balance-sheet of every branch is made up and sent to the bank, with a more detailed report. A special committee of the directors is appointed to examine those, and they go minutely through them, and weigh every outstanding debt, and strike off everything that is considered to be irrecoverable; they then consider in what degree the reports of the managers represent every other outstanding debt to be recoverable, either in full or in part; and when all that has been done, they add generally a sum to cover still any possible omission, and it is only then that the fair profits of the year are considered to be ascertained.

" Can you inform the committee how far your calculations, your annual calculations of bad and doubtful debts, have or have not been below or above the mark ?—In many instances our allowances have exceeded what has turned out to be the real loss; for, as I mentioned before, the directors, in order to be more secure, have been in the practice of making an additional deduction over all the deductions made by the officers at the branches.

" Have the proprietors any power under your deed of settlement of naming any auditors, or having any examination of those accounts, so as to verify their fidelity ?—We have no auditors, but there is a provision in the deed of settlement by which a certain number of proprietors may call for a further investigation of the accounts, if they are dissatisfied."

7.— *The Causes of its Prosperity.*

" Do you think there is anything peculiar in the construction of this bank which has insured its being correctly and well managed up to the present time, or that it has rather arisen from the ' happy accident ' of the directors who were selected having been honourable and correct men of business ?—I conceive the very first and indispensable thing was an exceedingly respectable board of directors formed in the first instance, and which has always been maintained. In the next place, that the system of accounting that was adopted, and the check on the operations of the different branches, which has not been departed from, has most materially contributed to that good result. In the next place, there was an exceedingly good field for banking when we commenced, for Ireland was very destitute of good banks at the time, the Bank of Ireland operations having been confined only to Dublin. Therefore, from all those concurring circumstances, I conceive the prosperity of the bank has resulted."

To these causes we may add one more, stated in the Report delivered by the directors to the proprietors in the year 1836, —the non-interference of the shareholders in the distribution of the profits:—

" To this desirable position the affairs of the bank have been conducted, as the directors have great pleasure in acknowledging, by the uniform support and continued approbation of the proprietors, who, far from manifesting any impatient desire to participate in the reserved profits, have always relied with confidence on the opinion of those by whom the working of the establishment was superintended, feeling assured that whenever such participation was clearly expedient, it would not be withheld."

The National Bank (formerly the National Bank of Ireland). —The Prospectus of this bank, issued in 1834, announced that it would be conducted on the " local shareholder principle."

" It is proposed that each branch shall have a separate capital proportioned to the extent of its business, one-half to be subscribed by resident shareholders, so as to identify their interest with their own establishment, and the other half to be subscribed by the National Bank of Ireland, whose connexion with each branch, whether its separate capital consists of 5,000*l.* or 50,000*l.*, will afford it the credit of whatever capital (however large) the National Bank of Ireland may have actually paid up at the time."

" The following are the terms and conditions of subscribing:—

" 1. That a company shall be formed in London, to extend to Ireland the benefit of a sound banking system.

" 2. That a bank be formed in each town in Ireland where practicable by law, and which offers a prospect of success to the operations of the company.

" 3. That the object of the London company shall be to connect itself with shareholders exclusively interested in the success of each local establishment.

" 4. That the principle of the bank shall be the division of profits of each bank with such local shareholders in Ireland. The capital of each branch to be subscribed equally by shareholders on the spot and the company in London.

" 5. That the capital of the London company shall be 1,000,000*l.*, in shares of 50*l.* each, to be called the original capital, which may be increased as the business of the company extends; but the premium, on any addition, to go to the first subscribers.

" 6. That the bank shall be formed as soon as half the capital is subscribed.

" 7. That the bank shall be managed by a board in London, consisting of twenty-four directors, in whom will be vested the supreme control.

"8. That each local bank shall be managed by a board of local directors, elected by the shareholders, subject to the approbation of the directors in London."

This principle was first announced to the public by the late Mr. Thomas Joplin. He attempted to introduce it into the National Provincial Bank of England, of which he was the managing director, and to the formation of which he had materially contributed. But the practical difficulties were found to be great. It was almost impossible to arrange the preliminaries to the satisfaction of all parties, and the principle was never brought into operation. Mr. Lamie Murray, who projected the National Bank of Ireland, was the secretary of the National Provincial Bank of England, and had adopted Mr. Joplin's views on the subject. When first established, therefore, the National Bank of Ireland acted on this principle; but after a few years the independent local banks with which it was connected consented to become branches of the head establishment.

Another peculiarity attended the formation of this bank. Its chief connexions lay among that political party in Ireland who advocated a Repeal of the Union, and the business of the bank is conducted with a view to embrace all classes irrespective of party or politics. In the provisional committee appeared the names of the late Daniel O'Connell, Esq., M.P., Maurice O'Connell, Esq., M.P., Fitz-Stephen French, Esq., M.P., James Grattan, Esq., M.P., and others of the same political views. The seat of government, however, like that of the Provincial Bank of Ireland, was fixed in London. One advantage resulted from connecting the heads of this party with an Irish joint-stock bank. There was an end to all *political* runs for gold. When a run afterwards took place, in consequence of the failure of the Agricultural Bank, Mr. O'Connell used all his influence to allay the excitement then occasioned. The chief office in Ireland is in Dublin, where, since the Act of 1845, it has issued its own notes.

The Report of 1848 states that the National Bank of Ireland had taken the business of the London and Dublin Bank.

"During the latter part of the year, it having been intimated to the directors that the London and Dublin Bank were desirous of dissolving that company, negotiations were entered into with the directors, which terminated in this establishment succeeding to its connexions in the towns of Dundalk, Carrickmacross, Wicklow, Kells, Athy, Mullingar, and Parsonstown, with every prospect of advantage to the bank. The whole of these localities are, with the exception of Parsonstown, within the circle from which all banks of issue, except the Bank of Ireland, had been excluded, until the extinction of the monopoly by the Banking Act of 1845."

We have already stated that this bank has commenced business in London as a London banker. It was at first supposed that this could not be legally done ; but upon investigation it was found that the prohibition to carry on business in London, and within sixty-five miles thereof, as Banks of Deposit, applied only to those Joint-stock Banks that issue notes in England, and not to the Banks of Issue in Ireland or Scotland.

At a special general meeting of the National Bank of Ireland, held October 20, 1855, for the purpose of taking into consideration a modification of the name of the bank, the chairman stated, that the desire of the proprietors, as well as the increase of business in London, seemed to necessitate a change of name that would not so exclusively apply to Ireland. After some observations, a resolution was passed unanimously, " That on and after the 1st of January next, 1856, the present name of the society be changed to that of ' The National Bank.' " [In 1864 the capital of the bank was increased by the issue of new shares to the extent of 500,000*l.*, and, by a resolution adopted in 1865, a further increase was made by the transfer of 300,000*l.* from reserve fund to capital account, making, with these additions, the present paid-up capital of the bank to be 1,500,000*l.* The bank has recently increased the number of its Irish branches, now seventy-one in all, besides its London head office and seven Metropolitan branches.]

The Hibernian Bank.—The Hibernian Joint-stock Bank was formed in the year 1824. The following account of the origin of this bank is given by John Robinson Pim, Esq., of Dublin :—

" A number of Roman Catholic gentlemen, finding they were continued to be excluded from the direction of the Bank of Ireland, met together, and obtained the signatures, not only of Roman Catholics, but of a number of others, amongst the rest myself, to the establishment of this bank. Many merchants signed it, as considering, that by having an opposition bank in such a city as Dublin, advantages would frequently be derived from it, and not altogether looking to the emolument which they should receive as subscribers to the bank, but looking at it as citizens generally. I myself never calculated on a very great deal of profit from it, except at a very remote period. Some of the individuals who undertook it came over to London, and they had expected to obtain the power of issuing notes, but they met with so much opposition from the Bank of Ireland,—there were some of the directors of the Bank of Ireland came over here in order to oppose it,—and the clauses which they intended to enable them to issue notes were expunged in the committee; but I state this only from hearsay."

Its nominal capital is 1,000,000*l.*, divided into 10,000 shares of 100*l.* each. 25*l.* per cent. has been paid upon each share, so that the money actually advanced amounts to 250,000*l.*

In the same year this company obtained an Act entitled, " An Act to enable the Hibernian Joint-stock Company, for the purpose of purchasing and selling annuities, and all public and other securities, real and personal, in Ireland, and to advance money and make loans thereof, on the security of such real and personal security, at legal interest, and on the security of merchandise and manufactured goods, to sue and be sued in the name of the governor or secretary for the time being."[*]

The preamble states, that—

"Whereas the commerce, and manufactures, and agriculture of Ireland have long laboured under great disadvantage, arising from the want of due command of capital; and that merchants and manufacturers have no means of procuring temporary advances of money on a deposit of their goods, when a slackness of demand arises; and whereas several persons have agreed to form themselves into a company, or partnership, under the name of the 'Hibernian Joint-stock Company,' and have subscribed or raised considerable sums of money in order to purchase and sell annuities and all public and other securities, real and personal, in Ireland; or to make loans and advances of money on the security thereof, and on the security of merchandise and manufactured goods, at legal interest, and to receive lodgments of money or deposits thereof; and great public benefit is expected to be derived to the trade, manufactures, and agriculture of Ireland, from the formation of such a company or partnership; and whereas difficulties may arise from time to time," &c.

It is enacted that this company may sue and be sued in the name of their governor or secretary. A memorial of the names of the governor, secretary, and members, and of the transfer of shares, to be enrolled in Chancery; and no actions to be

[*] Anno quinto Georgii IV. Regis, cap. 159.

brought by the company, under the authority of this Act, until such memorial shall have been enrolled. Execution upon any judgment against the governor or secretary may be issued against any of the members, who are to be reimbursed their expenses by the company.

The Royal Bank of Ireland.—The Royal Bank of Ireland was formed in the year 1836, and before opening made arrangements for taking the business of the private bank of Sir James Shaw & Co. At that time the law did not permit joint-stock banks, in Dublin, to accept bills drawn at less than six months after date, or to sue and be sued in the name of their public officers. These restrictions were removed by the Act of 1845. The Royal Bank attempted also at that time to obtain the power of issuing notes, but was not successful. The manager of the bank from its commencement has been Mr. Charles Copland, who had previously been a manager in the Provincial Bank of Ireland.

The Banks of Belfast.—There are three joint-stock banks at Belfast. The Northern Banking Company was formed in 1825, on a private bank which was called the Northern Bank. This was the first joint-stock bank in actual operation in Ireland. The Belfast Banking Company was formed on a private bank, which was called the Belfast Bank. The senior partner in this bank, John Holmes Houston, Esq., was examined as a witness before the Parliamentary Committee of 1826, on the abolition of small notes in Ireland. His evidence contains some interesting particulars respecting the state of banking in Belfast during the time he had been a partner in that bank. The Ulster Banking Company was formed in 1836. All these banks have branches extending throughout the north of Ireland. The prudence with which banking institutions have at all times been managed at Belfast, has no doubt greatly contributed, with other causes, to the prosperity of the north of Ireland.

The following joint-stock banks have ceased to exist in Ireland : —

1. The Agricultural and Commercial Bank of Ireland, formed in the year 1834, stopped payment in the latter end of the year 1836. It was afterwards resumed for a short time, and then finally closed. A full account of the reckless pro-

ceedings of this bank is given in the third volume of the *Bankers' Magazine.*

2. The London and Dublin Bank was formed in 1844, and merged in the National Bank of Ireland in the year 1848. This was not a bank of issue.

3. The Southern Bank of Ireland was formed at Cork after the failure of the Agricultural Bank of Ireland. It was .registered the 25th of March, 1837, opened in Cork in the month of July, and stopped payment in the following September.

[4. The Union Bank of Ireland, Limited. Established 1864.*]

Laws of the Currency in Ireland.—From what we have already said of the laws of the currency, those of our readers who are acquainted with Ireland will be able to judge beforehand of the revolutions of her circulation. Being purely an agricultural country, the lowest points will of course be in August or September, immediately before the harvest, and the commencement of the cattle and bacon trade. Then it rises rapidly, till it reaches its highest point in January, and then gradually declines. As an agricultural country, we should naturally expect that during the season of increase the circulation would expand most in the rural districts; and so we find that the circulation of the Bank of Ireland, in Dublin, expands very moderately—that of her branches, which are located chiefly in large towns, expands more—while the circulation of the joint-stock banks, which are located in the agricultural districts, receives the largest increase. Again, the purchases and sales of agricultural produce are known to be in small amounts; and hence the notes of the smallest denomination receive the largest relative increase. The annual changes of the Irish circulation are governed chiefly by the produce of the harvest, and the prices of agricultural products. These are the laws of the circulation of Ireland.

On this subject I may quote my own evidence before the Committee on Banks of Issue :—

"I have told the Committee that I was formerly manager of a joint-stock bank of issue in Ireland, and I have attempted to discover the laws which regulate the circulation of that

---

* Business transferred, within about three to four years, partly to the Munster Bank and partly to the Hibernian Bank.—EDITOR.

conntry, by ascertaining the highest and lowest amount of
he circulation in each year. This, which I have in my hand,
is a table, showing the circulation of the Bank of Ireland
(including branches), the separate circulation of the branches
alone, and the circulation of the Irish joint-stock and private
banks, on the last Saturday of April, August, and December,
of the years 1834 to 1839. It will be observed that those
periods are the same as those which I have referred to in the
circulation of the English country banks. The law of circulation appears to be different, but they agree pretty nearly in
this, that the lowest point is the latter end of August; but
the highest point in Ireland is generally the end of December
or the beginning of January, and from December, or the
beginning of January, it declines; so that the country circulation of England is advancing eight months and declining
four; but the circulation of Ireland is advancing four months
and declining eight.

"From whence is this table compiled?—From Appendix,
Nos. 32 and 33. This table shows that the circulation of
Dublin does not vary much; it shows that the circulation
of the branches of the Bank of Ireland varies more; and that
the circulation of the joint-stock and private banks in Ireland
varies considerably more.

A TABLE, *showing the* CIRCULATION *of the* BANK *of* IRELAND (*including
Branches*); *the Circulation of the Branches alone; and the Circulation
of the Irish Joint-stock and Private Banks; on the last Saturday of
April, August, and December, of the Years* 1834 *to* 1839.

I.—BANK OF IRELAND AND BRANCHES.						
	1834.	1835.	1836.	1837.	1838.	1839.
	£	£	£	£	£	£
April	3,922,300	3,798,600	3,614,100	3,332,300	3,398,400	3,536,400
August	3,452,800	3,198,700	3,123,500	2,921,600	3,055,800	2,981,800
December . . .	3,926,800	3,574,200	3,481,100	3,265,700	3,474,600	3,192,200

II.—BRANCHES OF THE BANK OF IRELAND.						
April				. . .	1,357,600	1,572,000
August	No separate account kept at this time.			1,056,200	1,257,600	1,211,900
December . . .				1,342,300	1,695,600	1,464,000

III.—JOINT-STOCK AND PRIVATE BANKS.						
April	1,386,165	1,517,648	2,083,431	1,798,724	2,366,774	2,568,377
August	1,140,654	1,264,572	1,928,900	1,480,240	1,881,906	1,982,122
December . . .	1,666,269	1,959,542	1,787,586	2,204,286	2,972,034	2,629,205

"It will be observed, that in the year 1836, with regard to the joint-stock banks, there was a departure from the law, which usually increases the Irish circulation very rapidly between the months of August and December; for in 1836 the Agricultural and Commercial Bank of Ireland stopped payment; that brought on a run for gold upon the other banks, and thus the circulation of those banks became reduced. This is the only year in which there is not a very considerable increase in the circulation of the joint-stock banks of Ireland between August and December.

"To what do you attribute this uniform increase of the Irish circulation towards December?—I attribute it to the trade in corn, and bacon, and cattle, which commences in the months of September and October in every year; the produce of the harvest commences to be brought to market in September; but the bacon is made in the beginning of October. The bacon must be made in cold weather, and therefore pigs are reared so as to be fit for killing by the 1st of October; and in the beginning of October the provision merchants send out their men to purchase pigs at the different markets, and they get notes from the bank. The cattle trade is conducted in the same way; men go to the market to buy pigs and cattle, and take them over to Bristol and Liverpool, but chiefly to Bristol from the part where I was. Those notes are chiefly issued in three ways. During the summer, the merchants, having their capital unemployed, lodged it as deposits in the bank; then, when the season for trade commenced, they drew out their deposits, in the form of notes. Afterwards, they brought us bills upon their factors in London, and our notes were issued in discounting those bills which they had drawn against the exportations of bacon and cattle. The dealers took their pigs and cattle over to Bristol, and sold them in the various markets and fairs in the west of England, and received the notes which were circulating in that district, and took them to Mr. Stuckey, and got a letter of credit upon me, payable on demand, for the amount. So that our notes were issued, in the first place, by the withdrawal of deposits; secondly, for the discounting of bills on London, drawn against the exports which were made; and thirdly, for the payment of letters of credit which had been obtained by the parties who had sold Irish cattle in the English markets.

The notes were, therefore, drawn out by the trade of the country, and of course it was not in our power to withhold issuing those notes, unless we wished to cramp the trade of the country."

Laws of the Currency in Ireland, since 1845.*—In the year 1845 an Act was passed for the regulation of bank notes in Ireland. The average amount of notes that had been in circulation during the year ending May 1, 1845 (6,354,494*l*.), was made the fixed or authorized issue. For any amount beyond its authorized issue, each bank was required to hold an equal sum in gold or silver coin, the silver not to exceed one-fourth of the whole. The Act came into operation on the 6th Dec. 1845, and from that period each bank has made returns to the Government, stating the average amount of notes in circulation during the preceding four weeks, distinguishing the notes under 5*l*. from those of 5*l*. and upwards, and stating the amounts of gold and silver coin it held in its vaults. These returns are made by all the banks of circulation in Ireland. These are—the Bank of Ireland, the Provincial Bank of Ireland, the National Bank, and the three banks in Belfast, viz., the Northern Banking Company, the Belfast Banking Company, and the Ulster Banking Company.

We possess these returns for every four weeks from Jan. 1846 to the present time. By adding together all the returns made during each year, and then dividing by thirteen, we obtain of course the average amounts in circulation from 1846 to the year 1851, inclusive. I have also added the proportion per cent. these averages bear to the certified circulation of 6,354,494*l*. The following are the average amounts of circulation :—

	Average Circulation.	Proportion to Certified Circulation.
1846	£7,259,948	114·25
1847	6,008,833	94·55
1848	4,828,992	76
1849	4,310,283	67·83
1850	4,512,444	71
1851	4,462,909	70·25

It appears that, if the authorized issue be represented by the number 100, the actual circulation for the six years, 1846

* This article is an abstract of a paper read before the Statistical Section of the British Association, at their meeting held at Belfast in the year 1852.

to 1851, inclusive, will be represented by the numbers 114, 94, 76, 67, 71, 70. The question naturally occurs to us— What is the cause of this great falling off in the annual circulation since the passing of the Act of 1845? In reply, we may observe that the annual productiveness of the harvest would affect the amount of notes in circulation. From the description of the harvests given in the annual reports of the Provincial Bank of Ireland, we learn that the years 1846 and 1848 were disastrous in regard to the produce of the harvest; and we consequently find, as we should naturally expect, a falling off in the following years in the circulation of bank notes. We may also observe, that a bad harvest in one year may, by the distress it produces, cause a less production of commodities in several following years, and hence there may be a less demand for bank notes. In a bad harvest the farmer consumes his own produce instead of selling it, and thus requires not the use of notes. If his potatoes are destroyed he will consume his grain. The distress of the farmer also diminishes the instruments of reproduction. If he has no potatoes he can rear no pigs. An abundant crop of potatoes produces in the following year an abundant crop of pigs, but a famine of potatoes will be followed by a famine of pigs; and hence the distress of one year may have the effect upon the circulation of notes in several succeeding years. After the failure of the potato crop in 1846, the exportation of swine was reduced from 480,827 in 1846, to 106,407 in 1847. The potato crop again failed in 1848. The number of swine exported in 1848 was 110,787; in 1849 it was only 68,053.

We may also observe, that a reduction in the quantity of commodities produced may be caused by a reduction in the number of producers, and this would occasion a less demand for bank notes. It appears, from the Census of 1841 and 1851, that, between these two periods, the population declined 1,659,330, or at the rate of 20 per cent.; and calculations have been made to show that the whole of this decrease had taken place since the year of the famine, 1846. Such a decrease, from whatever cause, must be attended with a decrease in the commodities produced and consumed by those individuals, and will consequently have occasioned a less demand for bank notes to pay for those commodities. If the lands previously occupied by this departed population remain uncultivated, there is a direct decrease in the agricultural produce. Such might be the effect where the occupants died. Emigration might produce an additional effect. The emigrants, before their departure, would change all their bank notes into gold to take with them, and thus would occasion a further reduction of the circulation. This decrease of the population occurred chiefly among those who had but small holdings in land. Those small cultivators are compelled to bring their produce to market immediately after the harvest, and hence the circulation rises in September and October. From these small holdings, too, the produce is brought to market in small quantities—"each man brings his sack of oats, or two or three pigs, to market"—and hence the circulation, thus occasioned, must consist chiefly of small notes. We may further observe, that the amount of notes which circulate in a country will also be affected by the quantity of commodities exported, and the quantity imported. The season in which there is the greatest export of commodities is the season of the highest circulation. But importation withdraws the notes previously in circulation. The effect of diminished exports and increased imports is referred to in the Reports of the Provincial Bank of Ireland, every year from 1847 to 1851; and Mr. Murray states, in his evidence before the Committee on Commercial Distress, that not only was the amount of notes reduced, but also that of silver.

Thus we find that the reduction in the amount of notes in circulation in Ireland has been preceded or accompanied by a reduction in the amount of commodities produced, occasioned by a reduced productiveness in the land actually cultivated, a destruction of the instruments of reproduction by the distress thus occasioned, a reduction in the number of producers by deaths and emigration, and the exportation of an increased portion of its capital in exchange for food. But there is another circumstance that concurs in powerfully producing the same effect—that is, the prices at which the commodities brought to market are sold.

The failure of the crops in Ireland led the late Sir Robert Peel to introduce "An Act to amend the Laws relating to the Importation of Corn." It is 9 & 10 Vict. cap. 22, and was passed June 26, 1846. A large reduction was made in the duty immediately; and it was enacted that, after the 1st day of

February, 1849, the duty on wheat, barley, oats, &c., should be only 1s. per quarter. And in consequence of the increased distress in Ireland, another Act was passed, in January, 1847 (9 Vict. cap. 1), to suspend, until the first day of the following September, all duties on the importation of corn. In consequence of these Acts, large importations took place, and the prices gradually declined. I have no means of ascertaining the average prices of grain throughout Ireland, but I have obtained from a London corn-merchant the average prices of wheat, barley, and oats, for each year from 1841 to 1851, and taking in each case the prices of the year 1845 as represented by 100, I have calculated the variations per cent. in the subsequent years. On comparing the years 1845 and 1851, we find that the circulation has declined 35·78 per cent., the price of wheat has declined 24 per cent., of barley 21·85 per cent., and of oats 17·40 per cent. If we compare the year 1841 with 1851, the decline of the circulation will only be at the rate of 16·7 per cent., while the price of wheat shows a decline of 40 per cent,, of barley 25 per cent., and of oats 17 per cent.

From the whole, we infer that the difference between the amount of bank notes circulating in a country at two distant periods cannot be regarded as any correct test of the condition of its inhabitants at those periods, unless we take into account all the circumstances by which that difference is attended— that the decline of the circulation of bank notes in Ireland, from the year 1845 to 1851, is no accurate measure of the distress that has existed in the country, as other causes besides distress have concurred in producing that effect—that in comparing the circulation of 1845 and 1851, we are making a comparison unfavourable to the country, as the year 1845 was a year remarkable for the high amount of its circulation—and that, [while the falling off between the years 1846 and 1851 was caused by the failure of the potato crop, which seriously affected production for some years, and the reduced price of grain, and also by emigration, yet in recent years, with increased production and largely increased value of nearly all kinds of agricultural produce, the circulation has again expanded, and for the four weeks ended 5th November, 1870, the total circulation of the Irish banks was 7,511,076l., which is higher than the amount already quoted as the average of the year 1846.]

Having considered the changes that have taken place in the annual amount of notes that have circulated in Ireland since the passing of the Act of 1845, I shall consider the monthly changes in the amount of the circulation.

Let us take up the returns, and look at any year we please, and we shall find that all the months vary from each other. Beginning at January, the amount of the circulation usually declines—slowly at first, but more rapidly in May, June, and July, until, by the end of August, we arrive at the lowest point. Then, in September, it begins to ascend, and goes on increasing till January, and then again declines till August. Now, let us inquire what are the laws which regulate these monthly variations. I stated that the annual variations were caused by variations in the quantity and price of agricultural produce. But, as no notes could be put into circulation until this produce is brought to market, the monthly circulation must depend upon the quantity of produce brought to market within the month. Now, it has been the custom in Ireland to commence bringing the produce to market immediately after the harvest. Hence arises the increase of the notes in September, and their further increase in the following months. But in the beginning of the year the landlords collect their rents, and receive from their tenants the notes for which this produce has been sold ; this brings the notes back to the bank, either to be placed to his credit (if he have an account there), or, otherwise, in exchange for a letter of credit on Dublin, or a bill on London. The circuit of a note, then, is this :—It is obtained from the bank by a corn-merchant, who pays it to a farmer for his corn, which he ships to England. The farmer afterwards pays the note for rent to his landlord, who brings it back to the bank. Every month the bank is issuing and retiring notes, but, from August to January, it issues more than it retires ; and hence the amount of notes in circulation increases, and from January to August it retires more notes than it issues, and hence the circulation falls.

We may notice another feature suggested to us by these Public Returns. We observe that a portion of the circulation consists of notes of 5*l.* and upwards, and another portion of notes under 5*l.* ; and it may be useful to inquire if these two classes of notes are subject to the same laws, and whether they rise and fall at the same time and in exact proportion to each other.

Viewing the monthly circulation, we observe that the small notes, like the large notes, are at their lowest amount about the month of August, and at their highest amount about January. But we observe, also, that from August the small notes increase more rapidly than the large ones, and after January they decline more rapidly; so that in every year the proportion of small notes in circulation is greater in January than in August. It may be observed, too, that the circulation of the Belfast banks includes a much larger proportion of small notes than is contained in the circulation of the other banks. To show this, it will be sufficient to analyse one of these returns. Upon the total circulation of all the banks, the proportion of small notes on the 7th of August, 1852, is 49·39 per cent.; upon that of the Bank of Ireland, 34·73 per cent.; the Provincial Bank, 58·82 per cent.; the National Banks, 59·93 per cent.; and the Belfast Banks, 86·55 per cent.

I have one feature more to notice in these returns—that is, the amount of gold and silver kept by the banks, in order to meet the payment of their notes. For several years past the Act of 1845 has not required the Irish banks to keep any amount of gold or silver, for they have always been below the authorized circulation; but another Act, passed in the year 1828, through the influence of Mr. Spring Rice—(Lord Monteagle)—requires that all notes should be payable in gold on demand at the place of issue. The gold and silver kept by the banks have only been to the amount that they deemed necessary or prudent for the purposes of business.

We observe from these returns that the annual average amount of gold and silver kept by all the banks has varied from 29 to 36 per cent. We observe, too, that in the years when the circulation has been low, the amount of gold and silver has been higher in proportion than in those years when the circulation has been high. Taking the average of years from 1847 to 1851, the *lowest* amount of gold, in proportion to its circulation, has been kept by the Bank of Ireland. The proportion varies from 24 per cent. in 1851, to 30 per cent. in 1849. The highest proportion has been kept by the Provincial Bank. It has varied from 38 per cent. in 1851, to 52 per cent. in 1849. We may also state that, in the monthly variations, the lower the circulation the higher the proportionate amount of gold and silver. This arises, it may be presumed, from the circumstance that the banks do not vary the amount of their gold and silver with every variation of the circulation. The proportion of silver to gold kept by all the banks, has varied from 20 to 33 per cent., but the proportion varies very much with different banks.

The amount of gold necessary to be kept against any given amount of notes in circulation is purely a question of management, and depends upon a variety of circumstances. The degree of public confidence the bank may have acquired, the excitable character of the population, the state of commercial credit, the facility of obtaining supplies, and the rapidity of communication with its branches, are all to be taken into calculation by a prudent banker. Gold can now be so readily obtained from England by means of steamboats, and distributed throughout Ireland by means of railways, that so large an amount may not be so necessary as formerly. The railways and the electric telegraph are useful to bankers, and present a striking instance of the utility of scientific discoveries to men of business.

Abolition of Small Notes.—The following is the report of the Select Committee of the House of Commons, made in 1826, respecting the abolition in Ireland of notes under 5*l.* :—

" With respect to the circulation of Ireland, the inquiries of your Committee have been less extensive than those which they have instituted with respect to Scotland.

" The first law in Ireland which restrained the negotiation of promissory notes, was an Act passed in the Irish Parliament in the year 1799.

" The preamble recites that various notes, bills of exchange, and drafts for money, have been for some time past circulated in lieu of cash, to the great prejudice of trade and public credit; and that many of such notes are made payable under certain terms, with which the poorer classes of manufacturers and others cannot comply, unless by submitting to great extortion and abuse. It adds, that the issue of such notes has very much tended to increase the pernicious crime of forgery; and the Act proceeds to apply to notes between the value of 5*l.* and 20*s.* similar restrictions to those which had been applied to such notes issued in England by the Act which passed in the year 1777. It permits, however, during the suspension of cash payments by the Bank of Ireland, the issue of bank-post bills, bills of exchange, and drafts under certain regulations, for any sums not less than three guineas. This Act did not extend to the Bank of Ireland.

" In 1805, this and some other Acts which had passed in the interim relating to the issue of small notes, were repealed ; and notes under 20*s.*, which had been previously admitted under certain regulations by the Act of 1799, were declared void.

" There is at present no law in force imposing any limitation to the period for which notes for a sum not less than 20*s.* may be issued in Ireland.

" A tolerably correct estimate of the amount of promissory notes, above and below 5*l.*, circulating in Ireland, may be formed from the subjoined returns made by the Bank of Ireland, and by other banks at present established in that country.

" Bank of Ireland notes.—An account of the average amount of the Bank of Ireland notes of 5*l.* and upwards (including bank-post bills) for the years 1820, 1821, 1822, 1823, 1824, and 1825 :—

Irish currency.
£   *s.*   *d.*

" Notes and post bills of 5*l.* and upwards 3,646,660 19 6

" An account of the average amount of the Bank of Ireland notes under the value of 5*l.* (including bank-post bills) for the years 1820, 1821, 1822, 1823, 1824, and 1825 :—

Irish currency.
£   *s.*   *d.*

" Notes and post bills under the value of 5*l.* ... 1,643,828 0 5

" It appears from the evidence that a practice prevails in Ireland of issuing notes for the payment of sums between one and two pounds, for three guineas, and other fractional sums.*

" Your Committee see no public advantage arising out of this practice, and they are of opinion that it ought to be discontinued, as it tends to dispense with the silver coin, and practically to exclude it from circulation.

" Your Committee hesitate, in the present imperfect state of their information, to pronounce a decisive opinion upon the general measures which it may be fitting to adopt with respect to the paper currency of Ireland.

" Although they are inclined to think that it would not be advisable to take any immediate step for the purpose of preventing the issue of small notes in Ireland, their impression undoubtedly is, that a metallic currency ought ultimately to be the basis of the circulation in that country.

" It will probably be deemed advisable to fix a definite, though not an early period, at which the circulation in Ireland of all notes below 5*l.* shall cease; and it is deserving of consideration, whether measures might not be adopted in the interim for the purpose of insuring such a final result by gradual, though cautious, advances towards it."

The following is a summary of the evidence given before the Committees of the two Houses of Parliament, as to the effect of abolishing the small note circulation in Ireland :—

1. Small currency is necessary to carry on the commercial transactions of the country.

---

* The Act 8 & 9 Vict. c. 37 (1845) prohibits the issue of notes for fractional parts of a pound, consequently the practice referred to has since been discontinued.—EDITOR.

JOHN ACHESON SMYTH, Esq., *Agent for the Belfast Bank at Londonderry.*

" In Lancashire, I believe all the raw materials are bought in large parcels, and by bills. In Ireland, the raw material is all bought in small parcels, and all in small notes. In Lancashire, there is only cash wanted to pay the workmen, but we want it both to pay the workmen and to buy the raw material. The provision and grain that we send to England are also bought in small notes, and we are reimbursed by drawing bills for our shipments."[*]

PIERCE MAHONY, Esq., *Solicitor to the Provincial Bank of Ireland.*

" If the banks were prevented issuing notes under the amount of 5*l.*, would any inconveniences arise in conducting the trade of the South of Ireland?—The trade of Ireland generally, and especially in the South of Ireland, would be greatly inconvenienced, and the growth of manufactures would be decidedly checked, if not destroyed, by such a measure. From the great subdivision of land in Ireland, and particularly in the South and West (where the population is almost exclusively agricultural), the produce is disposed of in small portions, scarcely ever representing 5*l.*, and almost universally under that amount. I am of opinion that the withdrawal of all notes under that amount would have the effect of curtailing the accommodation the banks now afford to the public to a ruinous extent, and that the trade of the country under such circumstances would not afford profitable employment for banking capital to any extent; and, therefore, I should anticipate the withdrawal of such establishments, except, perhaps, at Cork and Belfast. In the south and west of Ireland, from the nature of the provision and corn trade, the chief demand for notes or for gold commences in October, and continues until March, when that trade is nearly over for the season. From March until October the butter trade is almost the only one in the South and West of Ireland; and as that trade would not employ all the capital that is required in the winter season, the effect would be, if sovereigns were substituted for small notes, that the extra supply required for the corn, beef, and pork trade, must remain idle in the banker's chest, or be remitted at great risk and expense for employment elsewhere during the summer and autumn.

" Do you think, if a metallic circulation were adopted, that there would be a difficulty in maintaining that metallic circulation?—I do; because the trade in the south and west of Ireland is periodical; the remittances from those districts of Ireland would force the gold away at certain periods, and it must be returned at others, with considerable expense, to meet the trade of the country."[†]

2. A gold currency would be more inconvenient than notes, and would not be so well liked by the people.

---

[*] Commons' Report, p. 77.
[†] Ibid. pp. 250, 251.

LEONARD DOBBIN, Esq.,* *Agent for the Northern Banking Company of Belfast, at Armagh.*

" Do the people of the north of Ireland manifest any wish for gold in preference to notes, or for notes in preference to gold?—They decidedly prefer notes, and the weavers have refused to carry gold out of the market lately.

" Can you assign any reason for this preference?—There are many reasons that I could assign. The bank notes are now the established currency; the people are perfectly acquainted with them. If a man should lose notes, or a house be robbed, or if there is a forgery, it would be much better for them to trace notes than it would gold. I have often assisted poor people in tracing notes that were robbed, and forged notes, whereas the gold could not be traced so readily. Another reason I would give is this, guineas became light, and were troublesome to the people. When standing beam there was 1s. charged, and when lighter than standing beam 2s. 6d.; and when gold was scarce, and bank notes not a legal tender, the land agents refusing to take anything but gold, the tenants were obliged to pay from 1s. to 4s. on a guinea, discount. Some agents would only take gold." †

J. A. SMYTH, Esq., *Linen Merchant, and Agent for the Belfast Bank at Londonderry.*

" I am in the habit of employing my linen buyers to go to the country markets, and I must supply them with the week's money before they start, perhaps five hundred or a thousand pounds. They have to go through the interior of the country, and do not return for a week. They make their purchases all in small quantities, and it is more convenient for them to carry notes than gold." ‡

ARTHUR GUINNESS, Esq., *Director of the Bank of Ireland.*

" I conceive, that with the persons who handle the circulation of the country, there is a decided preference in favour of small notes over cash in every respect. I speak from mine own experience; for I remember perfectly well, before the restrictions upon cash payments, when gold was a great inconvenience in trade. I speak of those who handle the currency of the country, among whom I think the preference is in favour of the small notes, as more convenient, more portable, and less liable to counterfeit. I conceive these to form the general ground of preference."§

3. The profits of the banking establishments would be so much diminished, that they could not extend the same accommodation to the agricultural and commercial classes.

---

* This gentleman was afterwards agent for the Bank of Ireland at Armagh, and M.P. for that place.

† Commons' Report, p. 243.   ‡ Lords' Report, p. 7.

§ Commons' Report. p. 237.

W. P. LUNNEL, Esq., *Director of the Bank of Ireland.*

" If the notes under 5*l.* were prohibited, would the profits of the Bank of Ireland be materially affected by such prohibition?—I should expect that they would suffer: they must sacrifice a certain profit.

" Have you considered to what extent the profits of other bankers would be affected?—I should expect that the principal circulation of the country bankers is in small notes, and therefore in that proportion they would suffer."[*]

JOHN HOLMES HOUSTON, Esq., *Banker at Belfast.*

" If all the notes under 5*l.* were prohibited to be issued, would it be worth while, in your opinion, to keep the establishment of a bank at Belfast?—I do not think it would, except by carrying it on in the same manner as it formerly was—to keep a discount office, charging a commission on discounting bills, because 5*l.* notes would not circulate. Then our circulation would be so trifling it would not answer."[†]

H. A. DOUGLAS, Esq., *Director of the Provincial Bank of Ireland.*

" I consider the cash account system and the one-pound circulation so connected, that if the notes are withdrawn, it is understood that our establishment will not grant any further cash-credits. The business which we carry on, even if we charged a higher rate of interest, or a commission, would not be of sufficient magnitude to repay us for the expense of our establishment, independent of our notes. If the issue of small notes be withdrawn, then we cannot afford to allow interest on deposits."[‡]

4. **The abolition of small notes would prevent the investment of British capital in the present banking establishments.**

T. S. RICE, Esq., M.P. (LORD MONTEAGLE), *Director of the Provincial Bank of Ireland.*

" Is it your opinion, that if all notes under 5*l.* were abolished, a considerable inconvenience would arise in the ordinary traffic in Ireland?—I conceive that it would. I conceive that the first effect of the extinction of all notes below 5*l.* would be a much more considerable diminution of the general mass of the circulating medium in Ireland than in England.

" I fear extremely that if anything were to occur which materially diminished the profits of our establishment, it would have the effect of depriving us of one of the chief benefits of the establishment, namely, the support and control of British capitalists, and conducting the bank by British merchants, and upon British commercial principles. I conceive a rate of profit, rather higher than the average rate of profits, is essential to induce persons so circumstanced to engage in such a business, more particularly when it is considered that there is no limitation of responsibility by the grant of charters."[§]

[*] Lords' Report, p. 108.　　　　[†] Ibid. p. 35.
[‡] Ibid. pp. 24, 26, 27.　　　　[§] Ibid. pp. 47, 51.

5. The gold currency would be sent out of the country, whenever it bore a premium in England.

HENRY H. HUNT, Esq., *Local Director of the Provincial Bank of Ireland, at Waterford.*

" What do you think would be the consequence of a law which prohibited the issue of notes below 5*l.*, both by the Bank of Ireland and by any other banking establishment in Ireland ?—I should think it would be very hazardous indeed : I should very much apprehend that the gold circulation would at times be *withdrawn* in a very great degree *from the country,* whenever gold was wanted in London; for instance, A SMALL PREMIUM UPON A SOVEREIGN WOULD INDUCE A VAST QUANTITY OF THEM TO BE BROUGHT OUT OF IRELAND.

" Have you ever known instances of quantities of gold being brought over from Ireland to this country, and persons making a regular traffic of it ?—I have."*

6. The proposed measure would cause general distress, and prevent the progress of enterprise.

JOHN ROBINSON PIM, Esq., *General Merchant in Dublin.*

" The very idea of curtailing the currency under 5*l.* would have a tendency to discourage all adventure in Ireland at present. I should not, for one, be careful of placing money in any kind of machinery till the effect was tried. I fancy it would reduce property very much in that country,—and sometimes fancies are almost as bad as reality." †

Robert Murray, Esq., the chief officer of the Provincial Bank of Ireland, was examined as to the establishment of one Bank of Issue throughout Ireland. The following is his reply :—

" It would produce an entire revolution in the monetary affairs of Ireland. The committee will already have gathered, from the questions I have previously answered, that the produce is brought to market in very small quantities, and by a very large number, I had almost said an innumerable class of farmers; each man brings his sack of oats and two or three pigs to market. It would be almost impossible, in such a state of things, to regulate by one bank of issue the monetary affairs of Ireland, or to adapt it to its purposes as it is now situated."

It may be useful to trace the effects of the Act of 1845 (8 & 9 Vict. c. 37) upon the state of banking in Ireland, as compared with the effects of similar enactments in Scotland and England.

1. The limitation of issue in Ireland, as in Scotland, is not absolute. The banks may issue beyond · this limit, if they

* Commons' Report, pp. 73, 74. † Lords' Report, p. 19.

2 o .

retain an amount of gold and silver equal to this excess. In England the prohibition is absolute. The probable effect will be that these enactments will not lead to any permanent decrease of the circulation in Ireland or Scotland. The banks will merely import more gold when the circulation increases. In England it seems probable that the circulation will permanently decrease. Means will be employed to conduct banking operations with fewer notes, and these means will operate at all times—when the circulation is low, as well as when it is high.

The provision of the Act of 1845, which requires the banks of Scotland and of Ireland to keep an amount of gold equal to the notes in circulation beyond the fixed limits, tends, as we have observed, to restrict the granting of cash credits in Scotland. We doubt if it will have an equal effect in Ireland, simply because the cash-credits exist to only a limited extent. The Provincial Bank introduced the system in 1825, and no system could be better adapted to the state of the country. It would doubtless have greatly improved the condition and the habits of the people ; but the iniquitous runs for gold which, at the suggestion of reckless politicians, took place in 1828, 1830, 1831, and 1833, compelled the banks to restrict their operations. Had the banks remained without molestation, the whole of the agricultural districts of Ireland would probably by this time have had the benefits of this system, with the same beneficial results which have been realized in Scotland.

2. In Ireland these measures will not tend to produce so great an increase of gold as in Scotland. In Scotland the banks, previous to the passing of the Act, kept but a small amount of gold. But in Ireland the banks, from their liabilities to runs, have always kept large deposits of gold. The amounts required by the Act are not larger than those formerly kept in their vaults. It appears from the returns, that the Bank of Ireland has recently kept a smaller amount than before the passing of the Act. Hence their means of affording accommodation are not diminished ; and as they sustain no loss, they have no reason for increasing their charges. The Bank of Ireland and joint-stock banks, as a rule, allow interest only on deposit receipts.* The reason assigned by the Scotch banks

* Some of the banks in Dublin are understood to allow interest on current accounts in special cases, or under restriction as to the minimum balance which shall bear interest.—EDITOR.

was, that the operations on these accounts maintained in circulation a large amount of their notes. This will be no advantage if the bank must retain an amount of gold equal to this increase of notes in circulation.

3. The prohibition of new banks of issue has operated variously in the three countries. In Ireland it was beneficial; in Scotland it has been harmless; and in England it is injurious. The Agricultural Bank of Ireland caused considerable mischief. To prevent the recurrence of such evils, the most effectual way was to prohibit the formation of new banks of issue. Hereafter this restriction may become oppressive. Cork, and Limerick, and Waterford may become sufficiently wealthy to supply a banking capital, and may wish to form local banks. The local banks at Belfast have conferred great benefits on the north of Ireland. In Scotland the banks are sufficiently numerous; and, as they are allowed to unite, the authorized issue of notes is never likely to be less than it is. And although restrictions on banks are unsound in principle, they may not at present do any harm in Scotland. In England the restriction is injurious. Had we an unlimited power of forming new banks, many of those firms that now consist of not more than six partners would be merged in larger establishments. The number of banks would be less—the amount of their issues would probably be less—but they would attract a higher degree of public confidence, and their character and continuance would not be dependent upon the lives of individual partners.

4. Unions of banks in either Ireland or Scotland are not very likely, nor perhaps desirable. The banks are large, have a respectable capital, and enjoy the public confidence. In England, many banks are small, and have small capitals. Union among them would be highly beneficial. Yet such is the waywardness of legislation, that the Acts of 1844 and 1845 give facilities to unions in Ireland and Scotland, and restrict them in England. In Ireland and Scotland two banks of issue may unite, and the united bank have the united circulation. In England, if two banks of issue, either of which has more than six partners, should unite, the circulation of one or both of these banks would be lost.

5. The Act passed in 1844, for the regulation of joint-stock banks in England, was extended in 1846 to Scotland and Ireland, with the omission of the clause that rendered the

banks subject to the laws of bankruptcy. By a clause in these Acts, any bank for the formation of which proceedings had been taken before the 6th May, and which was actually in business on the 4th of July, must at the end of a year after the passing of the Act either retire from business or take a charter. The Preston Banking Company was in this case, and accordingly became a chartered bank. Out of London this is the only bank that has a charter under the Act in England. The Exchange Bank of Scotland was in a similar case, and on the 31st of December, 1846, it became a chartered bank. There is no bank of this kind in Ireland.

It was a special provision of this Act (Joint-Stock Banks Regulation Act) that no new joint-stock bank can be formed of a less nominal capital than 100,000*l*., and half the capital must be paid up before the commencement of business; that the assets and liabilities of the company must be published once at least in every month; and that at least one-fourth of the directors shall retire yearly, and shall not be eligible for re-election for at least twelve calendar months.

That provision of the Act which requires one-fourth of the directors to retire annually, and which declares them ineligible for election for one year, has been the subject of much discussion. The object of the Legislature appears to have been to prevent those evils which, in public companies of every kind, occasionally arise from the undue ascendency of individual directors. Practically, it may be injurious or advantageous to a bank, according to circumstances. On the one hand, it may deprive a bank of the services of its most useful directors for one year. And on their return, they may be less useful than heretofore, from being less acquainted with the transactions that have taken place during their absence. In small country banks it might not be easy to find other parties to take the places of the directors who had thus retired. On the other hand, it has been contended that the number of the directors, and consequently their influence, would thus be virtually increased—that, while on some occasions the most clever directors would be compelled to retire, at other times the least clever would retire, and their places might be better supplied—that the retirement of even the most clever might call forth the energies of the others, and thus the talents of the whole might be improved—that the plan tends to prevent the undue ascendency of any individual director, or of any knots or parties of directors, for any length of time—and that it is a convenient means of getting rid of an inefficient, injurious, or disagreeable director: for, when he is once out, it would be easy for the board, if so disposed, to prevent his re-election. By the charter of the Bank of Ireland, fifteen directors are chosen annually, and not above two-thirds of the directors of the preceding year can be re-elected.

6. There is another difference between Scotland and Ireland with reference to banking operations, though it does not arise from the above-mentioned Act. At the time of the union between England and Ireland, Ireland had her debts as well as England. And although England became liable for these debts, the dividends continued to be paid, and the transfers made in Dublin. Hence Government stock is bought and sold there in the same way as in London. Besides this, any party may purchase stock in Ireland, and have it transferred to England, or the reverse. The plan is this :—Any person holding stock may go to the Bank of England, either personally or by power of attorney, and get a ticket that will authorize him to have the same amount of stock put in to his name in Ireland. The stock in England is then transferred to the Commissioners for the Reduction of the National Debt. He may go to the Bank of Ireland in Dublin and reverse the operation. Several Acts of Parliament have been passed with reference to this subject. The last is the 25th Vict. c. 7, passed in the year 1862. When there is a great difference in the price of stocks in the two countries, operations of this kind may be very profitable.

This power of transferring Government stock from one country to the other has a tendency to equalise the price in both countries. It also serves the purpose of a medium of exchange. A transmission of stock has the same effect in rectifying the exchanges as a transmission of gold. And doubtless the exchanges between England and foreign countries might, to a great degree, be adjusted in the same manner.

There is a Stock Exchange in Dublin similar to that of London, established for the purchase and sale of Government stock, bank stock, railway shares, &c. No person can transact business there unless he has obtained a licence from the Lord Lieutenant. The number of these persons is at present about twenty-five. The borrowing and lending of money on stock are matters of daily occurrence. This is not always done through brokers. Individuals often effect these transactions directly with the banks. The general rule is that the lender shall have a margin of 5 per cent. on the value of the stock, and shall be entitled to call for additional security whenever the market price falls below that difference.

We have noticed the different meanings given to the word "circulation" in England, since the passing of the Act of 1844. By the Act of 1845, it is enacted that this word shall have the following meaning in Scotland and Ireland :—

"Section 17.—And be it enacted, That all bank notes shall be deemed to be in circulation from the time the same shall have been issued from any banker, or any servant or agent of such banker, until the same shall have been actually returned to such banker, or some servant or agent of such banker." *

The Exchanges between the Banks.

Since the Act of 1845—when other banks besides the Bank of Ireland acquired the power of issuing notes in Dublin—a system of clearing, or, as it is called, of exchanges, has been established, similar to that established in Edinburgh. The following is a copy of a clearing balance-sheet :—

BALANCES OF EXCHANGES WITH OTHER BANKS, ON _____, 18 .

DUE TO IT.		WITH	DUE BY IT.	
		Bank of Ireland.		
		Provincial Bank.		
		National Bank.		
		Ulster Bank.		

Here we may observe that all the banks that clear are banks of issue ; and the clearing in Dublin includes all the banks of issue in Ireland, although three of these banks have their head-

---

* It may be stated here that the circulation of the Issue Department of the Bank of England is always 14,000,000*l.* more than the amounts of gold and silver held in that department. The amount of the circulation in the hands of the public is found by deducting the amount of bank notes in the Banking Department from the amount of circulation of the Issue Department.

quarters in Belfast. Two of the Belfast banks clear by their agents. The Bank of Ireland is the agent for the Northern Banking Company, and the Ulster Bank has a branch in Dublin. It will be observed that the Bank of Ireland—the chartered bank—is a member of the clearing; and, in fact, the clearing is held daily, at two o'clock, in one of the rooms of that establishment. The differences are paid daily, like those at Edinburgh, in exchequer bills. The following are the amounts required to be held by each bank :—

					£
The Bank of Ireland	.	.	.	.	192,000
The Provincial Bank	.	.	.	.	100,000
The National Bank	.	.	.	.	80,000
The Ulster Bank	.	.	.	.	80,000
					£402,000

Those banks in Dublin that are not banks of issue are not members of the clearing. All the non-issuing banks, however, have accounts with the Bank of Ireland, and pay into that establishment the cheques they may have on the other banks. The issuing banks which attend the clearing have no account with the Bank of Ireland.

This system of clearing appears to work very satisfactorily. The following is an extract from a letter I received from an Irish banker on the subject :—

"The settlement of our 'exchange balances' in Dublin, through the use of exchequer bills, works very well. The great evil, *previously*, was, that when these balances were of magnitude, Dublin was such a limited money market, there was difficulty and expense in raising the needful quantity of Irish money for the purpose. If you anticipated the balance to be heavy against you, it was requisite to prepare some time *before*, and to have your funds lying idle and unproductive until the crisis arose. *Now*, we have exchequer bill interest for our surplus, and the power of replenishing our stock account whenever required by drawing on *London*, thus possessing the unbounded advantages of the greatest money market in the world. In point of fact, the arrangement has virtually changed the venue, and made *London* the actual and final place of settlement, through machinery worked in Dublin."

"*Regulations for making exchanges between the several banks in Ireland, at Dublin, and for settling the balances of such exchanges, at Dublin;* to take effect from and after the 8th day of December, 1845.

"1. The exchange shall be made daily at two o'clock, P.M.

" 2. The payments of the balances shall be made in exchequer bills, except for the fractional parts of 500*l.*, which may be paid in the notes of the particular bank debtor.

" 3. The exchequer bills shall be filled up in favour of the bank who may be the original holders,* and shall bear the distinguishing mark of ' Dublin Exchange Bills,' showing that they belong to the Dublin exchanges, and are not intended to be used for any other purpose, and shall be received *at par*, with the interest that may be due when the transfer takes place.

" 4. The amount of exchequer bills to be kept in the circle is fixed at 402,000*l.*, to be apportioned amongst the following banks in fixed sums, calculated in their respective amounts of circulation :—

| Bank of Ireland. | Ulster Bank. |
| Provincial Bank. | National Bank. |

The sums being once fixed, each bank is to maintain its quota at all times, as hereinafter provided.

" 5. Nine-tenths of the exchequer bills to be of 1000*l.*, and one-tenth of 500*l.*

" 6. The amount of exchequer bills held by each bank shall be stated every day in the Clearing-room.

" 7. It is expedient that no bank shall be obliged permanently to hold more exchequer bills than a surplus of one-third above the fixed amount, nor shall be allowed to reduce the amount held more than one-third below the fixed amount ; but as the exchequer bills will accumulate with some of the banks, and be required by others, it shall be imperative on the parties so situated to sell or buy exchequer bills ; that is to say, the bank holding the greatest amount of exchequer bills shall be bound to sell to the bank in want of them, what may be required for the legitimate purposes of the exchanges ; but it shall not be imperative on that party to sell a greater amount than what will reduce their stock to the original quota, and the purchaser shall be bound to take bills from those parties having the greatest proportionate amount of them beyond their respective original quota.

" 8. The preceding regulations will tend in a great degree to equalise the amount of exchequer bills ; but if exchequer bills shall nevertheless accumulate in the hands of a bank, so as to exceed their original quota by more than one-third, that party shall have the power to call upon the party or parties holding the smallest amount in proportion to their quota to purchase the excess—that is to say, the excess above their quota—plus one-third ; but it shall not be imperative on any party to take more than is required to bring up their stock to two-thirds of the original amount.

" In this way the fluctuation in the amount of exchequer bills amongst the different banks, which is an essential part of this arrangement, need never permanently exceed one-third more or one-third less than the original quota of each bank.

" The terms of purchase to be governed by the next regulation.

* They are not now filled up in favour of the bank who may be the original holders, but are stamped by each bank and are payable to bearer.—EDITOR.

" 9. The bank seeking to buy, or being called upon to buy, exchequer bills, from the bank or banks holding in excess of their quota, shall pay for the purchase by a Letter of Credit on their London correspondent, demandable on the fifth day after the date thereof, the purchaser paying 1s. 3d. per cent. on the amount of the Letter of Credit;* or to pay the amount in gold in Dublin, at the option of the holders of the bills.

" 10. The exchequer bills to be used for the Dublin exchanges are to be as nearly as possible divided into the two dates of March bills and June bills, which are to be exchanged at the Paymaster-General's Office here before due, and new ones to be provided, so as to keep up the stock in the circle; and no exchequer bills advertised to be paid are to be used in the exchanges.

" 11. Each bank is to be always liable to the income-tax on the interest of its original quota of exchequer bills, and no more; and the exchequer bills advertised to be renewed are, within a week after the Government notice appears in the *Gazette*, to be given up to the original holders, upon receiving other bills not advertised; failing which, a Letter of Credit on London, demandable on the fifth day from its date, subject to the charge as stated in No. 9, is to be given, or the amount to be paid in gold, at the option of the holders of advertised bills.

" 12. The exchanges are to be made at the Bank of Ireland, who undertake to pay those banks who are creditors in the exchange the exchequer bills or bills of exchange received from those banks who are debtors in the exchange; but the Bank of Ireland shall not be in any way responsible for the exchange transactions, or otherwise soever.

" 13. The statement of the balances after they are struck to be sent to their respective banks from the Clearing-room, by their clerks; and the clerks of bank creditors to be in waiting to receive the amount due to them at two o'clock.

" 14. Any bank a party to this agreement to have the power of withdrawing from it, and receiving back their exchequer bills at par, upon payment of them if needful, upon giving three months' notice.

" 15. No bank a party to this arrangement shall, after the 8th of December, 1845, directly or through any agent, demand gold from or pay gold to any other bank or banks parties to this arrangement, except as hereinbefore provided, unless under special agreement between any two of the banks they mutually arrange to pay and receive a sum of gold.

" It is assumed that each bank always has its statutory amount of gold; and if any bank be either in excess or deficiency in that amount, the export or import of gold must be borne by the bank seeking to diminish or increase its stock.

" Any violation of this regulation after the 8th of December, 1845, to be considered a virtual withdrawal of the bank who departs from this rule.

" N.B. The foregoing arrangements are to be subject to such alterations and amendments as may be required and agreed on by the several banks parties thereto, after the plan shall be in operation, and its working effect ascertained."

* Drafts or Letters of Credit are now granted without any charge beyond the five days allowed for the settlement.—EDITOR.

SECTION VII.

THE MORAL AND RELIGIOUS DUTIES OF BANKING COMPANIES.

———

" I implore the blessing of Divine Providence on our united efforts
to encourage the industry and increase the comforts of my people,
and to inculcate those Religious and Moral Principles which are the
surest foundation of our security and happiness."
                    SPEECH FROM THE THRONE, AUG. 9, 1845.

" Property has its Duties as well as its Rights."
                    THE LATE MR. DRUMMOND.

———

THIS is the age of public companies. The principle of association is one of the most powerful agents of modern times.
Whatever object we wish to accomplish—whether political or
commercial, literary or religious—the first step is to form a
society. Those joint-stock associations that involve the outlay
of capital with a view to profit, are called public companies,
and these form the subject of our present inquiries.

Public companies now occupy a distinguished place in our
social economy. We receive our education in schools and
colleges founded by public companies. We commence active
life by opening an account with a banking company. We insure
our lives and our property with an insurance company. We
avail ourselves of docks, and harbours, and bridges, and canals,
constructed by public companies. One company paves our
streets, another supplies us with water, and a third enlightens us
with gas. At home, numerous luxuries are brought within our
reach by different companies. And if we wish to travel, there
are railway companies, and steamboat companies, and navigation companies, ready to whirl us to every part of the earth.
And when, after all this turmoil, we arrive at our journey's end,
cemetery companies wait to receive our remains, and take
charge of our bones.

The question that now claims our attention is, whether these
powerful companies ought to be regarded as moral agents ?—
that is, whether they are capable of virtuous and vicious actions,
and, like individuals, are responsible to a Superior Power, who
will reward or punish them according to their works.

In examining this question, we shall propose the following inquiries :—

First.—Ought public companies, like individuals, to be regarded as moral agents, and therefore bound to perform moral and religious duties ?

Second.—What are those moral and religious duties which, as moral agents, public companies are bound to perform ?

Third.—What are those rewards or punishments which may be expected to follow the performance or non-performance of those duties ?

First.—We inquire, Ought public companies, like individuals, to be regarded as moral agents, and therefore bound to perform moral and religious duties ?

We assume, at the commencement of our inquiries, that mankind, *as individuals*, are moral agents, having had laws laid down for their government by a Superior Being, to whom they are responsible for their actions. They who deny this proposition (if such there be) are not the persons for whose perusal these pages are designed; and therefore we will not ask them to accompany us any further in our inquiries.

Assuming that mankind are responsible, as individuals, we propose to inquire whether public bodies, *as such*, are subject to the same responsibility. And here we would suggest the following considerations :—

1. Public companies are recognised as moral agents by the laws of the country in which they are established.

Public companies have, by law, the same rights as individuals; their property is protected by the same laws as that of individuals. Theft or fraud towards them is attended with the same punishment. They can sue and be sued in the same courts of justice. The military and naval forces protect them from external violence. They have the same commercial privileges, and can buy and sell and get gain. The improvements in the arts and sciences benefit them as well as individuals ; and whatever new laws are passed by the Legislature confers upon them the same benefits as upon individual citizens. Having the same rights, they have necessarily the same duties as individuals. Equality of privilege implies equality of moral obligation. Property has its duties as well as its rights ; and if the property which to-day is in the hands of an individual is transferred to-morrow into the possession of a thousand individuals, would it not carry with it the same amount of moral obligation ? Would not the possession of the property demand from the company the same duties towards their servants, their fellow-citizens, their country, and their God, which it previously demanded from the individual ? and would they not be equally bound to the exercise of justice, kindness, benevolence, and patriotism ? The success of public companies is often at the expense of individuals. Ought they not, then, to be called upon to perform the social duties of the classes they have annihilated ? On these principles the legislatures of all countries have imposed on public companies the same duties as on individuals ; and in case of violations of its laws, have rendered them subject to the same penalties. They have thus been recognised as moral agents.

2. Public companies are capable of sustaining many social relations which are the foundation of moral duties.

The social relations of public companies are various. They may be buyers or sellers—debtors or creditors—they may employ others, or be employed themselves—they may be receivers or bestowers of favour—they may be friends or enemies, neighbours or strangers—they may be wealthy or indigent—in prosperity or adversity—they may be influential or otherwise—they may be plaintiffs or defendants in a court of law, or be the accusing or the accused party in a criminal court. Every relationship implies a corresponding duty ; and we contend that public companies, in any of these relative positions, are bound to perform the same duties which the same relations would impose upon individuals.

3. Public companies sustain those relations to the Deity which imply an obligation to the performance of moral and religious duties.

We have considered public companies in their relation to the community in which they are established—in relations they may sustain to individual members of that or any other community ; we shall now consider them in their relation to the Deity. This forms the chief ground of moral and religious duty. Their relation to the Deity is a relation of dependence. It will not be denied, that for every talent necessary to conduct their operations, and for all the success which may attend their exertions, public bodies are as dependent as individuals upon the kindness of Providence. Every good and every perfect gift cometh down from the Father of Light.* Their relation to the Deity is also a relation of obligation. They have received favours—as recipients of favours it is their duty to be grateful, and this duty is the more obligatory in proportion to the greatness and condescension of their Benefactor. Their relation to the Deity is also a relation of responsibility. They possess wealth—influence—power. Providence never bestows these talents, without holding the parties on whom they are bestowed responsible for their proper use. Those who duly improve the talents with which Providence has entrusted them, will have those talents increased, and be rewarded by the Divine approbation. Those who neglect to use these talents, are held responsible for their neglect, and will be punished for their inactivity.† We have no reason to suppose that public companies are excluded from the general rules of the Divine administration. As far, then, as they are endowed with the same talents as individuals, so far must they be considered as subject to the same responsibilities. From these considerations we infer, that public companies, like individuals, are moral agents.

4. Public companies are analogous to other collective bodies who are acknowledged to be moral agents.

It will not be denied that a *nation* may declare an *unjust* war —may carry it on in a *cruel* manner—may treat a conquered nation with *oppression,* or may conduct a treaty of peace with *duplicity* and *fraud.* Nor will it be denied, that a nation may become immoral by the extinction of moral feeling in its rulers, and throughout the population.

If, then, nations are capable of performing virtuous or vicious actions, then are they moral agents; to be rewarded or punished according to their actions.

The Jewish history presents the most remarkable instance on record of a nation being rewarded for their righteousness and punished for their disobedience. The nations they conquered were subjected to the same discipline, and it is expressly stated that those nations were punished for their sins. And those who have studied the philosophy of history will have observed, that nations have risen and fallen in political greatness as they have risen and fallen in their observance of the principles of morality and religion.

* James i. 17.   † Luke xix. 13-26.

On this subject we might quote the language of historians, of moralists, of philosophers, and of theologians; but we prefer citing the language of a monarch, especially as that monarch is our own. Surrounded by her nobles, her senators, her councillors, her judges, her generals, and her admirals—Queen Victoria has declared from the throne, " RELIGIOUS AND MORAL PRINCIPLES ARE THE SUREST FOUNDATION OF OUR SECURITY AND HAPPINESS."

As, then, large bodies of men, like nations, are rewarded or punished in their collective capacity, for their virtuous or vicious actions, it would seem to follow, that smaller bodies of men, like public companies, may be subjected to the same moral discipline.

A public company, like a nation, is composed of a number of individuals who have a government for the regulation of their affairs, and whose acts are considered as the acts of the whole body. It is true that a public company is composed of a smaller number of persons than a nation, but that cannot affect the moral character of its actions. It is also true, that while a nation must always act through its government, a public company may, and often does, at the general meeting of its shareholders, act independently of its government; but neither can this alter its moral agency, for whether the form of government be aristocratical or democratical, the duties of a nation, or of a public company, remain the same.*

In opposition to this doctrine, it may be contended that, to render public bodies of men responsible in their collective capacity, would be destructive of personal or individual responsibility. But this is not the case. A nation may be punished for its national crimes, and yet the individual who may have caused these crimes may sustain an individual punishment. Thus Jeroboam, Ahab, and other kings of Israel, were individually punished, while, at the same time, the nation was also punished in its collective capacity. So a public company may be punished or rewarded for its actions while, at the same time, any individual who caused these actions may also be personally rewarded or punished. It may too be objected, that if a public company is to be punished, as such, for its acts, then all the

---

* In this discussion we consider public companies as corporations, and inquire what duties they, as corporations, owe to other parties. The several duties of directors, officers, and shareholders, do not lie within the range of our inquiries.

partners would share in the punishment, though many of them may have been quite innocent of the crime, To this we answer, that the same objection would apply to the doctrine of national responsibility.* It is not possible, in the case of a large body of men, for every individual to take part in its actions. The act of the authorized government, or of the majority of the members, must be regarded as the act of the whole community, and every individual must share in the prosperity or adversity resulting from such acts.

It may further be observed, that it is not inconsistent with the principles of the Divine government for persons to suffer for the wickedness, or to be rewarded for the righteousness, of those with whom they are socially connected. .

In our own day, we witness numerous instances of children possessing wealth, mental cultivation, and influence in society through the virtues of their parents. And, also, not a few cases of children being reduced to poverty and degradation through the vices of their parents. Children suffer through the conduct of their parents, and parents through the conduct of their children; masters by their servants, and servants by their masters. In fact, it is not possible for any individual, however obscure, to be either virtuous or vicious, without in some way promoting the happiness or misery of some person besides himself. It is, therefore, no valid objection to the doctrine of the moral responsibility of public companies, that it renders all the partners answerable for the conduct of the majority. In fact, human governments act upon this principle. If any company were to incur penalties to the state, those penalties would be enforced against the whole property of the company, though many individual partners might be quite unconscious of the offence by which those penalties were incurred.

The doctrine of collective responsibility in the present world might be still further confirmed by references to the punish-

---

* The logical reader need not be reminded, that in arguments from analogy it is a sufficient answer to an objection to show that the objection applies with equal force to the doctrine from which the analogy is drawn. Thus, in the text, the moral responsibility of nations is assumed as admitted by all parties, and, therefore, requiring no further proof. From the resemblance or analogy between the two cases, we infer the moral responsibility of public companies. It is, therefore, a sufficient answer to any objection against the latter doctrine, to show that it will equally apply to the former. Indeed, the more numerous the objections, if they will apply equally in both cases, the more the argument is strengthened, as they are confirmatory of the soundness of the analogy.

ments inflicted on particular cities. We will refer only to Nineveh and Jerusalem. In the former case an act of general humiliation obtained a remission, or at least a postponement, of the punishment due to their wickedness; and in the latter, their sin in rejecting the Gospel was visited with a signal punishment.

Before quitting this branch of our inquiry, we may notice one practical application of the doctrine of collective responsibility. It is, that every individual member of a public body, whether a nation, a family, or a company, should induce that body to walk in the path of uprightness. For should they not do so, he will have to bear a portion of the collective punishment, though he may not personally have taken any active part in the crime.*

SECONDLY.—Having shown that public companies are moral agents, and consequently bound to the performance of certain duties, we shall now inquire what are those duties which, as moral agents, public companies are bound to perform?

We shall not attempt to enumerate all these duties, but merely make a selection of the most important, and these we shall classify as, I. The duties of patriotism. II. The duties of social relationship. III. The duties of religion. IV. The duties of benevolence.

I. The duties of patriotism.

By the duties of patriotism, we mean those duties which a public company owes to the state. Patriotism is the love of one's country, or more properly the love of one's nation. Public spirit is a willingness to sacrifice a portion of one's time, property, or comfort, to promote the happiness of one's fellow-citizens. These are duties obligatory on every citizen,† and consequently binding on every collective body of citizens. We repudiate the doctrine that a public company has only to attend to the interest of its proprietors, regardless of the effect its measures may have on the public weal. This would be a violation of duty on the part of an individual, and still more so on the part of a public company. For they have received from the Legislature special privileges to enable them to carry on their operations. These privileges have been granted with a view to the promotion of the public interest. If, then, these privileges are employed to the injury of the public, then is

* Matt. xxiv. 19. † Ps. cxxxvii.; Neh i. 4; ii. 3; Rom. ix. 3.

there not merely a violation of the duty of citizenship, but a farther violation of duty by the misapplication of privileges conferred by the Legislature. "Unto whomsoever much is given, of him shall be much required; and to whom men have committed much, of him they will ask the more."* In proportion as the Legislature has conferred privileges, in such proportion it may be expected that they who have received these privileges, will be active in promoting the public interest. The possession of privileges implies an increased obligation to perform certain duties.

The first of these duties is to obey the laws. A public company should abstain from smuggling and all other illicit proceedings—should make correct returns to Government, and pay its fair proportion of the property-tax, and of all other duties. Another duty is to enforce the laws upon others. Individuals sometimes abstain from prosecuting frauds upon themselves, from a misapplied feeling of compassion, an unwillingness to incur odium, or the fear of expense; but none of these feelings are sufficient to justify a public company in abstaining from this duty. Such a course is injurious to the public, by holding out inducements to the commission of similar crimes. It is also the duty of public companies to support the cause of order and of due submission to constituted authorities—the rights of property —the supremacy of the law—the impartial administration of public justice—and to honour the constitutional government of the country, by whatever party it may be administered. Another duty is to conduct the affairs of the company on such a liberal, yet prudent scale of expense, as shall afford encouragement to the industry, trade, and fine arts of the country. Solomon says, "Prepare thy work without, and make it fit for thyself in the field, and afterwards build thine house."† Which means, if we understand it rightly, "Get your money before you spend it, but having got it, live in a scale of expense corresponding to your means—afterwards build thine house." Individuals may be justified in living much within their means, in order to provide for old age, or for the proper settlement of their children; but public companies cannot have such motives for conducting their establishments with an unsuitable economy. But, above all, it is the duty of a public company to maintain, in all its transactions, a high-toned morality. "Righteousness exalteth

* Luke xii. 48.   † Prov. xxiv. 27.

2 P

a nation."* A departure from moral rectitude is altogether inexcusable in a public company. As all their actions are presumed to be the result of previous deliberation, they cannot plead in excuse, as individuals do, the power of passion, the impulse of the moment, or the force of habit. In proportion to the weakness, or the absence of temptation, in such proportion would their conduct be the more criminal;† while their wealth and influence would render their example more extensively injurious to the public morality. If parties of high station in society depart from the strict rule of duty, those of inferior station will deviate still more widely. "If a ruler hearken to lies, all his servants are wicked."‡

II. The duties of social relationship.

The social duties of public companies are the same as those of individuals who maintain the same relations. These duties are clearly stated in the Holy Scriptures. The Bible is a code of laws—not a book of adjudged cases. It lays down the principles of human actions, but leaves the application of these principles to the dictates of reason and of conscience. We might read through the Bible, and not find a chapter headed "The duties of public companies." In this case we endeavour to ascertain, in the first place, what are the duties of individuals. Then we take the principles of these duties and apply them to the acts of public companies. The principles of moral duty undergo no change; but the circumstances of human society are perpetually changing, and hence the correct application of these principles is sometimes a matter of difficulty. We shall here, in the first place, state, in the language of Scripture, the principles of some of our social relationships, and then make a practical application of them. There are doubtless other principles we have not mentioned, and those we have mentioned may be applied, and are applied, in practice, to many other cases besides those specified.

1. These are the things that ye shall do: "SPEAK YE EVERY MAN THE TRUTH to his neighbour, execute the judgment of peace and TRUTH in your gates, and let none of you imagine evil in your hearts against his neighbour, and *love no false oath;* for all these are things that I hate, saith the Lord." §

* Prov. xiv. 34.　　　† Prov. vi. 30.
‡ Prov. xxix 12.　　　§ Zech. viii. 16, 17.

Insert no erroneous statements in your prospectus; make no incorrect calculations in order to deceive a parliamentary committee; circulate no unfounded rumours for the purpose of affecting the market value of your shares; and let your annual reports contain nothing but the truth.

2. Be honest and upright in all your dealings, let your charges be fair and just, and be sincere and straightforward in all your pecuniary transactions.

All promises or engagements must be faithfully kept, even when the performance is injurious to the interests of the company.

If any of the servants of a public company are found wanting in integrity, they should immediately be dismissed, and on no account be reinstated. And if any of their professional agents act dishonestly, even to benefit the company, they should not be employed again.

3. Banking companies should not take the accounts of disreputable parties; and a fraudulent bankrupt should not be allowed to reopen his account, even should he plead that, although he had cheated all his other creditors, he had not cheated his banker. In making advances, banking companies should consider the moral character of the party with whom they deal, as an element of their security, and should more readily afford accommodation to parties having such a character than to those who are without it.

Public companies should do nothing that would be considered dishonourable or disreputable in an individual member of the company. The moral character of an action cannot be changed by the number of persons who may commit it. Public companies should not listen to plans and schemes proposed for their adoption by parties known to be deficient in moral principle; nor should they hire agents to do what they would not do themselves.

4. Public companies should not speak unjustly or unkindly of each other. But this does not prohibit their speaking the TRUTH of each other on proper occasions, even when the truth may be unpleasant or injurious to the party about whom it is spoken. It may sometimes become the duty of a respectable and honourable company to expose the fraudulent and deceitful practices of other companies: we are not forbidden to bear witness—but only *false* witness—against our neighbour.

5. A public company should not meddle with politics, nor let the influence of the company be employed to produce any political change. It should not too frequently change the principles and maxims of its own government. Fixed rules and regulations are to a public company what habits are to an individual: they insure a uniformity of conduct, and are equally essential to success. A steady adherence to fixed principles is the surest road to prosperity. A restless discontent with moderate profits, and an attempt to get suddenly rich, by reckless speculation, has been the ruin of many companies as well as individuals. Nor should they change too often the terms on which they transact business with the public, as that occasions much inconvenience. Nor change too frequently the rate of their dividend, as that may lead to gambling in their shares. Better pay always the same rate of dividend, and let the surplus profit of one year be placed to a reserved fund to supply the deficiencies of future years.

6. In cases of dispute or litigation, do not let your judgment be blinded by self interest; but judge impartially, and do unto others as, in a similar case, you would wish to be done unto yourself. Use no means of hostility, or annoyance, or rivalry towards other companies which you would condemn as unjust or unfair were they used against yourself. Recommend to others no schemes, or speculations, or investments, in which you would not be willing to take any share yourself. Give no false testimonials of character, so as to induce others to employ parties whom you would not employ yourself. If you have received favours from other companies, or from individuals, do not let your thankfulness evaporate in mere votes of thanks, or acclamations of applause, but render to others the same tokens of gratitude which, under the same circumstances, you would expect to receive yourself: "All things whatsoever ye would that men should do unto you, do ye even so to them, for this is the law and the prophets."*

7. If there be a run on a banking company, the rival banking companies should render assistance, and not suffer a solvent bank to stop payment for want of temporary support. All hostile companies should render assistance to each other on the occurrence of calamities, to which all are liable. A railway company should not rejoice when accidents occur on a rival line; nor a

* Matt. vii. 12.

banking company when a rival bank has made a large amount of bad debts ; nor an assurance society when extensive fires or numerous deaths have absorbed the funds of a rival society ; nor a mining association when accidents have damaged the mines belonging to a rival association.

8. Do what is just though the law may not require it, and never have recourse to a legal quibble in order to baffle a just demand. Public companies should employ none but honourable men to plead any cause in which they may be engaged. Advocates who are noted for legal quibbling, attacking private character, or browbeating witnesses, should not be engaged ; and, more especially, the *standing counsel* of a public company should be a man of high moral and religious principles.

9. All the servants of the company who come into communication with the public should be instructed to behave with the utmost courtesy ; and if they do so, they are entitled to courtesy in return. No shareholder should address a servant of the company as if he were his own individual servant ; nor should he, in his transactions with the company, expect any undue attention or preference on account of his being a shareholder. When a company has occasion, in its annual report or public documents, to refer to the proceedings of other companies, it should always be done in the language of courtesy.

Be pitiful (full of pity).—In some cases life policies become forfeited through the inability of the parties to pay the premiums, and sometimes by the party meeting his death in a way that deprives his relations of all claim on the company. In cases like these, insurance companies should take all the circumstances into consideration, and *be pitiful.* When an honest tradesman fails, and his creditors agree to take a composition, the banking company should not refuse to accept the terms proposed, but should *be pitiful.* When the servant of a company has inadvertently committed an error, not involving any moral delinquency, let him not be too hastily dismissed, and thus placed for life in a lower condition, but *be pitiful.* When servants of the company, from sickness or old age, have become less effective than formerly, let arrangements be made for rendering their duties proportionate to their diminished strength. Recollect they were once young and healthy, and you had then the benefit of their services—do not treat them harshly now. *Be pitiful.*

10. " *Use hospitality one to another*, without grudging."[*]

It is proper that public companies, on particular occasions, such, for example, as the opening of a new line by a railway company, should entertain their friends and others connected with the company. Also, that the companies should use hospitality "one towards another." Social intercourse tends to promote friendly feelings; and a friendly feeling between the principal officers and members of different companies tends to promote a friendly feeling between the companies themselves. It is also a good practice to give an annual dinner to all the servants of the company. The words " without grudging " may suggest, that when the company can afford it, these entertainments should be given in a rather handsome style, without a too strict regard to economy. On these festive occasions, the humbler servants and others connected with the company should not be forgotten. " When thou makest a feast, call the poor, the maimed, the lame, the blind. And thou shalt be blessed, for they cannot recompense thee, for thou shalt be recompensed at the resurrection of the just."[†]

11. " Thou shalt *not oppress a stranger*, for ye know the heart of a stranger, *seeing* ye were strangers in the land of Egypt."[‡]

The principle of this suggestion is, that we ought to have compassion for all those who are in the same difficulties in which we formerly were ourselves. Those whom Providence has raised to a higher station than they or their fathers occupied, should entertain kindly feelings towards those who belong to the class from whence they have sprung. The same rule applies to public companies. Those which have overcome the difficulties of their formation, and become prosperous, should not employ any vexatious or oppressive means of preventing the growth of similar companies. Knowing the anxieties they experienced from the difficulties they ·had to encounter, they should not inflict similar anxieties upon others. Moses often enforces the duty of kindness towards servants and strangers, by reminding the Israelites that they had been strangers and bondsmen in the land of Egypt. In questions of morals, it is generally a safe guide to a correct judgment to put ourselves in the position of others, and to inquire what would then be our own feelings, and what kind of conduct we should wish, under such circumstances, to be adopted towards ourselves ? In the decision of such cases,

* 1 Pet. iv. 9.   † Luke xiv. 13, 14.   ‡ Exod. xxiii. 9.

it usually appears that the cultivation of the moral feelings has improved the intellectual faculties. A sound heart is less likely to go astray than a clever head. "The entrance of thy words giveth light : it giveth understanding unto the simple."*

12. "Masters, *give unto your servants that which is just and equal,* knowing that ye also have a Master in heaven."†

Be just in your appointments, and select those who are the most worthy and the best qualified for the duties they will have to discharge. *Be just in the amount of your remuneration ;* recollect that many of the servants of public companies have greater trusts and heavier responsibilities than the servants of individuals ; and in this case, it is just and equal that they be rewarded accordingly. *Be just in your promotions,* and let not merit be supplanted by patronage or favouritism. *Be just in the quantity of labour you exact.* Appoint a sufficient number of servants to do the work easily. Do not compel them to keep late hours, nor refuse reasonable holidays, for the purposes of health and recreation. *Be just in your reproofs.* "Forbear threatening."‡ Let not your censures or your punishments be more than proportionate to the offence ; and be as ready at all times to acknowledge the merits of your servants as to notice their defects. *Be just in your pensions,*—let your aged and worn-out servants be treated with respect and liberality. Recollect they were once young and healthy, and you had then the benefit of their services—do not treat them harshly now. All complaints, and all applications for increased remuneration or privileges, from the servants of public companies, should receive mature consideration ; and all refusals should be given with kindness and courtesy. Job, when reduced to distress, consoled himself with the reflection, that in his former prosperity, when he was the greatest of all the men of the East,§ he had not despised the cause of his man-servant or his maid-servant when they contended with him. Moses enacted, "Thou shalt not muzzle the ox when he treadeth out the corn ;"‖ and St. Paul has twice quoted this enactment,¶ to inculcate the lesson that we ought not to stint the remuneration, nor even the enjoyments of those by whose labour we profit. There is something touching in the following text :—"A certain centurion's

* Ps. cxix. 130. † Col. iv. 1.
‡ Eph. vi. 9. § Job xxxi. 13.
‖ Deut. xxv. 4. ¶ 1 Cor. ix. 9 ; 1 Tim. v. 18.

servant, *who was dear unto him,* was sick, and ready to die;"[*]
and the Psalmist has given us a lovely exhibition of the Divine
character in the words, "He hath pleasure in the prosperity of
his servant."[†]

Public companies have a right to expect that their servants
should not only be obedient during the official hours of business,
but that at all times their conduct should be such as will be
reputable to the company,—attempting to " please them well in
all things,"—" not answering again "—not objecting to obey any
lawful commands—"not purloining, but showing all good
fidelity,"—not misapplying the property with which they are
entrusted, not suffering the company to be defrauded or damaged
by other parties. " That they may adorn the doctrine of God
our Saviour in all things :" the servants of a public company are
exposed to observation and criticism, and its honourable reputation in the world will be affected by the estimate that may be
formed of their moral and religious character. Christian principle is of more importance than brilliant talents, and is more
highly respected, even by the ungodly. The personal character
of its servants is sometimes of greater value to a company than
their personal services, and can less easily be replaced. They
adorn the *doctrine* of Christianity when, from Christian motives,
they *practise* those virtues which are suitable to their several
stations.

14. " Pure religion and undefiled before God and the Father
is this, *to visit the fatherless and widows in their affliction,* and
to keep himself unspotted from the world."[‡]

Establish a fund for the relief of the widows and children of
the servants of the company. Such a fund is established by the
Bank of England, in the army and elsewhere, and why not by
all large companies? Mining and railway companies should
relieve the widows and children of those who meet with accidents
in their respective works. The word VISIT implies, that this
relief should be generous and kind; and the words, IN *their
affliction,* may suggest that it ought to be prompt and immediate,
not postponed till *after* their affliction.

15. "As we have opportunity, *let us do good unto all men,*
especially unto them who are of the household of faith."[§]

Let all your arrangements be adapted to promote the public

---

* Luke vii. 2.   † Ps. xxxv. 27.
‡ James i. 27.   § Gal. v. 10.

good, and more especially to benefit the moral and religious portion of the community. "He that diligently seeketh good procureth favour; but he that seeketh mischief, it shall come unto him."[*]

III. Having considered the duties of patriotism, and the duties of social relationship, we now come to the duties of religion.

By the duties of religion we mean the duties we owe directly to God. Those which are most applicable to public companies are, to acknowledge the hand of God—to promote his worship—and to reverence his Sabbaths.

In ancient Rome the merchants and bankers had a public procession every year to the temple of Mercury—who, by a strange association, was regarded as the god of merchants and of bankers, of thieves and of eloquence—to offer sacrifices for the blessings they had received; and, as the satirists said, to ask forgiveness for all the frauds and tricks they had practised in their trade during the past year.

In the Middle Ages, the public companies then formed took mottoes, many of which were expressive of religious feelings. Thus if we cast our eyes on our Royal Exchange, we shall see that the City motto is, "Domine, dirige nos," and that of the Mercers' Company is "Honor Deo." This would not be consistent with the manners of the present age, though we believe our public companies are as much disposed to implore Divine direction, and to render to God the honour of their success, as were any of the associations of former days.

We are not friendly to the introduction of religious matters, either by individuals or public bodies, into secular intercourse. We have no wish that our business meetings should commence with prayer, and conclude with the doxology. But surely there must be some way in which a public company may, consistently with our national character, and the manners of the age, express its reliance on Divine Providence, and its gratitude for the favours which Providence has conferred. Is there no way in which a public company may virtually utter the sentiments so beautifully expressed by David :—

" David blessed the Lord before all the congregation : and said, Blessed be thou, Lord God of Israel our father, for ever and ever. Thine, O Lord,

---

[*] Prov. xi. 27.

is the greatness. and the power, and the glory, and the victory, and the majesty : for all that is in the heaven and in the earth is thine ; thine is the kingdom, O Lord, and thou art exalted as head above all. Both riches and honour come of thee, and thou reignest over all ; and in thine hand is power and might ; and in thine hand it is to make great, and to give strength unto all. Now therefore, our God, we thank thee, and praise thy glorious name. But who am I, and what is my people, that we should be able to offer so willingly after this sort? for all things come of thee, and of thine own have we given thee ?"*

Another religious duty is, to support the public worship of God. Human legislation can enforce a small portion only of the moral and religious duties of mankind, and can never interfere until vice has grown into crime.† Religion extends her sway, not only over all the actions of man, but over the motives and springs of action.‡ Religious and moral principles implanted in the mind of the community are the only security for the performance of religious and moral duties, and the only means of acquiring the happiness which the performance of these duties tends to produce.

While we maintain, in the words of our motto, that " property has its duties as well as its rights," we maintain, with equal firmness, that property has its rights as well as its duties, and they who disregard its rights have no claim on the performance of its duties. But though the rights of property are as sacred as any other rights,§ yet they are the first to be disregarded among an immoral or an irreligious population. As a portion of the property class, therefore, public companies should support the extension of moral and religious principles, as a means of securing the safe and quiet enjoyment of their possessions. The maintenance of the public worship of God is one means of extending the knowledge and influence of these principles.

But apart from motives of interest, it is no less the duty of public companies, than of individuals, to promote the honour of

---

* 1 Chron. xxix. 10–14.

† Some writers on moral philosophy have divided the social rights of man into perfect and imperfect. The perfect rights can be enforced by human laws. The enactments referring to these rights are generally expressed in a negative form : " Thou shalt *not* kill ;" " Thou shalt *not* steal." The imperfect rights cannot be enforced perfectly by human laws. These enactments are generally positive. " Honour thy father and thy mother ;" " Thou shalt love thy neighbour as thyself." The fourth commandment has one of each kind : " Thou shalt do no manner of work ;" " Remember the Sabbath day to keep it holy."

‡ Exod xx. 17 ; Matt. xv. 19.　　　　　§ Mark. x. 19.

their Creator and Benefactor; and to diffuse among others those blessings that attend the discharge of religious obligations.

Public companies should not only give to all their servants the means of attending public worship, but they should also contribute towards its support in the district in which their operations are carried on. The houses and the lands they occupy, if not held by them, would probably be occupied by others who would thus contribute. It is, therefore, as much their duty as it is the duty of the other parishioners to provide the means of religious instruction for their neighbours. Contributions towards this object may not only be a suitable way of performing the duty to which we have referred,—that of acknowledging their obligations to the Divine Being, and of extending those principles by which their own property is rendered more secure,—but also of promoting the piety, and, consequently, the happiness, of all the members of the community, and of discharging a duty to which is distinctly attached the promise of temporal prosperity. "Bring ye all the tithes into the storehouse, that there may be meat in mine house, and prove me now herewith, saith the Lord of hosts, if I will not open you the windows of heaven, and pour you out a blessing, that there shall not be room enough to receive it."*

Another religious duty is to reverence the Sabbath-day.

Viewed only with reference to the present life, the institution of the Sabbath-day is one of the greatest blessings that religion ·has conferred upon man.

The design of the Sabbath is to insure an interval of bodily repose, more especially for the humbler classes of society;† to change the current of thought, and thus to preserve the mental powers in a state of vigour and freshness; to give leisure for reflection, and thus enable man to look above him, and around him, and within him, and consider his own character and destiny; and to furnish opportunity for the discharge of those duties of piety, of kindness, and of benevolence, which devolve upon him as a moral and religious being.

The institution of the Sabbath-day must not be regarded as diminishing the produce of annual labour. By improving the habits, and invigorating the mental powers, it increases the annual produce of labour, both in regard to nations and individuals. The labour of the Sunday tends not to wealth. It is

---

* Mal. iii. 10.   † Deut. v. 14.

not the man who " adds Sunday to the week " of toil, who employs that holy day in attending to his ordinary business or in making up his books—no, it is not he who is in the surest road to riches. It is the man who, when the Sunday dawns, feels his mind expand with new and exhilarating and ennobling associations; who, accompanied by his family, appropriately attired, pays his morning homage in the temple of religion, and passes the remainder of the day in works of charity or piety, or in innocent relaxations corresponding with the sanctity of the day—that is the man who, by improving the intellectual, the moral, and the social faculties of his mind, is adopting the surest means of acquiring wealth and respectability in the world.

They greatly err who imagine they are pleading the cause of the poor when they endeavour to remove the religious sanctions of the Sabbath-day. Should the mass of the population once entertain the impression that the observance of the Sunday is not required by religion, but is merely a matter of convenience or expediency, the poor will then have no security for cessation from toil. Reasons will soon be found, based apparently upon a regard for the poor, for increasing their labour. Let the Sunday be regarded no longer as a day of devotion, but merely as a day of pleasure, and it will soon become a day of toil.

IV. The last class of duties are the duties of benevolence.

By the duties of benevolence, we mean the duties we owe to the poor.

Throughout both the Old and the New Testament there is no duty more frequently enforced than this—nor one to the performance of which there is attached so many promises of temporal prosperity.

The rule by which public companies, as well as individuals, should regulate the amount of their contributions to religious and charitable purposes, is distinctly laid down in the Holy Scriptures—it is their ability.

"Every man shall give as he is able, according to the blessing of the Lord thy God, which he hath given thee.*—Thou shalt truly tithe all the increase of thy seed, that the field bringeth forth year by year.†—Upon the first day of the week let every one of you lay by him in store, as God hath prospered him."‡

The spirit of these instructions appears to be, that public companies should devote to religious and charitable purposes a

---

* Deut. xvi. 17.　　　　† Deut. xiv. 22.　　　　‡ 1 Cor. xvi. 2.

certain proportion of their annual profits. What that proportion should be, must be determined by each individual company. All public companies have the advantage of knowing the exact amount of their annual gains. " Be thou diligent to know the state of thy flocks, and look well to thy herds." The principle of this injunction is—balance your books every half-year, in order to ascertain the state of your affairs, and the amount of your profits. In all cases we think it better that a fixed sum should be set apart at the commencement of the year, rather than the amount should be regulated by the caprice of the moment. We think it a good practice, even for individuals, and especially for young men commencing life, to determine, like Jacob,* that a certain part of their future gains should be devoted to the cause of piety and benevolence. We are not friendly to religious vows, but we think every prudent man (and public companies are presumed to be assemblies of prudent men) should have fixed principles of action, and not let his discharge of pious and charitable duties depend on the impulse of the moment. " Every man according as he purposeth in his heart so let him give, not grudgingly or of necessity, for God loveth a cheerful giver."† This language seems to imply that the amount devoted to acts of charity should be the result of previous deliberation, and that those who have fixed the amount by a previous purpose, give with more cheerfulness than those whose minds present on every occasion a conflict between the suggestions of liberality and those of selfishness, and who grudgingly comply with the solicitations of others, or give as a necessity imposed on them by their social position.

We are no advocates for indiscriminate charity. We think that men of business (and of such our public companies are usually composed) should show the same prudence in the exercise of their charity as they would on other occasions; they should endeavour to ascertain the way of doing the most good with equal means, and look to the remote as well as to the immediate effects of their benevolence.

The first claim on their liberality is that of the parish or district in which the company conducts its operations. As the locality, if not occupied by a company, would probably be occupied by individuals, the company is morally bound to subscribe to the local charities as liberally as would be done by individuals

---

* Gen. xxviii. 22.   † 2 Cor. ix. 7.

of equal wealth. Another claim is, that of charities whose object has some connection with the object of the company, or which would relieve the distress of parties employed by the company.

There are also extraordinary cases, wherein, by a sudden visitation of Providence, there is general distress; such as when, by a revulsion of trade, large masses of men are thrown out of employment; or the occurrence of famine, pestilence, or fire. In these cases the appeal is not made to us in our local or professional character, but to our national feeling, or to our common humanity; and then public companies have the same duties to perform as would fall upon individuals of equal wealth. On the other hand, there are occasions wherein private charity is more useful than public charity; and it may become the duty of public bodies, as well as of individuals, to exercise their benevolence in secret.*

But it is not necessary that kindness to the poor should always take the form of almsgiving. It is often better to prevent poverty than to relieve it,—to give employment rather than money,—to grant a loan, than to bestow alms. And sometimes public companies can so construct their business arrangements, as, without any pecuniary sacrifice, greatly to promote the interest and the comfort of the humbler classes of the community. Public companies should also co-operate in endeavouring to raise the social condition of the poor, by diminishing the hours of labour, by relieving women and children from unsuitable or oppressive toil, and by extending among the rising population the benefits of religious education.

To remove the ignorance of the poor is a duty not less important than to relieve their distress.

The God of the Bible is described as " the God of knowledge ;" † and he has implanted in the minds of his creatures a

---

* Matt. vi. 1–4. It appears to us, that one of the least useful modes of benefiting the poor is that of permanent endowments. It seems much better that 1000*l.* were distributed immediately to the poor, than that this sum were invested in the Funds, and the interest doled out to the poor of distant generations. Let the benevolence of the present age relieve the distress of the present age; and let us hope that the benevolence of future ages will be equal to our own, and equally commensurate with the distress which may then exist. This immediate and broadcast charity seems to answer best to the scriptural description : " He hath dispersed abroad ; he *hath given* to the poor ; his righteousness [not his legacies] endureth for ever."—Ps. cxii. 9 ; 2 Cor. ix. 9.

† 1 Sam. ii. 3.

faculty for acquiring and increasing knowledge. The exercise and improvement of this faculty is as much a duty as the improvement of any other talent with which we are entrusted. And from the claims of our common humanity, and from the relation we all sustain to the same Creator,* it becomes our duty also to aid others in their pursuit of knowledge. The cultivation of our intellectual faculties does not diminish, but increases and refines our physical comforts—augments our social pleasure, by imparting to each individual additional claims to regard—exalts our devotional feelings, by unlocking more of the wisdom and goodness manifested in the works of God—and while the amiable, though injurious, aberrations of the moral and religious feelings are controlled by the judgment, the adjudications of reason on moral and religious questions are aided and guided by an instructed and enlightened conscience. It is quite possible for all these advantages to be extended to every individual in the community.

It is peculiarly the duty and the interest of the rich to educate the poor ; the morals of their children, and the comfort of their families, depend much on the religious education of their servants. Among an educated population, the rights of property—the effects of capital on the demand for labour, and the useful tendency of what are called luxuries—and the necessity for order and subordination in the state, will be better understood. In proportion as the mass of the population are instructed, will be the amount of national happiness and prosperity. Mighty is the monarch, great is the statesman, who can direct the united energies of a nation of cultivated minds. The education of the poor is a duty even more incumbent upon public companies than upon individuals. For it is to the inventions and improvements in science, often made by persons of the working class, that many of them owe their existence. Improvements in the application of steam have produced most of our present mining, and steamboat, and railway companies. Increased attention to statistics and the laws of mortality has multiplied our insurance companies. The general principle on which all our companies are founded—the power of association —is itself the offspring of modern science. Our public companies are triumphs of mind ; they denote a high degree of civilization, and exhibit most strikingly the command of man

* Mal. ii. 10 ; Acts xvii. 26.

over the elements of nature, as well as over the beasts of the field, and his power in compelling the inert properties of matter to become the active ministers of his will.

Great is the debt of gratitude due by all our public companies to the cause of mental cultivation ; and when these companies are computing the annual gains which from this source they have acquired, let them not forget that the Genius of Mental Cultivation, supported by Benevolence, Patriotism, and Religion, and attended by crowds of the uninstructed children of the indigent, stands at their door, and humbly asks payment of a portion of this debt.

Let them in part discharge this debt, by seeing that the children of their labourers, and the people of the district, are all supplied with the means of instruction. And afterwards, let them patronise those societies which have for their object the education of the children of the poor in other districts, and throughout the land. They should also, as far as it can be done with justice to others, give promotion to such of their servants as devote their leisure to the cultivation of their minds. The time is gone by when it was a reproach for a young man to be bookish, as he was supposed to abstract so much more time and attention from his official duties. It is now well known that the general cultivation of the intellectual powers renders them more effective in every operation in which they may be exercised. It is a great advantage to a public company to have educated servants.* Their superior knowledge is always useful—the mental discipline they have acquired improves their business habits—and, possessing within themselves a constant source of enjoyment, they are the less likely to indulge in those expensive pleasures which are the usual temptation to neglect and dishonesty.

* "It seems likely that a movement will continue to be made in favour of universal education. I think it desirable that bank managers and branch managers should aid this movement in their respective localities, and should support generally, by their assistance and influence, the formation of literary and scientific institutions. This would afford an outlet for any surplus energy of character that might remain after the hours of business, and enable them to promote the public good, without taking part in political or religious discussions. They would acquire for themselves much pleasurable and profitable amusement, would add to the usefulness and respectability of their character in public estimation, and thus be enabled to increase the influence of their respective establishments."—*A further Extract from the Letter quoted at page* 372.

SECTION VIII.

TEN MINUTES' ADVICE ABOUT KEEPING A BANKER.

1. A BANKER is a man who has an open shop, with proper counters, clerks, and books, for receiving other people's money in order to keep it safe, and return it upon demand.

2. The building or shop in which this business is carried on, is usually called in London a "Banking-house," but in Scotland, and in the country parts of England, it is called a "Bank." The word "bank" is also employed to denote the partnership or company who carry on the business of banking. Thus we say, the Bank of Scotland, the London and Westminster Bank, the Bank of Messrs. Coutts & Co.

3. When a company of this kind does not consist of more than six or eight partners, it is called a "Private Bank;" but when the company consists of several hundred partners, it is called in Scotland a "Public Bank," and in England a "Joint-stock Bank."

4. A private bank is usually managed by one or more of the partners, and all the partners are styled Bankers. A public bank is managed by a principal officer, who is usually styled a Manager. In England a bank-manager is not commonly called a banker; but in Scotland all managers of banks, and managers of branch banks, are called bankers. So mind, when I use the work "banker," you may apply it to either a private banker or to a bank-manager, whichever you please, as my observations will be as applicable to one as to the other. A banker is a man who carries on the business of banking; and whether he carries it on upon his own account, or as the agent of a public company, it appears to me to make no difference as to his claims to be called a banker.

5. It is the business of all these banks to receive other people's money, and to return it upon demand. And when any person puts money into one of these banks, he is said to have opened an account with the bank; and when he has thus opened an account, and continues to put in and draw out money, he is said to have a current account, or, in London phraseology, "to keep a banker."

6. In Scotland almost every man has an account of some

2 Q

sort with a bank. The rich man in trade has an account because of the facility of conducting his operations : the rich man out of trade has an account because he gets interest upon his lodgments, and he keeps his money in the bank until he has an opportunity of investing it elsewhere at a better rate of interest. The middle class of people have an account because of the convenience of it, and because they obtain the discount of their bills, and perhaps loans, on giving two sureties, which are called cash credits. The poorer classes lodge their small savings in the bank, because of the security, and because they get interest on the sums which are lodged.

7. But in London the practice of keeping an account with a bank is by no means so common as in Scotland. The London private banks are banks only for the rich. The bankers require that every person opening an account shall always have a sum to his credit; and if the sum thus kept is not what they deem sufficient, they will close the account. Hence the middle class of people in London have no banker at all, and the poorer class lodge their money in the savings banks, where they get interest, which they would not get from the London banker. It should also be stated, that besides keeping a sufficient balance, a party opening an account with a London banker is expected to give a certain sum every year to the clerks. This is called Christmas-money, and the object is merely to enable the banker to pay a less salary to his clerks, at the expense of his customers.

8. But within a few years, public or joint-stock banks have been established in London. These banks, or at least some of them, will allow you to open an account without promising to keep a large balance, or even any balance at all, provided you pay a small sum annually as a commission. This sum is fixed when you open the account, and it is about the same that you would be expected to give as Christmas-money to the clerks of a private bank. Hence people of moderate incomes, and those who can employ the whole of their capital in their business, are now able to keep a banker. These banks, too, give interest on deposits, whether the sums be large or small, as I shall hereafter explain.

9. The first public or joint-stock bank established in London was the London and Westminster Bank. The success of this bank has led to the formation of several others. You will observe,

that all banks which have branches conduct their business on the same terms at the branches as they do at the central office.

10. Since, then, the Scotch system of banking is established in London, why should not the keeping of a banker be as general in London as in Scotland? I have stated that, under the old system, those chiefly who were denied banking facilities were the middle class of people. Now, these people may be subdivided into two classes—those who are engaged in trade, and those who are not. I shall address myself, in the first place, to the former class.

11. Now, I ask you, why don't you keep a banker? You say you have been in business several years, and have never kept one. Of course, if no banker would take your account you could not do otherwise; but now there are bankers willing to take your account. But you say you can do without a banker. Of course you can. The question is, not whether by possibility you can do without a banker, but whether you cannot do better with one? But you reply, it would not be worth any banker's while to take your account. That is for his consideration, not for yours. The question for you to decide is, not whether your keeping a banker would be of use to him, but whether it would be of use to yourself. I shall point out to you some of the advantages.

12. In the first place, by keeping a banker, your money will be lodged in a place of security. You have now 50*l.* or 100*l.*, or perhaps sometimes 200*l.*, that you keep in your own house; you take it up into your bedroom at night, and when you go out on Sunday you carry it in your pocket. Now you may lose this money out of your pocket—the till may be robbed by your servants—or your house may be broken upon by thieves—or your premises may take fire and the money may be burnt. But even should you escape LOSS, you cannot escape ANXIETY. When you have a little more money than usual, you have fears and apprehensions lest some accident should occur. Now you will avoid all this trouble by keeping a banker.

13. The banker will not only take care of your money, but also of anything else you commit to his charge. You can get a small tin box with your name painted on it, and into this box you can put your will, the lease of your house, policies

of insurances, and any deeds or other documents that require particular care. You can send this box to your banker, who will take care of it for you; and you can have it back whenever you like, and as often as you like. If your premises are insured, it is clearly improper to keep the policy on the premises: for if the house be burnt, the policy will be burnt, too, and where then is your evidence of claim upon the insurance office?

14. Another advantage is the saving of time. When you receive money you will send it in a lump to the bank; and when you pay away money you will draw cheques upon the bank. Now to draw a cheque takes up much less time than counting out the money that you have to pay, and perhaps sending out for change because you have not the exact sum. Besides, you sometimes hold bills which, when due, you have to send for payment; now you can lodge these with your banker, who will present them for you. And when you accept bills, you will make them payable at your banker's instead of making them payable at your own house. Now in all these cases there is a great saving of time.; and, besides, your bills, from being made payable at a bank, will be considered more respectable.

15. Another advantage of keeping a banker is, that it will be a check upon your accounts. I need not speak to you, as a trader, of the importance of correct accounts. Your banker's book will be an authentic record of your cash transactions. If you make a mistake in your trade books, the banker's book will often lead to a detection of the error. If you have paid a sum of money, and the party denies having received it, you can refer to your banker's account, and produce your cheque, which is as good as a receipt. By means of a banker's account you could trace your receipts and payments, even after a number of years had elapsed; and hence disputed accounts could be readily adjusted, and error, arising from forgetfulness or oversight, be speedily rectified.

16. I could mention several other reasons why you should keep a banker.* But what I have said will be enough to induce you to make a trial; and when you have once opened an account, you will find so much convenience from it, that you will require no further reasons to induce you to continue it. If

* The reasons assigned here have a reference chiefly to London banking.

it should not answer your expectations, you can, whenever you please, close it again.

17. Now then, as you have made up your mind to keep a banker, the next thing is to determine at what bank you will open your account. On this point I must leave you to make your own choice. All the PUBLIC BANKS issue prospectuses containing the list of their directors, the amount of their paid-up capital, the names of the bankers who superintend their respective establishments, and their rules for transacting business. You can get a prospectus from each bank, compare them together, and please your own fancy. But if you have no other grounds for preference, I advise you to open your account with the BANK, or BRANCH BANK, that is NEAREST TO YOUR OWN PLACE OF BUSINESS. You will often have to go or send to the bank, and if it be a great way off, much time will be lost, and you will at times be induced to forego some of the advantages of keeping a banker rather than send to so great a distance. On this account, let your banker be your neighbour. Recollect, time is money.

18. There is no difficulty in opening an account. You will enter the bank and ask for the manager. Explain to him what you want to do. He will give you every information you may require, and you will receive a small account book, called a Pass-book, and a book of cheques. I advise you to keep these two books, when not in use, under your own lock and key.

19. You now require no further advice from me, as your banker will give you the most ample information respecting the way of conducting your account. Nevertheless, I may mention a point or two for your own government:—Do not depend entirely upon your banker's Pass-book, but keep also an account in a book of your own. Debit your banker with all cash you may pay into the bank, and credit him for all the cheques you may draw at the time you draw them. Send your Pass-book frequently to be made up at the bank, and when it returns, always compare it with your account-book. This will correct any mistake in the Pass-book. Besides, some of your cheques may not be presented for payment until several days after they are drawn, and if, in the meantime, you take the balance of the banker's Pass-book, you will seem to have more ready cash than you actually possess, and this may lead you into unpleasant mistakes.

20. When you lodge any money at the bank, always place the total amount of the cash, and your name, at full length, upon the outside of the parcel, or on a slip of paper. The cashier will then see at once if he agrees with your amount. This will save time and prevent mistakes.

21. Be always open and straightforward with your banker. Do not represent yourself to be a richer man than you are; do not discount with your banker any bills that are not likely to be `PUNCTUALLY` paid when due; and, should any be unpaid and returned to you, pay them yourself IMMEDIATELY. Do not attempt to OVERDRAW your account; that is, do not draw cheques upon your banker for more money than you have in his hands, without first asking his consent; and if you make him any promises, be sure that they be strictly performed. If you fail ONCE, the banker will hesitate before he trusts you again.

22. Should you be dissatisfied with anything connected with your account, make your complaint to the BANKER himself, and not to the clerks. Let all your communications be made in PERSON, rather than by LETTER. But do not stay long at one interview. Make no observations about the weather or the news of the day. Proceed at once to the business you are come about, and when it is settled, retire. This will save your banker's time, and give him a favourable impression of your character as a man of business.

23. If you are in partnership, besides opening an account with your banker in the names of the firm, you should open a private account for yourself, that your personal affairs may be kept separate from those of the partnership. Or if you are in an extensive way of business, and have a large family, it is advisable that you open a separate account with your banker in the name of your wife, that your trade payments and your household expenses may not be mixed up together in the same account. This is a good way of ascertaining the exact amount of your family expenditure.

24. If you are appointed executor or assignee to an estate, or become treasurer to a public institution or charitable society, open a separate account with your banker for this office, and do not mix other people's moneys with your own. This will prevent mistakes and confusion in your accounts. These separate accounts may be kept still more distinct by being

opened with another banker, or at another branch of the same bank.

25. There are a good many of the middle class of people who are not in trade, and I must now address them. Perhaps you are a clergyman, or a medical man, or you are in a public office, or are living on your rents or dividends. At all events, whatever you may be, I conclude you are not living beyond your means. If you are, I have not a word to say to you about keeping a banker; you will soon most likely, be within the keeping of a gaoler.

26. Several of the reasons I have given to the trader will also apply to you; but there is one that applies with much greater force—the tendency to insure accurate accounts. As you are not a man of business, I shall not advise you to keep an account of your receipts and your expenditure. I know you will do no such thing. Should you ever commence to do so, you will get tired before the end of the year, and throw the book aside. Now, if you keep a banker, he will keep your accounts for you; his Pass-book will show you the state of your accounts. All the money you receive you must send to the bank, and all your payments must be made by cheques upon the bank. If you want pocket-money, draw a cheque for 5*l.* or 10*l.*, payable to Cash, but by no means disburse any money but through your banker. Your book will be balanced every half-year. You will then see the total amount of your receipts during the half-year, and your various payments to the butcher, the baker, the tailor, &c. &c. The names to which the cheques are made payable will show you for what purpose they were given, and you should write these names in a plain hand, that the clerks may copy them correctly in the Pass-book. Now, if you look through your book once every half-year in this way, you will probably see occasion to introduce some useful reforms into your domestic expenditure. But if you are too lazy to do this, hand the book to your wife, and she will do it for you.

27. I shall now address another class of people. Perhaps you are a clerk, or a warehouseman, or a shopman, or a domestic servant. Well, you have no occasion to keep a banker; that is, you have no occasion to open a current account. But you have got a little money which you would like to put into a safe place, and upon which you would like to receive interest. Well, now, listen to me.

28. If the sum be under 10*l.*, or if the sum be above 10*l.*, and you are not likely to want it soon, put it into the savings bank ; you will receive interest for it at the rate of about 3*l.* for every 100*l.* for a year. But mind, you can only put money into the savings bank at certain hours in the week, when the bank is open, and you cannot put in more than 30*l.* in any one year, nor more than 150*l.* altogether, and you will receive no interest for the fractional parts of a pound sterling, and you cannot draw out any money without giving notice beforehand.

29. If, then, your money is more than 10*l.*, and you have already lodged 30*l.* this year in the savings bank, or 150*l.* altogether, or if you will have occasion to draw out your money without giving notice, then lodge it in one of the public banks. These banks are open every week-day from nine o'clock in the morning till four in the evening ; they will take lodgments of money to any amount, and interest will be allowed from the day it is lodged until the day it is drawn out ; and if the sum is under 1,000*l.* no notice is required. For all sums lodged on interest the bankers give receipts, called deposit receipts.

30. When you go to the bank to lodge upon interest any sum under 1,000*l.* you need not inquire for the manager. Hand your money to any clerk you may see standing inside the counter, and ask for a deposit receipt. You will be requested (the first time you go), to write your name and address in a book which is kept for that purpose, and then the deposit receipt will be given to you without any delay.

31. Mind, this deposit receipt is not transferable ; that is, you cannot lend it or give it to anybody else. When you want the money, you must take it yourself to the bank, and ask the cashier to pay you the amount. You will then be requested to write your name on the back of the deposit receipt ; the cashier will see that the signature corresponds with the signature you wrote in the book when you lodged the money, and will then pay you the amount and keep the receipt.

32. Although you cannot lodge upon a deposit receipt a less sum in the first instance than 10*l.*, yet, having lodged that sum, you can make any additions to it you please. Thus, if you wish to lodge 5*l.* more, you can take your 5*l.* note and your deposit receipt for 10*l.* to the bank, and get a new receipt for 15*l.* If, after having lodged 10*l.*, you wish to lodge 10*l.* more, you can get a separate receipt for the second 10*l.*, or have a new receipt

for 20*l.*, whichever you please ; and, observe, whenever any addition is made to a former receipt, the old receipt is cancelled, and the interest due upon it is either paid to you in money, or added to the amount of the new receipt, as may be most agreeable to yourself.

33. The rate of interest allowed upon the money you deposit in the bank will depend upon the value of money at the time —that is, upon the rate at which the bankers can employ it again. For the money you lend to the banker, he lends to other people. A part of the interest he receives from other people he gives to you who find the money. A part he keeps to himself for his knowledge and skill in employing the money safely and profitably. When he receives more interest from others, he will give you more. And when he receives less, he will give you less.

34. You will be surprised to find how the desire of lodging money in a bank will grow upon you. When you had the money in your pocket, you were anxious to find reasons for spending it. When you have placed it in the bank, you will be anxious to find reasons for not spending it. All habits are formed or strengthened by repeated acts. The more money you lodge in the bank, the more you will desire to lodge. You will go on making additions, until, at last, you will probably have acquired a sum that shall lay the foundation of your advance to a higher station in society.

35. Nor must you suppose that this desire to get and to save money is an improper one. That wealth is an evil is not the language either of Scripture or philosophy. It is true that wealth, like any other blessing, may be desired from improper motives, and sought by improper means, and such an ill-regulated desire may become the root of all evil. But it is not true that wealth honestly acquired has any tendency either to enervate the intellect, to corrupt the morals, or to impair the happiness of man. The fact is the reverse. Wealth is always represented in Scripture as a blessing, and though partaking of the uncertainty of all earthly blessings, it is a blessing to be received with thanksgiving, and to be employed in promoting the honour of God and the good of mankind.

" The philosophy which affects to teach us a contempt of money does not run very deep ; for, indeed, it ought to be still more clear to the philosopher than it is to the ordinary man, that there are few things in the world of greater importance. And so manifold are the bearings of money upon the lives and characters of mankind, that an insight which should search out the life of a man in his pecuniary relations, would penetrate into almost every cranny of his nature. He who knows, like St. Paul, both how to spare, and how to abound, has a great knowledge; for if we take account of all the virtues with which money is mixed up— honesty, justice, generosity, charity, frugality, forethought, self-sacrifice,— and of their correlative vices—it is a knowledge which goes near to cover the length and breadth of humanity : and a right measure and manner in getting, saving, spending, giving, taking, lending, borrowing, and bequeathing, would almost argue a perfect man."*

* Taylor's Notes on Life.

APPENDIX.

———◦◦———

JOINT-STOCK BANKS REGULATION.

(7 & 8 Vict. cap. 113—5th September, 1844.)

An Act to regulate Joint-Stock Banks in England.

No joint-stock bank established after the 6th May, 1844 (s. 1), to carry on business unless by virtue of letters patent granted according to this Act; but companies previously established are not to be restrained from carrying on their business until letters patent have been granted them, on their application as directed by this Act.

Before beginning to exercise the banking business, every such proposed company (s. 2) are to petition Her Majesty in council for letters patent; the petition to set forth the names and abodes of all the partners; the name and locality of the bank; the amount of capital stock not being less than 100,000*l.*, and the means by which it is to be raised; the amount paid up, and how invested; the proposed number of shares, and the amount of each share, not being less than 100*l.* This petition (s. 3) is to be referred to the Board of Trade; and, on their report that the provisions of this Act have been complied with, a charter is to be granted.

S. 4 prescribes the provisions of the deed of settlement, until which deed is executed (s. 5) all the shares subscribed for, and at least half the amount paid up, no company shall commence business.

The letters patent are to be granted for a term of years not exceeding twenty (s. 6), and the company will be by them incorporated, having a common seal, and being empowered to hold lands of such annual value as shall be expressed in the said letters patent; but such incorporation (s. 7) is not to limit the personal liability of the shareholders.

No action or suit (s. 8), by or against the company, to be affected by the plaintiff or defendant being a shareholder, but either of them to have the same action and remedy as though they were strangers; and every judgment or decree (s. 9) to be enforced against the property and effects of the company, and, subject to the provisions after-mentioned, upon the person, property, and effects of every shareholder, or former shareholder;

but execution (s. 10) against the company is to precede execution against any present or former shareholder, except where he would have been originally liable, or for which judgment is not obtained within three years of his having ceased to be a shareholder. Every person (s. 11) against whom execution has been issued, is to be reimbursed for all damages and costs by the company, or by contributions from the other shareholders, and, ss. 12 to 15 prescribe how such claims are to be enforced.

Within three months of the grant of the letters patent (s. 16), an account or memorial is to be made out in a form prescribed, setting forth all the particulars of the company, to be renewed in March, annually, and delivered to the commissioners of stamps and taxes, who are to register it, such register to be examined by any one on payment of 1*s.*, and a list of shareholders to be printed and exhibited by the company, occasional changes (s. 17) being notified by additional memorials. S. 18 prescribes the verification of the memorial, and s. 19 declares a certified copy of the same to be legal evidence, which copy the commissioners are to give (s. 20), on payment of 10*s.* All liabilities are to be continued (s. 21) according to last delivered memorial.

Bills and notes (s. 22) may be signed according to the deed of partnership, so that they be signed by one manager or director, declaring it to be on behalf of the company, but such manager not to be personally liable to any greater extent than any other shareholder.

Shares may be transferred (s. 23) by deed duly stamped, such transfer to be registered, and the entry endorsed on the deed, for which endorsement the company may charge a sum not exceeding 2*s.* 6*d.*, such transfer not to be made (s. 24) unless all calls have been paid ; and the company may close the transfer books (s. 25) for a limited time. Shares transmitted by death, bankruptcy, or other means than transfer (s. 26), are to be authenticated by a declaration ; and if by marriage or will (s. 27), by proofs of the same.

With respect to shares to which several persons may be jointly entitled (s. 28), any notice to the one who stands first on the register to be deemed sufficient, and for any money payable to a shareholder being a minor, or otherwise legally incapacitated (s. 29), the receipt of the guardians, &c., to be a sufficient discharge ; nor shall the company be bound (s. 30) to see to the execution of any trust, but the receipt of the party in whose name the share stands to be sufficient.

SS. 31 to 42 give power to the company to make calls, to enforce payment of the same, to declare the forfeiture of the shares, and to sell the same, giving previous notice of their intention ; but no more shares are to be sold than are sufficient for payment of the calls which may be in arrear.

S. 43 prescribes the method of serving notices or writs on the company.

Existing companies may continue (s. 44) their trades for a time not exceeding twelve months (unless for the purpose of closing their business); and then upon petition, as before prescribed (s. 45), to receive letters patent.

Agreements entered into with companies (s. 46) before their incorporation to be enforced as if made after, and in any pending suit, the court may direct the corporate name of the company to be substituted for that of the plaintiff or defendant representing such company, and no suit to be stayed by reason of such incorporation.

Power of suing and being sued (s. 47) in the name of any one of the public officers is given to all existing companies on complying with the provisions of the Act of 7 Geo. IV. c. 46, respecting returns and accounts; and s. 48 declares banking companies to be trading companies within the provisions of the 7 & 8 Vict. c. 3.

SS. 49 and 50 are the usual clauses of interpretation, and for amendment during the session.

BANKING (IRELAND).

(8 & 9 Vict. cap. 37—21st July, 1845.)

An Act to regulate the issue of Bank Notes in Ireland, and to regulate the repayment of certain sums advanced by the Governor and Company of the Bank of Ireland for public service.

THE first clause of this Act recapitulates the various Acts constituting the Bank of Ireland, and enumerates the various sums advanced by it to the Government, amounting to the sum of £2,637,069 4s. 8d., in return for the exclusive privilege of issuing notes in Dublin, or within fifty miles thereof, and then goes on to repeal so much of the Act of 21 & 22 Geo. III., Ireland, as prohibits any other body exceeding the number of six persons from issuing notes or bills payable on demand, or at any less time than six months, and authorises, from and after December 6, 1845, any persons exceeding six in number united or to be united in societies or partnerships, or for any bodies, politic or corporate, to transact or carry on the business of bankers in Ireland at Dublin, and at every place within fifty miles thereof, as freely as persons exceeding six in number as aforesaid may lawfully carry on the same business at any place in Ireland beyond the distance of fifty miles from Dublin; but every member of such partnership is to be responsible for the due repayment of all debts and liabilities.

S. 2. From and after the passing of this Act the debt is made chargeable upon the consolidated fund, and interest is to be paid on it to the corporation of the Bank of Ireland at the rate of 3½ per cent., amounting to £92,076 18s. 5d., in half-yearly payments, on January 5 and July 5, annually.

The Bank of Ireland (s. 3) undertakes to manage the public debt of Ireland, and to pay the dividends without any expense to the Government.

The Bank corporation (s. 4) may be dissolved any time after January 1, 1845, on repayment of the debt, and after a twelvemonth's legal notice.

S. 5 repeals so much of the 32 Geo. II. c. 14, s. 15 (Ireland), as prohibits public officers from being partners in banks, and s. 6 declares Bank of England notes to be not a legal tender in Ireland, but this is not to prevent their circulation in Ireland.

S. 7 prescribes the oaths to be taken to affirmations to be made by directors and members of the Bank of Ireland, which are to be only the oath of allegiance, the oath of qualification, and the oath of fidelity to the corporation.

All bankers claiming to be entitled to issue bank notes are to give notice (s. 8) to the commissioners of stamps and taxes, who shall ascertain if such person or persons were lawfully issuing bank notes in Ireland between May 1, 1844, and May 1, 1845, and the average amount circulated by them, and shall certify the same; they may then issue to the extent of the amount so certified, and the amount of gold and silver coin held by them in the proportion hereafter mentioned. No uncertified banker to issue bank notes. Where banks have become united between the periods mentioned (s. 9), the average amount is to be taken as that of the total amount. A duplicate of the certificate is to be published in the Gazette (s. 10), which publication is to be taken as evidence of the right to issue notes. Where banks have become united subsequently to the passing of this act (s. 11), the total amount is also to be the average.

Banks are permitted (s. 12), on making an agreement with the Bank of Ireland, to relinquish in its favour the right of issuing notes; but having done so, they are not allowed (s. 13) to resume the privilege.

After December 6, 1845, no bank (s. 14) to have in circulation a greater amount of notes, upon the average of four weeks, than the amount certified by the commissioners, and the monthly average of gold and silver held by it.

The issue of notes of less than 1*l.* (s. 15) is prohibited.

Banks are to render an account weekly (s. 16) in certain prescribed forms, a neglect of which, or rendering false returns, subjecting them to a penalty of 100*l.*

All bank notes issued (s. 17) are to be deemed bank notes in circulation.

The commissioners of stamps are to make a return (s. 18) every four weeks, to be published in the " Dublin Gazette."

S. 19 prescribes the mode of ascertaining the average amount of the bank notes of each banker in circulation, and of the gold and silver coin for every four weeks after December 5, 1845. The gold and silver coin (s. 20) to include only that held at the head offices, which are not to exceed four, of which not more than two are to be in one province, and the silver is not to exceed in amount one-fourth part of the amount of gold coin.

The commissioners are empowered (s. 21) to order the inspection, at all reasonable times, of all the books of bankers containing an account of their bank notes in circulation, and of their gold and silver coin; the penalty for refusing such inspection to be 100*l.*

All bankers (s. 22) other than the Bank of Ireland are to return their names, residences, and occupation, within fifteen days of the 1st of January in each year, to the stamp office, and in cases of partnership those of each member; such return to be published on or before the 1st of March, in the " Dublin Gazette." The penalty for a false return is 50*l.*

Any bank issuing in excess (s. 23), becomes liable to a penalty equal in amount to the sum by which the certified monthly circulation has been exceeded.

S. 24 declares notes for less than 20*s.* not negotiable in Ireland, and to be altogether null and void; but imposes a penalty of not more than 20*l.*, nor less than 5*l.*, for every offence in issuing such notes at the discretion of a justice of peace, who may determine in such matter. The note for 20*s.* and promissory notes (s. 25) for 20*s.*, or less than 5*l.*, made payable within twenty-one days, must be drawn in a certain form, or otherwise to be void, and may not be negotiated after the time limited for payment. Any person other than bankers issuing notes payable on demand for less than 5*l.* (s. 26), or uttering or negotiating (s. 27) promissory notes, bills of exchange, &c., transferable, to forfeit for every such note the sum of 20*l.* This, however (s. 28), not to extend to cheques on bankers.

SS. 29 and 30 prescribe the modes of recovering the penalties imposed by this Act, and for the suing of companies.

S. 31 contains a provision regarding an agreement between the Bank of Ireland and the Tipperary Joint-Stock Bank.

SS. 32 and 33 contain the interpretation of the terms used, and the usual provision for the amendment of the Act during the session, if needed.

BANKING (SCOTLAND).

(8 & 9 Vict. cap. 38—21st July, 1845.)

An Act to regulate the issue of Bank Notes in Scotland.

The first clause recites the title of the Act of 7 & 8 Vict. cap. 32, &c., regulating the issue of bank notes in England; and s. 10, which declares that no other person than a banker already issuing notes of May 1, 1844, should have power to issue bank notes in the United Kingdom in future; and goes on to enact that all bankers so claiming to be entitled to issue bank notes in Scotland shall give notice of such claim to the commissioners of stamps and taxes in London, who shall ascertain the average amount of their notes in circulation for the year preceding May 1, 1845, and certify the same. It shall then be lawful for such bankers to continue to issue to the same amount, together with an additional proportion, as hereafter prescribed, according to the amount of gold and silver coin in their possession at their principal place of business, and to no greater amount. Banks which may unite (s. 2) are to have the total amounts taken; and a duplicate of the certificate (s. 3) is to be published in the "London Gazette." S. 4 is to the same effect as s. 2.

The issue of notes for any fractional parts of a pound is by s. 5 prohibited.

The issue of each bank is limited (s. 6), from and after December 6, 1845, to amount certified by the commissioners, together with the average, taken every four weeks, of the gold and silver coin in their possession; a return of all which is to be made weekly (s. 7), in a prescribed form, distinguishing the amount of notes above and below 5*l.*, and the average amount of gold and silver coin held, under a penalty of 100*l.* for neglect or for rendering a false account. All bank notes to be deemed in circulation from the time they are issued until they are returned.

The commissioners (s. 9) are to make a monthly return, in a prescribed form, to be published in the " London Gazette."

SS. 10 to 21 correspond, with the necessary adaptation to Scotland, to ss. 19 to 29 of the Irish Act, with the exception of the prohibition in s. 20, of the places of issue being not more than four.

S. 22 is the interpretation clause; and s. 23 is the usual clause for alteration during the session.

BILLS OF EXCHANGE AND PROMISSORY NOTES.
(18 & 19 Vict. cap. 67—23rd July, 1855.)

An Act to facilitate the Remedies on Bills of Exchange and Promissory Notes, by the prevention of frivolous or fictitious Defences to Actions thereon.

FROM and after October 21, 1855, it is declared by s. 1 that all actions upon bills of exchange or promissory notes, commenced within six months after the same shall have become due and payable, may be by writ of summons, in a form prescribed and given in a schedule, and the plaintiff, on filing an affidavit of personal service, may at once, in case the defendant shall not have obtained leave to appear to such writ, sign final judgment in the form contained in another schedule, for any sum not exceeding the sum endorsed on the writ, together with interest and costs; but the defendant (s. 2), on showing a defence on the merits, is to have leave to appear. After judgment (s. 3), the court may, under special circumstances, set aside the judgment, and give leave to the defendant to defend the action. In any proceedings under this Act (s. 4), the judge may order the bill or note to be deposited with the officer of the court, and direct proceedings to be stayed until the plaintiff has given security for costs. Holders of dishonoured bills of exchange or promissory notes (s. 5) retain the same remedies as at present for the cost of noting bills for nonpayment. One summons (s. 6) may be issued by the holder of a bill of exchange against all or any of the parties to the bill, such summons to be deemed the commencement of proceedings, in like manner as if separate writs of summons had been issued. The Common Law Procedure Acts and Rules (s. 7) are incorporated with this Act; it applies (s. 8) to the Courts of Common Pleas, Lancaster, and Durham; and (s. 9) Her Majesty may, by an Order in Council, direct it to apply to all or any of the Courts of Record in England or Wales. It does not (s. 10) extend to Ireland or Scotland; and the short title (s. 11) is declared to be " The Summary Procedure on Bills of Exchange Act, 1855."

LIMITED LIABILITY.

(18 & 19 Vict. cap. 133—14th August, 1855.)

An Act for limiting the Liability of Members of certain Joint-Stock Companies.

BY s. 1 any joint-stock company to be formed under the 8 Vict. cap. 110 (other than an assurance company), with a capital to be divided into shares of a nominal value not less than 10*l*. each, may obtain a certificate of complete registration with limited liability, upon complying with the conditions following, in addition to doing all other matters and things now required in order to obtain a certificate of complete registration ; that is to say :—

" 1. The promoters shall state on their returns to the office for provisional registration, that such company is proposed to be formed with limited liability.

" 2. The word ' Limited' shall be the last word of the name of the company.

" 3. The deed of settlement shall contain a statement to the effect that the company is formed with limited liability.

" 4. The deed of settlement shall be executed by shareholders, not less than twenty-five in number, holding shares to the amount in the aggregate of at least three-fourths of the nominal capital of the company, and there shall have been paid up by each of such shareholders on account of his shares, not less than 20*l*. per cent.

" 5. The payment of the above per-centage shall be acknowledged in or indorsed on the deed of settlement, and the fact of the same having been *bonâ fide* so paid, shall be verified by a declaration of the promoters, or any two of them, made in pursuance of the Act 6 William IV. cap. 62."

Any joint-stock company (s. 2), now or hereafter registered, under the 8 William IV. cap. 43, or constituted under private Acts of Parliament (s. 3), may, with the consent of not less than three-fourths of its shareholders, on satisfying the registrars of its perfect solvency, and complying with the other regulations, obtain a certificate of limited liability. Every company so certified (s. 4) is to have its name legibly displayed at its place of business, and upon all bills of exchange, cheques, bills of parcels, &c.; and noncompliance (s. 5) subjects the company to a penalty not exceeding 5*l*. per day for not having the name on its premises, and of 50*l*., in addition to personal liability, on every person issuing a bill of exchange, cheque, bill of parcels, &c., without such name. Every increase in the amount of capital must be notified to the registrar (s. 6); and no increase will be registered unless it be proved to the registrar that a deed has been executed by shareholders of not less than 10*l*. each to the amount of three-fourths of the increased capital, and that not less than twenty per cent. of such increased capital has been paid up; and if any such increase be advertised or otherwise treated as part of capital before such registration, every director will incur a penalty of 50*l*. The members of a duly certificated company (s. 7) are freed from any personal liability beyond what

2 R

is afterwards provided. In case of execution or other process against the property of a company (s. 8), if it be not found sufficient, the process may be issued against any shareholders to the extent of the portions of their shares not then paid up; but no process to issue against any shareholder except by an order of the court, or of a judge of the court in which the action may have been brought. If the directors shall declare a dividend (s. 9) when the company is known to be insolvent, each director consenting thereto shall be jointly and severally liable, but not beyond the amount of the dividend so made : if any director be absent, or file an objection in writing with the clerk, he is to be exempt from liability. Notes or obligations of shareholders (s. 10) are not to be received in payment of calls, and no loans are to be made to them; and any officer receiving or making such, and the directors, are declared jointly and severally liable for all such sums, with interest, as may be deficient. The rights of creditors of existing companies (s. 11) are continued. The change of name of a company, under the regulations of this Act (s. 12), is not to affect the rights of such company or of other parties. When a company, acting under a certificate of limited liability (s. 13), has lost three-fourths of its subscribed capital, the trading is forthwith to cease, and the directors are to take proper steps for dissolving the company. Auditors (s. 15) are to be appointed for such companies, subject to the approval of the Board of Trade. Every pecuniary penalty (s. 16) to be deemed a debt to the crown, and recoverable accordingly. The Act does not apply to Scotland.

DRAFTS ON BANKER.

(19 & 20 Vict. cap. 25—23rd June, 1856.)

An Act to amend the Law relating to drafts on Bankers.

WHERE a draft on any banker, made payable to bearer, or to order on demand, bears across its face an addition, in written or stamped letters, of the name of any banker, or of the words "and company," in full or abbreviated, the same is to be paid only to or through some banker.

JOINT BANKING COMPANIES.

(20 & 21 Vict. cap. 49—17th August, 1857.)

An Act to amend the Law relating to Banking Companies.

THIS Act provides that no banking company whatever shall be registered under the Limited Liability Act; but where consisting of more than seven persons, must register under this Act if formed under the Joint-Stock Companies Acts 1856 and 1857. A neglect to register renders the companies unable to sue either in law or equity, or to make any dividend payable; and every director or manager becomes liable to a penalty of

5*l.* per day while unregistered, to be recovered by any person, whether a shareholder or not. Existing banking companies, who are not hereby required to be registered, are permitted to register themselves with the consent of a majority of the shareholders at a general meeting held for the purpose, and no fees are to be taken for registering any company under this Act which was in existence previous to its passing. The relations of the shareholders to each other, and their liabilities, are not affected by this Act, and suits and actions may be continued. Several Acts or parts of Acts, relating to the formation of banking companies are repealed, and it is enacted that any number of persons not exceeding ten, may carry on a banking business in partnership in all respects the same as any number of persons not exceeding six could do before the passing of this Act. S. 13, on the formation of new banking companies, is the most important. It provides that "seven or more persons associated for this purpose, may register themselves under this Act as a company other than a limited company, subject to this condition; that the shares into which the capital of the company is divided shall not be of an amount less than 100*l.* each; but not more than ten persons shall, after the passing of this Act, unless registered as a company under this Act, form themselves into a partnership for the purpose of banking, or if so formed, carry on the business of banking." Inspectors are not to be appointed by the Board of Trade to any company under this Act, unless applied for by one-third of the shareholders in number and value. S. 19 of "The Joint-Stock Companies Act" (19 and 20 Vict. cap. 47), not to apply to companies in Scotland. Property held in trust for any banking company shall on registration vest in such company. Any banking company that may have been registered as a limited company before the passing of this Act is not to be illegal, nor is the registration to be invalid, but any creditor or member of the company may petition the court to have it wound up, and the fact of being registered as a limited company shall be a sufficient cause for the order being issued; and the contributories are liable to contribute to the assets of the company to an amount sufficient to pay all debts and charges. The banks legally carrying on business before the passing of the Joint-Stock Companies Acts, and the Bank of England, are exempted from the provisions of this Act.

FRAUDULENT TRUSTEES, &c.
(20 & 21 Vict. cap. 54—17th August, 1857.)

An Act to make better Provision for the Punishment of Frauds committed by Trustees, Bankers, and other Persons intrusted with Property.

By s. 1, any person being a trustee either wholly or in part, either for any private person, or any public or charitable purpose, who shall, with intent to defraud, convert or appropriate any part of such trust fund to his own purposes; or any banker, merchant, attorney, or agent (s. 2), who shall, with intent to defraud, sell, transfer, or pledge any property intrusted to him for safe custody, or in any manner appropriate to his own use any such property; or any person (s. 3) under powers of attorney doing the like, are alike declared guilty of a misdemeanour. And any person (s. 4) being a bailee of any property, although he do not break bulk, so appropriating property, is declared guilty of larceny. Any person (s. 5) being a director, member, or public officer of any public company, so acting; or any such person (s. 6) keeping fraudulent accounts, or (s. 7) wilfully destroying, altering, or mutilating the books, papers, or securities, or making false entries; or (s. 8) making or publishing fraudulent statements, with intent to deceive any creditor or shareholder, or with intent to induce any person to become a shareholder or creditor; and any person (s. 9) knowingly receiving any chattel, money, or security, fraudulently acquired or disposed of, are alike declared guilty of a misdemeanour; the punishment for each misdemeanour (s. 10) to be penal servitude for three years, or imprisonment with or without hard labour for not more than two years, or by a fine, as the court shall award. No person (s. 11) to be exempt from answering questions in any court of law or equity, but such evidence is not to be admissible in any proceedings against them. No proceeding, conviction, or judgment (s. 12), under this Act, is to prevent or lessen any remedy in law or equity that may be otherwise available; but no conviction under this Act is to be received as evidence in any civil suit, nor affect any security given by any such trustee for the repayment of trust property misappropriated. No prosecution under this Act (s. 13) is to be commenced without the sanction of the Attorney-General, or, if a civil suit has been commenced, without the sanction of the judge of the court. If, upon the trial of any person under this Act, the offence proved (s. 14) amounts to larceny, he is not upon that account to be acquitted of a misdemeanour. In every prosecution (s. 15) for misdemeanour, the expenses of the prosecution to be allowed as in cases of felony; and (s. 16) no misdemeanour against this Act is to be tried at any court of general or quarter sessions. The word "trustee" is declared (s. 17) to include the heir, or personal representative of the trustee, all executors and administrators, liquidators under the Joint-Stock Companies Act, and assignees in bankruptcy. "Property" includes debts, legacies, and deeds or instruments giving a title to any property, as well as goods, money, &c. The Act (s. 18) is not to extend to Scotland.

DRAFTS ON BANKERS.

(21 & 22 Vict. cap. 79—2nd August, 1858.)

An Act to amend the Law relating to Cheques or Drafts on Bankers.

By s. 1 of this Act, the crossing of a cheque or draft on any banker is to be deemed a material part of such cheque or draft, whether crossed with the name of a banker or with two transverse lines with the words "and company," or any abbreviation thereof; and the banker on whom such cheque is drawn shall not pay the same to any other than the banker with whose name it is so crossed, or, if without a banker's name, to any other than a banker; but the lawful holder of a cheque uncrossed, or crossed with "and company" may (s. 2) cross the same with the name of a banker, and such crossing shall not afterwards be obliterated, but be deemed a material part of the cheque. Persons obliterating or altering such crossing (s. 3) with intent to defraud, are to be deemed guilty of felony, and on conviction, liable to the punishment inflicted for forgery. A banker, however (s. 4), is not to be responsible for paying a cheque which does not plainly appear to have been crossed, or to have been obliterated or altered, unless such banker shall have acted *malâ fide*, or been guilty of negligence in paying such cheque. By s. 5 banker is declared to include any person, persons, corporations, or joint-stock banks acting as a banker or bankers.

JOINT-STOCK BANKING COMPANIES.

(21 & 22 Vict. cap. 91—2nd August, 1858.)

An Act to enable Joint-Stock Banking Companies to be formed on the Principle of Limited Liability.

So much of the Joint-Stock Banking Companies Act, 1857, as prohibits a banking company from being formed under that Act with limited liability, is repealed by s. 1; but if the company issue notes in the United Kingdom, the limited liability is not to extend to them, but the shareholders are to be liable for the whole amount issued of such notes, in addition to the sum for which they may be liable as shareholders of a limited company. The registration of a banking company under the Act of 1857 (s. 2) not to prevent its re-registration under the present: provided (s. 3) that, thirty days previous to obtaining a certificate of registration with limited liability, notice be given to every person or firm who may have a banking account with the company, either personally or by letter by post, to the last known address, and in default of such notice, the unlimited liability will continue as respects such customers. Before availing itself of the provisions of this Act (s. 4), every company must publish a statement of its affairs in a prescribed form, containing the notice of limitation, the amount of capital of the company, the number of shares, the amount of calls paid up, the liabilities and the assets of the company, and a similar statement is to be prepared and exhibited in a conspicuous place of the office of such company, on February 1 and August 1 of every year, and each director is subjected to a penalty of 5*l.* for every day on which such exhibition is neglected. A company with limited liability (s. 5) is to be wound-up in the same manner and under the same jurisdiction as is provided for joint-stock banking companies in the Act of 1857.

˙EAST INDIA STOCK TRANSFER, &c.

(23 & 24 Vict. cap. 102—20th August, 1860.)

An Act to provide for the Management of East India Stock, and of the Debts and Obligations of the Government of India, at and by the Bank of England.

FROM and after August 1, 1860, the directors of the East India Company (s. 1) are to transfer the management of the capital stock of the Company, and the payment of the dividends thereon, to the Bank of England; the Bank to be remunerated (s. 2) by a sum as agreed upon by the Secretary of State for India, out of the revenues of India, to be paid at the same time as the amount due for dividends. Powers of attorney (s. 3) existing previous to December 31, 1860, not to be affected by this Act, and the Bank is authorised to act on any powers lodged with the East India Company. The Bank (s. 4) may require evidence of any dividend. The Secretary of State for India in Council is to pay (s. 5) to the Bank half-yearly, in December and June, the amount due as dividend on the capital stock; he may (s. 6) make such arrangements as may be deemed expedient, for payment of the debts and obligations of the Government of India, by the Bank of England; and (s. 7) he is also enabled to open accounts at the Bank of England for the payment of current accounts.

BANK OF ENGLAND PAYMENTS.

(24 Vict. cap. 3—22nd March, 1861.)

An Act to make further Provision respecting certain Payments to and from the Bank of England, and to increase the Facilities for the Transfer of Stocks and Annuities, and for other purposes.

THE first six clauses regulate and decrease the payments to the Bank of England for the management of the National Debt, and the Unredeemed Debt, and also regulate the balances to be retained by the Bank arising from unredeemed dividends and other unclaimed moneys. By s. 7 it is provided that, on closing the books for a certain number of days previous to the payment of dividends, the person in whose name the stock stands at the time of closing shall be entitled to the dividends then due, and in any transfer made after the books are so closed, the person accepting the same shall do so exclusive of the half-year's dividend then due. This provision, by s. 10, is also to apply to East India Stock. By s. 8 the re-transfer of stock on which dividends have been unclaimed for ten years to the Commissioners for the Reduction of the National Debt may be made by the Deputy Accountant-General, or the Assistant Secretary of the Governors, as validly as by the Accountant-General or Secretary of the Company for the time being.

STOCK CERTIFICATES TO BEARER. •

(26 Vict. cap. 28—8th June, 1863.)

An Act to give further Facilities to the Holders of Stock.

HOLDERS of any of the Government stocks are by this Act enabled to procure certificates of the same, in sums of not less than 50*l.*, or duplicates of 50*l.*, and not more than 1000*l.* These certificates may be made either payable to bearer, or to any person named, and to the certificates are attached coupons, entitling the bearer to receive the interest at the stated periods. From this interest the income-tax will be deducted. The fee for such certificate is not to exceed 5*s.* on every 100*l.* of stock, included in the certificate, and a proportional sum for any less amount. On changing a nominal certificate for one payable to bearer, one-half the original fee is payable; and on registering in the books of the Bank the stock included in the certificate, a fee not exceeding 5*s.* is to be charged. This will make stock almost as available as bank notes, with the advantage of bearing interest. The forging, or assisting to forge, any imitation of these certificates, or having in possession any portions of such plate, wood, or stone, prepared for such forgery, or knowingly uttering any such forged certificates, are declared to be punishable as felonies, with penal servitude for not more than fourteen, nor less than three years, or to be imprisoned for not more than two years, with or without hard labour or solitary confinement, at the discretion of the judge.

INDIA STOCK.

(26 & 27 Vict. cap. 73—28th July, 1863.)

An Act to give further Facilities to the Holders of India Stock.

THIS Act gives similar facilities to the holders of India Stock as are given to the holders of Government Stock by cap. 28, by the issue of certificates on payment of the like fees, and with the same punishments for forgery of them.

BANK-POST BILLS (IRELAND).

(27 & 28 Vict. cap. 86—29th July, 1864.)

An Act to permit for a limited Period Compositions for Stamp Duties on Bank-Post Bills of Five Pounds and upwards in Ireland.

THE Treasury, by this Act, is empowered to compound with bankers, as is now done in Scotland, for the stamp duty on bank-post bills, on the like terms and conditions, and with such security as the Commissioners are empowered to require in Scotland. The Act is for a period of three years.

BANK HOLIDAYS.

(34 Vict. cap. 17—25th May, 1871.)

An Act to make Provision for Bank Holidays, and respecting obligations to make Payments and to do other acts on such Bank Holidays.

BILLS due on Bank Holidays are payable on the following day, and also notice of dishonour shall be given on the day following such bank holidays.

No person shall be compellable to make payments on a bank holiday which he could not be compelled to make on Good Friday or Christmas Day.

Her Majesty, or the Lord-Lieutenant of Ireland in Ireland, may appoint special bank holidays by royal proclamation, and may alter the days of bank holidays by order in council.

The days fixed for bank holidays under this Act are as under :—In England and Ireland, Easter Monday, the Monday in Whitsun Week, the first Monday in August, and the 26th of December ; in Scotland, New Year's Day, Christmas Day—unless they fall on Sunday, when the following day is to be observed—Good Friday, the first Monday in May, and the first Monday in August.

INDEX.

THE END.

LONDON: PRINTED BY WILLIAM CLOWES AND SONS, STAMFORD STREET AND CHARING CROSS.

CPSIA information can be obtained
at www.ICGtesting.com
Printed in the USA
BVHW040756290819
556817BV00040B/2047/P